Advances in Software Engineering

Springer Science+Business Media, LLC

Hakan Erdogmus   Oryal Tanir
Editors

Advances in Software Engineering

Comprehension, Evaluation, and Evolution

 Springer

Library of Congress Cataloging-in-Publication Data
Erdogmus, Hakan.
    Advances in software engineering : comprehension, evaluation, and evolution / Hakan
Erdogmus, Oryal Tanir.
       p.   cm.
    Includes bibliographical references and index.

    1. Software engineering   I. Tanir, Oryal.   II. Title.
QA76.758 .E73   2002
005.1—dc21   00-047091

Printed on acid-free paper.

Production managed by Steven Pisano; manufacturing supervised by Erica Bresler.
Photocomposed pages prepared from the editors' Microsoft Word and TeX files.

9 8 7 6 5 4 3 2 1

SPIN 10776077

ISBN 978-1-4419-2878-8   ISBN 978-0-387-21599-0 (eBook)
DOI 10.1007/978-0-387-21599-0

Preface

Software engineering is a rapidly growing and changing field. Over the last decade, it has gained significant popularity, and it is now heralded as a discipline of its own. This edited collection presents recent advances in software engineering in the areas of *evolution*, *comprehension*, and *evaluation*. The theme of the book addresses the increasing need to understand and assess software systems in order to measure their quality, maintain them, adapt them to changing requirements and technology, and migrate them to new platforms. This need can be satisfied by studying how software systems are built and maintained, by finding new paradigms, and by building new tools to support the activities involved in developing contemporary software systems.

The contributions to the book are from major results and findings of leading researchers, under the mandate of the Consortium for Software Engineering Research (CSER). CSER has been in existence since 1996. The five founding industrial and academic partners wanted to create a research environment that would appeal to the applied nature of the industrial partners, as well as to advance the state of the art and develop fresh expertise. The research projects of the Consortium are partially funded by the industrial partners, and partially by the Natural Sciences and Engineering Research Council of Canada. Technical and administrative management of the Consortium is provided by the National Research Council of Canada—specifically by members of the Software Engineering Group of the Institute for Information Technology.

Software engineering research today overlaps with and borrows from many disciplines in social, pure, and engineering sciences, outside its traditional core disciplines of computer science and computer engineering. Examples are statistics, mathematics, economics, information management systems, systems engineering, cognitive science, sociology, and anthropology, to name a few. This many-faceted nature of the discipline is strongly reflected by the coverage of this book.

The book is organized into four parts: *Empirical Studies*, *Architectural Recovery*, *Maintainability*, and *Tool Support*. The central themes—*evaluation*, *comprehension*, and *evolution*—are present simultaneously in each of the parts and in most of the individual contributions.

The topics in the book will appeal to different groups of readers:

- students wishing to get an understanding of the state of the art,
- managers who want to appreciate issues related to legacy systems,
- software researchers who want better understanding of particular areas,
- practitioners who wish to see real-world examples,

- and software educators who are looking for thesis topics as well as a framework for industrial and academic collaboration.

For the field of software engineering to grow, it needs a proliferation and application of good ideas to produce novel solutions. We hope the readers will feel that this book provides some answers and plants seeds for future ideas to grow upon.

Acknowledgments

We would like to acknowledge the financial support provided to the Consortium for Software Engineering Research by the Natural Sciences and Engineering Council of Canada. We would also like to acknowledge the contributions made by the National Research Council of Canada and its staff and by the many Canadian Universities whose researchers and students have worked towards the betterment of the software engineering discipline. The industrial partners deserve special mention for having the vision to help create CSER, in addition to their financial, technical, and intellectual contribution.

We thank the reviewers for their excellent feedback, which helped improve the quality of the chapters. Last, but not least, we thank the authors who provided the content and who have patiently revised their work to satisfy the demands of this edited collection.

Contents

List of Contributors

Paula S.C. Alencar is a Research Associate Professor of Computer Science at the University of Waterloo in Canada. His research, teaching, and consulting activities have been directed to software engineering and formal methods in software engineering. Dr. Alencar has been a visiting professor at the University of Karlsruhe, at the Imperial College of Science and Technology, and at the University of Waterloo. Prior to his current position, he has held faculty positions at the Universities of Waterloo and Brasilia. He is principal or co-principal investigator with Donald Cowan on research grants from NSERC, CSER, CITO, IBM, and Sybase. He has published over 60 technical papers. He is a member of the IEEE, the IEEE Computer Society, ACM, CIPS, ACFAS, and AAAI. Prof. Alencar can be reached at palencar@csg.uwaterloo.ca.

Nicolas Anquetil received a D.E.A in computer science (artificial intelligence) from the University of Caen, France in 1988. He completed his Ph.D. in computer science at the University of Montreal in 1996, and worked at the University of Ottawa as a research associate and part-time professor. Since August 1999, Nicolas Anquetil has been a visiting professor at the Federal University of Rio de Janeiro. His research interests include reverse engineering, knowledge based approaches to software engineering, classification and theoretical fundations of the object model. Dr. Anquetil can be reached at anquetil@centroin.com.br or at nicolas@cos.ufrj.br.

M. Ajmal Chaumun earned his B.Sc. degree from Université du Québec, Hull, in 1993 and his M.Sc. degree from Université de Montréal in 1998. After his graduation, Chaumun worked as configuration management administrator at CGI, Inc. He is currently a software engineer at Ericsson Research, Montréal, Canada. He has published articles on software maintenance and reengineering in the IEEE Euromicro Conference. Mr. Chaumun can be reached at lmcajch@lmc.ericsson.se.

François Coallier is Chairman of the Consortium for Software Engineering Research (CSER). He is currently General Manager, Enterprise System Infratructure, at Bell Canada, where he is responsible for the management of the Intranet infrastructure and information systems process engineering. In addition, Mr. Coallier is the international Chairman of the Joint ISO and IEC subcommittee responsible for the elaboration of Software Engineering Standards (ISO/IEC JTCS/SC7). He is a member of the industrial consultative board of the Electrical and Computing Engineering department of École Polytechnique de Montréal. Mr. Coallier has a B.Sc. in Biology from McGill University, and a B.Eng. in engineering physics and a M.A.Sc in electrical engineering from Montreal's École Polytechnique. He is a Certified Quality Analyst (CQA) from the Quality Assurance Institute and a Fellow of the American Association for the Advancement of Science. He is the author of numerous publications on software quality and metrics. Mr. Coallier can be reached at Francois.Coallier@bell.ca.

Donald D. Cowan is a Distinguished Professor Emeritus of Computer Science at the University of Waterloo, and Director of the Computer Systems Group. He is the founding Chairman of the Computer Science Department at the university, and the author or co-author of over 200 papers and 15 books in computer/communications, software engineering, education, environmental information systems and mathematics. He is a founder and director of the Waterloo Foundation for the Advancement of Computing and the Waterloo Mathematics Foundation. He is a co-designer of the Waterloo Information Network (WIN), a prototype smart communities infrastructure. Prof. Cowan can be reached at dcowan@csg.uwaterloo.ca.

Michel Dagenais is a professor at École Polytechnique de Montréal, co-founder of the Linux-Quèbec user group, and moderator for the Usenet newsgroup comp.lang.modula3 FAQ and the Polytechnique Montréal Modula-3 programming environment. He authored or co-authored a large number of scientific publications in the fields of software engineering, structured documents on the Web, and object-oriented distributed programming for collaborative applications. In 1995-1996, during a leave of absence, he was the director of software development at Positron Industries where he was the chief architect for the Power911 call management system. Prof. Dagenais can be reached at michel.dagenais@polymtl.ca.

Khaled El-Emam is currently with the National Research Council in Ottawa. He is the editor of the IEEE TCSE Software Process Newsletter, the current International Trials Coordinator for the SPICE Trials, which is empirically evaluating the emerging ISO/IEC 15504 International Standard worldwide, co-editor of ISO's project to develop an international standard defining the software measurement process, and Knowledge Area specialist for the Software Engineering Process in the IEEE project to define the Software Engineering Body of Knowledge. He is also an adjunct professor at the School of Computer Science at McGill University, and an adjunct professor at the Department of Computer Science at the University of Quebec in Montreal. Previously, he worked on both small and large software research and development projects for organizations such as Toshiba International Company, Yokogawa Electric, and Honeywell Control Systems. Khaled El-Emam obtained his Ph.D. from the Department of Electronic Engineering, King's College, the University of London (UK) in 1994. He was previously the head of the Quantitative Methods Group at the Fraunhofer Institute for Experimental Software Engineering in Germany, a research scientist at the Centre de recherche informatique de Montréal (CRIM), and a research assistant in the Software Engineering Laboratory at McGill University. Dr. El Emam can be reached at Khaled.El-Emam@nrc.ca.

Hakan Erdogmus is an Associate Research Officer at the Institute of Information Technology, National Research Council of Canada. He joined IIT's Software Engineering Group in 1995. Dr. Erdogmus received a Ph.D. degree in telecommunications from the Institut national de la recherce scientifique, Université du Québec, in 1994, and an M.Sc. degree in computer science from McGill University, Montreal, in 1989. His research interests include software engineering economics, software architecture, design reuse, COTS-based systems, and formal methods. Dr. Erdogmus is a member of the ACM and the IEEE Computer Society. You can reach him at Hakan.Erdogmus@nrc.ca.

Patrick J. Finnigan is a staff member at the IBM Toronto Software Solutions Laboratory, which he joined in 1978. He received the M.Math. degree in computer science from the University of Waterloo in 1994, and is a member of the Professional Engineers of Ontario. He was a principal investigator, at the IBM Centre for Advanced Studies of the Consortium for Software Engineering Research (CSER) project. He is also Executive Director of CSER. He can be reached at finnigan@ca.ibm.com

Bob Fraser is the Information Development Manager for Electronic Commerce Development at the IBM Toronto Laboratory. After working several years of video game programming, he joined IBM in 1984 as a technical writer. He has worked on IBM's VisualAge Java and C++ products and now manages the Information Development team responsible for WebSphere Commerce Suite. He is a graduate of the Applied Computer Science program at Ryerson Polytechnic University. He can be reached at bfraser@ca.ibm.com.

Daniel M. German is a Ph.D. candidate with the Computer Science Department at the University of Waterloo. His research interests include documentation systems and software engineering with particular emphasis on hypermedia design approaches and formal methods. He can be reached at dmg@csg.uwaterloo.ca.

Dhrubajyoti Goswami received a B.Sc. degree in Physics (1987) from the University of Delhi, India, a B.E. degree in computer science and engineering (1990) from the Indian Institute of Science, Bangalore, and an M.Sc. degree in computer science (1995) from McGill University, Montreal, Canada. Currently, he is a Ph.D. candidate and a member of the Parallel and Distributed Systems (PADS) Group at the Department of Electrical and Computer Engineering, University of Waterloo, Canada. From 1990 to 1992, he worked with the Operating Systems Groups at DCM Data Products, New Delhi, and Altos India Ltd., the

R&D division of Pertech Computers Ltd., India. His research interests include parallel algorithms, algorithmic complexity theory, parallel and distributed computing systems, and theoretical computer science. Mr. Goswami can be reached at goswami@etude.uwaterloo.ca.

Francisco Herrera is an independent consultant specializing in User Centered Design and Usability. He has ample experience working with users in system integration and software development projects in Canada, the United States, and Mexico. He holds a Bachelor's degree in Mathematics and Computer Science from the National University of Mexico and a Master's degree in Computer Science from the University of Ottawa, Canada.

Richard C. Holt is a professor at the University of Waterloo. He was a professor at the University of Toronto from 1970 to 1997. His Ph.D. work on deadlock appears in many books on operating systems. Dr. Holt worked on a number of compilers such as Cornell's PL/C (PL/I) compiler, the SUE compiler, the SP/k compiler, and the Euclid and Concurrent Euclid compilers. He co-developed the S/SL parsing method, which is used in a number of software products. He is co-inventor of the Turing programming language, which is used in 50 percent of Ontario high schools and universities. He was awarded the CIPS 1988 national award for software innovation, the 1994-95 ITAC national award for software research, and shared the 1995 ITRC award for technology transfer. He is the author of a dozen books on languages and operating systems. He has served as Director of ConGESE, the cross-Ontario Consortium for Graduate Education in Software Engineering. His current area of research is in software architectures and visualization. Prof. Holt can be reached at holt@uwaterloo.ca.

J. Howard Johnson has been a research officer at the Institute for Information Technology, the National Research Council of Canada, in Ottawa since 1992. Before that he was a professor at the University of Waterloo and a methodologist and a manager of a systems development group at Statistics Canada. While a professor at the University of Waterloo, he became interested in studying algorithms for processing text. When he joined the Software Engineering Group in IIT, he applied these techniques to the process of software reverse engineering as part of a collaboration with teams from IBM, McGill University, University of Toronto, and University of Victoria sponsored by IBM and NSERC through several CRD grants. This project evolved into one of the founding projects of CSER and grew with the addition of more researchers from the University of Waterloo. Dr. Johnson can be reached at Howard.Johnson@nrc.ca.

Hind Kabaili is a Ph,D. student in software engineering at the Department of Computer Science and Operations Research at University of Montréal. She received an M.Sc. degree in computer science from Laval University, and an engineering diploma from Monastir National School of Engineering, Tunisia. She pursured her M.Sc. research at Centre de recherce informatique de Montréal. Currently, she is a research assistant with the SPOOL project, funded by Bell Canada and the Consortium for Software Engineering Research (CSER). During 1993, she was a member of the research staff at the Moroccan Royal Center for Space Detection, working on the Geographic Information Systems project. Mr. Kabaili can be be reached at kabaili@iro.umontreal.ca.

Ivan Kalas is a research staff member at the Centre for Advanced Studies, IBM Canada Laboratory. His research interests are in the area of object-oriented design, object-oriented concurrent systems, programming environments, and programming languages. He holds degrees in mathematics and physics, and a Master's degree in mathematical physics from the University of Toronto. He joined IBM in May of 1989.

Anatol W. Kark is the leader of the Software Engineering Group at the Institute for Information Technology, National Research Council of Canada. Prior to joining NRC in 1991 he was director of R&D at Philips Information System in Montreal. At Philips, Mr. Kark was responsible for the development of office automation applications, system software for enterprise PCs, and applications for Philips-Micom word processors. His interests include problem reports databases and their integration into software development and management environments. He is participating in the ISO/JTC1/SC7 work on software and system life cycle processes and supporting standards on configuration management and software project management. Anatol has served as Operations Manager for the Consortium for Software Engineering Research since its inception. As of May 2000, he assumed the position of Research Director of CSER. Mr. Kark can be reached at Anatol.Kark@nrc.ca.

Rudolf "Reudi" K. Keller is an associate professor in the Software Engineering Group (GÉLO) at the Department of Computer Science and Operations Research at University of Montréal (UdeM). Before joining the faculty at UdeM, he was for several years a researcher at Montréal's CRIM research institute. Dr. Keller has taught at the School of Computer Science at McGill University and at University of California at Irvine, where he was a postdoctoral fellow from 1989 to 1991. He received an M.Sc. degree in mathematics from the Swiss Federal Institute of Technology (ETH) at Zürich in 1983, and a Ph.D. degree in computer science from University of Zürich in 1989. His current research interests are object-oriented analysis and design, reverse engineering, design components and patterns, software quality, user interface engineering, business process modeling, and technologies for electronic marketplaces. Prof. Keller can be reached at keller@iro.umontreal.ca.

Scott Kerr is a research associate and Master's student at the Department of Computer Science, University of Toronto. He received his B.Sc. from the University of Toronto in 1996. He is presently working at the Centre for Advanced Studies at the IBM Toronto Laboratory as well as at the University of Toronto in the areas of conceptual modeling and software engineering. Scott can be reached at skerr23@hotmail.com.

Gregory Knapen obtained his Bachelor's degree from McGill University and his Master's degree from École Polytechnique de Montréal. He is currently working as a software developer at Actional (formerly Visual Edge, Inc). Gregory can be reached at gregory@visualedge.com.

Kostas Kontogiannis is an assistant professor at the University of Waterloo, Department of Electrical and Computer Engineering. He received a B.Sc. in mathematics from the University of Patras, Greece, an M.Sc. in computer science and artificial intelligence from Katholieke Universiteit Leuven, Belgium, and a Ph.D. in computer science from McGill University, Canada. His main area of research is software engineering. He is actively involved in several Canadian Centres of Excellence: the Consortium for Software Engineering Research (CSER), the Information Technology Research Centre (ITRC) of Ontario, and the Institute for Robotics and Intelligent systems (IRIS). Prof. Kontogiannis can be reached at kostas@swen.uwaterloo.ca.

Bruno Laguë is an Executive Consultant in the Quality Engineering and Research group at Bell Canada. This group is responsible for managing the technological risks inherent in the acquisition of high-tech products for Bell's telecommunications network. Bruno joined Bell in 1994, after three years of work at Bell-Northern Research (now Nortel Networks) as a software designer on the DMS100 telecom switch. Bruno obtained the "best thesis award" for his M.A.Sc. degree in Telecommunications in 1991 from École Polytechnique de Montréal. He obtained his Bachelor degree in computer/software engineering in 1989, also from EPM. Mr. Laguë can be reached at Bruno.Lague@bell.ca.

Timothy C. Lethbridge teaches software engineering at the University of Ottawa. His research interests include human-computer interaction, software design, software engineering tools, software engineering education and knowledge representation. He has been instrumental in the development of the undergraduate software engineering program at the University of Ottawa, one of the first in Canada. Lethbridge received his Ph.D. in computer science from the University of Ottawa in 1994; his thesis was on the topic of tools for knowledge management. Prior to that, Lethbridge worked at Bell-Northern Research (now Nortel Networks) and the Government of New Brunswick. You can visit his web page at http://www.site.uottawa.ca/~tcl or reach him at tcl@site.uottawa.ca.

François Lustman received a B.Sc. degree in electrical engineering and a Ph.D. in applied mathematics from University of Grenoble, France. He is currently professor at the Département d'informatique et de recherche opérationnelle, Université de Montréal, Canada. Before joigning UdeM, he spent fifteen years working in private and public organizations. He joined the university in

1981 and chaired the department from 1985 to 1989. He is a member of the GÉ-LO software engineering group. His present research interests are in software quality, evolvability, and in the use of formal methods for the specification and design of information systems. François Lustman has published one book on software project management, and several papers in compiler construction, medical databases, project management, information systems, software quality, and formal methods. Prof. Lustman can be reached at lustman@iro.umontreal.ca.

Johannes Martin is a Ph.D. candidate in the Department of Computer Science at the University of Victoria, British Columbia, Canada. He received a Master of Science degree from the Northern Illinois University in DeKalb, Illinois, USA. He received research fellowships from the Centre for Advanced Studies at the IBM Toronto Laboratory (CAS), where he has worked on research projects of the Canadian Consortium for Software Engineering Research (CSER). Johannes Martin's research interests include software engineering, migration, program understanding and visualization. He can be reached at jmartin@csr.csc.uvic.ca.

Ettore Merlo received his Ph.D. in computer science from McGill University (Montreal) in 1989 and his Laurea degree—summa cum laude—from the University of Turin (Italy) in 1983. He has been the lead researcher of the software engineering group at the Computer Research Institute of Montreal until 1993 when he joined École Polytechnique de Montréal, where he is currently an associate professor. His research interests are in software analysis, software reengineering, user interfaces, software maintenance and artificial intelligence. He has collaborated with several industries and research centers, in particular on software reengineering, clone detection, software quality assessment and architectural reverse engineering. Prof. Merlo can be reached at Ettore.Merlo@polymtl.ca.

Hausi A. Müller is a Professor in the Department of Computer Science at the University of Victoria, British Columbia, Canada. He is a Visiting Scientist with the Centre for Advanced Studies at the IBM Toronto Laboratory and the Carnegie Mellon Software Engineering Institute. He is a principal investigator of CSER, a Canadian Consortium for Software Engineering Research and the IRIS (Institute for Robotics and intelligent Systems) Network of Centres for Excellence. Together with his research group he investigates technologies to migrate legacy software to object-oriented and network-centric platforms. Dr. Müller's research interests include software engineering, software evolution, reverse engineering, software reengineering, program understanding, and software architecture. He is the General Chair of ICSE-2001, the IEEE/ACM International Conference on Software Engineering to be held in Toronto. He was a Program Co-Chair for ICSM-94, the IEEE International Conference on Software

Maintenance in Victoria, CASE-95, the IEEE International Workshop on Computer-Aided Software Engineering in Toronto, and IWPC-96, the IEEE International Workshop on Program Comprehension in Berlin. Dr. Müller is on the Editorial Board of IEEE Transactions on Software Engineering. You can reach him at hausi@csr.uvic.ca.

John Mylopoulos is a professor of computer science at the University of Toronto. His research interests include knowledge representation and conceptual modeling, covering languages, implementation techniques, and applications. Dr. Mylopoulos has worked on the development of requirements and design languages for information systems, the adoption of database implementation techniques for large knowledge bases, and the application of knowledge base techniques to software repositories. He is currently leading a number of research projects and is principal investigator of both national and provincial Centres of Excellence for Information Technology. Dr. Mylopoulos received his Ph.D. degree from Princeton University in 1970. His publication list includes more than 130 refereed journal and conference proceedings papers and four edited books. He is the recipient of the first-ever Outstanding Services Award given out by the Canadian AI Society (CSCSI), a co-recipient of the most influential paper award of the 1994 International Conference on Software Engineering, a Fellow of the American Association for AI (AAAI), and an elected member of the VLDB Endowment Board. He has served on the editorial board of several international journals, including the ACM Transactions on Software Engineering and Methodology (TOSEM), the ACM Transactions on Information Systems (TOIS), and the VLDB Journal and Computational Intelligence. Dr. Mylopoulos can be reached at jm@cs.toronto.edu.

Luis C.M. Nova is a postdoctoral fellow with the Computer Science Department at the University of Waterloo. His research interests include software engineering with emphasis on documentation systems, software design, object-oriented techniques, and formal methods. He can be reached at luisnova@csg.uwaterloo.ca.

Jean-Francois Patenaude received his computer engineering degree from École Polytechnique, Montréal, in 1997. He is currently pursuing his Master's degree in software reengineering, also at École Polytechnique. His research interests are related to software quality analysis. He now works at Bell Canada's Network Monitoring Center. You can reach Mr. Patenaude at patch@casi.polymtl.ca.

Stephen G. Perelgut received his M.Sc. degree in computer science from the University of Toronto in 1984. His research interests include compiler design and development, software engineering, software reuse, and electronic communications as they affect virtual communities. He is currently a full-time member of the IBM Centre for Advanced Studies and acting as both a principal investigator on the software bookshelf project as well as program manager for CASCON '97. Mr. Perelgut can be reached at perelgut@ca.ibm.com.

Gary Pianosi is the Vice-President of Product Development at the Waterloo Lab, Janna Systems, Inc., where he is responsible for product research and development. Gary is a 12-year veteran of the software industry, including over a decade of experience in the design and implementation of text database and document authoring systems. Previously, Gary was a co-founder of LivePage Corporation and was engaged in software research and development at the Waterloo Foundation for the Advancement of Computing. He began his career at the University of Waterloo's Computer Systems Group where he focussed on document authoring tools including an advanced SGML editing system. Gary earned a Bachelor of Mathematics degree in computer science from the University of Waterloo. Mr. Pianosi can be reached at garyp@janna.com.

Bruno R. Preiss received his B.A.Sc degree in engineering science (electrical engineering option) in 1982, his M.A.Sc degree in electrical engineering in 1984, and his Ph.D. degree in electrical engineering from the University of Toronto, Toronto, Canada. He is an associate professor in the Department of Electrical and Computer Engineering at the University of Waterloo, Ontario, Canada. He is a member of the Computer Communications Networks Group, the VLSI Research Group, and the Parallel and Distributed Systems (PADS) Group. His current research interests include parallel discrete-event simulation and multiprocessor and parallel processor computer architectures. Bruno R. Preiss is licensed as a Professional Engineer in the Province of Ontario, Canada. He is a member of the Canadian Society for Electrical and Computer Engineering, the Institute of Electrical and Electronics Engineers, and the Association for Computing Machinery.

Jamie Roberts is a member of the IBM Toronto Laboratory. He has been working on the research and development of many documentation products. Recently, he has been involved with the documentation for the IBM's Visual Age product suite. Jamie is currently working at the IBM Corporate level examining documentation issues. He has a B.A. and M.A. in English from the University of Waterloo. He is completing a Ph.D. in English at the University of Waterloo. He can be reached at robertsj@ca.ibm.com.

Sébastien Robitaille obtained his Bachelor's degree in physics and his Master's degree in computer science, both from the Université de Montréal. He is has been working as a software developer at Actional Corp. since May 2000. His Master's thesis was pursued as part of the SPOOL project on the topic of tool development to support object-oriented software comprehension. His major contribution to the SPOOL project was the development of a navigation-based technology, the Design Browser, whose purpose is to helps bridge the gap between software abstractions and implementations.

Guy Saint-Denis is currently pursuing a Master's degree at the Software Engineering Laboratory at the Université de Montréal, where he completed his Bachelor's degree in computer science in 1999. Prior to his studies in information technology, Guy freelanced as a camera-assistant in the film and television industry subsequent to completing a Bachelor of Fine Arts degree in still photography at Concordia University in 1989. His lifelong goal is to explore, discover, share, and, of course, have lots of fun along the way.

Reinhard Schauer is a software designer of Alcatel Carrier Internetworking Division, Canada. Previously, he was a research assistant at the Department of Computer Science and Operations Research of the University of Montréal, Canada, working on the architectural design of the SPOOL reverse engineering environment. Prior to this position, he was a Fulbright Scholar at Hawaii Pacific University, USA, from which he earned a Master's degree in information systems. He served as a research and project assistant in several industry collaborations of the University of Linz, Austria, from which he graduated with a Master's degree in Computer Science. Reinhard's interests in software engineering focus on object-oriented programming, reverse engineering, application frameworks, and database technologies. Reinhard Schauer can be reached at rschauer@newbridge.com.

Janice Singer conducts research in the field of empirical studies of software engineering. She is a member of the Software Engineering Group at the National Research Council of Canada. Her current projects are focused on the empirical study of patterns and studying the work practices of software engineers. She is also interested in qualitative research and ethical approaches to research. Dr. Singer received a Ph.D. in Cognitive Psychology from the University of Pittsburgh and a B.A. in Cognitive Science from the University of California, San Diego. She has held positions at Tektronix, Xerox, and IBM. Dr. Singer can be reached at Janice.Singer@nrc.ca.

Ajit Singh completed his B.Sc. degree in electronics and communication engineering (1979) at BIT, India, and his M.Sc. (1986) and Ph.D. (1991) degrees in computing science at University of Alberta, Canada. From 1980 to 1983, he worked at the R&D department of Operations Research Group, the representative company for Sperry Univac Computers in India. From 1990 to 1992, he was involved with the design of telecommunication systems at Bell-Northern Research (now Nortel Networks), Ottawa. Since 1993, he is a faculty member at Department of Electrical and Computer Engineering, University of Waterloo. Prof. Singh has published several research papers in the areas of software engineering, parallel computing, database systems, and   artificial intelligence. He can be reached at asingh@etude.uwaterloo.ca.

Martin Stanley is President and CEO of Techne Knowledge Systems, Inc., a startup company formed by a group of researchers from the universities of Toronto and Waterloo specializing in the development of tools for software re engineering. Mr. Stanley received his M.Sc. degree in computer science from the University of Toronto in 1987. His research interests include knowledge representation and conceptual modeling, with particular application to the building of software repositories. He is currently a part-time research associate in the Computer Science Department at the University of Toronto.

Oryal Tanir is Director of Business Engineering and Simulation at Bell Canada in Montreal and an adjunct professor at McGill University. He joined Bell Canada in 1986. As a researcher in Bell Canada, he has been exposed to many large systems such as telephony switches, data communication nodes, client server networks and real-time network surveillance systems. He has also managed and participated in several software research programs with various universities and government agencies. His research interests include software (systems) engineering, design-level reuse, computer architecture, discrete-event simulation, and concurrency models. He has published a book and numerous articles in the area of discrete-event simulation. He was the past chairman of the IEEE P1173 Working Group on standardization of simulation. He is a senior member of the Society for Computer Simulation and Society for Design Process Sciences. He is also a member of the Association for Computer Machines, and IEEE Computer and Communications Societies. Oryal is a registered Professional Engineer in Canada. He holds a Ph.D. and a Master's degree in electrical engineering from McGill University, Montreal. You can reach him at Oryal.Tanir@bell.ca.

Ivan Tomek is a professor of Computer Science in the Jodrey School of Computer Science, Acadia University, Canada. His main research interests include support for geographically dispersed work teams, in particular software development teams, interactive development environments, object-oriented programming and development methodologies, collaborative learning, collaborative virtual environments. Prof. Tomek can be reached at Ivan.Tomek@acadiau.ca.

Vassilios Tzerpos is a Ph.D. candidate at the University of Toronto. His research interests include software architecture, reverse engineering, and software clustering. His work has been published in various conference proceedings, such as the International Conference on Software Maintenance, the Working Conference on Reverse Engineering, and the International Workshop on Program Comprehension. He received his B.Sc. degree in electrical and computer engineering from the National Technical University of Athens, Greece in 1992, and his M.Sc. in computer science from the University of Toronto in 1995. Mr. Tzerpos can be reached at vtzer@cs.toronto.edu.

Kenny Wong is an assistant professor in the Department of Computing Science at the University of Alberta. His research interests include reengineering, program understanding, software architecture, software integration, and user interfaces. He is a member of the ACM, USENIX, and the IEEE Computer Society. Prof. Wong can be reached at kenw@cs.ualberta.ca.

List of Referees

Paulo S.C. Alencar
University of Waterloo

Daniel Amyot
University of Ottawa

Saida Benlarbi
Cistel Technology

Marsha Chechik,
University of Toronto

Lou Copertari
McMaster School of Business

Michel Dagenais
Ecole Polytechnique de Montréal

Khaled El-Emam
National Research Council of Canada

Hakan Erdogmus
National Research Council of Canada

Nick Graham
Queen's University

Pedro Henriques
Universidade do Minho

Ric Holt
University of Waterloo

Howard J. Johnson
National Research Council of Canada

Anatol W. Kark
National Research Council of Canada

Rudolf K. Keller
Université de Montréal

Barbara Kitchenham
Keele University

Gregory Knapen
Université de Montréal

Kostas Kontogiannis
University of Waterloo

Bruno Laguë
Bell Canada

Timothy C. Lethbridge
University of Ottawa

Steven D. Litvintchouk
The MITRE Corporation

Francois Lustman
Université de Montréal

Stephen A. MacKay
National Research Council of Canada

Serge Mankovski
Metamail, Inc.

Johannes Martin
University of Victoria

Alberto Mendelzon
University of Toronto

Ettore Merlo
École Polytechnique de Montréal

Hausi Müller
University of Victoria

Gail Murphy
University of British Columbia

Kumbasaray Ponnambalam
University of Waterloo

Jarrett Rosenberg
Sun Microsystems, Inc.

Janice Singer
National Research Council of Canada

Ajit Singh
University of Waterloo

Patrick Steyaert
MediaGeniX

Vassilios Tzerpos
University of Toronto

Susan Sim
University of Toronto

Mark Vigder
National Research Council of Canada

Michael Weiss
Carleton University

Hongwei Xi
University of Cincinnati

1
Introduction

Hakan Erdogmus
Oryal Tanir
Anatol W. Kark
François Coallier

1.1 Introduction

This edited collection reports on the projects, results, and directions of a collaborative Canadian software engineering research initiative. It is mandated by the organizational body of this initiative, the *Consortium for Software Engineering Research* (CSER). Section 1.4 provides more details about the Consortium.

Software engineering is still a maturing field. Its many facets and highly multidisciplinary nature make it both difficult and risqué to give a universally accepted definition. Thus, instead of attempting a definition, we provide an excerpt from the mission statement of the Software Engineering Group at the National Research Council of Canada. According to SEG, the goal of software engineering research is to "advance the state of software development to an engineering level by evaluating and improving the processes and technologies with which software is created, and demonstrating these processes and technologies through pilot projects and using both the engineering and the scientific approaches...."

This goal is sufficiently inclusive to cover the wide spectrum of issues addressed by the contributors of this collection. At the same time, we believe that it brings out the focal points. First, it implies that both process and technology are parts of the discipline. Second, it emphasizes the synergy between the engineering and the scientific approaches-between theory and empiricism-to tackle the underlying complex issues. As such, it hints at the increasingly multidisciplinary nature of the research.

Software engineering research today overlaps with and borrows from many disciplines in social, pure, and engineering sciences, outside its traditional core disciplines of computer science and computer engineering. Examples are statistics, mathematics, economics, information management systems, systems engineering, cognitive science, sociology, and anthropology, to name a few. This multifaceted nature of our discipline is strongly reflected by the coverage of this book.

The book is centered on three interrelated topics: *comprehension, evaluation, and evolution*. The choice of these topics is not incidental. Together they have constituted the core of CSER's research activities since its inception in 1996. Underlying the three topics is first and foremost the compelling need to understand software systems—both new and old—and how they are built and maintained. The topics consequently also address the need to assess these systems, to measure their quality, to maintain them, to adapt them to changing requirements and technology, to migrate them to new platforms, to discover new paradigms, and to build new tools to support all of these activities.

All contributions in this book have a CSER connection. However, the book is by no means a comprehensive account of all CSER research activities. The majority of the chapters originated directly from the different research groups and individual researchers within CSER. These contributions are officially connected to one or more CSER projects, and most are active as of this writing. Two have completed their term and are being pursued outside the structure of the Consortium. Two other contributions are peripheral to CSER, in that they are either partially funded or pursued outside while maintaining close ties with the Consortium.

Many overlaps and dependencies exist among the contributions, both in terms of the issues they tackle and their authorship. This situation is representative of the high level of synergy among the different research projects.

All contributions have undergone a stringent peer review process to maintain a high quality. The only exception is Chapter 18, which is an invited contribution. This work was included for historical reasons: it had a significant impact on the central themes and projects of the Consortium. The majority of its authors are still actively involved in many CSER projects, and continue to influence the evolution of the Consortium.

This book is targeted at both software practitioners and researchers. It contains information valuable to project managers and tool developers. Its organization around a central theme makes the individual parts suitable for use as reference material in a graduate seminar. Contributions range from survey articles to experience reports, from experimental studies to original research results. Their collective intent is to give the reader a snapshot of the state of the art in the *comprehension, evaluation,* and *evolution* of software systems.

1.2 Organization of the Book

The book is organized into four parts: *Empirical Studies, Architectural Recovery, Maintainability,* and *Tool Support*. The central themes—*comprehension, evaluation,* and *evolution*—are present simultaneously in each of the parts and in most of the individual contributions. Additionally, significant overlap exists among the different parts. The part titles indicate the focus of the contributions.

1.2.1   Part One: Empirical Studies

Part One, *Empirical Studies*, contains four chapters. It addresses an often-neglected aspect of software engineering research: empiricism. How do we know that the tools and methods being developed work? What can we learn from practicing software engineers? Chapters 2 and 5 attempt to answer the first question with a focus on quantitative techniques, while Chapters 3 and 4 attempt to answer the second question with a qualitative focus.

El Emam contributes a survey of object-oriented metrics in Chapter 2. This informative and comprehensive review dispels some common myths with an intelligent interpretation of the key results that the object-oriented metrics research has so far yielded. With more than 100 bibliographic references, it also doubles as a valuable account of the underlying literature.

Chapter 3 by Lethbridge and Singer describes the techniques that the authors have developed and used in their field studies of the work practices of software engineers. They identify and represent work patterns to help software engineers maintain large and complex systems. One of the conclusions they draw from their studies is that the efficiency and effectiveness of search tools is critical for dealing with large bodies of source code.

In Chapter 4, Lethbridge and Herrera report on their experience evaluating the usefulness of a particular software exploration tool in an industrial context. Again, their ultimate goal with this empirical study was to find ways to improve the efficiency of software maintenance for large systems by investigating how existing development tools are being used by practicing software engineers. This chapter highlights the factors that make the evaluation process difficult, and provides pointers for assessing the usefulness of complex development tools.

Chapter 5 deals with a common and controversial software development practice: *cloning*. Cloning, or producing new code by copying and modifying old code, is often cited as a significant driver of maintenance costs. In this chapter, Dagenais, Patenaude, Merlo, and Lagüe first describe a metrics-based approach to clone detection, and then report on the application of their approach to experiments performed on a number of large object-oriented systems. Their results confirm that modern software systems are also prone to cloning. They hypothesize that the extent of this practice depends on several factors unrelated to the programming language used.

1.2.2   Part Two: Architectural Recovery

Part Two, *Architectural Recovery*, attacks the problems associated with understanding and modernizing large software systems. It contains four chapters, ordered according to the level of abstraction with which they address program comprehension. The first chapter of this part describes an environment for reverse engineering based on the concept of *design patterns*. The second and third chapters discuss approaches to automatic *program clustering* as a way of remodularizing systems whose explicit architecture has been lost. The last chapter tackles a critical problem associated with the migration of non-object-oriented code to object-oriented code.

In Chapter 6, Keller et al. introduce the SPOOL reverse engineering environment. Their main hypothesis is that important design decisions and the thought processes of the designers often manifest themselves as recurring patterns of organization among design-level components, and that by extracting these patterns much can be gleamed about the system and its design rationale. The SPOOL environment is built upon this hypothesis.

In Chapter 7, Lethbridge and Anquetil provide a taxonomy for automatic clustering techniques, describe their main features, and discuss the criteria for their evaluation. Chapter 8, by Tzerpos and Holt, is a survey of automatic clustering techniques borrowed from other disciplines. While Chapter 8 overlaps with Chapter 7, Tzerpos and Holt focus exclusively on generic approaches and argue for their suitability in the software context.

The final chapter of Part Two, Chapter 9, presents an algorithm to convert non-object-oriented C programs with pointers to object-oriented Java programs with inheritance. In this chapter, Martin and Müller point out that the use of pointers in legacy systems written in such languages as C is a major problem. They argue that pointers often implicitly express inheritance relationships between structured data types. By detecting such usage of pointers in C programs, their algorithm is able to construct a Java-class hierarchy.

1.2.3   Part Three: Maintainability

Part Three, *Maintainability*, contains three chapters. Chapter 10, by Chaumun et al., addresses maintainability from the perspective of the potential repercussions that different kinds of changes may have on a system. The authors define a change model for the SPOOL environment of Chapter 6, and a technique to analyze the impact of the modeled changes for object-oriented systems. They also discuss the results of their experiments with large-scale systems to identify some design metrics (see Chapter 2) that affect changeability, and hence, maintainability.

In Chapter 11, Johnson links maintainability to the level of cloning in the code, as hypothesized in Chapter 5. However, his focus is on an alternative approach to clone detection, rather than on empirical validation of clone occurrences in existing systems. Johnson's approach to clone detection is based on the raw textual processing of the source code. This approach contrasts with the metrics-based approach of Chapter 5, which requires a set of metrics to be computed from an abstract representation of the code. As a result of its generality, text-based clone detection is in particular suitable for legacy software where parsers are not necessarily readily available to obtain the abstract representation otherwise required.

Unlike the previous two chapters, which address maintainability as a reverse engineering problem, Chapter 12 treats maintainability as a forward engineering problem. In this chapter, Goswami et al. describe an automated environment for generating parallel applications. They propose to alleviate the high level of complexity inherent in parallel programming by automatically generating part of the infrastructure code using packaged solutions. These packaged solutions are captured and encoded as design patterns. Thus the concept of *pattern* emerges once again in this chapter - albeit unlike in Chapter 6, it appears in its traditional forward engineering context.

1.2.4   Part Four: Tool Support

Part Four focuses on *Tool Support* for the *comprehension, evaluation*, and *evolution* of software systems. It contains six chapters. Chapters 13 and 14 describe the architecture of two successful reverse engineering environments. The two environments target systems that have been developed in different programming paradigms. Chapters 15 and 16, respectively, discuss the mechanisms to deliver software documentation to distributed software teams and collaborative work paradigms to support such teams. Chapters 16 and 17 address tool support for processing source code.

In Chapter 13, Schauer et al. expound on the design and implementation of the SPOOL environment (the goals and the underlying model of this environment are discussed in Chapters 6 and 10).

In Chapter 14, Finnigan et al. describe the Software Bookshelf, a software information management paradigm of historical importance that was developed at the IBM Toronto Labs. While SPOOL is designed for understanding object-oriented systems, the Software Bookshelf targets legacy systems typically written in non-object-oriented languages, with the aim of migrating such systems to more modern architectures.

The Software Bookshelf was one of the earliest development environments to suggest the delivery of information to software teams using a web-based interface. Chapter 15, by Alencar et al., builds upon this now widely popular information delivery mechanism. In this chapter, the authors tackle the usability and maintenance issues associated with publishing hyperlink documentation on the web, and then describe some approaches that are being employed to alleviate the underlying problems.

Web-based delivery of software documentation is one way in which geographically separated software teams can share information. However, delivery of information in a widely accessible form alone is not sufficient to allow distributed software teams to work on large software projects. Tomek investigates this question in Chapter 16. He introduces the concept of the *collaborative virtual environment* (CVE) and discusses the characteristics of such environments. After a survey of different types of CVEs, the chapter focuses on a particular

CVE —one that is text-based, high-performance, and easily deliverable on the web.

Most source code analysis and reverse engineering techniques rely on the availability of an abstract representation of the source code that captures the code's surface semantics. Examples are the clustering techniques discussed in Chapters 7 and 8, the change impact analysis model of Chapter 10, the metrics-based clone detection approach of Chapter 5, the code migration algorithm of Chapter 9, the SPOOL environment of Chapters 6 and 13, and the Software Bookshelf environment of Chapter 14. Therefore, *parsing*, the process of obtaining this abstract representation, is of paramount importance. The last two chapters attack central problems associated with parsing.

In Chapter 17, Knapen et al. address a problem often encountered in the industry: parsing under incomplete information. The question addressed is what to do when the source code is missing pieces required for successful compilation, but not necessarily for high level analysis of the source code? Their solution is a special parser that uses additional rules and type inference mechanisms to resolve the ambiguities resulting from the missing pieces.

In Chapter 18, Kontogiannis et al. attack another parsing problem: how to obtain abstract representations of the source code that are customized with respect to a user-defined model and that can easily be ported to various analysis tools. Their solution is a systematic methodology that allows the user to generate the desired representations. All this accomplished with the use of public-domain parser generators.

1.3   Abstracts

Chapter 2   Object-Oriented Metrics: Principles and Practice

Existing evidence suggests that the majority of faults in software systems occur in a small proportion of the system's components. Reliability can be increased, and rework costs reduced, if these components can be identified early. Subsequently, mitigating actions can be taken, such as a redesign or focused inspections and testing. For object-oriented systems, object-oriented metrics can serve as leading indicators of faulty classes. This chapter will provide an overview of object-oriented metrics, their rationale, and their utility in the identification of faulty classes. It presents empirical evidence as to which metrics have been found to be good leading indicators, and discusses metrics thresholds. Metrics thresholds, once identified, provide practical criteria for quality management.

*Chapter 3   Experiences Conducting Studies of the Work
Practices of Software Engineers*

The chapter describes various techniques for studying and representing the work of software engineers. The ultimate objective of the research addressed is to develop requirements for software engineering tools that will enable software engineers to more productively make changes to large legacy systems. However, to develop those requirements, the work practices of software engineers must be understood. The chapter discusses various techniques employed to observe work practices, analyze the resulting data, and produce graphical models of work patterns. In particular, it describes techniques that have been developed by the authors, such as synchronized shadowing and the use of Use Case Maps to represent work patterns. Finally, the chapter highlights some of the results of using these techniques in a real project. An important observation is that efficiently performing a search within source code is of paramount importance to software engineers when they work with large bodies of source code.

*Chapter 4   Toward Assessing the Usefulness of the TkSee
Software Exploration Tool: A Case Study*

One of the outputs of the CSER initiative has been the development of a software tool called TkSee. The TkSee tool allows software engineers to explore and understand source code. It has been serving as the infrastructure for various studies of program comprehension. It has also been used intensively by several practitioners inside Mitel Corporation. This chapter first provides a description of TkSee's capabilities and then discusses insights about its usability obtained during the field studies of the tool. This qualitative empirical study is intended to provide pointers to those who wish to assess the usability and usefulness of complex software products.

*Chapter 5   Comparison of Clones Occurrence in Java and
Modula-3 Software Systems*

Software engineers often build new subprograms by copying, or cloning, an existing piece of code with similar requirements, and then slightly modifying it. While this technique may be easier than extracting the common, reusable part and making it available in a library, it increases the system size and often leads to higher maintenance costs. The occurrence of clones is highly dependent on the system architecture, development model, language peculiarities, and software management practices. This chapter studies the occurrence of clones in large sets of object-oriented software libraries and programs, totaling over 1.1 million lines of code, in two different languages, Java and Modula-3. The factors that affect the clone detection accuracy and their frequency of occurrence are discussed. Comparisons are also made between systems written in the two languages.

Chapter 6   The SPOOL Approach to Pattern-Based Recovery of Design Components

Many reverse-engineering tools have been developed to derive abstract representations from source code. Yet most of these tools completely ignore recovery of the all-important rationale behind the design decisions that have led to its physical shape. Design patterns capture the rationale behind proven design solutions and discuss the trades-off among their alternatives. The authors argue that it is these patterns of thought that are at the root of many of the key elements of large-scale software systems, and that in order to comprehend these systems, we need to recover and understand the patterns on which they were built. The chapter presents the SPOOL environment for the reverse engineering of design components based on the structural descriptions of design patterns. It first gives an overview of the environment, then introduces a number of case studies, and finally discusses how pattern-based reverse engineering helped gain insight into the design rationale of some large-scale C++ software systems.

Chapter 7   Evaluation of Approaches to Clustering for Program Comprehension and Remodularization

When presented with a large legacy system which has little design information, an important approach to understanding and maintaining it is to automatically divide it into a more understandable set of modules or subsystems - a process called remodularization. This chapter reviews several remodularization approaches, which employ clustering technology. These approaches require making decisions that include which algorithms to use as well as which information to use as input to the algorithms. The chapter surveys several alternatives and presents some experimental evidence to help guide decision making. It also presents various approaches to evaluating the effectiveness of the existing approaches, including examining the coupling and cohesion of clusters, as well as the size of the largest cluster and the number of outstanding files.

Chapter 8   Automatic Architectural Clustering of Software

Early in the history of software engineering as a research field, it was recognized that the decomposition of a large software system into subsystems was essential for both the development and maintenance phases of a software project. In reality, however, software projects often fail to follow the principles of software engineering. This has given rise to architectural recovery that attempts to automatically remodularize, or cluster, a software system into meaningful subsystems. This chapter surveys current approaches to the clustering problem from researchers in the software engineering community. It focuses on the clustering techniques used in other disciplines, and argues that their utilization in a software context could lead to better solutions. The chapter concludes with research challenges and open problems of interest.

Chapter 9   Discovering Implicit Inheritance Relations in Non-Object-Oriented Code

In order to stay competitive in today's marketplace, businesses have to move some of their mission-critical legacy applications to web-based and network-centric platforms. Because of its wide acceptance as an available programming language on these kinds of platforms, Java is often cited as the language of choice for new systems. The size and complexity of legacy applications usually make it infeasible to rewrite the applications from the ground up, but require selected parts of the application to be migrated incrementally. A major obstacle in the migration of legacy systems written in C to Java is the extensive use of pointers in their source code. This chapter examines common usage patterns of pointers in C programs, shows how they implicitly express inheritance relationships between structured data types, and presents a formal approach to migrate such usage patterns to Java by creating an explicit class hierarchy.

Chapter 10   Design Properties and Evolvability of Object-Oriented Systems

One of the objectives of CSER's SPOOL project is to explore which properties of a design have the most impact on its evolvability. Evolvability of software is strongly related to the effort needed to identify and assess the impact of a change request. A systematic model to identify the impact boundaries at both the design and implementation level would reduce this effort and ease the difficult task of planning future releases. The authors have defined such a change impact model at the design level, and have carried it over to the implementation level using C++ as the target language. This chapter presents the change impact model of SPOOL. The authors show how this model has been used in experiments with large-scale object-oriented systems to identify some design properties that affect evolvability.

Chapter 11   Using Textual Redundancy to Study the Maintainability of Source Code

Large bodies of source code, documentation, and data have internal structure that results partly from the syntactic conventions of the representations and partly from the semantics of the application and its maintenance history. In particular, software systems will have multiple similar variants and versions corresponding to different platforms, sites, and points in time. Moreover, a single version will often have fragments of text copied from one place to another and modified to serve a new purpose. Although often shunned as a bad practice, this code cloning is to a certain extent inevitable, either because of the pragmatics of software maintenance or inadequate abstraction mechanisms in the representation language. This chapter discusses a purely text-based approach to clone detection. Since the approach does not rely on the extraction of a syntax tree to capture the surface semantics of the code, it is in particular suitable for legacy systems where parsers may not be readily available. It both contrasts and complements the approach used in the empirical study of Chapter 5.

Chapter 12   Building Parallel Applications Using Design Patterns

Parallel application design and development is a major area of interest in the domain of high-performance scientific and industrial computing. In fact, parallel computing is becoming an integral part of several major application domains - space, medicine, cancer and genetic research, graphics and animation, image processing, to name a few. With the advent of fast interconnected networks of workstations and PCs, it is now becoming increasingly possible to develop high-performance parallel applications using the combined computing powers of these networked resources, often at little or no extra cost. Consequently, high-speed networks and fast, general-purpose computers are contributing towards the mainstream adoption of parallel computing as an affordable alternative. However, parallel programs have inherent complexity over sequential code due to many low-level communication and synchronization details. To address this complexity, the authors propose a generic model for the design and development of parallel applications based on design patterns. These reusable components, *called parallel architectural skeletons*, hide most of the low-level details, thus enabling a developer to focus on application-level issues. The generic model enhances usability. The chapter describes an object-oriented, library-based implementation of the model in C++. The implementation is lightweight in that it does not necessitate any language extension. The skeleton library can be used as a building block for systematic, hierarchical development of parallel applications that are easier to maintain.

Chapter 13   The SPOOL Design Repository: Architecture, Schema, and Mechanisms

An essential part of reverse engineering is to represent the analyzed systems at a high level of abstraction, at the analysis or design level. End-user tools need access to this information, and thus a design repository is required for storing the analyzed systems. The SPOOL design repository was designed such that its schema would be resilient to change, adaptation, and extension, in order to easily address and accommodate new research projects. To this end, the authors have adopted the metamodel of the Unified Modeling Language (UML) as the basis of the SPOOL repository schema. In this chapter, they show how UML was used in reverse engineering by discussing the architecture and schema, as well as some of the key mechanisms, of the SPOOL design repository. The architecture is characterized by a suite of end-user tools, by the repository schema defining both the structure and the behavior of the repository, and by an object-oriented database as the persistent data store. The SPOOL repository mechanisms provide advanced functionality to end-user tools, supporting the traversal of complex object structures, the observation of models by views, and the accumulation of dependencies among high-level elements such as directories and files. The SPOOL repository constitutes a proof-of-concept of the implementation of the UML metamodel for reverse engineering purposes.

Chapter 14   The Software Bookshelf

Legacy software systems are typically complex, geriatric, and difficult to change, having evolved over decades and having passed through many developers. Nevertheless, these systems are mature, heavily used, and constitute massive corporate assets. Migrating such systems to modern platforms is a significant challenge due to the loss of information over time. This chapter reports on a landmark research project to design and implement an environment to support software migration. The project focused on migrating legacy PL/I source code to C++, with an initial phase of looking at redocumentation strategies. Recent technologies such as reverse engineering tools and World Wide Web standards now make it possible to build tools that greatly simplify the process of redocumenting legacy software systems.

The authors introduce the concept of a *software bookshelf* as a means to capture, organize, and manage information about a legacy software system. They distinguish three roles directly involved in the construction, population, and use of such a bookshelf: the *builder*, the *librarian*, and the *patron*. From these perspectives, they describe requirements for the bookshelf, as well as a generic architecture and a prototype implementation. The authors also discuss various parsing and analysis tools that were developed and integrated to assist in the recovery of useful information about a legacy system. Finally, they illustrate how a software bookshelf is populated with the information of a given software project and how the bookshelf can be used in a program understanding scenario. Reported results are based on a pilot project that developed a prototype bookshelf for a software system consisting of approximately 300K lines of code written in a PL/I dialect.

Chapter 15   Dynamic Documents Over the Web

Software and product information is more frequently being delivered as hypertext webs or documents because of the availability of the World-Wide Web and the associated communications infrastructure. However, this type of document, with its large number of files and hyperlinks, can become very complex and present significant usability problems for the creator, the maintainer, and the user. Because of this complexity, it becomes extremely difficult to implement and maintain dynamic aspects, such as views, of a document—a supposed advantage of a hyperlinked structure. In this chapter, the authors analyze the causes for these usability issues, and then describe some approaches that are being employed to address the underlying problems. They focus on how to make it easier to build, evolve, and use technical software documentation that is delivered via the web. In essence, their approach supports the separation of concerns for web-based documents into four orthogonal components: content, structure or organization, navigation, and presentation. They accomplish this separation by storing the information in databases and providing methods and tools to recreate the necessary views upon demand.

Chapter 16   Support for Geographically Dispersed
Software Teams

Globalization has the universal effect of distributing members of work teams, such as software development teams, geographically. This makes collaboration more difficult. Much recent research has been devoted to the exploration of means of alleviating the resulting problems. One of the approaches that seem most promising is based on the concept of a *collaborative virtual environment*. This contribution surveys the main concepts of collaborative virtual environments and describes work on a text-based virtual environment.

Chapter 17   Parsing C++ Code Despite Missing Declarations

This chapter addresses the problem of parsing a C++ software system that is known to compile correctly, but for which some header files are unavailable. A C++ program file typically depends on numerous included header files from the same system, a third party library, or the operating system standard libraries. It is not possible with a conventional parser to analyze C++ source code without obtaining the complete environment where the program is to be compiled. The authors study parsing ambiguities that result from missing header files. They propose a special parser that uses additional rules and type inference in order to determine the missing declarations. This new parser has reportedly achieved 100% accuracy on a large system with numerous missing header files.

Chapter 18   Toward Environment-Retargetable
Parser Generators

One of the most fundamental issues in software re-engineering is the representation of the source code at a higher level of abstraction than source text. Even though many researchers have investigated a variety of program representation schemes, one particular scheme, the Abstract Syntax Tree (AST), is of particular interest for its simplicity, generality, and completeness of the information it contains. This paper presents a methodology to generate Abstract Syntax Trees that conform to user-defined domain models that can be easily ported to different CASE tools, and that can be generated using public domain parser generators. The work reports on a prototypical tool that uses PCCTS and *flex* as a parser generator and a lexical analyzer, respectively. The resulting AST can be represented in terms of the conceptual modeling language Telos and can be used by various reverse engineering tools such as Rigi and Refine.

1.4   A Synopsis of CSER: Structure, Objectives, Principles, Results, and Directions

1.4.1   Background

Building and maintaining software products is an intellectual work performed by highly skilled professionals. The raw material for a successful and thriving software industry is thus principally the supply of highly qualified personnel.

The shortage of highly qualified personnel in the software industry is not a new phenomenon. In fact, statistics from around the world indicate that the problems facing the industry will become even worse in the coming years due to the explosive growth facing the software industry. Educational institutions cannot produce graduates fast enough.

Equally critical is the gap between the skills possessed by future software professionals and researchers produced by university graduate programs and the skills sought in these graduates by the software industry as well as by academic and research organizations. David L. Parnas emphasized this gap in a 1999 article, "Software Engineering Programs Are Not Computer Science Programs" (*IEEE Software*, November-December 1999).

The nature of academic computer science and software engineering research has shifted substantially over the past twenty years. In the past, the research was largely individualistic and long term, leading to scientific papers dubbed "research nuggets" by John Mylolpoulos of University of Toronto. The emphasis has since moved from research that is based on networking and large-scale collaboration, such as the Japanese Fifth Generation project or the European Union ESPRIT initiative, to research that is more team- and mission-oriented, and synergistic on a smaller, yet on a more effective scale.

These observations and a conviction that there is more to software production than the knowledge of data structures, programming languages, formal languages and computational complexity led to a series of meetings and brainstorming sessions among a number of groups from Canadian software and telecommunication industries, universities, and government laboratories. The result was the creation in June of 1996 of the Consortium for Software Engineering Research, or CSER.[1] The five founding industrial partners were Bell Canada, IBM Canada, Mitel Corporation, Nortel Networks and Object Technology International, Inc. Those partners have recently been joined by Sun Microsystems Canada. The founding academic partners were Acadia University, Université de Montréal, the University of Ottawa, the University of Toronto, the University of Waterloo, the University of Victoria, and the University of British Columbia. Recent university partners are Carleton University, the University of Alberta, and the École Polytechnique de Montréal.

The research projects of the Consortium are partially funded by the industrial partners and partially by the Natural Sciences and Engineering Research Council of Canada (NSERC)—a Canadian research funding agency. Technical and administrative management of the Consortium is provided by the National Research Council of Canada (NRC)—specifically by the members of the Software Engineering Group of the Institute for Information Technology.

Total funding for Phase 1 (1996-1999) of CSER was about 7.5 million Canadian dollars (about 4.7 million U.S. dollars) including in-kind industrial contributions. Phase 2 (1999-2002) funding presently stands at about 8 million Canadian dollars, with additional funding earmarked for projects under review.

1.4.2 Structure

CSER is an industry-directed organization. The industrial involvement is central to the concept, but it means much more than just providing funds for the researchers. Each of the industrial members takes the lead in defining the research projects and opens its development environment and proprietary software to the academic researchers. The industrial partners directly participate in the research activities by committing own employees.

This direct participation is the main difference between CSER style of collaborative research and more traditional research consortiums. It also makes the recruitment of new industrial partners in CSER more challenging than usual since the time of key employees is perceived by companies as being more precious than an equivalent cash contribution.

Another important CSER principle is the sharing of research results among industrial partners. Each research partner has access to the research results of all

---

[1]The creation of CSER was championed by Dr. W. Morven Gentleman, then with the National Research Council of Canada, Ottawa, and by Dr. Jacob Slomin, then with the the IBM Centre for Advanced Studies, Toronto.

CSER projects. This practice is facilitated by the fact that CSER research is pre-competitive in nature: industrial partners can significantly leverage their investment in CSER.

The industry orientation of CSER is also reflected in the governance of the Consortium. The Board of Directors manages the Consortium. It consists of the representatives of three industrial partners and two senior, non-funded academic appointees who represent university interests. A representative of NRC acts as Research Director, and a representative from NSERC's Partnership Program acts as Program Officer. These two positions have non-voting, observer status. An Executive Director handles legal and financial matters, and is assisted by an Operations Manager who deals with day-to-day issues.

The research projects of the Consortium are organized into two coherent themes. At the time of this writing, two themes were active:

1. *Empirical Evolution from Legacy Software to Modern Architectures* and
2. *Software Quality: Verification and Validation.*

Projects under each of the themes are directed by a Steering Committee, which consists of three members selected from the active projects. The Steering Committee reviews the progress and the direction of the research projects. It also reviews new proposals and applications. The Steering Committee then makes recommendations to the Board, which makes the final decisions.

Currently, the total CSER research effort, covering all contributions from all of the partners, stands at approximately 18 million Canadian dollars for five research projects from 1996 to 1999 and six research projects from 1999 to 2002.

1.4.3 Objectives and Principles

The objectives of CSER as stated in its charter are:

1. to focus university research and education on software engineering problems relevant to the industry,
2. to contribute through these research projects to the body of knowledge of the software engineering field,
3. to provide to its industrial and academic members an environment conducive to research, in which each research project will benefit from synergies with other projects, and
4. to improve the competence in the field of software engineering among university graduates through relevant educational programs and among current software professionals through dissemination of research results.

The research projects achieve these objectives by conforming to the strict requirements imposed on them. Each research project must:

1. be conducted at least partly in an industrial setting;
2. address industrial-scale problems using industrial-scale data; and
3. include empirical studies.

These requirements provide reciprocal benefits to the contributing research-ers: They give the researchers, both faculty and supported students, the oppor-tunity to spend time in the industrial laboratories, work with industrial-size and industrial-quality code that is hard to obtain otherwise, pursue real problems, and validate their results, thus increasing the quality and credibility of the re-search.

CSER is cognizant of the issues facing faculty members at the universities. Projects reconcile short-term goal-oriented research with longer-term higher-risk research. This approach creates an environment that nurtures innovation while addressing current problems.

A strong emphasis on continuity ensures the quality of the research and real-izes the desired impact on education and training. Continuity is present in the research programs, in the commitment of the industrial partners, and in the over-all project objectives.

Regular meetings are a key feature of the Consortium. All of the partici-pants—industry, university, and government researchers, as well as students—attend the general meetings held twice a year and usually hosted by an industrial member. The meetings provide a forum for the exchange of ideas, problems, and their solutions. CSER participants credit these meetings with maintaining both the quality and the progress of the research projects.

Each research project clearly identifies the benefits to the industrial partners, academic partners, CSER, and the software engineering community at large. The Consortium supports and encourages the incorporation of the generated knowledge into the academic curriculum. It is this feature that defines CSER's emphasis on education and training.

1.4.4   Results

Despite the very short time during which CSER has been in existence, it can claim many successes. Those successes and benefits are directly attributed to the stated objectives and principles.

First—as evidenced by this book - CSER has witnessed significant research results. It generated well over 100 publications and presentations directly attrib-utable to the individual projects. Many of those publications are co-authored with the industry partners. At least three academic partners - namely the Univer-sity of Ottawa, the University of Victoria, and the University of Waterloo - have been developing new software engineering curricula. At least 15 new courses throughout the participating universities originated from the CSER experience.

Dr. Timothy Lethbridge states that "CSER research directly influenced the design of the Software Engineering program in the School of Information Technology and Engineering at the University of Ottawa." He adds that CSER has provided him, as one of the principal designers of the program, "with direct access to top software companies and academics.... No other Canadian organization brings together the same kind of software engineering brainpower."

Second, some of the results of CSER research have found their way into the processes and methodologies by which industrial partners develop and maintain their software products. The industrial partners claim significant cost and time savings. Peter J. Perry, Head of the Strategic Technology Group at Mitel Corporation, comments on a tool developed by a CSER research team and field-tested at his organization:

> In the first of phase of CSER, we halved the time taken to get new staff productive from 12 to 18 months to 6 to 9 months. Commercial tools of similar function cost much more than the cost of the research to Mitel.

In addition to having specific problems solved, industry partners benefit from improved access to university researchers and their graduate students. Many industrial partners have hired the students who have worked on their CSER projects.

Third, CSER-sponsored students have been major beneficiaries. The consortium environment is an excellent setting for applied graduate work. CSER has provided funding for over 80 students. Students benefit from the exposure to many leading researchers and industry practitioners well beyond the capabilities of a single academic institution. CSER provides two opportunities for such exposure. On the one hand, students carry out some of their research at the company site, working alongside industry researchers. On the other hand, they participate in the semi-annual CSER meetings where they interact with the other CSER participants.

A great majority of these students have or will graduate with masters and doctoral degrees. CSER is proud of the fact that some of the Ph.D. graduates and post doctoral fellows progressed into lead researcher positions within the Consortium. Additionally, many more graduate and undergraduate students have been affected by the new and modified courses designed by CSER researchers.

Fourth, and possibly the most significant benefit of the Consortium, is a change in the attitudes both within the research community and among the industrial partners.

Initial meetings of CSER were characterized by rather narrow and inward-looking research reports. Since the problems encountered and the tools needed by the researchers to address these problems were very similar among the various projects, the discussions slowly converged toward the commonalties. The most recent semi-annual meeting took the form of a series of mini-workshops devoted to these common topics. The synergy was also demonstrated at the International Conference on Software Engineering held in June 2000. CSER researchers organized two of the collocated workshops, based on the issues that have directly originated from previous CSER meetings.

CSER has established a framework for collaboration that engenders trust and reciprocity. Not only are the university researchers exchanging ideas, but CSER industrial partners share proprietary software with the other CSER members. For example, IBM has agreed to make its VisualAge C++ Professional APIs available to all CSER participants. Similarly, Bell Canada licensed the use of its Datrix analysis suite for research purposes to all CSER participants. Moreover, some of the tools developed within an IBM-led project are being deployed at Mitel Corporation.

1.4.5   Directions

The first research theme—Empirical Evolution from Legacy Software to Modern Architectures—was selected after lengthy discussions. That selection was in part precipitated by the then impending Year 2000 problems. But the participants felt that the migration of software—whether due to changing user requirements, changing platforms, or other reasons—will dominate software industry for years to come.

Clearly, they have been proven right. The meteoritic rise of the World Wide Web and related technologies have caused a new wave of migration issues. We need to concern ourselves with new computing paradigms, new system architectures, and new applications enabled by an enormous increase in computing power. We now need to migrate not only code but also the whole wealth of enterprise assets encapsulated in the underlying data. Isn't the maintenance of very large websites merely an instance of the migration problem?

If we can be so bold, the recently created second theme of CSER research — Software Quality: Verification and Validation—will also endure. It is clear that software is ubiquitous. Software is written in massive amounts all over the world. User expectations of the functionality to be provided are growing at a much faster rate than our ability to provide that functionality. The user demands reliable, usable, and high-performance software. The research community is being challenged to develop tools and methodologies that would enable the software industry to fulfill these needs.

1.4.6   Conclusions

It is evident that the Consortium for Software Engineering Research has embraced the challenges that it originally set out. It has increased the number of university graduates with the right skills in order to meet software engineering industry needs. It has increased the capability of software professionals to address complex problems in software engineering and to keep abreast of changes in software technology. It has created strong linkages between industry personnel and university-based researchers, permitting the exchange of ideas and the fostering of solutions to industry driven problems. And finally, it has increased the number of academic resources and expertise in the software engineering practice.

Part I

Empirical Studies

2
Object-Oriented Metrics: A Review of Theory and Practice

Khaled El-Emam

2.1   Introduction

In today's business environment, competitive pressures demand the production of reliable software with shorter and shorter release intervals. This is especially so in commercial high-reliability domains such as telecommunications and the aerospace industry. One recipe for success is to increase process capability. There is recent compelling evidence that process capability is positively associated with productivity and quality. (Clark, 1997; El-Emam and Birk, 2000a, 2000b; Flowe and Thordahl, 1994; Goldenson and Herbsleb, 1995; Jones, 1999; Krishnan and Kellner, 1999). Quantitative management of software quality is a hallmark of high-process capability (El-Emam et al., 1998; Software Engineering Institute, 1995).

Quantitative management of software quality is a broad area. In this chapter we focus on only one aspect: the use of *software product metrics* for quality management. Product metrics are objective[1] measures of the structure of software artifacts. The artifacts may be, for example, source code or analysis and design models.

The true value of product metrics comes from their association with measures of important external attributes (ISO/IEC, 1996). An external attribute is measured with respect to how the product relates to its environment (Fenton, 1991). Examples of external attributes are testability, reliability and maintainability. Practitioners, whether they are developers, managers, or quality assurance personnel, are really concerned with the external attributes. However, they cannot measure many of the external attributes directly until quite late in a project's or even a product's lifecycle. Therefore, they can use product metrics as

---

[1] Objective means that if you repeatedly measure the same software artifact (and the artifact does not change), then you will get the same values. This is because in most cases the metrics are automated. The alternative is to have subjective metrics. Subjective metrics are not covered in this chapter.

leading indicators of the external attributes that are important to them. For instance, if we know that a certain coupling metric is a good leading indicator of quality as measured in terms of the number of faults, then we can minimize coupling during design because we know that in doing so we are also reducing rework costs.

Specifically, product metrics can be used in at least three ways:

- Making system-level predictions.
- Early identification of *high-risk* software components.
- The construction of preventative design and programming guidelines.

These uses allow an organization, for instance, to get an early estimate of quality, and to take early action to reduce the number of faulty software components.

Considerable effort has been spent by the software engineering research community in developing product metrics for both procedural and object-oriented systems, and empirically establishing their relationship to measures of important external attributes. The latter is known as the *empirical validation* of the metric. Once the research community has demonstrated that a metric or set of metrics is empirically valid in a number of different contexts and systems, organizations can take these metrics and use them to build appropriate prediction models and guidelines customized to their own context.

The objective of this chapter is to provide a review of contemporary object-oriented metrics. We start by describing how object-oriented metrics can be used in practice by software organizations. This is followed by an overview of some of the most popular object-oriented metrics, and those that have been studied most extensively. The subsequent section describes current cognitive theories used in software engineering that justify the development of object-oriented metrics. This is followed by a further elaboration of the cognitive theory to explain the cognitive mechanisms for metric thresholds. The empirical evidence supporting the above theories is then reviewed. The chapter is concluded with recommendations for the practical usage of object-oriented metrics, a discussion of the match between the empirical results and the theory, and directions for future research.

2.2   The Practical Use of Object-Oriented Metrics

In this section we describe how product metrics can be used by organizations for quality control and management.

2.2.1   Making System-Level Predictions

Typically, software product metrics are collected on individual components for a single system. Predictions on individual components can then be aggregated to give overall system level predictions. For example, in two recent studies using object-oriented metrics, the authors predicted the proportion of faulty classes in a whole system (El-Emam et al., 2001). This is an example of using predictions of fault-proneness for each class to draw conclusions about the overall quality of a system. One can also build prediction models of the total number of faults and fault density (Evanco, 1997). Similarly, another study used object-oriented metrics to predict the effort to develop each class, and these were then aggregated to produce an overall estimate of the whole system's development cost (Briand and Wuest, 1999).

2.2.2   Identifying High-Risk Components

The definition of a high-risk component varies depending on the context. For example, a high-risk component may be one that contains any faults found during testing (Briand et al., 1993; Lanubile and Visaggio, 1997), one that contains any faults found during operation (Khoshgoftaar et al., 1999), or one that is costly to correct after an error has been found (Almeida et al., 1998; Basili et al., 1997; Briand et al., 1993). Recent evidence suggests that most faults are found in only a few of a system's components (Fenton and Ohlsson, 2000; Kaaniche and Kanoun, 1996; Moller and Paulish, 1993; Ohlsson and Alberg, 1996). If these few components can be identified early, then an organization can take mitigating actions. Examples of mitigating actions include focusing defect detection activities on high-risk components by optimally allocating testing resources (W. Harrison, 1988), or redesigning components that are likely to cause field failures or be costly to maintain.

Early prediction is commonly cast as a binary classification problem.[2] This is achieved through a *quality model* that classifies components into either a high- or low-risk category. An overview of a quality model is shown in Figure 2.1. A quality model is developed using a statistical modeling or machine learning technique, or a combination of techniques. This is done using historical data. Once constructed, such a model takes as input the values on a set of metrics (M_1 ... M_k) for a particular component, and produces a prediction of the risk category (say either high or low risk) for that component.

A number of organizations have integrated quality models and modeling techniques into their overall decision making process. For example, Lyu et al. (1995) report on a prototype system to support developers with software quality models, and the EMERALD system is reportedly routinely used for risk assessment at Nortel (Hudepohl et al., 1996a, 1996b). Ebert and Liedtke describe the

---

[2] It is not, however, *always* the case that binary classifiers are used. For example, there have been studies that predict the number of faults in individual components (Khoshgoftaar et al., 1996) and that produce point estimates of maintenance effort (Jorgensen, 1995; Li and Henry, 1993).

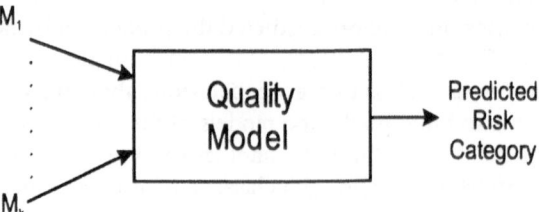

Figure 2.1. Definition of a quality model.

application of quality models to control the quality of switching software at Al-catel (Ebert and Liedtke, 1995).

In the case of object-oriented metrics, an example of a quality model was presented in a recent study using design metrics on a Java application (El-Emam et al., 2001). This model was developed using logistic regression (Hosmer and Lemeshow, 1989):

$$\pi = \frac{1}{1 + e^{-(-3.97 + 0.464 NAI + 1.47 OCMEC + 1.06 DIT)}} \qquad (2.1)$$

In the above equation:
- The variable π is the predicted probability that a class will have a fault.
- NAI is the total number of attributes defined in the class.
- $OCMEC$ is the number of other classes that have methods with parameter types of this class (this is a form of export coupling).
- DIT is the depth of the inheritance tree that measures how far down an inheritance hierarchy a class is.

NAI, $OCMEC$, and DIT are examples of object-oriented metrics. In fact, in this case, all of these metrics can be collected easily from high-level designs, and therefore one can in principle use this model to predict the probability that a class will have a fault at an early stage of development. A calibration of this model, described in El-Emam et al., (2001), indicated that if the predicted probability of a fault was greater than 0.33, then the class should be flagged for special managerial action (i.e., it would be considered to be high risk).

The metrics in the above example are class-level static metrics. Object-oriented metrics can also be defined at the method level or at the system level. Our focus here is only on class level metrics. Furthermore, metrics may be collected statically or dynamically.

Static metrics can be collected by an analysis of the software artifact. Dynamic metrics require execution of the software application in order to collect the metric values, which makes them difficult to collect at early stages of the design. The focus in this chapter is on static metrics.

2.2.3   Design and Programming Guidelines

An appealing operational approach for constructing design and programming guidelines using software product metrics is to make an analogy with conventional statistical quality control: identify the range of values that are acceptable or unacceptable, and take action for the components with unacceptable values (Kitchenham and Linkman, 1990). This means identifying thresholds on the software product metrics that delineate between *acceptable* and *unacceptable*. In summarizing their experiences using software product measures, Szentes and Gras (1986) state "the complexity measures of modules may serve as a useful early warning system against poorly written programs and program designs... Software complexity metrics can be used to pinpoint badly written program code or program designs when the values exceed predefined maxima or minima." They argue that such thresholds can be defined subjectively based on experience. In addition to being useful during development, Coallier et al. (1999) present a number of thresholds for procedural measures that Bell Canada uses for risk assessment during the acquisition of software products. The authors note that the thresholds result in 2 to 3 percent of the procedures and classes that are flagged for manual examination. Instead of thresholds based on experience, some authors suggest the use of percentiles for this purpose. For example, Lewis and Henry (1989) describe a system that uses percentiles on procedural measures to identify potentially problematic procedures. Kitchenham and Linkman (1990) suggest using the 75th percentile as a cut-off value. More sophisticated approaches include identifying multiple thresholds simultaneously, such as in Almeida et al. (1998) and Basili et al. (1997).

In an object-oriented context, thresholds have been similarly defined by Lorenz and Kidd (1994) as "heuristic values used to set ranges of desirable and undesirable metric values for measured software." Henderson-Sellers (1996) emphasize the practical utility of object-oriented metric thresholds by stating that "an alarm would occur whenever the value of a specific internal metric exceeded some predetermined threshold." Lorenz and Kidd (1994) present a number of thresholds for object-oriented metrics based on their experiences with Smalltalk and C++ projects.

Similarly, Rosenberg et al. (1999) have developed thresholds for a number of popular object-oriented metrics that are used for quality management at NASA GSFC. French (1999) describes a technique for deriving thresholds, and applies it to metrics collected from Ada95 and C++ programs. Chidamber et al. (1998) state that the premise behind managerial use of object-oriented metrics is that extreme (outlying) values signal the presence of high complexity that may require management action. They then define a lower bound for thresholds at the 80th percentile (i.e., at most 20% of the observations are considered to be above the threshold). The authors note that this is consistent with the common Pareto (80/20) heuristic.

2.3   Object-Oriented Metrics

Structural properties that capture interconnections among classes are believed to be important to measure (for example different types of *coupling* and *cohesion)*. This is because they are considered to affect cognitive complexity (see next section). Object-oriented metrics measure these structural properties. Coupling metrics characterize the static usage dependencies among the classes in an object-oriented system (Briand et al.,1999). Cohesion metrics characterize the extent to which the methods and attributes of a class belong together (Briand et al., 1998). In addition, *inheritance* is also believed to play an important role in the understandability of object-oriented applications.

A considerable number of such interconnected object-oriented metrics have been developed by the research community. For example, see (F. Brite e Abreu and Carapuca, 1994; Benlarbi and Melo, 1999; Briand et al., 1997; Cartwright and Shepperd, 2000; Chidamber and Kemerer, 1994; Henderson-Sellers, 1996; Li and Henry, 1993; Lorenz and Kidd, 1994; Tang et al., 1999). By far, the most popular of these is the metrics suite developed by Chidamber and Kemerer (1994) (known as the CK metrics). For historical reasons the CK metrics are the most referenced (Briand et al., 1999), and most commercial metrics collection tools collect these metrics. Another comprehensive set of metrics that capture important structural characteristics, namely different types of coupling, have been defined by Briand et al. (1997). These two sets of metrics have received a considerable amount of empirical study. A summary of the metrics can found in Table 2.1. Many of the metrics can be collected at the design stage of the life cycle. The table indicates which of the metrics can be collected accurately at the design phase. If the entry in the "Des" column is "Y," then the metric is typically available during design. Even though some of the metrics can be collected at design time, in practice, they are frequently collected from the source code during validation studies. Of the set shown, only the CK metrics suite currently is known to have a number of commercial and public domain analyzers (for Java, see CodeWork, 2000, Metameta, 2000, Power-Software, 2000b; and for C++, see Devanbu, 2000, ObjectSoft, 2000, Power-Software, 2000a)[3]. In addition there is at least one tool that can be used to collect the CK metrics directly from design documents (Number-Six-Software, 2000).

2.4   Cognitive Theory of Object-Oriented Metrics

A theoretical basis for developing quantitative models relating product metrics and external quality metrics has been provided in (Briand, Wuest, Ikonomovski,

---

[3] Note that this is not a comprehensive list of tools available on the market today. Also, please note that not all of the analyzers will collect all of the CK metrics; some only collect a subset.

and Lounis, 1998), and is summarized in Figure 2.2. This theory hypothesizes that the structural properties of a software component (such as its coupling) have an impact on its cognitive complexity. Cognitive complexity is defined as the mental burden of the individuals who have to deal with the component.

Table 2.1. Summary of object-oriented metrics.

Metric Acronym	Des	Definition
CBO	N	This is the coupling between object classes coupling metric (Chidamber and Kemerer, 1994). A class is coupled with another if the methods of one class use the methods or attributes of the other. In this definition, uses can mean as a member type, parameter type, method local variable type or cast. CBO is the number of other classes with which a class is coupled. It includes inheritance-based coupling (i.e., coupling between classes related via inheritance). A variant of CBO, known as CBO', excludes inheritance-based coupling (Chidamber and Kemerer, 1991).
RFC	N	This is the response for a class coupling metric (Chidamber and Kemerer, 1994). The response set of a class consists of the set M of methods of the class, and the set of methods invoked directly by the methods in M (i.e., the set of methods that can potentially be executed in response to a message received by that class). RFC is the number of methods in the response set of the class. A variant of RFC excludes methods indirectly invoked by a method in M (Chidamber and Kemerer, 1991).
DIT	Y	The depth of inheritance tree (Chidamber and Kemerer, 1994) metric is defined as the length of the longest path from the class to the root in the inheritance hierarchy.
NOC	Y	This is the number of children inheritance metric (Chidamber and Kemerer, 1994). This metric counts the number of classes that inherit from a particular class (i.e., the number of classes in the inheritance tree down from a class).
LCOM	N	This is a cohesion metric that was defined in Chidamber and Kemerer, (1994). It measures the number of pairs of methods in the class that have no attributes in common, minus the number of pairs of methods that do. If the difference is negative, the metric value is set to zero.

Table 2.1. *(continued)*.

WMC	Y[4]	This is the weighted methods per class metric (Chidamber and Kemerer 1994), and can be classified as a traditional complexity metric. It is a count of the methods in a class. It has been suggested that neither methods from ancestor classes nor *friends* in C++ be counted (Basili et al. 1996; Chidamber and Kemerer, 1995). The developers of this metric leave the weighting scheme as an implementation decision (Chidamber and Kemerer, 1994). Some authors weight it using cyclomatic complexity (Li and Henry, 1993). However, others do not adopt a weighting scheme (Basili et al., 1996; Tang et al., 1999). In general, if cyclomatic complexity is used for weighting, then WMC cannot be collected at early design stages. Alternatively, if no weighting scheme is used, then WMC becomes simply a size measure (the number of methods implemented in a class), also known as NM.
IFCAIC	Y	These coupling metrics are counts of interactions among classes. The metrics distinguish among the class relationships (friendship, inheritance, none), different types of interactions, and the locus of impact of the interaction (Briand et al., 1997).
ACAIC	Y	
OCAIC	Y	
FCAEC	Y	
DCAEC	Y	The acronyms for the metrics indicate what types of interactions are counted:
OCAEC	Y	
IFCMIC	Y	• The first or first two letters indicate the relationship:
ACMIC	Y	• A: coupling to ancestor classes;
OCMIC	Y	• D: coupling to descendents;
FCMEC	Y	• F: coupling to friend classes;
DCMEC	Y	• IF: inverse friend coupling; and
OCMEC	Y	• O: other (i.e., none of the above).
OMMIC	N	• The next two letters indicate the type of interaction between classes c and d:
IFMMIC	N	
AMMIC	N	• CA: there is a class-attribute interaction between
OMMEC	N	classes c and d if c has an attribute of type d.

Individuals that may be prone to cognitive complexity are the developers, testers, inspectors, and maintainers. High cognitive complexity leads to a component exhibiting undesirable external qualities, such as increased fault-

---

[4] Only the unweighted version of WMC is available during design. If weights are used, then this would depend on the characteristics of the weighting scheme. For example, cyclomatic complexity weights would certainly not be available during design.

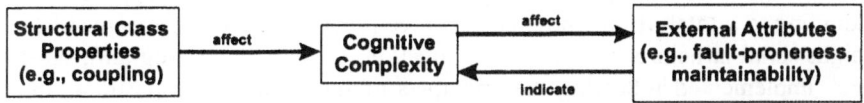

Figure 2.2. Theoretical basis for the development of object-oriented product metrics

proneness and reduced maintainability. Accordingly, object-oriented product metrics that affects cognitive complexity will be related with fault-proneness.

It should be noted that if a cognitive theory is substantiated, this could have important implications. It would provide us with a clear mechanism that would explain the introduction of faults into object-oriented applications.

2.4.1   Distribution of Functionality

In applications developed using functional decomposition, functionality is localized in specific procedures, the contents of data structures are accessed directly, and data central to an application is often globally accessible (Wilde et al., 1993). Functional decomposition is believed to make procedural programs easier to understand because such programs are built upon a hierarchy in which a top-level function calls lower-level functions to carry out smaller chunks of the overall task (Wiedenbeck et al., 1999). Hence tracing through a program to understand its global functionality is facilitated. This is not necessarily the case with object-oriented applications.

The object-oriented strategies of limiting the responsibility of a class and re-using it in multiple contexts results in a profusion of small classes in object-oriented systems (Wilde et al., 1993). For instance, Chidamber and Kemerer (Chidamber and Kemerer, 1994) found in two systems studied[5] that most classes tended to have a small number of methods (0-10), suggesting that most classes are relatively simple in their construction, providing specific abstraction and functionality. Another study of three systems performed at Bellcore[6] found that half or more of the methods are fewer than four Smalltalk lines or two C++ statements, suggesting that the classes consist of small methods (Wilde et al., 1993). Many small classes imply many interactions among the classes and a distribution of functionality across them.

In one experimental study with students and professional programmers, Boehm-Davis et al. (1992) compared maintenance time for three pairs of func-

---

[5] One system was developed in C++ and the other in Smalltalk.

[6] The study consisted of analyzing C++ and Smalltalk systems and interviewing the developers for two of them. For a C++ system, method size was measured as the number of executable statements, and for Smalltalk size was measured by uncommented nonblank lines of code.

tionally equivalent programs (implementing three different applications, amounting to a total of nine programs). Three programs were implemented in a straight serial structure (i.e., one main function, or monolithic program), three were implemented following the principles of functional decomposition, and three were implemented in the object-oriented style, but without inheritance. In general, it took the students more time to change the object-oriented programs, and the professionals exhibited the same effect, although not as strongly. Furthermore, both the students and professionals noted that they found that it was most difficult to recognize program units in the object-oriented programs, and the students felt that it was also most difficult to find information in the object-oriented programs.

Widenbeck et al. (1999) make a distinction between program functionality at the local level and at the global (application) level. At the local level they argue that the object-oriented paradigm's concept of encapsulation ensures that methods are bundled together with the data on which they operate, making it easier to construct appropriate mental models and specifically to understand the individual functionality of a class. At the global level, functionality is dispersed among many interacting classes, making it harder to understand what the program is doing. They supported this in an experiment with equivalent small C++ (with no inheritance) and Pascal programs where the subjects answered questions about the functionality of the C++ program more easily. They then performed an experiment with larger programs. The number of correct answers for the subjects with the C++ program (with inheritance) on questions about its functionality was not much better than guessing. While this study was done with novices, it supports the general notions that high cohesion makes object-oriented programs easier to understand and high coupling makes them more difficult to understand.

2.4.2   A Cognitive Model

Cant et al. (1995) have proposed a general cognitive theory of software complexity that elaborates on the impact of structure on understandability. At the core of the cognitive theory proposed is a human memory model that consists mainly of short-term and long-term memory.[7] In the same light, Tracz (1979) has claimed that "the organization and limitations of the human memory are perhaps the most significant aspects of the human thought process which affect the computer programmer." Hence, there is a view within the software engineering community that the human memory model is a reasonable point of departure for understanding structural properties on understandability.

---

[7] Tracz (1979) also discusses very-short-term memory, which plays a role in attention and perception. However, this does not play a big role in cognitive theories that are used to associate software product metrics to understandability. Neither does the concept of extended memory presented by Newell and Simon (1972). Therefore, they will not be discussed further.

Cant et al. argue that comprehension consists of both *chunking* and *tracing*. Chunking involves recognizing groups of statements and extracting from them information that is remembered as a single mental abstraction. These chunks are further grouped together into larger chunks forming a hierarchical structure. Tracing involves scanning through a program, either forwards or backwards, in order to identify relevant chunks. Subsequently, they formulate a model of cognitive complexity for a particular chunk, say D, which is the sum of three components: (1) the difficulty of understanding the chunk itself; (2) the difficulty of understanding all the other chunks upon which D depends; and (3) the difficulty of tracing the dependencies on the chunks upon which D depends. Davis (1984) presents a similar argument where he states that "any model of program complexity based on chunking should account for the complexity of the chunks themselves and also the complexity of their relationship."

In order to operationalize this model, it is necessary to define a *chunk*. Tracz (1979) considers a *module* to be a chunk. However, it is not clear what exactly a module is. Cant et al. (1995) make a distinction between elementary and compound chunks. Elementary chunks consist only of sequentially self-contained statements. Compound chunks are those that contain within them other chunks. Procedures containing a number of procedure calls are considered as compound chunks. At the same time, procedures containing no procedure calls may also be compound chunks. If a procedure contains more than one recognizable subunit, it is equivalent to a module containing many procedure calls in the sense that both contain within them multiple subchunks. Subsequent work by Cant et al. (1994) operationally defined a chunk within object-oriented software as a method. However, Henderson-Sellers (1996) notes that a class is also an important type of (compound) chunk.

One factor contended to have an impact on complexity is chunk familiarity (Henderson-Sellers, 1996). It is argued that chunks that are referenced more often (i.e., high export coupling) will be more familiar since they are used more often. Davis (1984) makes a similar argument for procedural programs. Therefore, when tracing other chunks more traces will lead to those with the highest export coupling. Furthermore, Henderson-Sellers (1996) applies the concept of cohesion to chunking by stating that a chunk with low cohesion will be more difficult to recognize since functions performed by the chunk will be unrelated, and hence more difficult to understand.

Henderson-Sellers (1996) notes that tracing disrupts the process of chunking. This occurs when it becomes necessary to understand another chunk, as when a method calls another method in a different class (method-method interaction), or when an inherited property needs to be understood. Such disruptions may cause knowledge of the original chunk to be lost. This then is contended to have a direct effect on complexity. In fact, tracing dependencies is a common task when understanding object-oriented software.

Cant et al. (1994) also performed an empirical study whereby they compared subjective ratings by two expert programmers of the complexity of understanding classes with objective measures of dependencies in an object-oriented system. Their results demonstrate a concordance between the objective measures of dependency and subjective ratings of understandability.

Wilde et al.'s (1993) findings are also concordant with this conclusion, in that programmers have to understand a method's context of use by tracing back through the chain of calls that reach it, and tracing the chain of methods it uses. Their findings were from an interview study of two C++ object-oriented systems at Bellcore and a PC Smalltalk environment. The three systems investigated span different application domains.

Related work on mental representation of object-oriented software provides further insights into the structural properties that are most difficult to understand. These works build on theories of text comprehension. Modern theories of text comprehension propose three levels of mental representation (Dijk and Kintsch, 1983; Kintsch, 1986). The first level, the *verbatim representation* consists of the literal form of the text. The second level, the *propositional textbase,* consists of the propositions of the text and their relationships. The third level, the *situation model* represents the situation in the world that the text describes. Pennington (1987a, 1987b) subsequently applied this model to the comprehension of procedural programs, where she proposed two levels of mental representation, the program model and the domain model, which correspond to the latter two levels of the text comprehension model above. The program model consists of elementary operations and control flow information. The domain model consists of data flow and program function information.

Burkhardt et al. (1997) applied this three level model to object-oriented software. For the situation model they make a distinction between a static part and a dynamic part. The static part consists of (a) the problem objects which directly model objects of the problem domain; (b) the inheritance/composition relationships between objects; (c) reified objects; and (d) the main goals of the problem. The dynamic part represents the communication between objects and variables. The static part corresponds to client-server relationships, and the dynamic part corresponds to data flow relationships. Based on this model, Burkhardt et al. performed an experiment. They asked their subjects to study an object-oriented application and then answer questions about it. Subsequently the subjects were asked to perform either documentation or a reuse task. The authors of the study found that the static part of the situation model is better developed than the dynamic, even for experts. Furthermore, there was no difference between experts and novices in their understanding of the dynamic part. Their findings suggest that inheritance and class-attribute coupling may have less of an impact on understandability than both cohesion and coupling.

Even though the above studies suggest that inheritance has little impact on understandability, within the software engineering community inheritance is strongly believed to make the understandability of object-oriented software difficult. According to a survey of object-oriented practitioners 55% of respondents agree that inheritance depth is a factor in understanding object-oriented programs (Daly et al., 1995). "Inheritance gives rise to distributed class descriptions. That is, the complete description for a class D can only be assembled by examining D as well as each of D's superclasses. Because different classes are described at different places in the source code of a program (often spread across several different files), there is no single place a programmer can turn to get a complete description of a class" (Leijter et al., 1992). While this argument is stated in terms of source code, it is not difficult to generalize it to design documents. The study by Wilde et al. (1993) indicated that, to understand the behavior of a method, one has to trace inheritance dependencies, which may be considerably complicated due to dynamic binding. A similar point was made by Leijter et al. (1992) about the understandability of programs in such languages as C++ that support dynamic binding.

In a set of interviews with 13 experienced users of object-oriented programming, Daly et al. (1995) noted that if the inheritance hierarchy is designed properly, then the effect of distributing functionality over the inheritance hierarchy will not be detrimental to understanding. However, it has been argued that there exists increasing conceptual inconsistency as one travels down an inheritance hierarchy (i.e., deeper levels in the hierarchy are characterized by inconsistent extensions or specializations of super classes) (Dvorak, 1994). Therefore inheritance hierarchies are likely to be improperly designed in practice. The study by Dvorak supports this argument. He found that subjects were more inconsistent in placing classes deeper in the inheritance hierarchy than they were in placing them lower levels in the inheritance hierarchy.

2.4.3 Summary

This section provided a theoretical framework to explain the mechanism by which object-oriented metrics could be associated with fault-proneness. If this hypothesized mechanism matches reality, then we would expect object-oriented metrics to be good predictors of external quality attributes, in particular, fault-proneness. In the subsequent sections, we will review the empirical studies that test these associations.

It must be recognized that the above cognitive theory suggests only one possible mechanism of what could impact external metrics. Other mechanisms can play an important role as well. For example, some studies have showed that software engineers experiencing high levels of mental and physical stress tend to produce more faults (Furuyama et al., 1994, 1997). Reducing schedules and many changes in requirements may induce mental stress. Physical stress may be a temporary illness, such as a cold. Therefore, cognitive complexity due to structural properties, as measured by object-oriented metrics, can never be the reason for all faults. For instance, the developers of a particular set of core functionality in a system may be placed under schedule pressure since there are many dependencies on their output. These developers may introduce more faults into the core classes due to stress.

It is not known whether the influence of object-oriented metrics dominates other effects. The only thing that can be stated reasonably is that the empirical relationships between object-oriented metrics and external metrics are not very likely to be strong. This is due to effects that are not accounted for, but as has been demonstrated in a number of studies, they can still be useful in practice.

2.5   Object-Oriented Thresholds

As noted in above, the practical utility of object-oriented metrics would be enhanced if meaningful thresholds could be identified. The cognitive theory described above can be expanded to include threshold effects. Hatton (1997) has proposed a cognitive explanation as to why a threshold effect would exist between *complexity* metrics and faults. [8]

Hatton argues that Miller (1957) shows that humans can cope with around 7 +/- 2 pieces of information (or chunks) at a time in short-term memory, independent of information content. He then refers to the text of Hilgard et al. (1971), where they note that the contents of long-term memory are in a coded form and the recovery codes may get scrambled under some conditions. Short-term memory incorporates a rehearsal buffer that continuously refreshes itself. Hatton suggests that anything that can fit into short-term memory is easier to understand and less fault-prone. Pieces that are too large or too complex overflow, involving use of the more error-prone recovery code mechanism used for long-term storage. In a subsequent article, Hatton (1998) extended this model to object-oriented development. If we take a class as a definition of a chunk, then if the class dependencies exceed the short-term memory limit, one can expect designers and programmers to make more errors.

2.5.1   Size Thresholds

A reading of the early software engineering literature suggests that when software components exceed a certain size, fault-proneness increases rapidly. This is in essence a *threshold effect*. For instance, Card and Glass (1990) note that many programming texts suggest limiting component size to 50 or 60 SLOC. A study by O'Leary (1996) of the relationship between size and faults in knowledge-based systems found no relationship between size and faults for small components, but a positive relationship for large components; again suggesting a threshold effect. A number of standards and organizations had defined upper limits on components size (Bowen, 1984), for example, an upper limit of 200 source statements in MIL-STD-1679, 200 HOL executable statements in MIL-STD-1644A, 100 statements excluding annotation in RADC CP 0787796100E,

---

[8] Hatton also suggests that components that are of low complexity do not use short-term memory efficiently, and that failure to do so also leads to increased fault-proneness. However, this aspect of his model has been criticised recently (El-Emam et al., 2000) and therefore will not be considered further.

100 executable source lines in MILSTAR/ESD Spec, 200 source statements in MIL-STD-SDS, 200 source statements in 'MIL-STD-1679(A), and 200 HOL executable statements in FAA ER-130-005D. Bowen (1984) proposed component size thresholds between 23-76 source statements based on his own analysis. After a lengthy critique of size thresholds, Dunn and Ullman (1979) suggest two pages of source code listing as an indicator of an overly large component. Woodfield et al. (1981) suggest a maximum threshold of 70 LOC.

Hatton (1998) argues that the concept of encapsulation, central to object-oriented development, lets us think about an object in isolation. If the size of this object is small enough to fit into short-term memory, then it will be easier to understand and reason about. Objects that are too large and overflow the short-term memory will tend to be more fault-prone.

2.5.2 Inheritance Thresholds

According to the above threshold theory, objects that are manipulated in short-term memory possessing inherited properties require referencing the ancestor objects. If the ancestor objects are in short-term memory then this tracing does not increase cognitive burden. However, if the ancestor objects are already encoded in long-term storage, access to long-term memory breaks the train of thought and is inherently less accurate. Accordingly, it is likely that classes will be more fault-prone if they reference inherited chunks that cannot be kept in short-term storage, and this fault-proneness increases as the extent of inheritance increases. An implication is that a certain amount of inheritance does not affect cognitive burden, it is only when inheritance increases beyond the limitations of short-term memory that understandability deteriorates. For example, Lorenz and Kidd (1994), based on their experiences with Smalltalk and C++ projects, recommended an inheritance nesting level threshold of 6, indicating that inheritance up to a certain point is not detrimental.

2.5.3 Coupling Thresholds

When there is a diffusion of functionality, then an object in short-term memory may be referencing or be referenced by many other objects. If each of these other objects is treated as a chunk and they are within short-term memory, then tracing does not increase cognitive burden. However, if more objects need to be traced than can be held in short-term memory, this requires retrieval (and pattern-matching in the case of polymorphism) of many other objects in long-term memory. Hence, the ensuing disruption leads to comprehension difficulties, and therefore greater fault-proneness. Therefore, one can argue that when the interacting objects overflow short-term memory, this will lead to an increase in fault-proneness. The implication of this is that a certain amount of coupling does not affect cognitive burden, until a non zero coupling threshold is exceeded.

2.6   Empirical Evidence

A considerable number of empirical studies have been performed to validate the relationship between object-oriented metrics and class fault-proneness. Some studies have covered the metrics that were described earlier in this chapter, (Basili et al., 1996; Briand et al., 1997; Briand et al., 2000; Briand et al., 1998; Tang et al., 1999).   Other studies validated a set of polymorphism metrics (Benlarbi and Melo, 1999), a coupling dependency metric (Binkley and Schach, 1998), a set of metrics defined on Shlaer-Mellor designs (Cartwright and Shepperd, 2000), another metrics suite (F. Brito e Abreu and Melo, 1996), and a set of coupling metrics (R. Harrison, Counsell, and Nithi, 1998). Other external measures of interest that have been studied are productivity (Chidamber et al., 1998), maintenance effort (Li and Henry, 1993), and development effort (Chidamber et al., 1998; Misic and Tesic, 1998; Nesi and Querci, 1998). However, here we will focus on the fault-proneness external measure.

It would seem that with such a body of work we would also have a large body of knowledge about which metrics are related to fault-proneness. Unfortunately, this is not the case. A recent study (El-Emam et al., 2001) has demonstrated a confounding effect of class size on the validity of object-oriented metrics. This means that if one does not control the effect of class size when validating metrics, then the results would be quite optimistic. The reason for this argument is illustrated in Figure 2.3. Class size is correlated with most product metrics, and it is also a good predictor of fault-proneness: *Bigger classes are simply more likely to have a fault.*

Empirical evidence supports an association between object-oriented product metrics and size. For example, in Briand et al., (2000) the Spearman rho correlation coefficients go as high as 0.43 for associations between some coupling and cohesion metrics with size, and 0.397 for inheritance metrics. Both results are statistically significant (at an alpha level of say 0.1).

Similar patterns emerge in other studies. One study by Briand et al. (1998) reports relatively large correlations between size and object-oriented metrics. In another study (Cartwright and Shepperd, 2000) the authors display the correla-

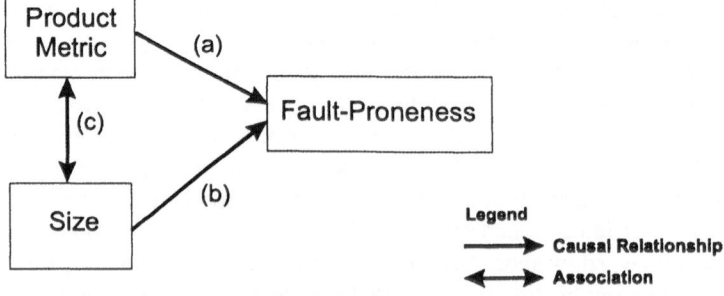

Figure 2.3. Illustration of confounding effect of class size.

tion matrix showing the Spearman correlation between a set of object-oriented metrics that can be collected from Shlaer-Mellor designs and C++ LOC. The correlations range from 0.563 to 0.968, all statistically significant at an alpha level 0.05. This result also indicates very strong correlations with size. In further support of this hypothesis, the relationship between size and defects is clearly visible in the study by Cartwright and Shepperd (2000), where the Spearman correlation was found to be 0.759 and statistically significant. Another study of image analysis programs written in C++ (R. Harrison et al., 1996) found a Spearman correlation of 0.53 between size in LOC and the number of errors found during testing, also statistically significant at an alpha level of 0.05. Finally, Briand et al. (2000) find statistically significant associations between six different size metrics and fault-proneness for C++ programs, with a change in odds ratio going as high as 4.952 for one of the size metrics.

A number of validation studies did not control for size (Binkley and Schach, 1998; Briand et al., 2000; Briand et al., 1998; R. Harrison et al., 1998; Tang et al., 1999). This means that if an association is found between a particular metric and fault-proneness, this may be due to the fact that higher values on that metric also mean higher size values. In the following sections, we therefore only draw conclusions from studies that *did* control for size, either statistically or experimentally.

2.6.1 Inheritance Metrics

As noted in Deligiannis and Shepperd (1999), the software engineering community has been preoccupied with inheritance and its effect on quality. Many studies have investigated that particular feature of the object-oriented paradigm.

An experimental investigation found that making changes to a C++ program with inheritance consumed more effort than a program without inheritance, and the author attributed this to the subjects finding the inheritance program more difficult to understand based on responses to a questionnaire (Cartwright, 1998). Another study by Cartwright and Shepperd (2000) found that classes with inheritance tend to be more fault prone. This suggests that, holding everything else equal, understandability of classes is stable when there is no inheritance, but falls if there is any inheritance.

In two further experiments (Unger and Prechelt, 1998), subjects were given three equivalent Java programs to modify, and the maintenance time was measured. One of the Java programs was *flat*, in that it did not take advantage of inheritance; one had an inheritance depth of 3; and one had an inheritance depth of 5. In an initial experiment, the programs with an inheritance depth of 3 on the average took longer to maintain than the flat program, but the program with an inheritance depth of 5 took as much time as the flat program. The authors attribute this to the fact that the amount of changes required to complete the maintenance task for the deepest inheritance program was smaller. The results for a second task in the first experiment and the results of the second experiment indicate that it took longer to maintain the programs with inheritance. This was attributed to the need to trace call sequences up the inheritance hierarchy in order to understand what a class is doing.

However, another study (Daly et al., 1996) contradicts these findings. The authors conducted a series of classroom experiments comparing the time to perform maintenance tasks on a flat C++ program and a C++ program with three levels of inheritance. The result was a significant reduction in maintenance effort for the inheritance program. An internal replication by the same authors found the results to be in the same direction, albeit the p-value was larger. This suggests an inverse effect for inheritance depth to the one described above.

More recent studies also reported similar contradictory results. Two studies found that there is a relationship between the depth of inheritance tree and fault-proneness in Java programs (El-Emam et al., 2001; Glasberg et al., 2000). However, two other studies found no such effect with C++ programs (El-Emam et al., 1999, 2000).

Overall, then, it seems that the evidence as to the impact of inheritance depth on fault-proneness is rather equivocal. This is usually an indication that there is another effect that is confounded with inheritance depth. Further research is necessary to identify this confounding effect and disentangle it from inheritance depth in order to assess the effect of inheritance depth by itself.

2.6.2   Coupling Metrics

The most promising results with object-oriented metrics were obtained using coupling metrics. A summary of three recent results is given Table 2.2. The "*" indicates that for this particular study ACMIC was not evaluated because it had too few observations that were non-zero, and hence lacked variation. It can be seen that both import and export coupling metrics tend to be associated with fault-proneness. The type of coupling depends on the system, likely a reflection of the overall design approach.

Table 2.2. Summary of validation results for coupling metrics.

	(El-Emam et al., 1999) (C++ system)	(El-Emam et al., 2001) (Java system)	(Glasberg et al., 2000) (Java system)
CBO	X	Not evaluated	Not evaluated
OCAEC	X	X	No association found
ACMIC	X	Not evaluated *	X
OCMEC	X	X	No association found
OMMEC	X	Not evaluated	Not evaluated
OCMIC	No association found	X	X
OCAIC	No association found	No association found	X

2.6.3   Cohesion Metrics

Three studies that evaluated the effect of cohesion, in the form of the LCOM metric, found no effect of cohesion on fault-proneness (Benlarbi et al., 2000; El-Emam et al., 1999; El-Emam et al., 2000). This is not surprising given that the concept of cohesion is not well understood.

2.6.4   Thresholds

A recent series of studies led by the author investigated thresholds for object-oriented metrics (Benlarbi et al., 2000; El-Emam et al., 2000; Glasberg et al., 2000). The first study demonstrated that an absence of size thresholds for object-oriented classes (El-Emam et al., 2000). The remaining two studies demonstrated that an absence of threshold effects for a subset of the metrics described earlier (Benlarbi et al., 2000; Glasberg et al., 2000). The results are consistent across all of the three studies: there are no thresholds for contemporary object-oriented metrics, including class size.

   Absence of thresholds does not mean that the claims of limits on short-term memory are not applicable to software engineering. However, the applicability of this cognitive model to object-oriented applications needs to be refined further. It is plausible that a *chunk* in the object-oriented paradigm is a method rather than a class. It is also plausible that dependencies between chunks need to be weighted according to the complexity of the dependency. These hypotheses require further investigation. The main result remains, however, that the existence of thresholds for contemporary object-oriented metrics lacks evidence.

   The existing object-oriented thresholds that have been derived from experiential knowledge, such as those of Lorenz and Kidd (1994) and Rosenberg et al. (1999) may, however, still be of some practical utility despite these findings. Even if there is a continuous (i.e., no threshold) relationship between these metrics and fault-proneness as we have found, if you draw a line at a high value of a measure and call this a threshold, classes that are above the threshold will still be the *most fault-prone*. The situation is illustrated in the left panel of Figure 2.4

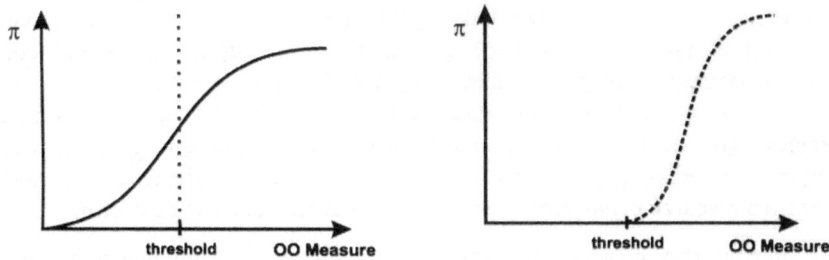

Figure 2.4. Different types of thresholds. An arbitrarily chosen threshold is illustrated on the left. A genuine threshold effect is illustrated on the right.

(where π is the probability of a fault). Therefore, for the purpose of identifying the most fault-prone classes, such thresholds will likely work. Classes with values below the threshold can still mean high fault-proneness, just not the highest.

Had a genuine threshold effect been identified, then classes with values below the threshold represent a *safe* region whereby designers deliberately restricting their classes within this region can have some assurance that the classes will have, everything else being equal, *minimal fault-proneness*. This genuine threshold effect is illustrated in the right panel of Figure 2.4.

2.7   Conclusions

This chapter reviewed contemporary object-oriented metrics, the theory behind them, and the empirical evidence that supports their use. The results obtained thus far can provide the basis for concrete guidelines for quality management in object-oriented applications. These can be summarized as follows:

- The most important metrics to collect seem to be those measuring the different types of export and import coupling. Most of these metrics have the advantage that they can be collected at the early design stages, allowing for early quality management. Assign your best people to work on classes with high values on the coupling metrics.
- If historical data is available, it would be even better to rank your classes by their predicted fault-proneness. This involves constructing a logistic regression model using the above coupling metrics (and a measure of size). This model would predict the probability of a fault in each class. Assign your best people to work on classes with the largest predicted fault-proneness.
- Other managerial actions that can be taken are larger and more experienced inspection teams for classes with high fault-proneness and development of more test cases for these classes. Given that these classes are expected to be the most fault-prone, such defect detection activities will help identify and remove these faults before the software is released.

It is clear from the above studies that we are not yet at the stage where precise prescriptive or proscriptive design guidelines can be developed. However, the findings so far are a useful starting point. The results do not, in general, contradict the cognitive complexity theory presented earlier. We did not find compelling evidence that the depth of inheritance tree is a major contributor to fault-proneness. However, this may be due to other ancestor-based coupling metrics being the main effect predicted by the theory rather than inheritance depth itself.

From a research perspective, the following conclusions can be drawn:

- Contemporary cohesion metrics tends not to be good predictors of fault-proneness. Further work needs to be performed at defining cohesion better, and developing metrics to measure it.

- The evidence as to the impact of inheritance depth itself on fault-proneness is equivocal. This is an issue that requires further investigation.
- No threshold effects were identified. This most likely means that the manner in which theories about short-and long-term human memory have been adapted to object-oriented applications needs further refinement.

In closing, it is important to note that the studies from which these recommendations were derived looked at commercial systems (i.e., not student applications). This makes the case that the results are applicable to actual projects more convincing. Furthermore, the studies focused only on fault-proneness. It is plausible that studies that focus on maintenance effort or development effort might give rise to different recommendations.

2.8   Acknowledgments

Discussions with Janice Singer and Norm Vinson have contributed towards improving the cognitive theory elements of this chapter. I also wish to thank them for providing directions through the cognitive psychology literature. Review comments from Hakan Erdogmus and Barbara Kitchenham have been very useful for making improvements to the chapter.

2.9   References

Abreu, F. B. e., and Carapuca, R. (1994). Object-oriented software engineering: measuring and controlling the development process. *In Proceedings of the 4th International Conference on Software Quality.*

Abreu, F. B. e., and Melo, W. (1996). Evaluating the impact of object-oriented design on software quality. *In Proceedings of the 3rd International Software Metrics Symposium, pp. 90-99.*

Almeida, M., Lounis, H., and Melo, W. (1998). An investigation on the use of machine learned models for estimating correction costs. *In Proceedings of the 20th International Conference on Software Engineering, pp. 473-476.*

Basili, V., Briand, L., and Melo, W. (1996). A validation of object-oriented design metrics as quality indicators. IEEE Transactions on Software Engineering, 22(10), 751-761.

Basili, V., Condon, S., El-Emam, K., Hendrick, R., and Melo, W. (1997). Characterizing and modeling the cost of rework in a library of reusable software components. *In Proceedings of the 19th International Conference on Software Engineering, pp. 282-291.*

Benlarbi, S., El-Emam, K., Goel, N., and Rai, S. (2000). *Thresholds for object-oriented measures*. NRC/ERB 1073. (National Research Council of Canada).

Benlarbi, S., and Melo, W. (1999). Polymorphism measures for early risk prediction. *In Proceedings of the 21st International Conference on Software Engineering, pp. 334-344.*

Binkley, A., and Schach, S. (1998). Validation of the coupling dependency metric as a predictor of run-time failures and maintenance measures. *In Proceedings of the 20th International Conference on Software Engineering, pp. 452-455.*

Boehm-Davis, D., Holt, R., and Schultz, A. (1992). The role of program structure in software maintenance. International Journal of Man-Machine Studies, 36, 21-63.

Bowen, J. (1984). Module Size: A standard or heuristic? Journal of Systems and Software, 4, 327-332.

Briand, L., and Wuest, J. (1999). *The impact of design properties on development cost in object-orientedsSystems*. ISERN-99-16. (International Software Engineering Research Network).

Briand, L., Basili, V., and Hetmanski, C. (1993). Developing interpretable models with optimized set reduction for identifying high-risk software components. IEEE Transactions on Software Engineering, 19(11), 1028-1044.

Briand, L., Daly, J., and Wuest, J. (1998). A unified framework for cohesion measurement in object-oriented systems. Empirical Software Engineering: An International Journal, 3, 65-117.

Briand, L., Daly, J., and Wuest, J. (1999). A unified framework for coupling measurement in object-oriented systems. IEEE Transactions on Software Engineering, 25(1), 91-121.

Briand, L., Devanbu, P., and Melo, W. (1997). An investigation into coupling measures for C++. *In Proceedings of the 19th International Conference on Software Engineering.*

Briand, L., Thomas, W., and Hetmanski, C. (1993). Modeling and managing risk early in software development. *In Proceedings of the International Conference on Software Engineering, pp. 55-65.*

Briand, L., Wuest, J., Daly, J., and Porter, V. (2000). Exploring the relationships Between design measures and software quality in object oriented systems. Journal of Systems and Software 51, 245-273.

Briand, L., Wuest, J., Ikonomovski, S., and Lounis, H. (1998). *A comprehensive investigation of quality factors in object-oriented designs: An Industrial case study*. ISERN-98-29. (International Software Engineering Research Network).

Briand, L., Arisholm, E., Counsell, S., Houdek, F., and Thevenod-Fosse, P. (1999). Empirical studies of object-oriented artifacts, methods, and processes: State of the art and future direction. Empirical Software Engineering: An International Journal, 4(4), 387-404.

Burkhardt, J.M., Detienne, F., and Wiedenbeck, S. (1997). Mental representations constructed by experts and novices in object-oriented program comprehension. In Human-Computer Interaction: INTERACT'97, pp. 339-346.

Cant, S., Henderson-Sellers, B., and Jeffery, R. (1994). Application of cognitive complexity metrics to object-oriented programs. Journal of Object-Oriented Programming, 7(4), 52-63.

Cant, S., Jeffery, R., and Henderson-Sellers, B. (1995). A conceptual model of cognitive complexity of elements of the programming process. Information and Software Technology, 7, 351-362.

Card, D., and Glass, R. (1990). Measuring software design quality. (Prentice-Hall, Englewood Cliffs, NJ).

Cartwright, M. (1998). An empirical view of inheritance. Information and Software Technology, 40, 795-799.

Cartwright, M., and Shepperd, M. (2000). An empirical investigation of an object-oriented software system. IEEE Transactions on Software Engineering, 26(2), 786-796.

Chidamber, S., Darcy, D., and Kemerer, C. (1998). Managerial use of metrics for object-oriented software: An exploratory analysis. IEEE Transactions on Software Engineering, 24(8), 629-639.

Chidamber, S., and Kemerer, C. (1991). Towards a metrics suite for object-oriented design. In Proceedings of the Conference on Object-Oriented Programming Systems, Languages and Applications (OOPSLA'91), pp. 197-211.

Chidamber, S., and Kemerer, C. (1994). A metrics suite for object-oriented design. IEEE Transactions on Software Engineering, 20(6), 476-493.

Chidamber, S., and Kemerer, C. (1995). Authors' reply. IEEE Transactions on Software Engineering, 21(3), 265.

Clark, B. (1997). The effects of software process maturity on software development effort. Unpublished PhD Thesis, University of Southern California.

Coallier, F., Mayrand, J., and Lague, B. (1999). Risk management in software product procurement. In K. El-Emam and N. H. Madhavji (Eds.), Elements of Software Process Assessment and Improvement. (IEEE CS Press).

CodeWork. (2000). JStyle. Available: http://www.codework.com/, 20th April 2000.

Daly, J., Brooks, A., Miller, J., Roper, M., and Wood, M. (1996). Evaluating inheritance depth on the maintainability of object-oriented software. *Empirical Software Engineering: An International Journal, 1*(2), 109-132.

Daly, J., Miller, J., Brooks, A., Roper, M., and Wood, M. (1995). Issues on the object-oriented paradigm: A questionnaire survey. EFoCS-8-95, Department of Computer Science - University of Strathclyde.

Daly, J., Wood, M., Brooks, A., Miller, J., and Roper, M. (1995). *Structured interviews on the object-oriented paradigm.* EFoCS-7-95, Department of Computer Science - University of Strathclyde.

Davis, J. (1984). Chunks: A basis for complexity measurement. Information Processing and Management, 20(1), 119-127.

Deligiannis, I., and Shepperd, M. (1999). A review of experimental investigations into object-oriented technology. *In Proceedings of the Fifth IEEE Workshop on Empirical Studies of Software Maintenance, pp. 6-10.*

Devanbu,P.(2000).*Gen++.*available: http://seclab.cs.ucdavis.edu/~devanbu/genp/, April 20th 2000.

Dijk, T. v., and Kintsch, W. (1983). *Strategies of discourse comprehension.* (Academic Press).

Dunn, R., and Ullman, R. (1979). Modularity is not a matter of size. *In Proceedings of the 1979 Annual Reliability and Maintainability Symposium, pp. 342-345.*

Dvorak, J. (1994). Conceptual entropy and its effect on class hierarchies. *IEEE Computer,* 59-63.

Ebert, C., and Liedtke, T. (1995). An integrated approach for criticality prediction. *In Proceedings of the 6th International Symposium on Software Reliability Engineering, pp. 14-23.*

El-Emam, K., Benlarbi, S., Goel, N., Melo, W., Lounis, H., and Rai, S. (2000). *The optimal class size for object-oriented software: A replicated study* NRC/ERB 1074. (National Research Council of Canada).

El-Emam, K., Benlarbi, S., Goel, N., and Rai, S. (1999). *A validation of object-oriented metrics.* NRC/ERB 1063. (National Research Council of Canada).

El-Emam, K., Benlarbi, S., Goel, N., and Rai, S. (2001). The confounding effect of class size on the validity of object-oriented metrics. IEEE Transactions on Software Engineering (to appear).

El-Emam, K., and Birk, A. (2000a). Validating the ISO/IEC 15504 measures of software development process capability. Journal of Systems and Software, 51(2), 119-149.

El-Emam, K., and Birk, A. (2000b). Validating the ISO/IEC 15504 measures of software requirements analysis process capability. IEEE Transactions on Software Engineering, 26(8), 541-566.

El-Emam, K., Drouin, J-N., and Melo, W. (1998). *SPICE: The theory and practice of software process improvement and capability determination.* (IEEE CS Press).

El-Emam, K., Melo, W., and Machado, J. (2001). The prediction of faulty classes using object-oriented design metrics. Journal of Systems and Software, 56(1), 63-75.

Evanco, W. (1997). Poisson analyses of defects for small software components. Journal of Systems and Software, 38, 27-35.

Fenton, N. (1991). *Software Metrics: A rigorous approach.* (Chapman and Hall).

Fenton, N., and Ohlsson, N. (2000). Quantitative analysis of faults and failures in a complex software system. *IEEE Transactions on Software Engineering,* 26(8), 797-814.

Flowe, R., and Thordahl, J. (1994). *A correlational study of the SEI's Capability Maturity Model and software development performance in DoD contracts.* Unpublished MSc Thesis, The Air Force Institute of Technology.

French, V. (1999). Establishing software metrics thresholds. *In Proceedings of the 9th International Workshop on Software Measurement.*

Furuyama, T., Arai, Y., and Iio, K. (1994). Fault generation model and mental stress effect analysis. Journal of Systems and Software, 26, 31-42.

Furuyama, T., Arai, Y., and Iio, K. (1997). Analysis of fault generation caused by stress during software development. Journal of Systems and Software, 38, 13-25.

Glasberg, D., El-Emam, K., Melo, and Madhavji, N. (2000). *Validating Object-Oriented Design Metrics on a Commercial Java Application,* Technical Report, NRC/ERB-1080 (National Research Council of Canada).

Goldenson, D. R., and Herbsleb, J. (1995). *After the appraisal: A systematic survey of process improvement, its benefits, and factors that influence success.* CMU/SEI-95-TR-009, Software Engineering Institute.

Harrison, R., Counsell, S., and Nithi, R. (1998). Coupling metrics for object oriented design. *In Proceedings of the 5th International Symposium on Software Metrics, pp. 150-157.*

Harrison, R., Samaraweera, L., Dobie, M., and Lewis, P. (1996). An evaluation of code metrics for object-oriented programs. Information and Software Technology, 38, 443-450.

Harrison, W. (1988). Using Software Metrics to Allocate Testing Resources. Journal of Management Information Systems, 4(4), 93-105.

Hatton, L. (1997). Re-examining the Fault Density - Component Size Connection. *IEEE Software*, 89-97.

Hatton, L. (1998). Does OO Sync with How We Think ? *IEEE Software*, 46-54.

Henderson-Sellers, B. (1996). *Object-Oriented Metrics: Measures of Complexity.* (Prentice-Hall).

Hilgard, E., Atkinson, R., and Atkinson, R. (1971). *Introduction to Psychology.* (Harcourt Brace Jovanovich).

Hosmer, D., and Lemeshow, S. (1989). *Applied Logistic Regression.* (John Wiley and Sons).

Hudepohl, J., Aud, S., Khoshgoftaar, T., Allen, E., and Mayrand, J. (1996a). EMERALD: Software metrics and models on the desktop. IEEE Software, 13(5), 56-60.

Hudepohl, J., Aud, S., Khoshgoftaar, T., Allen, E., and Mayrand, J. (1996b). Integrating metrics and models for software risk assessment. *In Proceedings of the 7th International Symposium on Software Reliability Engineering, pp. 93-98.*

ISO/IEC. (1996). *Information Technology - Software Product Evaluation; Part 1: Overview.* ISO/IEC DIS 14598-1. (International Organization for Standardization and the International Electrotechnical Commission).

Jones, C. (1999). The economics of software process improvements. In K. El-Emam and N. H. Madhavji (Eds.), *Elements of Software Process Assessment and Improvement.* (IEEE CS Press).

Jorgensen, M. (1995). Experience with the accuracy of software maintenance task effort prediction models. IEEE Transactions on Software Engineering, 21(8), 674-681.

Kaaniche, M., and Kanoun, K. (1996). Reliability of a commercial telecommunications system. *In Proceedings of the International Symposium on Software Reliability Engineering, pp. 207-212.*

Khoshgoftaar, T., Allen, E., Jones, W., and Hudepohl, J. (1999). Classification tree models of software quality over multiple releases. *In Proceedings of the International Symposium on Software Reliability Engineering, pp. 116-125.*

Khoshgoftaar, T., Allen, E., Kalaichelvan, K., and Goel, N. (1996). The impact of software evolution and reuse on software quality. Empirical Software Engineering: An International Journal, 1, 31-44.

Kintsch, W. (1986). Learning from text. Cognition and Instruction, 3, 87-108.

Kitchenham, B., and Linkman, S. (1990). Design metrics in practice. Information and Software Technology, 32(4), 304-310.

Krishnan, M. S., and Kellner, M. (1999). Measuring process consistency: Implications for reducing software defects. IEEE Transactions on Software Engineering, 25(6), 800-815.

Lanubile, F., and Visaggio, G. (1997). Evaluating predictive quality models derived from software measures: Lessons learned. Journal of Systems and Software, 38, 225-234.

Leijter, M., Meyers, S., and Reiss, S. (1992). Support for maintaining object-oriented programs. IEEE Transactions on Software Engineering, 18(12), 1045-1052.

Lewis, J., and Henry, S. (1989). A methodology for integrating maintainability using software metrics. *In Proceedings of the International Conference on Software Maintenance, pp. 32-39.*

Li, W., and Henry, S. (1993). Object-oriented metrics that predict maintainability. Journal of Systems and Software, 23, 111-122.

Lorenz, M., and Kidd, J. (1994). Object-Oriented Software Metrics. (Prentice-Hall).

Lyu, M., Yu, J., Keramides, E., and Dalal, S. (1995). ARMOR: Analyzer for reducing module operational risk. *In Proceedings of the 25th International Symposium on Fault-Tolerant Computing, pp. 137-142.*

Metameta. (2000). *Metameta Metrics.* Available: http://www.metamata.com, 20th April.

Miller, G. (1957). The magical number 7 plus or minus two: Some limits on our capacity for processing information. Psychological Review, 63, 81-97.

Misic, V., and Tesic, D. (1998). Estimation of effort and complexity: An object-oriented case study. Journal of Systems and Software, 41, 133-143.

Moller, K.-H., and Paulish, D. (1993). An empirical investigation of software fault distribution. *In Proceedings of the First International Software Metrics Symposium, pp. 82-90.*

Nesi, P., and Querci, T. (1998). Effort estimation and prediction of object-oriented systems. Journal of Systems and Software, 42, 89-102.

Newell, A., and Simon, H. (1972). Human Problem Solving. (Prentice-Hall).

Number-Six-Software. (2000). *Metrics one.* available: http://www.numbersix.com/metricsone/index.htm, April 20th 2000.

ObjectSoft. (2000). *ObjectDetail.* available: http://www.obsoft.com, 20th April 2000.

Ohlsson, N., and Alberg, H. (1996). Predicting fault-prone software modules in telephone switches. IEEE Transactions on Software Engineering, 22(12), 886-894.

O'Leary, D. (1996). The relationship between errors and size in knowledge-based systems. International Journal of Human-Computer Studies, 44, 171-185.

Pennington, N. (1987a).*Comprehension strategies in programming.* In Empirical Studies of Programmers, 2nd Workshop, pp. 100-113.

Pennington, N. (1987b). Stimulus structures and mental representations in expert comprehension of computer programs. Cognitive Psychology, 19, 295-341.

Power-Software. (2000a). *Krakatau for C/C++.* Available online at: http://www.power-soft.co.uk/.

Power-Software. (2000b). *Krakatau Java.* Available online at: http://www.power-soft.co.uk/.

Rosenberg, L., Stapko, R., and Gallo, A. (1999). *Object-oriented metrics for reliability.* Presented at the IEEE International Symposium on Software Metrics.

Software Engineering Institute. (1995). The capability maturity model: Guidelines for improving the software process. (Addison Wesley).

Szentes, J., and Gras, J. (1986). Some practical views of software complexity metrics and a universal measurement tool. *In Proceedings of the First Australian Software Engineering Conference, pp. 83-88.*

Tang, M.-H., Kao, M.-H., and Chen, M.-H. (1999). An empirical study on object oriented metrics. *In Proceedings of the Sixth International Software Metrics Symposium, pp. 242-249.*

Tracz, W. (1979). Computer programming and the human thought process. Software - Practice and Experience, 9, 127-137.

Unger, B., and Prechelt, L. (1998). *The impact of inheritance depth on maintenance tasks - detailed description and evaluation of two experiment replications* 19/1998. (Fakultat fur Informatik - Universitaet Karlsruhe).

Wiedenbeck, S., Ramalingam, V., Sarasamma, S., and Corritore, C. (1999). A comparison of the comprehension of object-oriented and procedural programs by novice programmers. Interacting with Computers, 11(3), 255-282.

Wilde, N., Matthews, P., and Huitt, R. (1993). Maintaining object-oriented software. IEEE Software, 75-80.

Woodfield, S., Shen, V., and Dunsmore, H. (1981). A study of several metrics for programming effort. Journal of Systems and Software, 2, 97-103.

3
Studies of the Work Practices of Software Engineers

Timothy Lethbridge
Janice Singer

3.1 Introduction

In this chapter we describe various techniques for studying and representing the work of software engineers[1] (SEs) and using the results to develop requirements for software engineering tools.

The ultimate objective of our research is to discover techniques that will enable software engineers to more productively make changes to large legacy real-time software systems. However, to achieve this objective we must understand software engineers' work practices. We describe various techniques we employed to observe work practices, analyze the resulting data, and produce graphical models of work patterns. In particular, we describe techniques that we have developed such as *synchronized shadowing* and the use of Use Case Maps to represent *work patterns*. Finally, we highlight some of the results of using these techniques in a real project: An important observation is that efficiently performing searches within source code is of paramount importance to the SEs when they work with large bodies of source code.

Our work began with collaboration between a computer scientist building tools for software maintainers (T. Lethbridge) and a psychologist (J. Singer) just hired in a software engineering research group. Although our research goal was to improve software maintainers' productivity, improving productivity was a very open-ended problem. It was not at all clear, when we began our work, what aspects of software maintenance could be most improved; it was even less clear what tools would be appropriate. However, since we both had a background in human/computer interaction, we were certain that we wanted to build *usable* tools for software maintainers.

---

[1] By *software engineers*, we are referring to people who perform software engineering work, but who may not be Professional Engineers in the legal sense.

Our first task involved a literature review. From the Empirical Studies of Programmers workshops, there were a few papers on software maintainers (e.g., Litman et al., 1996; Boehm-Davis et al., 1992). This research, primarily conducted from an information processing perspective, helped us understand individual processes in software maintenance. However, it was not clear how to take these results and build systems that could be used in real industrial practice with real software engineers. As Curtis (1986) appropriately asked about these types of studies, "By the way, did anyone study any real programmers?" meaning that the results might not apply in industrial practice.

There have been field studies in software design (Walz et al., 1993; Curtis et al., 1988; Kraut and Streeter, 1995), but again, it is not clear how design relates to maintenance. Also, these studies tended to look at larger issues that were not necessarily pertinent to building tools for individual software engineers.

Bendifallah and Scacchi (1987) did look at software maintenance as a form of articulation work. However, again, their work examines academic researchers and their maintenance of a relatively small tool. While Bendifallah and Scacchi's work assured us that the study of work practices was feasible in this field, it was not clear how their results would generalize to our target group of industrial maintainers.

This lack of relevant literature led us to broaden our emphasis from *usability* to *usefulness*. The questions of what do software maintainers do on a daily basis, in what activities are they involved, with what frequency, and using which tools, were all unanswered in the literature. Without this knowledge, we could not be sure about what would be useful tools for this domain. Thus, we went back to the literature. A review of the work of researchers in participatory design (e.g., Kyng and Mathiassen, 1997), distributed cognition (e.g., Hutchins, 1994), situated cognition (e.g., Suchman, 1987), and activity theory (e.g., Bannon and Bødker, (1991)[2] led us to believe that we could not ignore the context within which the work took place. Because of this, we decided to implement a field study in software maintenance (Singer and Lethbridge, 1998a; Lethbridge et al., 1997). This study used several ethnographic methods for data collection, including questionnaires, interviews, and observations. Following Glaser and Strauss' (1967) grounded theory approach, we were able to determine that software maintainers typically follow a *just-in-time comprehension* approach to program comprehension. That is, at any given time, they understood only the specific portion of the source code that would help them solve their current problem.

While we were closer to an answer about the usefulness of different software maintenance tools, we were unhappy with our methods of data collection and analysis. The difficulty of moving from field work to design requirements has been highlighted by other researchers (e.g., Button and Dourish, 1996; Blom-

---

[2] A comprehensive review of this literature will not be undertaken in this paper. Please refer to the individual papers and/or books for further information.

berg et al., 1996; Simonsen and Kensing, 1997)[3]. In fact, tools are now being created to help researchers record and represent their understanding of work (Pycock et al., 1998; Jordan et al., 1995).

Our dissatisfaction, however, focused not on adequate representations of the field, but rather on the fact that we felt we were collecting the wrong data. The field data was incomplete because software engineers were so quick that it was impossible to get all the actions recorded in observation sessions. Technical and practical issues did not allow us to videotape sessions. Additionally, our observations did not allow us to answer certain fundamental questions such as what is an individual's goal in doing a task, or how much time is spent on a task. Finally, the work required to represent the data was extreme. We spent over six months making transcripts and poring over them. While this might be appropriate in a research environment, it is entirely unfeasible in industry. These two concerns led us to develop both a new method for collecting data, *Synchronized Shadowing*, and a new method for representing it, using Use Case Maps (UCMs).

This chapter will discuss both of these innovations in the context of another field study that we subsequently implemented. We begin with a discussion of a general model of empirical studies in software engineering and situate our own observational field studies within this. Then we give more details about Synchronized Shadowing and our use of UCMs. We conclude with a case study showing how we applied these techniques to meet our objectives of building effective tools.

The methodology we developed as a result of our work is outlined in Figure 3.1. It combines synchronized shadowing with the use of Use Case Maps. We call it Work Analysis with Synchronized Shadowing (WASS).

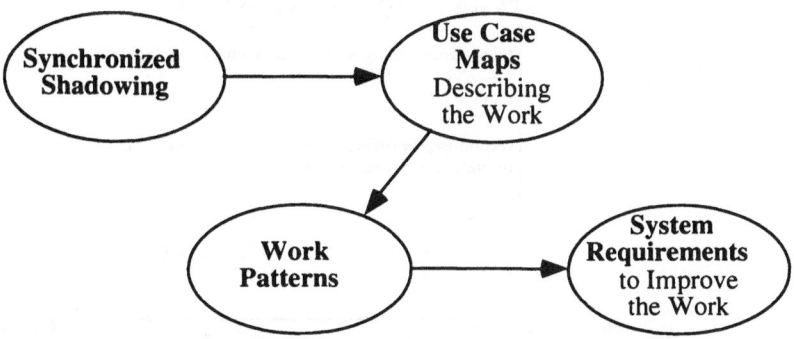

Figure 3.1. The Work Analysis with Synchronized Shadowing (WASS) methodology.

---

[3] Again, these references are in no way meant to be a comprehensive view, but rather an overview of current thinking.

3.2   An Overview of Approaches to Empirical Studies of Software Engineering Practices

Broadly defined, one calls a study *empirical* if it involves observing or measuring something. In analytical studies, in contrast, one deduces conclusions by applying logical and other mathematical reasoning to physical laws and other established facts. Since there are few unchallengable facts in the domain of software engineering processes, research in this domain will normally be empirical in nature.

Figure 3.2 shows a way of categorizing empirical studies of software processes using three dimensions: The environment, the degree of human contact, and the level of control. Most of the research discussed in this chapter falls close to the origin; it involves interactively gathering information about what people do in their natural work environments: We refer to all this as *work practices* studies.

3.2.1   Natural vs. Artificial Environments

The first dimension in Figure 3.2 distinguishes between field studies in natural work environments and studies performed in laboratory environments.

Field studies are conducted with practicing software engineers in the industry, whereas laboratory studies often involve groups of students in classroom or lab settings. Field studies often take more effort than laboratory studies. Relationships must be established with industrial companies, suitable software proj-

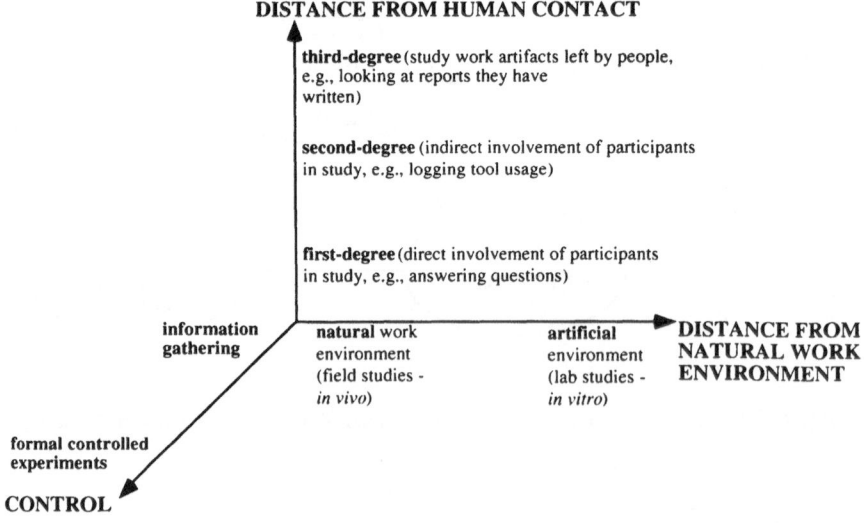

Figure 3.2. An approach to categorization of empirical studies of software processes.

ects and individual participants must be found, and the uncertain nature of the day-to-day activities of the company and its employees mean that the direction of the research is somewhat out of the researchers' hands (Lethbridge et al., 2000).

For the most part, studies of students performing software engineering tasks in laboratories are easier to conduct since there is a ready supply of students in university classes, and a faculty member can dictate their goals. While the conclusions of laboratory studies are useful, they are not as likely to be relevant to industrial practice since students lack experience and goals, and since their methods will not normally be the same as those of industrial practitioners.

One counter example is that Porter and Votta (1998) found no difference in results for professional vs. graduate student programmers. However their experiment was artificial in the sense that the exercises used were designed strictly for the experiment. It might be that people work differently with known materials than experimental ones. It is probably also true that graduate students are closer to professionals than undergraduates are in terms of their programming ability. Nonetheless, since we wanted to absolutely ensure our work was industrially relevant, the work discussed in this chapter falls in the field study category: We studied real programmers in real industrial environments.

3.2.2   Degree of Human Contact

The second way of categorizing empirical studies shown in Figure 3.2 relates to the degree of human contact that the technique involves.

We define *first-degree* empirical studies to be those involving human-to-human interaction between researchers and participants. Such techniques can include brainstorming, interviews, surveys, and observational studies.

We consider *second-degree* studies to be those where human processes are monitored, but where the researchers do not interact directly with the humans themselves, e.g., by gathering information automatically as people work.

Third-degree studies involve analysis of the artifacts resulting from work, e.g. source code, documents, and problem reports. The work reported in this chapter was first-degree (primarily observational studies), although we also used some second- and third-degree information.

3.2.3   Information-Gathering vs. Experimentation

The final dimension in Figure 3.2 contrasts *information-gathering studies* with *experiments*. Information gathering studies are suitable for generating hypotheses, while controlled experiments are more suitable for confirming or testing hypotheses.

In general, information-gathering studies are used to gather raw information about a phenomenon; the information may then be used to build a qualitative or quantitative model of the phenomenon. Techniques for producing qualitative models are discussed in detail by Glaser and Strauss (1967). Neuman (1997) and Denzin and Lincoln (1994) also give more detailed information on how to conduct qualitative studies.

Quantitative models can be used to develop hypotheses that can be tested in experiments. Experiments require the existence of a model and hypotheses about that model that are to be tested; formal experiments follow the scientific method rigorously and involve setting up some situation where extraneous variables are controlled, varying some independent variable(s), and measuring some dependent variable(s) in order to refute the null hypothesis.

In software engineering, it is usually very difficult to adequately control the extraneous variables, so true experiments are less widely used. However, there is one type of experiment that sits in the middle of this continuum and is useful in software engineering. Quasi-experiments are experiments where subjects are not randomly assigned to treatments. For instance, one could conduct a quasi-experiment on two different groups who had decided to implement two different programming processes. Here the two groups were not assigned randomly to the processes, but rather self-selected to them. For more information on quasi-experiments, see Cook and Campbell (1979).

Our studies of work practices are information-gathering in nature since we want to describe and model the work of software engineers.

3.2.4   Summary of the Three Dimensions of Empirical Studies

The three dimensions of empirical studies are largely orthogonal, with all points in space being possible, although not equally probable. For example, experiments are more likely to be performed in artificial environments where it is easier to control variables. Nevertheless it is possible to conduct large-scale experiments in an industrial context - for example, competitive development of a product by two teams that use different tools. In the above three-dimensional model of empirical studies, we have organized the types of empirical studies according to their data-generation phase, which we discuss in more detail in the next section. However, the resulting information must also be analyzed so conclusions can be drawn. This is usually the most time-consuming phase, since vast amounts of data can be generated, especially for information-gathering studies. Techniques for the analysis phase are discussed in section 3.4.

3.3   Techniques for Gathering Data in Observation Sessions

One of the techniques most widely used to understand work practices is observation. Shadowing is a form of observation where the observer moves around with the observee, recording what they are doing as they go about their normal daily routine. There are two big difficulties with shadowing: one is to effectively *capture* information; the other is to *analyze* the copious resulting data. To capture data, there are two widely used alternatives, simple note-taking or videotaping. Both require the output to be coded following the observation session before any analysis is undertaken. In this section we review these classic techniques, and then present our synchronized shadowing technique.

3.3.1 Note-Taking and Videotaping

Simple note-taking has two key problems: First, many details may be missed by the note-taker, partly because he or she may not notice all the nuances of what is going on, and partly because it is difficult to rapidly take accurate notes using a consistent format. Second, it is not feasible for the note-taker to record precise times when events occur, especially where action occurs quickly - the process of looking at his or her watch would cause the note-taker to miss an important activity.

Videotaping does not suffer from these problems since it allows one to record almost all details of a session. However, the process of coding can be very time consuming because one has much more data to work with.

There are some automatic logging tools that record precisely what occurs on the computer, such as every key press or every mouse click. These are impractical for our purposes, though, for two key reasons. First, they only record computer activity. We are interested in obtaining information about the work environment which includes situations when the participant looks at documentation, talks to neighbors, etc. The automatic logging tools do not capture this information. Second, because many programmers personalize their computer environment, the output of these tools in often difficult to interpret. For instance, the tools might tell you that a programmer is in Emacs, but they would not be able to interpret the macros that the programmer has set up to search for specific strings in Emacs. This makes these tools less useful in our context.

New tools are being developed that record the screen as well as the user's voice and synchronize them. We have not tried these tools because they have one fundamental problem in our context: Our software engineers move around from place to place, using different computers (e.g., in special hardware labs). We do not want to use observation techniques that interfere with the natural work processes.

3.3.2 Synchronized Shadowing

In our case, to make shadowing more practical, we developed an approach that has many of the advantages of videotaping, but without many of the drawbacks of note-taking. Our approach uses a program on a laptop computer to provide automated assistance to note-takers. The program improves the note-taking process in the following two ways:

- The note-taker can simply press one of many *buttons* to record an event that recurs frequently. This results in substantially increased note-taking speed, and hence fewer missed events. The notes will also be more consistent and hence faster to analyze since the buttons correspond to event categories: Much of the coding takes place at the time of observation. The meaning of the buttons can be preassigned following pilot studies, although adding new buttons dynamically during the observation session remains a possibility. Also, the note-taker can type other information after pressing any button, so nothing is lost from the ordinary note-taking process.
- Timing information is automatically recorded along with every button press, allowing for a level of accuracy in data analysis that would normally be available only by analyzing videotape.

Automated note-taking as described above can be very useful, but we developed the technique one step further: A single person using our program will still tend to miss much information. This makes sense because it is well known that when analyzing videotapes, one has to replay sections of the tape several times in order to notice all the details. We therefore arrange for *two* note-takers to participate in the shadowing, each using the automated note-taking program, but with different meanings for the buttons so they record somewhat different aspects of the work being observed. The two records are be merged after the session to form a more complete picture of what happened. A key process that makes this merging feasible is synchronizing the clocks of the two laptop computers so that proper sequences of events can be reconstructed - for this reason, we call our approach *synchronized shadowing* (Singer and Lethbridge, 1998).

It is very simple to create basic synchronized shadowing tools. For the event-recording buttons, we created macros in Microsoft Word that redefine certain keys (control sequences or function keys). Each such button adds a time stamp as well as an identifying string of characters to the current document. Before the observation session starts, we synchronize the computers' clocks. After the session we concatenate the documents and sort them. Figure 3.3 is the source code for two of the macros and Figure 3.4 illustrates the output of a session.

In addition to MS-Word macros, we have also created a more advanced synchronized shadowing tool, illustrated in Figure 3.5. This tool allows events to be nested within two levels of activities. For example, the highest level of activity might represent the primary task being performed; the second level might be the tool being used; and the events might be specific actions performed with the tool. Our new synchronized shadowing tool allows the user to dynamically add events, and manipulate various preferences. It provides similar output to that shown in Figure 3.4.

```
Public Sub MAIN()
Dim count_$
Dim counti
count_$ = WordBasic.[GetDocumentVar$]("statementNumber")
counti = WordBasic.Val(count_$)
counti = counti + 1
count_$ = Str(counti)
WordBasic.SetDocumentVar "statementNumber", count_$
WordBasic.InsertPara
WordBasic.Insert "* "
WordBasic.Insert count_$
WordBasic.Insert " - "
WordBasic.InsertDateTime DateTimePic:="H:mm:ss", InsertAsField:=0
WordBasic.Insert " "
End Sub

Public Sub MAIN()
WordBasic.ToolsMacro Name:="InsDate", Run:=1
WordBasic.Insert "GREP = "
End Sub
```

Figure 3.3. Two examples of MS-Word macros for automated note-taking while shadowing. The first inserts time, and the second inserts the time plus the keyword GREP; it is an example of one of many macros that would be bound to specific buttons.

```
 1 13:32:40 NEW-GOAL Friday, August 01, 1997 Jane Smith
 2 13:39:26 still explaining stuff
 3 13:39:52 UNIX ls cd
 4 13:40:12 EDITOR srh
 5 13:40:22 EDITOR quit
 6 13:40:28 GREP in system
 7 13:40:40 VIS at results
 8 13:41:02 EDITOR open found file
 9 13:41:33 EDITOR open empty
10 13:41:45 EDITOR copy
11 13:41:52 EDITOR paste
12 13:42:00 EDITOR save as xxdbllq.c
13 13:42:21 MODIFY part of query text
14 13:44:08 EDITOR save
15 13:44:12 MODIFY func name
16 13:44:38 EDITOR save
17 13:44:59 stop observing
```

Figure 3.4. Output of a synchronized shadowing session using MS-Word macros (lowercase text was typed by the person operating the program).

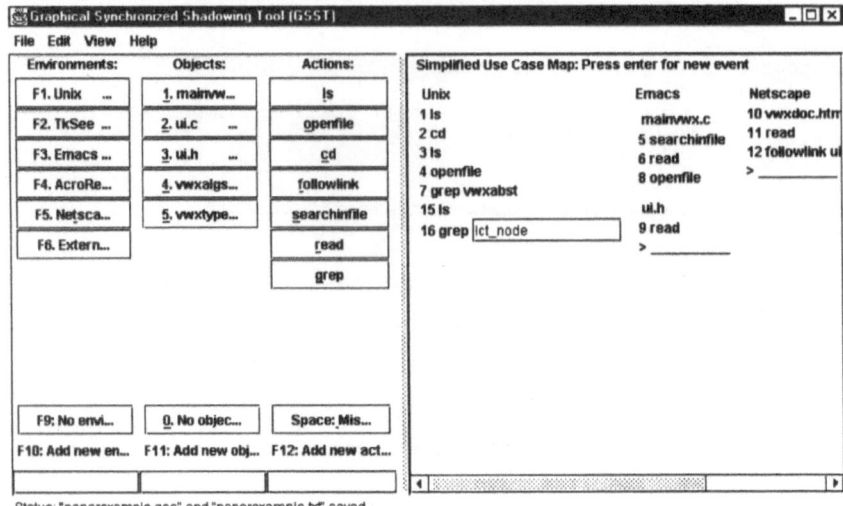

Figure 3.5. User interface of our second-generation Graphical Synchronized Shadowing Tool (GSST).

Synchronized shadowing is not perfect: The note-takers tend to vary the amount of time between the occurrence of an event and pressing the appropriate button. Timing, therefore is likely to be accurate only to the nearest 10 or 15 seconds, but this is adequate for our purposes.

3.4   Modeling Work to Develop Requirements

In this section we discuss how we use various techniques, including Use Case Maps (UCMs), to analyze the data obtained by synchronized shadowing. In the next section we provide a case study, illustrating the use of these techniques.

3.4.1   Coding Observational Data and Detecting Patterns

It is very difficult to analyze data that result from observational studies. The first step is to code, or categorize, all interesting events that occurred during the session. This is a subjective process normally requiring several iterations as the coders refine the coding scheme.

Once the raw observations are coded (at least preliminarily), there are two important approaches that can be used individually or together to obtain interesting information from the coded data:

- Counting occurrences of types events or summing the total amount of time spent on classes of activities. This can be useful to give an overall impression of how people spend their time. If one has enough data for different classes of people, one can discover differences among the classes.

- Detecting and modeling patterns of activities. This involves looking for repeating sequences and cycles that can be used to describe parts of the observed activity at a higher level of abstraction. Doing this is described in the paragraphs below.

The above approaches can be used synergistically. The counting and analysis of occurrences of these patterns can follow the process of modeling and building patterns. Similarly, the process of counting can lead to the development of patterns by pointing out the important types of events that should be included in those patterns.

A useful first step in discovering and representing patterns of activities is finding subsequences that are repeated frequently in the coded data. Several algorithms are known that can help with this. A basic approach simply divides an entire coded sequence of events into all possible subsequences of length n (called n-grams where n is normally at least 3) and counts the occurrences of each n-gram. Useful subsequences appear as the n-grams that occur most frequently. Even more interesting subsequences can sometimes be found by progressively increasing the value of n.

Exploratory Sequential Data Analysis (ESDA), (Sanderson et al., 1994) is another well-known technique that has been applied to describing software engineering processes (D'Astous and Robillard, 2000).

We found, however, that we wanted to go beyond merely finding patterns that are sequences of events. We sought a graphical technique that could show the context of each event and could more actively assist software designers to develop tools, as has been advocated by Bannon (1994) and Suchman (1995).

3.4.2   Use Case Maps

The Use Case Map (UCM) notation shows multiple sequences of localized events. By localized, we mean that each event occurs in a particular *context*. Contexts are shown as boxes. Sequences are shown as paths that wind from context to context, may form loops and may split into independent sequences or may merge. Events are points on the paths.

The UCM notation was originally invented by Buhr (Buhr 1998; Buhr and Casselman, 1996) to represent causal flows of responsibilities in real-time software systems. In such systems there are normally several parallel processes or tasks (paths), interacting with different subsystems (contexts) and involving interactions or computations (events).UCMs are also ideal, however, to represent the detailed flow of the tasks of a single person or a small group. As with computer systems, people work in parallel on multiple tasks (paths), work with various different tools, documents or other people (contexts), and perform series of actions (events).

Figure 3.6 shows a UCM that is being used to model a user's *particular* interaction with Unix and the Emacs editor. Later in the chapter we will show additional UCMs containing *generalized* patterns crystallized from observing many users.

To understand Figure 3.6, follow the numbered points along the path, and read the descriptions below:

- The circle is the start symbol.
- The user enters Emacs and opens a directory, the listing of which is shown as the first inner box. The user enters the context of this directory.
- The user employs an item from the directory listing to initiate the opening

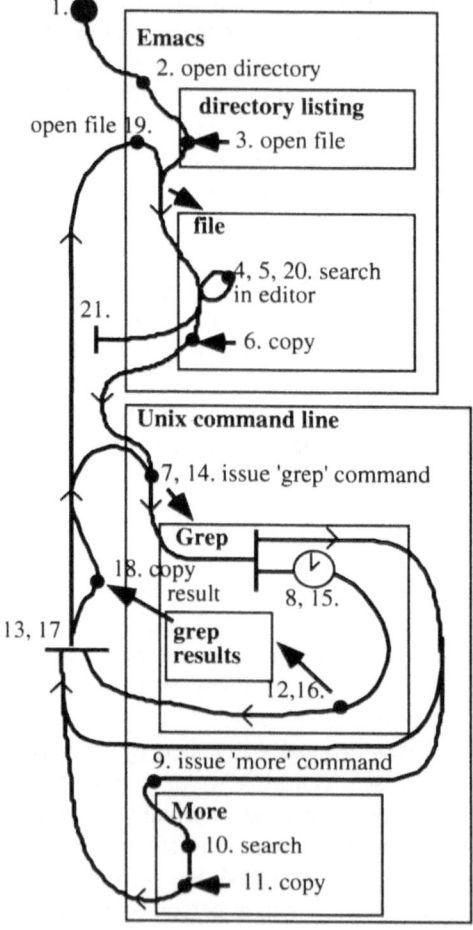

Figure 3.6. An example Use Case Map (UCM) shows the flow of work from context to context.

of a file. The bold arrows indicate information being taken to be used later.

- After entering the context of a file, the user performs a search.The user performs another search; the loop indicates repetition.
- The user places some information in the copy buffer, to be used later.
- After leaving Emacs and entering the context of the Unix command line, the user issues a *grep* command, using information in the copy buffer as the argument (represented again by the bold arrow).
- In the newly created *grep* context, the path forks. The upper path is that taken by the user who wishes to do something else while *grep* is executing. The lower path, with the clock symbol, is that taken by the computer that takes time to perform the *grep* (the clock symbol indicates a delay that could at some point be cancelled if the user gets tired of waiting).
- The user reenters a Unix command-line context and then issues a *more* command.
- The user searches using the *more* tool.
- The user copies some text from the information displayed by *more*.
- Meanwhile, the *grep* started earlier has completed and produced its results.
- The user now can get back to dealing with the *grep* results. The horizontal line indicates an *and-join* or *synchronization* in which the two subpaths (waiting for *grep* and the users activities while waiting) are reunited after *both* of them are completed.
- The user could do something with the *grep* results, but decides not to. Instead he ignores them and issues another *grep* command using the information copied earlier while performing *more*. The path converges with the path taken earlier using an *or-join*; the user will now repeat a subsequence performed earlier.
- There is a fork and a delay again during the execution of *grep*; the user again has the opportunity to do other things while waiting.
- As before, the results are eventually returned.
- The user waits at the and-join for the *grep* to be complete; this time he chooses not to work in the *more* program.
- This time, the user copies some text from the result.
- Instead of repeating *grep* for a third time, this time the user goes back to the Emacs context and opens a file using the contents of the copy buffer (taken earlier from the *grep* results) as a file name.
- The user searches in the file using Emacs as he did earlier.
- The user finishes his task, as shown by the line terminating the path.

The process of creating a UCM from synchronized shadowing data is relatively simple, although it is currently a manual process. Proceeding through the data sequentially, one draws path segments from event to event, drawing new contexts and placing events inside them as needed (the contexts need to be coded as part of the synchronized shadowing process). When a sequence is repeated, one makes the path form a loop (having previously detected repeated sequences as described above helps one anticipate such loops). We have found that after a small amount of rearranging, a readable UCM normally emerges.

If a UCM becomes too difficult to read, i.e., with too many events, contexts and paths, it can be split into several UCMs, each containing paths and contexts extracted from the large messy UCM. Doing this is how we discover *work patterns* in the UCMs: A work pattern is shown as a simplified UCM that contains paths that are followed very frequently, and typically involve just one or two contexts. UCMs provide a mechanism called *stubs* and *plug-ins* to facilitate this.

There are also other notations that can be used to model human work:

- data flow diagrams can, at a very high level, show the movement of information around a business;
- work-flow diagrams and Petri nets can show the sequences and dependencies among subtasks;
- and flow charts can show decision-making processes.

None of these notations, however, can clearly show at a detailed level both the context of the work and the multiple interacting threads of events. UML activity charts perhaps come closest to what we need. They can cope with multiple threads and contexts, but the current representation of contexts is limited to one dimension (the so-called *swimlanes*). UCMs display contexts in two dimensions, which is usually more understandable and supports hierarchies of contexts.

In this subsection, we have discussed how Use Case Maps can be used to represent work. Other researchers working on approaches to help people record and represent their understanding of work include Pycock et al. (1998) and Jordan et al. (1995). More information about use-case maps can be found at http://www.usecasemaps.org.

3.4.3   Requirements Development

The process described so far that involves developing *buttons* for synchronized shadowing, performing the shadowing, detecting patterns in the data, and drawing UCMs containing work patterns, should ideally be done in an *iterative* manner as a series of studies. Each step can help improve the other steps in the subsequent iterations; for example, the work patterns can give the researchers performing synchronized shadowing a better idea of what to look for.

The final, but certainly not least important, step in our process is taking the work patterns and interpreting them so as to discover potential software requirements. The essence of this process is examining the patterns looking for signs of inefficiency such as the following:

- Frequent sequences that can be automated.
- Frequent situations where the participant jumps back and forth between contexts, and where it might be possible to allow the required activity to all occur in only one context and thus eliminate context switching.

- Situations where the participant must frequently wait, due to system delays.
- Situations where the participant frequently makes mistakes because he or she has to rely on memory to transfer information or to perform similarly mentally taxing activities.

Each of these can lead to a requirement to reduce the inefficiency through improved software.

3.5   A Case Study: Empirical Studies at Mitel

This section presents a case study in which we applied synchronized shadowing and Use Case Maps to study and model the work patterns of software maintainers at Mitel Corporation, and then develop tools to make them more productive. The Mitel software engineers we studied were working on a large telecommunications system.

Before our first synchronized shadowing sessions, we studied the software engineers enough to discover the main types of events we would provide as buttons in the synchronized shadowing tool. Table 3.1 shows the set of control keys - which we used in place of buttons - that were used by one of the two note-takers. While the first note-taker recorded the individual actions that the programmers performed, the other note-taker focused more on their high-level goals while performing their actions. The programmers were asked to think out loud while performing their task. It was the job of the second note-taker to code this information, therefore his codes focused more on hypotheses and plans.

We conducted a total of nine synchronized shadowing sessions with eight software engineers, each session lasting about an hour. We attempted to coordinate our study of each SE so that it would occur at a time when the SE was performing what he or she considered typical work with source code.

Prior to meeting the participant to begin each session, we synchronized the

Table 3.1. Control sequences in Microsoft Word macros used by one of the observers during synchronized shadowing.

Control key	Description
^-v	VIS: Look at something
^-e	EDITOR: Issue an editor command
^-m	MODIFY: Write or modify some text
^-s	SEE: Issue a command in a software exploration tool
^-g	GREP: Run *grep*
^-t	TOOL: Work with some other tool.
^-u	UNIX: Type a command other than *grep*
^-z	NEW-GOAL: Start something completely new
^-space	Miscellaneous

clocks of the two computers. We also practiced using the synchronized shadowing interface to ensure that we were familiar with the coding scheme we had developed.

When the synchronized shadowing data was obtained, it was scanned manually for a short while to begin to find patterns. It was clear (as we had initially expected from earlier observations) that the vast majority of our participants' time was spent working in text editors or searching for various kinds of things.

Following the procedure outlined in Section 3.4, we worked our way through the data and developed a variety of UCMs that represent common work patterns. We found that the data coded during the initial synchronized shadowing sessions was coded at the level of detail we needed for the UCMs. Therefore we manually went back through the logs, looking at the free-form notes which had been added after each button press during synchronized shadowing. We were able to give more precise codes to each event; e.g., we needed to divide certain types of search into more detailed categories. The inter-rater reliability of this manual process was very high once we had agreed on the codes we wanted to use. For later synchronized shadowing sessions, we were able to add extra buttons to our tool and therefore reduce the need for subsequent manual analysis. The following are two examples of UCMs we generated from this work.

While exploring a series of files, our sample logs showed the participants doing three distinct types of activities: Searching for text, copying text (into the copy buffer) or merely reading the text. As for searching, it was done either using previously copied text or by manually typing the parameters. Users would jump repeatedly from file to file, using the contents of the copy buffer to transfer a piece of text from one file to use as a search parameter in another. Figure 3.7 shows the UCM we constructed to show this work pattern, in the context of a single file.

Figure 3.8 shows a second example UCM. In this case, the activity being

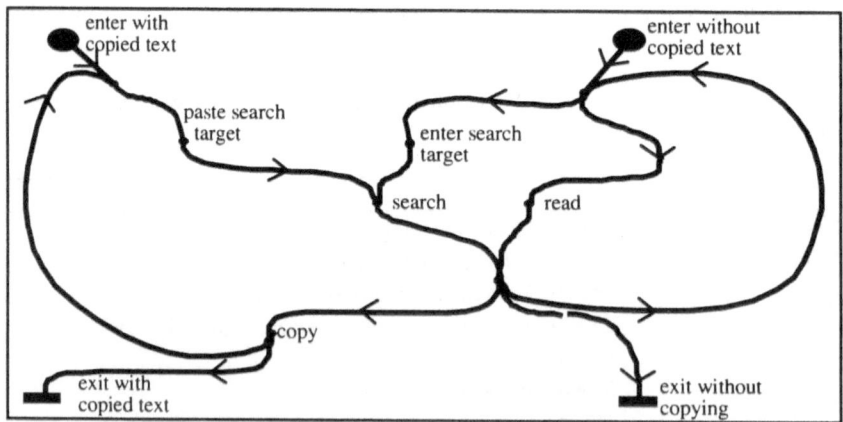

Figure 3.7. A Use Case Map showing an abstract view of the paths taken by users when exploring files (without editing).

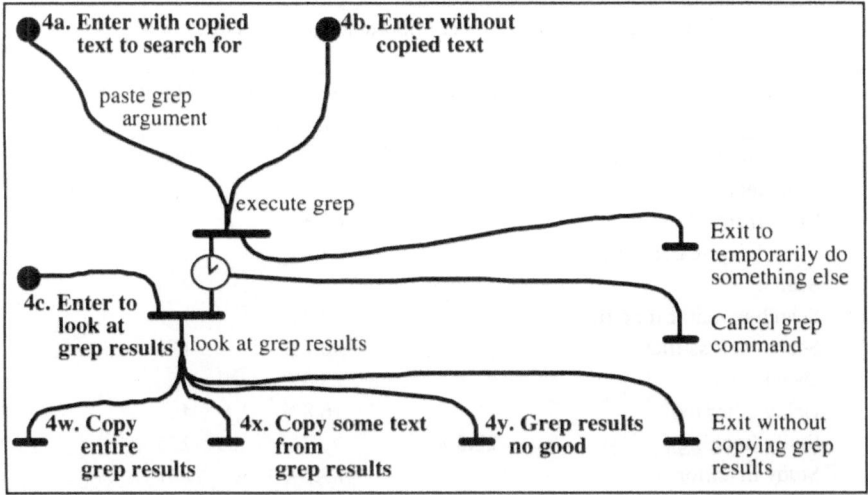

Figure 3.8. UCM showing possible paths when performing a search using *grep* (the clock symbol represents a period of waiting).

frequently performed is searching through multiple files using *grep*. The results of the searches are then manipulated. The figure illustrates all the possible paths that occur in this activity.

Important observations we make from Figures 3.7 and 3.8, as well as other UCMs not shown here are:

- Search within files, and search across files, are fundamental operations to the maintainers.
- Transfer of information from file to file and from tool to tool was most commonly performed by copying and pasting. There were two important sources of information to place into the copy buffer: text in a file and text in a search result. There were four different destinations into which the buffer would be pasted. These are; A file that is being edited, a file name to open, or a search parameter either in an editor or for *grep*.

We used a program to count the occurrences of the various categories and sequences of events in the UCMs. The results are presented in Tables 3.2 and 3.3. Of the 966 events recorded while performing synchronized shadowing, almost 30% involved searching, and almost 20% involved cutting and pasting.

Table 3.3 shows sequences where the user copies some text and then pastes it. It is clear that most of the time, when a maintainer selects some text in a file, he or she intends to use that as a search argument to find other occurrences of the text in the same file or in other files. Similarly, when a maintainer selects

Table 3.2. Frequencies of the most important categories of events.

Event types	Percent of total	Percent of subtotals	Number of events
Total number of events			966
Copy text	9.2%		89
Copy from file		66.3%	59
Copy from search results		34.8%	31
Search	28.3%		273
Search in editor (one file)		59.3%	162
Search across files		40.7%	111
Using *grep*		23.8%	65
Using other tool		16.8%	46
Study (reading)	28.5%		275
Study in editor		87.6%	241
Study search results		12.4%	34
Paste text	10.6%		102
Paste to modify text		7.8%	8
Paste to search in editor		32.4%	33
Paste to open file		22.5%	23
Paste to search across files		37.3%	38

text in a search result, it is generally the name of a file that he or she intends to open and study in more depth.

Analysis of the data shown above leads us to derive the following requirements for a software exploration tool we are developing called TkSee (Lethbridge and Anquetil, 1997; Lethbridge and Herrera, 2000).

- The tool should have a direct way to open a file from search results (e.g., by simply selecting some result)
- **Rationale:** 71% of copy operations performed on search results were performed in order to obtain a file name to open. This requirement would eliminate a considerable number of keystrokes or mouse movement (both issuing copy and commands, as well as actions required to exit the search results and enter).

Table 3.3. Copy-paste transitions

	Copy from file	Copy from search results
Paste to modify text	5.1%	16.1%
Paste to search in file	27.1%	9.7%
Paste to open file	1.7%	71.0%
Paste as search argument	47.5%	3.2%
Not immediately used	18.6%	0.0%

- The tool should have a simple command to automatically locate occurrences of whatever is in the copy buffer.
- **Rationale:** No matter what the source of copied text, users frequently used the copy buffer as the argument when performing a search in an editor. This requirement would save many paste operations and reduce the necessity to bring up a search dialog box.
- Add a command that allows the user to search for whatever is selected in the editor without doing a copy and then a paste.
- **Rationale:** 27.1% of copy operations from a file were immediately used to search in that file. This would speed this operation.
- In dialog boxes that initiate *grep*-like searches or searches within a file, prefill the box that specifies the argument with whatever text has just previously been selected in the editor and/or the search results.
- **Rationale:** This would reduce the need to do some copying.

The requirements above come from the data in Tables 3.2 and 3.3; thus it might be argued that we could eliminate the Use Case Map step and go straight from patterns in synchronized shadowing data, to tables, to requirements. The Use Case Maps however, had two critical roles: Firstly, we developed them iteratively as we performed pilot studies and improved our coding scheme (the set of buttons) for synchronized shadowing. As we saw patterns emerging, we drew the UCMs to obtain an understanding of which buttons should be present in our synchronized shadowing tool. Secondly, having the UCMs allows us to better explain the requirements.

Implementing the above requirements has allowed us to improve the functionality of TkSee considerably. TkSee's overall strengths include its integration of a variety of techniques for searching through source code (including the requirements illustrated above), its ability to allow maintainers to incrementally build models of aspects of the software, and its ability to support the manipulation and saving of search results and explorations. These features include those that our Use Case Maps tell us are the activities that maintainers perform most often.

3.6   Summary and Conclusions

We have described several techniques for performing observational field studies of people at work, and analyzing the resulting data. We applied these techniques to the work of software engineers in order to develop better tools for them; however, the techniques should be useful whenever one's objective is to understand work practices.

We situated our empirical study techniques in a three-dimensional space. On one axis, our techniques involve observation of people performing their everyday work; therefore, they can be called *field studies* as opposed to laboratory studies. On a second axis, our tools involve active observation involving direct contact with people as they go about their daily work, whereas other techniques might only indirectly observe people or else study the products of their work. On the third axis, our techniques involve information gathering for the purpose of constructing models; we make no attempts to run controlled experiments.

To gather data while observing software engineers at work, we use a note-taking approach as opposed to videotaping. However, since it is hard to be consistent when manually taking notes, we developed a technique we call synchronized shadowing whereby two people use clock-synchronized computers that are preprogrammed with buttons that record time-stamped annotations corresponding to different kinds of observed events. This technique allows us to gather reasonably accurate information in real-time that is already partially coded, hence analysis time is greatly reduced.

We build models from our synchronized-shadowing data using Use Case Maps (UCMs), a technique originally invented for modeling real-time systems, but which is ideally suited to model work practices. From the UCMs we can see work patterns, and from the work patterns we can deduce requirements for software tools. We call our combined approach WASS (Work Analysis from Synchronized Shadowing).

There remain some open research issues with our work: Firstly it would be nice to analyze the time consumed by the participants performing the work patterns, rather than just the sequences. We know, for example, that copying and pasting is performed very frequently, but it might be that other less time-consuming activities actually take more time. We would also like to use the technique in a wider context. Currently we have only used it in the one Mitel empirical study.

3.7   Acknowledgements

We thank the Mitel employees who participated in our studies. We also thank an anonymous reviewer for valuable suggestions and K. Teresa Khidir for helping polish the manuscript.

3.8   References

Bannon, L. (1994). Representing work in design. In L. Suchman (Ed.), *Representations of Work: A Symposium.* Monograph for proceedings of the 27th HICSS, January, Maui, Hawaii.

Bannon, L, and Bødker, S. (1991). Beyond the interface: Encountering artifacts in use. In J. Carroll (Ed.), *Designing Interaction: Psychology at the Human-Computer Interface.* Cambridge University Press: New York.

Bendifallah, S., and Scacchi, W. (1987). Understanding software maintenance work, *IEEE Transactions on Software Engineering,* 13(3), 311-323.

Blomberg, J., Suchman, L., and Trigg, R. (1996). Reflections on a work-oriented design project, *Human Computer Interaction*, 11, 237-265.

Boehm-Davis, D. Holt, R., and Schultz, A. (1992). The role of program structure in software maintenance, *Int. Journal of Man Machine Studies, 36*, 21-63.

Buhr, R.J.A (1998). Use case maps as architectural entities for complex systems, *IEEE Trans. Software Engineering,*. 24(12) Dec., 1131-1155.

Buhr, R.J.A and Casselman, R.S. (1996). *Use Case Maps for Object-Oriented Systems*, Prentice-Hall, Englewood Cliffs, NJ.

Button, G., and Dourish, P. (1996). Technomethodology: Paradoxes and Possibilities, In *Proc CHI '96; Human Factors in Computing Systems*, Vancouver, 19-26..

Cook, T., and Campbell, D. (1979) *Quasi-Experimentation: Design and Analysis Issues for Field Settings.* Rand McNally: Chicago, IL.

Curtis, W (1986) By the way, did anyone study any real programmers? In E. Soloway and S. Iyengar (Eds.). In *Proc. Empirical Studies of Programmers.* Norwood, NJ, pp. 256-262.

Curtis, B., Krasner, H., and Iscoe, N. (1988). A field study of the software design process for large systems, *Communications of the ACM,* 31(11), 1268-1287.

D'Astous, P., and Robillard, P. (2000). Protocol analysis in software engineering studies. *Empirical Studies in Software Engineering*, Khaled El-Eman and Janice Singer, eds., MIT Press.

Denzin, N.K and Lincoln, Y.S. (1994). *Handbook of Qualitative Research*, Sage Publications: Thousand Oaks, CA.

Glaser, B., and Strauss, A., (1967). *The Discovery of Grounded Theory: Strategies for Qualitative Research.* Aldine deGruyter: Hawthorne, NY.

Hutchins, E. (1994). *Cognition in the Wild*, MIT Press: Cambridge, MA.

Jordan, B., Goldman, R., and Sachs, P. (1995). Tools for the workplace, *Communications of the ACM,* 38(9), 42.

Kraut, R., and Streeter, L. (1995). Coordination in software development, *Communications of the ACM*, 38(3), 69-81.

Kyng, M., and Mathiassen, L. (1997). *Computers and Design in Context.* MIT Press: Cambridge, MA.

Lethbridge, T.C. and Anquetil, N. (1997). Architecture of a source code exploration tool: A software engineering case study, *University of Ottawa, Computer Science Technical report TR-97-07.*

Lethbridge, T.C. and Herrera, F. (2000). Towards assessing the usefulness of the TkSee software exploration tool: a case study, Elsewhere in this book..

Lethbridge, T., Singer, J., Vinson, N., and Anquetil, N. (1997). An examination of software engineering work practices. In *Proc. CASCON*, Toronto, October: IBM, 209-223.

Lethbridge, T.C., Lyon, and S., Perry, P. (2000). The management of university-industry collaborations involving empirical studies of software engineering, In *Empirical Studies in Software Engineering*, Khaled El-Eman and Janice Singer, eds., MIT Press.

Litman, D., Pinto, J., Letovsky, S. and Soloway, E. (1996). Mental models and software maintenance. In *Proc. Empirical Studies of Programmers: First Workshop*.

Neuman, W., L. (1997). *Social Research Methods: Qualitative and Quantitative Aproaches*. Allyn and Bacon: Boston, MA.

Porter, A., and Votta L. (1998). Comparing detection methods for software requirements inspections: A replication using professional subjects, *Empirical Software Engineering*, 3, 355-379.

Pycock, J., Palfreyman, K., Allanson, J., and Button, G. (1998). Representing fieldwork and articulating requirements through VR, In. *Proc CSCW*, Seattle, 383-392.

Simonsen, J., and Kensing, F. (1997). Using ethnography in contextual design, *Communications of the ACM*, 40(7), 82-88.

Singer, J., and Lethbridge, T. C. (1998a) Work practices as an alternative method to assist tool design in software engineering, *International Workshop on Program Comprehension*, Ischia, Italy, 173-179.

Singer, J., and Lethbridge, T.C. (1998). Studying work practices to assist tool design in software engineering. In *6th IEEE International Workshop on Program Comprehension*, Italy, 173-179. A longer version appears as: University of Ottawa, Computer Science Technical Report TR-97-08.

Sanderson, P.M., Scott, J.J.P., Johnston, T., Mainzer, J., Watanabe, L. M. and James, J.M. (1994). MacSHAPA and the enterprise of exploratory sequential data analysis (ESDA). *International Journal of Human-Computer Studies*, 41 (5), 633-681.

Suchman, L. (1987). *Plans and Situated Actions: The Problem of Human-Machine Communication*. Cambridge University Press: New York.

Suchman, L. (Ed.) (1995). Representations of work, *Special issue of the Communications of the ACM*, 38(9), 33-68.

Walz, D., Elam, J., and Curtis, B. (1993). Inside a software design team: Knowledge acquisition, sharing, and integration, *Communication of the ACM*, 36(10), 63-77.

4
Assessing the Usefulness of the TkSee Software Exploration Tool

Timothy C. Lethbridge
Francisco Herrera

4.1 Introduction

The goal of our research is to find ways to improve the productivity of software developers who are maintaining very large legacy systems. To help achieve this goal, we have developed a software tool called TkSee, which allows software engineers to explore and understand source code. This tool serves as the infra-structure for various studies of program comprehension, and is used intensively by several software developers inside Mitel Corporation. As researchers, the most important part of our mission is to evaluate the usefulness of the ideas we implement. In this chapter we present a case study in which we obtained insights about usability while trying to evaluate TkSee's overall usefulness. The intent of this chapter is to highlight the factors that made the evaluation process difficult, and to provide pointers to those who wish to assess the usefulness of complex software products.

4.1.1 Two Independent Factors Leading to Usefulness:
Utility and Usability

When developing a software system with innovative new capabilities, it is im-portant for developers to measure the usefulness of these capabilities so that future designs can be improved. This process may be made difficult, however, because some users might not *adopt* the system, while others might adopt the system but not exploit its functionality *as intended*. Failure to adopt the system may be due to the following reasons:

- they do not know that it exists;
- they are reluctant to change their work practices;
- they lack of time to learn the system;

- they have difficulty learning it;
- they experience minor annoyances with it, or
- it does not fit their task.

Failure to exploit functionality as intended may be because of the same reasons, or because the users do not learn it effectively.

The following two factors are necessary if a system is to be both adopted by users and useful to them:

1. The system's functionality must provide high *utility*; i.e., the system must have the raw computational capabilities and features that should, in principle, enable users to perform their work.
2. The system must have good *usability*; i.e., its design must ensure that users can easily learn and efficiently exploit its functionality.

This distinction between utility and usability is adopted from the work of Nielsen (1993) and the usability engineering community.[1] Both aspects of usefulness should be measured only in the context of particular groups of users and tasks. For example, utility can be seen as the fitness of the functionality to a certain task. Similarly, a system that a power-user finds usable might be quite unusable for an occasional user of the same system (and vice versa).

An important point to consider is that utility and usability, as defined above, are largely orthogonal. For example, imagine a spreadsheet program developed for statisticians with all the functional capabilities of Microsoft Excel, but in which editing a cell involved triple-clicking on the cell to select it and then pulling down a nested menu to open a dialog box containing the cell's contents. Such a program would have high utility (the needed ability to edit a cell is present), but low usability (users will have difficulties discovering the triple clicking and would be annoyed at not being able to directly type data in a cell). Conversely, imagine a second spreadsheet program that had exactly the same user interface as Microsoft Excel (widely recognized as being good), but which lacked statistical functions. Such a system would be low in utility for the statisticians, but high in usability. Neither system would be very useful, but each for a different reason.

Much software engineering work is biased away from usability and toward higher utility. The inventiveness and innovative thinking of most developers is oriented toward developing as many features as they can. As a result, usability considerations may be deferred, and then perhaps curtailed as deadlines loom.

---

[1] Note that the ISO 9241 definition of usability, "The effectiveness, efficiency and satisfaction with which specified users achieve specified tasks in particular environments," does not as readily allow one to make the distinction between utility and usability that we consider so important in this chapter. This is because the word "effectiveness" encompasses some aspects of utility.

This utility bias is often manifested as "feature bloat" - the availability of so many features, such that the system as a whole becomes so complex that usability becomes even worse than it otherwise might have been.

One of the main points we will emphasize in this chapter is that it is essential to view utility and usability as largely separate issues. Clearly seeing the distinction between them allows both to be improved. In particular, one's ability to measure utility can be significantly reduced by poor usability.

4.1.2   Assessing the Usefulness of a System

Developers should separately assess[2] both the utility and usability of systems in order to arrive at an overall assessment of usefulness.

Assessment of utility means evaluating the innovative computational or data-manipulation facilities that the new software is providing and that are supposed to help users achieve their goals. The objective of utility evaluation is to confirm whether the functionality implemented in the system actually helps users to achieve their goals better or whether it should be improved. In order to make such an assessment, developers typically give the system or a prototype to a group of users. The developers then gather information about any missing capabilities as well as ideas for improvements.

It is sometimes feasible to fully assess the utility of a proposed system during the review of its requirements, dispensing with a later assessment of the completed system. However, this is only realistic when developing simple systems in very well-understood domains. In the case of software that seeks to help users solve *complex* problems in *new* domains, it becomes imperative to assess the utility by actually having users use the system or a prototype. In the development of such software, it is typical that not even experts in the domain are able to clearly propose the required functionality. Hence requirements tend to originate from bright ideas, rather than systematic analysis of the problem. These must be validated by users who actually use the system.

The case study presented in this chapter discusses a program comprehension tool that is a typical example of a system for solving a complex problem: There is so far no well-recognized standard approach to program comprehension tool design, and the comprehension task itself is highly complex. The requirements for new features are therefore hypotheses that must be validated by their utility assessment.

Assessment of usability means evaluating factors such as the learnability and efficiency of use of the system, as well as how well the system guides the users through their task and provides them with feedback in response to their actions. These factors should be evaluated largely independently of utility. Later on in this chapter we will see that usability evaluation can be performed by having

---

[2] We use the words "assess" and "evaluate" interchangeably.

usability experts survey the system to look for violations of usability heuristics, or by observing users use the system.

As mentioned earlier, usability is often neglected in favor of utility. This can be particularly the case in complex systems for new domains, precisely because so many new functional ideas are being implemented. Unfortunately ignoring usability can undermine the ability of developers to accurately assess the utility. If the usability is poor, the users may not learn to efficiently use the functionality, may not learn parts of it at all, and may reject the system, saying it is not useful.

If users reject the system, the developers may blame the functionality when in fact it might have had excellent potential - with its excellence simply masked by poor usability. Since many developers are not well trained in software usability, they may not realize that usability is the real culprit in the failure.

Our thesis, therefore, is that usability must be formally assessed *before* attempting to evaluate the functionality of software. Failure to do this will make it impossible to accurately measure the underlying utility of implemented features, and may lead researchers to draw incorrect conclusions when certain features do not appear useful.

As part of our CSER research, we developed a code exploration tool called TkSee which is intended to help software engineers explore and understand source code more efficiently. The process we used for developing the tool was similar to the one described above: Research activities were undertaken to discover the needed functionality, which was then implemented, but without formal attention to usability. TkSee was given to a group of software engineers so that they could use it during maintenance of a large software system. Since an integral part of the research plan was to evaluate the utility of the various ideas we had implemented, we attempted to determine an appropriate approach for such an evaluation. We realized that TkSee had not been used as much as we had initially hoped and therefore we should start by exploring factors contributing to that situation. One of the issues we realized we should explore was TkSee's usability: We should explore how it had affected people's ability to learn and use the tool.

In the next section, we briefly explain the aspects of TkSee's functionality that we believe to be innovative and useful to its users. Following that, we look at some of the difficulties that arose as we set about evaluating the software. Most of these difficulties occurred because we had paid far more attention to utility than to usability.

4.2   Features of TkSee: Optimized Search and Hierarchical Management of Search Results

In this section, we outline the key functionality of TkSee and the process we used to develop the requirements for that functionality. The purpose of this section is to familiarize the reader with the context in which we performed the usability studies discussed in the next section.

The goal of our research is to improve the productivity of software developers who are working on large real-time software systems. We are working primarily with software systems and developers in Mitel Corporation, although we are also cooperating with others within CSER. We attempt to follow a disciplined approach to our research. This involves: (a) studying the work practices of the Mitel developers to discover what causes them the most difficulty; (b) designing tools that might reduce these difficulties; and (c) evaluating the tools to determine to what extent the difficulties have been reduced, and what resulting productivity increase has occurred.

Studies of software developers we performed prior to deploying TkSee identified two key challenges they face: Effectively searching through the code, and managing the results of searches. The developers we studied would normally use the Unix *grep* tool to search through the code; this is often very time-consuming since there are millions of lines of code. After obtaining results (lists of lines or *hits* which match a *grep* pattern) the developers would often perform further searches or other activities, and quickly lose track of earlier search results; they often, therefore, would tend to repeat the same searches. Also they often would want to search by name for what they knew to be either a variable, a type or a routine. *Grep*, on the other hand, is oblivious to syntax and returns any line that matches the search pattern (e.g., words in a comment, or variables when the developer is looking for a type). This results in excessively long lists of hits that take time to examine. When something interesting was found, the developer would often revert to old technology and write it down on paper, lest it be forgotten.

We also noted that the developers were using what we call a *just-in-time comprehension* strategy to solve problems. This is an opportunistic approach where developers follow chains of relationships, understanding just the minimum needed for the current subproblem, rather than systematically attempting to learn and understand entire components of the system.

These observations led us to design and implement the following features in TkSee: A hierarchy of software objects, instant access to the source code, and an unlimited hierarchical history of named hierarchies. We outline each of these features in Sections 4.2.1 through 4.2.3. Further details can be found in Lethbridge (2000) and Lethbridge and Anquetil (1997). A schematic view of TkSee is presented in Figure 4.1, while a screen-dump of the system as it existed prior to its first usability evaluation is shown in Figure 4.2. Figure 4.3, at the end of the chapter, shows the system following usability evaluation and also points out some more details of its design.

As mentioned at the beginning of this chapter, our goal in developing TkSee is to improve the productivity of the software developers. This may require us to merely help the developers do their current work faster; sometimes, however it requires us to restructure their tasks to a certain extent. When doing this we must, however, ensure that any restructuring does not scare them away from adopting our tools by forcing changes they do not have the time to learn.

4.2.1   A Hierarchy of Different Types of Software Objects Found While Searching

The hierarchy of software objects is shown as region B in Figure 4.1. The software objects are color-coded and can be such things as files, routines, variables, types, and lines in a file. The lines in a file are the same as the classic *grep* hits; part of our design philosophy was to provide the developers with a superset of functionality they had already. The ability to search for the other more specific software objects such as routines and variables means that developers are no longer limited to searching for whatever strings match their search pattern.

Indentation in the hierarchy represents any kind of relationship between the parent software object and the child (indented) software objects. Supported relationships include: "routine calls routine," "routine called by routine," "variable defined in routine," "type used in routine," "line found in file," etc. Specific icons distinguish among the relationships. Prior to the deployment of TkSee, the Mitel developers had visualized these relationships either in their heads or on paper. Users can perform many operations in the hierarchy: Some operations create a new hierarchy by performing general searches in the target system for any of the different types of software objects. Other operations allow subsets of the objects in the hierarchy to be extracted, or uninteresting objects deleted. Yet other functions allow the user to select several objects and ask to display related objects using indentation. Taken together, these operations were designed to provide those functions the Mitel developers appeared to need to more easily perform just-in-time comprehension.

4.2.2   Instant Access to the Source Code from Any Software Object in the Hierarchy

If a file, routine, or line of code is selected in the hierarchy (area B in Figure

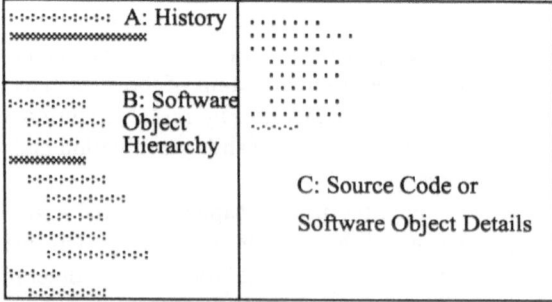

Figure 4.1. A schematic view of the TkSee main window.

4.1), then the actual code appears in area C of Figure 4.1. The number of key-strokes or other actions needed to access the code itself is thus minimized.

If a variable or type is selected in area B, then the definition of that variable or type and a list of places where it is used instantly appear in area C.

4.2.3   An Unlimited History of Named Hierarchies

The hierarchical history of named hierarchies is shown as area A in Figure 4.1. If a user creates a new hierarchy in area B, they never lose what was there. This is because the user can select earlier bookmarked hierarchies instantly in area A. New hierarchies, and hence bookmarks, are created whenever a new global search is initiated (e.g., searching for all files matching a pattern) or when the user asks to save a subset of some other hierarchy as a new hierarchy.

Unlike bookmarks in web browsers, no conscious action has to be taken to save a bookmark. All earlier hierarchies are always available, even those from previous sessions; also if a user backtracks to older bookmarks and then pro-ceeds forward again, no bookmarks are lost (an annoying problem in web browsers). The user can manually delete and rename bookmarks; the ability to rename bookmarks means that they can serve as *to-do lists*, for example, to re-mind the developer of a set of lines of code that need changing.

During design, there was some concern that the history of named hierarchies, being unlimited in size, might grow so large as to become confusing. In practice, this has not been the case. Users are readily able to identify the hierarchies that interest them and rapidly delete those of no further interest.

4.2.4   Other Features of TkSee

TkSee is designed to work extremely fast: A database is built from the compiled code to allow near-instant searches over millions of lines of code. The premise for this is that any time spent waiting for an answer represents lost productivity.[3]

TkSee is also designed to allow users to perform all their exploration within one window; this contrasts with some other software browsing tools that make use of many windows, each query often opening a new window. Our one-window design is intended to minimize the possibility of losing track of search results, although nothing stops the designer from opening two or more TkSee windows if he or she desires.

---

[3] The current system is designed for people trying to understand code; once changes are made, the database has to be rebuilt. This can take considerable time and is a drawback to our current tool that would need to be rectified if the tool were ever commercialized. In practice, however, users have not complained much since they tend to start modifying code only after thoroughly understanding what needs to be done.

In the above sections, we have outlined the key features of TkSee that we intend to subject to systematic evaluation as part of our research. There are, of course, many details that we have omitted because they are not central to our work, and are present in TkSee so it is a practical software exploration tool.

4.2.5   TkSee as One of Many Program Comprehension Tools

There are many software tools that shares the objectives, and some of the features, as TkSee. For example, commercial tools such as Source Navigator (Red Hat, 2000) (used to develop TkSee[4]) and Sniff+ (WindRiver, 2000) provide exploration based on relationships among different types of software objects. Research tools such as Rigi (Müller et al., 1993) and Software Bookshelf (Finnigan et al., 1997) provide powerful capabilities for visualizing software.

TkSee is not meant to compete with these tools, but rather to serve as an experimental testbed for various features, notably the indented list hierarchy and the history of editable and renamable bookmarked hierarchies. The fact that different tool developers have developed different features to solve similar problems suggests that determining which features are best is nontrivial. The onus is therefore on researchers to carefully evaluate the utility of each feature and derive conclusions that can be used in the design of future tools. As mentioned in the last section, the needed evaluation of functionality faces interesting challenges due to usability and user acceptance concerns. We will address these concerns in the next section.

4.3   Evaluation of the Usability of TkSee

In this section we continue the case study, discussing our experiences performing a usability evaluation of TkSee. For more details, the reader may consult Herrera (1999).

4.3.1   Usage Patterns Prior to the Usability Study

Early versions of TkSee were delivered to users in 1996; subsequent versions have been in continuous use ever since. Figure 4.2 depicts a screendump from the tool before the usability study. We discovered that we were not able to convincingly evaluate TkSee's functionality for two reasons: The tool was used by relatively few users, and those users only used a small subset of its features in the intended way.

---

[4] Some people have asked: Why do we not use TkSee to develop itself? We would like to do this in the future; however, we currently only have parsers to build databases of C, Pascal, and 68000 Assembler source code. TkSee is written in tcl/tk and C++.

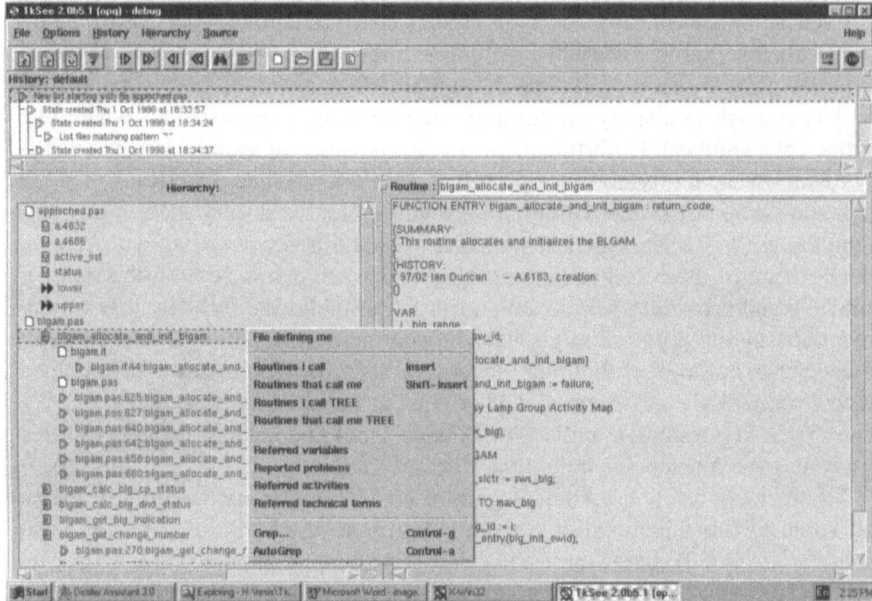

Figure 4.2. Example of TkSee prior to changes resulting from usability evaluation.

TkSee was made available to a team consisting of about 25 software developers. These people were performing a mix of new feature development and fixing defects. We did not notice any difference in the use of TkSee between feature developers and defect fixers. Both used the system to understand the code they were considering changing.

Only about 10 out of the 25 Mitel developers used TkSee for significant amounts of work over a two-year period. Of these ten, four adopted it with passion, using it almost constantly in their work, while the others used it for a while and then stopped or else used it only for very specific tasks. A large number of other users tried TkSee once or twice and then stopped, while many did not even try it.

We asked a sample of people what motivated them to use or not use TkSee. Most of the nonusers were happy with their existing tools and work practices, or else had felt that TkSee did not quite provide what they wanted. Some of the complaints of these latter users related to facilities that their existing tools provided but TkSee did not provide (e.g., information about binary executables and editing within the same window). However, in most cases the nonusers did not really understand the key features of TkSee either because it had not proved rapidly learnable or else because they had found some aspect of it difficult to understand. At some point during their learning attempts, many users had concluded that further learning was not worth additional investment of their very limited time.

Even among the heavy users of TkSee, many functions were hardly being used at all. An example of such a feature is *autogrep*. A user can take a relationship between two software objects in the hierarchy subwindow (region B of Figure 4.1) and ask to display the lines of code involved (e.g., the lines where one routine calls another). Unfortunately many users were not aware of the availability of such a capability nor what performing the operation really does.

It should be noted that we did not provide extensive documentation or training in the use of TkSee. Documentation consisted of a few web pages describing the operation of the commands; training consisted of demonstrating the tool periodically and providing help to anyone having trouble. We feel sure that a more proactive training program might have helped increase adoption to some extent; however, we do not feel that more extensive documentation would have helped much - we hardly ever observed anyone look at the existing documentation. We believe that, if possible, a tool such as TkSee should be made sufficiently usable so as not to need extensive training or documentation.

The fact that a few users had eagerly used TkSee was encouraging; it meant that some of the functionality was probably quite useful. Mitel reports (Lethbridge et al., 2000), based on informal observations, that some new hires who used TkSee took far less time than normal to become productive with maintaining Mitel software. However, we wanted to be scientific in our approach to evaluation of TkSee, and particularly when evaluating the utility of its individual features. The low adoption rate made us realize that it would not be possible to do this until more users efficiently used TkSee. A high adoption rate would have indicated that utility is high, but a low adoption rate could be blamed on either poor usability or poor utility (or both), and we did not know which was the case. To find out, we had to first evaluate and improve usability.

4.3.2   The Usability Study Process

In order to proceed, we designed and performed a usability study of TkSee. Two main techniques were applied in the study: (a) heuristic evaluation (Nielsen, 1992), and (b) think-aloud usability testing (Nielsen, 1993). We utilized user and task analysis (Hackos and Redish, 1998) to decide upon users and develop the tasks necessary for the think-aloud usability testing.

Heuristic Evaluation

The first approach we used is what Nielsen calls *heuristic evaluation*. We asked three evaluators to judge TkSee according to a list of usability guidelines found in Nielsen (1992, 1994). Each evaluator was asked to find as many deficiencies as they could by systematically examining TkSee. Table 4.1 shows a categorized summary of the 114 problems found by the evaluators. The main conclusion we can draw from this table is that the evaluators were able to find many problems in many different categories.

Table 4.1. Violations of Nielsen's usability guidelines found during heuristic evaluation of TkSee.

Usability guideline violated	Number of problems	
1. Use simple and natural dialogue	49	(43%)
2. Speak the users' language	20	(18%)
3. Minimize users' memory load	10	(9%)
4. Be consistent	15	(13%)
5. Provide good feedback	11	(10%)
6. Provide clearly marked exits	1	(1%)
7. Provide shortcuts or accelerators	2	(2%)
8. Provide good error messages[5]	0	
9. Prevent errors	5	(4%)
10. Provide good help and documentation	1	(1%)

The main difficulty with performing the heuristic evaluation was finding evaluators knowledgeable about usability. In the end, three people performed the evaluation and each person found different types of problems. One evaluator, for example, was an expert in usability but not in program comprehension. He found general usability problems which were not found by the other evaluators. These problems related to feedback, labeling, graphical design and so on. Another evaluator was already knowledgeable about TkSee and program comprehension and tended to point out capabilities that were missing (utility problems as opposed to usability problems) as well as incorrect behavior. The fact that the three evaluators found different, but intersecting, sets of problems confirm that multiple evaluators is important.

We consolidated the reports of the evaluators into a single report that was given to TkSee developers. This included a severity rating for the problems, as well as descriptions that were more comprehensive than provided by the evaluators. This stage was important since we needed to make it as easy as possible for the developers to understand the problems and systematically fix them. The process of reporting usability problems to developers is known to be particularly difficult and requires special considerations (Jeffries, 1994).

Since the developers were not knowledgeable about usability, they found some of Nielsen's guidelines difficult to understand. We therefore developed a more developer-oriented categorization scheme, which is found in Table 4.2. This categorization is designed to give developers a better idea about what they need to do to correct the problem. By using both categorizations, developers could more easily organize the solution of the problems.

This was the first time that TkSee and its developers were exposed to a usability evaluation. One hundred and fourteen usability problems were identified.

---

[5] As an exploration environment, where most user interaction is performed by selecting and issuing commands, TkSee has hardly any error messages.

Table 4.2. Types of problems found during heuristic evaluation of TkSee. A categorization designed to help developers understand usability issues.

Category of problem	Number of problems
1. Poor or missing feedback The software does not give the user adequate information about what has happened following an interaction which is a violation of guideline 5 in Table 4.1.	11 (10%)
2. Possible confusion Users may get confused by something such as certain behavior, situation, etc., and do not know what to do next or how to proceed.	14 (12%)
3. Possible misinterpretation Users may expect something such as a label, icon, menu item, command, etc., to mean one thing when it means something else.	11 (10%)
4. Poor labeling Other general problems with labeling.	6 (5%)
5. Lack of labeling A needed label is missing entirely.	2 (2%)
6. Lack of consistency A violation of guideline 4 in Table 4.1; could refer to consistency of any aspect of the UI including graphical design, labeling, dialog structure, feedback, etc.	15 (13%)
7. Poor graphical design Improvements are needed to layout, use of color, spacing, choice of fonts, aesthetics, etc.	9 (8%)
8. Unnecessary capability The UI would be better without the capability than with it.	5 (4%)
9. Lack of needed capability A capability is missing but users would expect to be present in order to perform their task; the problem may or may not relate directly to the UI.	11 (10%)
10. Lack of robustness A crash, hang, or inability to use a feature under certain conditions; the problem may or may not relate directly to the UI.	6 (5%)
11. Incorrect behavior The system fails to do what is expected; the problem may or may not be related directly to the UI.	2 (2%)
12. Nonoptimal interaction The way the users must interact to do something is not efficient.	22 (19%)

This number was much larger than expected so the TkSee developers were somewhat overwhelmed with the results. We worked with them in a series of meetings, helping them to understand each problem and to decide about suitable solutions. It proved essential in this process that the usability evaluator had considerable knowledge about TkSee.

We noticed it was difficult for them to understand the problems at an abstract level, and they required considerable time to see solutions that did not lead to other obvious usability problems, or to compare several proposed solutions. Insufficient knowledge about usability and about TkSee itself were the main causes of these difficulties. Many problems were also difficult to repair given the fact that TkSee is complex and was already implemented.

Prioritizing and organizing the problems became critical to developers. According to the original plan, developers were going to fix as many problems as possible prior to the think-aloud usability testing. In the end, only the most critical or quickly fixable problems were solved.

User and Task Analysis

User and task analysis was performed in preparation for think-aloud usability testing. The objective was to find a set of TkSee users that would provide as much information as possible for the least effort, as well as to determine an effective set of tasks. The process also served to gather information about how users had employed the tool. Aspects of this activity had been performed as part of the initial requirements gathering for TkSee, but a more detailed and precise approach was needed prior to usability evaluation.

In order to understand the types of users, we interviewed Mitel developers and managers and performed some field observations. We ended up classifying users in several dimensions: (a) their level of experience performing program comprehension in general; (b) their level of knowledge about the target software that is to be understood; and (c) their level of knowledge about TkSee.

The next step was to develop a very concrete set of tasks that we could ask the participants in think-aloud usability testing to perform. These tasks had to:

- Cover as many as possible of the work patterns (Lethbridge and Singer, 1997, 2000) typically performed during program comprehension. The work patterns would include performing various kinds of searches and manipulations of search results with different goals in mind.
- Involve the use of as many TkSee features as possible.
- Take 90 minutes maximum to complete.
- Give participants the opportunity to make some of their own choices about how to use TkSee. In other words we wanted to ensure that participants would have to think about how to use TkSee to accomplish a given task, not to be told precisely how to use it.

Our initial approach for generating the tasks was to work top-down, that is, to ask other TkSee users to give us suitable work scenarios that we could use as a basis for the concrete tasks. Unfortunately this approach did not work, because the TkSee users gave us goals that were just too abstract. For example, "Find out how many network interfaces can be active at the same time." Such a goal could be achieved in many different ways; what we really wanted were step-by-step scenarios at an intermediate level of detail so that we could plan the evaluation more precisely.

The approach we eventually adopted was bottom-up. We asked the TkSee users to give us *actual* examples of problems they had been faced with in the source code, along with step-by-step information about how the problems had been solved. These were embellished to arrive at a set of tasks that met all the above requirements.

In developing the tasks, there was a certain amount of risk that some participants in the think-aloud usability testing might already know the relevant sections of the code. In such a case they might not exercise TkSee as intended because they might be able to rely on their memory to provide answers instead of performing the tasks. We therefore phrased the tasks such that they required each participant to give a very detailed answer, for example, the exact number of uses of a variable. To complete a task, the participant also had to display something specific in a TkSee window and write down what they saw.

Think-Aloud Usability Testing

Think-aloud usability testing was used both to look for usability problems that TkSee users experience when learning and using the tool, and also to explore how efficiently the developers were capable of using its functionality. We observed ten developers performing the tasks prepared in the user and task analysis. We conducted a pilot study with first two participants (who happened to be TkSee developers) and then refined the tasks. The following discussion is based on results from the remaining eight Mitel participants.

Participants were requested to sign an informed-consent form after we explained to them the nature of the research. For those participants who had never used TkSee, each session was preceded by a 15-20 minute training session provided by Mitel support personnel.

The tasks were given to participants one at a time on index cards, and the participants were asked to verbalize their thoughts as they performed each task. An observer watched the participants, helped them when necessary, and kept rough notes. After each session, each participant discussed his or her experiences with the observer, and completed a short questionnaire. Each session lasted about 90 minutes and was videotaped.

Following the series of sessions, the notes and videotapes were analyzed and we arrived at a set of 72 usability problems. We categorized these problems using the same categories as in the heuristic evaluation; the results are in Tables 4.3 and 4.4.

Table 4.3. Violations of Nielsen's usability guidelines found during think-aloud usability testing of TkSee.

Usability guideline violated	Number of problems	
1. Use simple and natural dialogue	44	(61%)
2. Speak the users' language	9	(13%)
3. Minimize users' memory load	0	
4. Be consistent	1	(1%)
5. Provide good feedback	16	(22%)
6. Provide clearly marked exits	2	(3%)
7. Provide shortcuts or accelerators	0	
8. Provide good error messages	0	
9. Prevent errors	0	
10. Provide good help and documentation	0	

Table 4.4. Types of problems found during think-aloud usability testing of TkSee. The same categorization is used in Table 4.2.

Category of problem	Number of problems	
1. Poor or missing feedback	16	(22%)
2. Confusion	6	(8%)
3. Misinterpretation	8	(11%)
4. Poor labeling	6	(8%)
5. Lack of labeling	0	
6. Lack of consistency	1	(1%)
7. Poor graphical design	0	
8. Unnecessary element	2	(3%)
9. Lack of needed capability	7	(10%)
10. Lack of robustness	1	(1%)
11. Incorrect behavior	1	(1%)
12. Non optimal interaction	23	(32%)

We also categorized the problems according to whether they affected learn-ability only (25%), efficiency of use only (47%), or both (28%). In follow-up interviews, participants reported that while they thought TkSee was easy to learn, the learning process took considerable time. They also thought that TkSee was easy to use, but could be made more efficient for users.

A total of 53% of the problems had already been found in the heuristic evaluation (lower priority problems that had not yet been fixed). Finding the same problems again proved that the heuristic evaluation had uncovered legiti-mate problems, but we also showed that testing with users was essential to un-cover other types of problems. All eight participants encountered 7% of the problems. 14% of the problems were encountered by more than six and 43% of the problems were encountered by less than five. Finally, we noted that those five participants who were new to TkSee only noticed 20% of the problems while 7% were only noticed by the three experts.

Think-aloud evaluation was able to find more problems than heuristic evaluation in the "Use simple and natural dialog" and "Provide good feedback" categories. This stems from the fact that these categories tend to relate to dynamic behavior of the system, something that may be harder to evaluate using heuristics alone. On the other hand the heuristic evaluation found more problems than think-aloud evaluation in the "Minimize memory load," "Be consistent," and "Prevent errors" categories.

All the participants completed all the tasks; however, certain tasks were completed in very inefficient ways. Novices were not always able to discover the intended way the tool should be used, and experts had never learned certain useful features. For example, some tasks required looking for all the occurrences of a particular string in many files. The tool provided a feature for doing this in one step. However, none of the participants used that feature and, instead, completed the tasks in a much more cumbersome way.

An interesting side effect of think-aloud usability testing was that it served as an excellent training and awareness-raising approach in Mitel. TkSee users were willing to participate in the study even though they had been unwilling to explore the tool on their own. They were given tasks that exploited the power of the tool and had incentive to try to use the tool to accomplish them. At the end of each session, we instructed participants about how they could have achieved the tasks very efficiently. We saw that they then easily learned the features involved in solving the tasks and made comments such as "If at least somebody had told me about that feature before, I would have been using this tool for a long time." Having learned more about TkSee, the participants then encouraged other Mitel developers to learn to use the tool as well.

Having the videotapes was extremely helpful. Videotaping released the pressure of having to notice every problem in real-time; some problems were only noticed later upon reviewing the tapes. On the other hand, the analysis of the videos was tiring and very time-consuming. We had to spend about three to five times the duration of a video in order to analyze it.

As with the heuristic evaluation, communicating the problems to the TkSee developers was carefully planned. We prepared a report that summarized and categorized the problems and walked through this with the developers - showing them video clips of the problems to emphasize certain points and convince them of the seriousness. Following this, the developers implemented most of the recommended changes. Figure 4.3 shows TkSee following the changes.

4.3.3   The Impact of Usability Studies on the TkSee Development Team

In addition to discovering usability problems and helping train Mitel developers

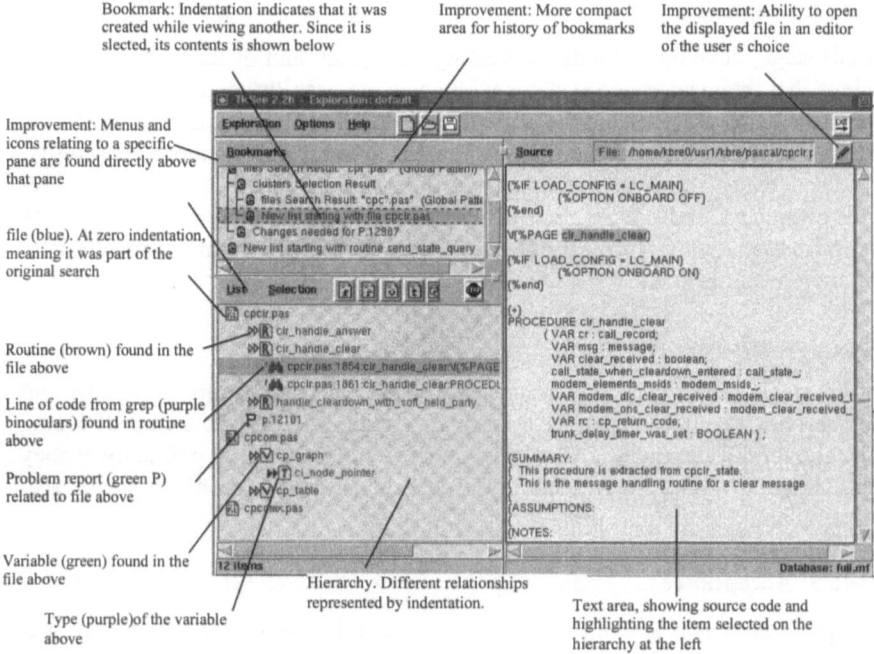

Bookmark: Indentation indicates that it was created while viewing another. Since it is slected, its contents is shown below

Improvement: More compact area for history of bookmarks

Improvement: Ability to open the displayed file in an editor of the user s choice

Improvement: Menus and icons relating to a specific pane are found directly above that pane

file (blue). At zero indentation, meaning it was part of the original search

Routine (brown) found in the file above

Line of code from grep (purple binoculars) found in routine above

Problem report (green P) related to file above

Variable (green) found in the file above

Type (purple)of the variable above

Hierarchy. Different relationships represented by indentation.

Text area, showing source code and highlighting the item selected on the hierarchy at the left

Figure 4.3. Example of TkSee showing some changes resulting from usability evaluation.

as discussed above, performing the usability study also helped raise awareness of usability among the TkSee development team.

TkSee had been developed in a university research environment following an informal and opportunistic development process. Features had been added by students and researchers when they had had bright ideas they wished to experiment with, hence it lacked complete documents describing its requirements, its design (except that of its database architecture (Lethbridge and Anquetil, 1997) and how to use it.

There was considerable staff turnover among TkSee developers because many were students. Also, almost none of the staff had any training in user interface design and usability. The newer staff was often not able to understand the tool or the purpose of certain features. They did not appreciate why certain user interface decisions had been made, or even that certain decisions were deliberate, hence they tended to make changes that were poor from a UI perspective and that led to usability problems.

Several authors describe the idea of stages of acceptance and commitment to user centered design in software projects (Bias and Mayhew, 1994; Ehrlich and Rohn, 1994). They explain that software projects can be in one of the following stages:

Stage 1. Skepticism

At this stage, developers focus on creating a large amount of functionality. They believe that they can create systems with adequate usability and that paying special attention to usability will be a waste of time. This was the stage in which the TkSee project appeared to be when we first set about trying to improve usability. We discovered that it was much better to focus initial usability activities at creating awareness and commitment to usability, rather than trying to obtain the best possible results. It would not be possible to achieve optimum results with skeptical developers.

Stage 2: Curiosity

At this stage, developers may admit that the system has usability problems, but are reluctant to do much about it, primarily because they are afraid of losing control over development. TkSee developers reached this stage gradually as they were shown the long list of usability problems and as the problems were carefully explained to them.

Stage 3: Acceptance

When this stage is reached, the developers accept the assistance of usability specialists and try to follow approaches that promote usability. By the end of the usability studies, the TkSee team had reached this stage; however, due to staff turnover there remained a tendency to slide back to earlier stages.

Stage 4: Partnership

At this stage, usability is considered critically important. Members of the design team, the managers and members of the user organization all work together to achieve usability, following a disciplined process. The TkSee team is still far from this stage - and indeed it is questionable whether it could or should ever be reached in a university research environment.

Even though the TkSee developers moved from skepticism to acceptance of usability, their insufficient knowledge about usability meant that they had to be helped in several ways. They had to be helped to understand usability problems, to see implications of inefficient solutions, to evaluate the effectiveness of different solutions, to prioritize the problems, and to decide how to fix the problems so that no new usability problems were introduced. This type of support was not always easy to give; producing the best results required experience on the part of the person performing the usability study.

4.4   Lessons Learned

The objective of this chapter has been to communicate insights we have learned while preparing to evaluate the usefulness of a software system. We have presented a program comprehension system called TkSee as a case study. Although the goal of our research has been to develop new approaches to program comprehension, we have realized that it is impossible to evaluate the usefulness of these approaches unless we separately consider two key aspects of usefulness: usability and utility. In this chapter, we have discussed usability evaluation, which we assert must precede functionality evaluation.

We found that particular challenges arose from the fact that we were studying usability in a complex domain where users perform creative problem solving. One of the most important consequences is that the usability evaluator needs to have considerable domain knowledge so as to be able to develop appropriate tasks and communicate effectively with both users and developers.

The creation of detailed tasks prior to the think-aloud usability study was very helpful. These tasks were used in the usability testing, but also helped TkSee developers test the system and design features planned for the future.

Due to the complex nature of program comprehension, determining the tasks for the usability testing became particularly difficult, primarily due to the different ways that TkSee users could approach the same problem.

We used both heuristic evaluation and think-aloud usability testing. This proved to be a good decision as both techniques yielded different sets of problems. In both techniques we used people with varied backgrounds, and again the different people found or ran into different problems. It proved particularly important to performing usability tests with Mitel software developers, TkSee's intended users.

Communicating effectively with TkSee's developers proved an essential part of the process: We found it necessary to carefully structure the list of problems found, and we developed a categorization scheme that helped the developer more clearly see the nature of the problem. We confirmed that the process of bringing developers from the stage of skepticism of usability to acceptance of effective usability processes requires methodical effort over a period of time.

Although the TkSee project addressed usability somewhat late, it was nevertheless much better than not having done anything. The usability studies produced immediate benefits: Before the study, for example, we only had a vague idea why many Mitel developers had not used the tool more. The study exposed many of the causes and brought to light many ideas to remedy the situation.

After the study, TkSee developers had a much clearer idea of what they should pay attention to in order to improve the tool. On the other hand, the advanced development status of the tool meant that not all the problems and improvements revealed by the study could be solved or implemented (we implemented all of the important problems and about 60% of the less important ones). We believe, however, that the usability study allowed us to make TkSee sufficiently usable so that we can now start to scientifically evaluate the utility of the aspects of its functionality that are at the core of our research.

4.5   Acknowledgements

We would like to thank the participants at Mitel as well as the TkSee developers for contributing to this work. We thank K. Teresa Khidir for helping make the chapter more readable.

4.6   References

Bias, R., and Mayhew, J. (1994). *Cost-Justifying Usability*. Academic Press, New York.

Ehrlich, K., Rohn, A. (1994). Cost justification of usability engineering: A vendor's perspective. In *Cost-Justifying Usability*, D. J. Mayhew and R. G. Bias Eds. Academic Press, New York, 73-110.

Finnigan, P., Holt, R., Kalas, I., Kerr, S., Kontogiannis, K., Muller, M., Mylopoulos, J., Perelgut, S., Stanley, M., and Wong, K (1997). The software bookshelf, *IBM Systems Journal*, 36(4) November, 564-593.

Hackos, J., and Redish, J. (1998). *User and Task Analysis for Interface Design*. John Wiley & Sons, New York.

Herrera, F. (1999). *A Usability Study of the TkSee Software Exploration Tool*, M.Sc. Thesis, School of Information Technology and Engineering, University of Ottawa, http://www.site.uottawa.ca/~tcl/gradtheses/fherrera/

Jeffries, R. (1994). Usability problem reports: Helping evaluators communicate effectively with developers. In *Usability Inspection Methods*. J. Nielsen and R. L. Mack, Eds. John Wiley & Sons, New York, 273-294.

Lethbridge, T.C. (2000). Integrated personal work management in the TkSee software exploration tool. In *Proc. 2nd Workshop on the Construction of Software Engineering Tools (COSET), ICSE 2000, Ireland*. (Published as a technical report by the School of Information Technology and Computer Science, University of Wollongong, Australia).

Lethbridge, T.C., and Anquetil, N. (1997). Architecture of a source code exploration tool: A software engineering case study. *University of Ottawa. Computer Science Technical Report TR-97-07*.
http://www.site.uottawa.ca/~tcl/papers/scet.html.

Lethbridge, T.C., and Singer J., (1997). Understanding software maintenance tools: Some empirical research. In *Workshop on Empirical Studies of Software Maintenance (WESS 97)*. Bari, Italy, October, 157-162

Lethbridge, T.C. and Singer, J. (2000). Experiences conducting studies of the work practices of software engineers, chapter 3 in this book.

Lethbridge, T.C., Lyon, S. and Perry, P. (2000). The management of university-industry collaborations involving empirical studies of software engineering. In El-Emam, K and Singer, J Eds, *Empirical Studies in Software Engineering*, MIT Press, to appear.

Müller, H., Mehmet, O., Tilley, S., and Uhl, J., (1993). A reverse engineering approach to subsystem identification, *Journal of Software Maintenance: Research and Practice*, 5(4), December, 181-204.

Nielsen, J. (1992). Finding usability problems through heuristic evaluation. In *Proc. ACM CHI '92*, 373-380.

Nielsen, J. (1993). *Usability Engineering*. AP Professional.

Nielsen, J. (1994). Heuristic evaluation. In *Usability Inspection Methods*. J. Nielsen and R. L. Mack, Eds. John Wiley & Sons, New York, 25-62.

Red Hat Corporation (2000). Source Navigator Web Page, http://www.cygnus.com/sn/.

WindRiver Corporation (2000). Sniff+ Web Page, (Formerly TakeFive Corporation), http://www.takefive.com/index.htm.

5
Clones Occurrence in Java and Modula-3 Software Systems

Michel Dagenais
Jean-François Patenaude
Ettore Merlo
Bruno Laguë

5.1   Introduction

Software engineers often build new subprograms by cloning (copying) an existing one with similar requirements, and then slightly modifying it. While this may be easier than factoring the common part out, and sharing it from a library, it increases the system size and often leads to higher maintenance costs. The occurrence of clones is highly dependent on the system architecture, development model, language peculiarities, and software management practices.

This chapter studies the occurrence of clones in large sets of object-oriented software libraries and programs, totaling over 1.1 million lines of code (LOC), in two different object-oriented programming languages: Java and Modula-3. The factors affecting the clone detection accuracy and their frequency of occurrence are discussed. Comparison is made between systems written in both languages.

5.2   Software Clones

In a single-programmer project, once a certain size is reached (e.g., usually about 10,000 lines of code), many frequent patterns (sorting, lexical analysis, list and table traversals) have been encountered and hopefully abstracted into reusable components. Further extensions may involve reusing these components and require relatively little new code. Occasionally, new reusable components may also be discovered and added.

This ideal situation is typically not fulfilled in large multiprogrammer projects with tight schedules. Clones may start to appear for any one of the following reasons:

- **Development time:** A software engineer clones a procedure when he needs similar functionality, instead of extracting the common reusable part. This practice is perceived as a quick solution; however, while it may be faster for the initial implementation, it often leads to code that is more expensive to maintain.

- **Communication:** A software engineer borrows code from a colleague, but cannot extract the common reusable part. Either he is not sufficiently knowledgeable about the cloned procedure, or he cannot convince the other software engineers involved to include this reusable procedure in the library and modify their code to use it.

- **Organizational structure and management factors:** A software engineer borrows code from another subsystem, but cannot avoid cloning because the other subsystem may not be modified; the other subsystem may belong to a different department or may not be modifiable. For example, it may be stored in nonvolatile memory in an embedded system, or frozen after a lengthy testing/qualification process.

- **Lack of information:** It may happen that two software engineers came up with similar procedures independently, thus leading to look-alikes more than clones. It would be beneficial to replace them with a reusable procedure. This sort of redundancy is typically much more difficult to detect as the procedures may achieve the same functionality with different apparent structures.

It is important to study the occurrence of clones in software systems in order to avoid code duplication whenever it is effective to do so (Laguë et al., 1997). Avoiding code duplication often helps reduce software maintenance costs and improves quality. Determining the development environment factors affecting the occurrence of the clones may make their prevention easier.

A cloning relation involves two procedures when one is a copy (perhaps slightly modified) of the other. Automatic procedures may be used for clone detection. They may miss some clones because they differ too much (false negative), and may report as *clones* procedures with similar structures that are not (false positive). Rejecting false positives requires examining manually the reported clones, while false negatives are more difficult to uncover. Once the cloning relations are identified, the reported clones are analyzed to determine their cause. This process may be used to:

- remove the clones to replace them with reusable components,

- add links between the clones to insure that they all get updated together, if applicable, when maintenance is required,

- or to better understand how to prevent new clones from occurring in extensions to the studied system, or in similar systems.

The next section discusses some of the clone detection experiments conducted in the past and reported in the literature. The following section details the large object-oriented systems studied in this paper and the underlying organizational structures of software development. It is followed by the results of the clone detection analysis performed. The chapter ends with a discussion of the results and suggestions for further investigations in this area.

5.3   Related Work

Several studies have been conducted to automatically identify cloned procedures (Baker, 1995; Church and Helfman, 1993; Horwitz, 1990; Jankowitz, 1988; Johnson, 1993; Kontogiannis et al., 1996; Laguë et al., 1997; Mayrand et al., 1996). The more recent systems (Kontogiannis et al., 1996; Laguë et al., 1997; Mayrand et al., 1996) have achieved a good compromise in terms of detection accuracy, and the ability to handle large systems with millions of lines of code.

An interesting scheme is used in (Laguë et al., 1997) in order to improve the detection accuracy for systems evolving over several versions. The metrics-based clone detection, where two procedures separated by a proximity metric value of less than δ_1 are identified as clones, is complemented by a study of clones identified in the previous version. Previously identified clones that still exist and that are less than δ_2 apart (where δ_2 is somewhat larger than δ_1) are kept as clones. This way, clones that are slowly diverging from one version to another, and would be missed because their metrics differ by more than δ_1, but less than δ_2, are properly identified.

Another approach to clone detection is to use program text directly without resorting to parsing first. Such an appraoch is described in Chapter 11 of this book. The text-based approach is particulary suitable for legacy software, where parsers and syntactic analyzers are not readily available.

In large systems, clones often represent more than 5% of the code and may in certain cases reach 20% (Mayrand et al., 1996). The proportion of cloned procedures varies significantly from one system to another; several factors may be involved such as the programming environment and software development policies, application domain, and programming language.

5.4   Experimental Context

While object-oriented programming started to enjoy recognition in the early eighties (Goldberg and Robson, 1983) and may be traced as far back as to the sixties, it came to widespread use gradually after 1992 with the popularity of C++ (Stroustrup, 1991). The lack of safety, garbage collection, and multithreading support in C++ led to the creation of Java (Gosling et al., 1996) in 1995. Java has most of the features found in Modula-3 (Nelson, 1991) and Ada95 (Barnes, 1996), but retains a C++ like syntax. Because of this recent widespread use, relatively few large object-oriented systems (developed over several years by multiple software engineers) are available for study.

5.4.1   Java

Despite Java's young age, several medium-sized systems with freely available source code were found:

- JDK (JDK, 1.1.5), a development kit from Sun Microsystems with 145,000 lines of code,

- SableCC (SABLECC, 2.5), CUP (CUP, 0.10g), ANTLR (ANTLR, 2.2.3), parser generators from McGill University, S. Hudson, and MageLang Institute, respectively, for a total of 74,000 lines of code,

- Swing (SWING, 1.0.2), KFC (KFC, 1.0b), user interface toolkits from Sun Microsystems, and K. Yasumatsu, with 215,000 and 57,000 lines of code respectively,

- HTTPClient (HTTPCLIENT, 0.3), a web browser developed by R. Tschalaer with 21,000 lines of code.

5.4.2   Modula-3

Modula-3 is a modern object-oriented language with modules, opaque types, objects, safety, exception handling, threads, and garbage collection. It comes with excellent libraries for graphical user interfaces, 3D graphics, network objects (remote method invocation), and stable persistent objects. It offers most of the same advanced features as Java (threads, safety, garbage collection) while retaining the efficiency and low-level capabilities of languages such as Ada95 and C++.

The SRC Modula-3 (Nelson, 1991) distribution, developed over the years at the DEC Systems Research Center, qualifies as a multiyear, multiperson, multiplatform project with a few major reorganizations.

- Its development started in Modula-2+ around 1984, and continued in Modula-3 since 1990, with several libraries being semiautomatically converted.

- At any given time, between 5 and 20 software engineers were involved developing applications and libraries.

- The system at one point ran on the experimental Firefly multiprocessor workstation, and was eventually ported to over 26 different platforms ranging from small 32-bit systems to 64-bit DEC Alpha processors, and running one of the numerous POSIX-like operating systems or Win32.

- The interface files in SRC Modula-3 (Modula-3, 3.6) amount to 4,565,355 characters in 123,337 lines. The implementation files contain 21,187 procedures/methods, 166,500 statements, for 16,236,505 characters in 493,519 lines. It is divided into 145 packages, 62 of which are programs, and the rest libraries.

5.4.3 Clone Detection

In Java, there are only methods, and thus no need to perform separate studies of procedures and methods. In Modula-3, there is no distinction between methods and procedures. Arbitrary procedures may be used as methods as long as their signature matches the corresponding method declaration (including the implicit *self* argument of the method declaration (Nelson, 1991)). The term procedure will refer to Java methods for the rest of this text.

The selected granularity for clone detection is thus the procedure. Cloned object types will appear as several cloned procedures, often in a single module. While in some cases portions of procedures may be cloned, their detection is much more difficult and was not attempted here.

Clone detection for Java and Modula-3 systems may be efficiently performed based on the proximity between a set of computed metrics. For each of n procedures, $p_i, i = 1, n$, a set of m metrics $pm_{i,j}, j = 1, m$, is computed. Two procedures are then reported as *detected clones* if the values of these metrics are *closer* than a given threshold. Unless the procedures are identical, manual verification is needed to confirm that the two procedures are indeed clones and could be shared. Proximity may be computed in different ways, such one metric at a time as absolute distance or as Euclidean distance (Kontogiannis et al., 1996; Mayrand et al., 1996). Pairwise comparisons between the metrics for tens of thousands of procedures would be expensive. Therefore, the values are sorted according to the *number of statements* metric, and each procedure is only compared to procedures with up to $\delta_{nbstatements}$ more statements. Then, for procedures within $\delta_{nbstatements}$ statements of each other, the other metrics are compared to see if they differ by less than δ_j. The clone detection procedure can accept absolute or relative values of δ for each metric.

As discussed in (Kontogiannis et al., 1996), a small number of weakly correlated metrics are very effective for clone detection. For each procedure, the number of statements, cyclomatic number, input variables, output variables, and local variables were used.

Other more cosmetic metrics such as average identifier length are quite effective at finding exact clones and rejecting procedures that just happen to have the same values for the structural metrics, such as size and number of variables. However, such metrics were not used because of the risk of falsely rejecting a real clone simply because the identifiers were systematically replaced (as often done in cloned undergraduate projects) (Jankowitz, 1988).

5.5   Results

The first experiment, shown in Table 5.1, examines how the number of detected clones varies with the procedure size. A minimum size of six statements was imposed. Indeed, small procedures are frequent and are more likely to have identical metrics. Even with this minimal size, both Modula-3 and Java analysis report multiple clones having metrics within 10% of one another. In Modula-3, 6,952 of the 21,187 procedures were involved in 78,418 pairs while in Java, 2,661 of 19,955 procedures were involved in 16,325 pairs.

For small sizes, the number of detected clones is extremely large, most of which are false positives, as will be seen later. This is explained by the very large number of small procedures, especially initialization procedures, and for which the metrics do not vary much.

An interesting element to notice is the higher number of detected clones for Java procedures with eight or nine statements. This peak is mostly due to a small procedure in SableCC, called *setNode*, which is reproduced in many places and accounts for 6,566 of the 9,624 reported clones. It is not surprising to find this in a parser generator, since there are many different node types, and that *setNode* procedure needs to be called with all these different node types.

The second experiment, in Figures 5.1 and 5.2, measures the variation of the number of detected clones with the difference δ_j allowed for each metric. The minimum size is ten statements. For the section with relative differences, the other metrics are allowed to be within 10%, and for the section with absolute differences, the difference allowed for the other metrics is 0.

In both languages the number of detected clones varies greatly with the size and the cyclomatic number. It is therefore important to appropriately select the maximum allowed difference. The possible reduction in false negatives is offset by the large number of additional false positives. Using relative differences is sensible for the number of statements as one may easily add a few statements to a large cloned procedure. The cyclomatic number, on the other hand, is a more fundamental structural measure and it may be preferable to use absolute differences. It leads to a more controlled increase in the number detected clones, as shown in Figures 5.1 and 5.2.

In Modula-3, the number of input and output variables is typically very small and relative differences are impractical for small discrete values. Furthermore, varying one parameter alone does not change much the number of detected clones because of correlations with the other metrics. The number of local variables has a greater impact than input or output variables on the number of detected clones. It is nevertheless smaller than the impact of the size or cyclomatic measures.

In Java, there are no VAR parameters, typically used as output variables. Therefore, a different metric was used: the number of nonlocal variables assigned or used by a procedure. The correlation between this metric and the number of input and local variables is weaker than between the number of input and output variables in Modula-3. Nonetheless, absolute differences seem preferable for thresh-

Table 5.1. Number of clone relations detected for different size ranges. For each size range, the number of procedures involved is computed. Some procedures, however, may be involved in cloning relations in neighboring size ranges (a 10% difference in size is allowed).

Number of	Clones detected		Procedures involved	
statements	M3	Java	M3	Java
6, 7	48,513	5,583	2,617	1,005
8, 9	13,106	9,624	1,591	785
10, 11	7,639	514	1,472	292
12, 13	4,183	198	1,066	165
14, 15	2,106	156	692	142
16, 17	769	100	486	84
18, 19	539	56	374	66
20, 21	400	23	270	27
22, 23	233	12	199	21
24, 25	158	20	143	17
26, 27	112	11	116	12
28, 29	299	1	104	2
30, 31	55	9	70	10
32, 33	48	3	63	6
34, 35	32	3	36	6
36, 37	24	0	37	0
38, 39	35	1	47	2
40, 41	38	0	44	0
42, 43	17	0	27	0
44, 45	13	0	22	0
46, 47	12	1	16	2
48, 49	9	0	15	0
50-59	55	6	52	9
60-69	11	3	16	6
70-79	4	0	8	0
80-89	0	0	0	0
90-99	3	0	6	0
100-109	1	0	2	0
110-119	1	1	2	2
120-129	2	0	4	0
130-...	1	0	2	0

Table 5.2. Modula-3: Identical clones c, near clones nc, and falsely reported clones (similar s, vaguely similar vs, and unrelated u) for various sizes.

Nb. of stmts.	c	nc	s	vs	u
6	0	0	0	0	20
8	0	0	0	0	20
10	0	0	0	0	20
12	0	0	0	14	6
14	0	0	0	1	19
16	0	0	0	0	20
18	1	0	0	0	19
20	0	0	0	0	20
24	1	0	0	0	19
28	9	0	0	0	11
32	2	0	0	0	18
40	11	1	0	0	8
50	7	0	0	7	6
60	5	1	0	8	6
120	2	0	0	1	0

olds on these metrics, and their impact on the number of detected clones is smaller than for the size and cyclomatic metrics.

The results from Figures 5.1 and 5.2 may be used to have a better feeling for the process of identifying potential clones. They illustrate the problem of false positives among small procedures, and outline the need to select appropriately the proximity thresholds for metrics. The subsequent results presented in this section directly address the more critical question of what and where are the real clones. They were obtained with a minimal size of six and each metric with a relative difference of less than 10%.

In Tables 5.2 and 5.3, for various sizes, the 20 first clones reported are sampled and their type is determined manually: identical, nearly identical, similar (worth sharing), similar structure, totally unrelated.

The proportion of false positives is larger for smaller procedures (more than 75%). Indeed, there are relatively few different combinations of number of variables, and cyclomatic number for small sizes; thus, numerous unrelated procedures have the same values by coincidence. Since small procedures account for most of the detected clones (in Modula-3, 78% of the 78,418 clones detected are of size between six and nine versus 93% in Java), a large proportion of the detected clones indeed consists of false positives.

Once again, as with the number of detected clones in Table 5.1, we see the effect of the SableCC setNode procedure in Table 5.3. Most of the true positives with eight statements are due to that procedure.

One aspect of Java that favors cloning is that it doesn't provide generic modules

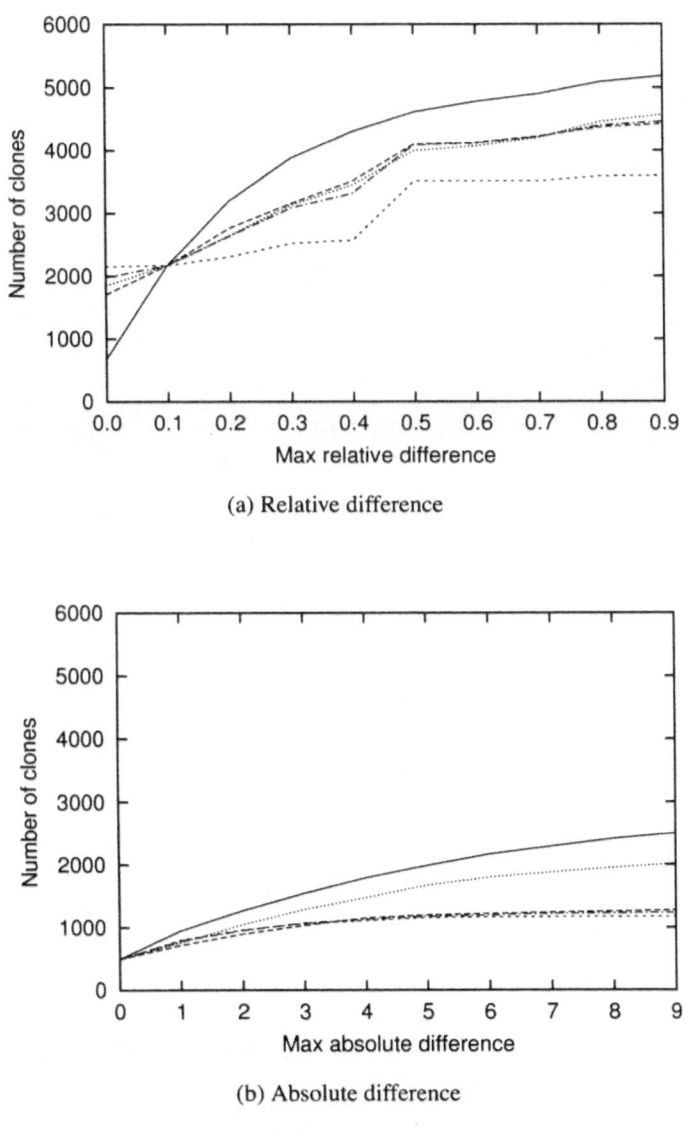

(a) Relative difference

(b) Absolute difference

statements ———
cyclomatic – – –
input var. – – – –
output var. ·········
local var. — · — ·

Figure 5.1. Java: Number of clones detected while varying the threshold for different metrics.

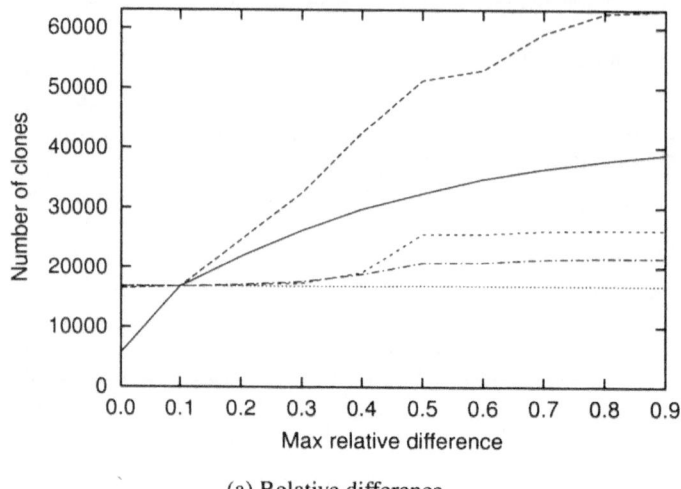

(a) Relative difference

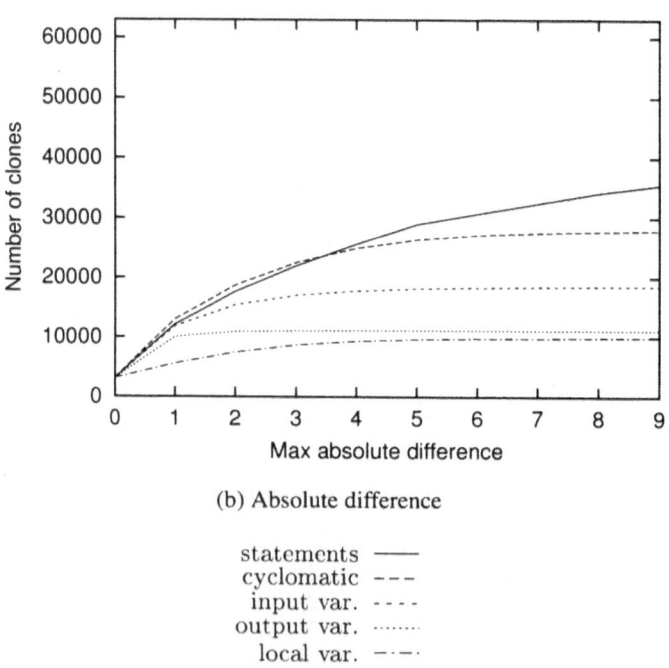

(b) Absolute difference

statements ——
cyclomatic - - -
input var. - - - -
output var. ·········
local var. —·—·

Figure 5.2. Modula-3: Number of clones detected while varying the threshold for different metrics.

or types. Because of this, many procedures are duplicated with only the type of some attributes being changed. Such clones were found in both small and large procedures. They account for at least 15% of the true positive clones.

Many clones are also found in the DebugGraphics class from Swing. Indeed, in debugging mode, the same special instructions need to be added at many places in the program, in order to produce tracing information.

Swing offers many *look-and-feel* choices for graphical user interfaces: Metal, Mac, Motif and Windows. More than 8% of the true positive clones in Table 5.3 are due to these look&feel variants.

In Modula-3, it is interesting to note that the module name and procedure name are probably the best indicators of cloning. Among the 78,418 clones detected, 2,251 have the same procedure name (*identifier*), and 279 have the same procedure and module name (*qualified identifier*, e.g., ModuleName.ProcedureName). Of these procedures with the same name, 1,803 were derived automatically, produced by code generators such as network objects or stub generators for stable objects. These are not part of the source code to maintain and may be ignored.

The remaining clones detected with the same procedure name, but not the same module name, are in large part false positives with generic names such as *Init, New, Pop, Setup, Check*, and *Eval*. Among 279 detected clones with the same *qualified identifier*, 272 have all metrics equal (and are all clones), and 7 have slight metrics differences (2 are clones and 5 have a similar structure).

In order to further investigate the importance of the name in the clone detection, the 167 clones detected with size 40 and larger were manually examined: all those without the same *qualified identifier* are false positives. The presence of real clones which don't have the same name (among the 76,000 detected clones without the same name) is more difficult to assess. While their proportion is definitely very low, a few with very similar structure, perhaps worth sharing, were found manually (with intimate knowledge of the system content): ParseName vs ParseCIName (case insensitive or not), and MeetH vs DifferenceH (2D regions intersection versus difference).

5.6   Discussion

When comparing the occurrence of clones between the DEC SRC Modula-3 distribution and the collection of Java systems, a number of factors need to be considered. Despite their different syntactic flavors (Pascal versus C-like), the two languages have many equivalent features. The differences in how procedures and types are grouped into interfaces and modules may affect the level of access control and encapsulation, but should not affect cloning significantly. The multiple interface inheritance mechanism in Java may help slightly avoiding clones. However, the most important feature for reducing clones may be generic modules, supported in Modula-3 but not yet in Java (the keyword `generic` is reserved for future use in Java).

Table 5.3. Java: Identical clones c, near clones nc, and falsely reported clones (similar s, vaguely similar vs, and unrelated u) for various sizes.

Nb. of stmts.	c	nc	s	vs	u
6	4	2	0	0	14
8	6	13	0	0	1
10	3	3	0	0	14
12	4	5	1	0	10
14	3	0	2	0	15
16	0	11	0	0	9
18	0	10	0	0	10
20	3	9	0	0	8
24	11	2	0	0	7
28	0	7	0	0	7
32	3	7	1	0	9
40	0	1	0	0	1
50	0	4	0	0	2
60	1	2	1	0	4
120	0	0	0	0	0

Another important factor explaining the differences in the occurrence of clones is the development environment. Indeed, DEC SRC Modula-3 was developed over several years by a small to medium team. Experimentation was encouraged, but a tight control was maintained over who could modify each package. By contrast, the Java packages studied were developed independently and simultaneously. Thus, no copying could take place across packages. Furthermore, these young packages have not yet gone through several reorganizations and developer turnover.

In Modula-3, the largest sources of real clones are in the packages Postcard and Webcard; Postcard is a mail/news client, and Webcard is a modified version, by another author, with an integrated Web client. From a maintenance point of view, Webcard should simply supersede Postcard. The next largest source of real clones are modules named TextExtras, RealRect, and RealInterval which are repeated in two or three packages. The effort of convincing the maintainers of the base libraries (where Text and Geometry operations reside) to incorporate these modules was presumably an obstacle. Colleagues of the auhtors of the modules simply copied these to their packages upon need, thus creating clones.

Interestingly, there are four clones of a procedure named QuickSort. They were probably created before the inclusion of *Generic* modules in Modula-3, and generic sorting facilities in the base library. Similarly, the 2D and 3D modules, the INTEGER and REAL modules, and the geometry modules have a lot in common and could be shared through the careful use of generic modules, which were not available when these modules were initially developed. In the following example,

Axis.T could be defined as X, Y for 2D and as X, Y, Z for 3D, and Length.T could be defined as INTEGER, REAL, or LONGREAL.

```
GENERIC INTERFACE
  Geometry(Axis, Length);

TYPE
  Point = ARRAY Axis.T OF Length.T;

  Rect = RECORD p1, p2: Point;
...
```

Several procedures with the same structure have a common origin but would require more work for sharing. The stubs generators for network and stable objects, the main program for m3build, m3ship, and m3where, the graphical programs columns and fours, and a few modules to add HTML markup to Modula-3 source code all have a similar structure, and were created by copy and modification. However, they fulfill different tasks and parameterizing the code to make it shareable may affect its readability negatively.

In the Java systems studied, as expected, few clones involve more than one system. Most of the clones occurred in closely related classes. It appears that some Java clones could be removed by proper encapsulation within higher level classes. Typical examples are the List and TableList classes that contain many nearly identical procedures. These two classes could be derived from a common ancestor class, sharing common procedures. In other cases, notably the highly cloned SableCC setNode, the procedures are too simple to be worth sharing. Finally, several clones could be removed through the use of generic modules, if such a facility existed in Java.

5.7   Conclusion

The number of real detected clones in SRC Modula-3 is not negligible (about 1% of 500,000 lines), but somewhat less than in other large systems studied in the literature (Laguë et al., 1997). In the Java systems analyzed, the cloning level is higher at 6% of the 512,000 lines. The level of cloning is a direct result of a system's history and development environment. SRC Modula-3 was developed in a research environment with emphasis on quality and novelty; thus, it was subject to time constraints to a much lesser extent. However, some of the code was developed through experimentation by cloning existing packages, but was not maintained later, providing little incentive to remove the clones.

Code duplication by lack of information is less likely in SRC Modula-3 than in other systems because of the high level of communication between the members of this relatively small group. However, the quality standards for the base libraries were such that several generally useful modules could not be included (because they did not fit these standards or by lack of time to perform a careful review). These were cloned in the few packages needing such functionality.

The larger occurrence of clones in the Java systems studied is surprising at first. Indeed, cloning is more likely in very large multiyear projects, than in smaller young packages such as the Java systems examined. A closer examination of the systems brings two plausible explanations. The development of the larger systems (JDK, Swing) was realized at Sun under considerable pressure, given the competitive and time sensitive commercial interests at stake. A second factor is the absence of generic modules in Java, which would have easily prevented a large number of clones.

As more studies on cloning appear in the literature, it may become possible to better isolate and measure separately the effect of system size, team composition, development environment, development history, programming language (C++, Ada95), and programming paradigm.

5.8   Acknowledgements

The financial support of Bell Canada, and of the Canadian National Science and Engineering Research Council, is gratefully acknowledged. The authors also wish to thank Gregory Knapen for his initial development of a Java parser and AST generator.

5.9   References

ANTLR (2.2.3). *Predicated-LL(k) Parser Generator*. MageLang Institute, http://www.antlr.org/.

Baker, S. (1995). On finding duplication and near duplication in large software systems. In *Proceedings of the Working Conference on Reverse Engineering*, Toronto, Canada.

Barnes, J. (1996). *Programming in Ada*. Addison-Wesley, Reading, MA.

Church, K. and Helfman, I. (1993). Dotplot: a program for exploring self-similarity in millions of lines of text and code. *Journal of Computational and Graphical Statistics*, 2(2): 153-174.

CUP (0.10g). *LALR Parser Generator for Java*. Scott E. Hudson, GVU Center, Georgia Tech, http://www.cs.princeton.edu/˜ appel/modern/java/CUP/

Goldberg, A. and Robson, D. (1983). *Smalltalk-80: The Language and its Implementation*. Addison-Wesley, Reading, MA.

Gosling, J., Joy, B., and Steele, G. (1996). *The Java Language Specification.* Addison-Wesley, Reading, MA.

Horwitz, S. (1990). Identifying the semantic and textual differences between two versions of a program. In *Proceedings of the ACM SIGPLAN Conference on Programming Language Design and Implementation*, White Plains, NY, 20-22 June, pages 234-245. *SIGPLAN Notices*, 25(6).

HTTPCLIENT (0.3). *Http client library.* Ronald Tschalaer, http://www.innovation.ch/java/HTTPClient/

Jankowitz, H. (1988). Detecting plagiarism in student Pascal programs. *Computer Journal*, 31(1):1-8.

JDK (1.1.5). *Java Development Kit.* Sun Microsystems, Inc.

Johnson, H. (1993). Identifying redundancy in source code using fingerprints. In *Proceedings of CASCON'93*, pp. 171-183, IBM Center for Advanced Studies, Toronto, Canada.

KFC (1.0b). *Kazuki Yasumatsu's Foundation Classes.* Kazuki Yasumatsu, http://ring.aist.go.jp/openlab/kyasu/

Kontogiannis, K., DeMori, R., Berstein, M., Galler, M., and Merlo, E. (1996). Pattern matching for clone and concept detection. *Journal of Automated Software Engineering*, 3:77-108.

Laguë, B., Proulx, D., Mayrand, J., Merlo, E., and Hudepohl, J. (November 1997). Assessing the benefits of incorporating function clone detection in a development process. In *Proceedings of the International Conference on Software Maintenance*, November, Bari, Italy.

Mayrand, J., Leblanc, C., and Merlo, E. M. (November 1996). Experiment on the automatic detection of function clones in a software system using metrics. In *International Conference on Software Maintenance*, pp. 244-253, Monterey, California.

Modula-3 (3.6). *Modula-3 Compiler for Unix, Windows/NT, and Windows 95.* Digital Equipment Corporation, http://www.research.digital.com/SRC/modula-3/html/srcm3.html

Nelson, G. (1991). *Systems Programming with Modula-3.* Prentice-Hall, Englewood Cliffs, NJ.

SABLECC (2.5). *Object-oriented compiler framework.* Etienne Gagnon, Sable Research Group, School of Computer Science, McGill University, http://www.sable.mcgill.ca/sablecc/

Stroustrup, B. (1991). *The C++ Programming Language*. Addison-Wesley, Reading, MA.

SWING (1.0.2). *SWING Component Set*. Sun Microsystems, Inc.,
http://www.javasoft.com/products/jfc/tsc/

Part II

Architectural Recovery

6
Pattern-Based Design Recovery with SPOOL

Rudolf K. Keller
Reinhard Schauer
Sébastien Robitaille
Bruno Laguë

6.1   Introduction

Automated tool support is crucial for the comprehension of large-scale, object-oriented software and involves compressing and clustering the vast amount of information that is contained in the source code. However, software comprehension demands more than the mere understanding of the static structure of the source code. The clear representation of the system's physical and logical structure is still insufficient for a developer to fully comprehend the purpose of a given piece of software (Beck and Johnson, 1994). Underlining this statement, Booch estimates that "it takes a professional programmer about 6-9 months to become really proficient with a larger framework," and he adds that "this rate increases rather exponentially to the complexity of software" (Booch, 1996). We agree with Beck and Johnson that one reason for this gigantic effort for software comprehension and evolution is that "existing design notations focus on communicating the what of designs, but almost completely ignore the why." They argue that comprehension of the rationale behind the design decisions is equally as much important as understanding of the software's structural and logical constituents. Yet, for the most part, current reverse engineering tools completely neglect recovery of the design rationale.

Design patterns capture the rationale behind recurringly proven design solutions and illuminate the trade-offs that are inherent in almost any solution to a nontrivial design problem. In forward engineering, the advantages of design patterns are widely accepted (Beck and Johnson, 1994), but in reverse-engineering their usefulness encounters strong resistance throughout both the pattern and the reverse-engineering communities (Buschmann et al., 1996). The main arguments are that patterns can be implemented in many different ways without ever being the same twice, and that the same structure may recur with widely different intents. In addition, existing studies that were aimed at detecting design patterns in existing software systems (Antoniol et al., 1998; Kraemer and Prechelt, 1996) failed to convey the usefulness of this approach to reverse engineering, considering the minimal results of recovered pattern instances. Nevertheless, it is these patterns of thought that comprise the rationale of many pieces of an existing software system, and to comprehend the software we need to recover these patterns, be it automatically or manually.

In the SPOOL project (Spreading Desirable Properties into the Design of Object-Oriented, Large-Scale Software Systems), a joint industry/university collaboration between the software quality assessment team of Bell Canada and the GELO group at the University of Montreal, we investigated methods and tools for software comprehension and for assessing software design quality, for instance, in respect to changeability (see Chapter 10). As part of the project, we have developed the SPOOL environment for design pattern engineering, which comprises functionality for design composition (Keller and Schauer, 1998), change impact analysis (see Chapter 10), and most importantly, support for the recovery of design patterns.

Note that with "support" we underline the purpose of the environment as an aid for gaining a pattern-based overview of the software system under investigation. It would be pretentious to argue that the environment itself can comprehend the rationale behind a design, "which would go far beyond the current state-of-the-art in artificial intelligence" (Brown, 1997). However, by generating appropriate views, it may lead a human analyzer to the recovery of the rationale behind some of its most critical parts. Using the environment, the analyzer can zoom into these design components[1] that resemble patterns, extract them as diagrams in their own right, contrast the pattern description with the implemented structures, or, in the case of a false positive, dismiss the existence of the automatically identified pattern instance.

In this chapter,[2] we apply our environment to the reverse engineering of design components that are based on some of the design pattern descriptions defined by Gamma et al. (1995). The purpose is to introduce pattern-based reverse engineering as a valuable technique for software comprehension and thus counter the widely held believe that design patterns are only meaningful in forward engineering. Applying our approach to several case studies extracted from in-

---

[1] Note that we introduced the term *design component* as the reification of design elements, such as patterns, idioms, or application-specific solutions, and their provision as software components (*JavaBeans*, *COM objects*, or the like), which are manipulated via specialization, adaptation, assembly, and revision. We refer to Keller and Schauer (1998) for further details on this approach to software composition. For the purpose of this chapter, we use the term *design component* as a package of structural model descriptions together with informal documentation, such as intent, applicability, or known-uses.

[2] This chapter is a revised and extended version of Keller et al. (1999).

dustrial, large-scale software, we show that pattern-based reverse engineering of design components is helpful for understanding software-in-the-large. In Section 6.2, we explain the architecture of the SPOOL environment. In Section 6.3, we describe the three C++ systems that we used for experimentation, present three case studies that show how we applied pattern-based reverse engineering of design components, and discuss the findings of our experiments. Section 6.4 compares our approach with related techniques. Section 6.5 concludes the chapter and provides an outlook into future work.

6.2   The SPOOL Reverse Engineering Environment

The SPOOL reverse engineering environment (Figure 6.1) uses a three-tier architecture to achieve a clear separation of concerns between the end-user tools, the schema and the objects of the reverse-engineered models, and the persistent

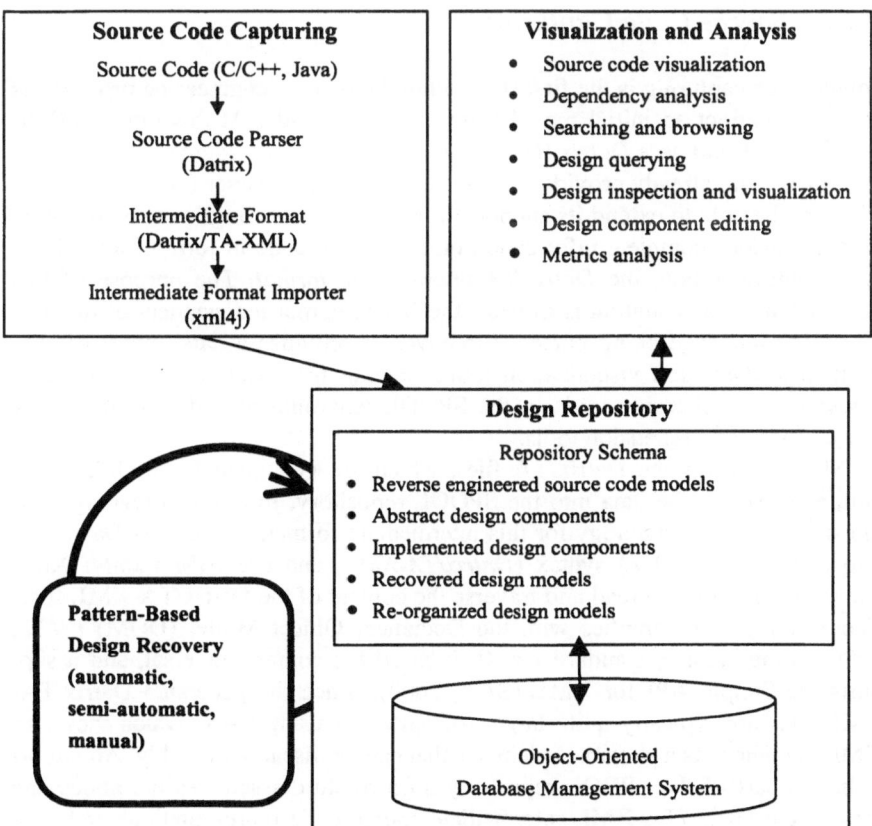

Figure 6.1. Overview of SPOOL reverse-engineering environment.

datastore. The lowest tier consists of an *object-oriented database management system*, which provides the physical, persistent datastore for the reverse-engineered source code models and the design information. The middle tier consists of the *repository schema*, which is an object-oriented schema of the reverse engineered models, comprising structure (classes, attributes, and relationships), behavior (access and manipulation functionality of objects), and mechanisms (higher-level functionality, such as complex object traversal, change notification, and dependency accumulation). We call these two lower tiers the SPOOL *design repository*. For a detailed description of the design repository, refer to Chapter 13. The upper tier consists of end-user tools implementing domain-specific functionality based on the repository schema, i.e., *source code capturing* and *visualization and analysis*.

In this section, we first describe the environment's techniques and tools for source code capturing. Then, we explain its functionalities for pattern-based design recovery and for design representation.

6.2.1   Source Code Capturing

Source code capturing is the first step within the reverse-engineering process. Its goal is to extract an initial model from the source code. At this time, SPOOL supports C++ and uses *Datrix* (Datrix, 2000) to *parse* C++ source code files. As the Datrix team already provides CSER members with a parser for Java, SPOOL will soon be able to extend its support for reverse engineering Java source code. Datrix provides complete information on the source code in form of an ASCII-based representation, the *Datrix/TA intermediate format*. The purpose of this intermediate representation is to make the Datrix output independent of the programming language being parsed. Moreover, it provides a data export mechanism to analysis and visualization tools, ranging from Bell Canada's suite of software comprehension tools to the SPOOL environment and to other CSER source code comprehension tools.

SPOOL parses the Datrix/TA files, which are generated for each compile unit, and *imports* the data into the SPOOL repository. In order to leverage off-the-shelf parsing technology for this intermediate format, we convert Datrix/TA into *XML* (W3C, 1998) syntax (*Datrix/TA-XML*) and use IBM's *xml4j* XML parser (IBM, 1999) to read and traverse the content of the Datrix/TA-XML files. The xml4j parser complies with the Document Object Model (DOM) (W3C, 1999) as the industry standard for XML-based file content traversal, and it supports the Simple API for XML (SAX, 2000). Since the generated Datrix/TA-XML files are typically quite large, we opted for using SAX, which views an XML document as a stream of elements that can be discarded quickly. An *import* utility as part of the SPOOL repository infrastructure assembles the nodes and arcs of the Datrix/TA-XML intermediate source code representations and constructs the objects of an initial physical model in the SPOOL repository. Note that we are currently working on substituting the Datrix/TA-XML representation by an XMI-based solution (XMI, 2000; Saint-Denis et al., 2000). At the current state of development, we capture and manage in the repository the source code information as listed in Table 6.1.

Table 6.1. Source code information managed in the SPOOL repository.

1.	*Files* (name, directory)
2.	*Classifier - classes, structures, unions, anonymous unions, primitive types* (char, int, float, etc.), *enumerations* [name, file, visibility]. Class declarations are resolved to point to their definitions.
3.	*Generalization* relationships [superclass, subclass, visibility].
4.	*Attributes* [name, type, owner, visibility]. Global and static variables are stored in utility classes (as suggested by the UML), one associated to each file. Variable declarations are resolved to point to their definitions.
5.	*Operations* and *methods* [name, visibility, polymorphic, kind]. Methods are the implementations of operations. Free functions and operators are stored in *utility* classes (as suggested by the UML), one associated to each file. *Kind* stands for *constructor, destructor, standard,* or *operator.*
5.1.	*Parameters* [name, type]. The type is a *classifier.*
5.2.	*Return types* [name, type]. The type is a *classifier.*
5.3.	*Call actions* - [operation, sender, receiver]. The receiver points to the class to which a request (operation) is sent. The sender is the classifier that owns the method of the call action.
5.4.	*Create actions.* These represent object instantiations.
5.5.	*Variable use* within a method. This set contains all member attributes, parameters, and local attributes used by the method.
6.	*Friendship relationships* between classes and operations.
7.	*Class and function template instantiations.* These are stored as normal *classes* and as *operations* and *methods,* respectively.

6.2.2 Pattern-Based Design Recovery

The purpose of pattern-based design recovery is to help structure parts of class diagrams to resemble pattern diagrams (see Figure 6.2, window 4). We envision three techniques to support this task: automatic design recovery, manual design recovery, and semiautomatic design recovery. Automatic design recovery relates to the fully automated structuring of software designs according to pattern descriptions, which are stored in the repository as abstract design components. We have implemented query mechanisms that can recognize the structural descriptions in the source code models, extract these from the source code, and visual-

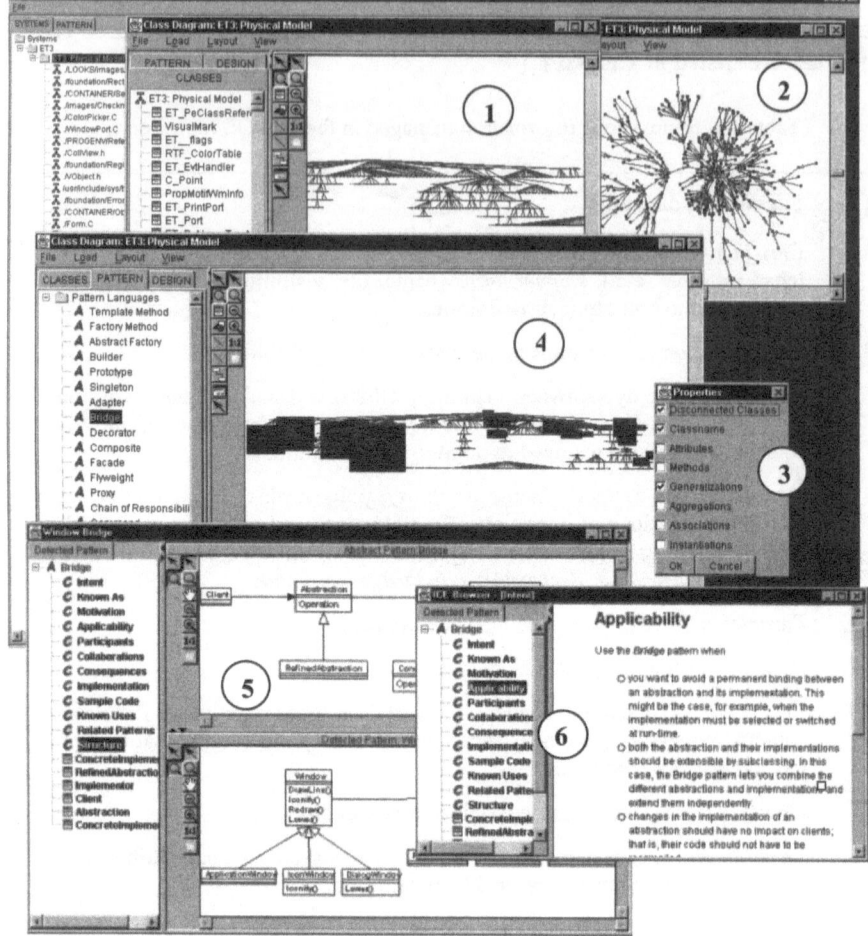

Figure 6.2. Graphic user interface of the SPOOL environment.

ize them within the class hierarchies. This technique will be further detailed in Section 6.3.

Manual design recovery relates to the structuring of software designs by manually grouping design elements, such as classes, methods, attributes, or relationships, to reflect a pattern. Our environment allows the developer to select model elements and associate them with the roles of the respective pattern elements. Manual design recovery gives the human analyzer the possibility to look at a model from his or her own perspective and cluster design elements to design components. It provides the flexibility that is necessary to group and communicate ad-hoc solutions as proto-patterns (Appleton, 1998), which may at some time even become patterns.

Semiautomatic design recovery combines both strategies, automatic and manual recovery. It may be implemented as a multiphase recovery process. The first phase consists of the automatic detection of low-level idioms or the general core of pattern descriptions. Subsequent phases match the identified instances with more specific implementation details, which may be provided interactively by the analyzer who is in control of the recovery process. He or she may interrupt recovery runs to confirm or decline the existence of a pattern occurrence, and to manually supply specifics that are not covered by the default recovery queries. At the current stage of development, we have implemented the techniques for automated and manual design recovery.

6.2.3   Design Representation

The purpose of design representation is to provide for the interactive visualization and analysis of source code models, abstract design components, and implemented components. It is our contention that only the interplay among human cognition, automatic information matching and filtering, visual representations, and flexible visual transformations can lead to the all-important why behind the key design decisions in large-scale software systems. To date, we have implemented and integrated tools (see Figure 6.1, "Visualization and Analysis") for the following:

- *Source code visualization* (visualizing classes, attributes, methods, operation calls, instantiations, friendship dependencies, type dependencies based on the types of parameters, operations and methods, and attributes),
- Interactive and incremental *dependency analysis* (the user may select a number of classes, files, or directories, and the system loads and visualizes the dependencies among these elements; see Section 6.4.3),
- Design investigation by *searching and browsing*, based on both structure and full-text retrieval, using the *SPOOL Design Browser* (Robitaille et al., 2000) (cf. Section 6.3.2),
- *Design querying* to classes that collaborate to solve a given problem,
- *Design inspection and visualization* within the context of the reverse-engineered source code models,
- *Design component editing*, allowing for the interactive description of design components, and
- *Metrics analysis* to conduct quantitative analyses on desirable and undesirable source and design properties.

Figure 6.2 illustrates the graphic user interface of the SPOOL environment. Windows 1 and 2 show the inheritance hierarchy of *ET++* (Weinand et al., 1989) (tree layout generated with *Dot* (Kontsofios and North, 2000) and spring layout generated with *Neato* (North, 2000)). Via the property sheet associated with such diagrams (window 3), all the other association relationships stored in the repository, such as instantiation or aggregation relationships, can be illustrated as well, in both separate and combined forms. Different colors distinguish the different kinds of association relationships. On the left hand side of each window, a tree view can be optionally displayed (windows 1, 4, 5, and 6) to convey in textual form the source code models, abstract design components, or implemented design components. Through a diagram's pop-up menu, design queries on the information contents of the current diagram can be launched, with subsequent visualization of the query results (window 4). In our environment, each of the supported abstract design components (the pattern like structures to be discovered) comprises a so-called reference class. This is the class in the component's structure diagram that is considered most characteristic of the component's nature.

Upon design recovery, we incrementally draw bounding boxes around the reference classes of the implementations of an abstract design component (window 4). In this way, a class that is the reference class for several of these implemented design components ("multiple reference class") will exhibit a taller bounding box than a class that is just part of a single component. Keeping the size of these bounding boxes constant during zooming leads to the effect that once their diagrams are sufficiently zoomed out (window 4), multiple reference classes will protrude from the diagram. The implemented design components can then be extracted into a separate diagram and related to the classes, methods, and attributes of their respective abstract design components (window 5), which in this study represent the descriptions of design patterns. The more informal constituents, such as intent, motivation, or applicability, can be viewed in the same or in separate diagrams (window 6). These informal descriptions are crucial for understanding the design, as they capture the rationale that may be at the root of the automatically identified design component.

Design representation also encompasses interactive description of design components. The SPOOL environment provides a class diagram editor based on the UML notation 1.1 (UML, 1997) for structural descriptions and an HTML editor for specifying the informal constituents of design components. Using these editors, the environment allows for the modeling, documenting, and storing of new abstract design components in the design repository. The environment also supports the refinement and generalization of existing abstract components. This is essential as design components can be rendered in different forms. For example, a design component representing an *Adapter* pattern can be refined into a *Class Adapter* or an *Object Adapter*, and similarly, a *Composite* may be specialized into a *Transparent Composite* or a *Safe Composite* component (Keller and Schauer, 1998).

The user interface of the SPOOL environment is implemented based on Java 1.2, the *JFC/Swing* components (Sun, 2000), and the graphic editor application framework *jKit/GO* (Instantiations, 2000). For visualizing the HTML code, the *ICEBrowser* (ICESoft, 2000) *JavaBeans* component is being used. To generate initial layouts of the system under investigation, we developed an interface to external layout generators. We integrated *Dot* (Kontsofios and North, 2000) for tree layouts and *Neato* (North, 2000) for spring layouts.

6.3   Applying Pattern-Based Reverse Engineering

The purpose of this section is to point out the importance of pattern-based reverse engineering of design components for the comprehension of large-scale software. We chose a case study approach to illustrate and discuss some of our findings when analyzing industrial systems. We have selected the following abstract design components, which we based on the corresponding descriptions in the pattern catalogue of Gamma et al. (1995): *Template Method, Factory Method,* and *Bridge.*

To assess the feasibility of pattern-based reverse engineering and the usefulness of the SPOOL environment, we analyzed the source code of three industrial C++ systems. Bell Canada provided us with two large-scale systems from the domain of telecommunications. For confidentiality reasons, we call these systems System-A and System-B. Our third test system is the well-known application framework ET++ 3.0 (Weinand et al., 1989), as included in the SNiFF+ development environment (TakeFive, 2000). Table 6.2 shows some size metrics for these systems. Note that header files from the compiler are included in these numbers.

In this section, we first show how we reverse-engineered the selected components in System-A, System-B, and ET++, respectively. Then, we discuss the three case studies.

Table 6.2. Size metrics of industrial systems.

	System-A	System-B	ET++
Lines of code	472,824	291,619	70,796
Lines of pure comments	60,256	71,209	3,494
Blank lines	80,463	90,426	12,892
# of files (.C/.h)	1,900	1,153	485
# of classes (.C/.h)	3,103	1,420	722
# of generalizations	1,422	941	466
# of methods	17,634	8,594	6,255
# of attributes	1,928	13,624	4,460
Size of the system in the repository	63.1 MB	41.0 MB	19.3 MB

6.3.1   Case Study #1: Template Method

"Template Methods define the skeleton of an algorithm in an operation, deferring some steps to subclasses" (Gamma et al., 1995). Template methods are often referred to as the characterizing building blocks of white box frameworks, which let clients extend the framework by overriding predefined hook methods that are called by the framework (Fayad and Schmidt, 1997). The rationale behind a Template Method is to make the steps of an algorithm easily exchangeable. The trade-off is that if not used with care, Template Methods can contribute to overly complex software, especially when the hook methods themselves are Template Methods deferring functionality to other hook methods. In large, framework-based application software, such as System-A, knowledge about the existence and location of Template Methods is crucial for the judicious evolution of the applications.

We reified the Template Method pattern (Figure 6.3 shows its structure) as an abstract design component, stored it in our repository, and associated it with a query that searches the source code models for the component's structure. The default implementation of the Template Method query traverses all classes (*AbstractClass*), goes into each method (*TemplateMethod*), looks up the operation call tree for local operation calls (*PrimitiveOperation*), and verifies if *PrimitiveOperation* is polymorphic. If all conditions are met, all relevant information is passed to a Design Component Builder object, which creates an Implemented Design Component containing references to the identified elements in the source code model. Note that through query options, the human analyzer can specify deviations from the default behavior of the query, for instance, to recover only those *TemplateMethods* in which *PrimitiveOperation* in *AbstractClass* is purely virtual (in the case of a C++ system), or to check if *PrimitiveOperation* is overridden by at least one other class (*ConcreteClass*) in the *AbstractClass'* subclass hierarchy.

Figure 6.4 illustrates the recovered Template Methods in one class tree of System-A (note that the reference class of Template Method is *AbstractClass*).

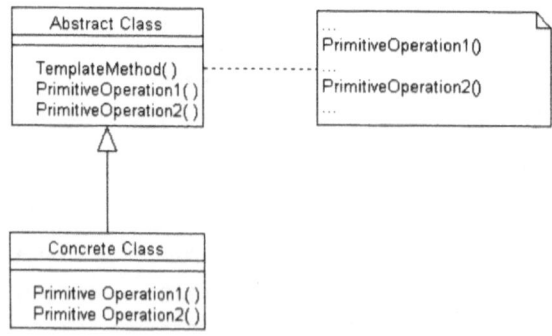

Figure 6.3. Structure of Template Method (Gamma et al., 1995).

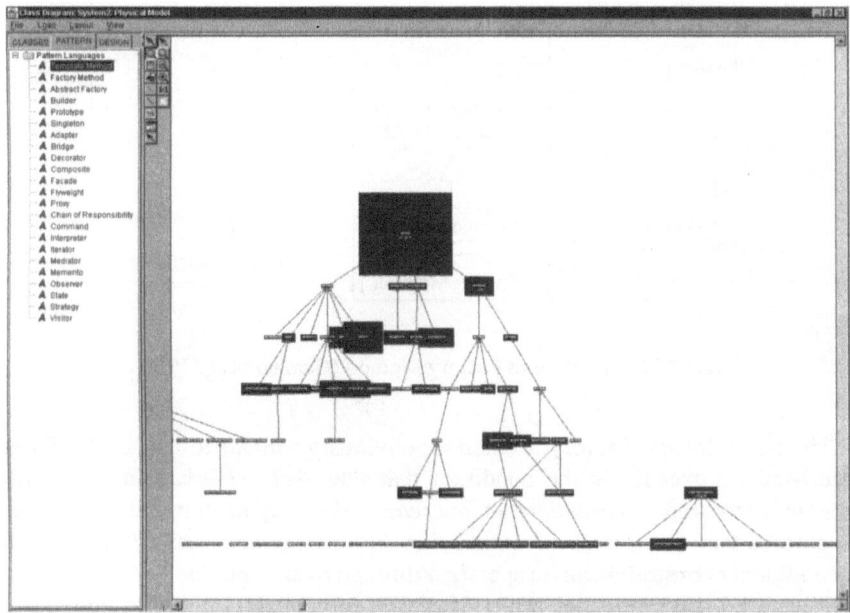

Figure 6.4. Template Methods in System-A.

This diagram clearly shows the key players within this part of the application, and conveys an impression of how many such mini-algorithms, which may be refined in subclasses, exist in the class tree. For instance, the main class, visible on top of the diagram, contains 43 Template Methods. More detailed information can be recovered by zooming into the diagram, showing operations and attributes, or by spawning another diagram that shows the implementation of one particular Template Method only.

It is our experience that knowledge on both the rationale and the existence of Template Methods is essential to develop an understanding on how to hook into the mechanisms that are enforced by a framework like architecture. Such knowledge may be of great help in flattening the learning curve of a framework.

6.3.2   Case Study #2: Factory Method

"Factory Methods define an interface for creating an object, but let subclasses decide which class to instantiate" (Gamma et al., 1995). Factory Methods are specialized Template Methods in that the *PrimitiveOperation* in the *Concrete-Class* instantiates a concrete product (see Figure 6.5). Factory Methods are often used when different objects have the same construction process. The construction algorithm is coded in the *Creator* class, and the steps that instantiate the objects are deferred to the subclasses.

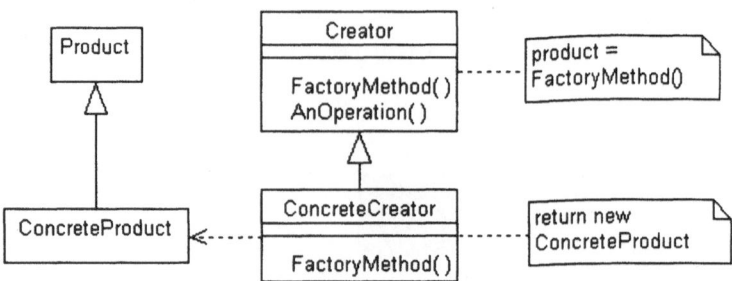

Figure 6.5. Structure of Factory Method (Gamma et al., 1995).

The query for the Factory Method is, obviously, similar to that of the Template Method, except for the condition that the *FactoryMethod* in *Concrete-Creator* is required to instantiate a *ConcreteProduct*. By default, the query does not enforce that *ConcreteProduct* be a subclass of another class (*Product*), but this additional constraint can be specified through query options.

Figure 6.6 illustrates the results of the Factory Method query as applied to System-B. The upper window shows the inheritance tree of all classes of System-B, which we laid out with Neato. Due to the high zooming ratio (the small points constitute large inheritance trees), the recovered design components protrude from the diagram. This is crucial information that can help find a basis for understanding a complex piece of software, which is presented in the lower window of Figure 6.6. We zoomed into the tallest bounding box and extracted the detailed information into a separate diagram (lower window). It illustrates a central *Creator* class, which defines 13 abstract *FactoryMethod* operations, and 57 subclasses, which implement these operations.

This automatically generated diagram provides essential information about the rationale behind the design of the system. The developers designed this part of System-B for easy extension with new classes. This was necessary as this part of the system deals with user interface forms and input tables, which by nature change very fast. The diagram also tells us that the designers decided to instantiate objects in the same classes that provide the functionality for their manipulation. In the example, a better solution would have been the use of an Abstract Factory, which "provides an interface for creating families of related or dependent objects" (Gamma et al., 1995). This would have provided for more flexibility as the manipulation functionality could have evolved independently from the object created by the factory. Thus, a different family of objects, which may reflect changed user requirements or a different user interface platform, could have been plugged into the class hierarchy without the need of subclassing existing classes. This would have reduced the number of classes from 57 to about 30, improving understandability and maintainability. This example illustrates pattern-based reverse engineering of design components as a technique that can

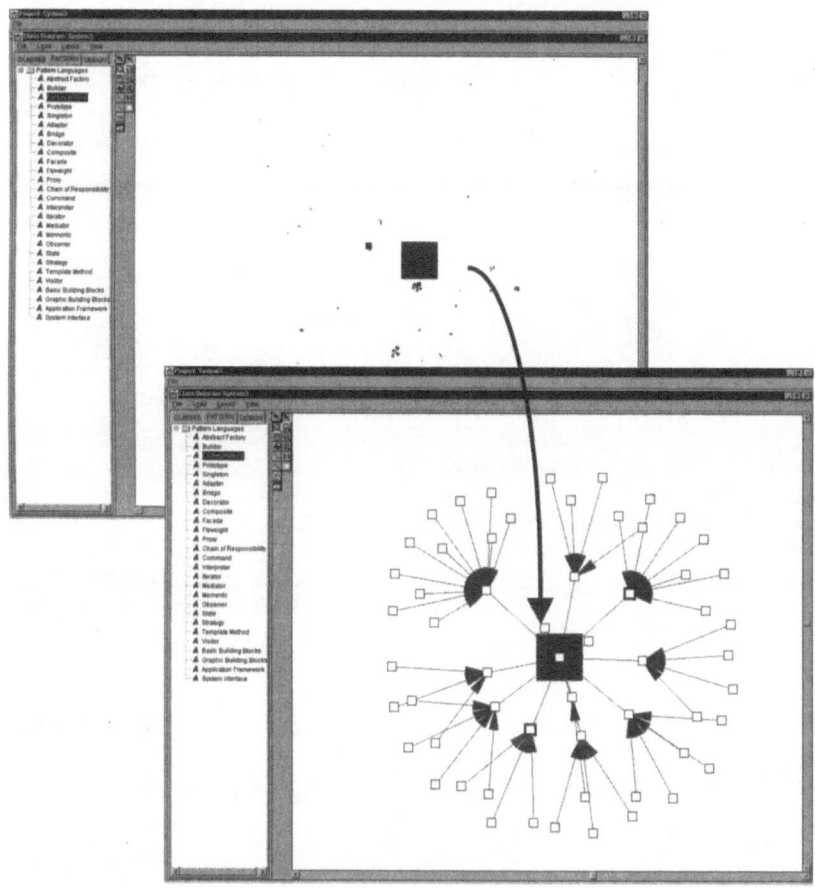

Figure 6.6. Factory methods in System-B: overview diagram (upper window); extracted Factory Methods (lower window).

help a human analyzer not only to comprehend a complex piece of software, but also to make substantial design improvements.

As a further example, window 1 of Figure 6.7 illustrates the occurrences of the *Factory Method* pattern in ET++. The user may want to inspect the recovered pattern instances by starting the design inspection tool (window 2). This diagram shows in its upper part the list of recovered Factory Method patterns, identified by the *Creator* class and the *FactoryMethod*. The middle part shows the selected Factory Method as a collaboration diagram. The example shows the class *ET_Object* with the method *GetObserverIter*, which calls the Factory-Method *MakeIterator* (top row). This method is overridden in five subclasses of *ET_Object* (middle row). Each of these implementations of *MakeIterator* instantiates different *Products* (bottom row). The lower part of the window shows the

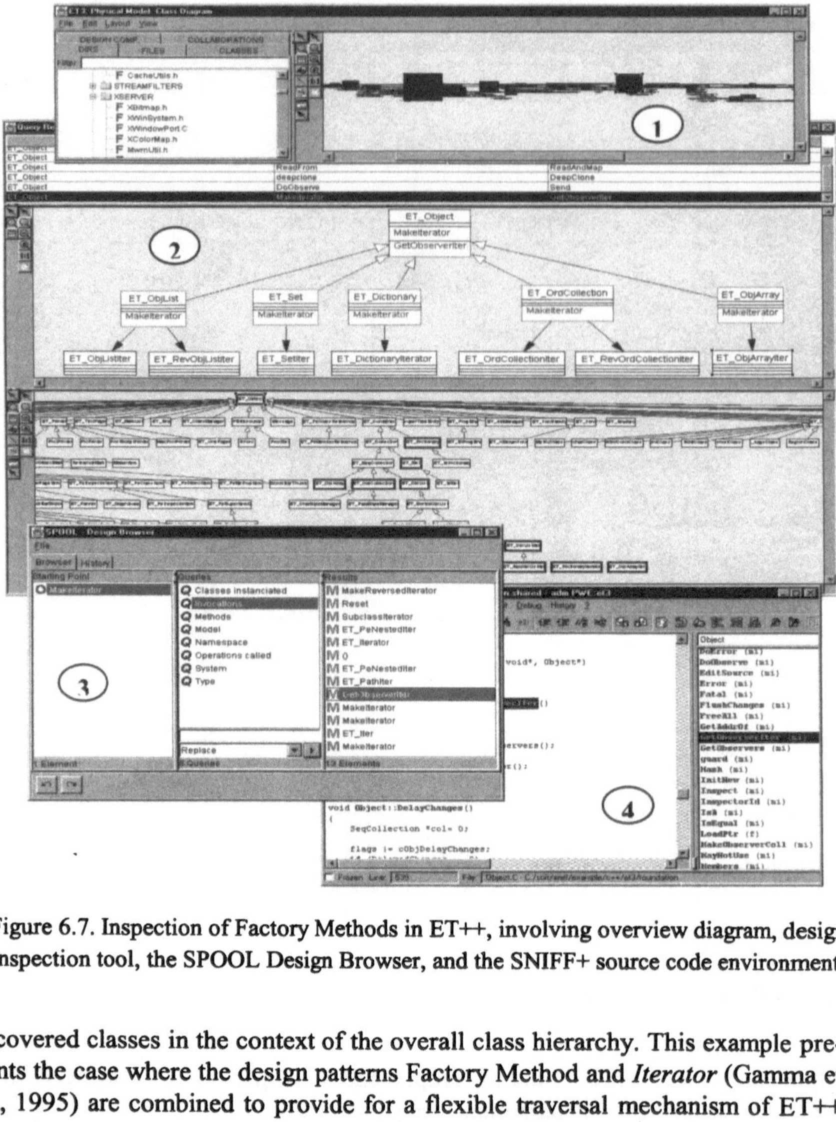

Figure 6.7. Inspection of Factory Methods in ET++, involving overview diagram, design inspection tool, the SPOOL Design Browser, and the SNIFF+ source code environment.

recovered classes in the context of the overall class hierarchy. This example presents the case where the design patterns Factory Method and *Iterator* (Gamma et al., 1995) are combined to provide for a flexible traversal mechanism of ET++ containers, such as lists, sets, dictionaries, collections, and arrays. Note that the SPOOL Design Browser with its structure and full-text retrieval functionality might have been used to hint at instances of the Iterator pattern (Robitaille et al., 2000).

The content of the design inspection diagram was automatically generated by the query for the Factory Method pattern. The diagram provides important information for program comprehension as it presents in a concise way all the classes that take on some role in a pattern-based collaboration. Note that in the physical file structure, these classes may be spread out over many directories and subsystems. Yet, the diagram falls short in conveying all the information a user might wish to obtain about the design fragment at hand. He or she might want to know, for instance, the classes and methods that invoke *MakeIterator*, or get information about the semantics of the method *GetObserverIter*, whose name alludes to its purpose of creating an Iterator of the *Observers* of a view element. A visual design inspection tool can never answer all of these questions.

The SPOOL Design Browser together with the SPOOL mechanism for integrating external tools provides the flexibility to obtain detailed knowledge as well as context information about the constituents of a recovered, pattern-based design. For example, the browser of window 3 shows all the methods from which *MakeIterator* is invoked, including the *GetObserverIter* method already identified in window 2. By invoking the *SNiFF+* environment (TakeFive, 2000), the user can then investigate and edit the retrieved elements directly in the SNiFF+ source code editor (window 4). This provides invaluable context information about how, in our example, a Factory Method is used.

6.3.3   Case Study #3: Bridge

The intent of a Bridge pattern is to "decouple an abstraction from its implementation so that the two can vary independently." (Gamma et al., 1995) The Bridge is a design technique that can avoid combinatorial explosion of class hierarchies if a domain concept in different variations can be implemented in multiple ways. If realized using inheritance, each variation would have a subclass for each of the possible implementations. To avoid this, the Bridge suggests separate class hierarchies for the abstraction and the implementation (Figure 6.8).

We include the Bridge as one of those patterns that demand human insight to be recovered from source code. The Bridge is a semantic concept that can have many forms of physical appearance in the source code. For instance, we have identified Bridges with Abstractions that are not subclassed, *ConcreteImple-*

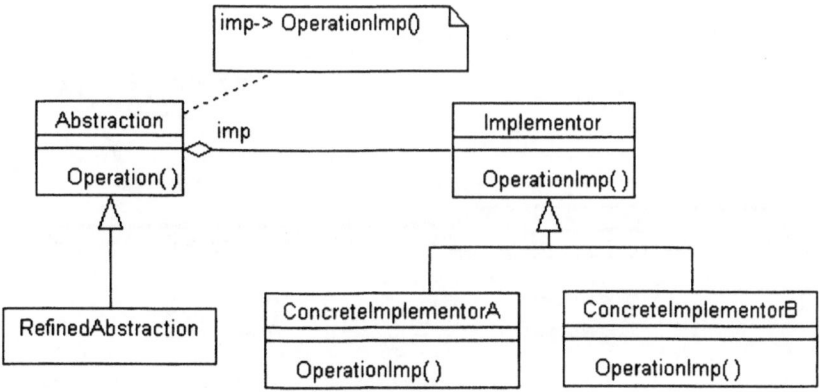

Figure 6.8. Structure of Bridge (Gamma et al., 1995).

mentors that do not have a common superclass, or *OperationImps* that constitute Template Methods (see Section 4.1) in which not *OperationImp*, but its hook method, is overridden. Our Bridge query captures these cases, and as an additional heuristic verifies that *Abstraction* and *Implementor* are not in the same path of the inheritance tree, which otherwise would be counter to the very intent of the Bridge. The final result was 46 Bridge-based design components in ET++, which not unsurprisingly included many false positives. It is our contention that the systematic discovery of the Bridge pattern within source code needs human insight into the problem domain of the software. However, as Figure 6.9 illustrates, a machine can generate appropriate diagrams that are of great value for the human analyzer to identify instances of the Bridge.

In the upper window of Figure 6.9, we illustrate all recovered Bridges in ET++. *Abstraction* serves as the reference class, which is decorated with a bounding box for each *Operation* that delegates functionality to a subclass of the abstract *Implementor* that is the target of the maximum number of delegations. More specifically, our default Bridge query looks for classes with an instance variable (imp) of a type *Implementor*. It then goes into the operation call tree of each method (Operation) in *Abstraction*, and verifies if the receiver of an operation call (*OperationImp*) is of type *Implementor* and is overridden by at least one subclass of *Implementor* (*ConcreteImplementor*). By default, we also allow that *OperationImp* be a Template Method, meaning that not *OperationImp* itself is overridden, but one of its polymorphic hook methods (see Case #1). We discovered many Bridge *Implementors* in industrial code that were based on Template Methods.

Our query reported 46 Bridge-based design components in ET++, yet most of the visualized Bridges had only up to three bounding boxes (i.e., operation calls to *Implementor*), meaning that most probably these automatically recovered

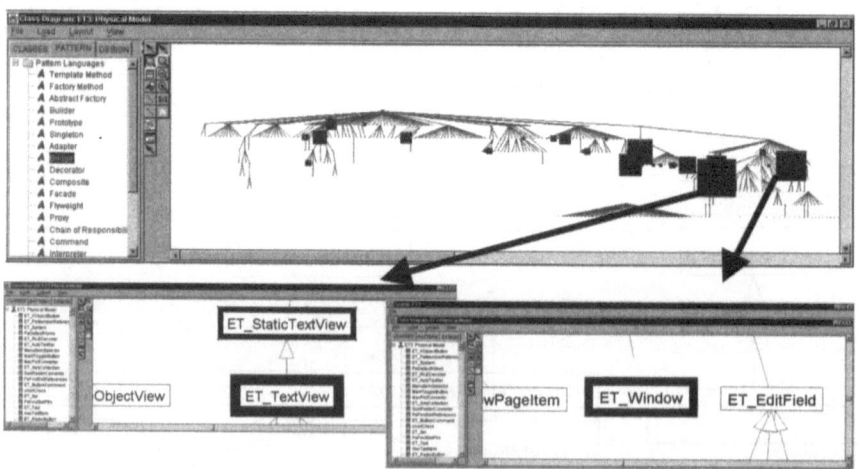

Figure 6.9. Bridges in ET++: overview diagram (upper window); *ET_TextView* class (lower left window); *ET_Window* class (lower right window).

implementations of Bridge reflect only its structure, but not its intent. Clearly visible in Figure 6.9 are a few reference classes with tall bounding boxes (right side of upper window). The lower windows of Figure 6.9 illustrate the three reference classes that exhibit the most bounding boxes. The lower left window shows *ET_TextView* with its superclass *ET_StaticTextView*, both delegating multiple methods to *ET_Text* (not displayed in Figure 6.9). The documentation of ET++ (Weinand et al., 1989) describes *ET_TextView* and *ET_Text* as the view and model of the MVC architectural design pattern, which is in this example applied to text handling. In other words, subclasses of *ET_TextView* provide different rendering strategies for instances of *ET_Text*, thus serving as the *Abstractions* for *ET_Text Implementors*, which is the very intent of the Bridge design pattern. The lower right window of Figure 6.9 shows the *ET_Window* class with 11 bounding boxes. Gamma et al. (1995) describe this case as one of the known uses of Bridge. In ET++, the *ET_WindowPort* class serves as the abstract *Implementor* for different kinds of windows, and *ET_XWindowPort* and *ET_SunWindowPort* as the *ConcreteImplementors*.

6.3.4 Discussion of Case Studies

The purpose of our work is to provide a technique that can supplement current reverse-engineering tools with the support to recover the all-important rationale behind the design decisions. We based this technique on design patterns and presented three case studies, each illustrating a different pattern on a different industrial system. Related studies on pattern detection (Antoniol et al., 1998; Kraemer and Prechelt, 1996) provided tables indicating numbers for the detected patterns and the true pattern implementations in the investigated systems. We argue that these numbers are misleading as they neither express quality of the analyzed software or the detection tool, nor convey the rationale behind the pattern-based design (see Section 6.4 for further discussion).

We believe in the strength of visualization and the integration of the human into the recovery process. Therefore, we selected a case study approach to convey the practicability of pattern-based reverse engineering. However, for comparison purposes, we summarize the results of our default recovery queries in Table 6.3.

Table 6.3. Implemented pattern-based design components.

	System-A	System-B	ET++
Template method	3,243	1,857	1,022
Factory method	247	168	44
Bridge	108	95	46

As the structures of Template Method (Figure 6.3) and Factory Method (Figure 6.5) unambiguously reflect the intent of the respective pattern, and in light of our rich software repository, which includes information on both operation calls and polymorphic methods, we can rely on the recovered design components for both patterns being correct. The Bridge pattern, on the other hand, requires human judgment. It is one of those patterns that can be implemented in many different ways. We captured some of these implementations, and, as case study 3 illustrates, used the technique of growing bounding boxes to visually identify those *Abstractions* that delegate many operations to an *Implementor*. In System-A, for example, the reference classes of 13 out of 108 discovered Bridge design components exhibited more than 5 bounding boxes; 6 of these were surrounded by more than 50 bounding boxes, which was clearly visible in the diagram. Four design components were real Bridge pattern implementations; the two others delegated many operations to another class, which provided much functionality, but did not have the semantics of an *Implementor* for the *Abstraction* of the considered component.

6.4   Related Work

Below, we will briefly review a number of studies dealing with the detection and the identification of design patterns. Also, we will discuss related work addressing fine-grained design recovery. Finally, we will reflect on the added value of our approach in the realm of documentation with patterns.

Several studies reported in the literature aim at detecting design patterns in object-oriented software based on structural descriptions. Kraemer and Prechelt (1996) developed a Prolog-based front-end to the Paradigm Plus CASE tool. They observed a precision ranging from 14 to 50 percent. Similar results are reported by Antoniol et al. (1998). However, as the number of patterns found in the analyzed software was close to zero, the precision factor has little significance. Moreover, both studies report that only the header files of C++ programs were analyzed, meaning that their experiments were conducted in the absence of information on function calls and object instantiations. Moreover, Kraemer and Prechelt (1996) do not report whether they considered polymorphism in their tool, and Antoniol et al. (1998) mention that they do not handle polymorphism, information that we consider indispensable for the identification of pattern like structures in source code models. Note that we consider the information currently managed by our repository (Table 6.1) as the minimum for serious recovery of pattern-based design components. Finally, we believe that only by the direct involvement of the human analyzer in the recovery process interesting pattern-based design components may be found.

Other studies that have influenced our work report on identifying patterns in existing software. Brown (1997) reviews the Gamma et al. patterns and provides an overview of how to identify each pattern in Smalltalk software. He discusses the difficulties of recovery of patterns in existing software, but also stresses the feasibility of detecting useful patterns in source code. Martin (1995) summarizes his experience when manually looking for patterns in existing software. Despite the fact that the application that his team investigated had been designed without any formal knowledge of patterns, they discovered that "in one or other form every pattern of Gamma et al. was used." Both studies convey the message that it is the human analyzer who needs to be in control of the detection process.

The recovery of design components has been subject of active research under varying terminology. Rich and Waters (1988) coin the term cliché for "commonly used combinations of elements with familiar name." Similarly, Baniassad and Murphy (1998) define conceptual modules as "a set of lines of source code that are to be treated as a logical unit." The difference between these techniques and pattern-based recovery of design components is in the level of abstraction. Whereas clichés and conceptual modules represent only small algorithms or data structures, patterns illustrate the complex relationships among the large pieces of software and, equally important, embody informal explications of the rationale behind the suggested designs. It is our contention that reverse engineering of large-scale software needs to put more emphasize onto discovering these well-known patterns of thought. Revisiting the statement of Johnson in our introduction, it is the rationale behind the design decisions (the why) that needs to be recovered to gain insight into more complex pieces of software. Clichés, conceptual modules, and alike cannot convey the why, but certainly are much needed building blocks for achieving more elaborate recovery of pattern-based design components.

Many authors have discussed the advantages of documenting software, and in particular frameworks, with pattern (Butler et al., 2000; Johnson, 1992; Odenthal and Quibeldey-Cirkel, 1997). Johnson brings their cause to the point: "Patterns can describe the purpose of a framework, can let application programmers use a framework without having to understand in detail how it works, and can teach many of the design details embodied in the framework" (Johnson, 1992). We claim that only the visualization of the implemented patterns in the context of the application under investigation will make documentation with patterns truly effective, elucidate the rationale behind the framework's design and make the applied patterns more tangible and understandable. In reverse engineering, pattern-based documentation of existing frameworks and large-scale software needs sophisticated tool support allowing the human analyzer to look at the software from different perspectives, and thus gain a more-encompassing picture of the complex relationships among the system's constituents.

6.5   Conclusion

Design patterns capture the subtle design decisions that have proven successful in many software development projects. They document the rationale behind the design, which is so important to understand when evolving a software system to meet the continuously changing requirements. Our experience when manually analyzing parts of two telecommunications software systems of Bell Canada confirm the findings of Martin that most of the design patterns of Gamma et al. (1995) are present in sizeable software systems (Martin, 1995). However, we also learned that the effort for the manual recovery of a significant number of design patterns in large-scale systems is infeasible, even with the use of state-of-the-art software comprehension tools, such as SNiFF+. Our study shows that effective pattern-based reverse engineering of sizable software systems is indeed feasible, but that it requires both support from pattern analysis tools and techniques, as well as the cognitive strength of the human analyzer.

In this chapter we have discussed the SPOOL environment for the pattern-based recovery of design components. We assessed our technology based on three case studies taken from industrial C++ software systems. The visualization technique of growing bounding boxes around the reference classes of pattern-based design components proved very helpful to gain an immediate understanding about the nature of the patterns in the software under investigation. In most cases, the size of the bounding box indicated if the recovered design component also carried the intent of the respective pattern. Advanced tool support comprising extraction of the design component into a separate diagram and design navigation helped verify the existence of the pattern.

Beyond extending the SPOOL environment with additional visual aids, we plan to work in five areas related to this study. First, we will continue conducting studies about specific design patterns and idioms, covering further patterns from the catalogue of Gamma et al. (1995) and beyond (Schauer et al., 1999; Keller and Schauer, 2000). Second, we wish to extend our repository to capture all major constructs of C++ and to cover additional programming languages. The schema of the repository will be based on multiple logical layers, each increasing the level of abstraction of the source code models. Third, we plan to supplement our current visualization technique, which is based on bounding boxes around the reference classes of pattern-based design components, with alternative techniques. This includes the UML-style pattern notation (UML, 1997) and component-specific rendering techniques. For example, to convey the essence of the *Layers* architectural pattern (Buschmann et al., 1996), its classes should be illustrated top-down according to their association with a layer, or, once jKit/GO (Instantiations, 2000) supports three-dimensional graphic objects, within three-dimensional space, each layer being a two-dimensional structure diagram and the connections among the layers being represented in the third dimension. Fourth, we aim to investigate the recovery of pattern-based design components with full-text, pattern-matching techniques. We believe that analyzing the names of identifiers and comments can retrieve much information about patterns. Fifth, we will integrate our environment with the suite of software comprehension tools of Bell Canada, including source code parsers for several programming languages, a tool for clone detection, and an environment for metric analysis. Such integration will provide the software quality assessment team of Bell Canada with an industrial-strength environment that can support them in the assessment of supplier software for maintenance and evolution.

6.6   Acknowledgments

We would like to thank the following organizations for providing us with licenses of their tools: Bell Canada for the source code parser Datrix; Lucent Technologies for the layout generators, Dot and Neato, as well as for the C++ source code analyzer *GEN++* used in the previous versions of SPOOL; and TakeFive Software for the SNiFF+ software development environment.

6.7   References

Antoniol, G., Fiutem, R., and Cristoforetti, L. (1998). Design pattern recovery in object-oriented software. In *Proceedings of the Sixth International Workshop on Program Comprehension*, Ischia, Italy, June 1998, pp. 153-160.

Appleton, B. (1998). Patterns and software: Essential concepts and terminology. On-line at http://www.enteract.com/~bradapp/docs/.

Baniassad, E. L. A. and Murphy, G. (1998). Conceptual module querying for software reengineering. In *Proceedings of the 20th International Conference on Software Engineering*, Kyoto, Japan, April 1998, pp. 64-73.

Beck, K. and Johnson, R. (1994). Patterns generate architectures. In *Proceedings of the 13th European Conference on Object-Oriented Programming*, Springer-Verlag, LNCS 821, pp. 139-149..

Biggerstaff, T. J. (1989). Design recovery for maintenance and reuse. *IEEE Computer*, 22(7):36-49, July 1989.

Booch, G. (1996). *Object Solutions: Managing the Object-Oriented Project*, Reading, MA: Addison-Wesley.

Brown, K. (1997). Design reverse-engineering and automated design pattern detection in Smalltalk. On-line at http://hillside.net/patterns/papers/.

Buschmann, F., Meunier, R., Rohnert, H., Sommerlad, P., and Stal, M. (1996). *Pattern-Oriented Software Architecture: A System of Patterns*, New York, John Wiley and Sons.

Butler, G., Keller, R. K., and Mili, H. (2000). A framework for framework documentation. *ACM Computing Surveys*, 32(1), Symposium on Object-Oriented Application Frameworks.

Datrix (2000). Datrix homepage, http://www.iro.umontreal.ca/labs/gelo/datrix/.

Fayad, M., and Schmidt, D. C. (1997). Object-oriented application frameworks. *Communications of the ACM*, 40(10):32-40.

Gamma, E., Helm, R., Johnson, R., and Vlissides, J. (1995). *Design Patterns: Elements of Reusable Object-Oriented Software*, Reading, MA: Addison-Wesley.

IBM (1999). IBM–alphaWorks, http://www.alphaworks.ibm.com/tech/xml/.

ICESoft (2000). ICESoft A/S, Bergen, Norway. ICEBrowser. Online documentation at http://www.icesoft.no/.

Instantiations (2000). jKit/GO online documentation. Instantiations, Tualatin, OR. On-line at http://www.instantiations.com/.

Johnson, R. (1992). Documenting frameworks using patterns. In *Proceedings of the Conference on Object-Oriented Programming: Systems, Languages and Applications*, Vancouver, B.C., October 1992, pp. 63-76.

Keller, R. K., and Schauer, R.. (1998). Design components: towards software composition at the design level. In *Proceedings of the 20th International Conference on Software Engineering*, Kyoto, Japan, April 1998, pp. 302-310.

Keller, R. K., Schauer, R., Robitaille, S., and Pagé, P. (1999). Pattern-based reverse engineering of design components. In *Proceedings. of the 21st International Conference on Software Engineering*, Los Angeles, May 1999, pp. 226-235.

Keller, R. K., and Schauer R. (2000). Towards a quantitative assessment of method replacement. In *Proceedings of the Fourth Euromicro Working Conference on Software Maintenance and Reengineering*, Zurich, Switzerland, February 2000, pp. 141-150.

Kontsofios, E., and North S. C. (2000). Drawing graphs with Dot. AT&T Bell Laboratories, Murray Hill, NJ. Available on-line at http://www.reasearch.att.com/sw/tools/graphviz.

Kraemer, C., and Prechelt, L. (1996). Design recovery by automated search for structural design patterns in object-oriented software. In *Proceedings of the Working Conference on Reverse Engineering*, Monterey, CA, November 1996, pp. 208-215.

Martin, R. (1995). Discovering design patterns in existing applications. In J. Coplien and D. C. Schmidt, Eds., *Pattern Languages of Program Design*, Addison-Wesley, pp. 365-393.

North S. C. (2000). *NEATO User's Manual*. AT&T Bell Laboratories, Murray Hill, NJ. On-line at http://www.research.att.com/sw/tools/graphviz/.

Odenthal, G., and Quibeldey-Cirkel, K. (1997). Using patterns for design and documentation. In *Proceedings of the 11th European Conference on Object-Oriented Programming*, Jyvaskyla, Finland, June 1997, pp. 511-529.

OMG (1998). Object Management Group (OMG). XML Metadata Interchange (XMI). Document ad/98-10-05, October 1998. Available on-line at ftp://ftp.omg.org/pub/docs/ad/98-10-05.pdf/.

Rich, C., and Waters R. (1988). The programmer's apprentice: A research overview. *IEEE Computer* 21(11):11-24.

Robitaille, S., Schauer, R., and Keller, R. K. (2000). Bridging program comprehension tools by design navigation. In *Proceedings of the International Conference on Software Maintenance (ICSM'2000)*, San Jose, CA, October 2000, pp. 135-141.

Saint-Denis, G., Schauer, R., and Keller, R. K. (2000). Selecting a model interchange format. The SPOOL case study. In *Proceedings of the Thirty-Third Annual Hawaii International Conference on System Sciences*, Maui, HI, January 2000.

Sax (2000). Sax 1.0: The simple API for XML. http://www.megginson.com/SAX/.

Schauer, R., Robitaille, S., Martel, F., and Keller, R. K. (1999). Hot spot recovery in object-oriented software with inheritance and composition template methods. In *Proceedings of the International Conference on Software Maintenance (ICSM'99)*, Oxford, Britain, August 1999, pp. 220-229.

Sun (2000). Sun Microsystems, Inc. Java Foundation Classes (JFC) documentation. http://www.javasoft.com/products/jfc/index.html.

TakeFive (2000). TakeFive Software. SNiFF+ dcumentation set. On-line at http://www.takefive.com/.

UML (1997). Documentation set version 1.1. http://www.rational.com.

W3C (1998). World Wide Web Consortium (W3C). Extensible Markup Language (XML) 1.0. W3C recommendation, February 1998, http://www.w3.org/TR/1998/REC-xml-19980210.

W3C (1999). World Wide Web Consortium (W3C). Document Object Model (DOM). W3C recommendation, June 1999. http://www.w3.org/TR/PR-DOM-Level-1.

Weinand, A., Gamma, A., and Marty, R.. (1989). Design and implementation of ET++, a seamless object-oriented application framework. *Structured Programming*, 10(2):63-87.

7
Approaches to Clustering for Program Comprehension and Remodularization

Timothy C. Lethbridge
Nicolas Anquetil

7.1   Introduction

When presented with a large legacy system which has little design information, an important approach to understanding and maintaining it is to automatically divide it into a more understandable set of modules or subsystems–a process called *remodularization*.

In this chapter we review several remodularization approaches that employ *clustering* technology. These approaches require making decisions that include which algorithms to use as well as which information to use as input to the algorithms (e.g., words in file names, use of global variables, etc.). Here we discuss several alternatives and present some experimental evidence to help guide decision making. We also present various methods to evaluate the effectiveness of the clustering approaches. These methods include examining the coupling and cohesion of clusters, as well as the size of the largest cluster created and the number of unclusterable singleton files that remain. In Chapter 8 of this volume, Tzerpos and Holt provide a discussion of the clustering problem focusing on automatic techniques that are also used in other disciplines.

Many legacy software systems are very difficult to understand and change. An important reason for this can be that they are not effectively divided into modules and subsystems. It can be useful to automatically rearrange the software into a new set of modules and subsystems, either in order to permanently restructure the system or to temporarily view it from an alternative perspective. We will refer to both tasks as remodularization.

Remodularization can be accomplished using clustering technology. In this chapter we hope to guide those who wish to try clustering, by presenting a review of many alternative approaches as well as the results of some experiments.

In Section 7.2, we present an overview of various algorithms for clustering, with an emphasis on hierarchical algorithms. In Section 7.3 we discuss how these algorithms can be evaluated. Then in Section 7.4 we discuss some experiments we have performed to help determine which algorithms are best for re-modularization.

7.2 Approaches to Clustering

Software engineers arrange software components into modules to reduce complexity, and promote reuse. For example, methods are arranged into classes; procedures and classes into files; and files into packages, directories and libraries, etc. In this chapter, we will describe how to use clustering algorithms for remodularization.

7.2.1   Coupling, Cohesion and Hierarchies: Characteristics of Good Modularization

The main purpose behind creating well-designed modules is to make the software easier to understand and therefore to change. In conventional software engineering practice, one recognizes the following as important characteristics of good modularization:

- Aspects of the software that are logically related are kept closer together and therefore easier to find and manipulate. This property is known as high cohesion.
- There are fewer linkages between diverse parts of the system; therefore, changes are more likely to have a more localized impact. This property is known as low coupling.
- Modules are organized into hierarchies of subsystems, with increasing abstraction as one moves upward towards the root. Modules that are lower in the hierarchy (closer to the leaves) have higher cohesion.
- One should avoid modules or subsystems that are either too large or too small. In other words, the hierarchy should be reasonably balanced.

   Coupling and cohesion tend to be inversely related: A module that has higher cohesion because it contains components that are closely related tends to have lower coupling. Low coupling and high cohesion make it easier to achieve information hiding, whereby the internals of a module need not be known by those who work only with the interface. Unfortunately, the coupling, cohesion and hierarchical organization of many software systems is often quite poor. This is due to reasons such as the lack of a directory hierarchy in older operating systems, the lack of knowledge about software architecture on the part of the original designers, and the undermining of the original modularization as many additions and alterations were made.

   Effective software remodularization therefore involves trying to rearrange software source code into a new, reasonably balanced, module hierarchy that has lower average coupling and higher average cohesion. One might also choose additional criteria to evaluate a potential remodularization, but we believe these are among the most important.

7.2.2   Manual and Automatic Approaches to Remodularization

There are two general approaches to remodularization: manual and automatic. The manual approach relies on the judgement of experts to rearrange the system. However, automatic approaches will often be superior in large systems because they may be more cost effective and reliable; in addition, human experts may not be available. In this chapter we will discuss automatic approaches.

Automatic and manual approaches can be combined: experts could evaluate several automatic clusterings and select the best, or the automatic approaches could use limited expert input as one of their decision-making criteria. Automatic clustering of software can be used for permanent remodularization, or to provide alternative and temporary views for a person who is trying to understand the software from a certain perspective.

No matter which approach is used, Clayton et al. (1998) points out that it is important to have a firm objective in mind when designing and evaluating a remodularization approach. The objective might be greater flexibility, higher cohesion, lower coupling, an object-oriented architecture, or some combination of these.

7.2.3   Overview of Automatic Clustering

Automatic clustering can be used in many disciplines to organize things into groups. For example, in biology it has been widely used to group organisms into species, genera, families, etc. The clustering literature is therefore very extensive. Wiggerts (1997) presents an overview of this literature and its application to remodularization. Lakhotia (1997) proposes a comparison framework for various aspects of clustering as applied to software remodularization.

The purpose of the current chapter is to shed additional light on clustering approaches so that better decisions can be made when applying them to remodularization. We do this, in part, by presenting some experimental results later in the chapter.

To apply automatic clustering, one needs to make several decisions:

What are the elements to be clustered together? In software remodularization, this is most frequently files, although routines or methods can also be clustered to create new files or classes. The latter is important in attempts to make systems more object-oriented (Girard et al., 1997).

What relationships between elements should be considered? There are many possibilities for software remodularization; this topic is explored in the next section.

How do we represent information about the elements and relationships?
We discuss this in Section 7.2.5.

What clustering algorithm should be used? There are several different classes of algorithms, and many alternatives within each class. These are discussed in Section 7.2.6. Some of these algorithms are also in common use in other disciplines. These *classical* clustering algorithms are also surveyed in Chapter 8.

7.2.4   Relationships for Clustering

An automatic clustering algorithm relies on evaluating the relationships among the elements to be clustered—in our case software components. Such an algorithm will try to keep related components in the same cluster, both to increase cohesion and at the same time to reduce coupling. Also, the clusters that are most closely related will be kept inside higher-level clusters, hence closer to the leaves of the hierarchy. Since there are many different kinds of relationships, and vast numbers of potential intercomponent links based on these relationships, choosing the best approach for automatic clustering requires considerable experimentation. The best approach will likely vary from one software system to another. The following are some of the categories of relationships among software components that automatic clustering tools may consider:

1. **Direct static *uses* relationships:** Two components are related if one uses the other in some way. For example, a file *includes* a file, a routine *calls* another, a file *contains routines that call routines* in another file, etc.

2. **Sibling static *uses* relationships:** Two components might be considered related if they both use some third thing. For example: two files *share the same included file*; two routines *call the same routine*, or *access the same global variable*, or *use the same type*, etc. The more things used in common by the components, the closer they are related.

3. **Dynamic relationships:** Two components might be considered related if execution traces show that they are used together to perform a particular operation at run time. The more frequently, and the closer in time, the two components appear together in a trace, the closer they can be considered related.

4. **Similar use of descriptive words:** Two components might be considered related if they contain the same words or phrases embedded in naming conventions and comments. The use of similar words implies they deal with similar abstract concepts. The more words or phrases shared by the comments or names of the components, the closer they are likely to be related. See Anquetil and Lethbridge (1999a) for an example of the application of this approach.

5. **History of common modification:** Two components might be considered related if they have been altered together in the past to effect a particular

change to the system. The more changes that have required altering both components, the closer they are likely to be related.

6. **Membership in a design pattern:** Two components might be considered to be related if they both participate in an instance of a design pattern, or both have the same role in several instances of the same design pattern. Well-understood design patterns for object-oriented code may be found in Gamma et al. (1994); however one may consider many other types of patterns. Examples of clusters built from patterns are: (1) All *adapters* might be considered related; (2) a particular *adapter* and *adaptee* might be considered related; (3) after defining a *utility* as a routine that has high fan-in, all utilities might be considered related (and hence put in a utility package).

Many of the most important relationships defined in the above list (categories 2 and 4, and many cases of 3, 5, and 6) are *similarity* relationships in the sense that the related elements share a particular property; we will exploit this fact later. Some categories (1, 2, 3, and 6) contain *formal* relationships between components: We define a formal relationship to be one that represents part of the implementation of the system. The behavior of the system would normally be different if such a relationship were different. Conversely, categories 4 and 5 contain *informal* relationships; however their informality does not mean that such relationships are less useful. *Design intent* is captured most strongly in categories 1 and 6 and also to a significant extent in categories 2, 3, and 4. Conversely, *emergent*[1] *properties* of design are captured in categories 5 and 3, and to a lesser extent in the others.

7.2.5   Combining and Representing Information About Entities and Relationships

A convenient way to represent information about the entities and relationships described above is to represent each entity as a vector of attributes. The more similar two vectors are, the more closely related will be the entities that the vectors describe. For example, if using the sibling static uses relationship "file inclusion," then the attributes set would be "all the files that might possibly be included." Vectors for each entity would be of equal length (the number of attributes) and each vector would contain "one" in those positions corresponding to files that are actually included by the entity, and "zero" otherwise. In this case, "file inclusion" would often be referred to as the *descriptive feature*.

Table 7.1 shows how information might be encoded for each of the categories of relationships listed in Section 7.2.4. Note that in many cases this encoding would result in extremely long vectors; hence, the clustering algorithms are

---

[1] Properties that may not have been expected or intended by designers, e.g., two data structures might be related because users tend to modify one then the other, or because maintenance requests always require changes to both.

Table 7.1. Representation of software entities as vectors of attributes that can then be compared for similarity.

Category of relationship	Possible attributes (vector elements)	What each attribute might represent so that the vectors can be compared for similarity
1. Direct static uses	For every interesting relationship, every *pair* of entities[a]	Whether the current entity is a member of the pair.
2. Sibling static uses	For every interesting relationship, every entity	The degree of relatedness between the current entity and the vector element entity. This can be a Boolean indicating the existence of a relationship or can be a count of the number of occurrences.
3. Dynamic	Every entity	Looking at execution traces, how close in time do the current entity and the vector element entity appear?
	Every time period in a trace, at some level of discretization	Whether the current entity appears in the time period, or the number of times it appears.
4. Similar use of words	Every interesting[b] word	Whether or not the word is used in the current entity, or the number of times it is used
5. History of modification	Each official change submitted to the configuration management system	Whether the current entity was changed, or a numeric value quantifying the extent of changes.
6. Membership in a pattern	For every interesting pattern, every entity	Whether the current entity participates in the pattern
	Every role in every interesting pattern	Whether the current entity plays the role.

[a]Since we intend to compare vectors element-by-element for similarity, the attributes must be such that the two related entities have the *same* attribute value when they are related. This necessitates representing *direct static uses relationships* as pairs of entities, meaning that these vectors would be prohibitively long. *Direct static uses relationships* are therefore unsuitable for this clustering approach, so an alternative approach, e.g., Bunch (Mancoridis et al., 1998), might be used.

[b]*Interesting* words can be a set of technical terms extracted automatically or semi-automatically from the system's comments; or can be all words except a predetermined set of common English words (stop words).

typically computationally expensive. Also, many of the vectors will be sparse, with most elements "zero" or "false." Although in the table completeness, encoding *direct static uses relationships* are shown as similarity vectors, this is not practical because the vectors would be prohibitively long—*sibling static uses relationships* can be used instead.

When clustering, it is common to just use one type of relationship; however, at the cost of longer vectors and hence greater computing time, one can combine information from several relationships. Two issues can then arise: conflicts and redundancy.

First, it is necessary to handle *conflicts* among the categories of relationships: For example, what should one do if a *static uses relationship* (relationship category 1 or 2, above) says that two components are closely related, while the history of common modification (category 5) suggests they are not? In this case, the overall similarity might be merely moderate, which may not be what is wanted. An approach might be to give absolute priority to some relationships.

Secondly, one has to handle *redundancy* in the relationships. For example imagine two files, where one includes another (i.e., a *direct static uses relationship*). They will likely refer to some of the same symbols (a *sibling static uses relationship*), have similar words in their comments (informal knowledge) and have been modified at the same times in the past.

Performing clustering in the presence of all this redundancy can cause algorithms to take much more computing time than necessary, so it might be a good idea to discover which relationships have the least mutual redundancy and choose to use just those. On the other hand, the redundancy could have a reinforcing effect on clustering decisions: If several relationships agree that two components are related, then perhaps it is more certain that they should be in the same cluster.

7.2.6   Clustering Algorithms

In the previous three subsections, we have discussed the software elements and their relationships that can be used for clustering, as well as how they can be represented as attribute vectors. In this section, we survey a few approaches to clustering that make use of these vectors.

It is important to understand that these algorithms do not *discover* some hidden or unknown structure in a system; instead they *impose* a structure on the set of entities they are given. They decide to ignore some links and favor others; a decision based on such factors as the metrics used to compute similarity between two vectors or the sub-lgorithms used to group similar entities together. The structures imposed by the different algorithms have different qualities; only a few may be useful to software engineers. Several classes of algorithms can be used to generate clusters; these are discussed in the next three subsections.

Hierarchical Clustering Algorithms

Hierarchical clustering algorithms start by imagining the elements are arranged in an n-dimensional space, where n is the number of elements in each vector. Some hierarchical algorithms are *agglomerative*; these seek the most similar elements or existing clusters in this space and place them together in a new, larger, cluster. The algorithms continually build larger and larger clusters in this manner until all elements are in one large supercluster with the individual elements being the leaves of the hierarchy. It is also possible for hierarchical algorithms to work in reverse, starting with all elements in one cluster and finding an appropriate way to split each cluster into subclusters, based again on distance in n-space.

Hierarchical algorithms differ depending on their choice of two key subalgorithms: The metric used to compute the similarity of vectors, and the linkage rule used to join together two clusters whose elements vary in similarity. We will outline these issues in Sections 7.2.7 and 7.2.8, respectively. The experiments we report in Section 7.4 are primarily based on hierarchical clustering algorithms.

Partitioning Algorithms

Partitioning algorithms create a set of clusters that form a partition of the element set. There are many flavors of them: They may start with a fixed number of clusters and put each element in one of these; or they may start with no cluster at all and create new ones as new elements are inserted that cannot be joined to any existing cluster, etc. One tool using such an algorithm is Bunch (Mancoridis et al., 1998). It is based on a hill-climbing algorithm that tries to maximise overall cohesion and minimize overall coupling. For comparison, we will present a few results from using Bunch in Section 7.4.

Concept Analysis Algorithms

Starting with attribute vectors, concept analysis algorithms build a lattice whose nodes are called concepts, and which can be converted to clusters. A concept contains a set of elements and is described by a set of attributes. A concept that is the parent of several concepts has just those attributes that are valid for all the child elements. The top, or supremum, concept contains all the elements, but most likely has no attributes since nothing is likely to be true for all elements. The bottom, or infimum, concept contains the empty set of elements as well as all attributes.

Concept analysis generates the complete set of concepts that are possible given the vectors. Unfortunately, this set will normally be vast. To be useful to a software engineer there has to be some way to pick a subset of intermediate-sized clusters. One feature of concept analysis is that an element can be in more than one of the resulting clusters; this may or may not be useful.

Examples of applications of concept analysis to software remodularization include Kuipers and van Deusen (1999); Lindig and Snelting (1997); and Siff and Reps (1997).

7.2.7 Similarity Metrics

Similarity metrics are used in clustering to compute the closeness between two vectors. Here we present an overview of some alternative such metrics; see Anquetil and Lethbridge (1999b) or Sneath and Sokal (1973) for more details.

Three important categories of similarity metrics are as follows:

Association Coefficients

Association coefficients consider each attribute as a binary value and compute similarity based on the number of zeros or nonzeros in each vector. Several different formulas can be used, based on the following four quantities: $a=\|X \cap Y\|$, $b=\|X \backslash Y\|$, $c=\|Y \backslash X\|$ and $d=\|F \backslash (X \cup Y)\|$, where X and Y are the two vectors being compared and F is a vector of all-ones. Popular association coefficients include:

- Simple-matching: $1 - ((a + d)/(a + b + c + d))$
- Jaccard: $1 - (a/(a + b + c))$
- Sørensen–Dice: $1 - ((a + d)/2a/(2a + b + c))$

Distance Coefficients

Distance coefficients consider each attribute to be a scalar value. Popular distance coefficients include:

- Taxonomic: $\sqrt{\sum_{i=1}^{\|F\|} (x_i - y_i)^2}$

- Camberra: $\sum_{i=1}^{\|F\|} (|x_i - y_i|/(x_i + y_i))$

  where x_i and y_i are elements of X and Y.

Correlation Coefficients

Correlation coefficients compute a value on a +1 to -1 scale, which is then mapped to a 0.1 similarity scale. The linear correlation coefficient is widely used in statistics.

The *Zero* Problem

Choosing an appropriate metric requires experimentation, and the appropriate choice depends strongly on the type of vector. An important problem that must be resolved is dealing with sparcity, i.e., the very large numbers of zeros in the vectors; some vectors may, in fact, be all zeros. If two vectors have zero for the same attribute, it does not mean that they should be considered more similar. For example, the fact that routine x and routine y do not call routine z is of very little interest; what is important is if they both call routine w.

A good association coefficient such as Sørensen—Dice and Jaccard will counter zero problems by only considering the presence of *ones*. The formulae for computing correlation are also somewhat immune to the zero problem. On the other hand, the simple matching and distance coefficients do not work very well, in the latter case because vectors with zero for many attributes will naturally be closer together in n-space.

7.2.8   Linkage Rules

We have described above how one might compute the similarity (or conversely the distance) between two individual *elements*. Agglomerative hierarchical algorithms then use *linkage rules* to compute distance between successively larger *clusters*. Imagine the scenario shown in Figure 7.1, where we want to create a new cluster by combining the closest two of the three existing clusters. In order to compute the overall distance, d, between a pair of clusters the following are several alternative linkage rules we can use, where $d_{i,j}$ is one of the distances between a member of one cluster and a member of the other (i and j iterate over the members the two clusters whose distance is being computed):

- Single linkage: d = min(di,j). This is the closest-neighbor rule and favors noncompact but more isolated clusters, hence it should encourage low coupling. In Figure 7.1, the closest members of C2 and C1 are closer than the closest members of C3 and C1; hence C1 and C2 would be joined into a larger cluster.
- Complete linkage: d = max(di,j) This is the furthest-neighbor rule and favors compact but less-isolated clusters, hence it should encourage high cohesion. Referring to Figure 7.1, C1 and C3 would be joined if this rule were used.
- Weighted average linkage: d = average(di,j). This is a compromise between single and complete linkage.
- Unweighted average linkage: This is similar to the weighted average, but deals more fairly with the situation where the members of the clusters are

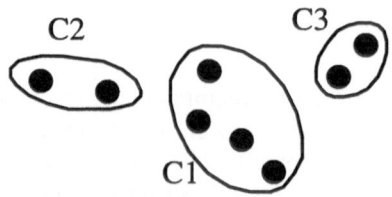

Figure 7.1. Three example clusters used to illustrate linkage rules.

themselves clusters with unequal numbers of elements. It gives each element equal weight (the weighted average linkage rule, on the other hand, results in the elements of smaller clusters being given more weight).

7.3   Approaches to Evaluating Clustering

In the last section we discussed a large number of options that one can use when performing clustering. In this section, we discuss three criteria for evaluating a clustering approach:

1. The *expert* criterion that compares an automatic remodularization to one created by experts,
2. The *design quality* criterion that uses both coupling and cohesion metrics,
3. The *algorithm behavior* criterion that evaluates size and inclusiveness of the clusters generated by the algorithms.

These evaluation criteria are best used together. An algorithm should give good results for all three.

The three evaluation criteria work on a *partition* of the element set, whereas, our experiments generate a *hierarchy*. In order to convert hierarchies to partitions, we chose to *cut* the hierarchy of clusters at various heights and use the evaluation criteria separately for each cut. The heights vary from zero, where all clusters contain a single element, to one, where all elements are gathered into one big cluster. This method proved useful in analyzing the dynamics of the cluster hierarchy, that is to say, how the evaluation criteria behave as the clusters get bigger and bigger.

7.3.1   The Expert Criterion

When evaluating a clustering algorithm using the expert criterion, one compares the clusterings produced by the algorithm to modularizations created by human designers, who we call experts. If the expert modularizations for several systems are very *similar*, or congruent, to those produced by the algorithm being evaluated, then we conclude that the algorithm has good properties. If the expert modularization is very *different* from what the algorithm generates, then we can conclude that either the algorithm is poor, or else has divided the system in a different (but not necessarily bad) way.

To obtain expert modularizations, we could ask experts to cluster systems manually. However, this would not be necessary in the case of systems where a good modularization is captured in a configuration management system or a directory hierarchy. We can use these existing modularizations to calibrate our algorithms, which will then be used to cluster those systems that are not well modularized.

There are several approaches to determine the similarity, or congruence, between two different module hierarchies, each containing the same elements. Here we discuss two such approaches.

Comparison of Pairwise Distance Measures (PDMs)

Lakhotia and Gravley (1995) summarize the method of comparing pairwise distance measures. For each pair of elements in a cluster hierarchy, one first computes d, the distance between the elements. The distance can be calculated as the shortest path between the elements in a graph representing the hierarchy of clusters, although several alternative methods are also available. The distance would be zero if the elements were in the same cluster, and large if the only enclosing cluster was the *root* cluster containing all others. The distance is expressed as a value from 0 to 1, where 1 would be used for the maximum possible path length.

The following equation illustrates how, for each pair of elements z_i and z_j, one can sum the differences between the pairwise distances in cluster hierarchies 1 and 2. The congruence would be equal to 1 for identical hierarchies.

$$congruence = 1 - \sum_{i=1}^{n1} \sum_{j=1}^{n2} |d_1(z_i, z_j) - d_2(z_i, z_j)|$$

Lakhotia and Gravley outline several alternative equations that can be used, each more complex than the one shown here; however, the principle of all such equations is similar.

Comparison of *Intra* and *Inter* Pairs

Instead of comparing entire hierarchies, one can compare two sets of clusters —where a set of clusters is a cut across a hierarchy at some level as described earlier, or where it is the result of a nonhierarchical clustering approach. A pair of entities is *intra* if both are members of the same cluster and *inter* if they are members of different clusters.

The information-retrieval metrics *precision* and *recall* can then be used to compare the sets of pairs. Precision is the percentage of intra pairs proposed by the automatic clustering method, which are also, intra in the expert set of clusters. Recall is the percentage of intra pairs in the expert set, which are also intra in the automatic set. For more details about this approach, see Anquetil and Lethbridge (1999b).

7.3.2   The Design Quality Criterion

The design quality criterion for evaluating a clustering algorithm relies on measuring coupling and cohesion. There are several ways of doing this, but one of the simplest is based on the same attribute vectors and similarity functions we described in Section 7.2.

Cohesion can be computed as the average similarity of all the *intra* pairs (see Section 7.3.1 for a definition of these), while coupling is the average similarity of all the *inter* pairs. As with the clustering methods themselves, the choice of entities and relationships for the vectors is important, as is the choice of similarity measure (Patel et al., 1992; Kunz and Black, 1995).

When using a design quality approach it is important to use different attributes for evaluation than were used for clustering; otherwise one is guaranteed artificially good results. For example, one could use vectors where the attributes are "common calls to routines" to compute the coupling and cohesion of a clustering scheme that is based on "common uses of words in file names."

7.3.3   The Algorithm Behavior Criterion

Clustering algorithms can result in sets of clusters with two key undesirable properties. These properties express imbalances in the sizes of the clusters, and can be illustrated using astronomical analogies (Hutchens and Basili, 1985).

- One excessively large cluster (a black hole): This occurs when an algorithm decides to keep adding elements to one single cluster without creating any additional clusters, that is, sucking them all into the black hole. A good metric to capture the tendency for this to happen is the size of the largest cluster (in a given cut through the cluster hierarchy), as a percentage of the total number of elements. The ideal value of this metric is near $1/n$, where n is the number of clusters in the cut; at this value, the clusters in the cut have nearly equal size.
- Many leftover unclustered elements (a gas cloud): This occurs when some subset of the elements are clustered into a hierarchy, but many elements are left out. A suitable metric is the number of unclustered elements, expressed as a percentage of the total number of elements; the ideal value is zero.

More details of these properties can be found in Anquetil and Lethbridge (1999b). Examples of the application of the various algorithms are presented in the following section.

7.4   Results of Experiments

We conducted a series of experiments to determine which of the various algorithms described in Section 7.2 worked best for software remodularization. Due to space limitations, we present here only a shortened overview of the selected results. More detailed results and additional information can be found in Anquetil and Lethbridge (1999b), and interested readers are encouraged to visit the web site at http://www.site.uottawa.ca/~anquetil/Clusters/.

We experimented with four different systems, the Linux kernel (available at http://www.kernel.org/), Mosaic version 2.6 (at ftp://ftp.ncsa.uiuc.edu/Mosaic/

Unix/source), gcc version 2.8.1 (at http://www.gnu.ai.mit.edu/software/gcc/gcc.html), and a substantially large proprietary telecommunications system. Basic metrics about these systems has been tabulated in Table 7.2. for the reader's convenience.

We used files of source code as our entities to be clustered; these do not count *include* files. We used the seven types of attributes for our vectors that are shown in Table 7.2. Five of the attributes were *sibling static uses relationships*: uses of global variables, types, and macros as well as calls to routines and inclusions of files. The remaining two attributes captured informal information—the words found in identifiers (Anquetil and Lethbridge, 1999a) and the words found in comments.

Table 7.2. The four systems used in our experiments. The last seven lines are the attributes we used in our experiments.

	Gcc	Mosaic	Linux	Telecom System
Lines of code	460K	140K	600K	2M
Files (entities)	215	225	875	1,817
Global variables	684	152	770	12,982
Types	209	323	906	6,586
Macros	1,710	1,292	8,827	N/A[a]
Called routines	1,753	1,091	1,904	7,306
Included files	129	262	457	1,655
Words in identifiers	4,739	3,821	11,111	7,105
Comment words	6,072	5,967	14,431	12,446

[a] Macros are treated as function calls by the parser that processes this system.

7.4.1   The Zero Problem with Attributes

As discussed in Section 7.2.5, it is best to compose the descriptive vectors from attributes that are less likely to have values equal to zero. One problem with such attributes is that some of the similarity metrics do not work well when there are many zeros. However, an even worse problem occurs when a vector is composed of all zeros. The problem is that two entities with such vectors cannot be distinguished, no matter what algorithm is used.

Table 7.3 shows that *global variables* and *called routines* were most prone to the above mentioned zero problem. This makes intuitive sense, since it is generally considered to be quite good practice to avoid the use of global variables, and many low-level utilities will not call other routines. On the other hand, the informal features tended to not have the zero problem. This was due to the fact that it was normally possible to find usable technical terms in the identifiers or the comments.

Table 7.3. Percentages of elements (files) that had vectors of all zeros when particular attributes were used as a basis for clustering.

Attribute	Gcc	Mosaic	Linux	Telecom System	Mean
Types	23	24	21	19	22
Global variables	44	65	53	28	48
Called routines	33	29	42	38	36
Included files	18	12	24	21	19
Macros	22	12	27	N/A	20
All of the above formal attributes	8	6	10	12	9
Words in identifiers	4	0	0	15	5
Comment words	3	1	6	2	3

7.4.2 Overall Evaluation of Attributes

Figure 7.2 shows how the use of different attributes affected the performance of clustering. The four graphs in this figure contain curves generated from Mosaic using hierarchical clustering with the Jaccard similarity metric and complete linkage. For comparison, we also present the results for Bunch in Table 7.4.For the design criterion graphs, the "words in identifiers" and "all formal" attribute vectors performed the best for cohesion. Both also performed better than Bunch.[2] "Words in comments" clearly performed worse. The differences for coupling are not significant.

For the expert criterion graphs, again the "words in identifiers" and "all formal" attribute vectors performed similarly and seem overall the best, while "words in comments" has good recall. Among the individual formal features, "file inclusion" is good while "variable use" has good precision.

General conclusions from these results are that it is important to use more than one type of attribute, and to consider using formal attributes.

7.4.3 Evaluation of Linkage Rules

Figure 7.3 illustrates the effect of applying different linkage rules when combining clusters into larger clusters (described in Section 7.2.8). The x-axis shows clusters generated by cutting the cluster hierarchy at various heights. All four graphs in Figure 7.3 were generated from Linux, using included files as attributes and the linear correlation coefficient as the similarity metric.

As expected, complete linkage gave the best cohesion, but the least good

---

[2] Due to the need for further experiments, we cannot conclude from this data that Bunch, or non-hierarcical algorithms in general are poor; instead we can only say that hierarchical algorithms are comparable.

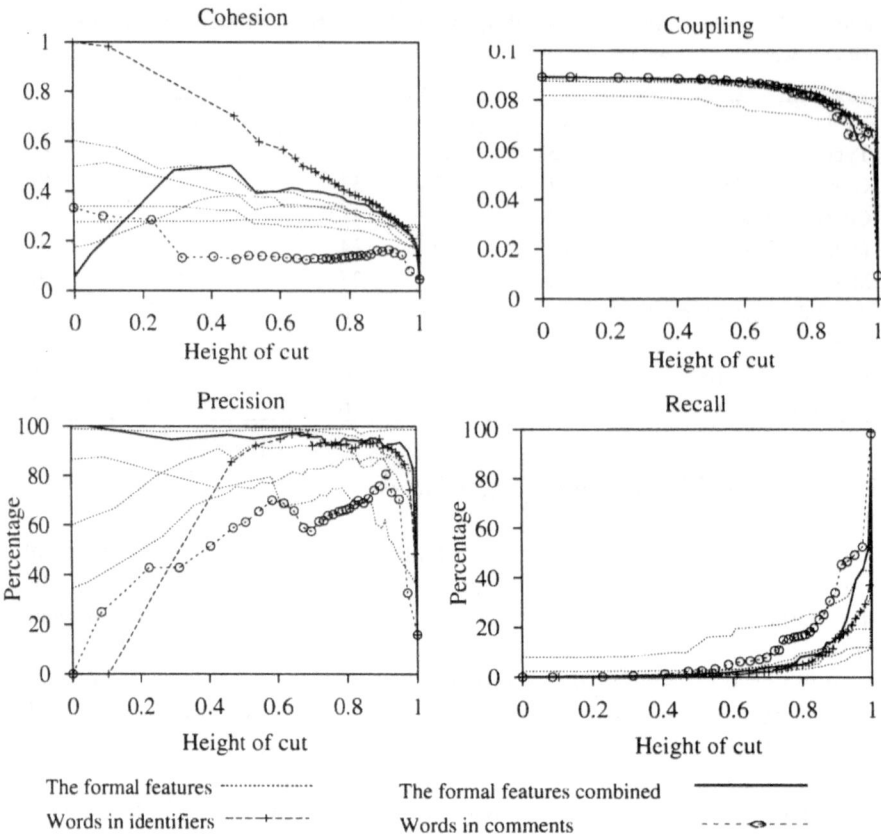

Figure 7.2. Evaluation of several different types of attributes using design and expert criteria.

coupling, single linkage gave the opposite effect, and the other two linkage rules gave intermediate effects. The choice of linkage rule should therefore depend on which design quality appears more important.

Table 7.4. Evaluation of several types of attributes using design and expert criteria (Mosaic) with the Bunch tool (Mancoridis et al., 1998).

Descriptive feature	Cohesion	Coupling	Precision	Recall
All formal	0.235	0.080	0.956	0.233
Variable use	0.252	0.094	0.748	0.021
Macro use	0.242	0.075	0.921	0.281
Routine call	0.267	0.090	0.967	0.078
File inclusion	0.236	0.081	0.890	0.197
Type use	0.263	0.080	0.888	0.190

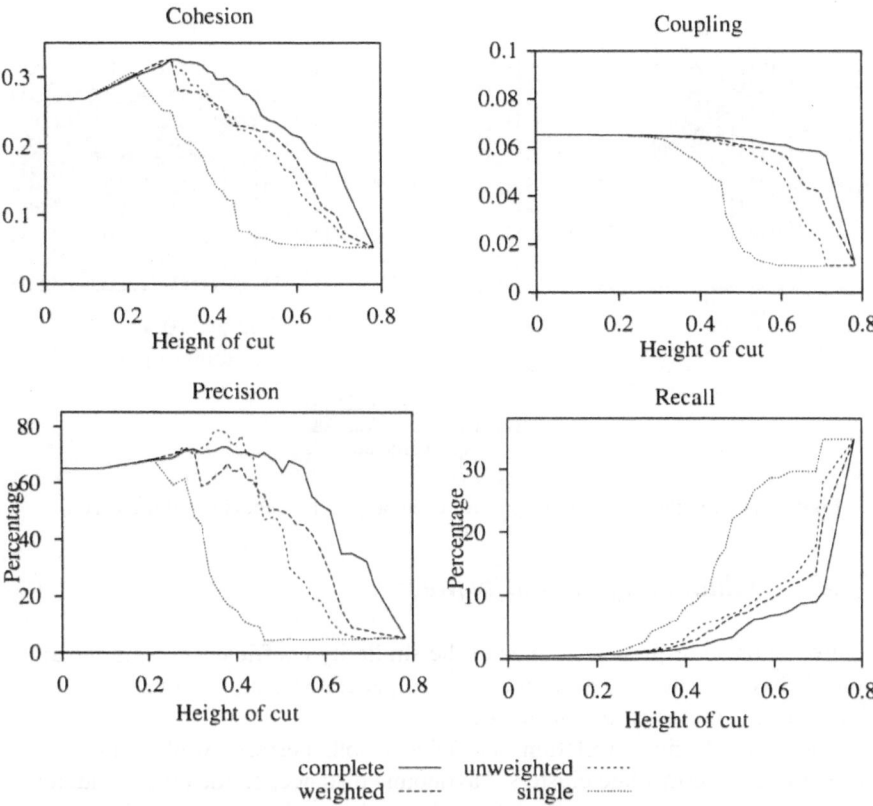

Figure 7.3. Comparison of linkage rules using design and expert criteria (Linux)

There was also a similar contrast between complete linkage and single link-age when using the expert evaluation criteria (inter-intra pairs method). Com-plete linkage, in general gave significantly better precision (i.e., the files it grouped together tended also to be grouped together by experts). However it produced worse recall (i.e., it failed to group together many of the pairs of files that were grouped together by experts).

Figure 7.4 applies the algorithm behavior criterion to the complete and single linkage rules. The larger the black area on the graphs, the better the algorithm is behaving. This is due to the fact that it is generating clusters of intermediate size.

In the case of Figure 7.4, complete linkage performs significantly better than that of single linkage. These graphs were generated from gcc, using routines as the attributes and the Jaccard similarity metric. Note that the *x*-axis has been foreshortened.

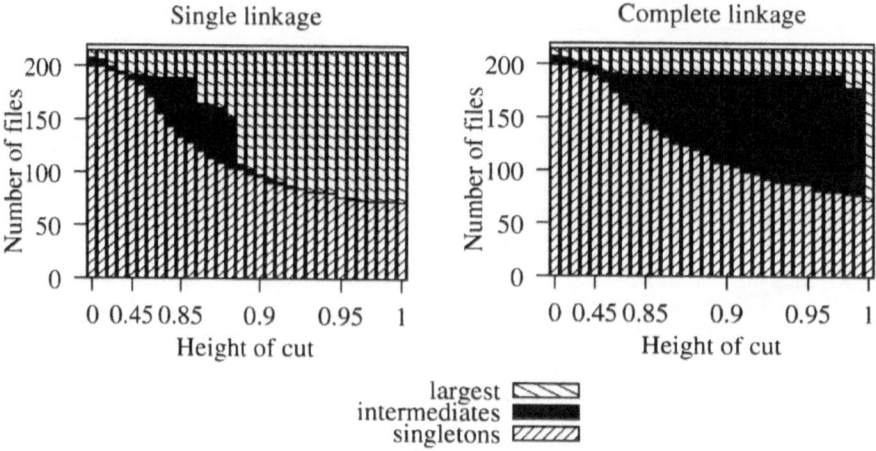

Figure 7.4. Comparison of linkage rules using algorithm behavior criteria (gcc).

7.4.4 Evaluation of Similarity Metrics

Figure 7.5 presents graphs of three of the similarity coefficients, using the algorithm behavior criteria. These graphs were generated from Mosaic using complete linkage and the *macro* attributes.

The Jaccard and correlation coefficients both perform well, with a large black area of intermediate clusters. Taxonomic distance, on the other hand, tends to fall into a *black hole* pattern: It has a large cluster that at some point captures all the intermediate clusters.

The results for the Bunch tool are 32 singleton clusters, 159 elements in intermediate clusters, and 39 in the largest cluster. This is very similar to the better cuts in the hierarchical clustering approaches.

7.5   Summary and Conclusions

In this chapter we have reviewed many of the decisions that have to be made when designing a hierarchical clustering algorithm for remodularization of software. We also presented evaluation criteria and experimental data to illustrate the effect of various decisions. The evaluation criteria included design qualities (coupling and cohesion), comparison with expert modularizations, and the tendency of the algorithm to produce a balanced set of clusters.

Several general algorithm approaches are available for clustering. We compared hierarchical algorithms to a nonhierarchical tool called Bunch and concluded that the hierarchical algorithms perform at least as well. However, they might be favored because they produce a hierarchy of clusters instead of just a

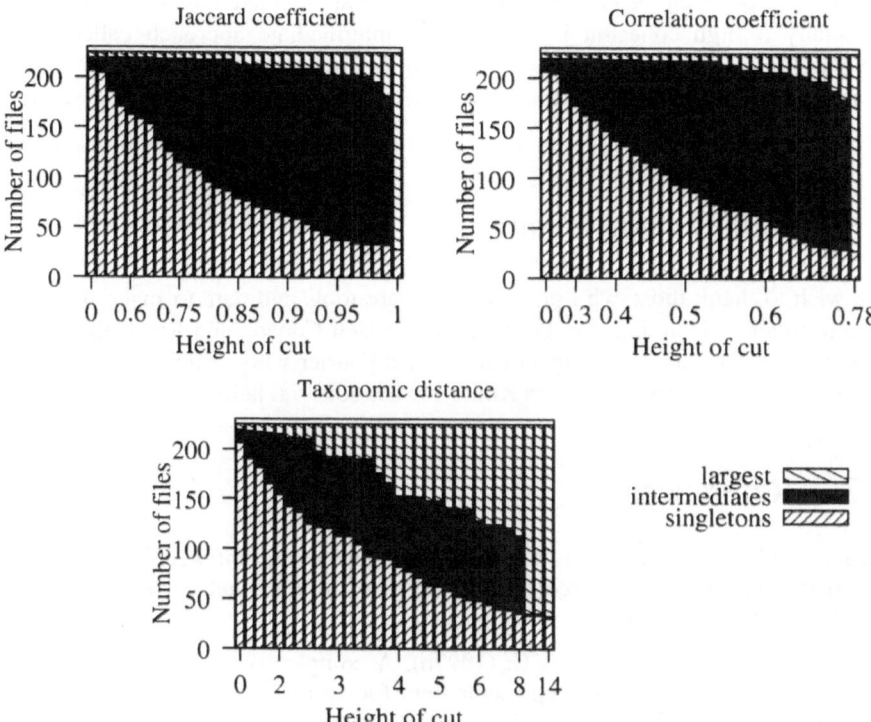

Figure 7.5. Comparison of three similarity metrics using algorithm behavior criteria (Mosaic).

simple set. When given a hierarchy, it is still necessary to make cuts at one or more levels to arrive at useful sets of modules or subsystems: Cutting in the upper half of the hierarchy gives the best results.

A key choice in designing a clustering algorithm is which sources of information will be used to make decisions about the elements to put together. We conclude from our experiments that one should make use of several sources of information (e.g., uses of data types, uses of global variables, as well as file inclusions), and consider using informal information such as the words found in comments and the names of identifiers. Hierarchical algorithms require that these sources of information be composed into vectors—one vector per entity being clustered.

The hierarchical algorithms make use of similarity metrics to compare vectors. Several such metrics are available, but we found the Jaccard and correlation coefficients had the best performance.

Finally, the algorithms require one to choose rules for combining clusters into larger ones. The rules dictate whether the nearest (single linkage) or farthest (complete linkage) elements in two clusters should be used when determining the distance between the clusters. We conclude that complete linkage is the best, especially if high cohesion is a goal. The intermediate approach called *unweighted linkage* might be better if coupling is important. Single linkage tends to result in a black hole phenomenon, where the algorithms build one single large cluster.

7.6   Acknowledgements

We wish to thank those who provided software tools and data to make this research possible, including the Datrix group at Bell Canada and Ric Holt at the University of Waterloo. We also thank Cedric Fourier who participated in early phases of this work and K. Teresa Khidir for her editorial help.

7.7   References

Anquetil, N., and Lethbridge, T.C. (1999a). Recovering software architecture from the names of source files, *J. Software Maintenance: Research and Practice,* 11(3), 201-221.

Anquetil, N., and Lethbridge, T.C. (1999b). A comparative study of clustering algorithms and abstract representations for software remodularization, In *Proc. Working Conference on Reverse Engineering*, IEEE, Atlanta, pp. 235-255.

Clayton, R., Rugaber, S., and Wills, L. (1998). On the knowledge required to understand a program, *In Proc. Working Conference on Reverse Engineering.* IEEE, Oct. 1998, 69-78.

Gamma, E., Helm, R., Johnson, R., and Vlissides J. (1994). *Design Patterns: Elements of Reusable Object Oriented Software*, Reading, MA: Addison-Wesley.

Girard, J-F., Koschke, R., and Schied, G. (1997). Comparison of abstract data type and abstract state encapsulation detection techniques for architectural understanding, In *Proc. Working Conference on Reverse Engineering.* IEEE, Oct., 66-75.

Hutchens, D. H., and Basili, V. R. (1985). System structure analysis: Clustering with data binding, *IEEE Transactions on Software Engineering*, 11(8), August, 749-757.

Kuipers, T., and van Deusen, A., (1999). Identifying objects using cluster and concept analysis, In *Proc. 21st International Conference on Software Engineering*, ACM, May, 246-55.

Kunz, T., and Black, J.P. (1995). Using automatic process clustering for design recovery and distributed debugging, *IEEE Transactions on Software Engineering*, 21(6), June, 515-527.

Lakhotia, A. (1997). A unified framework for expressing software subsystem classification techniques, *J. of Systems and Software,*. 36(3), March, 211-231.

Lakhotia, A., and Gravley, J. M. (1995). Toward experimental evaluation of subsystem classification recovery techniques. In *Proc. Working Conference on Reverse Engineering*, Toronto, 262-269.

Lindig, C., and Snelting, G. (1997). Assessing modular structure of legacy code based on mathematical concept analysis. In *Proc. 19th International Conference on Software Engineering, ICSE'97*, May, 349-359.

Mancoridis, S., Mitchell, B. S., Rorres, C., Chen, Y., and Gansner, E. R. (1998). Using automatic clustering to produce high-level system organizations of source code. In *Proc. 6th International Workshop on Program Comprehension*. IEEE Computer Society, June, pp. 45-52. See also http://www.mcs.drexel.edu/~serg/

Patel, S., Chu, W., and Baxter, R. (1992). A measure for composite module cohesion, In *Proc. 14th International Conference on Software Engineering*, ACM, 38-48.

Siff, M., and Reps, T. (1997). Identifying modules via concept analysis. In *Proc. International Conference on Software Maintenance*, Oct. 1997, IEEE Computer Society, 170-79

Sneath, P. H. A., and Sokal, R. R. (1973). *Numerical Taxonomy*, W.H. Freeman and Company, San Francisco.

Wiggerts, T. (1997). Using clustering algorithms in legacy systems remodularization. In *Proc. Working Conference on Reverse Engineering*. IEEE, October, 33-43.

8
Automatic Architectural Clustering of Software

Vassilios Tzerpos
Richard C. Holt

8.1   Introduction

The definition of the term *large software* is constantly changing, as the size of software systems continues to increase rapidly. What DeRemer and Kron called a large system in their classic paper on programming-in-the-large (1976), would probably be classified as a medium-sized, if not small-sized, system today. Advances in hardware technology concerning the size, speed, and cost of primary and secondary storage, as well as the advent of modern programming languages and object-oriented programming, have allowed the size of software systems to increase significantly in the last decade.

When a system becomes large, it is very hard to ensure that its structure is the intended one. Moreover, the original documentation, if it exists at all, becomes outdated as the system evolves, since the developers are usually busy trying to meet the next deadline. The fact that developers often discontinue their association with such large projects intensifies the problem, since they take a lot of the knowledge about the system with them.

These factors contribute to the transformation of a piece of software into what is known as *legacy* code or software, namely a piece of code that one uses but does not necessarily understand. The drawbacks of having legacy code in a software system become obvious when the time comes to alter its functionality, to adapt it to a new hardware platform or operating system, or to improve its performance. One needs to understand the code once again.

Even systems that are still under development are impacted by these problems. Parts of the system might become legacy code, if only because they have not been maintained for some time. Also, large projects often hire new people who must be brought up to speed, but the seasoned developers are often too busy to help with this. If the documentation is obsolete, then a newcomer is at a loss as to where to start, and cannot know the full impact of a potential modification on the rest of the system.

Clearly, a solution to all these problems is required. If one could derive a decomposition of a large software system into meaningful subsystems in an automatic (or semi-automatic) way, then much of the effort required to understand and to improve a software system would be alleviated. At the same time, this capability would enable one to remodularize legacy code, as well as to identify candidate subsystems for extraction of reusable components.

Automatic clustering techniques described in the literature claim that they can do exactly this—detect the natural groups (or *clusters*) in a collection of entities, such as procedures or source files. However, none of these algorithms has been shown to be effective on large systems. Further research is required in order to reveal the best approach to the problem of decomposing a software system.

Since research on clustering began long before the term software was coined, many techniques are already in use in other disciplines. In this chapter, we will argue that these techniques (heretofore called *classic* clustering techniques) can be used effectively in a software context, once they have been adapted to fit the peculiarities of this specific problem domain.

The structure of the rest of this chapter is as follows. Section 8.2 is a survey of current approaches to the software clustering problem by researchers in the software community. A more detailed discussion of general approaches to clustering can be found in Chapter 7 of this book; here we will focus on automatic clustering using classical techniques. In this light, Section 8.3 first presents clustering techniques from other disciplines. In Section 8.4, we explain why we think classic clustering techniques would be appropriate for the software version of the problem. Section 8.5 outlines research challenges and open problems of interest. Finally, Section 8.6 presents our conclusions.

8.2 Previous Work on Software Clustering

8.2.1 Knowledge-Based vs. Structure-Based Approaches

A common approach to the problem of understanding a software system and recovering its design is the *knowledge-based* approach. In the *bottom-up* version of this approach, one attempts to reverse-engineer and understand small fragments of the source code, using preexisting domain knowledge. One then combines these fragments in an effort to understand the system as a whole, thus determining its design. This approach has been shown to work well with small systems.

When dealing with large systems, however, this approach does not perform as effectively. One of the reasons is that the size of the knowledge base is becoming prohibitively large. Other reasons are outlined by Neighbors (1996): "Knowledge-based understanding of large system semantics [is] currently too difficult for three reasons: absence of a robust semantic theory, lack of problem domain specific semantics, and knowledge spreading in the source code."

For these reasons, the software clustering community mainly adopts *structure-*

based approaches. In these approaches, the decomposition of a software system is determined by looking at syntactic interactions (such as *call* or *fetch*) between entities (such as procedures or variables). In this case, the problem of clustering a software system can be thought of as the partitioning of the vertex set of a graph, where the nodes are defined as procedures or variables, and the edges as relations between these entities.

The rest of this section presents a survey of important publications in the field of software clustering, as well as some of the recent approaches to the problem.

8.2.2   Early Work

In one of the early works in software clustering, Belady and Evangelisti (1981) recognized the need to automatically cluster a software system in order to reduce its complexity. They also presented a first approach to doing this for a specific system. In addition, they provided a measure for the complexity[1] of a system after it has been clustered. Their approach, however, only works with a specific kind of system, and they did not validate their complexity measure. A point of interest is that they did not extract information from the source code, but rather from the system's documentation.

Subsequent to this work, Hutchens and Basili (1985) performed clustering based on *data bindings*. A data binding was defined as an interaction between two procedures based on the location of variables that are within the static scope of both procedures. They defined different kinds of data bindings, from simplistic and easy to compute (e.g., a data binding between two procedures p and q exists, if there exists a variable that belongs in the static scope of both procedures) to sophisticated and hard to compute (e.g., the data binding only exists if control flow might be given to procedure q after the value of the common variable has been set by p). On the basis of the data bindings, a hierarchy is constructed from which a partition could be derived.

An interesting feature of their paper is that they compared their structures with the developer's mental model with satisfactory results. They also raised the important issue of *stability*; when the system changes slightly, how is the clustering affected? Finally, they recognized that it might be necessary to disregard certain information, such as omnipresent nodes, in order to get a clearer view of the structure of a software system.

One of the most active researchers in the area of software clustering in the early 1990s was Schwanke. His papers (Schwanke et al., 1989; Schwanke and Platoff, 1989; Schwanke, 1991) and his tool (called ARCH) addressed the problem of automatic clustering in an innovative way. Although his approaches were not tested against a large software system, they showed promise.

---

[1]Complexity here refers to how difficult it is to understand a system after it has been clustered in a specific way.

One of Schwanke's main contributions was that he added to the classic low-coupling and high-cohesion[2] heuristics by introducing the *shared-neighbors technique* (Schwanke and Platoff, 1989) in order to capture patterns that appear commonly in software systems. This refers to identifying subsystems that are not comprised of resources cooperating to implement a specific functionality, but rather of resources providing similar functionality, such as the routines of a math library.

Furthermore, his maverick analysis (Schwanke, 1991) enabled him to refine a partition by identifying components that happened to belong to the wrong subsystem, and placing them in the correct one. He also attempted to provide names and descriptions for automatically generated clusters, but not very convincingly.

Choi and Scacchi (1990) presented an approach to finding subsystem hierarchies based on resource exchanges between modules. The complexity of their algorithm is $O(n^2)$, which is better than Schwanke's $O(n^3)$, but still probably too high for large systems. It appears to perform well on small examples, but its ability to scale up is questionable.

Müller has also been involved in the automatic clustering problem (Müller and Uhl, 1990; Müller et al., 1993). His approaches tend to be semi-automatic, meaning that they are meant to help a designer perform clustering on a software system. He introduces the important principles of *small interfaces* (the number of elements of a subsystem that interface with other subsystems should be small compared to the total number of elements in the subsystem) and of *few interfaces* (a given subsystem should interface only with a small number of the other subsystems).

8.2.3 Recent Work

The last couple of years have seen a renewed interest in the problem of clustering a software system automatically. The main reason for this is the rapid growth of Reverse Engineering as a research field, largely due to the Year 2000 and Euro conversion[3] problems. Understanding large software has become a very important issue and clustering can help deal with it.

Lakhotia (1997) introduced a unified framework for expressing software clustering techniques. Realizing that the techniques in the software clustering literature have been presented using different terminology and symbols, he proposed a framework consisting of a consistent set of terminology, notation, and symbols, which can be used to describe the input, output, and processing performed by these techniques. Several existing techniques have been reformulated to conform to this framework.

---

[2]*Low coupling* is a software engineering principle that requires that interactions between subsystems should be as few as possible. *High cohesion* is a related principle that requires that interactions should be kept as much as possible within a subsystem.

[3]Financial software in Europe had to be modified in order to accommodate the common currency.

Neighbors (1996) attempted to identify subsystems with the ultimate goal of hand extraction of reusable components. He looked at compile-time and link-time interconnections between components and tried different approaches. The approaches that were successful were based on naming and on reference context. His results were validated by the developers of the system on which he experimented.

An interesting alternative approach was presented by Anquetil and Lethbridge (1997). Instead of looking at structural information, such as procedure calls or data references, they only looked at the names of the resources of the system. Their experiments produced promising results, but their approach has the obvious drawback that it relies on the developers' consistency with the naming of their resources. In Chapter 7 of the present book, Lethbridge and Anquetil discuss in more detail both their technique and other clustering techniques not covered here.

Bowman and Holt introduced the term *ownership architecture* (1999). They argued that the organization of system developers into teams can help one understand a software system, and that such a structure is often congruent to the system's concrete architecture. An extensive case study involving the Linux operating system was presented to corroborate their conjecture.

Finally, various researchers have recently started looking at techniques used in other disciplines in order to come up with a better solution to the automatic clustering problem.

Wiggerts (1997) presented a survey of techniques used by the cluster analysis community and attempted to reuse them for system remodularization. His future plans include clustering a software system in "a more or less" object-oriented way.

Several researchers attempted to use concept analysis in order to identify subsystems (Lindig and Snelting, 1997; van Deursen and Kuipers, 1999). Their experiments demonstrated that concept analysis could be helpful in certain reverse-engineering scenaria, such as object identification.

Mancoridis et al. (1998) treated clustering as an optimization problem and employed genetic algorithms in order to overcome the local optima problem of hill-climbing algorithms, which are commonly used in clustering problems. His experiments demonstrate encouraging results and fast performance.

8.2.4   Observations

By examining the literature on software clustering, one can draw interesting observations. First, most researchers seem to agree on structural-based criteria and naming conventions as being the most promising approaches. However, there exists a variety of different interactions between modules that are used as the basis to decide which resources depend on which modules. Isolating the interactions that are appropriate for the software clustering problem, and determining the properties that make them so, are problems that need more study.

Another observation is that none of the approaches has been tested extensively against large software systems.[4] This omission becomes more interesting when one considers that these approaches were developed with such systems specifically in mind. It is not clear whether these approaches scale up to large systems.

Also, validation of an approach against more than one system is required. Many researchers present results that demonstrate that their algorithm performs very well for a given software system. It would be interesting to see how the algorithm performs on a number of systems, since an algorithm can be specifically tuned to perform well on a particular system.

Finally, the issue of performance is very important. Most graph partitioning problems are shown to be NP-complete (Garey and Johnson, 1979) or NP-hard. The approaches presented above, however, are heuristic approaches that attempt to reduce this complexity to polynomial upper bounds. What kind of complexity is acceptable for large systems remains to be seen.

A more detailed description of open problems and research challenges can be found in Section 8.5. In the next section, we present popular cluster analysis approaches that have been used to solve clustering problems found in other disciplines.

8.3   Classic Clustering Techniques

8.3.1   Background

Cluster analysis has been used in a number of different disciplines[5] in order to solve a wide spectrum of problems. Its objective is to find algorithms and methods for grouping or classifying objects. Many diverse techniques have been developed in order to discover structure within complex bodies of data.

Computer science has also benefited from clustering techniques. For example, the data base community uses clustering to group related entities together in relational (Silberschatz et al., 1997), as well as object-oriented data bases (Tsangaris and Naughton, 1991). Data mining also employs similar techniques in order to cluster spatial and multidimensional data (Ng and Han, 1994; Zhang et al., 1996).

In this section, we will present the most important cluster analysis techniques found in the literature. Since these techniques are used in many disciplines, there is considerable confusion of terminology. For example, the raw material to be clustered has been called point, item, data unit, subject, object, element, entity and many other terms. We will use the term *object*. Also, the aspects of the objects that we look at in order to decide on the appropriate clustering have been called variables, attributes, characters, or features. We will use the term *feature*.

---

[4] A large system refers to an industrial system with a size of order of magnitude close to a million lines of code.

[5] Examples include psychology, biology, statistics, social sciences, and various fields of engineering.

8.3.2   Similarity Measures

One of the first things that a clustering approach usually does is to decide on what grounds two objects will be judged to be similar. Moreover, one needs a measure that will decide which pair of objects are more similar than any other pair. The answer to this problem is a *similarity measure*.

Similarity measures can be divided in two groups, depending on the kind of information that serves as their input. We distinguish the following kinds of information:

1. *Relations between the objects.* In this case, the problem can be represented as a graph, where the nodes are the objects and the edges are the relations. If we have more than one relation, then the graph will have multiple kinds of edges.

   Common similarity measures that deal with cases like this are based on the number of edges connecting two objects, the length of the shortest path between two objects, or the weight that different kinds of edges might have. Whether the graph is directed or undirected is also a factor.

2. *The score of the objects on different features.* In this case, similarity is usually measured by *association coefficients*. These are expressed in terms of the number of features that are present for each object. For this reason, association coefficients assume binary features (i.e., reflecting whether a feature is either present or not). The following table is used in order to calculate various coefficients between object i and object j:

	Object j **1**	Object j **0**
Object i **1**	a	b
Object i **0**	c	d

   In the above table, a is the number of features that are present for both objects, b the number of features present only for object i, and so on. Different coefficients treat 0-0 matches (their number is given by d) differently and also put different weightings on any of the four entries of the table. The most common coefficients are:

   - the *simple matching coefficient*, defined as: $\frac{a+d}{a+b+c+d}$
   - the *Jaccard coefficient*, defined as: $\frac{a}{a+b+c}$

   An extensive study of coefficients can be found elsewhere (Anderberg, 1973).

Other similarity measures that are found in the literature include distance measures (usually Euclidean or Manhattan), correlation coefficients, and probabilistic measures (based on the assumption that agreement on rare features is more important than agreement on frequent ones).

ALL   **ONE**

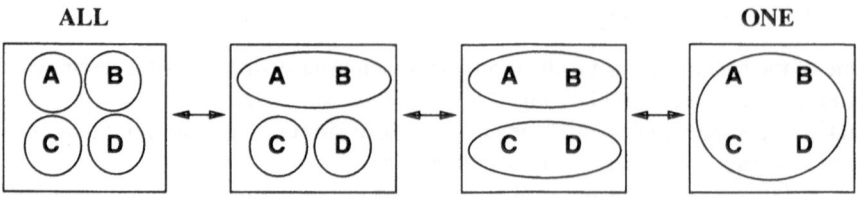

Figure 8.1. An example partition sequence.

8.3.3 Algorithms

Once the similarity measure has been decided upon, an appropriate algorithm has to be chosen as well. The majority of the algorithms found in the literature can be categorized into one of the following three categories: *hierarchical* algorithms, *partitional* algorithms, and *graph-based* algorithms. We will present each category in detail.

Hierarchical Algorithms

These algorithms produce a nested sequence of partitions. In one end of this sequence is the partition where each object is in a different cluster (we will call this partition ALL), and in the other end the partition where all the objects are in the same cluster (we will call this partition ONE). At each step through this sequence two of the clusters are joined together. Figure 8.1 shows an example partition sequence for four objects A,B,C, and D.

A common representation for a hierarchical structure is that of a dendrogram. Figure 8.2 presents the dendrogram for the example partition sequence.

However, different partitions in a sequence like the one shown in Figure 8.1 are not of equal importance. Actually, one is usually interested in a small number of them (maybe only one). This is usually referred to as finding cut points for the dendrogram. Factors that influence the selection of a cut point are usually a priori knowledge on the expected structure, or prechosen parameters such as the maximum number of clusters allowed, or the maximum number of objects in a cluster.

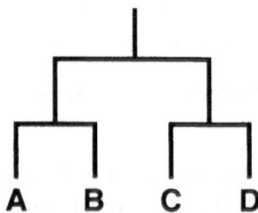

Figure 8.2. The dendrogram for the example partition sequence.

Hierarchical algorithms are divided into two categories, agglomerative and divisive:

1. *Agglomerative (or bottom-up)*. These start with partition ALL and iteratively join the most similar clusters based on the similarity measure. An interesting point of debate between researchers is how to compute similarity between a newly formed cluster and the rest of the already formed clusters. This is called the *update rule* problem.

   Many different solutions exist for it. The most common include the single-link update rule (the similarity of the newly formed cluster to an existing cluster C is the *maximum* of the similarities of its constituents to C), and the complete-link update rule (the similarity of the newly formed cluster to an existing cluster C is the *minimum* of the similarities of its constituents to C).

2. *Divisive (or top-down)*. These start with partition ONE and try to iteratively split it until we reach partition ALL. Such algorithms, however, suffer from excessive computational complexity, as one has to look at an exponential number of partitions at every step. This is the main reason why these algorithms are not very popular.

Partitional Algorithms

Partitional algorithms usually work by starting with an initial partition and trying to modify it in an attempt to optimize a criterion that represents the quality of a given partition. What constitutes a good criterion is an interesting problem. It usually has to do with the domain on which one tries to cluster. For example, a criterion could be a mathematical expression that is maximized when the cohesion of the clusters is maximized.

The challenge that partitional algorithms face is the combinatorial explosion of the number of possible partitions. Even for a small number of objects the number of possible partitions is astronomical. For example, there are 34,105 partitions of ten objects into four clusters, but this number explodes to approximately 11 million if the objects are increased to 19.

The usual workaround to this problem is to start with an initial partition (chosen randomly or based on some heuristics) and attempt to optimize the chosen criterion by modifying that partition in an appropriate way. These algorithms (called hill-climbing algorithms) do converge (Anderberg, 1973), but usually to local optima. Therefore, the choice of the initial partition is crucial for the success of the algorithm.

Perhaps the best-known partitional algorithm is ISODATA (Anderberg, 1973). Its effectiveness is based on the successful initial choice of value for seven parameters that control factors such as the number of expected clusters, the number of objects in a cluster, etc. The algorithm then proceeds to iteratively improve on an initial partition by joining and splitting clusters, depending on how close to the chosen parameters the actual values for the current partition are. Several variations of this method exist in the literature.

Graph-Based Algorithms

A particular class of algorithms that is of interest are the ones that are based on graph properties. Different categorizations of these techniques exist, depending on the perspective one chooses (Corneil and Woodward, 1978; Wiggerts, 1997). We distinguish the following categories:

- *Minimum Spanning Tree (MST) algorithms.* These algorithms begin by finding an MST of the given graph. Next, they either iteratively join the two closest nodes into a cluster (hierarchical agglomerative version) or split the graph into clusters by removing inconsistent edges (partitional version). The definition of an inconsistent edge varies, but they are usually considerably larger than the rest of the edges on the MST.

- *Clique algorithms.* These algorithms start with the maximal complete subgraphs (cliques) of the given graph, and either define them as clusters, or use them as the basis for other algorithms.

- *Local connectivity algorithms.* The number of edge or vertex disjoint paths of a specified length between two points is the criterion used in these algorithms in order to decide which objects (or nodes in this case) are similar enough to be in the same cluster. For example, instead of only using edges (paths of length 1) as an indication of closeness, one could also use paths of length 2 (Vaswani, 1968).

- *Aggregation algorithms.* These algorithms select sets of nodes and collapse them into aggregate nodes, which can be used as clusters or can be input for a new iteration to find higher level aggregates. Graph reduction is an aggregation technique that is based on the notion of the neighborhood of a node (von Laszewski, 1993). Bicomponents and strongly connected components have also been used for this purpose (Botafogo and Schneiderman, 1991).

- *Heuristic approaches.* As mentioned before, the large number of possible partitions makes the problem of graph partitioning almost impossible to solve optimally. Heuristic approaches attempt to search the space of possible solutions in a clever way in order to come as close to the optimal solution as possible in a reasonable amount of time. For example, the Kernighan-Lin method (1970) attempts to overcome the local optima problem of hill-climbing algorithms by choosing to go downhill for a while in the hope of finding a taller hill in the next few steps.

8.3.4   Observations

By examining the literature on cluster analysis, one can draw some interesting observations. First, researchers agree that "a classification is neither true or false" (Everitt, 1993). This means that no particular partition can be the ideal answer to the problem of classifying a large number of objects. Based on different points of view, one can come up with two different, but equally valid, decompositions of the same set of objects. Some classifications, however, are more useful than others. It is the job of the cluster analysis researcher to find what factors determine the usefulness of a particular clustering.

Another observation is that "the multitude of alternatives makes it difficult to say that a particular measure and a specific method are clearly superior selections for treating the problem at hand" (Anderberg, 1973). On any given problem, a large group of different methods will give practically the same results, while perhaps a few other methods will give distinctively different results. A theoretic explanation of the behavior of different methods does not exist, however.

Finally, looking back at the literature on software clustering, we see that some cluster analysis techniques have indeed been used by software researchers. Hutchens and Basili (1985) used a hierarchical agglomerative method in order to perform their clustering. Schwanke and Platoff (1989) defined binary features in the same way as defined earlier in this section. Mancoridis et al. (1998) used a hill-climbing optimization approach similar to the one presented in Section 8.3.3.

It remains to be seen whether the software community will adopt more cluster analysis techniques. The next section explains why we think this would be a good idea.

8.4   Classic Techniques for Software Clustering

We believe that the software community can benefit from the cluster analysis techniques available. As explained at the end of the previous section, many software researchers are reinventing these techniques. It would be beneficial if the software community adopted and adapted the already well-studied algorithms of cluster analysis.

One of the main reasons why we think this would be a good idea, is that the peculiarities of software as a clustering domain could be used to alleviate a lot of the problems facing classic clustering techniques. For example, with software we already have a rather good idea of what a cluster should look like. Software Engineering principles such as *information hiding* (Parnas, 1972), or *few interfaces* could guide the clustering process toward a desirable solution. Also, since our goal is usually to understand a software system, we can cluster to different levels of proximity[6] depending on our perspective. Therefore, specifying the number

---

[6]Proximity, in the cluster analysis literature, refers to how close to the data we look,

of clusters is not a big problem for software clustering. Furthermore, a software system can have more than one valid view, which is what different clustering algorithms can give us.

Another interesting issue in the cluster analysis literature is that of *clustering tendency*. Most clustering algorithms can be accused of imposing a structure on a set of data, even if no structure exists. In this case, it is possible that the structure presented as the final solution is an artifact of the algorithm used, rather than a natural grouping of the objects in question. With legacy software however, this need not be a problem. As it has been noted (Wiggerts, 1997), any structure is better than no structure, since one needs to start somewhere. Besides, one would hope that even the most badly written piece of code would have some structure.

In their classic text on *Algorithms for Clustering Data*, Jain and Dubes (1988) present a framework for a cluster analysis project, which is divided into seven steps. To demonstrate that it would also fit the software clustering problem, we present it in a software context (the titles are theirs, but the explanations ours):

1. *Data collection*. This refers to extracting the relevant information from the source code. A critical issue here is what kind of information one needs to extract.

2. *Initial screening*. The data extracted from the source code usually requires some massaging before it can be used. As noted in Hutchens and Basili (1985), certain information may have to be deleted as it might interfere with the clustering process, e.g., omnipresent nodes[7] (Müller and Uhl, 1990).

3. *Representation*. This refers to choosing the appropriate similarity measure. It is usually based on the type of information available, the experience of the investigator, and the insight of system experts. In the case of software clustering, there exists a wealth of different software metrics (Adamov and Baumann, 1987; Kontogiannis, 1997) that could be used for this purpose.

4. *Clustering tendency*. This step checks if the available data have a natural tendency to cluster or not. As explained before, this is not a problem in a software context.

5. *Clustering strategy*. The algorithm to be used and the value of any parameters in it are chosen during this step. It is up to the investigator to decide on the most appropriate algorithm. Comparative studies between different existing algorithms would facilitate the process of choosing or developing effective algorithms.

---

that is, are we trying to find a few or a lot of clusters?

[7]This refers to nodes (typically procedures in the software case) with a large in- or out-degree. In the software case, this might correspond to library routines, the interactions with which are not necessary in order to decide on the structure of the rest of the system.

6. *Validation*. Formal techniques for the validation of a partition exist, but in a software context there are usually alternative methods available. Developers associated with the examined software project can compare the partition obtained from the automatic clustering approach with their own mental model of the structure of a system. Also, in the case of legacy software, empirical studies could evaluate whether the clustering actually helped in the understanding of the system.

7. *Interpretation*. This refers to comparing results with other studies, drawing conclusions, and getting ideas for improvements on any of the previous steps.

In the next section, we will present open problems and research challenges a researcher in the field of software clustering might have to face.

8.5   Research Challenges

Throughout this chapter, we have mentioned various problems facing researchers in software clustering and presented the reasons that make these problems difficult. In this section, we present an organized list of open problems that pose interesting challenges to the researchers in the area:

- It is not clear which kinds of relations between software objects are appropriate from a clustering point of view. Procedure calls and data references are commonly used, but what about relations such as source inclusion (Carmichael et al., 1995) or type references? Should they be used, and if so, with equal weight to other relations or not? The field is in need of a theory of dependencies that characterizes such relations.

- Another interesting research issue is the selection of appropriate algorithms. A comparative study tested on a number of systems is long overdue. It is possible that certain algorithms are best suited for a particular type of software system. A categorization of algorithms and the types of software for which they work best would be beneficial to the software clustering field.

- There exists a gap between the structures obtained by the software clustering researchers and the ones presented by the software architecture community (Garlan and Shaw, 1993; Shaw and Garlan, 1996). Closing this gap is not easy, as a compromise has to be found between the automatic approaches of the clustering community, and the supervised ones of the software architecture community (Harris et al., 1995).

- Clustering approaches need to be tested on large systems, as success on small systems does not guarantee effective scaling up to large systems. Obtaining access to large systems is not easy, but it can be done, and it is crucial for the validation of candidate approaches. Many open source systems appear to be promising candidates for the creation of a benchmark for different algorithms. An updated version of the proposed subject programs is needed (Lakhotia and Gravley, 1995).

- Most software approaches currently present static views of the structure of a software system. However, most large systems are complex enough to require more elaborate views, such as dynamic views. This is certainly an important challenge for the software clustering community.

- The issue of stability is also important. Minor changes to the software system should not drastically affect its generated structure. A study of the types of structures generated by different algorithms and their stability would be very interesting (such studies exist for graph theoretic approaches (Corneil and Woodward, 1978; Raghavan and Yu, 1981)).

- A related issue is that of incremental clustering. Assuming that a satisfactory partition of a software system exists, how do we update this structure when the software system changes, and how do we do it in a way that still reflects the actual structure of the system and causes the least possible modification? An approach to this problem has already been presented by Tzerpos and Holt (1996).

- Software is a peculiar clustering domain since the developers that are associated with the system being examined can provide a lot of help. Integrating information obtained from the developers with the automatic approaches described in this paper is an important challenge (Tzerpos and Holt, 1996).

The aforementioned problems pose interesting challenges to researchers, and suggest that the software clustering field is a fertile one for research.

8.6   Conclusion

The goal of this chapter was threefold:

- to present the state of the art in the research of software clustering,

- to survey classic clustering techniques and show that they can be utilized in a software context, and

- to demonstrate that the software clustering field has research potential.

In Section 8.2, we presented the most important approaches to the software clustering problem, and outlined their advantages and disadvantages. In Section 8.3 we surveyed cluster analysis approaches that have been used in other disciplines, and in Section 8.4, we argued that they could be used effectively in a software context. Finally, in Section 8.5 we presented a number of open problems in the area of software clustering.

We believe that further research on the problem of decomposing a software system automatically is very important, and that it will benefit not only the research community, but also the people involved in the development of large software systems.

8.7   References

Adamov, R. and Baumann, P. (1987). *Literature Review on Software Metrics.* Institut für Informatik der Universität Zürich.

Anderberg, M. R. (1973). *Cluster Analysis for Applications.* New York: Academic Press, Inc.

Anquetil, N. and Lethbridge, T. (1997). File clustering using naming conventions for legacy systems. In *Proceedings of CASCON 1997,* pp. 184-195, Toronto, Canada.

Botafogo, R. A. and Schneiderman, B. (1991). Identifying aggregates in hypertext structures. In *Proceedings of Hypertext 91,* pp. 63-74, December, San Antonio, TX.

Bowman, I. T. and Holt, R. C. (1999). Reconstructing ownership architectures to help understand software systems. In *Proceedings of the Seventh International Workshop on Program Comprehension,* pp. 28-37, Pittsburgh, PA.

Carmichael, I. H., Tzerpos, V., and Holt, R. (1995). Design maintenance : Unexpected architectural interactions. *International Conference on Software Maintenance,* pp. 134-137, Nice.

Choi, S. C. and Scacchi, W. (1990). Extracting and restructuring the design of large systems. *IEEE Software,* January: 66-71.

Corneil, D. G. and Woodward, M. E. (1978). A comparison and evaluation of graph theoretical clustering techniques. *INFOR, The Canadian Journal of Operations Research and Information Processing,* 16:74-89.

DeRemer, F. and Kron, H.H. (1976)   Programming-in-the-large versus programming-in-the-small. *IEEE Transactions on Software Engineering*, 2(2):80-86.

Everitt, B. S. (1993). *Cluster Analysis*. New York: John Wiley & Sons.

Garey, M. R. and Johnson, D. S. (1979). *Computers and Intractability*. New York: W. H. Freeman and Co.

Garlan, D. and Shaw, M. (1993). An introduction to software architecture. In Ambrola V. and Tortola, G. (eds.), *Advances in Software Engineering and Knowledge Engineering*, Series on Software Engineering and Knowledge Engineering, Vol. 2, pp. 1-39. Singapore: World Scientific.

Harris, D. R., Reubenstein, H. B., and Yeh, A. S. (1995). Reverse engineering to the architectural level. In *International Conference on Software Engineering*, pp. 186-195, Seattle, WA.

Hutchens, D. H. and Basili, V. R. (1985). System structure analysis: Clustering with data bindings. *IEEE Transactions on Software Engineering*, 11(8):749-757.

Jain, A. and Dubes, R. (1988). *Algorithms for Clustering Data*. Englewood Cliffs, NJ: Prentice-Hall.

Kernighan, B. W. and Lin, S. (1970). An efficient heuristic procedure for partitioning graphs. *Bell Systems Technical Journal*, 49:291-307.

Kontogiannis, K. (1997). Evaluation experiments on the detection of programming patterns using software metrics. In *Proceedings of the Fourth Working Conference on Reverse Engineering*, pp. 44-55, Amsterdam.

Lakhotia, A. (1997). A unified framework for software subsystem classification techniques. *Journal of Systems and Software*, pp. 211-231.

Lakhotia, A. and Gravley, J. M. (1995). Toward experimental evaluation of subsystem classification recovery techniques. In *Proceedings of the Second Working Conference on Reverse Engineering*, pp. 262-269.

Lindig, C. and Snelting, G. (1997). Assessing modular structure of legacy code based on mathematical concept analysis. In *Proceedings of the 19th International Conference on Software Engineering*, pp. 349-359, Boston, MA.

Mancoridis, S., Mitchell, B., Rorres, C., Chen, Y., and Gansner, E.R. (1998). Using automatic clustering to produce high-level system organizations of source code. In *IWPC '98, IEEE Proceedings of the 1998 International Workshop on Program Comprehension*, pp. 45-53, Ischia, Italy.

Müller, H. A., Orgun, M. A., Tilley, S. R., and Uhl, J. S. (1993). A reverse engineering approach to subsystem structure identification. *Journal of Software Maintenance: Research and Practice*, 5:181-204.

Müller, H. A. and Uhl, J. S. (1990). Composing subsystem structures using (k,2)-partite graphs. In *Conference on Software Maintenance*, pp. 12-19, 26-29 November, San Dieg0, CA.

Neighbors, J. M. (1996). Finding reusable software components in large systems. In *Proceedings of the Third Working Conference on Reverse Engineering*, pp. 2-10, Monterrey, CA.

Ng, R. T. and Han, J. (1994). Efficient and effective clustering methods for spatial data mining. In *Proceedings of VLDB 94*, pp. 144-155, September 12-15, Santiago de Chile.

Parnas, D. (1972). On the criteria to be used in decomposing systems into modules. *Communications of the ACM*, 15:1053-1058.

Raghavan, V. V. and Yu, C. T. (1981). A comparison of the stability characteristics of some graph theoretic clustering methods. *IEEE Transactions on Pattern Analysis and Machine Intelligence*, 3(4):393-402.

Schwanke, R. W. (1991). An intelligent tool for re-engineering software modularity. In *Proceedings of the 13th International Conference on Software Engineering*, pp. 83-92, Austin, TX.

Schwanke, R. W., Altucher, R., and Platoff, M. A. (1989). Discovering, visualizing, and controlling software structure. *ACM SIGSOFT Software Engineering Notes*, 14(3):147-150.

Schwanke, R. W. and Platoff, M. A. (1989). Cross references are features. In *Second International Workshop on Software Configuration Management*, pp. 86-95. ACM Press.

Shaw, M. and Garlan, D. (1996). *Software Architecture: Perspectives of an Emerging Discipline*. Englewood Cliffs, NJ: Prentice-Hall,.

Silberschatz, A., Korth, H., and Sudarshan, S. (1997). *Database Systems Concepts*. New York: McGraw-Hill.

Tsangaris, M. S. and Naughton, J. F. (1991). A stochastic approach for clustering in object bases. In *Proceedings of SIGMOD 91*, pp. 12-21, Denver, CO.

Tzerpos, V. and Holt, R. C. (1996). A hybrid process for recovering software architecture. In *CASCON 1996*, pp. 1-6, November 12-14, Toronto, Canada.

Tzerpos, V. and Holt, R. C. (1997). The orphan adoption problem in architecture maintenance. In *Proceedings of the Fourth Working Conference on Reverse Engineering*, pp. 76-82, October 6-8, Amsterdam.

van Deursen, A. and Kuipers, T. (1999). Identifuing objects using cluster and concept analysis. In *Proceedings of the 21th International Conference on Software Engineering*, pp. 246-255, May 16-12, Los Angeles, CA.

Vaswani, P. K. T. (1968). A technique for cluster emphasis and its application to automatic indexing. *Information Processing*, 68(2):1300-1303.

von Laszewski, G. (1993). A collection of graph partitioning algorithms. Technical Report SCCS 477, Northeast Parallel Architectures Center, Syracuse University, NY, April.

Wiggerts, T. A. (1997). Using clustering algorithms in legacy systems remodularization. In *Proceedings of the Fourth Working Conference on Reverse Engineering*, pp. 33-43, Amsterdam.

Zhang, T., Ramakrishnan, R., and Livny, M. (1996). Birch : An efficient data clustering method for very large databases. In *Proceedings of SIGMOD 96*, pp. 103-114, Montreal, Canada.

9
Discovering Implicit Inheritance Relations in Non-Object-Oriented Code

Johannes Martin
Hausi Müller

9.1 Introduction

The evolution of the *Internet* and, in particular, *electronic commerce* on the Internet boosted the acceptance of *Java* as *the* programming language for the *World Wide Web* with the *Java Virtual Machine* (JVM) as the virtual hardware platform.

In order to stay competitive in today's marketplace, many businesses have to move some of their mission critical legacy applications to web-based and network-centric platforms. Because of its wide acceptance as a programming language on these platforms, Java is the language of choice for the new systems. The size and complexity of the legacy applications to be moved to the new platform usually make it infeasible to redesign and rewrite the applications from the ground up, but require selected parts of the application to be incrementally migrated to the new platform and therefore to Java.

A major obstacle in the migration of legacy systems written in C and similar programming languages to Java is the extensive use of *pointers* in their source code. Java supports pointers only in the very limited form of *references*. While almost no type checking of pointers is enforced by C compilers, Java implements strict type checking for references that allows conversion only between *compatible* reference types (such as classes that are related through inheritance).

In this chapter, we examine a common usage pattern of pointers in C programs, show how it implicitly expresses inheritance relationships between structured data types, and present a formal approach to migrate such usage patterns to a programming language such as Java by creating an explicit class hierarchy. Section 9.5.3 presents a tool that assists the software engineer in this task.

9.2   Related Work

Several researchers have addressed the problem of identifying classes during the migration of legacy systems to object-oriented platforms. A common approach is to use data structures in the legacy system as basic building blocks for classes and to add functions that operate on these structures as methods to those classes (Canfora et al., 1996; Liu and Wilde, 1990; Livadas and Johnson, 1994; Yeh et al., 1995). Kontogiannis et al. (1998) apply this technique in the migration of the IBM compiler back end from a PL/I derivative to C++.

A different approach is to use design documents of the legacy systems such as structure charts and data-flow diagrams to recover a possible object-oriented architecture of the legacy system (Gall and Klösch, 1995; George and Carter, 1996).

Cimitile et al. (1997) center the identification of classes around persistent data stores, such as files or tables in a database, with functions as candidate methods for these classes.

Object-oriented programming languages greatly facilitate reuse by providing generalization and specialization features, such as inheritance. While the above publications show how to identify distinct classes within a system, they do not take advantage of generalization or specialization features of the target programming languages. It is worthwhile to examine how commonalities and relationships of structures in a legacy system can be used to design class hierarchies in the target system.

The considerations in this chapter are similar to some research done in the *refactoring* community (Opdyke, 1992; Brown et al., 1998; Fowler et al., 1999). Opdyke (1992) defines refactorings as behavior preserving reorganization plans for source code. He discusses the foundations and applications of selected refactorings in depth, but does not present techniques to identify sections of code that will benefit from refactoring. He explicitly excludes type casts from his considerations.

9.3   Motivation

Object-oriented programming became popular in the late eighties and early nineties with the availability of programming languages such as Smalltalk (Goldberg and Robson, 1983), C++ (Stroustrup, 1986), and later Java (Gosling et al., 1996a). Some programmers adopted object-oriented ideas while still working with non-object-oriented languages, in fact, research continues on how to express object-oriented features in procedural languages such as C (Di Mare, 1999). While implementations of these features in C may not look as elegant as in C++, they are possible. In fact, the original C++ front end *cfront*, written by Stroustrup (1986), transliterates C++ code into C code that emulates many C++ features using pointers. This C code is then compiled into object code.

While comparing C source code automatically transliterated from C++ to C source code written by developers of procedural systems, we found similarities in the data and control structures used. Moreover, we could manually convert the procedural code to object-oriented code quite easily. From these experiments the question arose: As it is possible to transliterate C++ source code to C, is it also possible to discover intentional and even unintentional object-oriented structures in C code, using the inverses of some of the mappings used in the transliteration from C++ to C? If true, this would help immensely in the migration of procedural legacy systems to object-oriented platforms. For our further experiments, we focused on one aspect of object-oriented languages: polymorphism.

Object-oriented programming languages such as C++ provide a variety of means for expressing polymorphism. One way to express polymorphism in the procedural language C is to use pointers and *type casts* (type conversion operators) between pointers to different data structures. In this chapter, we examine how type casts in C source code have been used to express polymorphism, show how the same kind of polymorphism can be better expressed in an object-oriented language, and show how software engineers can benefit from the implicit object-oriented structures during the migration of a legacy system from C to an object-oriented programming language.

9.4   Migration Example

9.4.1   Example Code

Figure 9.1 shows a simple example of a C program using distinct data structures and type casts to express specializations of a data structure. The specialized data structures (`Manager` and `Worker`) contain all the fields of the base data structure (`Employee`) as well as additional fields. Whenever pointers to variables of type `Manager` or `Worker` are allocated, their *state variable* `employeeKind` is initialized to identify the variables' runtime type. The program accesses the variables using pointers of type `Employee` for general processing. For computations particular to the specialized data structures, the program determines the runtime type of the variable using the state variable, and casts it to a pointer of the specialized type (`Manager` or `Worker`).

A large number of similar techniques have been used to express specializations and generalizations like this. In some cases, the specialized data structures contain the base data structure (rather than containing the same fields). Sometimes, data structures are padded with extra variables to ensure that all have the same size. In other cases, *unions* are used to group related data structures. Stroupstrup's *cfront* C++ front end transliterates a class hierarchy into data structures similar to the ones in our example.

```
enum { WORKER, MANAGER };
struct Employee {
  int employeeKind;
  char name[20];
  char extension[4];
};
struct Manager {
  int employeeKind;
  char name[20];
  char extension[4];
  int numUnderlings;
  struct Employee* underlings;
};
struct Worker {
  int employeeKind;
  char name[20];
  char extension[4];
  struct Manager* manager;
};
void showEmployee(struct Employee *e) {
  printf("%s", e->name);
  switch (e->employeeKind) {
    case WORKER:
      {
        struct Worker* w = (struct Worker*) e;
        printf(" is managed by %s.\n",
               w->manager->name);
      } break;
    case MANAGER:
      {
        struct Manager* m = (struct Manager*) e;
        printf(" manages %d employees.\n",
               m->numUnderlings);
      } break;
  }
}
```

Figure 9.1. Example of related data structures and their use in a C program.

9.4.2 Traditional Migration Approach

When using data structures in the C source as basic building blocks for the Java classes and adding functions that operate on these data structures as member methods for these classes, a software engineer might convert the C data structures into Java classes and add the showEmployee() function as a member method show() to the Employee class. The signature of showEmployee() clearly indicates that it is an operation on the Employee class.

This solution has two significant drawbacks:

- The `Employee`, `Manager`, and `Worker` classes are very tightly coupled, since the `show()` member method of `Employee` directly accesses the fields of the other classes.

- The type casts within the `show()` member method of `Employee` are illegal in Java (they are possible in C++).

To solve this problem, the software engineer would probably add `show()` member methods to the `Manager` and `Worker` classes containing partial copies of the original `showEmployee()` function. While this approach solves the problem by producing legal Java source code, the duplication of source code is an undesired feature. There might also be side effects on other parts of the program: for example, an array of `Employee` class objects cannot contain `Worker` objects.

9.4.3 Migration Through Identification of Inheritance

Clearly, we need to find a better solution for this migration problem. The similarity of the data structures in our examples and the type casts between them suggest that they are closely related. Our domain knowledge supports this observation: managers and workers *are* employees. This suggests that we should model our target classes in a way that explicitly states this relationship, namely by using inheritance.

Figure 9.2 shows a transformation of the example from Figure 9.1 using classes related to each other by inheritance. Class `Employee` continues to contain the fields for the general data structure, but classes `Manager` and `Worker` *inherit* these fields from `Employee` rather than redefining them. Traditional rationale is used to transform the `showEmployee()` function into a `show()` member method of the `Employee` class. The program still uses type casts, but these casts are between classes that are explicitly related through inheritance and therefore legal in a Java program.

Figure 9.3 shows a further transformation of the example from Figure 9.1, building on the basic transformation from Figure 9.2. To decrease coupling between the classes and increase coherence within the classes, the `show()` member method of `Employee` has been split; it now contains only the code common for all employees. The new `show()` member methods of `Manager` and `Worker` handle the specialized cases.

Further analysis of the code revealed that the `employeeKind` variable is a constant for any given class, and its value has no meaning except for differentiating the distinct classes. Therefore, the Java comparison operator `instanceof` (Gosling et al., 1996b) can be used instead of the `employeeKind` variable (it is not needed at all in our example code, but it may be needed in other parts of the program).

```
class Employee {
  static final int WORKER = 0;
  static final int MANAGER = 1;

  int employeeKind;
  String name;
  String extension;

  void show() {
    System.out.print(name);
    switch (employeeKind) {
      case WORKER:
        {
          Worker w = (Worker) this;
          System.out.print(" is managed by ");
          System.out.print(w.manager.name);
          System.out.println(".");
        }
        break;
      case MANAGER:
        {
          Manager m = (Manager) this;
          System.out.print(" manages ");
          System.out.print(m.numUnderlings);
          System.out.println(" employees.");
        }
        break;
    }
  }
}
class Manager extends Employee {
  int numUnderlings;
  Employee[] underlings;
}
class Worker extends Employee {
  Manager manager;
}
```

Figure 9.2. Transformation of code from Figure 9.1.

9.5   Formalization, Implementation, and Evaluation

9.5.1   Algorithm

We formalized the transformation from Figure 9.1 to Figure 9.2 in an algorithm (Figure 9.5). In the notation of the algorithm, we use a number of abbreviations and primitive operations for artifacts in the subject system's source code; they are

```
class Employee {
  String name;
  String extension;

  void show() {
    System.out.print(name);
  }
};

class Manager extends Employee {
  int numUnderlings;
  Employee[] underlings;

  void show() {
    super.show();
    System.out.print(" manages ");
    System.out.print(numUnderlings);
    System.out.println(" employees.");
  }
}

class Worker extends Employee {
  Manager manager;

  void show() {
    super.show();
    System.out.print(" is managed by ");
    System.out.print(manager.name);
    System.out.println(".");
  }
}
```

Figure 9.3. Further transformation of code from Figure 9.1.

explained in Figure 9.4.

First, all type casts between nonprimitive data structures in the program have to be analyzed (Figure 9.5, Step 1). The algorithm iterates over all relevant type cast expressions and records the relations between source and target data structures.

As mentioned in Section 9.4.1, in some cases extra variables are used to pad all data structures to have the same size. Therefore, the algorithm checks which fields in the data structures are actually referenced by the program (Figure 9.5, Step 2). Besides from such padding fields, the algorithm also identifies fields that are no longer used in the program, and can thereby help in the detection of errors in the code (if those fields really should be referenced) or the removal of dead code (if those fields are no longer needed).

Finally, the groups of related structures as identified by the analysis of type casts are transformed to class hierarchies, with the base classes containing the common fields, and the subclasses containing the specialized fields. Only those fields that are actually used in the program are included in the classes built (Figure 9.5, Step 3). In our experiments, we consider two fields common to two data structures, if they have the same type, name, and position in the data structures. Other definitions of common fields are possible: the fields' names could be phonetically or semantically compared, or compatible rather than identical field types could be considered as criteria for commonality.

Once the hierarchy has been built, candidate member methods for the classes can be found using traditional methods (see Section 9.2). The further transformation from Figure 9.2 to Figure 9.3 cannot be automated as easily as the first transformation. A tool would have to follow the control and data flow of the program

castSet	the set of all type cast expressions that involve only nonprimitive types.
typeSet	the set of all nonprimitive types defined.
fieldAccessSet	the set of all field access expressions (a field access expression in the algorithm refers to an expression that denotes a field of a structure, such as e.name or e→name in C).
ce.destType	the destination type of the cast expression ce.
ce.sourceType	the source type of the cast expression ce.
fe.field	the field involved in the field access expression fe.
t.fieldSet	the set of all fields of type t.
t.fieldReferenced[f]	true, if field f of t is ever referenced.
t.destTypeSet	a set of types that is to contain, after completion of the algorithm, all nonprimitive types the type t is cast to.
t.sourceTypeSet	a set of types that is to contain, after completion of the algorithm, all nonprimitive types the type t is cast from.
commonFields(S)	a function that returns the set of common fields of all types in set S.
relatedTypes(S)	a function that returns a set of types in set S related through type casts (as determined in steps 1 and 2 of the algorithm).
similarTypes(S, F)	a function that returns subsets of set S whose member types share fields other than the fields in set F.
createClass(F, b)	a function that creates a class containing the fields in set F, with base class b.
createClass(t, b)	a function that creates a class from type t (using the fields and name of the type), with base class b.

Figure 9.4. Conventions for the notation of the algorithm.

```
/* Step 1: Analyze type casts */
for t in typeSet do
  t.destTypeSet := ∅
  t.sourceTypeSet := ∅
end for
for ce in castSet do
  add ce.destType to ce.sourceType.destTypeSet
  add ce.sourceType to ce.destType.sourceTypeSet
end for

/* Step 2: Check for use of fields within structures */
for t in typeSet do
  for f in t.fieldSet do
    t.fieldReferenced[f] := false
  end for
end for
for fe in fieldAccessSet do
  t.fieldReferenced[fe.field] := true
end for

/* Step 3: Build class hierarchy */
for s in relatedType(typeSet) do
  build level of class hierarchy(s, NULL)
end for

proc: build level of class hierarchy(S, base)
  F := commonFields(S)
  if ( ∃ t: t.fields = F ) then
    newBase := createClass(t, base)
  else
    newBase := createClass(F, base)
  end if
  for s in similarTypes(S) do
    build level of class hierarchy(s, newBase)
  end for
```

Figure 9.5. Algorithm for inheritance detection.

to convert. Program slicing techniques could be used to achieve this. Opdyke's investigation and formalization of *subclassing and simplifying conditionals* provides a good starting point for further work in this area (Opdyke, 1992).

9.5.2   *Efficiency Considerations*

When dealing with algorithms that are to be used on large software systems, it is important to consider the computational complexity of these algorithms to make sure they will perform adequately. We will examine the three algorithms we introduced in this respect, using the following definitions:

- C_n, complexity for algorithm n.

- n_{casts}, number of type cast expressions between non primitive types.

- n_{access}, number of field access expressions.

- n_{types} number of structured data types.

- $n_{related}$, maximum number of types in a set of related structured types.

Step 1 This algorithm examines every type cast expression in a program exactly once. For every type cast between nonprimitive data types, a data type is added to two sets of data types. Assuming a complexity of $\log n$ for the insertion of an element into a set, we get

$$C_1 = n_{casts} \log n_{related}$$

Experience with legacy systems and examination of object-oriented class libraries suggest that the number of data types in a set of related data types is relatively small and does not rise significantly as the subject system grows. We can therefore replace the logarithmic expression by a constant:

$$C_1 = n_{casts}$$

Step 2 This algorithm sets a flag for every field access expression.

$$C_2 = n_{access}$$

Step 3 The recursive implementation of this algorithm suggests that it is rather inefficient. However, a closer look at the algorithm reveals that every data structure in the program is processed at most once:

$$C_3 = n_{types}$$

Overall, the complexity of our algorithms depends *linearly* on the size of the subject system.

9.5.3   Tool Implementation

In real applications, related classes, and the degree of their relationships may not be as easily identifiable as in our simplified example, for several reasons:

- The related classes may be contained in different source files or even subsystems.

- The software engineer might not have sufficient domain knowledge to make an association between two different data structures.

- The type casts that support the association of distinct data structures are typically spread across many source files and are hard to spot. Tools such as the *grep* utility can help to find *explicit* type casts. Since traditional C compilers do not enforce the use of type casts, many of these casts may be *implicit* and therefore extremely hard to find.

Modern C compilers keep track of the type of pointers and warn the programmer of implicit type conversions. This suggests that a C compiler can be used to identify *all* type casts between pointer types in a program and thus help in the identification of possible type hierarchies in the source code. Unfortunately, it is usually quite difficult to use an existing C compiler for tool development, since the C compilers' internal data structures and interfaces are rarely accessible and documented for tool writers.

The IBM VisualAge-for-C++ product ships with two different C++ compilers: a traditional command line driven compiler that can be used with traditional build utilities such as *make*, and an incremental compiler that is built into the IBM VisualAge-for-C++ development environment (IDE, also referred to by its IBM project name *Montana* (Soroker et al., 1997; Karasick, 1998; Martin, 1999). The IDE and its incremental compiler provide a novel means for tool writers to extend the environment. The compiler's internal data structures (the *CodeStore*) are very well documented and designed to be used by tool writers. By using these data structures and support routines, a tool writer can significantly reduce the complexity of the tools to develop while saving a great amount of time.

IBM VisualAge-for-C++ provides for several ways to interface with the compiler. Tools can extend the compiler by introducing code transformation or optimizations at compile time, or query the CodeStore for information on the program compiled once the compilation is finished. These tools can run either stand alone or be integrated into the IDE to provide new views and query facilities to the users. For our research, we wrote and tested a stand alone tool implementing the algorithms presented earlier by querying the CodeStore after completed compilation and then integrated it into the IDE. The complete tool consists of only about 1500 lines of code, of which about 400 provide the integration into the IDE.

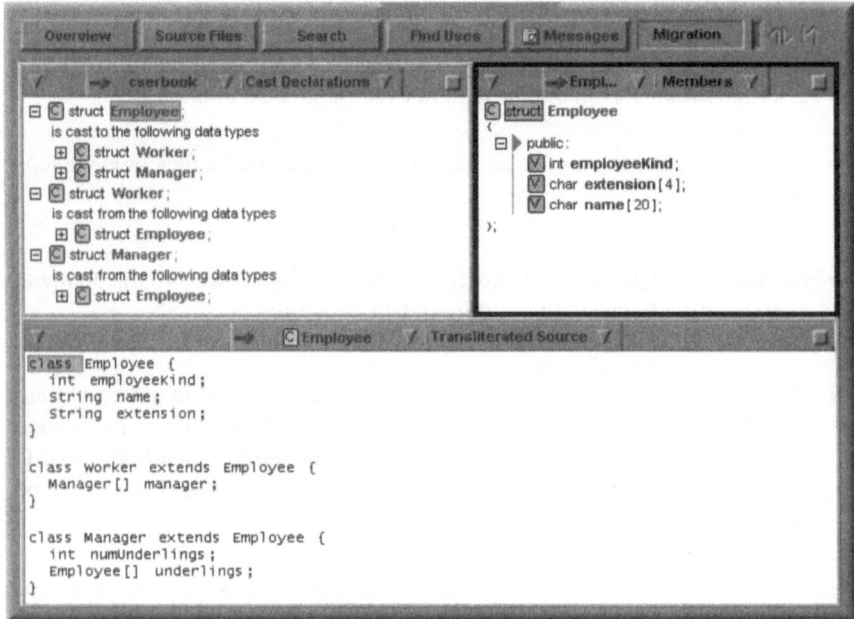

Figure 9.6. Migration tool. Transliteration of data structures.

9.5.4   Case Studies

For a first case study and to verify the correct operation of our tool, we created a VisualAge-for-C++ project and compiled our example program within the VisualAge-for-C++ IDE. We then opened the *migration page* we implemented (Figure 9.6). In the top left window, this page shows all data structures that have type cast relationships to other data structures. For each of these data structures, it also shows which data structures are directly related to it. Upon the selection of one of the data structures, the top right window displays the current C language implementation of that data structure, the bottom window displays the Java class hierarchy built using the type cast relationships.[1]

Closer examination of the transliterated source shows a difference between the manual and the automatic transliteration: in the version produced by the tool, manager in the Worker class is an array. Our simple tool cannot determine whether the pointer in the original source is used as a reference to a Manager or as an array of Managers. The software engineer has to use his domain knowledge ("every worker has exactly one manager"), or a more sophisticated tool needs to

---

[1]The algorithm we presented correctly identified the underlings field of the Manager data structure as unused and therefore removed it in the transliteration. Since a complete application would use this field, we added another function to our program that accesses this field.

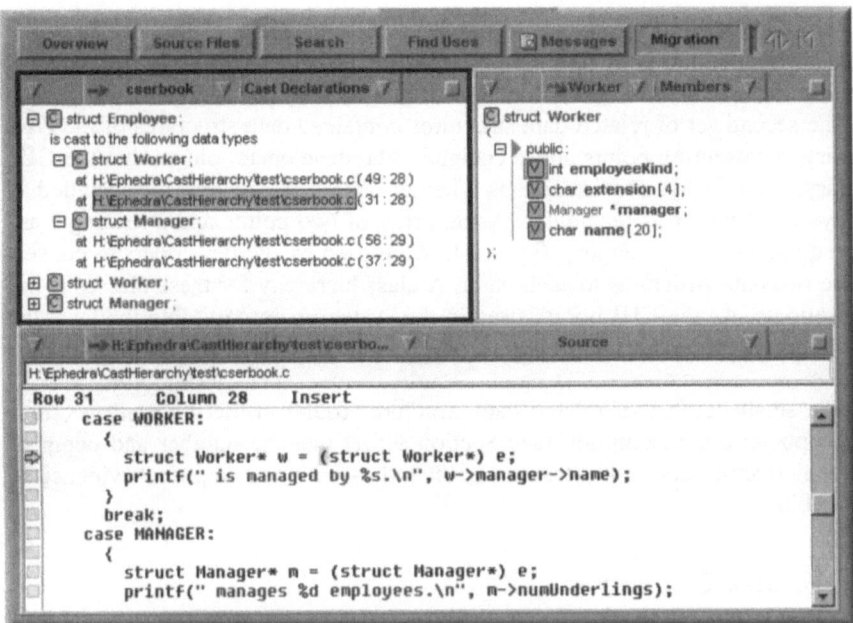

Figure 9.7. Migration Tool. Analysis of type casts.

be built that checks in what contexts the manager pointer is used. This is only one of the problems to be solved in the conversion of data types from C to Java, we won't discuss these further since they are beyond the scope of this chapter.

The view can also be used to determine where in the source code type casts have been applied to data types (Figure 9.7). The software engineer can use this information to locate parts of the source code that can be coded more elegantly in Java by exploiting the class hierarchy that has been built (as in Figure 9.3). The standard set of views and search tools in the VisualAge-for-C++ IDE can be used to further explore the code and the usage of the data structures of interest.

For a second case study, we examined a 30,000 line music notation program with a graphical user interface (GUI), written in a mix of C and C++. Since the program was usually built using a traditional compiler and makefiles, we first had to import the source files into the VisualAge IDE. Thanks to the relatively small size of the system (35 source files, only two link targets), this was not a problem. After successful compilation of the system in VisualAge, our tool identified two sets of related data structures by following the type casts between these data structures. It determined the common fields of the data structures and proposed a class hierarchy. Moreover, it eliminated a number of fields that were not referenced by any routines of the program. The developers had named these fields "unused". This suggests that the findings of our tool were indeed correct.

We presented our results to the developers of the system. They informed us that one of the sets of related data structures contained the central data structures of the system. The developers mental model of the relationships of these data structures agreed with the hierarchy proposed by our tool. If the system was to be moved to Java, a conversion of the data structures as proposed by the tool would be likely.

The second set of related data structures contained data structures of the GUI library, representing points and rectangles. The developers told us that the GUI library is not always consistent as to whether rectangular regions are specified as arrays of points or as rectangles. As an array of two points and a rectangle are stored identically in memory, type casts were used by the developers to convert these two data structures to each other. A class hierarchy for these classes is not appropriate. As the GUI library used in the system is not available for Java, the GUI part of the system will have to undergo major changes for a migration to Java.

The small number of related data structures found in the program we studied supports our assumption (see Section 9.5.1) that the number and depth of class hierarchies does not increase significantly—but more empirical evidence is desirable.

9.5.5   Tool Usability

For a tool to be usable on a large legacy system, it is important that the tool not only performs the automated tasks reasonably fast, but also visualizes the results adequately. If the results are voluminous, the tool has to support filtering and search facilities. The VisualAge-for-C++ IDE implements various kinds of search tools and a few filters. While the built-in filters are not powerful enough to simplify the complexity of a large project, the IDE's API enables the users to create their own advanced filters that can be targeted at the subject system.

As our tool is based on the incremental C++ compiler of the VisualAge IDE, some work is required to import a *makefile* based system into the IDE. If the system requires legacy libraries that are not supported by VisualAge-for-C++, it might be difficult or infeasible to import the system into the IDE. Efforts by other compiler writers to expose and document interfaces of their compilers would constitute a major advantage for tool developers.

Our tool was designed to *support* the software engineer in the migration and restructuring of source code, not to magically transliterate all the code. The involvement of software engineers in the process is important: they will have to decide which of the restructurings proposed by the tool will improve the quality and maintainability of the code sufficiently to justify a change toward an object-oriented architecture.

9.6   Research Challenges

We showed how type conversion operators can be used to detect relations between data types in a C program. Another method to express relations of data types is to use *unions*. It should be possible to use considerations similar to the ones presented here to build inheritance hierarchies by examining these unions in C programs. Further research should combine both approaches.

The examination of *function pointers* promises to be useful, too. Within data structures, they have often been used to work around the lack of virtual functions in non object-oriented languages. Once class hierarchies have been built, it should be possible to eliminate the need for function pointers by using virtual methods.

Results gained from research into program slicing could be used for increasing coherence within the classes build by splitting functions operating on objects of several classes into specialized member methods for each of these classes (as in the conversion of `show( )` in Figure 9.3). Program slicing tools should also be able to detect state variables and help in their replacement through type comparison operators such as Java's `instanceof` operator.

The tool presented only addresses the detection of inheritance in related data structures. Traditional techniques for identification of member methods for classes, as well as results from the research challenges should be integrated into the tool. Refactoring tools provide additional valuable features.

9.7   Conclusions

Migration of legacy systems written in procedural programming languages to object-oriented platforms is a problem many businesses currently face. In this chapter, we presented a migration strategy that not only allows legacy code to be ported to object-oriented platforms, but also exploits some of the object-oriented features of the target platform. We presented a tool that helps the software engineer in employing this strategy in the migration process. There are still many open questions and possibilities in both research and automation of migration to object-oriented technology. Our approach answers some of these questions in a way that can be automated and therefore proves feasible and valuable for mass software change.

9.8   References

Brown, W. J., Malveau, R. C., McCormick, H. W., and Mowbray, T. J. (1998). *Antipatterns: Refactoring Software, Architectures, and Projects in Crisis.* New York:John Wiley and Sons.

Canfora, G., Cimitile, A., and Munro, M. (1996). An improved algorithm for identifying reusable objects in code. *Software Practice and Experiences*, 26(1):24-48.

Cimitile, A., Lucia, A. D., Di Lucca, G. A., and Fasolino, A. R. (1997). Identifying Objects in Legacy Systems. In *Proceedings of 5th IEEE International*

Workshop on Program Comprehension, pp. 138-147, May 28-30, Dearborn, MI.

Di Mare, A. (1999). C Iterators. Technical Report, Universidad de Costa Rica. http://www.di-mare.com/adolfo/p/c-iter.htm.

Fowler, M., Beck, K., Brant, J., Opdyke, W., and Roberts, D. (1999). *Refactoring: Improving the Design of Existing Code*. New York: Addison-Wesley-Longman.

Gall, H. and Klösch, R. (1995). Finding objects in procedural programs: an alternative approach. In *Proceedings of 2nd IEEE Working Conference on Reverse Engineering*, pp. 208-216, July 14-15, Toronto, Canada.

George, J. and Carter, B. D. (1996). A strategy for mapping from function-oriented software models to object-oriented software models. *ACM Software Engineering Notes*, 21(2):56-63.

Goldberg, A. and Robson, D. (1983). *Smalltalk-80: The Language and Its Implementation*. Reading, MA: Addison-Wesley.

Gosling, J., Joy, B., and Steele, G. (1996a). *The Java Language Specification*. Reading, MA: Addison-Wesley.

Gosling, J., Joy, B., and Steele, G. (1996b). Type Comparison Operator "instanceof", In *The Java Language Specification*, Section 15.19.2, Reading, MA: Addison-Wesley.

Karasick, M. (1998). The Architecture of Montana: An Open and Extensible Programming Environment with an Incremental C++ Compiler. In *Proceedings of the Conference on Foundations of Software Engineering*, November 3-5, Orlando, FL.

Kontogiannis, K., Martin, J., Wong, K., Gregory, R., Müller, H., and Mylopoulos, J. (1998). Code Migration Through Transformations: An Experience Report. In *Proceedings of CASCON '98*, November 30-December 1, Toronto, Canada.

Liu, S. and Wilde, N. (1990). Identifying objects in a conventional procedural language: an example of data design recovery. In *Proceedings of IEEE Conference on Software Maintenance*, pp. 266-271, San Diego, CA.

Livadas, P. E. and Johnson, T. (1994). A new approach to finding objects in programs. *Journal of Software Maintenance: Research and Practice*, 6:249-290.

Martin, J. (1999). Leveraging IBM VisualAge for C++ for Reverse Engineering Tasks. In *Proceedings of CASCON '99*, November 8-11, Toronto, Canada.

Opdyke, W. F. (1992). *Refactoring Object-oriented Frameworks*. Ph.D. thesis, University of Illinois at Urbana-Champaign. http://st.cs.uiuc.edu/pub/papers/refactoring/opdyke-thesis.ps.Z

Soroker, D., Karasick, M., Barton, J., and Streeter, D. (1997). Extension Mechanisms in Montana. In *Proceedings of the 8th IEEE Israeli Conference on Computer Systems and Software Engineering*, June 18-15, Herzliya, Israel.

Stroustrup, B. (1986). *The C++ Programming Language*. Reading, MA: Addison-Wesley.

Yeh, A. S., Harris, D. R., and Rubenstein, H. B. (1995). Recovering abstract data types and object instances from a conventional procedural language. In *Proceedings of Second IEEE Working Conference on Reverse Engineering*, pp. 227-236, July 14-15, Toronto, Canada.

Part III

Maintainability

10
Design Properties and Evolvability of Object-Oriented Systems

M. Ajmal Chaumun
Hind Kabaili
Rudolf K. Keller
François Lustman

10.1 Introduction

Over the years, cumulative data have shown that maintenance is a major cost concern—as a matter of fact, a growing cost concern (Pigoski, 1997). The maintainability of a system seems to have much influence on the ease or difficulty to implement changes. A consensus has emerged among the research community that the maintainability of a software system is dependent on its design (Rombach, 1990), in the procedural paradigm as well as in the object-oriented paradigm.

In ISO 9126, maintainability has four components, namely, analyzability, testability, stability, and changeability (ISO, 1992). In application areas such as telecommunications, software systems are evolving constantly at unprecedented rates. There are organizations that do not develop the software they operate, but purchase it. These organizations are not directly interested in testability or diagnosis, but in the software's ability to sustain an on-going flow of changes. In this research, the focus will be on that single aspect of maintainability, i.e., changeability. In the SPOOL project (cf. Chapters 6 and 13), we are investigating the dependency between the changeability of software systems and their design.

One way of assessing changeability is to assess the impact of changes (change impact analysis). The approach we have taken is both analytical and experimental. It involves defining a systematic change impact model that is more complete and general than those presented in the literature, and applying it on industrial software systems to assess their changeability.

In Section 10.2 of this chapter, we present work that is related to maintainability and changeability. The change impact model, and its application to C++, are described in Section 10.3. A first case study for testing the practicality of the model was carried out on a medium-sized C++ industrial software system, and is presented in Section 10.4. The lessons learned from this case study led us to improve our experimental environment and to define and carry out a more advanced experimentation. Thus, an attempt to find correlations between change impacts and design metrics was successfully performed on three large software systems. The experiment is detailed in Section 10.5, and its results are discussed in Section 10.6. Section 10.7 concludes the chapter and provides an outlook into future work.

10.2   Software Maintenance and Design Properties

Design characterization is mostly done through metrics. A conventional distinction is made between architectural or high-level design and algorithmic or low-level design, and according to Rombach (1990), the former has more influence on maintainability than the latter. In the realm of object-oriented design, numerous design metrics have been published (Abreu, 1994; Chidamber and Kemerer, 1994; Lorenz, 1993). One suite of object-oriented design metrics has been proposed by Chidamber and Kemerer (Chidamber et al., 1998; Chidamber and Kemerer, 1994; Chidamber and Kemerer, 1994) and progressively refined. The suite (called C&K metrics later in this chapter), theoretically well-grounded, comprises of four interclass metrics—DIT (depth of inheritance tree), NOC (number of children), CBO (coupling between objects), and RFC (response for a class) and two intraclass metrics, WMC (weighted methods per class) and LCOM (lack of cohesion in methods).

Several studies were conducted to validate the metrics and to relate them to some maintenance or some maintainability property. Li and Henry, took five of the above metrics (CBO was excluded), added three of their own (DAC, number of ADTs defined in a class; MPC, message-passing coupling; and NOM, number of methods), and tested that set on two commercial object-oriented systems numbering 39 and 70 classes. They were able to conclude that there is a strong relationship between the metrics and maintenance effort (expressed in number of lines changed). Later on, they restricted themselves to the metrics available from design documents, and were able to draw the same conclusions (Li and Henry, 1993). Basili et al. (1996) were interested in a specific part of maintenance, i.e., fault detection and fault proneness. Experiments on eight systems developed by students showed that, individually, the C&K metrics were related to the probability of fault detection and that, globally, they were also good indicators of faulty modules.

Some studies on the relationship between design and maintainability were based on other design metrics. Hsia et al. (1995) for example, studied the effect of architecture on maintainability. On two systems designed by students, the authors measured maintainability (adding new features) and its relationship to architecture, namely the broadness of the inheritance trees. It turned out that maintainability is better for systems with broader trees, i.e., shallower inheritance trees. Briand et al. (1997) defined 18 coupling measures between classes and studied their significance in predicting fault-proneness in several industrial systems on which they had gathered maintenance data. They were able to conclude that some of the coupling metrics were significant predictors of fault-proneness.

Less work has been conducted on the matter of change impact. Han (1997) developed an approach for computing the change impact on design and implementation documents. Artifact dependencies involve inheritance, aggregation and association. Change impact is identified based on the value of a Boolean expression. However, software changeability is not really assessed. Kiran et al. (1997) compared the maintainability of software systems in the functional paradigm and in the object-oriented paradigm. They used programs developed by students and defined sets of changes, which were implemented by graduate students. Results suggest that the maintenance effort is less important in the object-oriented paradigm than in the functional paradigm. In particular, the impact of the set of changes considered is more localized in the object-oriented paradigm than in the functional paradigm.

Kung et al. (1994) was interested in the system wide impact of changes for regression-testing purposes. They defined a classification of changes (broadly, data, method, class, and library) and impacts resulting from the changes and based on three links: inheritance, association, and aggregation. They defined formal algorithms to calculate all the impacted classes including ripple effects. Li and Offutt (1996) proposed also algorithms for calculating the complete impact of changes made in a given. They were interested in the effects of encapsulation, inheritance, and polymorphism on the impact.

This literature survey can be summarized as follows. Most of the results presented above are derived from the study of small commercial systems or of systems developed in course assignments. Based on these experiments, a growing body of evidence suggests that the design has an influence on the maintainability, and that the C&K metrics, for example, may be considered as maintainability indicators.

Changeability has been studied less than both test detection and the overall maintenance effort. In particular, there is no evidence that design has an influence on changeability. Moreover, most of the change impact studies in the literature propose incomplete models. For example, Kiran et al. (1997) considered only inheritance, aggregation and association but not invocation and friendship. Li and Offutt (1996) did not consider changes in inheritance links, nor virtual methods. The association and aggregation links were not fully covered in their impact calculation algorithms either. Kung et al. (1994) did not consider the impact of data change and of method change because others had already covered it.

In summary, most results on the influence of design on changeability come out of small systems, and the change impact models we found in the literature are incomplete or not systematic.

10.3   Change Impact Model

Our goal in the SPOOL project was to define a list of changes and a change impact model as complete and systematic as possible. The model should be language-independent, i.e., be situated at the design level. Also, it should allow for the concise and systematic impact calculation by using a formal approach. Finally, it should be applicable on industrial strength software systems with hundreds or even thousands of classes.

10.3.1 Conceptual Model

Model Overview

The model considers a system at the design level. A software system is then viewed as composed of a set of classes. A class, in addition to being an artifact in its own right, includes a set of variables (the instance variables) and a set of methods. Also, classes are linked together by conceptual links.

By definition, what is called a change is a unique change to a single component, class, variable, or method. It has been stated that interclass links seem to have more importance than intraclass links. It has therefore been decided to consider intraclass change impact as a whole, but to concentrate the investigation on the impact of a change on other classes.

Once a change is applied to a class or to one of its constituents, other classes may be impacted if they have some link with the changed class. The impacted classes will be defined by their links with the changed class. It is worthy to note that only classes having a direct link with the changed class will be considered. This means that at this stage, our model will not take into account the ripple effect of a change. Finally, by definition, the impact of a change is the set of classes directly impacted by the change. The nature of the impact is not considered, the main reason being that it is often impossible to define completely the nature of the impact.

Changes

We define a change to a system as one to any of the three components. Examples are the addition of a variable, change in a method's scope from public to protected, or the removal of the relationship between a class and its parent. The main changes to object-oriented systems at the design level are identified. They are categorized according to the component they affect, and a total of 13 changes are identified (see Table 10.1).

As a matter of fact, some changes may be refined. One example is the case of the change in method scope, which may be refined into change in method scope from public to private, from public to protected, and so on. Another example is the method signature change that may be refined into seven different

Table 10.1. Changes to an object-oriented system at the design level.

Component	Change definition
Variable	Change variable type
	Change variable scope
	Add variable
	Delete variable
Method	Change method return type
	Change method implementation
	Change method signature
	Change method scope
	Add method
	Delete method
Class	Change inheritance structure
	Add class
	Delete class

changes. But for the sake of simplicity, these refined changes are not reported in Table 10.1.

Links

Once a change is applied to a class or to one of its components, other classes may be affected if they have some link with the changed class. A link is of any of the following types: association (**S**), aggregation (**G**), inheritance (**H**), and invocation (**I**).

- Association means that one class is referencing data variables of another class.
- Aggregation between two classes is established when a class definition is based on objects of the other class.
- Inheritance between two classes means that the derived class can benefit from whatever has already been defined in the base class.
- When methods defined in one class are being invoked by methods in another class, this is referred to as invocation.

The links are unidirectional. The class at the origin of the link is dependent on the class at the end. In our model, the changed class is always at the end of the link. For example, the inheritance link means that the changed class is the base class and the impacted class is the derived class, or in the association class, that the impacted class makes reference to the changed class.

The links are independent from each other, and any number and types of links may be found between two classes.

In addition to the impact on other classes, a change may create some impact within the changed class itself. For example, a change in the type of a variable of one class leads to an impact in all the methods in the same class that use that variable. An artificial link called *local* (**L**) is introduced to denote such impact.

Impact

The impact of a change, i.e., the set of classes directly impacted, depends on two main factors. First, different types of change lead to different sets of impacted classes. For example, the change in the type of a variable has an impact in all the classes referencing this variable, whereas the addition of a parent to a class may cause impact in at least all derived classes.

Given a type of change, the type of link between classes is the second main factor to influence the impact result. Consider a change in the scope of a method from public to protected. Classes that invoke this method will be impacted, but classes that are derived from the changed class will not. Note that more than one type of link between the changed class and an impacted class can be involved in the calculation.

Thus, for a given change ch_i in class Cl_j, the set of impacted classes is defined by a set expression, written with Boolean operators, in which the variables stand for the links. For example, the impact formula for such a hypothetical change may be given by

$$Impact\ (Cl_j, ch_i) = \mathbf{SH'} + \mathbf{G},$$

meaning that classes that are in association (**S**) with, and not derived (**H•**) from, the changed class Cl_j, or classes that are in aggregation (**G**) with Cl_j are impacted. As examples, the change impact formulae for a change to each of the three component types are as follows:

1. *Impact* (variable deletion) = **S** + **L**
2. *Impact* (method scope change from public to protected) = **H•IF•**
3. *Impact* (deletion of nonabstract class) = **S** + **G** + **H** + **I**

10.3.2 Application to C++

Design documents, if available, are often not consistent and do not reflect the reality of the system. In fact, the only document we can be sure to truly correspond to the running system is the source code. The industrial systems targeted for experimentation and provided by our project partner are written in the C++ language. For these reasons, it was decided to map the conceptual model into the C++ language.

In C++, a software system is viewed (e.g., at the conceptual level) as a set of classes, each class including a set of variables and a set of methods. Changes are also considered one at a time and only direct impact will be considered, not any ripple effect.

Changes

Only syntactic, static changes are considered. If a change is made to a class, the system has to be recompiled. If it compiles successfully, it means that there is no impact. This means that only static properties of the source code are considered. Impact arising at run-time due to polymorphism is not addressed. Neither are semantic issues that may arise from the change. This is because it might be difficult to assess them by an automatic processing of the source code.

The following illustrate some changes considered:

1. The code change from "class c2: public c1" to "class c2: protected c1" corresponds to a change in inheritance derivation for class c2.
2. The code change from "void m (void)" to "void m (int a)" represents a signature change in method m.
3. The code change from "int v;" to "double v;" represents a change in the type of variable v.

The list of 13 changes identified at the design level (see Table 10.1) was extended to address the code level and the specificity of C++. For instance, the change "variable change from *static* to *nonstatic*" was introduced. Another example of a refined change is the "variable scope change" which may be sub-classified as six changes:

1. From public to private
2. From public to protected
3. From protected to private
4. From protected to public
5. From private to public
6. From private to protected.

Changes are handled one at a time. For example, for the code transformation "class c2: *c1, c0* {...}" to "class c2 {...}", we say that *c2* has deleted parent *c1* followed by *c2* has deleted parent *c0* instead of *c2* has deleted parents *c1* and *c0*. We also consider the changes to be non-overlapping, i.e., a change to a method or to a variable component is not also a change to the class component that comprises the method or variable under consideration.

The final list, presented in Table 10.3, contains a total of 66 changes, comprising 12 changes for variable, 35 for method, and 19 for class components.

Links

The next step is to establish which links are represented in C++ and how to identify them. The four links (**S, G, H,** and **I**) in the conceptual model are encountered in C++. In addition, a fifth link, friendship (**F**), which does not exist at the design level but is an integral part of the language, was introduced. These five links are described below with examples. We consider *C1* as the class to be changed and look for potential impact in class *C2*, with *C2* being linked to *C1*. Comments in the source text are inserted using the double slash (*//*). Note that the "local" link (*L*) is considered conceptual and occurs, when the changed class coincides with the impacted class.

(S) Association

```
class C2 {
  ...
  C2_m1( ) {
    // C1_v1 is a var. of C1.
    // o1 is a global object
    // or global object
    // reference of C1.
    ...C2_v1 = o1.C1_v1;

    // o1ptr is a global
    // object pointer of C1.
    ...C2_v1 = o1ptr->C1_v1;
  }
  ...
  // C1_v1 is used in
  // parameter list.
  C2_m2 (..., o1.C1_v1, ...);
  C2_m3 (..., o1ptr->C1_v1, ...);
};
```

(H) Inheritance

```
// private inheritance.
// (protected, public:
// similarly)
class C2: private C1 {...};
```

(F) Friendship

```
class C1 {
  ...
  // C2 can access any member
  //of C1.
  friend class C2;
  ...
};
```

(G) Aggregation

(i) *by reference*:

```
class C2 {
  ...
  // b is a declared
  // variable of type
  // pointer to C1.
  C1 * b;
  // In constructor,
  C2::C2() {
    // b is dynamically
    // created.
    b = new C1();
  }
  ...
};
```

(ii) *by value*:

```
class C2 {
  ...
  // An instance of C1 is
  // part of C2.
  C1 b;
  ...
};
```

(I) Method Invocation

```
Class C2 {
  ...
  // o1 is either a global
  // object or  an object
  // reference of C1.
  o1.C1_m (...);
  // o1 is a global object
  // pointer of C1.
  o1->C1_m (...);
  ...
};
```

Impact

To calculate the impact of a change, a truth table is set up for that change with the five links appearing in the top (see Table 10.2). Each row represents one configuration of these five links (present or not). Depending on the combination

Table 10.2. Top part of truth table for variable scope change from public to private.

Links of Class C2 with C1					Impact on class C2
S	G	H	I	F	(I: impact, X: no impact)
Y	Y	Y	Y	Y	X
Y	Y	Y	Y	N	I
Y	Y	Y	N	Y	X
Y	Y	Y	N	N	I
Y	Y	N	Y	Y	X
Y	Y	N	Y	N	I
Y	Y	N	N	Y	X
Y	Y	N	N	N	I
Y	Y	Y	Y	Y	X

of links corresponding to the row, there is impact (**I**) or not (**X**), and the row is marked accordingly in the "Impact" column. It is worth mentioning that in some cases, it is not known whether there is impact or not (uncertain impact) until the corresponding piece of code is closely examined. For example, consider the change in the return type of a pure virtual method. Derived classes may or may not define the method. If the method is not defined in a derived class, there is no impact. But, if the method is being defined in a derived class then, there is impact in that method definition. Only by looking at the derived class definition can one determine whether there is impact or not. This type of impact (uncertain impact) has been treated as certain impact for the purpose of impact calculation.

In some cases, it may happen that the state underlying a row cannot exist, and the row is marked with "-". For example, when there is a change in the return type of a pure virtual method, the rows in which **G** appears cannot be investigated since the abstract class can be instantiated as an object (**G**). For each row, the appropriate Boolean expression is derived and reduced, if possible, and the term "**L**" is appended if there is local impact. For example, for a deletion of a nonabstract class in the class inheritance structure (code change from "class c2: *c1*, c0 {…}" to "class c2: c0 {…}"), the corresponding expression is **H + F + L**, which implies there is impact in derived classes (**H**), in friend classes (**F**), and locally (**L**), too. It may also happen that a change triggers another change (triggered change) to occur. For example, addition of a pure virtual method in a nonabstract class results in a triggered change since the class is now turned abstract. To indicate a triggered change, a note to the final expression is added, in the form *ie (change id)*—"ie" stands for impact expression and "change id" refers to the triggered change).

For each of the 66 identified changes, its impact has been calculated (see Table 10.3). For illustration, consider the change in variable scope from public to private (code change from "*public*: int v;" to "*private*: int v;"). From the change's truth table (Table 10.2), the respective *canonical expression* is derived, for example:

Table 10.3. Impact result for all changes ($C++$).

Change Id	Change description	Impact expression	Local impact
v.1.1	Variable value change	-	-
v.1.2	Variable type change	S	L
v.1.3	Variable addition	-	-
v.1.4	Variable deletion	S	L
v.1.5	Variable scope change		
v.1.5.1	Public -> Private	SF'	-
v.1.5.2	Public -> Protected	SH'F'	-
v.1.5.3	Protected -> Private	SHF'	-
v.1.5.4	Protected -> Public	-	-
v.1.5.5	Private -> Public	-	-
v.1.5.6	Private -> Protected	-	-
v.1.6	Variable change (*Static/Non static*)		
v.1.6.1	Static -> Non static	S	L
v.1.6.2	Non static -> Static	-	-
m.2.1	Method change (*Static/Non static*)		
m.2.1.1	Static -> Non static	I	L
m.2.1.2	Non static -> Static	-	L
m.2.2	Method change (Pur/Non virtual)		
m.2.2.1	Virtual -> Non virtual	-	-
m.2.2.2	Non virtual -> Virtual	-	-
m.2.2.3	Virtual -> Pure virtual	S + G + H + I	L
m.2.2.4	Non virtual -> Pure virtual	H + *ie*(3.1.1)	L
m.2.2.5	Pure virtual -> Virtual	H + *ie*(3.1.2)	L
m.2.2.6	Pure virtual -> Non virtual	H + *ie*(3.1.2)	L
m.2.3	Method return type change		
m.2.3.1	Non pure virtual method	I + *ie*(3.1.2)	L
m.2.3.2	Pure virtual method	H	L
m.2.4	Method implementation change	-	L
m.2.5	Method signature change		
m.2.5.1	Non pure virtual method	I	L
m.2.5.2	Pure virtual method	H	L
m.2.6	Method scope change		
m.2.6.1	Public -> Private		
m.2.6.1.1	Non virtual method	IF'	-
m.2.6.1.2	Virtual method	IF'	-
m.2.6.1.3	Pure virtual method	-	-
m.2.6.2	Public -> Protected		
m.2.6.2.1	Non virtual method	H'IF'	-
m.2.6.2.2	Virtual method	H'IF'	-
m.2.6.2.3	Pure virtual method	-	-
m.2.6.3	Protected -> Private		
m.2.6.3.1	Non virtual method	HIF'	-
m.2.6.3.2	Virtual method	HIF'	-

Table 10.3. (continued)

m.2.6.3.3	Pure virtual method	-	-
m.2.6.4	Protected -> Public		
m.2.6.4.1	Non virtual method	-	-
m.2.6.4.2	Virtual method	-	-
m.2.6.4.3	Pure virtual method	-	-
m.2.6.5	Private -> Public		
m.2.6.5.1	Non virtual method	-	-
m.2.6.5.2	Virtual method	-	-
m.2.6.5.3	Pure virtual method	-	-
m.2.6.6	Private -> Protected		
m.2.6.6.1	Non virtual method	-	-
m.2.6.6.2	Virtual method	-	-
m.2.6.6.3	Pure virtual method	-	-
m.2.7	Method addition		
m.2.7.1	Pure virtual method	$S + G + H + I + F$	-
m.2.7.2	Virtual and non virtual method	$I + ie(3.1.2)$	L
m.2.8	Method deletion		
m.2.8.1	Pure virtual method	$ie(3.1.2)$	-
m.2.8.2	Virtual and non virtual method	$I + ie(3.1.1)$	L
c.3.1	Class change (*Abstract/Non-abstract*)		
c.3.1.1	Non abstract -> Abstract	$G + H + I$	L
c.3.1.2	Abstract -> Non abstract	H	L
c.3.2	Class friendship relation change		
c.3.2.1	Add friend	-	-
c.3.2.2	Delete friend	$F(S + G + H + I)$	-
c.3.3	Class deletion		
c.3.3.1	Non-abstract class	$S + G + H + I$	-
c.3.3.2	Abstract class	$S + H + I$	-
c.3.4	Class inheritance derivation		
c.3.4.1	Public -> Private	$F'(S + I)$	-
c.3.4.2	Public -> Protected	$H'F'(S + I)$	-
c.3.4.3	Protected -> Private	$HF' (S + S'G + S'I)$	-
c.3.4.4	Protected -> Public	-	-
c.3.4.5	Private -> Public	-	-
c.3.4.6	Private -> Protected	-	-
c.3.5	Class inheritance (*Virtual/Non virtual*)		
c.3.5.1	Virtual -> Non virtual	-	L
c.3.5.2	Non virtual -> Virtual	-	L
c.3.6	Class addition	-	-
c.3.7	Class inheritance structure		
c.3.7.1	Add abstract class	$S + G + H + I + ie(3.1.1)$	L
c.3.7.2	Add non abstract class	H	L
c.3.7.3	Delete abstract class	$H + F + ie(3.1.2)$	L
c.3.7.4	Delete nonabstract class	$H + F$	L

$$SGHIF' + SGHI'F' + SGH'IF' + SGH'I'F' +$$
$$SG'HIF' + SG'HI'F' + SG'H'IF' + SG'H'I'F'.$$

Reducing this expression yields **SF'**, meaning there is impact in classes that are in association (**S**) with the changed class, i.e., referencing the variable, but which are not friends (**F'**) of the changed class.

For 25 of the 66 changes there is no impact whatsoever (neither in other classes nor locally), for 4 changes there is only local impact, for 37 changes there is impact in other classes, and for 11 changes there is a triggered change.

10.4   Proof of Concept Implementation

10.4.1 Rationale

There were three reasons for performing this implementation:

- to see if the change impact model could be implemented and applied to an industrial-strength software system;
- to explore the architecture of such a change impact calculator;
- to make on attempt to find some relations between impact of changes and some design property.

Because it was meant to be mostly a proof of feasibility experiment, it was decided to limit its scope. The architectural environment should require the minimum amount of work to be set up, only one change would be considered, and only one design property would be probed for relationship with impact.

10.4.2 Definition of Experiment

The test system provided by our project partner is a decision support system for telecommunications. For confidentiality reasons, it is called System-B in this chapter. It is written in C++ and comprises 1420 classes. However, it could not be analyzed in its entirety in a single parse due to lack of memory. The work was performed on 85% of the system.

The change considered was the method signature change; the Boolean expression of its impact is **I**, meaning there is impact in classes where the method is invoked. The size of the impact set was calculated for the method signature change on every method defined in a targeted class, summed for all the methods defined in that class, and divided by the number of methods of that class. In the rest of the chapter, this average value will be called "change impact." The impact results were twofold: the number of classes impacted, and the number of lines impacted. These results were used in further calculations to estimate the mean and standard deviation of the change impact for the whole system. The design property considered for relationship with the impact was the number of methods of a class. More specifically, it was the WMC metric, which in our experiment is equal to the number of methods defined in a class. The relationship tested was defined by the following hypothesis:

> For the test system, there is a relationship between the WMC metric and the change impact of the method signature change as defined above.

The prototype environment is illustrated in Figure 10.1. Queries are defined to calculate the impact expressions. These queries are themselves contained in scripts, i.e., high-level specifications written in GEN++, the C++ implementation of GENOA (Devanbu, 1992). Analyzers are generated from the scripts. The change type and the changed component are specified as input to a front-end application written in C++. Once the input is validated, the front-end determines which analyzers are to be invoked, based on the type of the given change. The test system is compiled into an abstract semantics graph, a language-independent view of the source code, using the AT&T C++ front-end. The abstract semantics graph consists of nodes that represent program elements such as

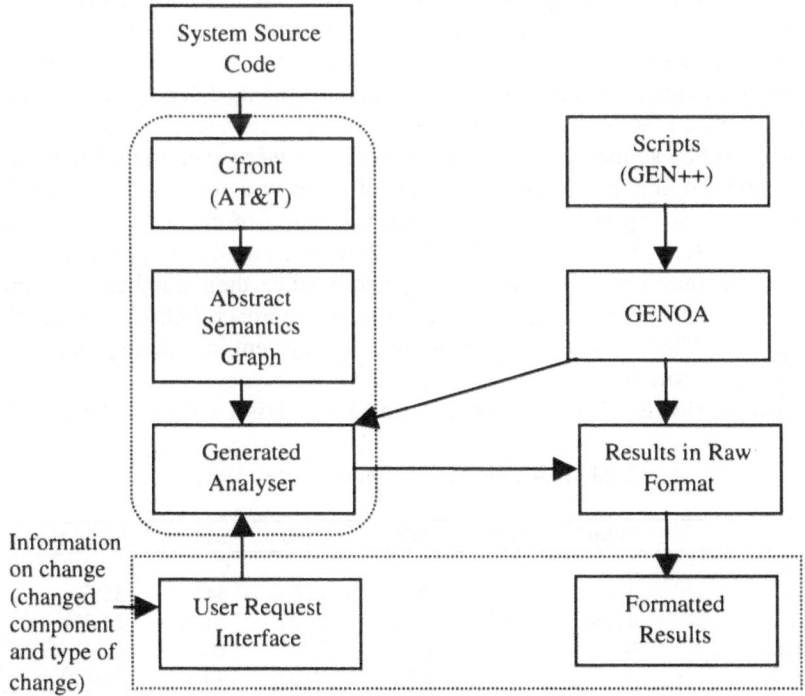

Figure 10.1. Prototype of change impact model (C++).

expressions, statement, and the like. The analyzer runs over the abstract semantics graph gathering the information specified in the script. The output comprises the line number, class name and file name of the impact, which is sent back to the front-end application.

After performing intermediary calculations on all results received, the front-end application stores the final results in ASCII format. The front-end application can be invoked interactively or in batch mode via a shell script.

10.4.3   Tests and Results

Experimental approach

At first, during the experimentation stage of the work, some descriptive statistics on the test system were produced. They are presented in Table 10.4. The system has quite a flat inheritance hierarchies (refer to DIT column in Table 10.4) and a majority of classes with a small number (less than 20) of methods. These results are similar to the observations of others (Basili et al., 1996; Chidamber and Kemerer, 1994; Li and Henry, 1993). But there exist a few outlier classes with a large number (more than 100) of methods including the one with 172 methods. This seems to be a sign of poor object-oriented practice, and we contend that these classes should have been further decomposed into smaller units.

The second step consisted in calculating the impact for the method signature change. This could not, however be carried out as planned. The time required to parse the system amounted to about 14 minutes per change impact computation for each method signature change. Given that there were over 14,000 methods in the system, computing the impact for all of them was realistically impossible. Instead of obtaining results for the whole population of classes, a more modest approach, based on sampling, had to be taken. The population of the 1044 system classes may be considered heterogeneous since their number of methods varies from 1 to 172! So, the stratified sampling approach (Alalouf et al., 1990) was applied. This caused the breaking up of the system into three groups based on the WMC criterion:
- Group I (lowest WMC values) contains those classes with 1 or 2 methods.

Table 10.4. Summary of metrics for test system.

	WMC	DIT[a]	NOC	CBO	RFC	LCOM
Min.	1	0	0	0	0	0
Max.	172	8	29	437	541	3587
Mean	13.50	2.87	0.88	11.71	24.10	27.61
Median	8	2	0	7	10	0
Std Dev.	17.82	2.27	2.41	20.57	40.26	216.20

[a] DIT refers to the maximum path length from a class to the root class of the inheritance tree.

- Classes in Group II (middle-range WMC values) have no less than 3 and no more than 29 methods.
- The remaining classes, that is, those with at least 30 methods, were found in Group III (highest WMC values).

There were 109, 837, and 98 classes in Groups I, II, and III, respectively. For Group I, the experiment was carried out on all the 109 classes. However, for Group II and III, we focussed on 30 randomly selected classes in each group. In Group II, the selected classes were split equally among those with 12, 13, and 14 methods (classes with mean number of methods in the whole system are those with 13 methods). In Group III, the class with the maximum number of methods was also included in the test sample.

The hypothesis (relationship between WMC and impact of method signature change) was tested twice on the stratified samples, first by correlation analysis and, second, by the analysis of variance (ANOVA) (Matel and Nadeau, 1988). In the ANOVA test, a null hypothesis H_0 was formulated, stating that the mean change impact is equal in all three samples. The hypothesis would either be accepted or rejected. In case of rejection, the alternative hypothesis H_1 (which implies that for at least two samples, the mean change impact differs) would be accepted.

Results

Descriptive statistics of the impact results for both classes and lines are summarized in Table 10.5 below. In Group III, there is no class with null impact. In both Groups I and III, one single class yields the maximum values for class and line impact; in Group II, however, these values result from two different classes. The mean value for class and line impact increases through Group I to III.

The estimate variance of each sample (the three groups) was calculated by using the stratified sampling approach. The three estimate variances were then used to compute the estimate mean of the whole system. With 95% confidence, the mean value lies between 0.54 and 0.99. The standard deviation of the change impact was also estimated for the whole system by combining the three samples into one, and the value was found to be between 1.52 and 1.89. The sample cor-

Table 10.5. Descriptive statistics of the impact results for the three groups.

	Group I (1-2 methods)		Group II (3-29 methods)		Group III (30+ methods)	
Classes: Total (Tested)	109 (109)		837 (30)		98 (30)	
Impact	Class	Line	Class	Line	Class	Line
Min	0.00	0.00	0.00	0.00	0.04	0.17
Max	19.50	125.50	3.54	11.54	7.12	8.24
Mean	0.30	1.35	0.77	1.86	1.31	2.75
Median	0.00	0.00	0.48	0.72	1.24	2.49
Std Dev.	1.90	12.03	0.79	2.61	1.27	1.94

relation coefficient between the two variables, the WMC metric, and the measured change impact was also calculated, and found to be somewhat weak, 0.21. A scatterplot revealed two outlier classes. Once the outliers were removed, the correlation coefficient rose to 0.55.

In the variance analysis approach (ANOVA), the null hypothesis we wanted to test was

$$H_0: \mu_1 = \mu_2 = \mu_3$$

μ_1, μ_2 and μ_3 represent the mean values of the change impact for the three groups. The variance within each group and between different groups was computed. The calculated F_0 (4.607) was found to be greater than the Fisher value, F_α (3.050). Details of the intermediate results may be found in Chaumun et al. (1999).

Interpretation

The estimate mean of the change impact (less than 1) provides an interesting result. It can be said that a method signature change to the system implies, on the average, not more than one class being impacted. In other words, this system can readily absorb a method signature change. However, two outliers classes are pinpointed as classes that should be of concern for the method signature change because of their high impact value.

From the impact results, two anomalies are noted. Surprisingly enough, there were classes with 14 methods, but with null impact. Those classes were closely examined and found to contain mostly virtual methods. Since we perform static analysis of the source code, invocation of these methods may have been "rerouted" elsewhere. The second anomaly is the excessive impact (7.12 and 19.50), which are well above the mean value of 0.56 for the 3 samples combined) associated with two classes, one of which has only two methods.

The correlation analysis shows a very weak (0.21) correlation between the WMC metric and the change impact. When the two outliers classes (with excessive impact) were omitted, the correlation went up to a somewhat stronger level of 0.55. But we should be cautious because only a sample of the test system has been used.

The ANOVA test confirmed that correlation result. We obtain a value (4.607) greater than the Fischer value (3.050). This means that we have to reject the null hypothesis H_0 and accept the alternative hypothesis H_1 which, implies that the mean of the change impact differs for at least two samples. We conclude that there is indeed a relationship between the WMC metric and the change impact of the method signature change for the test system.

The calculation of the estimate of the mean value of the change impact and the correlation analysis were performed again with impacted lines replacing impacted classes. Our findings based on the class impact results were confirmed by the line impact result.

10.4.4 Lessons Learned

There were positive results in the validation.

- The impact model can be implemented and is a useful tool to investigate change impact.
- The descriptive analysis of the impact has brought out interesting results on the system. It has, for example, shown that on the average, the considered software may easily absorb a method signature change.
- It has also enabled us to find those classes that would potentially create problems if a method signature change would have to be carried out.
- It has shown that a relationship, although a tenuous one, seems to exist between WMC and the impact of a method signature change. This result was considered as a stimulus to investigate further and broader.

On the negative side, mainly system size and the computation approach caused problems.

- First and foremost, system size is a problem in empirical studies of software systems. As mentioned above, there was not enough memory to store the whole of the system.
- The number of classes, an indicator of size, had an impact not only on computing time, but also on statistical methodology. As reported in Section 10.4.3, the time required to compute one change impact was so high that we could not apply the change to all classes. As a result, the statistical analysis could not be performed on the complete population, but only on a sample, and the statistical methodology had to be adjusted accordingly.
- The prototype system also posed some problems. Each change impact had to be programmed by a separate script that would be processed by GENOA to generate an analyzer (see Figure 10.1). That analyzer would parse the whole system each time it was called upon to look up information.
- Finally, when performing the post-mortem of the experiment, it was realized that some methodological aspects were specific to the change considered and could not be carried over to other changes. The case in point was the definition of how to measure impact. In our case, it was decided that for each class, the impact would be the average number of impacted classes by a change to each method's signature. But, for another change such as change to a class structure, this definition might be inappropriate.

The lessons learned can be summarized as follows:

- The system under study should be parsed only once to capture and store the abstract data representation for possible retrieval later.

- The experimentation environment should be able to handle and process efficiently large software systems.
- For any change, what is called impact and how to calculate this impact must be defined beforehand.
- The change impact computation should require little programming effort and should be efficient even for large systems.

10.5. Experiment

10.5.1 Objectives

The lessons, positive and negative, drawn from the validation test were put to good use, and more ambitious objectives could be set for the experiment. They can be summarized in one word: generality. The experiment was directed at finding results that could be more general than just one change or one system or one design property. More specifically, the objectives included the following:

- to find results that would apply to more than one change;
- to find results applicable to more than one software system, and if possible, applicable to all systems;
- to find relationships with several design properties defined by metrics.

10.5.2 Software Environment

The new environment, depicted in Figure 10.2 was designed to address the problems encountered in the validation test. It provides a repository-based solution (see Chapter 13). The test system source code is parsed by a parsing tool,

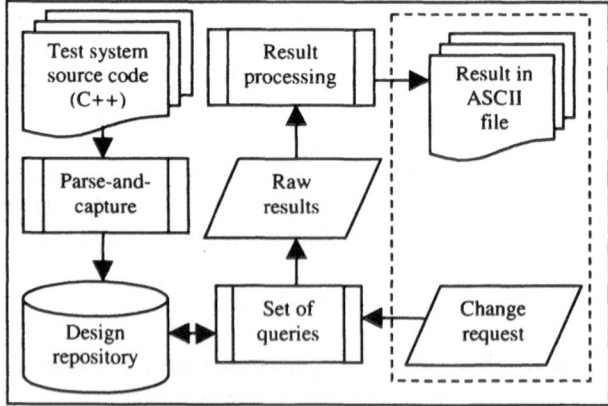

Figure 10.2. Environment for change impact calculation.

e.g., a compiler. GEN++, the C++ implementation of *GENOA* [11], was used in this extraction process. The parsed information contains data about all the classes and links in the system. This information is captured and fed into a design repository. The schema of the design repository is based on our extended UML (Unified Modeling Language) metamodel 1.1 (Rumbaugh et al., 1999). The object-oriented database management system *POET 5.1* (Poet, 1999) serves as the repository backend, with the schema being represented as a Java 1.1 class hierarchy. Change requests are batch-processed using a flexible report generator mechanism. They typically contain information on the change type as well as on the target class, methods, and variables. This triggers a set of queries corresponding to the specified change. The code in these queries uses the change request information as parameters to interrogate the repository. Raw results are fetched and processed into ASCII files. The ASCII files obey a specific format that can readily be transferred into spreadsheet programs such as Excel for further statistical processing.

10.5.3 Definition of Study

Test Systems

In order to broaden the scope of the expected results, the changeability of three different systems was assessed. These systems vary in class size and application domain. The first test system is *XForms*, which can be freely downloaded from the web (Xforms, 1998). It is a graphical user interface toolkit for X window systems. It is the smallest of the test systems (see Table 10.6). *ET++*, the second test system, is a well-known application framework (Weinand et al., 1989). The version used in the experiment is the one included in the SNiFF+ development environment (TakeFive, 1999). The third and largest test system is *System-B* from Bell Canada (see Section 10.4.2). It is used for decision making in telecommunications. Table 10.6 provides some size metrics for these systems. Note that header files from the compiler are included in the numbers shown in the

Table 10.6. Size metrics of test systems.

	XForms	ET++	System-B
Lines of code	7,117	70,796	291,619
Lines of pure comments	764	3,494	71,209
Blank lines	1,009	12,892	90,426
# of effective classes	83	584	1,226
# of classes	221	722	1,420
# of files (.C/.h)	143	485	1,153
# of generalizations	75	466	941
# of methods	450	6,255	8,594
# of variables	1,928	4,460	13,624
Size in repository	2.9 MB	19.3 MB	41.0 MB

lower part of the table (last six rows), whereas the numbers in the upper part (first four rows) represent the system that was effectively investigated in the study.

Changes and Impacts

There are 37 changes that generate some impact in other classes. Testing all of them would have been complete but time and effort consuming, and a staged approach was decided upon. The first step, presented here, involved the selection of a set of changes as representative as possible. Six changes were selected, according to the following criteria:

1. There should be at least one change for each component (variable, method, and class).
2. A selected change should have an impact in at least one other class (according to our model, there are 29 changes with no such impact).
3. The impact expression should be different for any pair of changes; since otherwise, we would have obtained duplicate results.
4. The selected changes should be of practical relevance, that is, they should be able to be exercised in practice.

Table 10.7 lists the six changes considered and their corresponding impact expression.

Table 10.7. Investigated changes with impact expressions.

Change	Impact expression	Impact definition
Variable type change	$S + L$	Average of impact for each variable change
Variable scope change from public to protected	SH'F'	Average of impact for each variable change
Method signature change	$I + L$	Average of impact for each method change
Method scope change from public to protected	H'IF'	Average of impact for each method
Class derivation change from public to protected	H'F' (S + I)	Impact
Addition of abstract class in class inheritance structure	$S + G + H + I + L$	Impact

Methodology

The aim of the experiment was to find design properties that would be indicators of a system's changeability. More precisely, the objectives were to find correlation between the size of the impact sets and some design property described by a metric. The metrics in the C&K suite were considered prime candidates. However, due to the specificity of the changeability property, four additional metrics, derived from the NOC and CBO metrics, were considered. NOC the number of direct descendants of a class and CBO is "approximately equal to the number of couples with other classes (where calling a method or instance variable from another class constitutes coupling)" (Chaumun et al., 1999). Below, we present the four metrics, together with the rationale for their consideration.

- *NOC* (Number of Children in sub tree):* when some component of a class is changed, it may affect not only its children, but also the whole sub tree of which the changed class is the root.

- *CBO_NA (CBO No Ancestors: same as CBO, but the coupling between the target class and its ancestors is not taken into consideration):* the coupling between the target class and its ancestors, taken into consideration by CBO, is irrelevant for change impact, since the ancestors of the target class will never be impacted. To eliminate such "noise," ancestors are excluded in CBO_NA.

- *CBO_IUB (CBO Is Used By: the part of CBO that consists of the classes using the target class):* the definition of CBO merges two coupling directions: classes using the target class and classes used by the target class. For changeability purposes, the former seems more relevant than the latter one, hence the split.

- *CBO_U (CBO Using: the part of CBO that consists of the classes used by the target class):* introduced as a consequence of CBO_IUB, to cover the part of CBO not considered by CBO_IUB.

In summary, nine metrics were considered—five C&K metrics (WMC, DIT, NOC, CBO, RFC) and four changeability-oriented refinements of the C&K metrics (NOC*, CBO_NA, CBO_IUB, CBO_U).

Experimental Procedure

The nine design metrics, as introduced in the previous section, were extracted from the test systems. Next, for each of the six changes considered and each of the test systems, its test set, that is, the set of classes for which the change is applicable, was computed. For example, when considering the method scope change from public to protected, only classes with at least one public method were included in the test set. Then, for each class in each test set, the change impact for the given change was calculated, i.e., the number of classes that would be impacted. Once the metrics and impact data were collected, the correlation between each change impact and each design metric was investigated for all the classes involved in the test sets. In each case, the correlation coefficient was calculated, and scatter plots were produced. Outlier points were removed and the correlation coefficient was computed again.

10.6   Results

10.6.1 Observations on the Test Systems

Table 10.8 presents the statistics for the nine metrics considered in this study.

For all metrics except those related to inheritance, there is wide variation from one system to another. This is not true of DIT, NOC, and NOC*: all systems have the same median values, 2 for DIT, and 0 for NOC and for NOC*. A median of 0 for NOC and for NOC* means that for the three systems, half the classes are leaves. Based on this and on the mean values of NOC (around 0.8), it can be stated that the classes that do have children have on the average less than two children. Furthermore, a median of 2 in the three systems for the depth of inheritance tree means that half the classes have 2 or fewer ancestors. Because our results are across three widely different systems, we advance the hypothesis that, in general, inheritance is used in a limited way, much less than its potential benefits would suggest. Note that Chidamber et al. (1998) found the same limited use of inheritance and guessed that programmers traded reuse potential for simplicity of understanding.

Each of the six changes was applied to each test system. The impact values are presented in Table 10.9.

The values vary from one system to another, from one change to another, and no general conclusion can be drawn on the impact of a given change. Comparison between changes, however, yields some results. Based on both mean values and median values, a classification of changes by impact comes out. Among the six changes investigated, the most expensive one, across systems, is the addition of an abstract class in the inheritance structure of a class. On the other hand, the least expensive one is to change the scope of a method from

Table 10.8. Descriptive statistics of the three test systems.

System		WMC	DIT	NOC	NOC*	CBO	CBO_NA	CBO_IUB	CBO_U	RFC
XForms (83 classes)	Min.	0	0	0	0	0	0	0	0	0
	Max.	23	4	14	60	20	20	19	9	45
	Mean	4.48	2.39	0.82	2.57	4.13	3.16	0.98	3.16	6.52
	Median	2	2	0	0	4	3	0	4	2
	Std. Dev.	5.27	1.55	2.35	9.63	3.18	3.18	3.07	1.97	9.90
ET++ (584 classes)	Min.	0	0	0	0	0	0	0	0	0
	Max.	105	8	56	361	301	301	293	76	746
	Mean	10.04	2.09	0.78	2.09	24.48	22.5	5.01	19.80	90.65
	Median	6	2	0	0	24	21.5	0	21	36.5
	Std. Dev.	12.94	1.78	3.40	16.79	25.37	24.56	20.96	16.01	128
System-B (1226 classes)	Min.	0	0	0	0	0	0	0	0	0
	Max.	166	9	29	266	707	707	707	93	2735
	Mean	11.98	3.02	0.88	3.42	32.49	29.36	7.06	25.77	171.0
	Median	7	2	0	0	21	18	1	17	47
	Std. Dev.	15.75	2.46	2.53	18.52	36.15	34.97	29.49	23.96	290.0

public to protected. This might have been expected, considering their impact expressions (see Table 10.7).

10.6.2 Relationships between Impact and Design Metrics

The correlation coefficients are presented in Table 10.10. Note that numbers in parentheses represent coefficients that were obtained after removing some outliers. In the case of CBO_IUB, the biggest ratios of outliers/data points were 2/37 (Change #1, *XForms*), followed by 4/502 (Change #3, *ET++*), and 6/1052 (Change #5, *System-B*). From these correlation results or lack thereof, the following conclusions were drawn.

A General Design-Level Changeability Indicator

For all systems, and for all changes but one, CBO_IUB is strongly or very strongly correlated with the change impact. Given the broadness of this result (six changes, three systems of small, medium, and large size), it may be concluded that CBO_IUB is a good indicator of changeability in a system. In fact, our experimentation confirms the common-sense property, which to our knowledge has not been proved: the more a class is used through invocation of its methods and outside references to its variables, the larger the impact of a change to such a class. Note, however, that the values of CBO_IUB vary considerably from one system to another (see Table 10.8).

Table 10.9. Change impact results for the three test systems.

Change	System	# of classes in test set	Min.	Max.	Mean	Median	Std. Dev.
Variable type change	XForms	37	1	20	1.78	1	3.17
	ET++	416	1	81	2.02	1	5.97
	System-B	707	1	32	1.46	1	1.85
Variable scope change from public to protected	XForms	1	-	-	-	-	-
	ET++	65	0	80	3.78	0.67[a]	12
	System-B	72	0	52	1.84	1	6.21
Method signature change	XForms	70	1	3.67	1.19	1	0.49
	ET++	502	1	17.64	1.46	1	1.26
	System-B	1 221	1	38.60	1.77	1	2.06
Method scope change from public to protected	XForms	70	0	267	0.18	0	0.48
	ET++	496	0	16.64	0.40	0	1.19
	System-B	1 174	0	37.39	0.60	0	1.79
Class deriv. change from public to protected	XForms	65	0	4	0.32	0	0.89
	ET++	458	0	281	3.71	0	16.46
	System-B	1 052	0	291	4.42	0	20.03
Add. of abstract class in inherit. structure	XForms	65	0	4	0.32	0	0.89
	ET++	458	0	281	3.71	0	16.46
	System-B	1 052	0	291	4.42	0	20.03

[a] Note that the impact values are calculated as averages (see Section 10.5.2), and hence medians need not be an integer.

Table 10.10. Correlation coefficients for the three test systems.

Change	System	WMC	DIT	NOC	NOC[a]	CBO	CBO_ NA	CBO_ IUB	CBO_ U	RFC
Variable type change	XForms	0.31	-0.04	0.97	0.96	0.56	0.60	0.71 (0.94)	0.15	0.10
	ET++	0.21	-0.12	0.47	0.55 (0.91)	0.55	0.57	0.71 (0.85)	0.09	0.01
	System-B	0.03	-0.01	0.48	0.22	0.12	0.13	0.13	0.01	0.02
Variable scope change from public to protected	Xforms[b]	NA	NA	NA	NA	NA	NA	NA	NA	NA
	ET++	0.18	-0.22	0.09	0.09	0.55	0.55	0.61 (0.87)	-0.22	0.04
	System-B	.07	-0.12	-0.06	0.01	0.21	0.22	0.31 (0.73)	0.00	0.07
Method signature change	XForms	0.22	-0.47	0.16	0.33 (0.69)	0.44	0.48	0.54 (0.72)	-0.30	0.10
	ET++	0.30	-0.24	0.43	0.35 (0.41)	0.56	0.59	0.76 (0.85)	-0.16	0.02
	System-B	0.23	-0.24	0.32	0.34 (0.40)	0.48	0.52	0.74 (0.81)	-0.17	0.02
Method scope change from public to protected	XForms	0.21	-0.46	0.14	0.31	0.39	0.43	0.49 (0.78)	-0.29	0.09
	ET++	0.21	-0.24	0.22	0.06	0.43	0.46	0.63 (0.82)	-0.19	-0.03
	System-B	0.23	-0.24	0.09	0.07	0.46	0.50	0.72 (0.75)	-0.18	0.02
Class deriv. change from public to protected	XForms	0.32	-0.43	0.06	0.23	0.24	0.28	0.34 (0.89)	-0.24	0.17
	ET++	0.42	-0.11	0.53	0.30	0.70	0.73	0.96	-0.01	0.12
	System-B	0.52	-0.11	0.10	0.08	0.40	0.44	0.81 (0.93)	-0.05	0.16
Add. of abstract class in inherit. structure	XForms	0.23	-0.28	0.57	0.91	0.57	0.63	0.74 (0.91)	-0.24	0.09
	ET++	0.38	-0.14	0.62	0.63 (0.79)	0.64	0.67	0.85 (0.98)	-0.05	0.09
	System-B	0.39	-0.16	0.22	0.55 (0.70)	0.68	0.72	0.92	-0.08	0.12

[a] Corresponds to the correlation coefficient after removal of outliers.

[b] Only one class had public variables in XForms, and no statistics were calculated.

The original CBO metric is not a changeability indicator, which can easily be explained: it puts together the classes using the changed class and those used by the changed class. That second component introduces noise with respect to change impact.

Impact and Inheritance

Hsia et al. (1995) found that systems with deeper inheritance trees required more maintenance work than those with shallower ones, based on systems developed by students in class assignments. If the result were valid for industrial systems, one could have expected that some correlation would be found between DIT and the impact of all changes or at least of some changes. As can be seen in Table 10.10, such is not the case. Based on the changes tested here, the hypothesis that DIT influences changeability cannot be sustained. One explanation might be that even if such a correlation exists, industrial systems are too shallow for the DIT property to show enough variability.

10.7 Conclusion

The SPOOL project deals with the many aspects of changeability and design. In the work presented here, the goal was to find relationships between changeability and design properties described by metrics. The findings had to be applicable to industrial-strength software. The approach taken was both theoretical and empirical. First, a model of software changes and change impacts was defined at the conceptual level, and subsequently adapted to the C++ language. Then a proof of feasibility attempt, conducted on an industrial-strength system, yielded several useful lessons. The most important lesson is that system size is a major problem in empirical studies, and that has a major impact on experimental protocols. Based on these learned lessons, an experiment was set up for relating design metrics to change impact size. Three software systems of increasing sizes were experimented upon. The metrics defined by Chidamber & Kemerer were tested as candidate changeability indicators as were several refinements of these metrics, specifically geared towards changeability detection. The experiment was successful. It showed a high correlation, across systems and across changes, between changeability and the access to a class by others through method invocation or variable access. On the other hand, our results could not support the hypothesis that the depth of the inheritance tree has some influence on changeability. Note that this lack of correlation is counter to the results found by Hsia et al. (1995). Furthermore, earlier results on the morphology of industrial systems (Chidamber and Kemerer, 1994) were confirmed: the use of inheritance is rather limited, which may explain the negative result.

The hypothesis that design properties are related to the size of the impact set has received a first confirmation and encourages us to pursue this matter further. In a first step, we will try to consolidate the results obtained so far. More evidence will be sought by increasing the batch of changes and the set of test systems. Also, an attempt will be made to give practical value to the results found here, that is, to design a procedure for estimating the changeability of a system, based on the value of CBO_IUB. This would enable the potential buyer of a software system to assess its evolvability or to locate those parts of the system, which will be more difficult to change. A further step will involve the attempt to upgrade the concept of change, from atomic programming change as defined presently, to the more realistic one of change request, involving several changes to several classes, and to define the impact set of a change request. Relationships between design properties and the impact set of a change request will be sought by experiments on industrial-strength systems. If they are successful, the hypothesis that design properties have an influence on evolvability will be closer to confirmation.

10.8   References

Abreu, F. B. (1994). Object-oriented software engineering: measuring and controlling the development process. In *Proceedings of the 4th International Conference on Software Quality*, Washington DC, USA.

Alalouf, S., Labelle D., and Menard J. (1990). *Introduction à la statistique appliquée*. Addison-Wesley.

Basili, V. R., Briand L. C., and Melo W. L. (1996). A validation of object-oriented design metrics as quality indicators. *IEEE Transactions on Software Engineering*, 22(10): 751-761.

Briand, L. C., Devanbu P., and Melo W. (1997). An investigation into coupling measures for C++. In *ICSE97*, Boston, MA, pp. 412-421.

Chaumun, M. A. (1998). *Change Impact Analysis in Object-Oriented Systems: Conceptual Model and Application to C++*. Master's thesis, Université de Montréal, Canada, November 1998.

Chaumun, M. A., Kabaili, H., Keller R. K., and Lustman, F. (1999). A change impact model for changeability assessment in object-oriented software systems. CSMR99, *Proc. Third European conference on Software Maintenance and Reingineering*, Amsterdam, The Netherland, pages 130-138, March, , 1999.

Chaumun, M. A., Kabaili, H., Keller, R. K., Lustman, F., and St-Denis, G. (2000). Design properties and object-oriented software changeability. Accepted, CSMR2000, *Fourth European Conference on Software Maintenance and Reingineering*, Zurich, Switzerland, pages 45-54, February, 2000.

Chidamber, S. R., Darcy D. P., and Kemerer C. F. (1998). Managerial use of metrics for object-oriented software. In *IEEE Transactions on Software Engineering*, 24(8): 629-639.

Chidamber, S. R. and Kemerer C. F. (1991). Towards a metrics suite for object-oriented design. In *Proceedings OOPSLA*, Phoenix, AZ, pp. 197-211.

Chidamber, S. R. and Kemerer C. F. (1994). A metrics suite for object-oriented design. In IEEE *Transactions on Software Engineering*, 20(6): 476-493.

Devanbu, P. T. (1992). GENOA - a customizable, language- and front-end independent code analyzer. In *Proceedings of the 14th International Conference on Software Engineering*, pp. 307-317, Melbourne, Australia.

Han, J. (1997). Supporting impact analysis and change propagation in software engineering environments. In *STEP97*, London, England, pp. 172-182.

Hsia, P., Gupta, A., Kung, C., Peng, J., Liu, S. (1995). A study of the effect of architecture on maintainability of object-oriented systems. In ICSM95, Nice, France, pp. 4-11.

ISO 9126 Information Technology (1992). Software product evaluation : quality characteristics and guidelines for their use, International Organization for Standardization, Geneva, 1992.

Kazman, R., Abowd, G., Bass, L., and Clements, P. (1996). Scenario-based analysis of software architecture. In IEEE Software, Vol. 13, No. 6, pages 47-55, November 1996.

Kiran, G. A., Haripriya S., and Jalote P. (1995). Effect of object orientation on maintainability of software. In *ICSM97*, Bari, Italy, pp. 114-121.

Kung, D. C., Gao, J., Hsia, P., Lin, J., Toyoshima, Y. (1995). Class firewall, test order, and regression testing of object-oriented programs. In *Journal of Object-Oriented Programming*, Vol. 8, No. 2, pages 51-65, May 1995.

Kung, D., Gao, J., Hsia, P., Wen, F., Toyoshima, Y., and Chen, C. (1994). Change impact identification in object oriented software maintenance. In *ICSM94*, Victoria, B.C., Canada, pages 202-211, September 1994.

Li, W. and Henry S. (1993), Object-oriented metrics that predict maintainability. *Journal of Systems and Software*, 23: 111-122.

Li ,W., Henry, S., Kafura, D., Schulman, R. (1995). Measuring object-oriented design. In *Journal of Object-Oriented Programming*, Vol. 8, No. 4, pages 48-55, July/August 1995.

Li, Li (1998). *Change Impact Analysis for Object-Oriented Software*. Ph.D. thesis, George Mason University, Virginia, USA, 1998.

Li ,Li and Offutt J. A. (1996). Algorithmic analysis of the impact of changes to object-oriented software. In *ICSM96*, pp. 171-184.

Lindvall, M. (1997). *An Empirical Study of Requirements-Driven Impact Analysis in Object-Oriented Software Evolution*. Ph.D. thesis, Linköping University, Sweden, 1997.

Lorenz, M. (1993). *Object-Oriented Software Development: A Practical Guide*. Englewood Cliffs, NJ: Prentice-Hall.

Matel, J-M. and Nadeau R. (1998). *Statistique en gestion et en économie*. Gaëtan Morin Éditeur, Montréal, Canada.

Munson, J. C. and Elbaum S. G. (1998). Code churn: A measure for estimating the impact of code change. In *Proceedings of the International Conference on Software Maintenance (ICSM'98)*, Bethesda, MD, pp. 24-31.

Pigoski, T. M. (1997). *Practical Software Maintenance*. New York: John Wiley & Sons.

Poet Software Corporation (1999). POET Java ODMG Binding. On-line documentation, San Mateo, CA, 1999. Available at http:://www.poet.com.

Rombach, H. D. (1990). Design measurement: some lessons learned. In *IEEE Software*, 7(2): 17-25.

Rumbaugh, J., Jacobson I., and Booch G. (1999). *The Unified Modeling Language Reference Manual*. New York: Addison-Wesley.

TakeFive GESMBH (1999). SNiFF+ documentation set. Salzburg, Austria. 1999. Available on-line at: http://www.takefive.com.

Weinand, A., Gamma E., and Marty R. (1989). Design and implementation of ET++, a seamless object-oriented application framework. In *Structured Programming*, 10(2): 63-87.

Xforms (1998). Graphical user interface toolkit for X. 1998. Available on-line at http://bragg.phys.uwm.edu/xforms.

11
Using Textual Redundancy to Study the Maintainability of Source Code

J. Howard Johnson

11.1 Introduction

Reverse engineering and design recovery attempt to reconstruct abstractions from legacy program sources (Biggerstaff, 1989; Chikofsky and Cross, 1990) as a prelude to migrating systems to new platforms or in support of maintenance activities for software evolution. Many of the techniques employed for this purpose take the source for the system as a whole, and, after a large analysis stage, provide a view of the structure to help with understanding, navigation, or assessing the impact of change.

One particular technique looks for parts that are the same with the hope that the structure revealed will provide useful insight. Large bodies of source code, documentation, and data often have long repeated sections of content as a result of maintaining multiple variants for different platforms or multiple versions across time. By analyzing the structure of these repetitions, useful information can be gleaned about the maintenance history and prospects for future maintainability.

One approach to this problem involves looking at the system as a compiler would by parsing it and constructing abstract syntax trees that capture the surface semantics of the code (Buss and Henshaw, 1991; Buss and Henshaw, 1992; Whitney et al., 1995). This approach has the advantage of being able to look under the surface of the code and analyze its meaning as a programmer would see it; however, much of the surface structure of the code has been lost since comments, indentation structure, manifest constants, macro calls, and inclusion structures disappear before compilers attempt lexical analysis. Furthermore, for legacy systems, parsers often do not exist in a form that can be used for constructing these abstract syntax trees.

By recognizing that text processing algorithms can be applied in these situations, a large body of existing technology can be brought to bear. These approaches have a different set of tradeoffs and have strengths likely to complement the parsing-based ones. For example, they tend to be much lighter weight and often scale up better since they spend less time pondering over each byte. They also treat the body of source directly in the form expressed by the authors with comments, formatting, and the manifest constants, macro calls, and inclusions that are present before preprocessing. They also can handle multiple versions and variants in a graceful way without requiring knowledge of the build process or having access to special header files.

Between 1993 and 1998 work was done in the Software Engineering Group at the Institute for Information Technology on an approach to understand the structure of the large bodies of text that make up a large software system. The goal of the work was to find all exact matches occurring in a body of source and use data analysis to extract meaning from the results. This approach guarantees that it finds all matches having particular characteristics. It is often the lack of a match that is most informative. The collection of matches is re-expressed in a form that allows quite flexible summarization of their structure. This structure is especially important when very large sources are studied.

Looking for all short matches can be a problem. In this study, the minimum line length is set to ten. Experimentation with different values has demonstrated that this number is small enough to find the kinds of matches that are interesting without causing an explosion of fine-level detail that can be distracting for a high-level study of a body of source.

Of course, it is possible to preprocess the text or postprocess the matches, and aim for approximate matches rather than exact matches. However, there is a surprising amount of utility in discovering all exact matches of the rather short length of ten lines.

The following sections provide an outline of the methods and their application to problems in software maintenance. Section 11.2 discusses the issue of textual redundancy in source and what it signifies from a software maintenance point of view. Section 11.3 provides a summary of the approach. In Section 11.4 an example based on gcc is used to show a small-scale application of the approach. Section 11.5 considers the case of analyzing a gigabyte of source associated with 13 versions of Mozilla to demonstrate a large-scale analysis. Section 11.6 provides a summary and concludes the chapter.

11.2   Redundancy in Source

Text in different files can be similar for several reasons. Two of these are of particular interest from a software maintenance point of view: software cloning and change (or lack of change) between versions of a system. A particular example of software cloning occurs in some approaches to the management of multiple configurations.

11.2.1   Software Cloning

Maintenance of large software systems under pressure often leads to a phenomenon referred to as software cloning. It is often easier to copy and modify an existing piece of code rather than making the original code handle the new function as well as all previous functions. This cut-and-paste activity can happen for code fragments of a few lines or for modules of thousands of lines. It can happen in procedural code or in declarations. It can happen in documentation.

Software cloning has a number of negative effects on software maintenance:

- Red herrings and dead code can be created.

- If the component that was copied is subsequently discovered to have a defect, the defect probably should be repaired in the other clones. These clones must be found and the impact of the correction assessed in each context.

- Errors in the systematic renaming can lead to unintended aliasing, resulting in latent bugs.

- The bulk of the code grows much faster than it would by extending the functionality of the existing module to meet the new requirement.

Software cloning is not all bad. It addresses quite well a short-term goal of quicker and more reliable change. It is also sometimes necessary because the programming language employed lacks an appropriate abstraction mechanism. Whether cloning is good or bad, the understanding of a large source depends on the discovery and analysis of copied and modified code. This is the motivation for tools for clone detection.

Since a common approach to understanding source is to perform lexical analysis on it, followed by some semantic analysis, it is natural to look for clones as subtrees of the syntax or semantic trees that match in all or in part. This approach has the advantages that it can be combined easily with other semantic analysis and that it also identifies common recurring code fragments or clichés. Buss et al. (1994) used this approach in their work. A number of software metrics are calculated for each subtree and a clone is signaled if the metrics all agree or differ from one another by less than a given threshold. Such a metric-based approach is discussed in Chapter 5.

Another approach similar to that discussed here is that of Baker (1992). She calculates a position tree for the whole of the source and uses the information contained in it to identify large matches. The approach described here has a slightly different view about matches and is designed to scale up to much larger sources than can likely be handled using position trees.

11.2.2   Change in Large Systems

In the natural evolution of large systems, the content of individual files changes, large files split into smaller ones, files are renamed, and directories are reorganized. These introduce confusion for the maintainer, since things are not where they were before. The maintainer needs to be able to visualize how the present system relates to his or her understanding of a previous version.

Change also shows where activity is going on to remove bugs or enhance functionality. To identify the important parts of the system for maintenance purposes it is useful to consider what has been changed previously.

Identifying change for both of these reasons can be supported usefully by tools, especially in large systems.

11.2.3   Support for Multiple Configurations

Large systems are usually expected to run in more than one environment. There are several strategies for maintaining a number of similar but different versions of modules. One such strategy involves maintaining separate files for each variant, only one of which is used in any specific system build.

Understanding the structure of these multiple configurations can be important for maintenance since modifications may affect the environments in different ways.

11.3   Overview of Method

The basic form of the method considers the source as a collection of files each made up of a sequence of lines. The files are identified by name and version and the lines within each file are identified by line numbers. The name and version tags may have further structure provided by a file system hierarchy or source management system but are considered as sufficient for identifying and locating the content for browsing or maintenance.

A *snip* is a sequence of lines occurring within a file and are said to *match* another snip if it agrees byte for byte with it. The task is then to find all informative matches within the body of text, organize this information, and extract information that is useful for further study of the source. To improve the efficiency of finding all matches, a method (Johnson, 1993) based on the string searching algorithm of Karp (1986) and Rabin (1987) is employed.

Matches that are very short can happen by chance and are unlikely to be informative, so it is useful to put a lower limit on the size of the match to be detected. For the purpose of the following discussion this bound has been set to ten lines. We then have a very good chance of obtaining almost all informative matches while eliminating the bulk of accidental matches. It is also low enough that many situations where text has been modified during cloning are also found since ten identical lines often occur in the neighborhood.

The situation is made more complicated because matches can involve more than two locations in the text. In such cases, it often happens that the matches are not all the same length. It is harder to manage and analyze the data if this problem is not properly addressed. The solution undertaken in this research employs two processes: *combining* and *splitting*.

Combining allows adjacent matches to merge into a larger match if they are incident on exactly the same files. We can then combine matches of ten lines into larger ones when appropriate.

Splitting occurs when a collection of overlapping matches has a more complicated pattern of file incidence. The match is broken up into smaller matches each of which has a consistent pattern of file incidence.

After application of these processes, raw matches are resolved into an equivalent set of snips and matches such that the following conditions hold:

1. No two snips overlap.

2. The collection of snips covers the text.

3. Matches can be identified as a collection of two or more snips with identical content.

4. If we extend the concept of match to include collections with a single unmatched snip, then the collection of matches covers the text.

The result of this analysis is a form of data that is much easier to record and to use for further study.

11.3.1   Data Model

The data model, illustrated in Figure 11.1, provides a framework for match information. Boxes indicate entity types and arrows indicate relationships. A solid arrow indicates an aggregation relationship and points from the element to the aggregate. If the arrow is single, the element belongs to exactly one aggregate and we have a functional (many-to-one) relationship. If the arrow is double, the element can belong to more than one aggregate and the relationship is many-to-many. A dotted arrow is a one-to-one relationship that identifies an element in the class pointed to, with each element from the class at the tail of the arrow.

The two main entity types of interest are snips and matches, shown at the bottom of the diagram. The entity type *file* is used to collect together snips that constitute a file. Each snip is associated with exactly one file and participates in exactly one match. In addition files and matches can be considered as aggregations of snips because of the way they are defined. Because snips do not overlap and collectively cover the files, a file may be viewed as the aggregation of snips that belong to it. Similarly, because matches are defined as one or more snips sharing the same content, a match may be viewed as an alternative aggregation of snips.

On the left side of the diagram is the file system view of files. Each file is in a unique directory, and each directory has a unique parent, indicated by the arrow pointing from the directory type to itself. The unique root of the directory is signaled by the incoming arrow to the directory type. This model does not

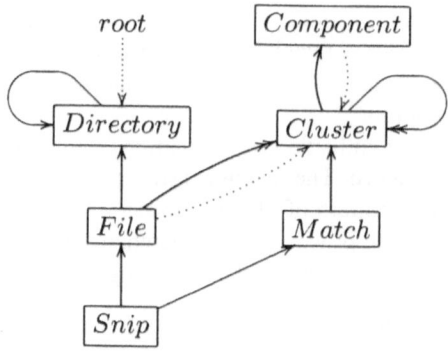

Figure 11.1. Combined data model.

handle hard links, symbolic links, or aliases directly. For simplicity, structurally identical files are treated the same as files that result from copying.

In order to collect together matches in a sensible manner, the concept of cluster is introduced. A *cluster* is the collection of files that have snips participating in a match. Thus each match uniquely identifies a cluster that has exactly the files touched by that match. This cluster aggregates all of the matches that touch exactly this set of files.

Clusters are also aggregations of files although files can belong to more than one. The dotted arrow identifies the singleton cluster with the file it contains.

A *component* is a collection of clusters with the following property: For any two clusters in the collection, either the clusters overlap or they belong to a sequence of clusters such that each consecutive pair of clusters in the sequence overlap. The strength of this concept is that the set of components partitions files in such a way that files in separate components are totally unrelated as far as matches are concerned. The dotted arrow from component to cluster identifies the component with the cluster containing all of the files in that component.

The aggregation relation from cluster to itself recognizes that each cluster is a collection of files and therefore the clustered are related by set containment. In other words, the aggregate cluster contains all the clusters that form subsets of it.

Because the subsets relation on clusters is quite large in typical cases, it is often useful to calculate the transitive reduction of it. The *transitive reduction* of a transitive relation is the smallest subset of the relation whose transitive closure equals the original relation. In simpler words, if $C_1 \subset C_2$ and $C_2 \subset C_3$, then a transitive relation also contains $C_1 \subset C_3$. The transitive reduction removes the $C_1 \subset C_3$. Reduction can lead to a substantially smaller dataset as is shown later.

A *Hasse diagram* of a transitive relation is one that shows only arcs in the transitive reduction and is commonly used for visualizing small partial orders. An example of a Hasse diagram appears in the next section.

11.3.2   Using the Data

The preceding analysis yields a database conforming to the given data model and providing detailed information about the source. There are several ways that this information can be used.

The most obvious is an alternative method for navigating the source. If a cursor is located at some line in the source, the containing snip is identified. From the snip, we can move up in the match hierarchy to the match set. From there we can move up to the cluster for that match or down to another snip in the same match set. At each point the local environment can be shown.

A prototype system based on this idea was built (Johnson, 1996) and proved to be a useful first step in studying how matches occur in a file context. In particular, this system could display, for each cluster, all of the content of a file in that cluster that participated in matches associated with that file or higher in the cluster hierarchy. Basically, it showed a skeleton of the file that was in common with all of the files in the cluster. It was possible to go up to superclusters or down to subclusters to explore the structure of the match.

Figure 11.2 shows the beginning of an example cluster page from this prototype. The cluster is named "0.C" and represents a singleton cluster for the file "A/fx80.h." It is located in component "0" and has immediate super-clusters "0.CI" and "0.CE." After some summary statistics about this cluster, the snips of the file are shown. The first four lines are in common with the cluster "0.CI" which is immediately above "0.C" in the cluster graph. Lines 5–17 constitute the boilerplate shared by cluster "0.A-KM-Q," which is three levels up in the cluster containment graph.

This idea can be further developed as a tool that generalizes the Unix tool *diff*.

Another approach is to classify the clusters in some way and compute summary statistics for metric purposes or focus in on clusters with particular properties to study cloning. One particular method involves comparing the cluster containment relation with the file system hierarchy by encoding the cluster to the lowest common ancestor directory in the file system. The match size measures associated with the directory nodes then indicate how much matching is occurring among subtrees as opposed to how much is within specific subtrees. Matching among subtrees suggests either a coupling such as cloning between subsystems or the result of a reorganization where a subtree has been moved from one subsystem to another. Work on this method is underway (Johnson, 1995), and there are interesting variations yet to explore.

An extreme form of classifying clusters is by component. When the analysis yields many components, it is possible to study the components by the type of structure they exhibit. In a multiversion system, components that span only different versions of the same file can be easily summarized with a few statistics. Energy can be focused on those components that have more complex structure and probably exhibit more interesting behavior.

The next section shows the re-analysis of such a component obtained as part of

Cluster 2: 0.C=>A/fx80.h

Previous Next

Content of File A/fx80.h

View Snip Summary for File A/fx80.h

Directory:
/x/ta/A
File size:
54909
File size (without internal matches):
54907
Log (base 2) of file size (without internal matches):
15.74
Super Clusters (by decrease in log match size):
0
    0.CI
-1.53
    0.CE
Component:
Component 0

(Hash 189) 0.CI **(up 1 level)**

```
1  /* Definitions of target machine for GNU compiler.  Alliant FX version.
2     Copyright (C) 1989 Free Software Foundation, Inc.
3     Adapted from m68k.h by Paul Petersen (petersen@uicsrd.csrd.uiuc.edu)
4     and Joe Weening (weening@gang-of-four.stanford.edu).
```

(Hash 103) 0.A-KM-Q **(up 3 levels)**

```
5
6  This file is part of GNU CC.
7
8  GNU CC is free software; you can redistribute it and/or modify
9  it under the terms of the GNU General Public License as published by
10 the Free Software Foundation; either version 2, or (at your option)
11 any later version.
12
13 GNU CC is distributed in the hope that it will be useful,
14 but WITHOUT ANY WARRANTY; without even the implied warranty of
15 MERCHANTABILITY or FITNESS FOR A PARTICULAR PURPOSE.  See the
16 GNU General Public License for more details.
17
```

Figure 11.2. Example cluster summary and navigation page.

an earlier study (Johnson, 1994a; Johnson, 1994b).

When many versions or variants are available, significant matching is expected to occur. Modelling may predict certain kinds of patterns that should occur. By comparison with the data, anomalies can be detected and studied. If, for example, snapshots of a system are taken periodically, the changes can be easily made to stand out from the bulk of unchanging content. Similarly, multiplatform systems can be studied as variations on a common theme with the differences highlighted.

There are also opportunities for visualization. For example, showing part of a Hasse diagram of clusters can provide easily understandable information about the structure of a match. Some preliminary work has been done (Johnson, 1994b), but there are still many new ways of showing structure in a visual form that can be explored.

11.4   A Small Example from GCC

A small example demonstrates how analysis can be done. A collection of eight files from gcc 2.3.3 and nine files from gcc 2.5.8 have been selected and are listed in Table 11.1. These exhibit significant cloning and renaming with a complex match structure. Each name is abbreviated using a two-character alias in which the first character identifies the file name and the second distinguishes the version. Thus, the alias *3* identifies the 3b1.h files, *c* identifies the crds.h files, *f* the fx80.h files and so on. The alias *3A* indicates the 3b1.h file from gcc 2.3.3 and *3B* indicates the 3b1.h file from gcc 2.5.8, and so on for the others.

This system is a collection of configuration files that tailor the GNU C compiler for a number of platforms based on the Motorola 68000 architecture. The configuration directory has a large collection of configuration files since gcc has been ported to many platforms during its long history. Cloning is quite common among configuration files since platforms often are extremely similar with small differences. The usual approach to configuring a new platform is to take an existing working configuration, copy it, and make the necessary enhancements.

This collection of files arose as part of a larger study (Johnson, 1994b) as one of many components, but have been reanalyzed here.

The following summary statistics were calculated:

- The 17 files made up of 14,891 lines and 545,953 characters.

- After analysis, 849 snips were identified in 345 match sets.

- These matches formed 70 clusters in 1 component.

Table 11.2 shows how large these files are and how much they participate in the matches of the full set. The size column indicates the true size measured in bytes. Unique size gives the size in bytes after internal matches have been removed.

The other two columns summarize the extent to which each file participates in matches with other files. The private part occurs only in the given file, whereas the

Table 11.1. A collection of files from gcc 2.3.3 and gcc 2.5.8.

Alias	Full path
3A	gcc2.3.3/config/3b1.h
cA	gcc2.3.3/config/crds.h
fA	gcc2.3.3/config/fx80.h
hA	gcc2.3.3/config/hp320.h
6A	gcc2.3.3/config/m68k.h
mA	gcc2.3.3/config/mot3300.h
nA	gcc2.3.3/config/news.h
tA	gcc2.3.3/config/tower-as.h
fB	gcc2.5.8/config/fx80/fx80.h
3B	gcc2.5.8/config/m68k/3b1.h
cB	gcc2.5.8/config/m68k/crds.h
dB	gcc2.5.8/config/m68k/dpx2.h
hB	gcc2.5.8/config/m68k/hp320.h
6B	gcc2.5.8/config/m68k/m68k.h
mB	gcc2.5.8/config/m68k/mot3300.h
nB	gcc2.5.8/config/m68k/news.h
tB	gcc2.5.8/config/m68k/tower-as.h

shared part occurs also in at least one other file. The large values for the shared part signal a large amount of internal matching. These two columns have internal matches removed. As a result, they sum to the unique size column.

The largest part of the matches is, of course, between similarly named files from the two versions. Table 11.3 measures the extent of these matches. The aliases shown have the version qualifier removed for brevity. Thus, 3 is used to indicate the collection containing versions $3A$ and $3B$, and similarly for the others. Since d has only one version dB, the data in this case is the same as for the previous table.

In Table 11.3, size indicates the number of bytes that occur in matches that include all versions. The private part of the size occurs only in these versions and not in files with different names, whereas the shared part occurs in each of the versions and also in a differently named file. Again, all of these numbers represent the size after internal duplicates have been removed, and again private plus shared equals the total size.

All of the sizes in Table 11.3 for two-version files are less than or equal to the corresponding shared values from Table 11.2 since all of the bytes must occur in all versions. The reason that the two values need not be equal is that matches can occur between single versions as we will see later.

Table 11.4 shows the remaining 45 clusters with their sizes and private and shared parts defined analogously. The aliases for these clusters are formed by combining the aliases of all of the elements. If a file has all versions included, the alias contains the single-letter alias representing all versions.

Table 11.2. File sizes and measure of sharing.

Alias	Size	Unique size	Private	Shared
3A	16933	16933	596	16337
cA	22062	22062	1442	20620
fA	54909	54907	217	54690
hA	22413	22413	2395	20018
6A	65837	65538	3945	61593
mA	28185	28185	2669	25516
nA	16253	16253	2112	14141
tA	23581	23581	2010	21571
fB	55053	55051	223	54828
3B	17682	17681	686	16995
cB	22465	22465	1704	20761
dB	34232	34232	30162	4070
hB	22876	22876	2858	20018
6B	72169	71868	10508	61360
mB	29764	29763	3762	26001
nB	17443	17443	3302	14141
tB	24096	24096	1963	22133

Table 11.3. Sharing of content between versions.

Alias	Name	Size	Private	Shared
3	3b1.h	16,337	6,790	9,547
c	crds.h	20,566	13,869	6,697
d	dpx2.h	34,232	30,162	4,070
f	fx80.h	54,644	32,670	22,974
h	hp320.h	20,018	12,727	7,291
6	m68k.h	61,161	40,972	20,189
m	mot3300.h	25,296	11,712	13,584
n	news.h	14,141	9,254	4,887
t	tower-as.h	21,571	11,553	10,018

Table 11.4. Clusters sorted by private size.

Alias	Size	Private	Shared	Alias	Size	Private	Shared
f,6	18,596	17,915	681	3B,cB	4,331	195	4,136
3,c,f,h,m,n,t,d	2,129	2129	0	fB,6B	18,795	184	18,611
3,m,t	6,206	1,924	4,282	mB,tB	8,982	175	8,807
3,m	8,396	1,824	6,572	h,m,t	4,861	148	4,713
m,t	8,353	1,538	6,815	h,m,n	4,410	115	4,295
c,6,m	1,975	1,295	680	3B,mB	8,900	76	8,824
h,t	6,031	1145	4,886	c,6	2,044	69	1,975
h,m	5,700	724	4,976	h,6A	739	59	680
3,c,f,h,6,m,n,t	680	680	0	3,cA,m	3,688	54	3,634
c,m	5,636	678	4,958	n,d	3,622	53	3,569
3,h,m,n,t,d	3,184	542	2,642	fA,6A	18,969	46	18,923
3,c,h,m,n,t,d	2,642	513	2,129	3,t,mB	6,247	41	6,206
3,c	4,136	502	3,634	n,t	4,358	38	4,320
c,f	3,298	489	2,809	c,m,t,d	2,671	29	2,642
h,m,n,t	4,295	431	3,864	t,mB	8,420	26	8,394
3,f,h,m,t,d	2,547	418	2,129	h,n,t,d	3,209	25	3,184
3,t	6,636	389	6,247	f,6B	18,611	15	18,596
3B,mB,tB	6,634	387	6,247	f,6,t	681	1	680
h,n,d	3,569	360	3,209	3,h,n	3,865	1	3,864
f,6A	18,923	327	18,596	m,t,d	3,632	1	3,631
3,c,m	3,634	312	3,322	c,mA	5,637	1	5,636
6,m	2,204	229	1,975	h,mA	5,701	1	5,700
3,mA	8,614	218	8,396				

In terms of the discussion in the previous section, the totals are calculated for the clusters and then summed for all clusters meeting a particular criterion. The shared part of t is the sum of the private parts of clusters that contain t and something else. There are 18 of these listed in Table 11.4.

Table 11.4 is listed in descending order by the size of the private part. Clearly the most interesting cluster in this table is f,c with a private part of 17,915 bytes. By itself it accounts for almost all of the shared parts for both f and 6 and provides strong evidence that extensive cloning has been done. It is likely that one of these files is a clone of the other or they are both clones of a file that as since disappeared.

If we look at the source for f, line 3 acknowledges that it is based on 6 (see Figure 11.2). However, we can get more information about the nature of the cloning from the clusters themselves. Table 11.5 collects all of the clusters that involve a version of f and a version of 6.

There is also information about the direction of cloning. Notice that there is private content in common between both copies of f and each individual copy of 6. There is no private content in common between both copies of 6 and each separate copy of f. This suggests that f is cloned from 6 since 327 bytes of 6

Table 11.5. Sharing between fx80.h and m68k.h.

Alias	Size	Private	Shared
f,6	18,596	17,915	681
3,c,f,h,6,m,n,t	680	680	0
f,6A	18,923	327	18,596
fB,6B	18,795	184	18,611
fA,6A	18,969	46	18,923
f,6B	18,611	15	18,596
f,6,t	681	1	680

removed or changed between versions of 6 were preserved in f. The absence of this phenomenon in the other direction strongly supports this conclusion.

Upon inspection of the files it is observed that the 327 bytes of 6 removed correspond to five separate changes made that weren't reflected in f. The 15 bytes that occur in the later version of 6 and not the earlier are an artifact resulting from other maintenance activity on 6. This kind of inconsistent updating of clones is exactly the problem with this strategy for code maintenance.

The information in Table 11.3 has a rather complex structure. Figure 11.3 shows a Hasse diagram with the seven biggest clusters. Since $3,c,f,h,m,n,t,d$ is everything except dB, this long name is abbreviated as $\overline{6}$. In addition to the large matches involving f and 6, there are a number of other interesting matches that interact in a complex manner.

What is the significance of 680 bytes occurring in $3,c,f,h,6,m,n,t$ but not in dB? After further inspection of the source, it is quickly discovered to be 17 lines of boilerplate at the beginning of each file but erroneously omitted from d. The first 13 of these lines are shown in Figure F2 as lines 5–17 of f. The other clusters of Figure 11.3 show other obvious sharing of code.

11.5 A Large Example: Mozilla

In early 1998, Netscape decided to make its proprietary code Open Source (Stanek, 1999). Now a large commercial body of source is available for study. Since Mozilla continues to be developed, the open source community needs to be coordinated, and does so through the web site at http://www.mozilla.org/. In their words they describe what Mozilla is:

> Mozilla is an open-source web browser, designed for standards compliance, performance, and portability.

Mozilla is large. The Milestone 12 release of December 21, 1999 has 18,611 files and a total size of 113,488,492 bytes. There are 1,246,683 lines of C++ code

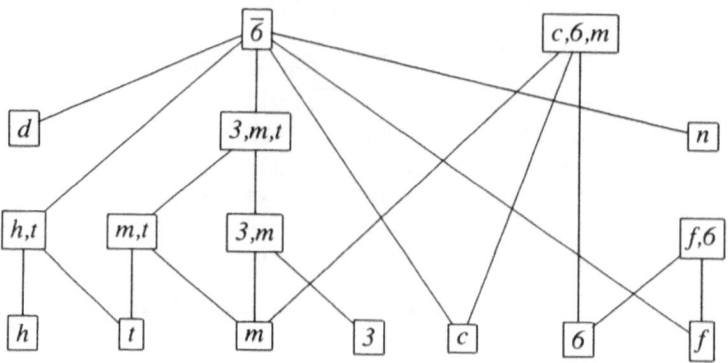

Figure 11.3. Hasse diagram for the seven largest clusters.

in 2,467 files, 491,024 lines of C code in 921 files, and 504,647 lines of C/C++ headers in 3,355 files. The remaining 11,868 files composed of code, make files, project files, graphics, documentation, test data, and other text and binary files split into 697,845 lines.

For this exercise, we look at Milestones 3–15 available from the Mozilla web site. The following results were obtained:

- There are 200,738 files composed of 33,614,023 lines and 1,258,288,054 characters.

- If only one snip from each matched set is counted, the size reduces to 4,400,126 lines and 213,567,578 characters.

- There are 4,450,928 snips that make up 373,569 match sets.

- There are 119,487 clusters in 19,874 components.

- The cluster containment graph has 1,856,746 arcs; this reduces to 212,054 after transitive reduction.

- 35% of the lines and 26% of the characters first appear in Milestone 3.

- 22% of the lines and 28% of the characters appear in only one Milestone; 17% of the lines and 11% of the characters appear in all 13 Milestones.

- 83% of the lines and 88% of the characters appear in clusters with a file path across all Milestones; 15% of the lines and 10% of the characters appear in clusters with exactly two file paths.

- Of the clusters having one path, 26% of the lines and 31% of the characters occur in one Milestone; 11% of the lines and 21% of the characters appear in two Milestones; 12% of the lines and 7% of the characters appear in all 13 Milestones.

Table 11.6. Components of redundancy for major Mozilla subdirectories.

Subdirectory	Among	Within	Ratio
xpcom	92,772	13,1133	0.707
include	8,865	29,516	0.300
jpeg	1,310	34,481	0.038
mailnews	11,688	483,022	0.024
xpfe	4,256	203,812	0.021
config	503	27,516	0.018
netwerk	1,908	118,026	0.016
nsprpub	599	40,123	0.015
lib	740	52,677	0.014
xpinstall	1,109	79,402	0.014
db	117	8,974	0.013
network	1,418	120,767	0.012
rdf	1,465	142,333	0.010

- Of the clusters that participate in Milestone 15, 11% of the lines and 12% of the characters occur in a singleton cluster; 65% of the lines and 68% of the characters belong to files that have not changed their file path; 7% of the lines and 6% of the lines have been moved in the directory tree between Milestones without apparent cloning; 10% of the lines and 8% of the characters showed matches in previous Milestones but not in Milestone 15. This leaves 7% of the lines and 6% of the characters that have some kind of matches occurring in Milestone 15.

There is a lot more exploration to be done on a source tree as large as Mozilla, but one more example shows the kinds of things that are possible with this approach. Table 11.6 shows a comparison of matches (measured as number of lines) that occur among the subdirectories of first-level Mozilla directories with matches that occur within these subdirectories by identifying the least common ancestor of all of the paths for each cluster. If this least common ancestor path is, for example "…/mozilla/xpcom/io," then all of the matching in this cluster is within a subdirectory of "xpcom." On the other hand, if the answer is "…/mozilla/xpcom" then the matching in this cluster involves different files or subdirectories directly under "xpcom." The ratio of of these values gives a strong indication of movement or cloning among these subdirectories, suggesting areas worthy of further investigation.

Table 11.6 shows the subdirectories with a ratio over 0.01. Each of these is worthy of more detailed study using the same techniques recursively or using techniques described in the previous section.

11.6   Conclusions

The analysis of textual redundancy is a promising tool for understanding the structure of cloning and reorganization in large bodies of source code. It can handle multiple versions and variants easily. It is language independent and insensitive to parsing errors or lack of knowledge of the build structure. With the power of modern computers, it appears to scale up well enough and provides an interesting overall view of redundant structure.

An alternative to the textual approach is described in Chapter 5. This apprach is suitable under different situations, and promises to be effective for clone detection in contemporary systems.

There is much that needs to be done. More work on data analysis techniques are likely to yield real benefits. Work on new visualization techniques for the masses of information obtained also will be quite useful. Integrating this exact-matchbased approach with parsing-based and approximate-match-based approaches should be able to provide a better view of source code than can any of them alone.

11.7   References

Baker, B. S. (1992). A program for identifying duplicated code. In *Proceedings of Computing Science and Statistics: 24th Symposium on the Interface*, College Station, TX, March 18-21.

Biggerstaff, T. J. (1989). Design recovery for maintenance and reuse. *Computer*, 22(7):36-49.

Buss, E., De Mori, R., Gentleman, M., Henshaw, J., Johnson, H., Kontogiannis, K., Müller, H., Mylopoulos, J., Paul, S., Prakash, A., Stanley, M., Tilley, S., Troster, J., and Wong, K. (1994). Investigating reverse engineering technologies: The CAS program understanding project. *IBM Syst. Journal*, 33(3):477-500.

Buss, E. and Henshaw, J. (1991). A software reverse engineering experience. In Gawman, A., Pachl, J., Slonim, J., and Stilman, A., editors, *Proceedings of the 1991 Centre for Advanced Studies Conference (CASCON '91)*, pp. 55-73, IBM, Toronto, October 28-30.

Buss, E. and Henshaw, J. (1992). Experiences in program understanding. In Botsford, J., Ryman, A., Slonim, J., and Taylor, D., editors, *Proceedings of the 1992 Centre for Advanced Studies Conference (CASCON '92)*, pp. 157-189, IBM, Toronto, November 9-12.

Chikofsky, E. J. and Cross II, J. H. (1990). Reverse engineering and design recovery: A taxonomy. *IEEE Software*, 7(1):13-17.

Johnson, J. H. (1993). Identifying redundancy in source code using fingerprints. In Gawman, A., Gentleman, W. M., Kidd, E., Larson, P.-Å., and Slonim, J., editors, *Proceedings of the 1993 Centre for Advanced Studies Conference (CASCON '93)*, pp. 171-183, IBM and NRC, Toronto, October 24-28.

Johnson, J. H. (1994a). Substring matching for clone detection and change tracking. In *Proceedings of the Internation Conference on Software Maintenance (ICSM)*, pp. 120-126, Victoria, British Columbia, September 19-23.

Johnson, J. H. (1994b). Visualizing textual redundancy in legacy source. In Botsford, J., Gawman, A., Gentleman, M., Kidd, E., Lyons, K., and Slonim, J., editors, *Proceedings of the 1994 Centre for Advanced Studies Conference (CASCON '94)*, pp. 9-18, IBM and NRC, Toronto, October 31-November 3.

Johnson, J. H. (1995). Using textual redundancy to understand change. In Bennet, K., Bockus, D., Gentleman, M., Johnson, H., Kidd, E., Slonim, J., and Stilman, A., editors, *Proceedings of the 1995 Centre for Advanced Studies Conference (CASCON '95)*, CD-ROM, IBM and NRC, Toronto, November 7-9).

Johnson, J. H. (1996). Navigating the textual redundancy web in legacy source. In Bauer, M., Bennet, K., Gentleman, M., Bockus, D., Burnside, P., Hoffman, E., James, A., Krmpotic, J., Rintjema, L., Stilman, A., Johnson, H., Lyons, K., and Slonim, J., editors, *Proceedings of the 1996 Centre for Advanced Studies Conference (CASCON '96)*, CD-ROM, IBM and NRC, Toronto, November 12-14.

Karp, R. M. (1986). Combinatorics, complexity, and randomness. *CACM*, 22(2):98-109.

Karp, R. M. and Rabin, M. O. (1987). Efficient randomized pattern-matching algorithms. *IBM J. Res. Develop.*, 31(2):249-260.

Stanek, W. R. (1999). *Netscape Mozilla Source Code Guide*. Netscape Press.

Whitney, M., Kontogiannis, K., Johnson, J. H., Bernstein, M., Corrie, B., Merlo, E., McDaniel, J. G., Mori, R. D., Müller, H. A., Mylopoulos, J., Stanley, M., Tilley, S. R., and Wong, K. (1995). Using an integrating toolset for program understanding. In Bennet, K., Bockus, D., Gentleman, M., Johnson, H., Kidd, E., Slonim, J., and Stilman, A., editors, *Proceedings of the 1995 Centre for Advanced Studies Conference (CASCON '95)*, pp. 262-274, IBM and NRC, Toronto, November 7-9.

12
Building Parallel Applications Using Design Patterns

Dhrubajyoti Goswami
Ajit Singh
Bruno R. Preiss

12.1   Introduction

Parallel application design and development is a major area of interest in the domain of high-performance scientific and industrial computing. In fact, parallel computing is becoming an integral part in several major application domains such as space, medicine, cancer and genetic research, graphics and animation, image processing, to name a few. With the advent of fast interconnecting networks of workstations and PCs, it is now becoming increasingly possible to develop high-performance parallel applications using the combined computing powers of these networked resources, at no extra cost. Contrast this to the situation until the early 90s, where parallel computing was mostly confined only to special-purpose parallel computers that were unaffordable by small research institutions. Nowadays, high-speed networks and fast general-purpose computers are aiding in the mainstream adoption of parallel computing at a much more affordable cost.

However, parallel computing is not simple. The complexity arises due to the accumulation of many intricate details related to low-level parallelism, on top of the sequential code. As an aid to handling some of these complexities, this research proposes a generic model for designing and developing parallel applications through the employment of reusable parallel computation patterns.

The concept of design patterns has been extensively studied and used in the context of object-oriented software design. Patterns in this context describe strategies for solving recurring design problems in systematic and general ways (Gamma et al., 1994). Similar ideas are being explored in other disciplines of computing as well. For instance, ACE (the Adaptive Communication Environment) is an object-oriented toolkit that implements various network-level patterns to simplify the development of concurrent, event-driven communication software (Schmidt, 1994).

In the parallel computing domain, design patterns describe recurring parallel computational problems of similar structure and communication-synchronization behavior, and their solution strategies. Examples of such recurring patterns are: static and dynamic replication, divide and conquer, data parallel pattern with various topologies, compositional framework for irregularly structured control-parallel computation, systolic array, singleton pattern for single-process single- or multi-threaded computation.

12.1.1   Pattern-Based Approaches in Parallel Computing

The exploration of design pattern concepts in the parallel programming domain is not new. Starting with the late 80s, several pattern-based systems have been built with the intention of facilitating parallel application development through the use of some of these ready-made, reusable components. These earlier systems include Code (Browne et al., 1989) and Frameworks (Singh et al., 1991). Some of the recent systems based on similar ideas that are worth mentioning are: Enterprise (Schaeffer et al., 1993), Code2 (Browne et al., 1995), HeNCE (Browne et al., 1995), Tracs (Bartoli et al., 1995), and DPnDP (Siu and Singh, 1997).

Frameworks was one of the earliest systems specifically designed to restructure existing sequential programs to exploit parallelism on workstation clusters. Patterns in Frameworks are called templates, which are at a different level of abstraction than the parallel patterns mentioned previously in this section. In Frameworks, an application consists of modules which interact with one another via mechanisms similar to remote procedure calls (RPCs). A module's interconnections with other modules are specified by an input template, an output template, and a body template. Developers create modules by selecting appropriate templates and application procedures. Arbitrary process graphs could be created by interconnecting resulting modules.

Enterprise was an improvement over Frameworks in several aspects. Patterns in Enterprise are at a much higher level of abstraction than in Frameworks. The three-part templates in Frameworks are combined into single units in Enterprise and are called *assets*, which are named to resemble operations in a human organization. For example, the asset named *department* represents a master-slave pattern in the traditional parallel programming terminology. A fixed collection of assets is provided by the system which can be combined to create an asset diagram to represent the parallel program structure.

Code, Code2 and HeNCE are all based on visual programming techniques to aid the programmer develop his parallel structure graphically through the use of nodes and arcs that represent computations and interactions respectively. Code is one of the pioneers of the idea of a two-step development process. During the first step, programmers design the various sequential components, and then, during the second step, compose them into a parallel structure. The graphs in Code depict data-flow pattern of computation. Each node in Code could itself be another data-flow graph. Thus it supports reuse of other data-flow graphs by allowing recursive embedding of graphs. As a major distinction between Code and HeNCE, graphs in HeNCE depict control flow. In addition, HenNCE supports patterns with replication, pipeline, loop and conditional constructs.

Tracs is another graphical development system, however with some new concepts. Application development in Tracs consists of two distinct phases: the definition phase and the configuration phase. During the definition phase, the user defines the three basic components of an application: the message model, the task model and the architecture model. The architecture model defines the software architecture of the parallel application in terms of message and task models. An architecture model defined during this phase can be saved in a user-defined library for later use. During the configuration phase, the programmer constructs the complete application from the basic components, either defined during the definition phase or selected from the system libraries or both. Evidently, Tracs is one of the first systems known to us that is based on the idea of extensibility by providing support for an extensible library of user-defined architecture models.

Unlike the design-level patterns in the object-oriented domain (Gamma et al., 1994), the previous systems in parallel computing support patterns not only at the design level but also at the implementation level. In other words, the design-level patterns are also pre-implemented, similar in concept to frameworks in the conventional software engineering terminology.

12.1.2   Limitations of the Previous Approaches

Though the idea of design- and implementation-level patterns hold significant promise, in practice, most of the pattern-based approaches mentioned previously suffer from severe limitations. Some of these limitations include: limited usability, lack of flexibility, and limited extensibility.

Most systems support only a limited set of patterns in ad hoc ways. There is no generic or canonical model of a pattern, which in turn substantially hampers the usability of the approach. Usability is also hampered by the lack of a clear-cut methodology for composing various patterns in a single application. Besides usability, there are two other important aspects: flexibility and extensibility. Most of the systems are hard-coded with a limited and fixed set of patterns, and often there is no clear way to add new patterns to the system when required (leading to lack of extensibility). Furthermore, if a certain desired parallel pattern is not supported by a system, often there is no alternative but to abandon the system (leading to lack of flexibility). The interested reader can refer to the comprehensive paper by Singh et al. for a detailed look at the desirable characteristics and the shortcomings of different pattern-based approaches in parallel computing (Singh et al., 1998).

Tracs (Bartoli et al., 1995) is one earlier system that addresses the issue of extensibility. However, the type of extensibility realized inside Tracs is restrictive. For example, in Tracs a user can graphically create a 5-slave master-slave pattern and save it inside the library for future use. However, a generic master-slave pattern could have been more useful for this purpose.

Complete graphical representation of parallel applications, as in many of the previously mentioned approaches, also has its limitations. As one of these limitations, graphs alone may not be enough to convey the *behavior* of an application. For instance, the graphical representation of a 2-D data-parallel mesh and a systolic array pattern might look structurally identical. But these two patterns differ significantly in their behavioral aspects, which may not be conveyed in a graph.

DPnDP (Siu and Singh, 1997) is the first system known to us that addresses both the issues of flexibility and extensibility. Unfortunately it concentrates only on the structural aspects of a pattern and ignores the behavioral aspects (such as the parallel computation model and the communication-synchronization behavior inside a pattern) altogether. Despite its limitations, DPnDP was a good learning experience and it set up the initial stage for this research.

12.1.3 Approach

This research proposes a generic (pattern- and application-independent) model for realizing and using parallel design patterns, useful for solving network-oriented parallel applications. The model is based on the popular message-passing paradigm, which makes it suitable for a cluster of interconnected workstations or PCs. The structural and behavioral attributes associated with a parallel design pattern are abstracted in an application-independent manner. These application-independent abstractions hide most of the low-level details that are commonly encountered in any parallel application development (problem decomposition and distribution, process/thread creation, process-processor mapping, communication and synchronization, data packing and unpacking, load balancing, etc). The set of abstracted attributes is generic for all patterns.

The term *parallel architectural skeleton* is used to imply an pattern's physical realization that is application independent. A parallel architectural skeleton can be regarded as a building block that contains the necessary ingredients for constructing application-specific virtual architectures, suitable for solving problems that conform to a specific parallel computing pattern or a collection of patterns.

In the rest of the discussion, the term *parallel architectural skeleton* is abbreviated to *architectural skeleton*, or simply *skeleton*.

Each architectural skeleton is a reusable component that hides the low-level, application-independent details related to the implementation of a particular parallel design pattern. Separating and pre-packaging those application-independent details from application code enables a user to reuse the same skeleton again and again for different applications that follow similar patterns. Furthermore, it liberates the user from the additional burden of many of the low-level details and instead enables him to concentrate more on application-specific issues.

In contrast to the other pattern-based approaches in parallel computing, this approach is based on a generic model which guides a user to systematically compose his application in a hierarchical fashion. The model is generic because it can be described in a way independent of patterns and applications. Genericity enhances usability.

The model turns out to be an ideal candidate for object-oriented style of design and implementation. It is currently implemented as a C++ template library without necessitating any language extension. The C++-implementation enables a user to design and develop his parallel applications using a mainstream programming language, without the extra burden associated with the learning of a new language or a new methodology. As discussed later, the object-oriented and the library-based approach has an extra benefit towards extensibility.

The library of skeletons supplies the reusable building blocks which encapsulate the structural and behavioral attributes associated with the network-oriented patterns in parallel computing. The hierarchical compositional model, discussed in the next section, enables a user to systematically compose his application using the desired patterns which can interact with one another via standard interfaces and using both low- and high-level communication-synchronization protocols. The inherent presence of a hierarchy and standard interfaces for patterns make it possible to refine parts of an application without affecting the rest (hierarchical refinement is discussed in a later section of the chapter). Most of the attributes associated with the skeletons are parameterized where the parameters depend on the needs of an application. Consequently, they enable the same skeleton or a set of skeletons to be reused in different applications that follow identical patterns but are not necessarily similar in other aspects. All these of issues make the architectural skeleton approach unique in comparison with the other pattern-based approaches in parallel computing.

12.2   The Architectural Skeleton Model

A *parallel architectural skeleton* is a set of attributes that encapsulate the structure and behavior of a pattern in parallel computing in an application-independent manner. The attributes are parameterized, where the parameters depend on the needs of an application. The user extends a skeleton by specifying the parameters associated with the attributes, as needed by the application at hand. Figure 12.1 illustrates the various phases of application development using parallel architectural skeletons. As shown in the figure, different extensions of the same skeleton can result in somewhat different *abstract parallel computing modules* (abbreviated to *abstract module*). An abstract module is yet to be filled in with application code. Once an abstract module is supplied with application code, it results in a *concrete parallel computing module* (abbreviated to *concrete module*, or simply, *module*). A parallel application is a systematic collection of mutually interacting, instantiated modules.

An abstract module inherits all the properties associated with a skeleton. Moreover, it has additional components that depend on the application. In object-oriented terminology, an architectural skeleton can be described as the *gener-*

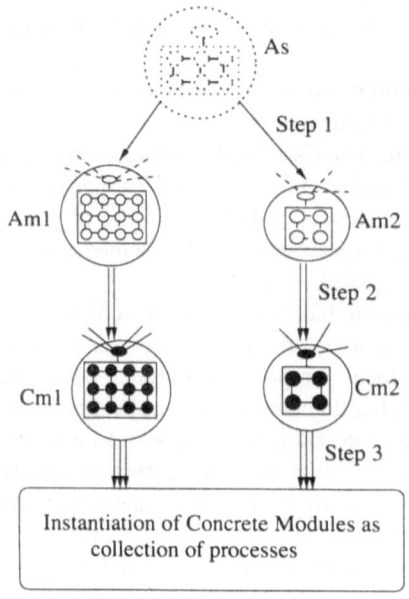

Legend:

Step 1: Extend
Step 2: Add Application Code
Step 3: Instantiate

As: An Architectural Skeleton
Am: An Abstract Module
Cm: A Concrete Module

Figure 12.1. Relationships between a parallel architectural skeleton, an abstract module and a module.

alization of the structural and behavioral properties associated with a particular parallel pattern. An abstract module is an application-specific *specialization* of a skeleton.

Figure 12.2 illustrates the anatomy of an abstract module (in this case, the module extends the data-parallel architectural skeleton designed for 2-D mesh topology). An architectural skeleton is formally defined as follows:

Definition. A *parallel architectural skeleton*, As, is an application-independent abstraction comprised of the set of generic attributes $\{Rep, BE, Topology, P_{Int}, P_{Ext}\}$. An *abstract module* is an application-specific extension of a skeleton. Let Am be such an abstract module that extends the skeleton As. The various attributes inherited by Am (from As) are described as follows:

- *Rep* is the representative of Am. When filled in with application code, *Rep* represents the module in its action and interaction with other modules.

- *BE* is the back-end of Am. Formally, $BE = \{Am_1, Am_2,..., Am_n\}$, where each Am_i is itself an abstract module. The notion of modules inside another module results in a tree-structured hierarchy. Am, at the root of this tree, is the *parent* and each Am_i is its *child*. Modules Am_i and Am_j belonging to the same back-end are *peers* of one another.

- *Topology* is the interconnection-topology specification of the modules in-

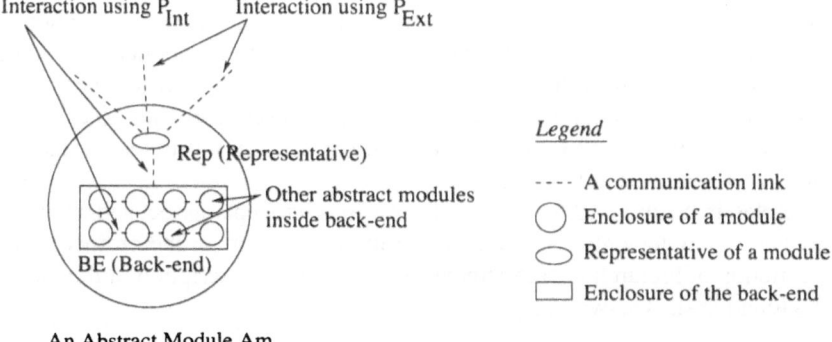

Figure 12.2. Diagrammatic representation of an abstract module.

side the back-end (*BE*), and their connectivity specification with *Rep*.

- P_{Int} is the internal communication-synchronization protocol of Am and its associated skeleton, As. The internal protocol is an inherent property of the skeleton, and it captures both the parallel computing model of the corresponding pattern and the topology. Formally, P_{Int} is defined as a set of primitive commands. Using the primitives inside P_{Int}, the representative of Am can interact with the modules in its back-end, and a module in the back-end can interact with its peers.

- P_{Ext} is the external communication-synchronization protocol of Am and is defined as a set of primitive commands. Using the primitives inside P_{Ext}, Am can interact with its parent and the peers. Unlike P_{Int}, which is an inherent property of the skeleton, P_{Ext} is adaptable. In other words, Am adapts to the context of its parent by using the internal protocol of its parent as its external protocol.

Though an abstract module is an application-specific specialization of an architectural skeleton, it is still devoid of any application code. User writes application code for an abstract module using its communication and synchronization protocols, P_{Int} and P_{Ext}. A code-complete abstract module is called a *concrete parallel computing module*, or simply a *module*. A parallel application is a hierarchical collection of instances of such modules.

Parent-child relationships among modules result in a tree-structured hierarchy. A parallel application can be viewed as a hierarchical collection of modules, consisting of a *root* module and its children forming the sub-trees. This tree is called the *HTree* of the application. For example, in a `Master-Slave` application, the `Master` module forms the root of the hierarchy, and the dynamically replicated children `Slave` modules form the sub-trees. In another application consisting of the three modules `Producer`, `Worker` and `Consumer`, a *composite module* that extends the *composite skeleton* forms the root of the hierarchy, and its three children (`Producer`, `Worker` and `Consumer`) form the sub-trees.

The concept of *HTree* is important, because the object-oriented implementation dynamically constructs the hierarchy associated with an application, while completely hiding it from the user. A *singleton module*, which resembles a single process in conventional parallel computing and consequently has no children, forms a leaf in the hierarchy. *HTrees* are diagrammatically illustrated for the examples discussed in Section 12.5.

Examples in Section 12.5 illustrate the various concepts associated with the model and its implementation, including examples of some of the protocols and an illustration of hierarchical refinement. A more formal description of the model can be found in the Goswami (2000).

12.3   An Object-Oriented Implementation

This section discusses some key issues related to the present object-oriented implementation of the model. Goswami et al. (1999b) provide additional details regarding the object-oriented features of the implementation.

The model has been currently implemented using an industry standard C++ compiler (SunCC, V 4.1) without any language extension. MPI (Gropp et al., 1994), the proposed standard message passing interface, is used as the underlying communication-synchronization library. There are several vendors who are currently working toward an implementation of the MPI standard (presently at release 2.0) as proposed by the MPI forum (MPIF). The current implementation of the model uses LAM 6.1, initially developed at the Ohio Supercomputing Center and now maintained and extended at the University of Notre Dame, USA. LAM (Local Area Multicomputer) is an MPI programming, development, and debugging environment for heterogeneous computers on a network. It implements the complete MPI-1 standard and many of the MPI-2 features.

A textual interface based on a specification language whose parser is implemented in Perl (Wall et al., 1996) helps the user in the various stages of application development. The textual interface is parsed to produce the front-end C++ code which is subsequently compiled and linked with the skeleton library to generate the executable. However it must be emphasized here that the use of a specification language is not a language extension. It merely helps the user to bypass certain laborious C++-related details that can easily be handled by Perl scripts. An expert in C++, for example, may want to directly develop his application in the language of his expertise without going through the specification-language phase.

Other important features of the implementation include: (1) the use of C++ operator-overloading to implement certain primitive operations inside protocol classes; and (2) the use of marshaling and unmarshaling mechanisms whereby the data attributes of an entire object can be marshaled, shipped over a communication link, and then unmarshaled, without the usual hassles of data packing and unpacking. These features will be discussed in Section 12.5.

Figure 12.3 illustrates the high-level class diagram behind the design of the

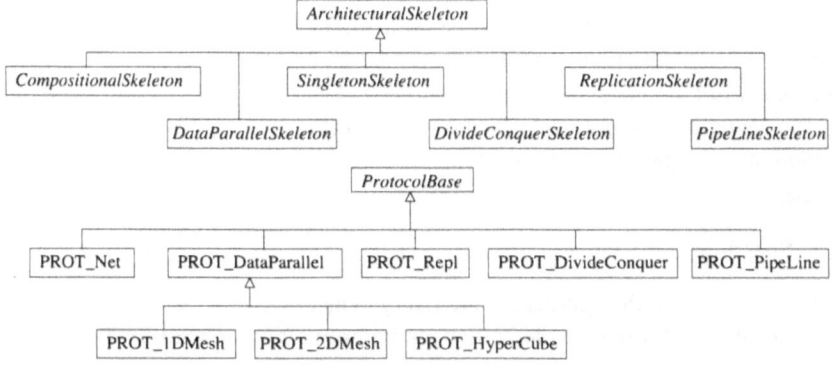

Figure 12.3. High level class diagram of the skeleton library.

skeleton library. It uses the standard UML (Booch et al., 1999) notation. For simplicity, the figure does not illustrate the relationships between the skeleton classes and the various protocols. The various attributes and the methods associated with each class, and the formal parameters, in the form of templates, associated with each inherited skeleton class are not shown.

It is worth mentioning here that the library of architectural skeletons exhibits the characteristics of a *framework* in the conventional software engineering terminology. In that context, the skeleton-library could also be called *a framework for developing network-based parallel applications*.

12.4   Selected Patterns in Parallel Computing

Before demonstrating the model and its implementation, we present two of the patterns that are used in the examples. These two patterns are frequently encountered in parallel computing. They are the dynamic replication pattern and the composite pattern. The description of the patterns is general, that is, they are not discussed exclusively from the perspective of the model. The subsequent section will illustrate the physical realization of these patterns within the boundaries of our approach.

In what follows, we use a commonly accepted pattern format (Meszaros and Doble, 1997).

12.4.1   Dynamic Replication of Modules

Context: Your design and development of a parallel application has to deal with a situation where a sequential computing module has to work collectively with a group of other modules. The sequential module may not be in pace with the other modules. This will definitely slow down the entire application if the other modules need to rely on its outcome. Accordingly, it might be necessary to replicate the workload of the sequential module to speed-up its performance.

Problem: Find a convenient methodology to replicate the workload of the out-of-pace sequential module so that the other modules in the application are not affected in any significant respect.

Forces:

- Speed-up is the biggest consideration here.

- Some parts of the application are likely to be developed by others. You need to handle your part of the bottleneck without affecting their work.

- Not all applications are suitable for replication. For example, the workload of a module can be easily replicated if (1) it performs some repeated computation, say inside a loop; (2) each iteration is independent; and (3) communication does not occur in the middle of a computation phase. Replication is achieved by assigning the workload of each iteration to a separate module, thus overlapping their executions in time. This situation is most frequently encountered when the modules in question form a pipeline. Each pipeline stage performs some repeated computation which can easily be replicated, at least theoretically.

- Automatic replication is not easy to implement. An efficient implementation has to deal with issues like dynamic distribution of workload and balancing of system load without compromising performance. For example, if the CPUs are already overloaded, further replication will in fact degrade performance.

Solution: The solution will depend on the particular context. For the user of the architectural skeleton library, the solution will be to use the *replication skeleton* that implements a dynamic replication pattern. The user replaces the out-of-pace sequential computing module with a *replication module* that extends the replication skeleton, and then distributes the work load of the original sequential module to dynamically replicated `Worker` modules, where each `Worker` is a child of the replication module. A `Worker` can be a sequential module (also called a singleton module in the context of this model). Since each `Worker` exclusively deals with its parent, the replication module, and the interface of the replication module with the rest of the modules remain unchanged from before (in the context of this model), the other modules are unaffected by this change. An example is provided in the next section.

12.4.2 *Support for Hierarchical Pattern Composition*

Context: A parallel application module that you are developing involves several patterns in parallel computing. The patterns must be interconnected in a particular fashion to produce a desired topology. The interconnected patterns need to interact with one another; they may engage in interaction behaviors, including collective communication (scatter, gather, and reduce types of operations) and peer-to-peer broadcasting. The application module that you are developing will itself be a part of a bigger, more complex parallel application.

Problem: How do you achieve hierarchical pattern composition?

Forces: The following issues need consideration while choosing a solution:

- Flexibility is one of the mandatory requirements of all pattern-based approaches in parallel computing. The approach should be flexible enough to enable a user to intermix patterns as desired, or enable him to bypass patterns in order to build applications from scratch. Flexibility often enhances usability.

- An efficient implementation of hierarchical pattern composition is a fairly complicated issue. One of the factors that need consideration is the dynamic load-balancing of the composed modules in the processor-cluster, where each module might contain other modules as well. Dynamic load balancing is itself a major research interest. Note that a load imbalance might cause severe performance degradation, which may mask off any possible gain.

Solution: Again, the solution depends on the precise context. For instance, for the user of an architectural skeleton library, the solution will be to take advantage of the *composite skeleton* that implements a composite pattern. The user extends the skeleton appropriately to create an abstract module, or the *composite module*. Each of the patterns to be composed is realized as a module in this model's context, and it becomes a child of the composite module. By default, the composed children modules inside the composite module form an all-to-all interconnection topology. The internal protocol, PROT_Net, of the composite skeleton supports the desired communication-synchronization requirements of the composed modules. Note that the composite module can itself be a part of another module. Each abstract module becomes concrete as soon as it is code-complete. An example is provided in the next section.

12.5   Examples

The following examples illustrate the concepts behind the architectural skeleton model, discussed in Section 12.2 as well as the various issues related to its implementation and use. The examples will be revisited in a later section while analyzing the software engineering related aspects of the model and its implementation.

12.5.1   Hello World

This first example simply prints the string "Hello World." A single process structure is suitable for this purpose, which can be realized using the *singleton skeleton*. As a property of this skeleton, any module that extends it contains only the representative, and the back end of the module (*BE*) is empty. Consequently, the internal protocol, P_{Int}, is not required and hence it is an empty set. For the same reason, the topology attribute is also void.

The following code segments illustrate the user's portion of the code in the specification language:

```
// My simple sequential program.
MyModule EXTENDS SingletonSkeleton
{
    Rep {
        printf ("Hello World\n");
    }
}
```

Though it looks quite trivial, the example demonstrates many important aspects of the model and its implementation. MyModule is a parallel computing module that extends the singleton skeleton. Rep corresponds to the representative of the module. When Rep is empty, what we have is an abstract module. Filling in of Rep with application code (in this case, inserting the code for printing the string "Hello World") results in the concrete module, MyModule. Recall that an abstract module is a module without application code.

The back end of MyModule is empty (that is, the module exclusively contains the representative) and hence its internal protocol, P_{Int}, is undefined. The module resembles a single process in the conventional parallel computing terminology. As a standalone module, MyModule has no parent and hence its adaptable external protocol, P_{Ext}, is also void in this case. The module is both the root and the leaf of the single-node *HTree*.

The specification language parser, implemented in Perl, translates the previous code to the following C++ code, inserted in the file Pmain.cc:

```
// Automatically generated file: Pmain.cc.
#include "BasicDef.h"
#include "VoidClass.h"
#include "SingletonSkeleton.h"
// Global definitions will go below:
//---------------------------------------
//---------------------------------------
// Generated code for module: "MyModule"
class MyModule : public SingletonSkeleton <Void>
{
public:
    MyModule() {};
    virtual void Rep() {
        printf ("Hello World\n");
    }
    // Miscellaneous local definitions go below:
    //---------------------------------------
```

```
};
void Pmain()
{
  MyModule TopLevel_524;
  TopLevel_524.Run();
}
```

The automatically generated file, `Pmain.cc`, is subsequently compiled and
linked with the skeleton library to produce the executable, which finally runs on a
cluster of workstations or PCs.

The specification language and its parser merely reduce some of the laborious
and monotonous coding, and implicit details (for instance, choosing the right protocols) on the part of the user. If desired, the user can simply write his application
in pure C++ syntax, thus bypassing the specification language phase.

As the generated code segments suggest, C++ templates are used to realize certain statically configurable parameters associated with the attributes. For instance,
in the previous code, the sole template parameter associated with the singleton
skeleton corresponds to its adaptable external protocol, P_{Ext}. The value `Void` of
the parameter implies that the external protocol is undefined.

12.5.2   A Graphics Animation Application

The following example further elaborates the model and its implementation. It illustrates an irregular composition of modules using the *composite skeleton*. Moreover, it emphasizes on issues like refinement and also illustrates some of the useful features of its present object-oriented implementation (such as automatic data
marshaling and unmarshaling mechanisms; use of operator overloading in C++ to
implement certain primitive operations inside protocol classes).

Let us consider the graphics animation program (Singh et al., 1998) consisting
of three modules: `Generate`, `Geometry` and `Display`. The program takes
a sequence of graphics images, called frames, and animates them. `Generate`
computes the location and motion of each object for a frame. It then passes the
frame to `Geometry`, which performs actions such as viewing transformation,
projection and clipping. Finally, the frame is passed to `Display`, which performs
hidden surface removal and anti-aliasing. Then it stores the frame onto the disk.
After this, `Generate` continues with the processing of the next frame and the
whole process repeats.

One way of implementing this application is as follows. The implementation
uses the *composite skeleton* and the *singleton skeleton*. The composite skeleton
implements the composite pattern, discussed in the previous section. Here, the
`Root` composite module (that is, `Root` extends the composite skeleton) forms
the root of the hierarchy. The three children of `Root` are `Generate`, `Geometry`
and `Display`, and they form the subtrees. Initially each of the three children is
a singleton module, and hence is a leaf of the hierarchy (refer to Figure 12.4(a)).
By default, the three child modules form an all-to-all interconnection topology.

The internal protocol, P_{Int}, associated with the composite skeleton is /break
PROT_Net = {Send(...), Receive(...), Broadcast(...), Spawn(...),...}. PROT_Net be-
comes the external protocol (that is, P_{Ext}) for each of the three children (refer to
Section 12.2).

`GenerateGeometry` and `GeometryDisplay` are user-defined classes
whose data attributes can be marshaled, shipped over a communication link and
then unmarshaled, without the usual hassles of data packing and unpacking. Their
constituent data members are either system defined wrappers of standard data
types or other user defined types. The example also illustrates the use of C++
operator overloading as an alternative way for implementing and using certain
primitive operations inside PROT_Net (for instance: Send(...), Receive(...)).

```
// ***********************************************************
GLOBAL {
// Any global definition may go here.

#include "geom.h"
#define MAXIMAGES 120

// The following defines a marshal-able class.
class GenerateGeometry : public UType {
  Int imageNumber; // "Int" is a System defined
                   // marshalable wrapper for "int"
  ObjTable table;  // "ObjTable" is a marshalable
                   // class defined in "geom.h"
public:
  // Marshal() "this" object
  virtual void Marshal()
//   {imageNumber.Marshal(); table.Marshal();};
  // Unmarshal "this" object
  virtual void UnMarshal()
//   {imageNumber.UnMarshal(); table.UnMarshal();};
  // Constructor(s) etc...
  ...
};

// Another marshalable class definition.
class GeometryDisplay : public UType {
  Int imageNumber;
  Int nPoly;
  PolyTable table; // "PolyTable" is another marshalable
                   // class defined in "geom.h"
public:
  virtual void Marshal() {imageNumber.Marshal();
        nPoly.Marshal(); table.Marshal();};
  virtual void UnMarshal() {imageNumber.UnMarshal();
        nPoly.UnMarshal(); table.UnMarshal();};
  // Constructor(s) etc...
  ...
}
}
// ***********************************************************
// The "Root" module (root of  the  hierarchy).
// Has three children: Generate, Geometry and Display.
Root EXTENDS CompositionalSkeleton
{
```

```
    CHILDREN = Generate, Geometry, Display;
    Rep {
    // Representative code goes here. In this case, the
    // representative has no functionality (it is empty).
    // If needed, Rep can interact with the three children
    // using primitives inside internal protocol PROT_Net.
    }
}
// **********************************************************
// The "Generate" module extends the singleton skeleton.
Generate EXTENDS SingletonSkeleton
{
    // A singleton module can have no children.
    Rep {
        // The representative code goes here.
        int image;
        GenerateGeometry Work;
        for (image = 0; image < MAXIMAGES ; image++){
            ComputeObjects (Work);
            Geometry << Work;
        // The above operation is a member primitive of the
        // external protocol: PROT_Net. An alternative
        // option is to use: Send(Geometry, Work, context).
        }
    }
    // All local definitions go below:
    LOCAL {
        void ComputeObjects(GenerateGeometry& Work)
        {
        // User code for "ComputeObjects" goes here.
        }
    }
}
// **********************************************************
// The "Geometry" module.
Geometry EXTENDS SingletonSkeleton
{
    Rep {
        int image = 0;
        GenerateGeometry Work;
        GeometryDisplay Frame;
        for (image = 0; image < MAXIMAGES ; image++){
            Generate >> Work;
        // The above operation is a member primitive of the
        // external protocol: PROT_Net. An alternative option
        // is to use: Receive(Generate, Work, context).

            DoConversion(Work, Frame);
            Display << Frame;
        }
    }
    LOCAL {
        // local definition of DoConversion(...) goes here.
    }
}
// **********************************************************
// The "Display" module.
Display EXTENDS SingletonSkeleton
{
```

```
Rep {
    int image;
    GeometryDisplay Frame;
    for (image = 0; image < MAXIMAGES ; image++) {
        Geometry >> Frame;
        DoHidden(Frame);
        WriteImage(Frame);
    }
}
LOCAL {
    // Local definitions of DoHidden(...) and
    // WriteImage(...) go here.
}
}
// ****************************************************
```

As in the previous example, the specification language parser automatically generates the front-end C++ file Pmain.cc, which is subsequently compiled and linked with the skeleton-library to generate the executable.

12.5.3   Hierarchical Refinement

It is generally the case that Display module, which performs actions such as hidden surface removal and anti-aliasing, is the most time intensive of the three children modules. Consequently, the singleton Display module is replaced with another module, of identical name, that extends the *replication skeleton*. The replication skeleton implements the replication pattern (refer to the previous section).

The work load of the new Display module is now distributed among dynamically replicated Worker modules, each of which is a child of Display. The internal protocol, P_{Int}, for the replication skeleton is PROT_Repl. Consequently PROT_Repl becomes the external protocol for each replicated child Worker.

Note that none of the other modules is affected by this change. This type of localized replacement, whereby a subtree of the original *HTree* is replaced with another without affecting the rest, is called a *refinement*. The change in the implementation is illustrated next.

```
// The refined "Display" module.
Display EXTENDS ReplicationSkeleton
{
    //The dynamically replicated children of "Display"
    CHILDREN = Worker;
    Rep {
        int image = 0;
        int success;
        GeometryDisplay Frame;
        while (True){
            success = True;
            while ((image < MAXIMAGES) && success){
                Geometry >> Frame;
                // The above operation is a member primitive
                // of the external protocol, PROT_Net.
                image++;
                success = SendWork(Frame);
```

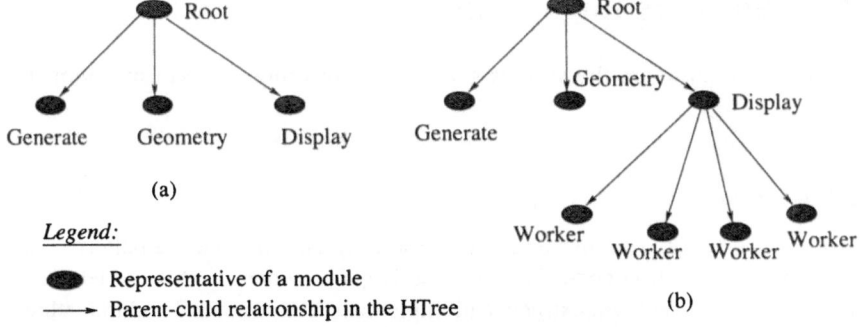

(a)

Legend:

● Representative of a module

——➤ Parent-child relationship in the HTree

(b)

Figure 12.4. HTree before and after refinement.

```
                // The above operation is a member primitive
                // of the internal protocol PROT_Repl.
        }
        if (!success) {// Do it myself, if unsuccessful
                        // in assigning it to a worker.
            DoHidden(Frame);
            WriteImage(Frame);
        }
        if (image == MAXIMAGES) break;
    }
    }
    LOCAL {
    // Local definitions of DoHidden() and WriteImage()
    // go here. They can also be defined globally
    // since these  methods are used in more than one module
    // one module.
    }
}

// Each replicated "Worker" module
Worker EXTENDS SingletonSkeleton
{
    Rep {
        GeometryDisplay Frame;
        ReceiveWork(Frame);
        // The above operation is a member primitive of
        // the external protocol, PROT_Repl.
        DoHidden(Frame);
        WriteImage(Frame);
    }
    LOCAL {
        // Local definitions of DoHidden(...) and
        // WriteImage(...) go here.
    }
}
```

Figure 12.4(a) illustrates the *HTree* before refinement. Figure 12.4(b) illustrates the modified *HTree* after refinement. Note that only the subtree with Display at its root is affected by this change.

12.6   Software Engineering Issues

This section focuses on the various software engineering related aspects of the model.

12.6.1   Reuse

There are two types of reuse we can talk about: (a) reuse of code for patterns, and (b) reuse of application code. The first one is quite evident in this model, since each architectural skeleton extracts and implements the structural and the behavioral attributes associated with a pattern in an application-independent manner. The various parameters associated with these attributes (dimensions of a mesh, width of a divide-conquer tree, and selection of appropriate protocols) enable the same skeleton to be configured to the needs different applications as abstract parallel computing modules. The abstract modules become concrete with the insertion of application code.

Regarding the reuse of application code, it is a known fact that parallel application code is nothing but sequential code with embedded parallelism constructs (calls to primitive methods belonging to various protocol classes). In fact, a parallel application can be viewed as a restructuring of the original sequential code with embedded parallelism constructs. A smart restructuring enables chunks of the original sequential code to be reused. In the graphics animation example, the procedures $DoHidden(...)$, $DoConversion(...)$ and $WriteImage(...)$ are reused, except for minor changes related to the passed parameter type(s), from the original sequential code. Moreover, these reused procedures constitute the majority of the overall application code.

12.6.2   Genericity

Rather than being ad hoc, each architectural skeleton is defined in a generic fashion that is, in a pattern- and application-independent manner with its universal set of attributes. Many useful patterns in parallel computing are realized within the generic model (see Figure 12.3). Each parallel computing module can interact with other modules via standard interfaces (i.e., the representatives), a well-defined set of protocols and using a universal set of rules. The generic approach enhances usability.

12.6.3   Composition Using Patterns

A parallel computing module can contain other modules inside its back end, and thus pattern composition is an inherent property of the model. The *composite skeleton* supports irregular composition of patterns inside the back end, with no restriction on the types of patterns that can be composed (refer to Section 12.4).

Thus, a composite module, which is an extension of the composite skeleton, can contain other composite modules as well. Standard interfaces for all modules and a well-defined adaptation rule make pattern composition feasible.

12.6.4   Hierarchical Refinement

The same set of characteristics of the model that facilitates pattern composition also supports hierarchical refinements of an application. A parallel computing module can be viewed as a black box, where the only part visibile from the outside world is the action of the module, its interface, and its interaction with other modules. As long as these three factors remain unaffected, the module can always be replaced by another module without affecting the rest of the application.

Hierarchical refinement is already illustrated for the graphics animation example in Section 12.5.2, where the singleton `Display` module is refined to a dynamically-replicated module of identical name. Figure 12.4 illustrates the affect of refinement on the hierarchy.

12.6.5   Separation of Concerns

Also known as *separation of specifications*, separation of concerns is a desirable characteristic of all pattern-based approaches. Extracting those components of patterns that are application independent into architectural skeletons leads to a clear separation between application code and application-independent issues. The application-independent components hide most of the low-level details related to process and topology creation, process-processor mapping, communication and synchronization, load balancing, data marshaling and unmarshaling, and numerous other issues. These pre-packaged components are tested to be reliable, provided they are used correctly. Thus, separating these low-level concerns enables the user to concentrate on application-related issues.

12.6.6   Flexibility

Flexibility is one of the major concerns associated with all pattern-based approaches (Singh et al., 1998).

MPI (Gropp et al., 1994) is known to be extremely flexible because of its proven applicability in solving a vast majority of parallel applications known to us at this moment. Often, different solution strategies can be combined in solving an application using MPI. Within the framework of our model, flexibility can be achieved if many of the features of MPI could be supported. This is the main idea behind the composite skeleton and its associated protocol, PROT_Net. The composite skeleton, with the help of its internal protocol PROT_Net, can support many of the useful features of the MPI programming model, and can be used to substitute patterns if an application demands so. Moreover, a composite module is like any other module from the model's perspective, and thus can be used in conjunction with the other patterns supported by the model. This could provide added flexibility to the user.

12.6.7   Extensibility

As mentioned previously, lack of extensibility is another major concern associated with most pattern-based approaches (Singh et al., 1998). Most of these systems are hard-coded with a limited and fixed set of patterns, and often there is no clear way to add new patterns to the system when required.

In contrast, the architectural skeleton approach is intended to be extensible. A couple of factors favor extensibility: (1) the generic approach helps in setting the standard for the various components of a skeleton and their individual functionality. It also sets the standard for pattern composition, interface and interaction. Contrast this with an ad hoc set of skeletons, where adding anything new will only be through sheer brute force technique. (2) The object-oriented and library-based approach favor extensibility. Object-oriented features like polymorphism enable new skeleton classes to be extended from the skeleton base class or from the existing skeleton classes. While designing and implementing a new skeleton, the implementer need to systematically fill in a pre-specified collection of virtual methods.

12.7   Proof of Concept: Experiments and Results

A set of experiments were conducted to assess the system. The set of experiments can be sub-divided into two main categories: performance measurement and software quality measurement.

12.7.1   Performance Measurement

A collection of non-trivial and useful parallel applications were implemented, using both the architectural skeleton approach and direct implementation in MPI. In each case, the speed-up ratio was measured with respect to the best possible sequential application. The underlying hardware was a cluster of Sun Sparc workstations connected with a low-speed Ethernet network. Theoretically, speed-up depends on the granularity (that is, the ratio of computation time to communication overhead) of an application. Significant speed-up was observed for high-granularity applications. For instance, using a cluster of 10 processors, an improvement factor of 6.5 was achieved for a certain image processing algorithm. The observed performance difference with MPI is within 5%, which can be mainly attributed to the fact that the skeleton library is implemented as an extremely thin layer on top of MPI. A detailed discussion about the experiments and the results is beyond the scope of this paper. The interested reader can refer to Goswami et al. (1999a,1999b) and Goswami (2000).

12.7.2   Software Quality Measurement

A comprehensive study was performed to assess the software quality related aspects of the system. The concept of software metrics is well established and a variety of software metrics have been used over time to measure the qualities of software products. In this study, some candidate metrics for measuring software qualities, especially complexity, were collected (e.g., Halstead software science metrics (Halstead, 1977), McCabe's cyclomatic complexity metrics (McCabe and Butler, 1989)). The experiments involved architectural skeletons, Frameworks (Singh et al., 1991), Enterprise (Schaeffer et al., 1993) and direct implementations using MPI. The study suggests that the use of skeletons significantly lowers software complexity as compared to code written from scratch using MPI. Again, a detailed discussion of the study is beyond the scope of this chapter. The interested reader can refer to the works of Ladan and Singh (Tahvildari, 1998; Tahvildari and Singh, 2000).

12.8   Conclusion and Future Directions

The paper presents a generic model for designing and developing parallel applications, and is based on the idea of design patterns. The model is an ideal candidate for implementation using object-oriented techniques. The object-oriented approach has been used to build an application-independent library of skeletons, while keeping in mind extensibility as one of the major issues. Other issues of equal importance were flexibility, reusability, separation of concerns, inherent support for hierarchical pattern composition, and hierarchical refinement.

The present set of architectural skeletons supports those patterns for coarse-grain message-passing computation. They can yield good performance in a networked MIMD environment. Research is in progress to incorporate new skeletons to this environment.

12.9   References

Bartoli, A., Corsini, P., Dini, G., and Prete, C. (1995). Graphical design of distributed applications through reusable components. *IEEE Parallel and Distributed Technology*, 3(1):37-50.

Booch, G., Rumbaugh, J., and Jacobson, I. (1999). *The Unified Modeling Language User Guide*. Addison-Wesley, Reading, MA.

Browne, J., Azam, M., and Sobek, S. (1989). Code: A unified approach to parallel programming. *IEEE Software*, 6(4):10-18.

Browne, J., Hyder, S., Dongarra, J., Moore, K., and Newton, P. (1995). Visual programming and debugging for parallel computing. *IEEE Parallel and Distributed Technology*, 3(1):75-83.

Gamma, E., Helm, R., Johnson, R., and Vlissides, J. (1994). *Design Patterns: Elements of Reusable Object-Oriented Software*. Addison-Wesley, Reading, MA.

Goswami, D. (2000). *Parallel Architectural Skeletons: The Re-Usable Building Blocks in Parallel Applications*. PhD thesis, Department of Electrical and Computer Engineering, University of Waterloo. In preparation.

Goswami, D., Singh, A., and Preiss, B. (1999a). Architectural skeletons: The re-usable building-blocks for parallel applications. In *1999 International Conference on Parallel and Distributed Processing Techniques and Applications (PDPTA'99)*, Las Vegas, NV.

Goswami, D., Singh, A., and Preiss, B. (1999b). Using object-oriented techniques for realizing parallel architectural skeletons. In *The Third International Symposium on Computing in Object-oriented Parallel Environments (ISCOPE'99)*, San Francisco, CA. In Lecture Notes in Computer Science, Vol. 1732, pp 130-141.

Gropp, W., Lusk, E., and Skjellum, A. (1994). *Using MPI: Portable Parallel Programming with the Message-Passing Interface*. MIT Press, Cambridge, MA.

Halstead, M. (1977). *Elements of Software Science*. Elsevier North-Holland.

McCabe, T. and Butler, C. (1989). Design complexity measurement and testing. *Communications of the ACM*, 32(12):1415-1425.

Meszaros, G. and Doble, J. (1997). A pattern language for pattern writing. In *Pattern Languages of Program Design-3*, Software Patterns Series. Addison-Wesley, Reading, MA.

Schaeffer, J., Szafron, D., Lobe, G., and Parsons, I. (1993). The enterprise model for developing distributed applications. *IEEE Parallel and Distributed Technology*, 1(3):85-96.

Schmidt, D. (1994). ACE: an object-oriented framework for developing distributed applications. In *Proceedings. of the Sixth USENIX C++ Technical Conference*, Cambridge, MA.

Singh, A., Schaeffer, J., and Green, M. (1991). A Template-Based Approach to the Generation of Distributed Applications Using a Network of Workstations. *IEEE Transactions on Parallel and Distributed Systems*, 2(1):52-67.

Singh, A., Schaeffer, J., and Szafron, D. (1998). Experience with parallel programming using code templates. *Concurrency: Practice and Experience*, 10(2):91-120.

Siu, S. and Singh, A. (1997). Design patterns for parallel computing using a network of processors. In *Sixth IEEE International Symposium on High Performance Distributed Computing*, pp. 293-304.

Tahvildari, L. (1998). Assessing the impact of using design-pattern-based systems. Master's thesis, Department of Electrical and Computer Engineering, University of Waterloo.

Tahvildari, L. and Singh, A. (2000). Impact of using pattern-based systems on the qualities of parallel applications. In *Proceedings of the International Conference on Parallel and Distributed Processing Techniques and Applications (PDPTA'2000)*, Las Vegas, NV.

Wall, L., Christiansen, T., and Schwartz, R. (1996). *Programming Perl*. O'Reilly & Associates.

Part IV

Tool Support

13
The SPOOL Design Repository: Architecture, Schema, and Mechanisms

Reinhard Schauer
Rudolf K. Keller
Bruno Laguë
Gregory Knapen
Sébastien Robitaille
Guy Saint-Denis

13.1 Introduction

The landscape of reverse engineering is rich in tools for the recovery, quantification, and analysis of source code. Most of these tools, however, cover only a small slice of what the notion of *reverse engineering* promises: "a process of analyzing a subject system to (a) identify the system's components and their interrelationships and (b) create representations of a system in another form at a higher level of abstraction" (Chikofsky and Cross, 1990). These tools hardly take into account that reverse engineering is a process of collaborating activities, rather than a focused task of investigating some specific software property. To be effective, the process of reverse engineering demands that tools communicate and that infrastructure support be provided for their coordination. In the SPOOL project, we have developed and integrated a suite of tools in which each tool addresses a different task of reverse engineering yet allows for easy transfer of the gathered information to other tools for further processing (cf. Chapter 6). At the core of such tool collaboration lies the SPOOL repository.

The SPOOL reverse engineering environment (Figure 13.1) uses a three-tier architecture (Tsichritzis and Klug, 1978; Fowler, 1997) to achieve a clear separation of concerns between the end-user tools, the schema and the objects of the reverse engineered models, and the persistent datastore. The lowest tier consists of an *object-oriented database management system* which provides the physical, persistent datastore for the reverse engineered source code models and the design information. The middle tier consists of the *repository schema*, which is an object-oriented schema of the reverse engineered models, comprising structure

(classes, attributes, and relationships), behavior (access and manipulation functionality of objects), and mechanisms (higher-level functionality, such as complex object traversal, change notification, and dependency accumulation). We
call these two lower tiers the SPOOL *design repository*. The upper tier consists
of end-user tools implementing domain-specific functionality based on the repository schema. This includes tools for the parsing of the source code and its
transformation into the repository schema (*source code capturing*) as well as
tools for the *visualization and analysis* of the source code models. Refer to
Chapter 6 for details about the upper tier and for information on the research that
we conducted based on the SPOOL reverse engineering environment.

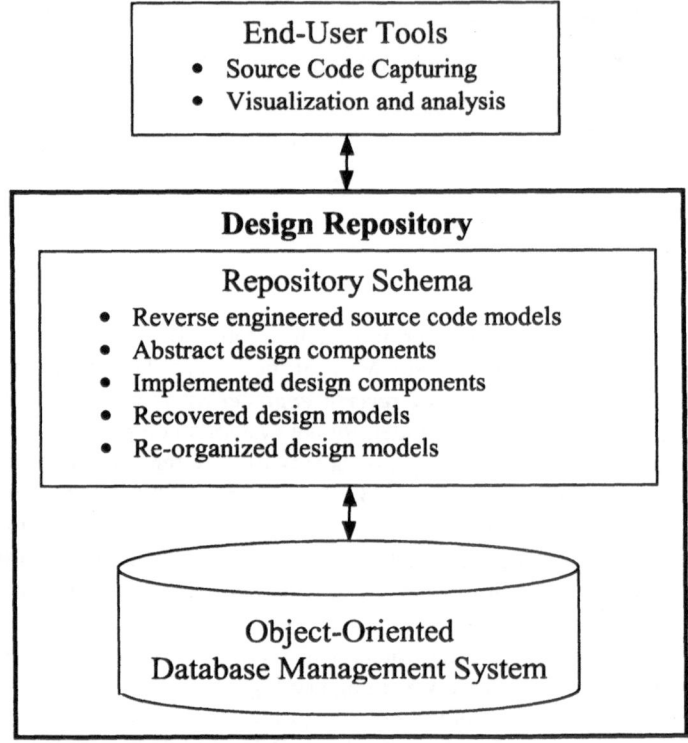

Figure 13.1. Overview of SPOOL reverse engineering environment.

At the core of the SPOOL reverse engineering environment is the SPOOL
design repository, which consists of the repository schema and the physical data
store. The repository schema is an object-oriented class hierarchy that defines
the structure and the behavior of the objects that are part of the reverse engi-

neered *source code models*, the *abstract design components* that are to be identified from the source code, *the implemented design components*, and the *recovered and re-organized design models*. Moreover, the schema provides for more complex behavioral mechanisms that are applied throughout the schema classes, which includes uniform traversal of complex objects to retrieve contained objects, notification to the views on changes in the repository, and dependency accumulation to improve access performance to aggregated information. The schema of the design repository is based on an extended version of the *UML metamodel 1.1* (UML, 1997). We adopted the UML metamodel to the end of reverse engineering as it captures most of the schema requirements of the research activities of SPOOL. This extended UML metamodel (or SPOOL repository schema) is represented as a *Java 1.1* class hierarchy, in which the classes constitute the data of the *MVC-based* (Buschmann et al., 1996) SPOOL reverse engineering environment.

The object-oriented database of the SPOOL repository is implemented using *POET 6.0* (POET, 2000). It provides for data persistence, retrieval, consistency, and recovery. Using the precompiler of POET 6.0's *Java Tight Binding*, an object-oriented database representing the SPOOL repository is generated from the SPOOL schema. As POET 6.0 is ODMG 3.0 (ODMG, 2000) compliant, its substitution of POET 6.0 for another ODMG 3.0 compliant database management system would be accomplishable without major impact on the schema and the end user tools.

In the remainder of this chapter, we first detail the architecture of the SPOOL repository. Next, we explain the SPOOL repository schema and its relation to the UML metamodel, discussing the schema's top-level, core, relationship, behavior, and extension classes. Furthermore, we describe three of the key mechanisms of the repository, that is, the traversal of complex objects, model/view change notification, and dependency management. Finally, as a conclusion, we reflect on the use of the UML metamodel as the basis of the SPOOL repository schema, and provide an outlook into future work.

13.2 Repository Architecture

The major architectural design goal for the SPOOL repository was to make the schema resilient to change, adaptation, and extension, in order to address and accommodate easily new research projects. To achieve a high degree of flexibility, we decided to shield the implementation of the design repository completely from the client code that implements the tools for analysis and visualization. The retrieval and manipulation of objects in the design repository is accomplished via a hierarchy of public Java interfaces, and instantiations and initializations are implemented via *an Abstract Factory* (Gamma et al., 1995). Figure 13.2 illustrates the architecture of the SPOOL design repository.

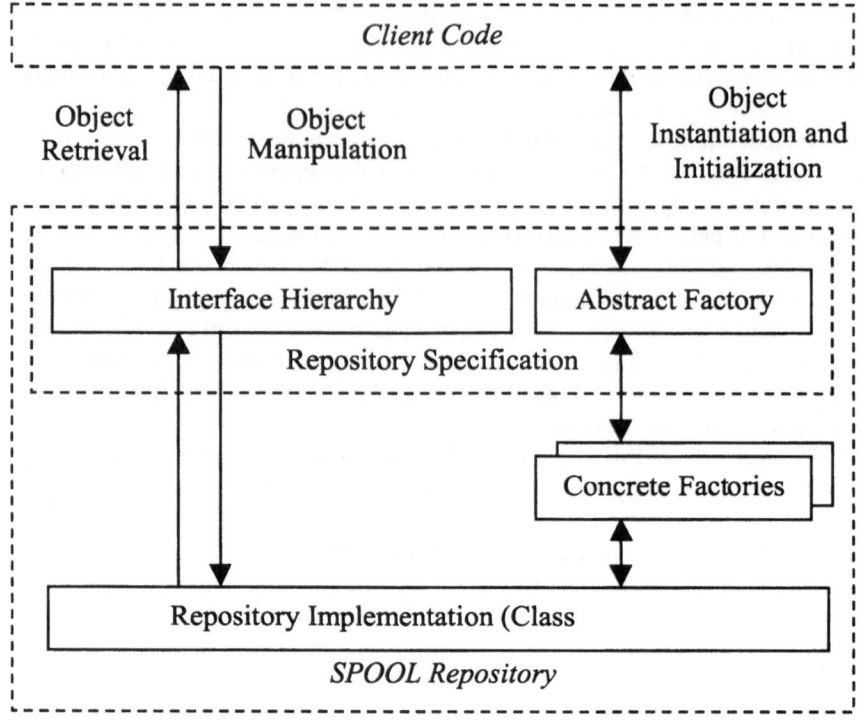

Figure 13.2. SPOOL repository architecture.

The *interface hierarchy* specifies the semantics of the *retrieval* and *manipulation* functionality of the SPOOL repository. Binding the *client code* to interfaces instead of classes yields the benefit that the client code remains unaware of the concrete types and the implementation of the objects it instantiates. This permits changes in the *repository implementation* without affecting the client code, neither at compile nor at run-time, as long as the implementation adheres to the specification of the interfaces. The *Abstract Factory* provides hook methods for object *instantiation* and *initialization*. Instead of instantiating directly the classes of the repository implementation, the client code requests the instantiation of repository classes from the Abstract Factory class, whose subclasses, the *Concrete Factories*, will perform the actual instantiation of the respective classes. The use of the Abstract Factory design pattern proved very helpful as both the instantiated class and the initialization code can vary among the hook methods of the different Concrete Factories. In this way, the access to the SPOOL repository can easily be adapted, in order to meet application-specific needs.

Figure 13.3 shows an excerpt of the interface hierarchy of SPOOL, which defines *IfcModelElement* to be the parent interface of *IfcOperation*, *IfcClass*, and *IfcFile*. These interfaces are implemented with an abstract *ModelElement* as the superclass and *Operation*, *Class*, and *File* as the respective concrete subclasses. The *Client* code is only bound to the interfaces of the hierarchy (not shown in Figure 13.3) and to the Abstract Factory *AbstractModelFactory*, which provides the hook methods *makeOperation*, *makeClass*, and *makeFile* for the instantiation of the respective concrete ModelElement classes. The actual instantiation is encoded in the Concrete Factory class *ModelFactory*, in which, for example, *makeClass* returns an instance of the repository class *Class*.[1]

This design provides to the SPOOL environment the flexibility needed for corrective changes without any effect on the client code, for simplifying testing, and for the adaptation of the repository to client specific requirements. Due to the decoupling of the client code from the repository's implementation code, corrective changes or refactoring measures in any of the classes that implement the repository will not affect the client code, as long as the changes do not violate the expectations of the client code on the interface. For testing purposes, a new implementation of, for example, *Class* (*TestClass*) could be instantiated in a new subclass of the factory *ModelFactory* (*TestModelFactory*) which inherits all instantiation and initialization code from the established *ModelFactory* and may redefine only *makeClass* to instantiate *TestClass* instead of *Class*. The client

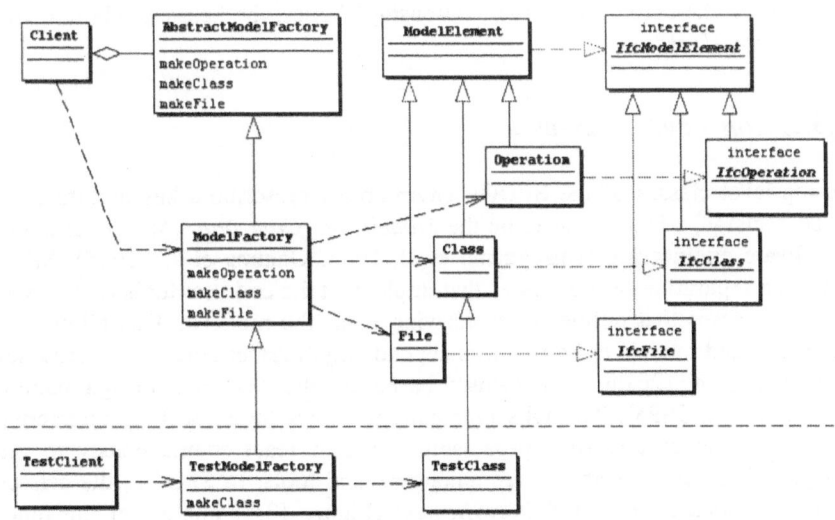

Figure 13.3. Decoupling of client code from SPOOL repository implementation.

---

[1] Note the difference between the notion of *Class* as used in (a) the repository schema to represent the structure and behavior of the reverse engineered system classes and (b) in the Java programming language as the metaclass of all Java classes.

code can then be tested easily by just changing the model factory from *Model-Factory* to *TestModelFactory*. A similar solution may be applied in the case in which a specific client of the repository demands functionality that is not implemented in the default version of the repository. Providing the client with a domain-specific ModelFactory can avoid many changes in the client code that would be inevitable if the client code were directly coupled to the repository's implementation.

13.3 Repository Schema

The schema of the SPOOL repository is an object-oriented class hierarchy whose core structure is adopted from the UML metamodel. Being a metamodel for software analysis and design, the UML provides a well-thought-out foundation for SPOOL as a design comprehension environment. However, SPOOL reverse engineering starts with source code from which design information should be derived. This necessitates extensions to the UML metamodel in order to cover the programming language level as far as it is relevant for design recovery and analysis. In this section, we present the structure of the extended UML metamodel that serves as the schema of the SPOOL repository. This includes the top-level classes, the core classes, the relationship classes, the behavior classes, and the extension classes.

13.3.1 Top-Level Classes

The top-level classes of the SPOOL environment prescribe a key architectural design decision, which is based on the *Model/View/Controller (MVC)* paradigm of software engineering (Buschmann et al, 1996; Gamma et al., 1995). MVC suggests a separation of the classes that implement the end user tools (the views) from the classes that define the underlying data (the models). This allows for both views and models to be reused independently. Furthermore, MVC provides for a change notification mechanism based on the *Observer* design pattern (Gamma et al., 1995). The Observer pattern allows tools, be they interactive analysis or background data processing tools, to react spontaneously to the changes of objects that are shared among several tools. In SPOOL, the classes *Element, ModelElement,* and *ViewElement* (Figure 13.4) implement the functionality that breaks the SPOOL environment apart into a class hierarchy for end-user tools (subclasses of *ViewElement*) and a class hierarchy for the repository (subclasses of *ModelElement*). The root class *Element* prescribes the MVC based communication mechanism between ViewElements and ModelElements. In the following, we describe these three core classes of SPOOL in more detail.

"An *Element* is an atomic constituent of a model" (UML, 1997). It is the abstract superclass from which all SPOOL classes inherit, be they part of the user

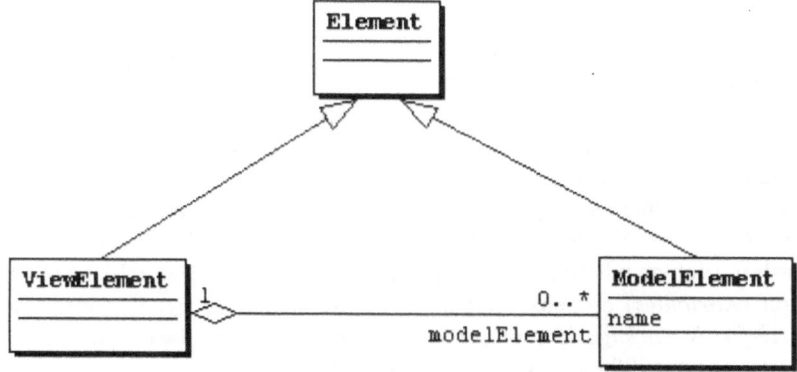

Figure 13.4. SPOOL repository schema: Top-level classes.

interface or part of the repository schema. Like other well-known object-oriented framework architectures, such as Smalltalk and *ET++* (Weinand et al., 1989), the top-level *Element* class provides both the *Subject* and the *Observer* interfaces of the MVC architectural design pattern, allowing in principle every SPOOL object to observe any other SPOOL objects. Note that the design and programming guidelines of SPOOL prohibit that ModelElements observe the state of ViewElements. In SPOOL, dependencies emanate always from the ViewElement class hierarchy towards the ModelElement class hierarchy and *never* vice versa.

"A *ModelElement* is an *Element* that is an abstraction drawn from the system being modeled. Contrast with *ViewElement*, which is an Element whose purpose is to provide a presentation of information for human comprehension" (UML, 1997). Each ModelElement has a name, which must be unique in the namespace (see Core Classes) in which it is embedded. The class hierarchy of ModelElement represents the SPOOL repository schema. It comprises classes that represent the structure and behavior of both the reverse engineered source code models and the higher-level abstractions of the systems that are recovered by the visualization and analysis tools.

"A *ViewElement* is a textual and/or graphical projection of a collection of *ModelElements*" (UML, 1997). The ViewElement class is the abstract root class of the SPOOL tools, which provides the abstract functionality and specifications for rendering of user interface objects, be they complex diagrams or primitive graphic objects. A ViewElement holds on to the ModelElements that provide the data for the visual or textual representation. Upon notification of a change in ModelElements, implemented via the observation mechanism in Element, the ViewElement fetches the relevant data from the respective ModelElements and redraws the relevant parts of its representation.

13.3.2 Core Classes

The core classes of the SPOOL repository schema adhere to a large extent to the classes defined in the core and model management packages of the UML meta-model. These classes define the basic structure and the containment hierarchy of the ModelElements managed in the repository (see Figure 13.5). At the center of the core classes is the *Namespace* class, which owns a collection of ModelElements. A *GeneralizableElement* defines the nodes involved in a generalization relationship, such as inheritance. A *Classifier* provides *Features*, which may be structural (*Attributes*) or behavioral (*Operations* and *Methods*) in nature (see Figure 13.6). A *Package* is a means of clustering ModelElements. In the following, we will detail the Namespace and the Feature classes.

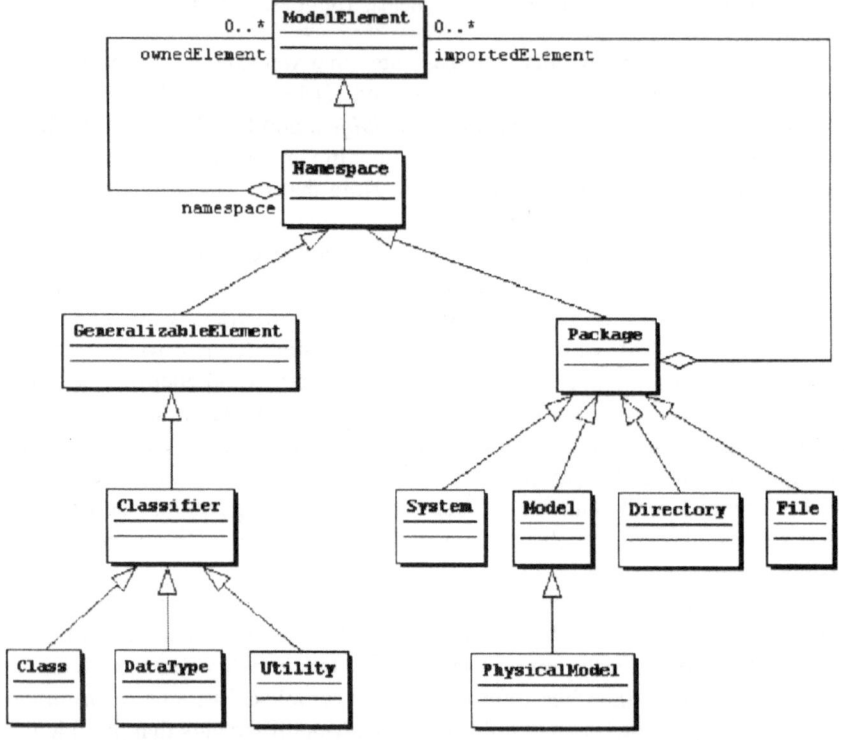

Figure 13.5. SPOOL repository schema: Namespace classes.

"A *Namespace* is a part of a model that contains a set of ModelElements each of whose names designates a unique element within the namespace" (UML, 1997). A Namespace may be viewed as a container for ModelElements, which themselves may be Namespaces. The Namespace defines an owning (or exis-

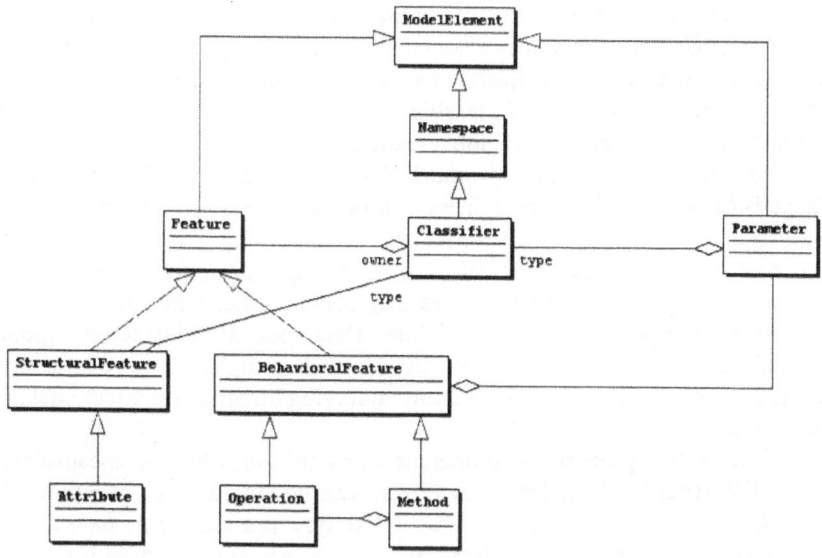

Figure 13.6. SPOOL repository schema: Feature classes.

tence) relationship to these ModelElements, meaning that the contained ModelElements cease to exist if the containing Namespace is deleted from the repository. Examples of Namespaces are classes, unions, files, directories, or whole systems. In SPOOL, the Namespace provides much functionality for retrieval and traversal of complex source code structures, such as directories, which may contain other directories or source code files, which in turn contain classes, which are the containers for methods and attributes, and so forth. As an example of such a traversal routine, the Namespace method *allContainedElements (Method.class)* applied to a whole reverse engineered system returns all methods that are somewhere contained in any class stored in any file of any subdirectory of the system at hand.

"A *GeneralizableElement* is a ModelElement that may participate in a generalization relationship" (UML, 1997). GeneralizableElements are the end points of a Generalization relationship. Refer to the Relationship classes described below for further details on generalization hierarchies. Subclasses of GeneralizableElement are Classifier, an abstract superclass for classes, unions, interface, and alike, and Package, which may be a whole system, a directory, or a file.

"A *Classifier* is an element that describes behavioral and structural features; it comes in several specific forms, including class, data type, interface, component, and others that are defined in other metamodel packages" (UML, 1997). In SPOOL, the Classifier implements all access mechanisms to its features, which are attributes, operations, and methods. Being a subclass of Namespace, Classifier inherits the storage, retrieval, and manipulation functionality for its features from Namespace. Moreover, it allows for nested Classifiers, such as the inner or anonymous classes of Java. A key role in the SPOOL repository plays the *Utility* subclass of Classifier. It serves as a container for all non-member behavioral and structural features, which are declared or defined outside the namespace of a class. Again, being a subclass of Classifier, Utility reuses all repository functionality for the management of such global features.

"A *Package* is a grouping of model elements" (UML, 1997). In SPOOL, Package is the superclass for containers of ModelElements. For example, a typical containment hierarchy of a reverse engineered model starts with a system, which contains physical and logical models. A *PhysicalModel* consists of *Directories* or *Files*, where the Directories may contain other Directories or Files. Files may be composed of Classes, Unions, Datatypes, a Utility for the global code, and alike. The traversal functionality for such complex package structures is inherited from Namespace, which allows querying direct and indirect package containment.

"A *Feature* is a property, like operation or attribute, which is encapsulated within a Classifier" (UML, 1997). A feature can be structural or behavioral in nature. *StructuralFeatures* are *Attributes* whose type is a Classifier. *BehavioralFeatures* can be *Operations* or *Methods*, and they are associated with a set of *Parameters*, which also include the return parameter. In object-oriented literature there is much confusion about the difference between Operations and Methods and, very often, these two notions are used synonymously. However, there is a significant difference between these two notions. The UML defines an Operation as a service that can be requested from an object of a class and a Method as the implementation of an Operation. Whereas an Operation constitutes a specification, a Method provides the executable body of the algorithm implementing the specification. Every Method must have exactly one Operation, which can be inherited from supertypes in the generalization hierarchy. An Operation can be implemented multiple times within its subtype hierarchy.

13.3.3 Relationship Classes

"A relationship is a connection among model elements" (UML, 1997). The UML introduces the notion of Relationship as a superclass of Generalization, Dependency, Flow, and Association for reasons of convenience, so that tools can refer to any connections among ModelElements based on the same supertype (Figure 13.7).

"A *Generalization* is a taxonomic relationship between a more general element and a more specific element. The more specific element is fully consistent with the more general element (it has all of its properties, members, and relationships) and may contain additional information" (UML, 1997). In SPOOL, classes, interfaces, and packages can participate in a generalization relationship, since they all are GeneralizableElements (see section Core Classes). It is common knowledge that classes and interfaces can be organized in form of a generalization hierarchy; however, it is less obvious that packages can participate in a

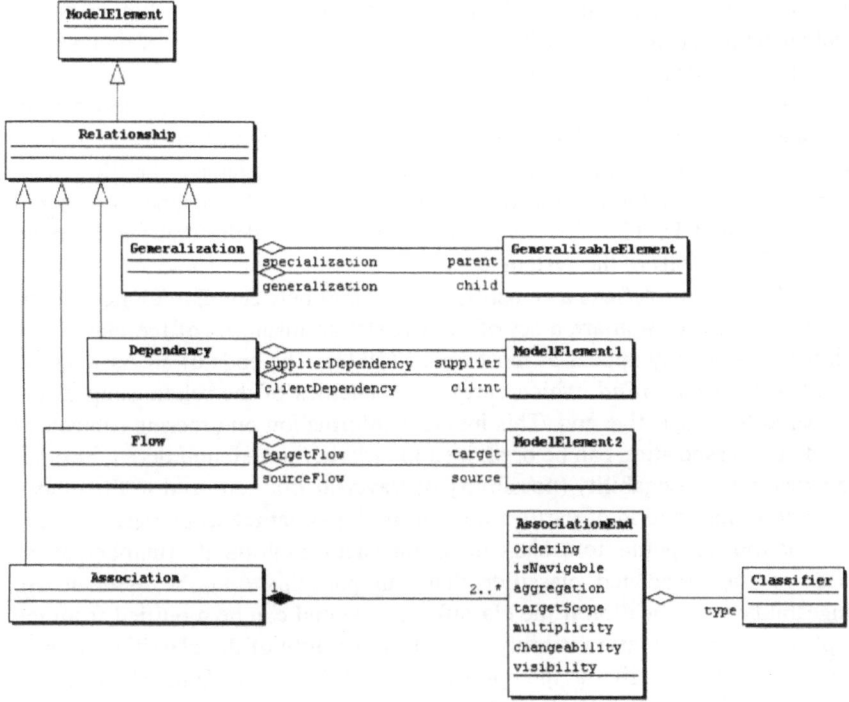

Figure 13.7. SPOOL repository schema: Relationship classes.

generalization hierarchy, too. The purpose of organizing packages in form of a generalization hierarchy is to show design solutions at multiple levels of abstraction. In SPOOL we use package generalization to structure design patterns (Keller et al., 1999). For example, the *Composite* design pattern may be implemented as a *Safe Composite* or a *Transparent Composite*, each having its strength and pitfalls. Refer to Gamma et al. (1995) for more details. At a certain level of design comprehension, however, these differences can or should be ignored, to be able to keep a global overview of the system at hand and not get bogged down into design details.

"A *Dependency* states that the implementation of functioning of one or more elements requires the presence of one or more other elements" (UML, 1997). The UML specifies the modeling of Dependencies as a *client/supplier* relationship between ModelElements and associates to each of the two participating ModelElements the Dependency that serves as the *supplier* (*supplierDependency*) and the one that serves as the *client* (*clientDependency*), respectively. Examples of dependencies as stated by the UML are Bindings, Abstractions, Usage, or Permissions (UML, 1997). We implemented the UML dependency mechanism to allow SPOOL tools to analyze and store semantic relationships among the model elements in the repository. Conforming to the UML metamodel, we also use dependencies to store some structural relationships between model elements, such as friendship relationships among classes of a reverse engineered C++ system.

"A *Flow* is a relationship between two versions of an object or between an object and a copy of it" (UML, 1997). A Flow is directed, it emanates from a source towards a target. In the SPOOL repository, we implement the Flow relationship to provide a foundation for version management for reverse engineered source code models. The objective is to store only the delta that has changed between two versions of the system at hand.

"An *Association* defines a semantic relationship between classifiers. The instances of an association are a set of tuples relating instances of the classifiers. Each tuple value may appear at most once" (1997). The ends of an Association are called *AssociationEnd*, which carry the semantics of the relationship to the classifier at the respective end. This includes information on ordering (objects at the end of an association can be organized in ordered, sorted, unordered, or other data structures), navigability (possibility of traversal from one end to the other), aggregation (designation of part/whole relationships), target scope (specification if the relationship points to a class or an instance), multiplicity (number of instances of the associated classifier that can participate in the association), changeability (specification if the classifier at one end can be modified from the one of the other end), and visibility (specifies visibility of the classifier at association end to the classifier at the opposite end). Refer to the UML (UML, 1997) for more details on the semantics of these attributes. Note that the derivation of Associations and the attributes of the AssociationEnds is not a straightforward task. The goal of the SPOOL reverse engineering environment is to provide human-controlled tool support to this end.

13.3.4 Behavior Classes

The behavior classes of the SPOOL repository implement the dynamics of the reverse engineered system. It is important to understand that the UML metamodel takes a forward engineering perspective and focuses on software analysis and design, rather than on the reverse engineering of source code. Therefore, the UML metamodel does not aim to encompass and unify programming language constructs.

The purpose of analysis and design is to specify what to do and how to do it, but it is the later stage of implementation in which the missing parts of a specification are filled to transform it into an executable system. However, the UML is comprehensive in that it provides a semantic foundation for the modeling of any specifics of a model. For example, the UML suggests State Machine diagrams (similar to Harel's Statechart formalism (Harel, 1988)) to specify the behavior of complex methods, operations, or classes. To cite another example, collaboration diagrams can be used to specify how different classes or certain parts of classes (that is, roles) have to interact with each other in order to solve a problem that transcends the boundaries of single classes.

In SPOOL, we look at a system from the opposite viewpoint, that is, from the complete source code, and the goal is to derive these behavior specification models to get an improved understanding of the complex relationships among a system's constituents. For this purpose, we included in the SPOOL repository the key constructs of the behavior package of the UML metamodel, including the Action and Collaboration classes presented below. However, we modified certain parts to reduce space consumption and improve performance.

Action Classes

"An *Action* is an executable atomic computation that results in a change in state of the system or the return of a value" (Booch et al., 1999). The SPOOL repository uses Actions to describe the internals of a method. Figure 13.8 shows the corresponding diagram.

The UML metamodel embeds Actions into State Machines and Collaborations, which would result in an extra StateMachine object for each method of the reverse engineered system. In SPOOL, we provide a shortcut and save the set of Actions directly with the Method and provide access as well as manipulation routines for Actions as part of the SPOOL schema class Method. This improves performance of many queries on the SPOOL repository as it avoids indirection

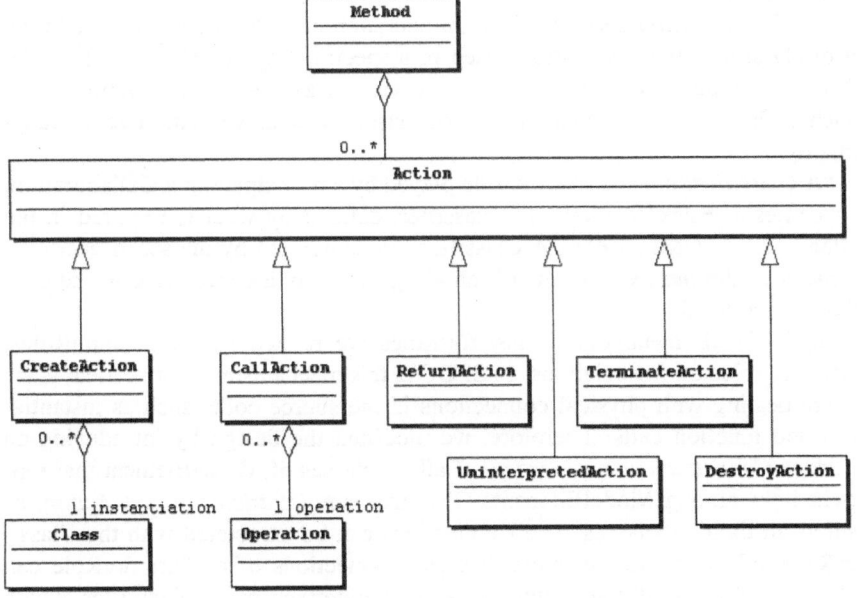

Figure 13.8. SPOOL repositoy schema: Action classes.

via StateMachine objects. Furthermore, the UML specifies many different subclasses of Action, which include *CreateAction, CallAction, ReturnAction, TerminateAction, UninterpretedAction,* and *DestroyAction* (UML, 1997). We implemented all of these classes, but as the SPOOL analysis tools that we implemented so far are based on CreateActions and CallActions only, we do not import all this information into the SPOOL repository. This reduces the overall size of the physical datastore, which in turn improves the performance of many analysis tools. Note that at any time objects instantiating any of the Action subclasses can be imported, as the integrated Datrix parsers (Datrix, 2000) generate all the necessary information. Such an extension would not affect the existing SPOOL visualization and analysis tools.

Collaboration Classes

One of the key goals of the SPOOL reverse engineering environment is to provide support for the extraction of predefined design concepts, such as the structures of design patterns, from source code. We call the design concepts to be recovered abstract design components and the recovered instances of these design concepts implemented design components. The notion of design component alludes to the fact that these conceptual fragments of the overall design are managed as entities that may be used as the building blocks in a compositional design process (Keller and Schauer, 1998). In SPOOL, we implemented a simplified version of the Collaboration package defined by the UML metamodel (Figure 13.9).

"A *Collaboration* describes how an operation or a classifier is realized by a set of classifiers and associations used in a specific way" (UML, 1997). In the UML metamodel, a Collaboration can be viewed as a set of interacting roles, which define the communication among classes to achieve some overall functionality.

"A *ClassifierRole* is a specific role played by a participant in a Collaboration. It specifies a restricted view of a classifier, defined by what is required in the collaboration" (UML, 1997). A ClassifierRole is defined by the set of *available Features* of the *base* Classifier, which altogether play a certain role in the Collaboration at hand.

In the UML metamodel, ClassifierRoles are related by AssociationRoles, which are roles on Associations. In SPOOL, this mechanism is not needed, since we are dealing with physical connections in the source code, such as instantiations and function calls. Therefore, we modified the design by introducing an interface *Connection* as a supertype of all subclasses of ModelElement that represent links among ModelElements. This includes *Relationship* and *Action*, as well as all their subclasses. The Connections can be associated with the ClassifierRoles of Collaboration. Note that the Connections of a ClassifierRole can only be a subset of all the Connections that are defined by the Classifier, which is the base of the ClassifierRole.

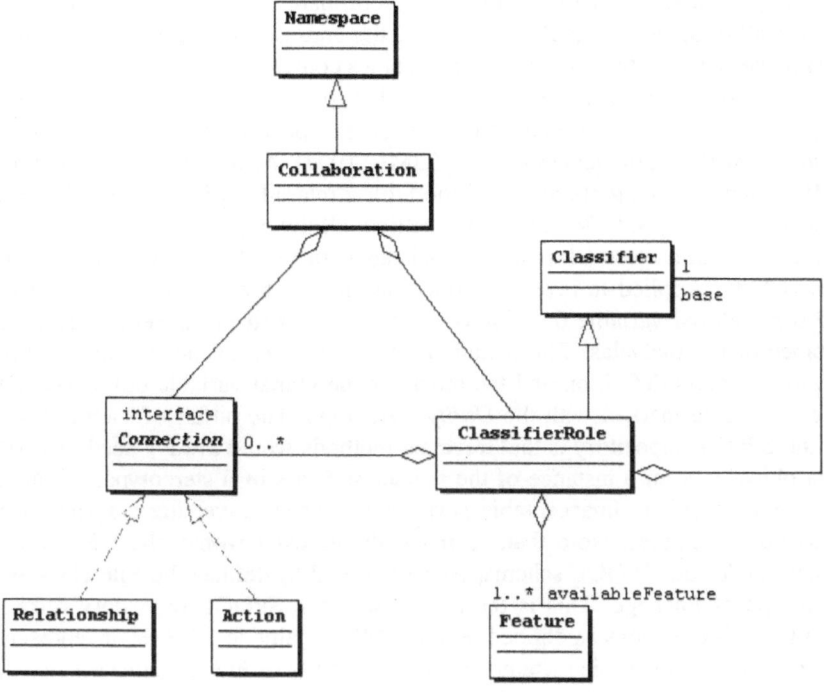

Figure 13.9. SPOOL repositoryschema: Collaboration classes.

13.3.5 Extension Classes

The UML metamodel suggests two approaches to metamodel extension; one is based on the concept of TaggedValues and the other on the concept of Stereotypes. In SPOOL, we have only implemented the former approach (Figure 13.10) since Stereotypes as defined in the UML metamodel would not scale to meet the performance requirements of the SPOOL repository.

"A *TaggedValue* is a (Tag, Value) pair that permits arbitrary information to be attached to any ModelElement" (UML, 1997). In programming languages, the concept of TaggedValue is known under the notion of property. Using Tagged-Values, the end-user tool can plug into any ModelElement any tool-specific data.

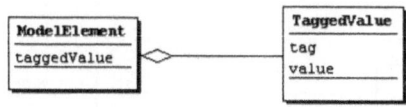

Figure 13.10. SPOOL repository schema: TaggedValue extension class.

This may include information on color, layout, paths, aliases, and the like. The interpretation of the TaggedValue is up to the end-user tool, and different tools must make sure that they use the TaggedValues consistently.

"The *Stereotype* concept (Figure 13.11) provides a way of classifying (marking) elements so that they behave in some respects as if they were instances of new *virtual* metamodel constructs" (UML, 1997). As a concrete example, the UML metamodel suggests to model the Utility (classifiers for non-member features) as a stereotyped *Class*. In such a setting, Utility objects would be instances of the UML metaclass Class and associated with the Stereotype object of the name Utility. Applied to reverse engineering, a C++ file with a class definition and some global variable definitions would be mapped in the repository as an instance of the metaclass File containing two instances of the metaclass Class, one for the class definition and the other for the global variable definition. The latter would be marked with the *Utility* stereotype. The pitfall of such a design for the SPOOL repository is that traversal methods would always need to verify if an object is a pure instance of the metaclass Class or a stereotyped instance. This would result in unacceptable performance when traversing a system with thousands of classes. Note that, to make things even worse, the UML metamodel, unlike the SPOOL schema, (see Figure 13.5) defines the File class as a stereotype of Package. This is the reason why the SPOOL repository refrains from using Stereotypes as defined by the UML metamodel. Rather, it represents all extensions to the basic metamodel, such as Utility or File, as subclasses of the metaclass Namespace. Thus, each ModelElement has an unambiguous type of its metaclass, and the Namespace traversal methods can use the Java *instanceof* operator to identify the type of a ModelElement.

13.4 Repository Mechanisms

To be usable and reusable as the backend for a diverse set of interactive reverse engineering tools, the SPOOL repository implements a number of advanced mechanisms. The *traversal mechanism* defines how to retrieve objects of certain types from a complex object containment hierarchy. *The observation mechanism* defines model/view change notification that goes beyond the Observer pattern.

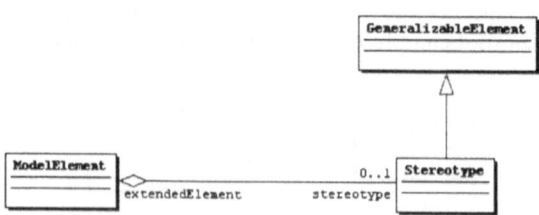

Figure 13.11. SPOOL repository schema: Stereotype extension class.

The *dependency mechanism* allows for compression of the vast amount of dependencies among ModelElements for fast retrieval and visualization.

13.4.1 Traversal Mechanism

In SPOOL, the Namespace serves as a container for a group of ModelElements (Figure 13.5). Consequently, it defines methods that traverse complex object structures and retrieve ModelElements of a given type. For example, to identify all classes of a system, all files in all subdirectories of the system at hand must be checked for instances of the metatype Class. Unlike the objects in text-based repositories (Wong and Müller, 1998; Holt, 1997), the objects in SPOOL's object-oriented database are typed and can be queried according to their types. SPOOL allows for the identification of the type of an object merely by using the Java *instanceof* operator or the reflective *isInstance* operation of the Java class *Class*. Hence, metaclass types can be provided as parameters to the retrieval methods of Namespace, which then recursively traverse the containment hierarchy of the namespace at hand and examine each ModelElement whether it is an instance of that type. If this is the case, the ModelElement is added to a return set, which is passed through the recursive traversal. The following code snippet shows the implementation of the method *allContainedElements* of the SPOOL repository class Namespace.

```
public void allContainedElements(Class aMetaClass, Set returnSet) {
    // elements() returns an iterator over the direct content
    // of a namespace
    Enumeration enum = elements();
    while (enum.hasMoreElements()) {
        ModelElement modelElem = (ModelElement) enum.nextElement();
        if (aMetaClass.isInstance(modelElem))
            returnSet.add(modelElement);
        if (modelElem instanceof Namespace)
            ((Namespace) modelElem).
                    allContainedElements(aMetaClass, returnSet);
    }
}
```

The above version of *allContainedElements* accepts two parameters, the first specifies the type of the instances of ModelElement to be retrieved and the second accepts a Set in which the retrieved ModelElements are to be returned. For each ModelElement of the Namespace to which *allContainedElements* is applied, this method first verifies if the ModelElement at hand is an instance of the type passed as parameter; if so, it is added to the return set. Then, it checks if the ModelElement is itself an instance of a Namespace, in which case *allContainedElements* is recursively applied to this sub-Namespace. Recall that the SPOOL repository schema is an object-oriented class hierarchy and, therefore, traversal and retrieval operations can also use abstract superclasses or interfaces to identify ModelElements of any of the derived subclasses. This is very helpful for SPOOL tools to query the content of the repository. In many cases, there is no need to change the client code if the repository schema is, for example, extended with a new leaf class. Client code that is bound to the interface of an abstract superclass of the SPOOL repository schema will automatically receive objects of the new subclass.

13.4.2 Observation Mechanism

A general goal of the design of the SPOOL repository is to serve as the backend for interactive reverse engineering tools. Multiple end-user tools should be able to work in parallel without sacrificing data consistency. This calls for a change notification mechanism that informs running tools about manipulations in the repository. Hence, SPOOL is based on the Model/View/Controller architectural design pattern (Buschmann et al., 1996), which separates the user interfaces (the ViewElement class hierarchy) from the application data (the ModelElement class hierarchy) and allows for the synchronization of multiple user interfaces on the same data.

Applying MVC out of the textbook to the vast amount of data that is typically stored in the SPOOL repository would soon degenerate overall performance due to considerable runtime overhead for model/view coordination (Vlissides, 1998). For example, ET++ (Weinand et al., 1989), a small-sized C++ application framework for graphic user interfaces of about 70,000 lines of C++ source code contains about 600 classes with 7,000 methods. If we loaded all of these 600 classes with all 7000 methods into a class diagram, and applied the pure Observer design pattern to coordinate the views with possible model changes, this would result into 7,600 graphic representations each hooked into their model counterparts upon creation of a system's class diagram. Vice versa, when the class diagram is closed, these views would need to be removed again from their respective models. As another example, consider source code clustering tools, which usually shift many classes and other model elements around in the system to be re-organized. Their performance would greatly suffer from a model that generated thousands of change notification messages for each removal of a ModelElement from one Namespace and its subsequent addition to another Namespace. In theory, the SPOOL repository would allow such a strategy, but in practice this is only feasible for small-sized diagrams, where message passing does not lead to a performance bottleneck.

In SPOOL, we implemented another strategy for model/view change notification. Diagrams as a whole, such as the tree directory diagram (left part of Figure 13.12) and the class diagram (right part of Figure 13.12), are hooked into the namespaces that they represent, which is in the given case the whole system ET++ (Weinand et al., 1989). When a ModelElement of any part of the system is

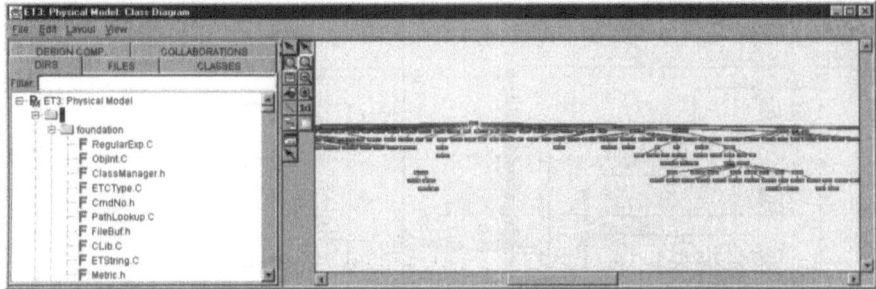

Figure 13.12. View synchronization via SPOOL's observation mechanism.

updated or a ModelElement is added or removed, the SPOOL repository propagates notification of the change to all containers of this ModelElement. If a view observes any of these containers it will be notified of the change. In Figure 13.12, for instance, if a method is deleted from any class, the SPOOL repository generates a change event indicating this update, and propagates it along the container path, which includes the class, the file of the class, all directories in which this file is contained, the physical model that holds the reverse engineered code, and finally the system as the outermost container. As the tree directory diagram and the class diagram are hooked into the system, they receive this event, which includes information about what and where the event occurred. As a result, each diagram can identify the changed element in its containment hierarchy and execute the appropriate update on its visual representation. This avoids the problem of too many runtime links between models and observers; however, it does not address the problem that every change results in an event that is separately passed on to the observing views.

The manipulation of ModelElements in the SPOOL repository is performed based on transactions. To guarantee consistency among end-user tools, the SPOOL repository caches all change events in what SPOOL calls aggregate event sets. These sets aggregate all changes of the SPOOL repository within a transaction. When the transaction is finished, all view elements that hook into one of the changed model elements or any of its containers are notified of the change and receive the set of changed model elements they are observing. Normally, such aggregate event sets can significantly reduce message passing between models and views.

13.4.3 Accumulated Dependency Mechanism

An important requirement of the SPOOL repository is to provide information on dependencies between any pair of ModelElements within interactive response time. Figure 13.13 illustrates this requirement in more detail.

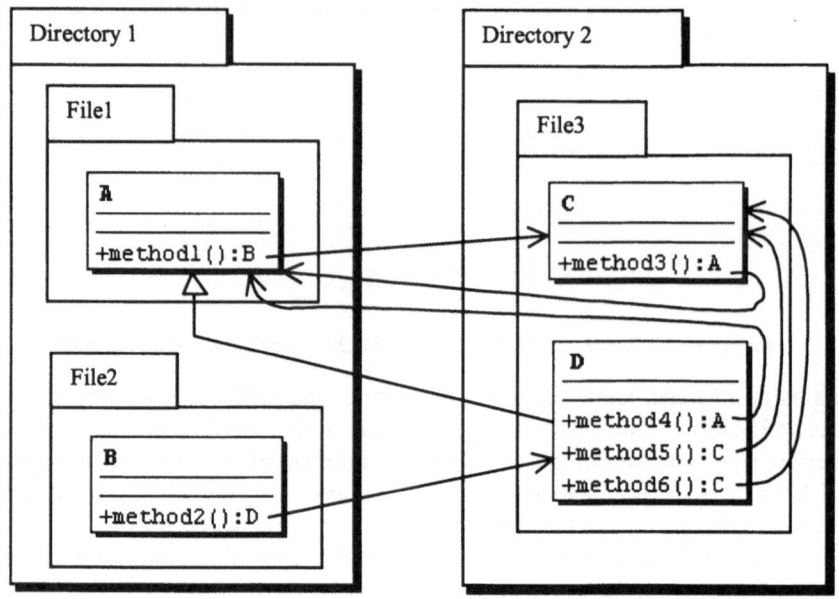

Figure 13.13. Dependencies between Model Elements.

The directory *Directory1* of Figure 13.13 consists of the two files *File1*, which contains the class *A*, and *File2*, which contains the class *B*. Directory *Directory2* consists of the file *File3*, which contains the two classes *C* and *D*, where *D* is a subclass of *A*. The return type of the method *method1* is *C*, the return type of the method *method2* is *D*, the return type of the methods *method3* and *method4* is *A*, and the return type of the methods *method5* and *method6* is *C*. In this diagram, there are seven connections among ModelElements. Six connections are defined by the return types (*ReturnType* connection) of the methods, and one connection is defined for the generalization relationship (*Generalization* connection) between *A* and *D*. According to the above mentioned requirement, end-user tools should be able to identify, within interactive response time, whether there are any connections between, say, the two top-level directories *Directory1* and *Directory2*, the directory *Directory1* and the method *method3* of class *C*, or the file *File2* and the class *D*, and display them in dependency diagrams.

Figure 13.14, for example, shows such a dependency diagram for the top-level directories of the system ET++ (Weinand et al., 1989). A property dialog box can be opened to inspect the nature of a specific dependency. In Figure 13.14, for instance, the dependency between the directories *CONTAINER* and *foundation* includes 13 generalization connections, 50 feature type connections (types of attributes and return types of operations and methods), 541 parameter type connections, 5 class instantiation connections (*CreateAction*), 498 operation

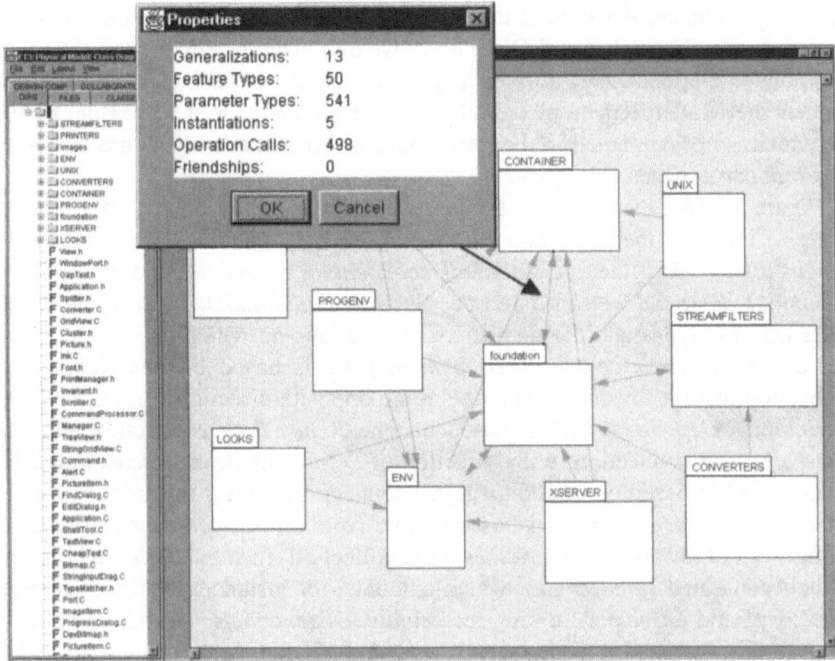

Figure 13.14. SPOOL dependency diagram with dialog box for inspection of properties.

call connections (*CallAction*), and 0 friendship connections. On demand, the dialog can also be invoked for each direction of a dependency.

A straightforward approach to identify dependencies among ModelElements would be the traversal of the whole object structure at run-time. However, applied to reverse engineered software with directories that contain hundreds of files, this approach would require batch processing. A radically different approach would be to store each and every dependency among ModelElements as separate dependency objects, which would result in an unmanageable amount of dependency data. In the small example of Figure 13.13, this would amount to an overall of 36 dependency objects. Hence, the solution that we adopted in SPOOL constitutes a trade-off between run-time efficiency and space consumption.

In SPOOL, we capture and accumulate dependencies at the level of Classifiers (for instance, classes, unions, or utilities). Accumulation refers to the fact that we store for each dependency its types together with the total number of primitive Connections on which each type is based. Given a pair of dependent Classifiers, we generate a so-called *AccumulatedDependency* object, which captures this information for the dependencies in the two directions. To be able to identify dependencies between higher-level namespaces, such as directories, files, or packages, without much lag time, we store the union of all AccumulatedDependencies of all contained Classifiers of a given Namespace redundantly with the

Namespace. Hence, if we want to identify, for example, dependencies between the directories *Directory1* and *Directory2*, we only need to iterate over the set of AccumulatedDependencies of *Directory1* and look up for each element of the set whether the ModelElement at the other end of the element at hand (that is, the one which is not contained in the Namespace under consideration) has as one of its parent namespaces *Directory2*.

Figure 13.15 illustrates the *AccumulatedDependencies* of our previous example. *A* includes the *AccumulatedDependencies* #1 and #2, *B* the *AccumulatedDependency* #3, *C* the *AccumulatedDependencies* #1 and #4, and finally *D* the *AccumulatedDependencies* #2 and #3. Each *AccumulatedDependency* is designated with the types and the number of connections on which it is based, in either direction. The *AccumulatedDependency* #1 is based on one *ReturnType* connection from *A* towards *C* and one in the opposite direction from *C* to *A*, the *AccumulatedDependency* #2 is based on one *ReturnType* connection and one *Generalization* connection in the direction of *D* towards *A*, the *AccumulatedDependency* #3 is based on one *ReturnType* connection from *B* towards *D*, and the *AccumulatedDependency* #4 is based on two type *ReturnType* connections emanating from *D* towards *C*. All *Namespaces* collect all *AccumulatedDependencies* of their contained *Namespaces*, which amounts, for instance, for the directories *Directory1* and *Directory2* to the *AccumulatedDependencies* #1, #2, and #3, for *File1* to the *AccumulatedDependencies* #1 and #2, for *File2* to the *Accumulat-*

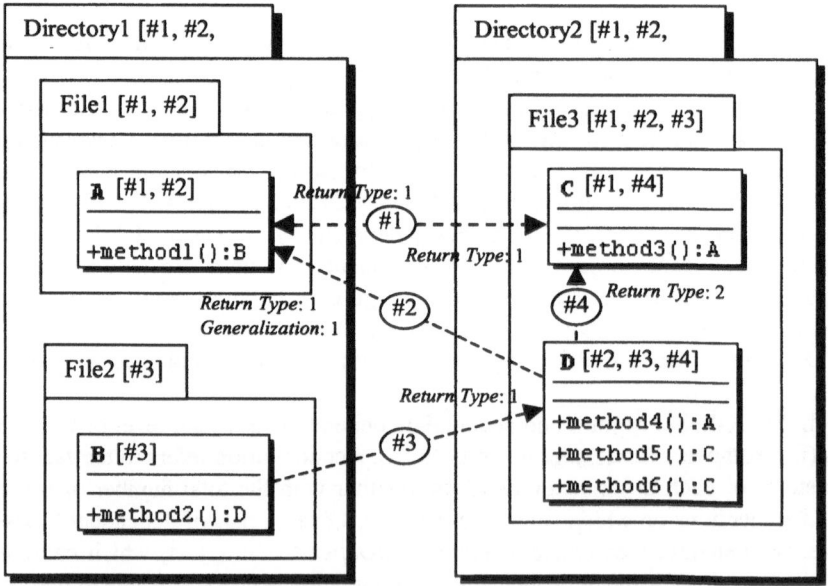

Figure 13.15. Accumulated Dependencies between Model Elements.

edDependency #3, and for *File3* to the *AccumulatedDependencies* #1, #2, and #3.

13.5 Conclusion

The authors of the UML, Booch, Jacobson, and Rumbaugh, acknowledge that "reverse engineering is hard; it's easy to get too much information from simple reverse engineering, and so the hard part is being clever about what details to keep" (Booch et al., 1999). Reverse engineering is the human-controlled process of transforming the flood of detailed information contained in source code into structural and behavioral models at higher levels of abstraction. These are meant for easy comprehension of complex system interrelations, and the UML with its nine different kinds of diagrams was designed to this end. The authors of the UML emphasize that the purpose of the UML is not to provide a mere notation for forward engineering; rather, the UML was devised both "to allow models to be transformed into code and to allow code to be re-engineered back into models" (Booch et al., 1999).

The UML is hardly accepted in the reverse engineering community. Demeyer et al. have articulated some reasons for the "why not UML" (Demeyer et al., 1999). We wholeheartedly agree that there is a lack of complete and precise mappings of programming languages to the UML. However, we consider this as a challenge for researchers, rather than a reason for abandoning the UML. With its Stereotype extension mechanism, the UML does provide constructs to capture the many details of source code written in different programming languages. The issue at hand is to define unambiguously how to map the various UML constructs to source code constructs and to provide tool support for the traceability in both directions. A second argument of Demeyer et al. against the UML is that it "does not include dependencies, such as invocations and accesses" (Demeyer et al., 1999). This constitutes yet another misconception in the reverse engineering community about the UML. All too often, the UML is looked at as a notation for structure diagrams only, and all other diagrams are rather neglected. Yet, the behavior package of the UML metamodel provides a precise specification of the method internals. However, a critique against the UML may be that the behavioral package is too heavyweight to be directly applicable to reverse engineering. It is impossible to generate and store for each method a StateMachine object together with all its internal objects. In SPOOL, we implemented a shortcut solution for the representation of the bulk of the methods. We associated Actions directly to methods instead of generating StateMachines, which consist of Actions that are invoked by Messages. Refer to the UML for further details on the structure of StateMachines (Booch et al., 1999). We do, however, allow StateMachines to be reverse engineered and stored for methods or classes of interest.

The UML has several advantages. First, the UML metamodel is well documented and based on well-established terminology. This is of great help to convey the semantics of the different modeling constructs to tool developers. Second, the metamodel is designed for the domain of software design and analysis, which is the target of the reverse engineering process. The UML introduces constructs at a high level of granularity, enabling the compression of the overwhelming amount of information that makes source code difficult to understand. Third, the UML metamodel is object-oriented, meaning that the structure, the basic access and manipulation behavior, and complex mechanisms can be separated from end-user tools and encapsulated in the repository schema. Fourth, the UML defines a notation for the metamodel constructs, thus providing reverse engineering tool builders guidelines for the visual representation of the model elements.

Adopting the UML in the SPOOL environment has proven to be one of the most important and beneficial decisions of our project. In this chapter, we have described how the UML can be matched to reverse engineering, and what benefits can be reaped. We are not aware of any other implementation of the UML metamodel for reverse engineering purposes; the SPOOL repository constitutes a proof-of-concept of such an implementation.

In our future work on the SPOOL design repository, we will aim to provide complete and precise mappings between the constructs of the UML-based SPOOL repository schema and the four programming languages C, C++, Java, and a proprietary language deployed by Bell Canada. We will also increase the information content of the SPOOL repository in respect to dynamic behavior. As discussed previously, a balance between space consumption and fast response time needs to be sought. One solution that we will investigate is parsing the source code of methods on the fly when querying, for example, control flow information. A third area of work will be to provide Web-based access to the repository, which will allow our project partners to remotely check in source code systems and immediately use SPOOL tools to query and visualize the repository content.

13.6 References

Booch, B., Jacobson, I., and Rumbaugh, J. (1999). *The Unified Modeling Language User Guide*. Addison-Wesley, Reading, MA.

Buschmann, F., Meunier, R., Rohnert, H., Sommerlad, P., and Stal, M. (1996). *Pattern-Oriented Software Architecture - A System of Patterns*. John Wiley and Sons, New York.

Chikofsky, E. J., and Cross, J. H. II (1990). Reverse engineering and design recovery: A taxonomy. *IEEE Software*, 7(1):13-17, January 1990.

Datrix (2000). Datrix homepage. Bell Canada. On-line at <http://www.iro.umontreal.ca/labs/gelo/datrix/>.

Demeyer, S., Ducasse, S., and Tichelaar, S. (1999). Why unified is not universal. UML shortcomings for coping with round-trip engineering. In *Bernhard Rumpe, editor, Proceedings UML'99 (The Second International Conference on the Unified Modeling Language)*. Springer-Verlag, New York, 1999. LNCS 1723.

Fowler, M. (1997). *Analysis Patterns. Reusable Object Models*. Addison-Wesley, Reading, MA.

Gamma E., Helm, R., Johnson, R., and Vlissides, J. (1995). *Design Patterns: Elements of Reusable Object-Oriented Software*. Addison-Wesley.

Harel, D. (1988). On visual formalisms. *Communications of the ACM*, 31(5):514-530, May 1988.

Holt, R. C. (1997). Software Bookshelf: Overview and construction. March 1997. On-line at <http://www-turing.cs.toronto.edu/pbs/papers/>.

Keller, R. K., and Schauer, R.. (1998). Design components: towards software composition at the design level. In *Proceedings of the 20th International Conference on Software Engineering*, Kyoto, Japan, pages 302-310, April 1998.

Keller, R. K., Schauer, R., and Lague, B. (1999). Pattern-based reverse engineering of design components. In *Proceedings. of the 21st International Conference on Software Engineering*, Los Angeles, CA, pages 226-235, May 1999.

ODMG (2000). Object Data Management Group (ODMG). On-line at <http://www.odmg.com>.

POET (2000). Poet Java ODMG binding, on-line documentation. Poet Software Corporation. San Mateo, CA. On-line at <http://www.poet.com>.

Tsichritzis, D. and Klug, A. C. (1978). The ANSI/X3/SPARC DBMS framework report of the study group on dababase management systems. *Information Systems*, 3(3):173-191, Pergamon Press Ltd.

UML (1997). Documentation set version 1.1. Available at <http://www.rational.com>.

Vlissides, J. (1998). Pattern Hatching. Design Patterns Applied. Addison-Wesley, Reading, MA.

Weinand, A., Gamma, A., and Marty, R.. (1989). Design and implementation of ET++, a seamless object-oriented application framework. *Structured Programming*, 10(2):63-87, February 1989.

Wong, K. and Müller, H. (1998). Rigi user's manual, version 5.4.4, University of Victoria, Victoria, Canada. On-line at <ftp://ftp.rigi.csc.uvic.ca/pub/>.

14
The Software Bookshelf

Patrick Finnigan
Richard C. Holt
Ivan Kalas
Scott Kerr
Kostas Kontogiannis
Hausi A. Müller
John Mylopoulos
Stephen G. Perelgut
Martin Stanley
Kenny Wong

14.1 Introduction

Legacy software systems are typically complex, geriatric, and difficult to change, having evolved over decades and having passed through many developers. Nevertheless, these systems are mature, heavily used, and constitute massive corporate assets.

Migrating such systems to modern platforms is a significant challenge due to the loss of information over time. As a result, we embarked on a research project to design and implement an environment to support software migration. In particular, we focused on migrating legacy PL/I source code to C++, with an initial phase of looking at redocumentation strategies.

Recent technologies such as reverse engineering tools and World Wide Web standards now make it possible to build tools that greatly simplify the process of redocumenting a legacy software system. In this chapter we introduce the concept of a software bookshelf as a means to capture, organize, and manage information about a legacy software system.

We distinguish three roles directly involved in the construction, population, and use of such a bookshelf: the builder, the librarian, and the patron. From these perspectives, we describe requirements for the bookshelf, as well as a generic architecture and a prototype implementation. We also discuss various parsing and analysis tools that were developed and integrated to assist in the recovery of useful information about a legacy system. In addition, we illustrate how a software bookshelf is populated with the information of a given software project and how the bookshelf can be used in a program-understanding scenario. Reported results are based on a pilot project that developed a prototype book-shelf for a software system consisting of approximately 300K lines of code written in a PL/I dialect.

Software systems age for many reasons. Some of these relate to the changing operating environment of a system, which renders the system ever less efficient and less reliable to operate. Other reasons concern evolving requirements, which make the system look ever less effective in the eyes of its users. Beyond these, software ages simply because no one understands it anymore. Information about a software system is routinely lost or forgotten, including its initial require-ments, design rationale, and implementation history. The loss of such informa-tion causes the maintenance and continued operation of a software system to be increasingly problematic and expensive.

This loss of information over time is characteristic of legacy software sys-tems, which are typically complex, geriatric, and difficult to change, having evolved over decades and having passed through many developers. Neverthe-less, these systems are mature, heavily used, and constitute massive corporate assets. Since these systems are intertwined in the still-evolving operations of the organization, they are very difficult to replace.

Organizations often find that they have to re-engineer or refurbish the legacy code. The software industry faces a significant problem in migrating this old software to modern platforms, such as graphical user interfaces, object-oriented technologies, or network-centric computing environments. All the while, they need to handle the changing business processes of the organization as well as urgent concerns such as the "Year 2000 problem."

In the typical legacy software system, the accumulated documentation may be incomplete, inconsistent, outdated, or even too abundant. Before a re-engineering process can continue, the existing software needs to be documented again, or *redocumented*, with the most current details about its structure, func-tionality, and behavior. Also, the existing documentation needs to be found, consolidated, and reconciled. Some of these old documents may only be avail-able in obsolete formats or hard-copy form. Other information about the soft-ware, such as design rationale, may only be found in the heads of geographically separated engineers. All of this useful information about the system needs to be recaptured and stored for use by the re-engineering staff.

As a result of these needs, we embarked on a research project to design and implement an environment to support software migration. In particular, we fo-cused on migrating legacy PL/I source code to C++, with an initial phase of looking at redocumentation strategies and technologies. The project was con-ducted at the IBM Toronto Centre for Advanced Studies (CAS) with the support of the Centre for Software Engineering Research (CSER), an industry-driven program of collaborative research, development, and education, that involves leading Canadian technology companies, universities, and government agencies.

Technologies improved over the past few years now make it possible to build tools that greatly simplify the process of redocumenting a legacy software system. These technologies include reverse engineering, program understanding, and information management. With the arrival of nonproprietary World Wide Web standards and tools, it is possible to solve many problems effectively in gathering, presenting, and disseminating information.

These approaches can add value by supporting information linking and structuring, providing search capabilities, unifying text and graphical presentations, and allowing easy remote access. We explore these ideas by implementing a prototype environment, called the *software bookshelf*, which captures, organizes, manages, and delivers comprehensive information about a software system, and provides an integrated suite of code analysis and visualization capabilities intended for software re-engineering and migration.

We distinguish three roles (and corresponding perspectives) involved in directly constructing, populating, and using such a bookshelf: the *builder*, the librarian, and the patron. A role may be performed by several persons and a person may act in more than one role. The builder constructs the bookshelf substrate or architecture, focusing mostly on generic, automatic mechanisms for gathering, structuring, and storing information to satisfy the needs of the librarian. The builder designs a general program-understanding schema for the underlying software repository, imposing some structure on its contents. The builder also integrates automated and semi-automated tools, such as parsers, analyzers, converters, and visualizers to allow the librarian to populate the repository from a variety of information sources.

The *librarian* populates the bookshelf repository with meaningful information specific to the software system of interest. Sources of information may include source code files and their directory structure, as well as external documentation available in electronic or paper form, such as architectural information, test data, defect logs, development history, and maintenance records.

The librarian must determine what information is useful and what is not, based on the needs of the re-engineering effort. This process may be automatic and use the capabilities provided by the builder, or it may be partly manual to review and reconcile the existing software documentation for on-line access. The librarian may also generate new content, such as architectural views derived from discussions with the original software developers. By incorporating such application-specific domain knowledge, the librarian adds value to the information generated by the automatic tools. The librarian may further tailor the repository schema to support specific aspects of the software, such as a proprietary programming language.

The *patron* is an end user of the bookshelf content and could be a developer, manager, or anyone needing more detail to re-engineer the legacy code. Once the bookshelf repository is populated, the patron is able to browse the existing content, add annotations to highlight key issues, and create bookmarks to highlight useful details. As well, the patron can generate new information specific to the task at hand using information stored in the repository and running the integrated code analysis and visualization tools in the bookshelf environment. From the patron's point of view, the populated bookshelf is more than either a collection of on-line documents or a computer-aided software engineering (CASE) toolset. The software bookshelf is a unified combination of both that has been customized and targeted to assist in the re-engineering effort. In addition, these capabilities are provided without replacing the favored development tools already in use by the patron.

The three roles of builder, librarian, and patron are increasingly project- and task-specific. The builder focuses on generic mechanisms that are useful across multiple application domains or re-engineering projects. The librarian focuses on generating information that is useful to a particular re-engineering effort, but across multiple patrons, thereby also lowering the effort in adopting the bookshelf in practice. The patron focuses on obtaining fast access to information relevant to the task at hand. The range of automatic and semi-automatic approaches embodied by these roles is necessary for the diverse needs of a re-engineering effort. Fully automatic techniques may not provide the project - and task-specific value needed by the patrons.

In this chapter we describe our research and experience with the bookshelf from the builder, librarian, and patron perspectives. As builders, we have designed a bookshelf architecture using Web technologies, and implemented an initial prototype. As librarians, we have populated a bookshelf repository with the artifacts of a legacy software system consisting of approximately 300,000 lines of code written in a PL/I dialect. As patrons, we have used this populated bookshelf environment to analyze and understand the functionality of a particular module in the code for migration purposes.

In the next section, we expand on the roles and their responsibilities and requirements. The subsequent section outlines the overall architecture of the bookshelf and details the various technologies used to implement our initial prototype. We also describe how we populated the bookshelf repository by gathering information automatically from source code and existing documentation as well as manually from interviews with the legacy system developers. A typical program-understanding scenario illustrates the use of the software bookshelf. Our research effort is also related to other work, particularly in the areas of information systems, program understanding, and software development environments. Finally, we summarize the contributions of this experience, report our conclusions, and suggest directions for future work.

14.2 The Software Bookshelf Metaphor

Imagine an ideal scenario: where the developers of a software system have maintained a complete, consistent, and up-to-date written record of its evolution from its initial conception to its current form; where the developers have been meticulous at maintaining cross references among the various documents and application-domain concepts; and where the developers can access and update this information effectively and instantaneously. We envision our software bookshelf as an environment that can bring software engineering practices closer to this scenario, by generally offering capabilities to ease the recapture of information about a legacy system, to support continuous evolution of the information throughout the life of the system, and to allow access to this information through a widely available interface.

Our software bookshelf directly involves builder, librarian, and patron roles, with correspondingly different, but increasingly project- and task-specific, responsibilities and requirements. The roles are related in that the librarian must satisfy the needs of the patron, and the builder must satisfy the needs of the librarian (and indirectly the patron). Consequently, the builder and librarian must have more than their own requirements and perspectives in mind.

14.2.1 The Builder

The bookshelf builder is responsible for the design and implementation of an architecture suitable to satisfy the information gathering, structuring, and storing needs of the librarian. To be relatively independent of specific re-engineering or migration projects, the builder focuses on a general conceptual model of program understanding. In particular, the schema for the underlying software repository of the bookshelf needs to represent information for the software system at several levels of abstraction (Lee and Harandi, 1993; Ning, 1989; Arango et al., 1985).

The levels are:

- *Physical.* The system is viewed as a collection of source code files, directory layout, build scripts, etc.
- *Program.* The system is viewed as a collection of language-independent program units, written using a particular programming paradigm. For the procedural paradigm, these units would include variables, procedures, and statements, and involve data and control flow dependencies.
- *Design.* The system is viewed as a collection of high-level, implementation-independent design components (e.g., patterns and subsystems), abstract data types (e.g., sets and graphs), and algorithms (e.g., sorting and math functions).
- *Domain.* The domain is the explanation of "what the system is about," including the underlying purpose, objectives, and requirements.

At each level of abstraction, the software system is described in terms of a different set of concepts. These descriptions are also interrelated. For instance, a design-level concept, such as a design pattern, (Gamma et al., 1995) may be implemented using one or more class constructs at the program level, which correspond to several text fragments in various files at the physical level.

The builder also integrates various tools to allow the librarian to populate the bookshelf repository. Data extraction tools include parsers that operate on source code or on intermediate code generated by a compiler. File converters transform old documents into formats more suited to on-line navigation. Reverse engineering and code analysis tools are used to discover meaningful software structures at various levels of granularity. Graph visualizers provide diagrams of software structures and dependencies for easier understanding. To aid the librarian, the builder elaborates the repository schema to represent the diverse products created by these types of tools.

The builder has a few primary requirements. Since the information needs of the librarian and patron cannot all be foreseen, the builder requires powerful conceptual modeling and flexible information storage and access capabilities that are extensible enough to accommodate new and diverse types of content. Similarly, the builder requires generic tool integration mechanisms to allow access to other research and commercial tools. Finally, the builder requires that the implementation of the bookshelf architecture be based on standard, nonproprietary, and widely available technologies, to ensure that the bookshelf environment can be easily ported to new platforms without high costs or effort. In this paper we describe our experiences in using object-oriented database and Web technologies to satisfy these and other requirements.

14.2.2 The Librarian

The librarian is responsible for populating the bookshelf repository with information specific to the software system. The librarian weighs the usefulness of each piece of information based on the needs of the re-engineering or migration project. The gathered information adds project-specific value and lowers the effort of the patron in adopting the bookshelf environment. The bookshelf content comes from several original, derived, and computed sources:

- *Internal*—the source code, including useful prior versions; the librarian can capture this information from the version control and configuration management system and the working development directories
- *External*—information separated from the source code, including requirements specifications, algorithm descriptions, or architectural diagrams (which often becomes out-of-date or lost when the code changes); the librarian can recover this information by talking to the developers who know salient aspects of the history of the software
- *Implicit personal*—information used by the original developers, including insights, preferences, and heuristics (which is often not verbalized or documented); the librarian can recover this information by talking to the developers and recording their comments

- *Explicit personal*—accumulated information that the developers have maintained personally, including memos, working notes, and unpublished reports (which often becomes lost when a developer leaves); the librarian can often recover this information by accessing a developer's on-line data-bases, along with a roadmap on what can be found
- *References*—cross-referenced information, such as all the places where a procedure is called or where a variable is mentioned (which is valuable for recovering software structure, but time-consuming and error-prone to maintain manually); the librarian can usually recover this information by using automated tools
- *Tool-generated*—diverse information produced by tools, including abstract syntax trees, call graphs, complexity metrics, test coverage results, and performance measurements (which is often not well integrated from a presentation standpoint); the librarian need not store this information in the bookshelf repository if it can be computed on demand

The librarian organizes the gathered information into a useful and easily navigable structure to the patron and forms links between associated pieces of information. The librarian must also reconcile conflicting information, perhaps in old documentation, with the software system as seen by its developers. Finding both implicit and explicit personal information is critical for complementing the tool-generated content. All these difficult processes involve significant application-domain knowledge, and thus the librarian must consult with the experienced developers of the software to ensure accuracy. For the patron, the bookshelf contents will only be used if they are perceived to be accurate enough to be useful. Moreover, the bookshelf environment will only have value to the re-engineering effort if it is used. Consequently, the librarian must carefully maintain and control the bookshelf contents.

The librarian has a few primary requirements. The librarian requires tools to populate and update the bookshelf repository automatically with information for a specific software system (insofar as that is possible). These tools would reduce the time and effort of populating the repository, releasing valuable time for tasks that the librarian must do manually (such as consulting developers) or semi-automatically (such as producing architectural diagrams).

The librarian requires the bookshelf environment to handle and allow uniform access to diverse types of documents, including those not traditionally recorded (e.g., electronic mail, brainstorming sessions, and interviews of customers). Finally, the librarian requires structuring and linking facilities to produce bookshelf content that is organized and easily explored. The links need to be maintained outside of the original documents (e.g., the source code) to not intrude on the owners of those documents (e.g., the developers).

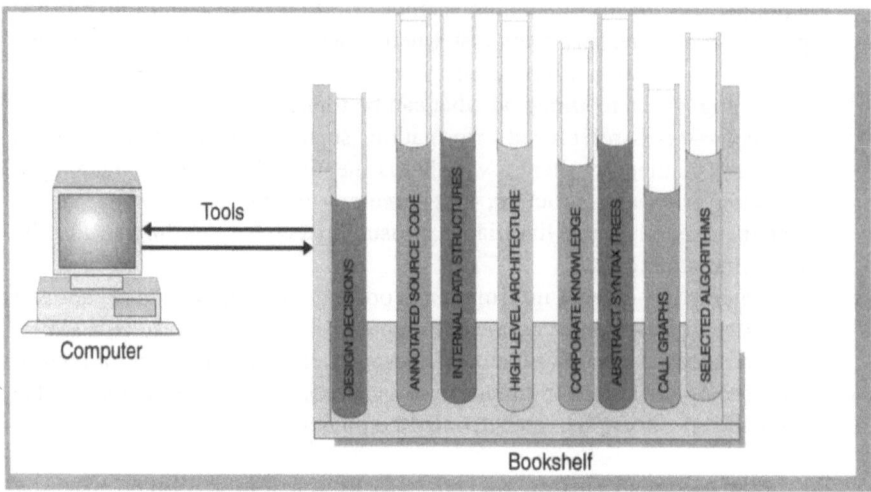

Figure 14.1. A populated software bookshelf environment.

14.2.3 The Patron

The patron is an end user who directly uses the populated bookshelf environment to obtain more detail for a specific re-engineering or migration task. This role may include the developers who have been maintaining the software system and have the task of re-engineering it. Some of these patrons may already have significant experience with the system. Other patrons may be new to the project and will access the bookshelf content to aid in their understanding of the software system before accepting any re-engineering responsibilities. In any case, the patron can view the bookshelf environment as providing several entities that can be explored or accessed (see also Figure 14.1):

- *Books*—cohesive chunks of content, including original, derived, and computed information relevant to the software system and its application domain (e.g., source code, visual descriptions, typeset documents, business policies)
- *Notes*—annotations that the patron can attach to books or other notes (e.g., reminders, audio clips)
- *Links*—relationships within and among books and notes, which provide structure for navigation (e.g., guided tours) or which express semantic relationships (e.g., between design diagrams and source code)

- *Tools*—software tools the patron can use to search or compute task-specific information on demand
- *Indices*—maps for the bookshelf content, which are organized according to some meaningful criteria (e.g., based on the software architecture)
- *Catalogs*—hierarchically structured lists of all the available books, notes, tools, and indices
- *Bookmarks*—entry points produced by the individual patron to particularly useful and frequently visited bookshelf content

For the patron, the populated bookshelf environment provides value by unifying information and tools into an easily accessible form that has been specifically targeted to meet the needs of the re-engineering or migration project. The work of the librarian frees the patron to spend valuable time on more important task-specific concerns, such as rewriting a software module in a different language. Hence, the effort for the patron to adopt the bookshelf environment is lowered. Newcomers to the project use the bookshelf content as a consolidated and logically organized reference of accurate, project-specific software documentation.

The patron has a few major requirements. Most importantly, the bookshelf content must pertain specifically to the re-engineering project and be accurate, well organized, and easily accessible (from possibly a different platform at a remote site). The patron also requires the bookshelf environment to be easy to use and yet flexible enough to assist in diverse re-engineering or migration tasks. Finally, the patron requires that the bookshelf environment not interfere with day-to-day activities, other than to improve the ability to retrieve useful information more easily. In particular, the patron should still be able to use tools already favored and in use today.

14.3 Building the Bookshelf

With builder, librarian, and patron requirements in mind, the builder designs and implements the architecture of the bookshelf environment to satisfy those requirements. In this section we describe our experience, from a bookshelf builder perspective, with a bookshelf architecture that we implemented as a proof-of-concept. The architecture follows the paradigm proposed by Van der Linden and Muller (1995), where a system is composed of a set of building blocks and components (Kozaczynski et al., 1995).

Our client—server architecture consists of three major parts: a user interface, an information repository, and a collection of tools (see Figure 14.2). The client-side user interface is a Web browser, which is used to access bookshelf content. The server-side information repository stores the bookshelf content, or more accurately, stores pointers to diverse information sources. The repository is based on the Telos conceptual modeling language (Mylopoulos et al., 1990), is implemented using DB2[1] (DATABASE 2), and is accessed through an off-the-shelf Web server. Client-side tools include parsers to extract information from a variety of sources, scripts to collect, transform, and synthesize information, as well as reverse engineering and visualization tools to recover and summarize information about software structure. These major parts are described in more detail later in the section.

Our architecture uses Web technologies extensively (see Table 14.1 for acronyms and definitions). In particular, these technologies include: a common protocol (HTTP), integration mechanisms (CGI, Java[2]), a common hypertext format (HTML), multimedia data types (MIME), and unified access to information resources (URL). These standards provide immediate benefits by partly addressing some requirements of the builder (i.e., tool integration, nonproprietary standards, and cross-platform capabilities), the librarian (i.e., uniform access to diverse documents and linking facilities), and the patron (i.e., easy remote access).

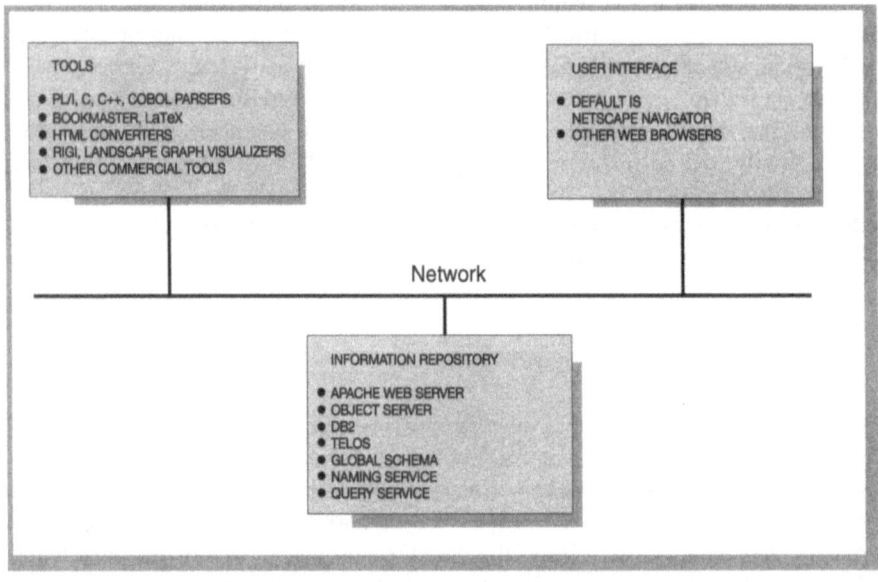

Figure 14.2. Builder perspective of the implemented bookshelf architecture.

---

[1] DB2 and DATABASE2 are trademarks or registered trademark of International Business Machines Corporation.

[2] Java is a trademark or registered trademark of Sun Microsystems, Inc.

Table 14.1. Web technologies.

Item	Description
Common Protocol	The Web is founded on a client-server architecture. The clients and servers run independently, on different machines in different control domains. They communicate through a common protocol, the *HyperText Transfer Protocol* (HTTP). The connections are stateless; once the transaction with the client is completed, the server forgets the communication context. Version 1.1 of the HTTP protocol supports persistent connections that allow multiple transfers before the connection closes. To be served, a client issues a request to one of the servers, and the server analyzes the request, performs the requested operation (e.g., GET, POST, PUT), and generates a response.
Unified Access	The servers provide controlled access to information resources they manage. The resources are accessed by clients via links called *uniform resource locators* (URLs) that designate the location and the identity of the desired resource.
Multimedia Data Types	The data associated with requests and responses are typed using the *Multipurpose Internet Mail Extensions* (MIME). The unit of transfer between the client and the server is a MIME document, which is a typed sequence of octets.
Common Hypertext Format	The *HyperText Markup Language* (HTML) defines a composite document model. The document may contain references to other documents that are rendered in line by the client (e.g., tags, pictures, audio, video). In addition to these, the document may contain links to external documents (or parts thereof). If the type of a document is text/HTML and the document contains links to other documents, each one of these is handled in a separate transfer.
Integration Mechanism	The *Common Gateway Interface* (CGI) defines a mechanism that allows a Web server to launch and convey requests to arbitrary external programs.

Many nonproprietary components are available off-the-shelf, including Web browsers, Web servers, document viewers, and HTML file converters, which can reduce the effort of building a software bookshelf architecture. Consequently, the use of Web technologies provides significant value to the bookshelf builder. In addition, the Web browser is easy to use and—we can assume today—immediately familiar to the patron. This lowers the startup cost and training effort of the patron in adopting the populated bookshelf environment.

14.3.1 User Interface

The patron navigates through the bookshelf content using a Web browser, which may transparently invoke a variety of tools and scripts. The patron can browse through books or notes by simply *clicking* (a selection using a mouse button) on any links. We implemented a hypermedia link mechanism to support relationships between various pieces of content. This mechanism allows the librarian to provide the patron a choice among possible destinations. For instance, clicking on a procedure name in a source code file may present a list of options, including the definition of the procedure in source code, its interface declaration, its position within a global call graph, the program locations that call it, and its internal data and control flow graphs. Once the patron chooses an option, a particular view of the procedure can be presented by the browser or by one of the integrated presentation tools in the bookshelf environment. This *multiheaded* link mechanism thus offers the librarian added flexibility in organizing and presenting access to bookshelf content.

We chose Netscape Navigator[3] as the default Web browser for the bookshelf environment, but any comparable browser should suffice. The browser must, however, support Java (Gosling et al., 1996) directly since this is used as a client-side extension mechanism. In particular, this mechanism enables any browser that connects to the Web server to be transparently extended to handle various data objects in the information repository.

Navigator also supports remote invocation features to allow tools to tell it to follow a URL. In following the URL, Navigator accesses the Web server to retrieve requested content from the information repository. For example, a tool can present a map of the bookshelf content as a graph, where clicking on a node would invoke Navigator to go to the corresponding book or note. These features also allow, for example, a code editor to request the browser to display details about a selected software artifact. This ability benefits the patron by making the bookshelf content readily and transparently accessible from the patron's development environment.

14.3.2 Information Repository

To track all the different information sources and their cross references, the bookshelf environment contains an information repository that describes the content of the bookshelf. Access to the information repository is through a Web server. A module of this server is an object server, which is a mediator to a persistent object store. The object server and object store constitute the implementation of the repository.

---

[3] Netscape Navigator is a trademark or registered trademark of Netscape Communications Corporation.

The structure for the stored data is specified using an object-oriented conceptual modeling language. By using object-oriented database technology, the bookshelf builder can provide the necessary capabilities to represent and structure highly interrelated, fine-grained data. The librarian especially needs these capabilities to express and organize software artifacts and dependencies. Furthermore, our particular choice of technology supports dynamic updates to the data schema, to allow extension to new and unforeseen types of content. Consequently, our use of object-oriented database technology provides a major benefit by satisfying some requirements of the builder (i.e., powerful conceptual modeling and extensibility to new types of content) and the librarian (i.e., structuring and linking facilities).

Meta-Data Repository

The information repository generally stores descriptions about pieces of bookshelf content (such as location) along with the links among the pieces. Since these descriptions constitute data about other data, they are called *meta-data* (Seligman and Rosenthal, 1996).

The repository explicitly stores the meta-data, not necessarily the data themselves. The actual data are left in files, databases, physical books, etc. This indirect approach is necessary since the actual data can be too large to store or too complex to fully model. Nevertheless, this detail only concerns the builder and librarian. The patron perspective is that bookshelf content is somehow delivered by the bookshelf repository.

Our repository design provides three basic capabilities for the builder and librarian: an information model, global schema, and persistent storage. The information model provides facilities for modeling the meta-data and is analogous to a data model for a database. The global schema consists of classes describing the kinds of information to be stored. This schema serves as a foundation for modeling the software implementation domain (by the builder) and modeling the application domain (by the librarian). In addition, the shared nature of this schema enables data integration for various tools. The persistent storage contains a populated instantiation of the schema.

Web Server

The Web server provides an interface for accessing information in the repository. It does so by delivering the appropriate data to the requesting tool or acting directly as an information conduit. The Web server accepts HTTP requests and maps them using the repository meta-data into appropriate actions for accessing the actual content. This approach allows the server to journal all requests. The server can also cache requests, to allow specific optimizations for accessing distributed content. In our bookshelf implementation, we use the freely available

Apache Web server.[4] The only additional requirement is that the server support CGI.

Object Server and Store

The repository is implemented by an object server and object store. The object server is an in-memory facility that offers caching, query, and naming services, built as an Apache Web server module for more efficient performance (see Figure 14.3). (An earlier, slower prototype used CGI and Tcl scripts to connect the Web server and repository.) The object store provides persistence for content description objects using DB2. The object server communicates with the object store through messages implemented with UNIX[5] sockets. The single communication channel between the object server and store ensures consistency. In addition, all queries and updates can be performed in the local workspace of the object server, thereby increasing performance. The object server can update the store according to whatever schedule is appropriate, depending on hardware availability, security issues, and usage patterns.

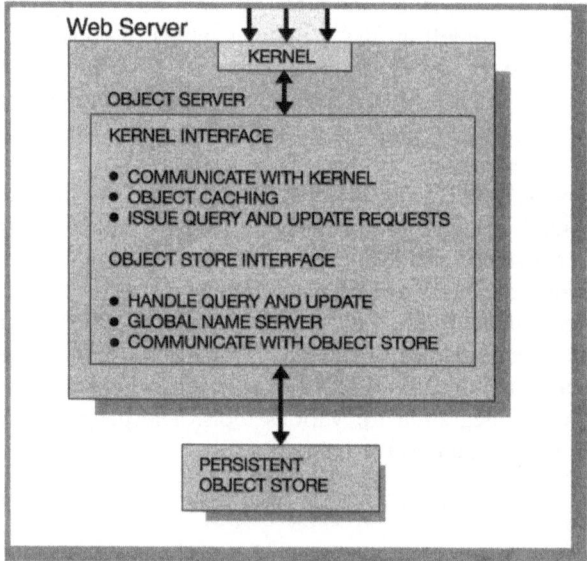

Figure 14.3. Bookshelf repository subsystems.

---

[4] The Apache HTTP Server Project is a collaborative software development effort aimed at creating a commercial-grade source-code implementation of an HTTP Web server. Information about the project can be found at the Internet World Wide Web site http://www.apache.org.

[5] UNIX is a trademark or registered trademark of X/Open Co., Ltd.

Information Modeling

The information model is based on the conceptual modeling language Telos (Mylopoulo et al., 1990) which offers facilities for organizing information in the repository using generalization, aggregation, and classification. These facilities are all necessary to satisfy the information structuring needs of the librarian.

In our experience, program-understanding and re-engineering tasks require a high level of flexibility in structuring information and forming semantic associations. Telos also provides constructs for representing meta-data using meta-classes and meta-attributes. For example, links from a procedure to *called* procedures would be stored as part of the meta-description of a procedure. An interpreter/compiler for Telos is built into the object server.

Schema

The repository does not impose a predefined view of the data it is representing. Rather, a customized schema needs to be built for each application domain. This customization is a significant task and it is necessary for the builder to reduce the work of the librarian. Figure 14.4 shows some of the design-level metaclass definitions. In our customization we have tried to prepare a generally global

```
MetaClass Design
    in DesignClass
    isa Realization
    with
    isRealizedByAttribute
        isRealizedBy : Implementation

    isPartOfAttribute
        isPartOf : Design
    hasPartsAttribute
        hasParts : Design

    isContainedInAttribute
        isContainedIn : Design
    containsAttribute
        contains : Design
end

MetaClass System
    isa Design
    ...
end

MetaClass Subsystem
    isa Design
    with
    isPartOfAttribute
        isPartOf : System
    hasPartsAttribute
        hasParts : Subsystem
    ...
end

MetaClass Algorithm
    with
    descriptionAttribute
        pseudoCode : PseudoCode
        specification : Specification
        text : AlgorithmText
    ...
end
```

Figure 14.4. Schema details for the design level.

schema that is applicable to a variety of program-understanding projects. This schema mirrors the levels of software abstraction previously outlined and includes meta-classes defining the kinds of objects that can reside in the object store.

According to these design-level definitions, a `System` is a subclass of `Design` and may have `Subsystems` as parts (with `isPartOfAttribute`). Design-level classes (`Design` and its subclasses) are realized by one or more program-level classes (`Implementation` and its subclasses). This is expressed by the `isRealizedByAttribute` of `Design`. For example, a specific `Subsystem` is a design that could be realized as a set of files. Finally, an `Algorithm` can be described by `PseudoCode`, a `Specification`, or in `AlgorithmText`.

Analogous definitions apply for the program and physical levels. Relevant metaclasses for the program level include `Implementation`, `ProgrammingConstruct`, and `Statement`. Similarly, `Storage`, `FileSystem`, `StorageFile`, and `Directory` are some of the classes for the physical level. Figure 14.5 shows these different levels of the schema.

Link Mechanism

A multiheaded hypermedia link is implemented by accessing a repository object that describes possible destinations for the link. This description depends on the classes that the object instantiates. The possible destinations can be different for different types of objects (e.g., procedures versus variables) and can be further

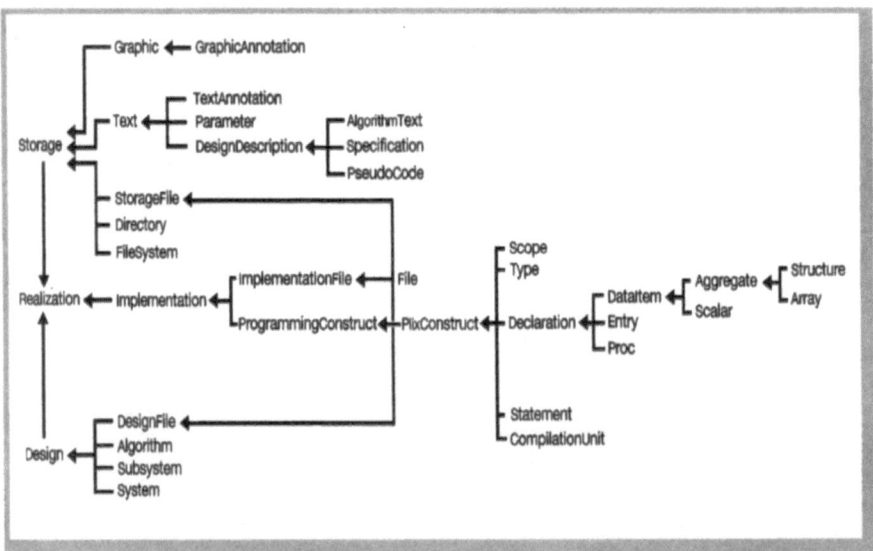

Figure 14.5. Schema overview: the basic classes at the design, implementation, and storage levels. Nodes represent meta-classes and arcs represent is-a relations.

individualized for particular objects. In Telos terms, these multiheaded links are supported by multiple attributes within multiple attribute categories. For example, while browsing a procedure object, the patron may want to see different views of the procedure and its relationship to the rest of the software. By accessing the attributes in the `defaultView` and `availableView` categories, the patron can navigate to a source code view of the procedure or a text file explaining the implemented algorithm (see Figure 14.6).

Name Translation Service

The repository integrates the content found in disparate information sources. A particular procedure may be mentioned many times in different source code files and other documentation. For this procedure, there should only be a single object in the store, with appropriate attributes describing where the procedure is defined, mentioned, called, etc. Consequently, one common problem of data integration is reconciling the multiple names used for the same entity. At one extreme, a tool may have an inflexible mechanism that requires a unique name for each entity it manipulates. At the other extreme, a tool may simply manipulate the entities without any concern for their meaning. In addition, the implementation domain may impose restrictions on the names of entities. For example, the rules of a programming language usually require that all global procedures have unique names.

To deal with these needs, our repository provides an integrated name trans-

```
SimpleClass proc_1
  in Proc
  with
  URL
    : "http://CSER/projects/boundary.html"
  name
    : "proc_1"
  defaultView
    HTMLSourceView : proc_1_1;
  availableView
    AlgorithmView : proc_1_3;
      //algorithm
    ProcCalledByView : proc_1_2;
      //called procedures
    FullCallGraphView : proc_1_26;
      //entire call graph
    NearCallGraphView : proc_1_27;
      //neighborhood call graph
    FarCallGraphView : proc_1_28;
      //far call graph
    ProcToVarView : proc_1_29
      //accessed variables
  end
```

Figure 14.6. Specific detail of the repository schema showing how attribution is used to represent hyperlinks.

lation service for use by the bookshelf tools. This service is implemented by giving each entity a unique object identifier and by maintaining a mapping between this identifier and the form of name needed by a tool. This service provides additional capabilities, aside from easing data integration. In particular, this service is a basis for a general, name-based query service for use by the tools. This query service is used to support virtual links that implicitly connect entities or dynamic links that are created on demand. For example, consider a patron reading through a text document that describes the major algorithms used in a software system. This document predates the creation of the software and has almost no explicit hyperlinks. If the patron highlights a word representing the common name of an algorithm, the viewing tool could query the repository for all entities that use this name. Using the result, the tool can present the patron with a number of navigation options for further exploration of how this algorithm is implemented in the software. These navigation paths are dynamic. If it happens that these paths are useful, they can be made explicit and static, without changing the original document.

Adding New Content

By design, the information repository is easily extensible with new data or types of data. In the former case, the repository creates new objects describing the new data, with appropriate pointers to the location of the data. The new data are immediately available to all tools. A tool can dynamically query the repository, fetch information about the new data, and display them to the patron. The latter case for a new type of data requires changes to the schema to describe the class of information being added to the repository.

The schema itself is dynamic. That is, the schema can be extended, contracted, or modified without changing the representation of existing objects or the tools that manipulate those objects. This flexibility allows, for example, a new type of view to be added to the procedure class without affecting any of the actual procedure instances or any of the display tools that already operate on these instances. Another use of a dynamic schema is to create user-defined views to organize and capture implicit personal information.

14.3.3 Tools

Our bookshelf environment is based on an open architecture, which allows a variety of tools to be integrated. Tools that populate the bookshelf repository are generally independent, communicating with each other using files and to the bookshelf Web server using standard Web protocols. These common protocols also provide the necessary integration mechanism for the Web server to export meta-data or data to external tools. These tools may use this information to locate the appropriate input files and derive new information that is stored either separately as a file, directly in the repository, or in some combination of the two.

For example, a code analyzer might scan the intermediate representation of a set of program files, and calculate various complexity metrics. The results could be stored in a local file, with an entry made in the repository describing the new information and its location. In this example, the tool takes care of storing its output in a file, but updates to the repository are sent to the bookshelf Web server via Web protocols.

Adding Tools

A web browser provides only a single kind of access point into the bookshelf contents. Additional presentation tools that also access the repository are needed and should be integrated within the bookshelf architecture using Web protocols. For example, suppose that a patron wants to edit a source code segment while also viewing an annotated version of the source in the Web browser. The patron clicks on a button on the Web page to launch the patron's favorite code editor to process the appropriate source code file. One way of implementing this feature with Web protocols is the following. The button is tied to a URL which, when clicked, causes the Web server to run a CGI script. This script encapsulates the name of the desired file using a special MIME type. The encapsulated data are sent from the server to the browser as a response. The browser recognizes these data as having a special type, and launches the appropriate helper application on the data. The helper application processes the data as a file name, consults the patron's preferences, and launches the preferred code editor to process the desired file. Such an approach relaxes the requirement for a detailed tool-modeling notation usually found in other software engineering environments (Valetto and Kaiser, 1995). In any case, a CGI script or helper application mediates between a tool and the repository, translating between the specific form required by the tool and the form required by the Web server.

Tighter integration with the bookshelf environment can be achieved by making a tool fully HTTP-aware (i.e., capable of sending and receiving HTTP requests and responses). If this is done, the tool is able to communicate with other tools and the repository more efficiently. An important step for integrating a specific tool is to describe its capabilities in terms of what kinds of views it can display (using MIME types) and what kinds of information it supplies (using the repository schema).

Dynamic Content

There is a need for live, specialized, computed views as bookshelf content (Zachmann, 1987; Sowa and Zachman, 1992). It is not possible to prefabricate all the views one might want and store them directly as static HTML pages or graphic images. There are a number of server-side solutions for creating dynamic pages. Web authors often use CGI scripts or Web server modules to construct content dynamically. Also, a meta-language of preprocessing and transformation directives can extend HTML to provide more dynamic pages. Server Side Includes (SSI) are a primitive form of such a meta-language.

In addition to the server-side approaches, there are also client-side strategies that operate from the Web browser, including helper applications, plug-ins, Java applets, and JavaScript[6] handlers. Helpers are independent programs that can provide sophisticated views. Plug-ins are software components that conform to an interface for communicating with the browser and drawing into its windows. Java applets are platform-neutral programs fetched over the network and run on a Java-enabled browser. JavaScript handlers are scripts that are triggered on certain events, such as the clicking of a link. These scripts are embedded in HTML pages and are interpreted by JavaScript-enabled browsers. All of these strategies are flexible for presenting interactive views of bookshelf data. However, some strategies may be easier to exploit than others.

To gain experience with tool integration strategies, we decided to focus on two extremes: tight and loose integration. For tight integration, the tool is essentially reimplemented in the new setting (e.g., rewritten as a Java applet). For loose integration, the tool needs to be programmable and customizable, to adapt and plug into the new setting. An annotated bibliography on different strategies for software engineering environment integration can be found in Brown and Penedo (1992). In the past, we had developed software visualization tools that employed graph-oriented user interfaces (i.e., Landscape (Penny, 1992), Rigi (Müller and Klashinsky, 1988), and SHriMP (Storey et al., 1996)). Given our experience with these tools and the opportunity to compare these visualization techniques within the Web paradigm, we decided to integrate Landscape and Rigi into the bookshelf environment.

Integrating Landscape Views

The Landscape tool (Penny, 1992) produces diagrams, called landscapes, of the global architecture of the target system (Chase, 1996). In each diagram, there are boxes that represent software entities such as subsystems, modules, or files. Arrows connecting the boxes represent dependencies, such as calls to procedures or references to variables. These diagrams are created semi-automatically—based on software artifact information extracted automatically using parsers, together with system decomposition information collected manually from the developers through interviews. A later section in this paper illustrates how a patron uses these diagrams to obtain high-level overviews of the target software.

The original version of the Landscape tool was stand-alone. For the bookshelf environment, a new landscape tool was written as a Java applet. This applet displays landscape diagrams, to provide convenient navigation through the structure of the software from diagram to diagram, and to access related bookshelf content.

---

[6] JavaScript is a trademark or registered trademark of Sun Microsystems, Inc.

Integrating Rigi Views

Rigi is a visualization tool for exploring and understanding large information spaces. The user interface is a graph editor that is used to browse, analyze, and modify a graph that represents the target information space. The tool is end-user programmable and extensible using the Tcl scripting language (Ousterhout, 1994), allowing user-defined views of graphs, integration with external tools, and automation of graph editing operations (Tilley et al., 1994). Also, Rigi is designed to document software architecture and to compose, manipulate, and visualize subsystem structures according to various criteria (Müller et al., 1993).

To exploit its reverse engineering and software analysis capabilities, the Rigi tool was integrated into the bookshelf environment. The basic idea was to allow Rigi to render views constructively, based on information stored in the repository. This is an advance over approaches that only retrieve static, ready-made images. By building views dynamically, the patron can filter immaterial artifacts, emphasize relevant components, and customize the views to the analysis task at hand. The views are live and manipulable. Also, changes to the software being re-engineered are easily reflected without requiring batch updates to statically stored images.

Like Landscape, the Rigi system could be tightly integrated with the bookshelf environment by rewriting the user interface in Java. However, the programmability of Rigi allows for a loose integration strategy that requires no changes to the editor. Rigi was connected to the bookshelf environment using a CGI script and a helper application, both written in Perl (Wall et al., 1996). Access to Rigi and its constructive views from the bookshelf Web browser had to be as simple as following a URL. Consequently, we specified a special form of URL that invokes the CGI script with a sequence of keyword/value pairs. These pairs specify required parameters, including project name, domain model, database, version, user identification, session data, display host, computational host, requested view, and context. The CGI script parses the pairs and sends the parameters to the helper application as a custom MIME type. The helper converts the parameters into Tcl and generates a custom configuration file, as well as a startup script that is used to launch Rigi to produce the view. If Rigi is already running, then the helper conveys the requested view in a file that Rigi periodically polls.

In our experience, the time needed to convey the request to Rigi is short, compared to the time needed to compute and present the requested view in a window. Since constructive views are computed by another process possibly on another machine, there are no memory problems or security limitations incurred by rendering these views within the browser using plug-in modules or Java applets. This integration strategy is generic and can be readily adapted for any stand-alone analysis tool that is end-user programmable or provides a comprehensive application program interface.

There are many strategies for integrating a tool with a Web browser. We explored two specific approaches: loose integration using CGI scripts, which allows for fast prototyping, and tight integration using Java applets, which allows for a common "look-and-feel."

Parsers

The librarian requires tools to populate the bookshelf repository from existing information sources automatically, insofar as that is possible. For example, the files that belong to a software project are stored, typically, in one or more directories in a file system. The process of converting these files to HTML can be automated by "walking" the directory structure and converting the files based on their content types. Of particular interest are parsers, tools used to extract data about software artifacts and dependencies automatically. Source code files are parsed at various levels of detail according to program-understanding needs. For example, a simple parser might extract procedure calls and global variables, whereas a complete parser might generate entire abstract syntax trees.

Our use of parsers is for program-understanding purposes rather than code generation, and so the focus is primarily on extracting useful information, not all the details that would be needed for code compilation. Information useful for program understanding includes procedures (their definitions and calls) and data variables (their definitions and usage). In the implemented bookshelf environment, the parser output is processed through further code analysis to establish links among related code fragments, compile cross references of procedures and global variables, drive visualization tools, generate architectural diagrams, produce metrics on structural complexity (McCabe, 1976; Halstead and Maurice, 1977), locate cloned fragments of code, and determine data and control flow paths. Since the parsers collect the locations of the extracted artifacts, the detailed analyses can be linked to the relevant fragments of code.

A simple source code parser was developed using emacs macros (Stallmann, 1981) and is currently used to parse procedure definitions and calls, and variable declarations and references. Because this parser analyzes the program source, HTML tags can be inserted in the annotated source code output at appropriate points, such as around a procedure definition. Hypertext links are generated automatically from these references using indirection (i.e., the repository maintains a mapping of references to tags), and HTML pages are generated automatically with resolved HTML tags. The parser can be extended to link the annotated code to other documentation. Similarly, external comments and notes can be attached to relevant code fragments.

A series of prototype parsers were also developed to parse two alternative program representations generated by a compiler front-end processor we were using: the cross-reference listing and the intermediate language representation. As bookshelf builders, our goal was to obtain some level of language independence by using these forms of input in some combination. In addition, parsers for these inputs are easier to write due to the limited syntax. The cross reference listing requires only a simple parser, but the reported data are selective and the format of the listing is language- and compiler-dependent. Some information is also missing, such as procedure-to-procedure calls.

These problems can be overcome by parsing the intermediate language representation. For a family of IBM compilers, this representation is shared across multiple languages, hardware, and operating system platforms. The representation can provide detailed information to determine static control flow and, to some degree, information to calculate complexity metrics. In particular, this information includes variable type definitions, function parameter declarations, function return types, and active local and global variables. Nevertheless, in our experience, parsing only this representation is not enough since some of the information is lost. For example, the structure of file inclusions is not maintained and names of data elements generated by the front-end processor may not accurately match the variables names from the original source. Still, the approach handles the entire compiler family sharing the intermediate representation. To demonstrate this, we applied the parser to the intermediate representations of both PL/I dialect and C source code.

14.3.4 Shortcomings and Lessons Learned

The initial prototype of the bookshelf environment served as a testing ground that helped us understand where Web technologies worked well (e.g., ready access, ease of use, and consistent presentation) and where more sophisticated approaches were needed. The prototype became a vehicle for bringing together a diverse set of reverse engineering tools and techniques.

Our experience with the prototype exposed several issues with building a bookshelf using Web technologies. First, the advantage of a universally understood Web browser interface degenerates rapidly as more interactive techniques are used to give the degree of control and flexibility required for sophisticated re-engineering needs. Second, the separation between the client side and the server side introduces sharp boundaries that must be dealt with to create a seamless bookshelf environment to the patron. For example, since a client and the server run most often on different machines and file systems, there is a problem when mapping access rights between the client and server contexts. Third, the connections are stateless (as mentioned in Table 14.1). This creates a communication overhead when composing documents for viewing in the Web browser. Finally, no mechanism is provided for session management and version control.

The initial prototype has several limitations. First, adding a new tool required the builder to write a handcrafted CGI script, which takes some effort. Second, repository access was slow for the patron, because of the communication mechanisms used (i.e., UNIX pipes and interpreted Tcl scripts). Third, there were no security provisions to support selective access to read and possibly edit bookshelf content among patrons. Finally, maintaining a populated bookshelf repository in the face of multiple releases of the target software was another problem not addressed. Some support for multiple releases has been added to later versions of the prototype and this support is being evaluated.

14.4   Populating the Bookshelf

With patron requirements in mind, the librarian populates the bookshelf repository with project-specific content to suit the needs of the re-engineering or migration effort. In this section, from a librarian perspective (see Figure 14.7) we describe our experience in populating the initial bookshelf prototype with a target software system. This target software is a legacy system that has evolved over twelve years, contains approximately 300K lines of highly optimized code written in a dialect of PL/I, and has an experienced development team. This system is the code optimization component of a family of compilers. In this paper, the name used to refer to this system is SIDOI.

14.4.1 Gathering Information Manually

As with many legacy systems, important documentation for SIDOI existed only in hard-copy versions that were filed at the back of some developer's shelf. One

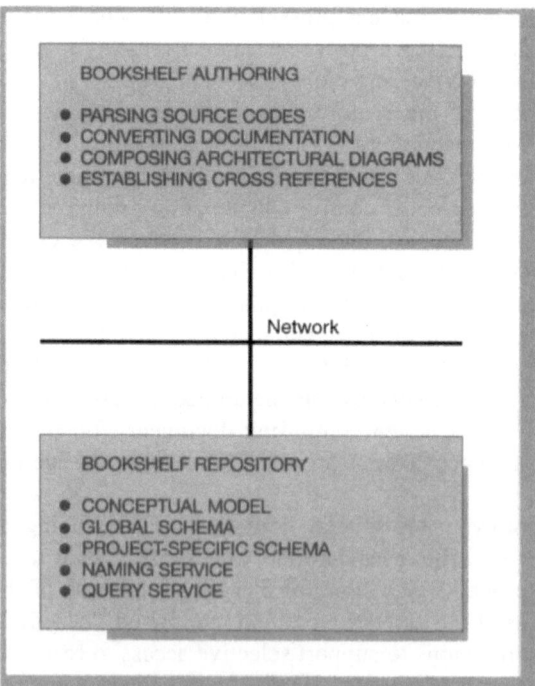

Figure 14.7. Librarian perspective of bookshelf environment capabilities.

major need was to discover these documents and transform them into an electronic form for the software bookshelf. Consequently, over a one-year period, the members of the bookshelf project interviewed members of the development team, developed tools to extract software artifacts and synthesize knowledge, collected relevant documentation, and consequently converted documents to more usable formats.

Most of the information for the bookshelf repository was gathered or derived automatically from existing on-line information sources, such as source code, design documents, and documentation. However, some of the most valuable content was produced by interviewing members of the development team.

Recovering Architectures

The initial view of the legacy system was centered around an informal diagram drawn by one of the early developers. This diagram showed how the legacy system interfaced with roughly 20 other major software systems. We refined this architectural diagram and collected short descriptions of the functions of each of these software systems. The resulting diagram documented the external architecture of the legacy system. At roughly the same time, the chief architect was interviewed, resulting in several additional informal diagrams that documented the high-level, conceptual architecture (i.e., the system as conceived by its owners). Each of these diagrams was drawn formally as a software landscape.

The first of these diagrams was simple, showing the legacy system as composed of three major subsystems that are responsible for the three phases of the overall computation. The diagram also showed that there are service routines to support these three phases, and that the data structure is globally accessed and shared by all three phases. There were also more detailed diagrams showing the nested subsystems within each of the major phases. Using these diagrams, with a preliminary description of the various phases and subsystems, we extracted a terse but useful set of hierarchical views of the abstract architecture.

After some exploration with trying to extract the concrete architecture (i.e., the physical file and directory structure of the source code), we found it more effective to work bottom-up, collecting files into subsystems, and collecting subsystems into phases, reflecting closely the abstract architecture. This exercise was difficult. For example, file-naming conventions could not always be used to collect files into subsystems; roughly 35 percent of the files could not be classified. The developers were consulted to determine a set of concrete subsystems that included nearly all of the files. The concrete architecture contained many more subsystems than the abstract architecture.

In a subsequent, ongoing experiment, we are recovering the architecture of another large system (250K lines of code). In this work we have found that the effort is much reduced by initially consulting with the architects of the system to find their detailed decomposition of the system into subsystems and those subsystems into files.

ILI Data Structure

The intermediate language implementation (ILI) data structure represents the program being optimized. The abstract architecture showed that understanding ILI would be fundamental to gaining a better understanding of the whole system. As a result, we interviewed the developers to get an overview of this data structure and to capture example diagrams of its substructures. This information is documented as a bookshelf book that evolved with successive feedback from the developers (see Figure 14.8). This book provides descriptions and diagrams of ILI substructures. The developers had repeatedly asked for a list of *frequently asked questions* about the ILI data structure, and so one was created for the book.

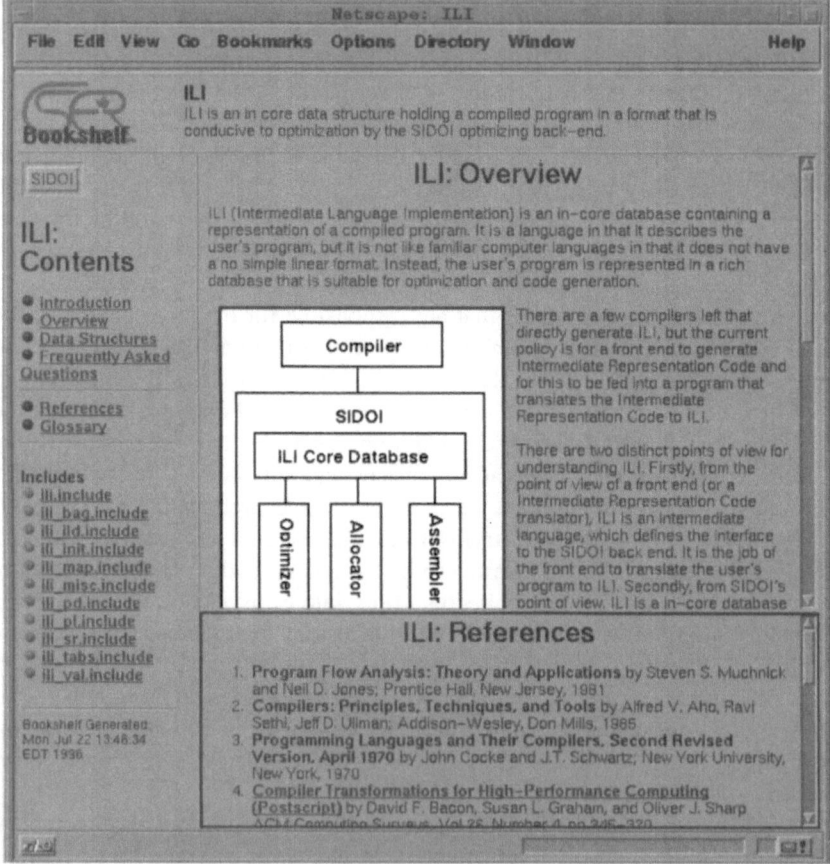

Figure 14.8. Bookshelf view representing the documentation on the key ILI data structure.

Effort

In addition to the initial work of extracting the architectural structure of the target system, one significant task was getting the developers to write a short overview of each subsystem. These descriptions were converted to HTML and linked with the corresponding architectural diagrams for browsing. Since there are over 70 subsystems, this work required more than an elapsed month of a developer's time. We collected relevant existing documents and linked them to the browsable concrete architecture diagrams. In some cases, such as when determining the concrete architecture, we required developers to *invent* structures and subsystem boundaries that had not previously existed.

In our experience, the bookshelf librarian would need to acquire some application-domain expertise. In many legacy software projects, the developers are so busy implementing new features that no time or energy is left to maintain the documentation. Also, the developers often overlook parts of the software that require careful attention. Thus, the librarian must become familiar with the target software and verify new information for the bookshelf repository with the developer.

Reducing Effort

We were constantly aware, while manually extracting the information, that this work is inherently time consuming and costly. We evolved our tools and approaches to maximize the value of our bookshelf environment for a given amount of manual work. It is advantageous to be selective and load only the most essential information, such as the documentation for critical system parts, while deferring the consideration of parts that are relatively stable. The bookshelf contents can be refined and improved incrementally as needed.

In a subsequent experiment with another target system, we have been able to do the initial population of its bookshelf much faster. Our support tools had matured and our experience allowed us to ignore a large number of unprofitable information extraction approaches from the first target system.

14.4.2 Gathering Information Automatically

Several software tools were used to help create and document the concrete architecture. To facilitate this effort, the parser output uses a general and simple file format. This format is called Rigi Standard Format (RSF) and consists of tuples representing software artifacts and relationships (e.g., procedure P calls procedure Q, file F includes file G). These tuple files were the basis of the diagrams of the concrete architecture. A relational calculator called Grok was developed to manipulate the tuples. To gain insights into the structure of this information, the Star system (Mancoridis and Holt, 1995) was used to produce various diagram layouts. The diagrams were manually manipulated to provide a more acceptable appearance for patrons.

Valuable information about the software was found in its version control and defect management system. It provided build-related data that was used to create an array of metrics about the build history of the project. The metrics included change frequency, a weighted defect density, and other measurements relating to the evolution of each release. A set of scripts was written that queried the version control system, parsed the responses, and gathered the desired metrics that can be used by different tools to generate views of the evolution of the software.

14.5 Using the Bookshelf

Re-engineering or migration tasks are generally goal-driven. Based on a desired goal (e.g., reducing costs, adding features, or resolving defects) and the specific task (e.g., simplifying code, increasing performance, or fixing a bug), the patron poses pertinent questions about the software and answers them in part by consulting the bookshelf environment data (see Figure 14.9). To illustrate the use of the software bookshelf, we introduce a scenario drawn from our experience with the SIDOI target system. The scenario illustrates the use of the bookshelf environment during a structural complexity analysis task by a patron who is an experienced developer.

In this scenario, the patron wishes to find complex portions of the code that can be re-engineered to decrease maintenance costs. In particular, one subsystem called DS has been difficult to understand because it is written in an unusually

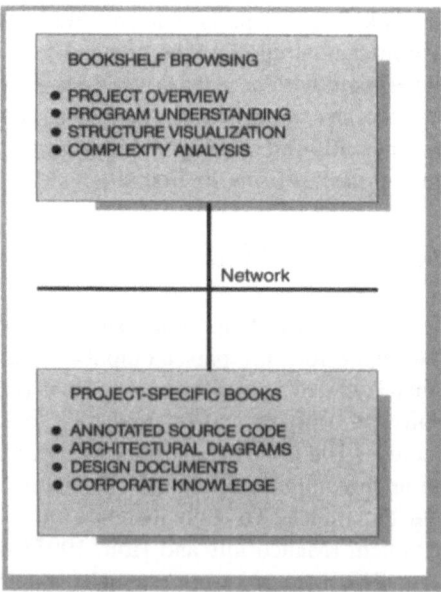

Figure 14.9. Patron perspective of a populated bookshelf environment.

different style. Other past developers have been reluctant to change DS because of its apparent complexity (despite reports of suspected performance problems). Also, there may be portions of DS that can be rewritten to use routines elsewhere that serve the same or similar function. Reducing the number of such cloned or redundant routines could simplify the structure of DS and ease future maintenance work. The information gathered, while studying the complexity of DS, will help to estimate the required effort to revise the subsystem.

14.5.1 Obtaining an Overview

The patron is unfamiliar with DS and decides to use the bookshelf environment to obtain some overview information about the subsystem, such as its purpose and high-level interactions with other subsystems. Starting at the high-level, architectural diagram of SIDOI (see Figure 14.10), the patron can see where DS

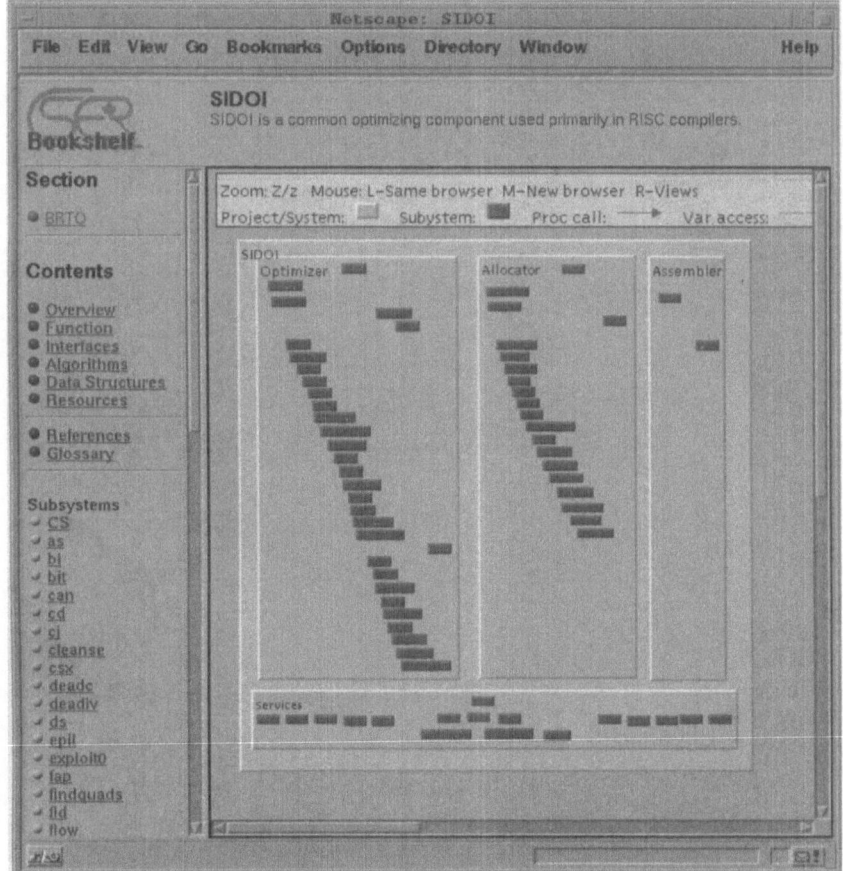

Figure 14.10. High-level architectural view of the SIDOI system.

fits into the system. This diagram was produced semi-automatically using the Landscape tool, based on the automatically generated output of various parsers. Since nested boxes express containment, the diagram (in details not shown here) indicates that DS is contained in the optimizer subsystem. For clarity, the procedure call and variable access arcs have been filtered from this diagram. The patron can click on a subsystem box in this diagram or a link in the subsystem list in the left-hand frame to obtain information about a specific subsystem. For example, clicking on the DS subsystem link retrieves a page with a description about what DS performs, a list of what source files or modules implement DS, and a diagram of what subsystems use or are used by DS (see Figure 14.11). The diagram shows that DS is relatively modular and is invoked only from one or more procedures in the PL/I file `optimize.pl` through one or more procedures in the file `ds.pl`.

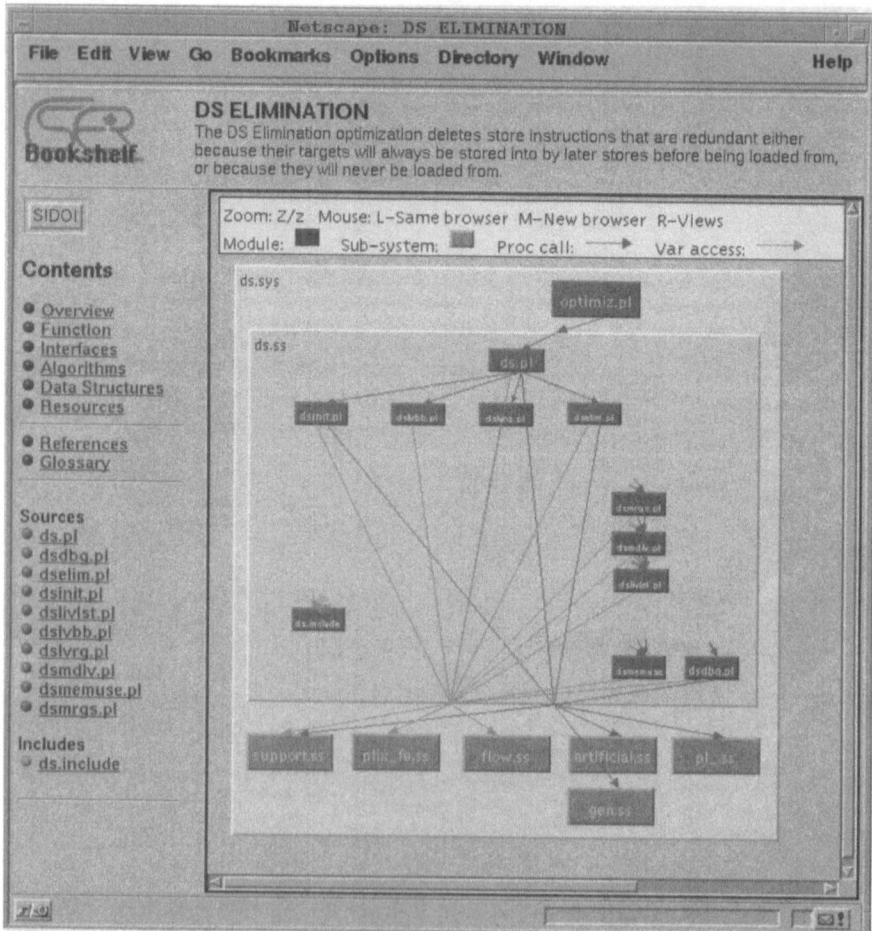

Figure 14.11. Architectural view of the DS subsystem.

The page also offers links to other pages that describe the algorithms and local data structures used by DS. The algorithm description outlines three main phases. The first phase initializes a local data structure, the second phase performs a live variable analysis, and the third phase emits code where unnecessary stores to variables are eliminated. The data structure description is both textual and graphical, with "clickable" areas on the graphical image that take the patron to more detailed descriptions of a specific substructure. These descriptions are augmented by important information about the central ILI data structure of SIDOI. After considering potential entry points into the DS subsystem, the patron decides to navigate systematically along the next level of files in the subsystem: `dsinit.pl`, `dslvbb.pl`, `dslvrg.pl`, and `dselim.pl`.

14.5.2 Obtaining More Detail

The patron can click on a file box in the previous diagram or a file link in the list on the left-hand frame to retrieve further details about a particular source file of DS. For example, clicking on the `dsinit.pl` file link provides a list of the available information specific to this file and specific to the DS subsystem (see Figure 14.12).

The available views for a given file are outlined below.

- *Code redundancy view.* This view shows exact matches for code in the file with other parts of the system, which is useful for determining instances of cut-and-paste reuse and finding areas where common code can be factored into separate procedures.
- *Complexity metrics view.* This view shows a variety of metrics in a bar graph that compares this file with other files in the subsystem of interest.
- *Files included view.* This view provides a list of the files that are included in the file.
- *Hypertext source view.* This view provides a hypertext view of the source file with procedures, variables, and included files appearing as links.
- *Procs declared view.* This view provides a list of procedures declared in the file.
- *Vars fetched and vars stored views.* These views provide a list of varibles fetched or updated in the file.

In general, clicking on a file, procedure, or variable in the diagram or set of links produces a list of the available views specific to that entity. Views appear either as lists in the left-hand frame, as diagrams in the right-hand frame, or as diagrams controlled and rendered by other tools in separate windows. Figure 14.13 shows a diagram generated by Rigi with the neighboring procedures of procedure `dsinit`. The patron can rearrange the software artifacts in the diagrams

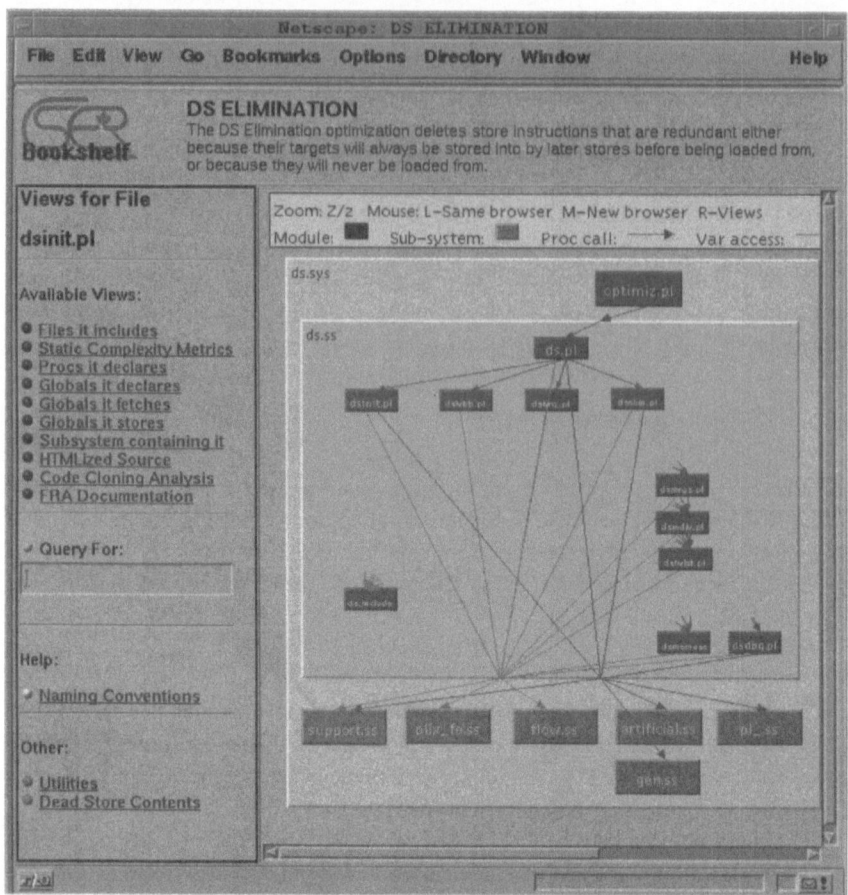

Figure 14.12. Available views for the dsinit.pl module.

and apply suitable filters to hide cluttering information. The capabilities of the Rigi tool are fully available for handling these diagrams.

Other, more flexible navigation capabilities are provided. For instance, the patron can enter the name of a software artifact in the query entry field of the left-hand frame. This search-based approach is useful for accessing arbitrary artifacts in the system that are not directly accessible through predefined links on the current page. Also, the Web browser can be used to return to previously visited pages or to create bookmarks to particularly useful information.

14.5.3 Analyzing Structural Complexity

While focusing on the DS module, the patron decides that some procedure-specific complexity measures on the module would be useful for determining

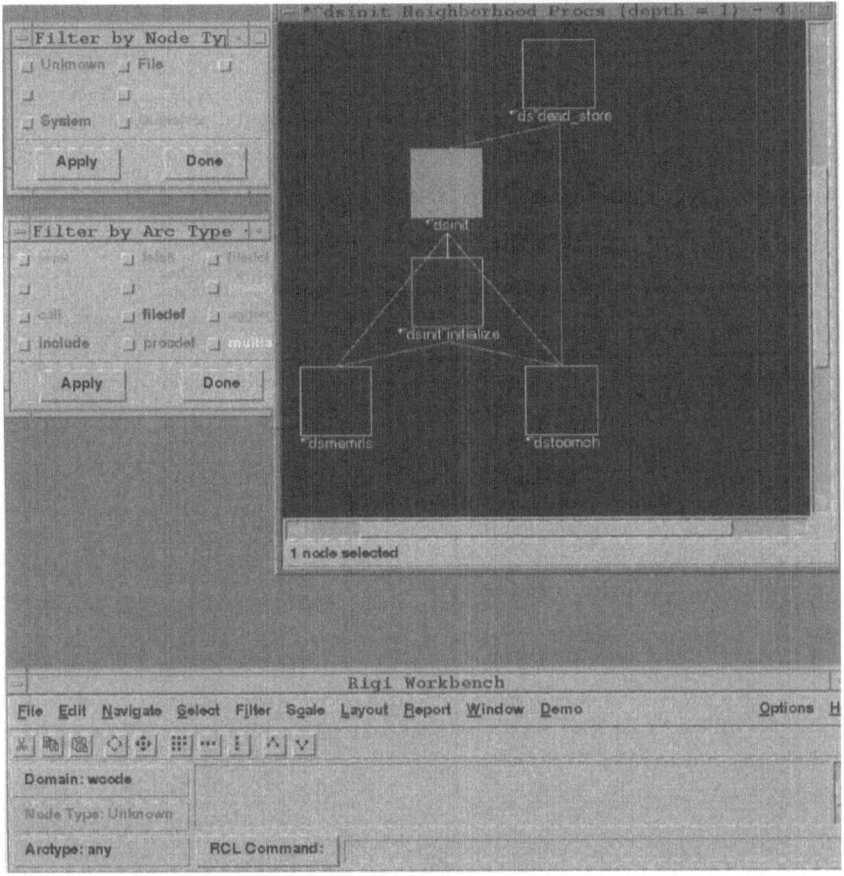

Figure 14.13. Call graph with the neighboring procedures of procedure dsinit.

areas of complex logic or potentially difficult-to-maintain code (see Figure 14.14). Such static information is useful to help isolate error-prone code (McCabe, 1976; Kafura and Reddy, 1987; Curtis et al., 1979; Buss, 1994). The bookshelf environment offers a procedure-level complexity metrics view that includes data- and control-flow-related metrics, measures of code size (i.e., number of equivalent assembly instructions, indentation levels), and fanout (i.e., number of individual procedure calls).

To examine areas of complex, intraprocedural control flow, the cyclomatic complexity metric can be used. This metric measures the number of independent paths through the control flow graph of a procedure. The patron decides to consider all the procedures in DS and compare their cyclomatic complexity values. This analysis shows that dselim, initialize, dslvbb, and dslvrg have values 75, 169, 64, and 49, respectively.

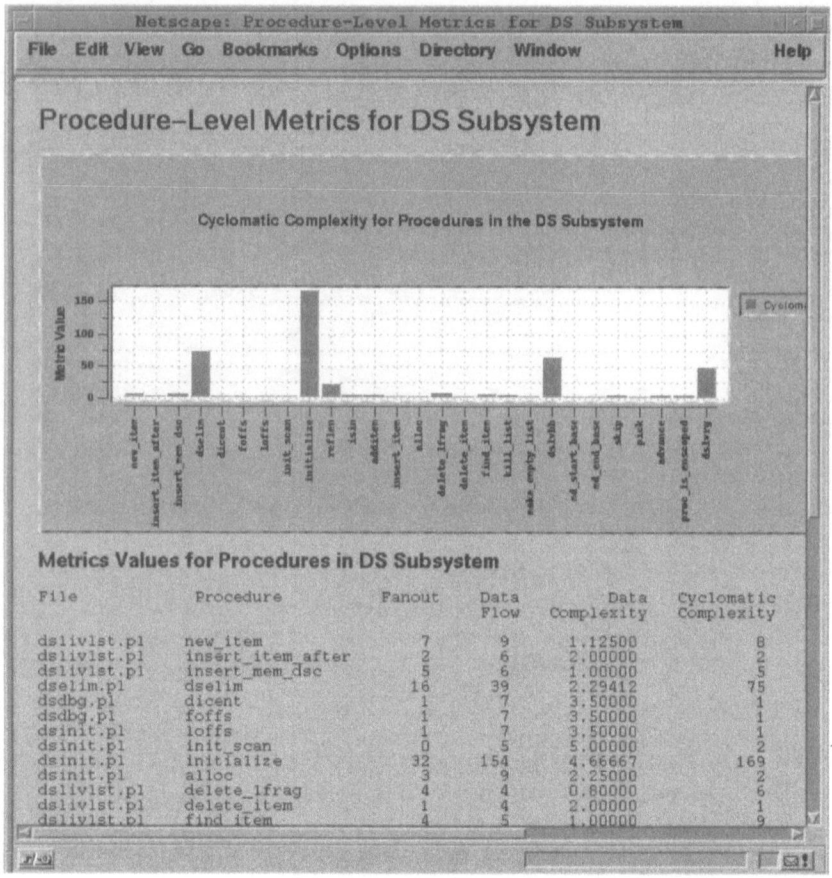

Figure 14.14. Procedure-specific metrics for the DS subsystem.

14.5.4 Finding Redundancies

Using the code redundancy and source code views in the bookshelf environment, the patron discovers and verifies that procedures dselim and dslvbb are nearly copies of each other. Also, procedure dslvrg and dslvbb contain similar algorithmic patterns. Code segments are often cloned through textual cut-and-paste edits on the source code. Some of the clones may be worth replacing by a common routine if future maintenance can be simplified. The amount of effort needed depends on the complexity measures of the cloned code. With a pertinent set of bookshelf views, the re-engineering group can weigh the benefits and costs of implementing the revised code.

After completing the whole investigation, it is useful to store links to the discoveries in some form, such as Web browser bookmarks, guided tour books, footprints on visited pages, and analysis objects in the repository. Such historical information may help other developers with a similar investigation in the future.

14.6 Related Work

In this section, we discuss related work on integrated software environments, parsing and analysis tools, software repositories, and knowledge engineering.

14.6.1 Integrated Software Environments

Tool integration encompasses three major dimensions: data (i.e., exchanging and sharing of information), control (i.e., communication and coordination of tools), and presentation (i.e., user interface metaphor) (Schefstrom and Van den Broek, 1993). Data integration is usually based on a common schema that models software artifacts and analysis results to be shared among different tools. For example, in the PCTE system (ECMA, 1990), data integration is achieved with a physically distributed and replicated object base. Forming a suitable common schema requires a study of functional aspects related to specific tool capabilities and organizational aspects in the domain of discourse. Control integration involves the mechanics of allowing different tools to cooperate and provide a common service. In environments such as Field (Reiss, 1990) and SoftBench (Cagan, 1990), tools are coordinated by broadcast technology, while environments based on the Common Object Request Broker Architecture (CORBA) standard (OMG, 1991) use point-to-point message passing. Furthermore, control integration involves issues related to process modeling and enactment support (Curtis et al., 1992),   computer-supported cooperative work (CACM, 1991), cooperative information systems (CACM, 1997), and distributed computing. Presentation integration involves look-and-feel and metaphor consistency issues.

The software bookshelf tries to achieve data integration through a meta-data repository and Telos conceptual model, control integration through Web protocols and scripting, and presentation integration through the Web browser hypertext metaphor. Kaiser et al. recently introduced an architecture for World Wide Web-based software engineering environments (Kaiser et al., 1997). Their OzWeb system implements data integration through subweb repositories and control integration by means of groupspace services. In addition, there are several existing commercial products such as McCabe's Visual Reengineering Toolset BattleMap (McCabe, 1995), which offers a variety of reverse engineering and analysis tools, visualization aids, and a meta-data repository. By and large, these environments are not based on the technologies selected for our bookshelf implementation. In particular, our work is distinguished through an open and extensible architecture, Web technology with multiheaded hypermedia links, a powerful and extensible conceptual model, and the use of off-the-shelf software components.

14.6.2 Parsing Tools

Many parsing tools and reverse engineering environments have been developed to extract software artifacts from source files (Arnold, 1993). The Software Refinery (Kotik and Markosian, 1989) parses the source and populates an object repository with an abstract syntax tree that conforms to a user-specified domain model. Once populated, the user can access, analyze, and transform the tree using a full programming and query language. PCCTS is a compiler construction toolkit that can be used to develop a parser (Parr, 1996). The output of this parser is an abstract syntax tree represented by C++ objects. Analysis tools can be written using a set of C++ utility functions. GENOA provides a language-independent abstract syntax tree to ease artifact extraction and analysis (Devanbu, 1992). Lightweight parsers have emerged that can be tailored to extract selected artifacts from software systems rather than the full abstract syntax tree (Murphy et al., 1996; Murphy and Notkin, 1996). For the software bookshelf, our parsers convert the source to HTML for viewing or extract the artifacts in a language-independent way by processing the intermediate language representation emitted by the compiler front-end processor.

14.6.3 Analysis Tools

To understand and manipulate the extracted artifacts, many tools have been developed to analyze, search, navigate, and display the vast information space effectively. Slicing tools subset the system to show only the statements that may affect a particular variable (Weiser, 1984). Constructive views (Wong, 1993), visual queries (Consens et al., 1992), Landscapes (Penny, 1992), and end-user programmable tools (Tilley et al., 1994) are effective visual approaches to customize exploration of the information space to individual needs. Several strategies have emerged to match software patterns. GRASPR recognizes program plans, such as a sorting algorithm, with a graph parsing approach that involves a library of stereotypical algorithms and data structures (clichés) (Wills and Rich, 1990). Other plan recognition approaches include concept assignment (Biggerstaff et al., 1994) and constraint-based recognition (Quilici, 1994). Tools have been developed for specific analyses, such as data dependencies (Selby and Basili, 1991), coupling and cohesion measurements (Choi and Scacchi, 1990), control flow properties (Arnold, 1993), and clone detection (Kontogiannis et al., 1996; Johnson, 1996; Baker, 1995). On the commercial front, several products have been introduced to analyze and visualize the architecture of large software systems (Olsem, 1997).

14.6.4 Software Repositories

Modeling every aspect of a software system from source code to application domain information is a hard and elusive problem. Software repositories have been developed for a variety of specialized uses, including software development environments, CASE tools, reuse libraries, and reverse engineering systems. The information model, indexing approach, and retrieval strategies differ considerably among these uses. The knowledge-based LaSSIE system provides domain, architectural, and code views of a software system (Devanbu et al., 1991). Description logic rules (Devanbu and Jones, 1997) relate the different views and the knowledge base is accessed via classification rules, graphical browsing, and a natural language interface. The Software Information Base uses a conceptual knowledge base and a flexible user interface to support software development with reuse (Constantopoulos et al., 1995). This knowledge base is organized using Telos (Mylopoulos, 1990) and contains information about requirements, design, and implementation. The knowledge base can be queried through a graphical interface to support the traversal of semantic links. The REGINA software library project builds an information system to support the reuse of commercial off-the-shelf software components (Nagl, 1996). Their proposed architecture also exploits Web technology.

14.6.5 Knowledge Engineering

Related areas in knowledge engineering include knowledge sharing (Patil et al., 1992), ontologies (Gruber, 1993), data repositories (Bernstein and Dayal, 1994), data warehouses (Hammer, 1995), and similarity-based queries (Jagadish et al., 1995; Jurisica and Glasgow, 1997)). Meta-data have received considerable attention (e.g., (Klas and Sheth, 1994)) as a way to integrate disparate information sources (Seligman and Rosenthal, 1996). Solving this problem is particularly important for building distributed multimedia systems for the World Wide Web (WWW5, 1996). Atlas is a distributed hyperlink database system that works with traditional servers (Pitkow and Jones, 1996). Other approaches to the same problem focus on a generic architecture (e.g., through mediators (Wiederhold, 1995)). The software bookshelf uses multiheaded links and an underlying meta-data repository to offer a more flexible, distributed hypermedia system.

In general, the representational frameworks used in knowledge engineering are richer in structure and in supported inferences than those in databases, but those in databases are less demanding on resources and also scale up more gracefully. The bookshelf repository falls between these extremes in representational power and in resource demands. Also, the bookshelf repository is particularly strong in the structuring mechanisms it supports (i.e., generalization, aggregation, classification, and contexts) and in the way these are integrated into a coherent representational framework.

14.7 Conclusions

This chapter introduced the concept of a software bookshelf to recapture, re-document, and access relevant information about a legacy software system for re-engineering or migration purposes. The novelty of the concept is the technologies that it combines, including an extensible, Web-based architecture, tool integration mechanisms, an expressive information model, a meta-data repository, and state-of-the-art analysis tools. The paper describes these components from the perspectives of three, increasingly project-specific roles involved in directly constructing, populating, and using a software bookshelf: the builder, the librarian, and the patron. Moreover, we outline a prototype implementation and discuss design decisions as well as early experiences. In addition, the paper reports on our experiences from a substantial case study with an existing legacy software system.

The software bookshelf has several major advantages.

First, its main user interface is based on an off-the-shelf Web browser, making it familiar, easy-to-use, and readily accessible from any desktop. This aspect provides an attractive and consistent presentation of all information relevant to a software system and facilitates end-user adoption.

Second, the bookshelf is a one-stop, structured reference of project-specific software documentation. By incorporating application-specific domain knowledge based on the needs of the migration effort, the librarian adds value to the information generated by the automatic tools.

Third, reverse engineering and software analysis tools can be easily connected to the bookshelf using standard Web protocols. Through these tools, the bookshelf provides a collection of diverse redocumentation techniques to extract information that is often lacking or inconsistent for legacy systems.

Fourth, the bookshelf environment is based on object-oriented, meta-data repository technology and can scale up to accommodate large legacy systems.

Finally, the overall bookshelf implementation is based on platform-independent Web standards that offer potential portability for the bookshelf. Using a client-server architecture, the bookshelf is centralized for straightforward updates yet is highly available to remote patrons.

We consider the software bookshelf useful because it can collect and present in a coherent form different kinds of relevant information about a legacy software system for re-engineering and migration purposes. We also demonstrated that it is a viable technique, because the creation of a large software bookshelf can be completed within a few months by librarians who have access to parsers, converters, and analysis tools. Moreover, the viability of the technique is strengthened in that the bookshelf environment requires little additional software and expertise for its use, thanks to adopting ubiquitous Web technology.

Despite some encouraging results, there are additional research tasks to be completed to finish evaluating the bookshelf technique.

First, we are currently validating the generality of the technique by applying it to a second legacy software system. Such a study will also provide a better estimate of the effort required in developing new bookshelves and provide useful insight to bookshelf builders.

Second, we wish to study techniques that would allow bookshelf patrons to extend and update bookshelf contents, as well as adding annotations at public, private, and group levels. This study would ensure that the technology does indeed support the evolution of a bookshelf by its owners and end users.

Third, we are working on mechanisms for maintaining consistency of the bookshelf contents and for managing the propagation of changes from one point, for example, a source code file, to all other points that relate to it.

Fourth, the bookshelf user interface is sufficiently complex to justify a user experiment to evaluate its usability and effectiveness.

Finally, we are currently studying extensions to the functionality of the bookshelf environment so that it supports not only redocumentation and access, but also specific software migration tasks.

14.8 Acknowledgments

The research reported in this paper was carried out within the context of a project jointly funded by IBM Canada and the Canadian Consortium for Software Engineering Research (CSER), an industry-directed program of collaborative university research and education, involving leading Canadian technology companies, universities, and government agencies.

This project would not have been possible without the tireless efforts of several postdoctoral Fellows, graduate students, and research associates. Many thanks go to: Gary Farmaner, Igor Jurisica, Iannis Tourlakis, and Vassilios Tzerpos (University of Toronto); Johannes Martin, James McDaniel, Margaret-Anne Storey, and James Uhl (University of Victoria); and Morven Gentleman and Howard Johnson (National Research Council).

We also wish to thank all the members of the development group that we worked with inside the IBM Toronto Laboratory for sharing their technical knowledge and insights on a remarkable software system.

Finally, we gratefully acknowledge the tremendous contributions of energy, diplomacy, and patience by Dr. Jacob Slonim in bringing together the CSER partnership and in launching this project.

14.9 References

Arango, G., Baxter, I., and Freeman, P. (1985). Maintenance and Porting of Software by Design Recovery. In *CSM-85, Proceedings of the Conference on Software Maintenance*, Austin, TX, IEEE Computer Society Press, November 1985, pages 42-49.

Arnold, R. (1993). *Software Reengineering*. IEEE Computer Society Press, NY.

Baker, S. (1995). On Finding Duplication and Near-Duplication in Large Software Systems. In *Proceedings of the Working Conference on Reverse Engineering (WCRE)*, Toronto, Ontario, IEEE Computer Society Press, July 1995, pages 86-95.

Bernstein, P. and Dayal, U. (1994). An Overview of Repository Technology. *International Conference on Very Large Databases*, Santiago, Chile, September 1994.

Biggerstaff, T., Mitbander, B., and D. Webster. (1994). Program Understanding and the Concept Assignment Problem. *Communications of the ACM*, 37(5), May 1994, pages 72-83.

Brown, A. and Penedo, M. (1992). An Annotated Bibliography on Software Engineering Environment Integration. *ACM Software Engineering Notes*, 17(3), July 1992, pages 47-55.

Buss, E. (1994). Investigating Reverse Engineering Technologies for the CAS Program Understanding Project. *IBM Systems Journal*, 33(3), August 1994, pages 477-500.

CACM (1991). Collaborative Computing. *Communications of the ACM*, Special Issue, December 1991.

CACM (1997). Mylopoulos, J. and Papazoglou, M. (Editors). Special Issue on Cooperative Information Systems. *IEEE Expert*.

Cagan, M. R. (1990). The HP SoftBench Environment: An Architecture for a New Generation of Software Tools. *Hewlett-Packard Journal*, 41(3), June 1990, pages 36-47.

Chase, M. (1996). Analysis and Presentation of Recovered Software Architectures. In *Proceedings of Working Conference on Reverse Engineering (WCRE)*, Monterey, CA, IEEE Computer Society Press, November 1996, pages 153-162.

Choi, S. C. and Scacchi, W. (1990). Extracting and Restructuring the Design of Large Systems. *IEEE Software*, 7(1), January 1990, pages 66-71.

Consens, M., Mendelzon, A., and Ryman, A. (1992). Visualizing and Querying Software Structures. In *Proceedings of the 14th International Conference on Software Engineering (ICSE)*, Melbourne, Australia; IEEE Computer Society Press, May 1992, pages 138-156.

Constantopoulos, P. et al. (1995). The Software Information Base: A Server for Reuse. *Very Large Data Bases Journal*, 4, pages 1-43.

Curtis, B., Kellner, M., and Over, J. (1979). Measuring the Psychological Complexity of Software Maintenance Tasks with the Halstead and McCabe Metrics. *IEEE Transactions on Software Engineering*, SE-5, March 1979, pages 96-104 .

Curtis, B., Kellner, M., and Over, J. (1992). Process Modeling. *Communications of the ACM*, 35(9), September 1992, pages 75-90.

Devanbu, P. (1992). GENOA—A Customizable Language- and Front-End Independent Code Analyzer. In *Proceedings of the 14th International Conference on Software Engineering* (*ICSE*), Melbourne, Australia, IEEE Computer Society Press, May 1992, pages 307-317.

Devanbu, P. and Jones, M. (1997). The Use of Description Logics in KBSE Systems. *ACM Transactions on Software Engineering and Methodology*, 6(2), April 1997.

Devanbu, P. (1991). Lassie: A Knowledge-based Software Information System. *Communications of the ACM* 34(5), May 1991, pages 34-49.

ECMA (1990). *ECMA: Portable Common Tool Environment*, Technical Report ECMA-149, Geneva, Switzerland.

Gamma, E., Richard, H., Johnson, R. and Vlissidos, J. (1995). *Design Patterns: Elements of Reusable Object-Oriented Software*, Addison-Wesley Publishing Co., Reading, MA.

Gosling, J., Joy, B. and Steele, G. (1996). *The Java Language Specification*, Addison-Wesley Publishing Co., Reading, MA.

Gruber, T. (1993). A Translation Approach to Portable Ontology Specifications. *Knowledge Acquisition* 5, No. 2, March 1993, pages 199-220.

Halstead, M. and Maurice, H. (1977). *Elements of Software Science*, Elsevier North-Holland Publishing Co., New York.

Hammer, J. (1995). The Stanford Data Warehousing Project. *IEEE Data Engineering Bulletin*, June 1995.

Jagadish, H., Mendelzon, A., and Milo, T. (1995). Similarity-based Queries. In *Proceedings of the Fourteenth ACM SIGACT-SIGMOD-SIGART Symposium on Principles of Database Systems* (*PODS*), San Jose, CA, May 1995, pages 36-45.

Johnson, H. (1996). Navigating the Textual Redundancy Web in Legacy Source. In *Proceedings of CASCON '96*, Toronto, Ontario, November 1996, pages 7-16.

Jurisica, I. and Glasgow, J. (1997). Improving Performance of Case-based Classification Using Context-based Relevance. *International Journal of Artifi-*

cial Intelligence Tools, special issue of IEEE ITCAI-96 Best Papers 6, No. 3&4.

Kafura, D. and Reddy, G. (1987). The Use of Software Complexity Metrics in Software Maintenance. *IEEE Transactions on Software Engineering*, SE-13(3), March 1987, pages 335-343.

Kaiser, G. et al. (1997). An Architecture for WWW-based Hypercode Environments. In *Proceedings of the 19th International Conference on Software Engineering (ICSE)*, Boston, MA, IEEE Computer Society Press, May 1997, pages 3-13.

Klas, W. and Sheth, A. (Editors). (1994). Special Issue: Metadata for Digital Media. *ACM SIGMOD Record*, 23(4), December 1994.

Kontogiannis, K. et al. (1996). Pattern Matching for Clone and Concept Detection. *Journal of Automated Software Engineering*, 3, pages 77-108.

Kotik, G. and Markosian, L. (1989). *Automating Software Analysis and Testing Using a Program Transformation System.* Reasoning Systems Inc., 3260 Hillview Avenue, Palo Alto, CA 94304.

Kozaczynski, V. et al. (1995). Architecture Specification Support for Component Integration. In *Proceedings of the Seventh International Workshop on Computer-Aided Software Engineering (CASE)*, Toronto, Canada, IEEE Computer Society Press, July 1995, pages 30-39.

Lee, H. and Harandi, M. (1993). An Analogy-based Retrieval Mechanism for Software Design Reuse. In *Proceedings of the 8th Knowledge-Based Software Engineering Conference*, Chicago, IL, IEEE Computer Society Press, pages 152-159.

Mancoridis, S. (1996). *The Star System*, Ph.D. thesis, Department of Computer Science, University of Toronto, 10 King's College Road, Toronto, Ontario, Canada M5S 3G4.

Mancoridis, S. and Holt, R. (1995). Extending Programming Environments to Support Architectural Design. In *Proceedings of the Seventh International Workshop on Computer-Aided Software Engineering (CASE)*, Toronto, Ontario, IEEE Computer Society Press, July 1995, pages 110-119.

McCabe (1995). *Visual Reengineering Toolset*, 5501 Twin Knolls Road, Suite 111, Columbia, MD 21045. More information can be found at the Internet World Wide Web site http://www.mccabe.com/visual/reeng.html.

McCabe, T. (1976). A Complexity Measure. *IEEE Transactions on Software Engineering* SE-2, pages 308-320.

Müller, H. and Klashinsky, K. (1988). Rigi—A System for Programming-in-the-Large. In *Proceedings of the 10th International Conference on Software Engineering (ICSE)*, Raffles City, Singapore, IEEE Computer Society Press, April 1988, pages 80-86.

Müller, H. et al. (1993). A Reverse Engineering Approach to Subsystem Structure Identification. *Journal of Software Maintenance: Research and Practice*, 5(4), December 1993, pages 181-204

Murphy G. and Notkin, D. (1996). Lightweight Lexical Source Model Extraction. *ACM Transactions on Software Engineering and Methodology*, April 1996, pages 262-292.

Murphy, G., Notkin, D., and Lan, S. (1996). An Empirical Study of Static Call Graph Extractors. In *Proceedings of the 18th International Conference on Software Engineering*, Berlin, Germany, IEEE Computer Society Press, March 1996, pages 90-100.

Mylopoulos, J. et al. (1990). Telos: Representing Knowledge About Information Systems. *ACM Transactions on Information Systems*, 8(4), October 1990, pages 325-362.

Nagl, M. (Editor). (1996). *Building Tightly Integrated Software Development Environments: The IPSEN Approach*, Lecture Notes in Computer Science 1170, Springer-Verlag, Inc., New York.

Ning, J. (1989). *A Knowledge-based Approach to Automatic Program Analysis*, Ph.D. thesis, Department of Computer Science, University of Illinois at Urbana-Champaign.

Olsem, M. (1997). *Software Reengineering Assessment Handbook*, United States Air Force Software Technology Support Center, 00-ALC/TISEC, 7278 4th Street, Hill Air Force Base, Utah 84056-5205.

OMG (1991). Object Management Group, Inc. *The Common Object Request Broker: Architecture and Specification*, Framingham Corporate Center, 492 Old Connecticut Path, Framingham, MA 01701, December 1991.

Ousterhout, J. (1994). *Tcl and the Tk Toolkit*, Addison-Wesley Publishing Co., Reading, MA.

Parr, T. J. (1996). *Language Translation Using PCCTS and C++: A Reference Guide*, Automata Publishing Company, 1072 South De Anza Blvd., Suite A107, San Jose, CA 95129.

Patil, R. et al. (1992). The DARPA Knowledge Sharing Effort: Progress Report. In *Proceedings of the Third International Conference on Principles of Knowledge Representation and Reasoning*, Boston.

Penny, P. (1992). *The Software Landscape: A Visual Formalism for Programming-in-the-Large*, Ph.D. thesis, Department of Computer Science, University of Toronto.

Pitkow, J. and Jones, K. (1996). Supporting the Web: A Distributed Hyperlink Database System. Fifth International World Wide Web Conference (WWW96), Paris, May 1996.

Quilici, A. (1994). A Memory-based Approach to Recognizing Programming Plans. *Communications of the ACM*, 37(5), May 1994, pages 84-93.

Reiss, S. (1990). Connecting Tools Using Message Passing in the Field Environment. *IEEE Software*, 7(3), July 1990, pages 57-66.

Schefstrom, D. and Van den Broek, G. (1993). *Tool Integration: Environments and Frameworks*, John Wiley & Sons, Inc., New York.

Selby, R. and Basili, V. (1991). Analyzing Error-Prone System Structure. *IEEE Transactions on Software Engineering*, SE-17(2), February 1991, pages 141-152.

Seligman, L. and Rosenthal, A. (1996). A Metadata Resource to Promote Data Integration. In *IEEE Metadata Conference*, Silver Spring, MD, IEEE Computer Society Press, April 1996.

Sowa, J. F. and Zachman, J. A. (1992). Extending and Formalizing the Framework for Information Systems Architecture. *IBM Systems Journal*, 31(3), 590-616.

Stallman, R. (1981). Emacs: The Extensible, Customizable, Self-Documenting Display Editor. In *Proceedings of the Symposium on Text Manipulation*, Portland, OR, June 1981, pages 147-156.

Storey, M.-A. et al. (1996). On Designing an Experiment to Evaluate a Reverse Engineering Tool. In *Proceedings of the Working Conference on Reverse Engineering (WCRE)*, Monterey, CA, IEEE Computer Society Press, November 1996, pages 31-40.

Tilley, S. et al. (1994). Programmable Reverse Engineering. *International Journal of Software Engineering and Knowledge Engineering*, 4(4), December 1994, pages 501-520.

Valetto, G. and Kaiser, G. (1995). Enveloping Sophisticated Tools into Computer-Aided Software Engineering Environments. In *Proceedings of the Seventh International Workshop on Computer-Aided Software Engineering (CASE)*, Toronto, Ontario, IEEE Computer Society Press, July 1995, pages 40-48.

Van der Linden, F. and Muller, J. (1995). Creating Architectures with Building Blocks. *IEEE Software*, 12 (6), November 1995, pages 51-60.

Wall, L., Christiansen, T., and Schwartz, R. (1996). *Programming Perl*, O'Reilly and Associates Inc., 101 Morris Street, Sebastopol, CA 95472.

Weiser, M. (1984). Program Slicing. *IEEE Transactions on Software Engineering*, SE-10(4), July 1984, pages 352-357.

Wiederhold, G. (1995). The Conceptual Technology for Mediation. *International Conference on Cooperative Information Systems*, Vienna, May 1995.

Wills, l. and Rich, C. (1990). Recognizing a Program's Design: A Graph-Parsing Approach. *IEEE Software*, 7(1), January 1990, pages 82-89.

Wong, K. (1993). Managing Views in a Program Understanding Tool. In *Proceedings of CASCON '93*, Toronto, Ontario, October 1993, pages 244-249.

WWW5 (1996). Fifth International World Wide Web Conference, Paris, May 1996.

Zachman, J. A. (1987). A Framework for Information Systems Architecture. *IBM Systems Journal*, 26(3), pages 276-292.

15
Dynamic Documents Over the Web

Paulo Alencar
Don Cowan
Daniel German
Luis Nova
Bob Fraser
Jamie Roberts
Gary Pianosi

15.1 Introduction

In general, software engineering practice includes document production as one of the activities that software developers need to perform during the software development process. According to Pressman (1992), most software development organizations spend a substantial amount of time developing documents, and in many cases the documentation process itself is quite inefficient. Pressman also mentions that it is not unusual for a typical software engineering organization to spend as much as 20 or 30 percent of all its software development effort on producing documentation. Thus, automated support for document presentation and production provides an opportunity for the developers to save time and effort and, consequently, to improve productivity.

However, the organization of most current online documentation systems is similar to that found in hardcopy manuals. The structure is rigid and navigation techniques are limited. The document topics are organized in a sequence of chapters that are subdivided into a number of sections and subsections. These sections are further connected through hyperlinks. Additional browsing techniques available in these systems include an index of topics or a query system that supports searching for a given string across the collection of documents.

Today, with the diversity of publishing formats and user profiles, we must devise a system that allows us to "author once, publish many." Information that was once delivered in a rigid software-specific format may have to be converted a few months later. Thus, having a system that allows an easy transition to a different presentation, structural, or publishing format is crucial for software documentation (Stieren, 1997).

15.1.1 Using the Internet and the Web

The accessibility of the World Wide Web (WWW) and the Internet/Intranet has produced a paradigm shift in the way product information can be stored, distributed and presented. Product information, formerly delivered in hardcopy and softcopy books, is now being delivered as hypertext webs or documents tagged with HTML and accessible through a Web browser. This new paradigm has generated numerous tools to author and maintain documents with embedded tags.

The Internet as a world wide interconnected collection of networks allows individuals or groups in almost any type of organization to interchange data. Access to data can be provided to anyone on the Internet independent of the location of the user and the data. Because of the Internet's exponential growth a large percentage of individuals who would like to exchange documents have that capability (Tanenbaum, 1996).

The WWW is one such set of data. The Web consists of a vast collection of documents, and uses the Internet infrastructure to provide access to documents stored in different machines all over the world. These documents are called pages. Pages may have links that refer to other pages located at different locations. Users can activate a link and jump to the referred page. The strings of text that are links to other pages are called hyperlinks. As individual pages may contain not only text but also hyperlinks, they are referred to as hypertext or hypertext pages. When the hypertext pages are mixed with other media, such as audio or video, the result is called hypermedia. Web pages are built from text strings delineated or marked with tags from languages called markup languages, such as HTML (Hypertext Markup Language). These text strings refer to text, graphics, hypermedia content, and links to other Web pages. Web pages are viewed with a program called a browser.

Putting large information libraries into hypertext webs presents many new challenges for document designers and writers. The information itself must be designed for easy and usable online access, a process that involves organizing information into independent, distinct topics. The result is often a web of information containing thousands of files.

At IBM, we have experience creating webs of product information for several VisualAge products that exceed 10,000 files. The size of these webs creates enormous building and maintenance problems for the writers, and corresponding search and navigation issues for the users. To solve these problems, we looked for new approaches for creating, maintaining, and delivering large information webs.

15.1.2 Our Approach to Dynamic Documentation

In this chapter we address the problem of how to make it easier to build, evolve, and use technical software documentation that is delivered via the Web.

In essence, our approach is to provide support to separate the different concerns of Web-based documents into four orthogonal components: content, structure, navigation, and presentation. The proposed support is basically provided by storing the information in databases and providing methods and tools to handle multiple document views and related navigation issues.

The objective of this research project is to investigate and propose models that address the documentation needs of IBM within this new Web and Internet-based world. The proposed documentation model is being prototyped using LivePage Enterprise software (Janna Systems Inc., 1999). This software stores documents tagged with SGML-compliant languages in SQL databases. The LivePage software also has a number of integrated tools including a server mechanism that supports SQL statements embedded in documents and dynamic presentation of documents on the Web.

In this way, we would enable users of IBM products to navigate and search easily through large databases of product information, which will be dynamic and customizable and may be distributed across an Intranet or the Internet. In addition, we would simplify the construction and maintenance of these databases so that the creators of product information may concentrate on content and usability instead of issues related to managing large files. The University of Waterloo, Janna Systems, and the IBM Canada Laboratory are performing this research, which aims at implementing the approach described in this section.

In the next section we describe the challenges faced when building, maintaining, delivering, and using large documents distributed over the WWW. Among other issues, we examine the impact of tagging or markup languages and the underlying storage models. In Section 15.3, we briefly outline the underlying document model that constitutes the basis for the work presented in this chapter. In Section 15.4, we describe how our approach has been implemented; and the results of applying this approach to some technical documents. We close the chapter with discussions of future and related work.

15.2 Building, Maintaining and Using Hyperlinked Documents

Documents created for delivery using the WWW normally use a number of hyperlinked files tagged with HTML. As these documents grow they become extremely difficult to manage and maintain because of the number of files and links. For example, producing, maintaining and using paper documents for complex software systems such as IBM's DB2 involves about 20 large manuals. These documents have to be made available for different operating environments and in several national languages. Moreover, it has been argued that maintaining a large Web site for such documentation is similar to and as complex a task as maintaining a large software system (Brereton et al., 1998).

Because of the inherent complexity of the document the maintainer can not easily or correctly modify or add features. For example, it is difficult to add as a new feature a "role" tag that is not visible but that defines a set of users that can access the document. Thus, it is not unusual for document features not to be implemented in a timely manner or not to work. Further, the user will find it almost impossible to augment the documentation, a practice, which is becoming more common as software systems are constructed from components. For example, suppose that a software company needs to include a document component in its existing software documentation about how the software works with a new operating system. Adding this component may not be possible because of the existence of inconsistent document parts.

A typical hyperlinked HTML document is constructed from individual text files formed through hyperlinks into a large web or network of pages. There is usually some implied hierarchical structure resembling a table of contents. This structure is usually implemented as a set of hyperlinks or table of contents (TOC) radiating from the main or home page. In addition, the hyperlinks are used to connect related concepts together into a knowledge structure. There are a number of issues to be addressed in adding material or modifying material in such a document. Tasks such as relating content to a file name, adding or moving a page within the structure all become quite complex.

Modifying existing Web pages is quite difficult. How do we find the correct context in a large Web space consisting of files with simple names? It is very difficult to map the contents of substantial text files into names. Adding new pages is also a problem. The page or file name must be added to the existing table of contents; this operation may cause a series of update operations. Deleting a page is similarly complex, not only must the page be removed from the appropriate tables of contents, but all hyperlinks that use this page as a destination from the TOC or as part of the knowledge structure must be found and modified. The problems described here only relate to a single view of a document; the problems increase dramatically when multiple TOCs must be maintained because dynamic and conditional views of a document are required.

Because current Web-based documentation systems rely on files as the storage model, there is little underlying additional structure or language to support features such as access control and a history or audit trail.

Maintenance of a documentation system is an expensive operation that is labor-intensive and requires a large investment in highly paid personnel. Many Web sites become stale or out of date because of this requirement for investment.

Searching a Web document is also a complex operation. An index of all the important words and terms in the set of Web pages must be compiled, so that a local search can be performed.

So far we have discussed only a single author, maintainer or user. How can a document be shared so that the integrity of the document is maintained? In other words how do we prevent multiple authors/maintainers from modifying a document at the same time? How do we ensure that all changes are backed up, so we can recover from disasters or errors?

The tagging language HTML is also a problem; it is not easily extensible. The developer of the Web browser fixes these languages and merges both the structural and presentation aspects of the language into a single tag thereby removing flexibility. Besides not allowing distinct tags to handle structure and presentation, it is not possible to add new tags to deal with additional features such as rating a Web site or limiting the users that can access a specific page depending on their roles.

Most of the issues illustrated in this section are related to separation of concerns and extensibility. These are issues usually addressed in software engineering, but only beginning to be examined in the context of document systems (Halasz and Schwartz, 1994; Isakowitz et al., 1995; Garzotto et al., 1993; Schwabe and Rossi, 1995; German et al., 1999). Most tools to support authoring and maintenance of HTML documents focus on the file as the main entity. The authors of these tools pay almost no attention to the fact that these types of documents are just a visual representation of more abstract entities that are interrelated, and the modification of one entity might require changes in another.

Because files are just simple lists with no underlying structure and associated programming language, they are not easily extended to include new structures. The markup language for describing the document is similarly limited and not extensible, and describes a mixture of structure, navigation and appearance. The following list categorizes some of the common problems of HTML documents that arise from these considerations:

- *Consistency.* Since every page is independent, information common to several pages has to be repeated, presenting a potential consistency problem.[1]
- *Organization or structure.* The organization of an HTML document is bound when the files are created. Restructuring is expensive and requires splitting, collating, renaming or deleting files, and also updating links among files.
- *Navigation.* Since the navigational structure is embedded in the files, it is difficult to find and modify navigational links.
- *Presentation.* Information is not isolated from its presentation.[2] If the presentation of pages needs to change, that information has to be changed on a file-by-file basis.

---

[1] Some HTTP servers support "server-side includes", which are directives to the server that are replaced by the contents of a given file or the result of an executable program. This technique only partially addresses the problem of consistency at a high performance price, since the directive is executed every time the node is requested.

[2] Cascading Style Sheets are trying to solve this problem partially at the file level.

- *Referential Integrity.* When the name, hyperlink or Uniform Resource Locator (URL) (Berners-Lee et al. 1994) of a resource changes, all the links pointing to that resource have to be updated. This problem exists at both the global level, where the author does not have control over the documents pointing to the local information from an external site, and at the local level.
- *Extensibility.* Files do not have the associated tools and structures that make them easy to extend their capabilities. Similarly the tagging languages are limited in scope.

The apparent simplicity of the tagging systems and the file structures being used for document systems has a substantial cost. The author of a document mixes together different design concerns indiscriminately, and then stores the result in multiple files. Because of this integration, it is difficult to change a document's presentation, structure, and content without a complete and complex rewrite. In addition, because there is no clear distinction among these disparate concepts, a document designer often considers the navigational and organizational structure first, followed by presentation, and finally, if there is any time left, the content. Ideally, this process should be reversed: write the content, define the presentation, and then impose a navigational structure.

Many of the issues described can be resolved with database systems and more powerful tagging languages. In the next two subsections we briefly describe extensible tagging languages, and then describe in general terms how databases can be used to address many of the issues associated with creation, maintenance, and use of text-based documentation systems.

15.2.1 Tagging Languages

As mentioned earlier, a markup language (also known as a tagging language) is the language used for writing Web pages. Essentially, a markup language describes how to format documents. The term "markup" applies when copyeditors used to tell typographers which fonts to use. Therefore, markup languages contain explicit commands for formatting. These languages use tags to indicate the start and the end of a formatting mode. For example, in HTML, <B> means start boldface mode, and </B> means leave boldface mode. Other well known examples of markup languages are TeX and Troff.

Tagging languages can be divided into general-purpose and domain-dependent schemes. In the former, the tags have a generic meaning; an H1 tag in HTML represents the biggest type of title tag available. However, this type of tag does not specify whether the tag is the title of a book, the title of a poem, or the name of a country. The only information specified is that the text enclosed by the tag is sufficiently important to render it with a large font and in bold. Domain-dependent schemes are created to reflect the structure of the document: a book is divided into chapters and the chapters into sections. Each one can have a title. Paragraphs, quotations, citations, foreign words-each can be separately marked with a specific tag type.

Generic languages such as HTML have been extensively used because they are easier to implement since the browser knows the language being rendered for presentation. SGML (Goldfarb, 1990) and its newer derivative XML (W3 Consortium, 1997) are meta-languages in that they are used to define domain-specific tagging languages. These meta-languages with an accompanying grammar or document type definition (DTD) (Goldfarb, 1990) define the language. In other words they define the tag types and their use. The accompanying style languages such as XSL (Microsoft Corporation, 1998; W3 Consortium, 1998) and DSSSL (Adler, 1994) provide the flexibility to expand the syntax and semantics of documentation systems and support the separation of the presentation of the document from the other design concerns.

Including more information about the structure of a document benefits both the authoring and browsing processes. The author does not have to make style decisions such as the size of the header for a particular part of the text or whether quotations should be displayed with underscores or italics. Instead, the author can concentrate on the content and the proper use of tags. In a subsequent step, the document can be translated into a generic tag language—such as HTML—or it can be viewed by using a more sophisticated browser that takes as input the DTD, a style-sheet that specifies how to render each tag in the language and the document. The way the document is displayed can then be easily changed, either by the designer or by the reader. Furthermore, searching can be more precise, since the search engine can take advantage of the structure of the document.

15.2.2 Databases for Storage of Text

A database is a data repository that provides access to a large number of data elements, which in our case are related to documents. In the case of a relational database, the repository stores a structured collection of tabular data. The data is accessed through query language statements. The use of a query language hides the complexity of the sophisticated processing required to implement queries.

Relational and object-oriented databases can be used to store the objects found in documentation. The stored elements are segments of text and objects to which they refer (e.g., pictures, graphics, audio or video clips and programs). What are the advantages of using a database over the use of multiple files?

A database can be viewed as a single file containing various structures or meta-data relating all the objects or tables. Extra structures can be imposed upon the database to capture relationships that are not inherent in the document. Although such structures can also be added to files, the languages and tools to support these structures must also be constructed, whereas languages such as SQL, and supporting tools are an inherent part of a database system. We mention some specific examples of useful structures in the following paragraphs.

We have noticed that almost all hyperlinks in a document fall into four categories; structural or organizational, circular, star, and index. Structural links are used to organize a document into a hierarchy resembling a book. Circular, star and index links form knowledge structures. Circular and star links connect similar concepts together. Circular links form a chain, while star links point to a common destination or concept. Index links are the reverse of star links, in that they are usually presented as part of an index table and connect the concept in the table to all its references. Since hyperlink structures can be categorized, the relationship among hyperlinks can be captured in database structures. This structure can then be scanned to detect missing destinations, or reflect deleted or additional hyperlinks. Multiple organizational structures can also be maintained supporting different views of a document.

A history could be included in the database that included comments about modifications to the data or the date of the most recent changes. Such a structure would allow an author or user to find and track the most recent changes to a document. The aforementioned structures can be used to separate organization and navigation from content, thereby addressing issues related to separation of concerns. Such structures also make it easy to support referential integrity and consistency. In effect the ability to add structures with supporting languages such as SQL or embed those languages in other programming languages makes a highly extensible open environment.

Databases support common functions such as security, backup and replication. The security model in most databases has been well tested over time. Security can be used to lock database structures in order to implement check-in and check-out facilities. Such techniques are essential in managing author interaction in a multi-author document. Backup structures are also inherent in most database systems and are essential in implementing disaster control. Replication facilities support distribution of information across computing platforms.

Storing and manipulating text containing a markup language such as SGML or XML is only valuable if the text can be delivered in manageable chunks similar to those provided by a traditional Web-based system. In the next section we describe the LivePage system and illustrate how it uses database technology to store and deliver Web pages.

15.3 The Underlying Hypermedia Model

Currently, there are several methodologies for hypermedia document development such as Schwabe and Rossi's Object-Oriented Hypermedia Design Model, OOHDM (Schwabe and Rossi, 1995); Isakowitz et al.'s Relational Management Methodology, RMM (Isakowitz et al., 1995); Lange's Object Oriented Design Method, EORM (Lange, 1995); Garzotto et al.'s Hypermedia Design Model, HDM (Garzotto et al., 1993). These methodologies are, primarily, guidelines to be followed during the design process. They also specify the characteristics of the deliverables that are created at each of their stages. These products are usually informally specified in the sense that they do not have a formal syntax or formally defined semantics.

In particular, OOHDM defines a four-step building process, where each step focuses on a specific design concern of a large hypermedia application. Based on this methodology, German et al. (1999) defined a formal system that separates the different tasks faced during the application design process. In this respect, a hypermedia document is defined according to four different concerns: content, structure, navigation, and presentation. These concerns can be viewed as four orthogonal axes in a design space.

Such a design model requires an implementation tool that closely follows these concerns. LivePage Enterprise software was chosen as the implementation platform because of its ability to represent the four different hypermedia concerns separately. While content, structure, and navigation are represented in different relational tables, presentation is defined by means of style files, which are dynamically attached to the document being delivered.

15.4 Implementing the Document System

In a previous section, we have proposed that database systems are an appropriate storage model for tagged text, and support the separation of the different concerns of hypermedia design.

15.4.1 A Base Implementation

We have developed a base implementation (Janna Systems Inc., 1999; Zobel et al., 1991) of our model that satisfies most of the specified requirements, and uses a relational database system. Figure 15.1 illustrates a simplified view of this implementation; details are presented in the next subsections.

The System Implementation

In this implementation we initially embed text, hyperlinks, and references to objects into a single document. We distinguish or "separate" them by tagging conventions using an SGML-compliant tagging language. Thus, if we move to a different entity storage model, we will be able to separate the three types of information easily.

Once the document is complete, we verify it against a grammar or document type definition (DTD) before loading the document into a single relational (SQL) database.

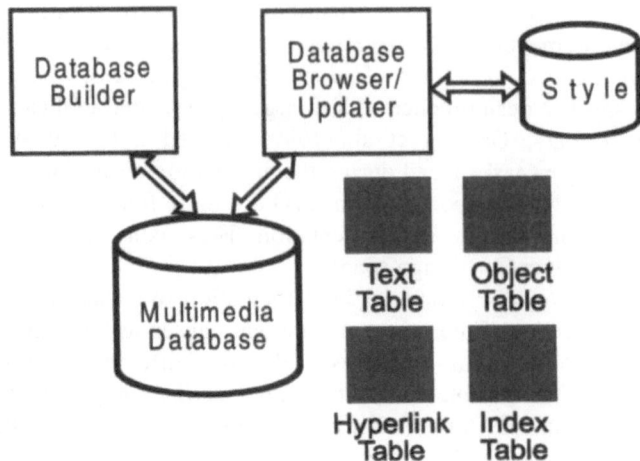

Figure 15.1. The base implementation.

Each fundamental tagged structure[3] or document component is loaded into a single field in a relational database table and given a unique identifier. There are three separate tables for text, objects and hyperlinks. In addition, every word in the document is also placed in an index to facilitate searching when the database is browsed. Optionally, every structure tag can be placed in the same index to facilitate searching for words within specific tagged structures. An author can also create specialized indices by defining the words and phrases that form its content. The various objects such as graphics, video and sound, and links to external programs are stored directly in the object table as "blobs" with the appropriate attributes. The tables for the tagged text, hyperlinks, objects and index are identified and collectively labeled as a multimedia database.

The Toolkit

The basic LivePage toolkit is provided to support creation (the database builder), maintenance (the updater), and browse and query (the browser) of the database. Builder functions, namely the verification against a DTD and creation of the database tables are described earlier. We consider documents as trees (Mackie and Zobel, 1992), and the updater allows a substructure (subtree) to be moved, deleted, modified or replaced within the document. While this sub-structure is being changed, the corresponding section of the database can be locked in order to maintain database integrity. Since we use SQL database tech-nology, the database can be created, updated, and browsed using SQL state-

---

[3] Apart from certain exceptions, a fundamental tagged structure will contain no tagged substructures.

ments. However, the LivePage tools provide an interface that makes the application of the SQL statements transparent.

The database builder and updater are primarily tools for the database administrator or author, while the browser is a tool for the general user to examine the database. The browser supports linear browsing, forward and backward hyperlinks, and object activation. The functions of the database builder and updater are presented through a uniform user interface so documents can be created and modified seamlessly.

The browser also supports queries. The queries can be Boolean or simple where the results of the simple query are presented in relevance order with the most relevant result presented first. The simple query can be an English sentence.

Text stored in the database can be extracted and modified using most commercially available structured text editors. Similarly objects stored in the database can be extracted using the updater and can be created or modified using appropriate authoring tools.

Tools such as the browser and updater allow the client to view the document stored in the database. However, the document contains only content, structural and navigation information. Presentation or style information is contained in a separate style repository and is loaded into the browser or updater when it is invoked.

Connecting to the World Wide Web

The base implementation described previously allows local access to documents but does not support access through the WWW. The LivePage toolkit contains two other mechanisms for this purpose. Figure 15.2 illustrates the architecture of a dynamic distributed document database system accessible over the WWW. Users accessing a WWW browser such as Netscape or Microsoft Explorer request a WWW page from a WWW server. Using the CGI, NSAPI or Microsoft ISAPI protocol, the WWW server passes the request to the LivePage Server module that then accesses a database of WWW pages tagged with SGML or XML. The specific WWW page that was requested is retrieved from the database and then transformed into HTML by the LivePage server, and returned through the WWW server to the WWW browser for presentation.

The transformation shown in Figure 15.2 proceeds in two steps. First the SGML or XML document is transformed into HTML. After this transformation the document is augmented with HTML code and other language commands to achieve a specific appearance. A typical presentation would contain a "Table of Contents" (TOC) and navigation buttons. The automatic generation of a TOC and the navigation buttons relieves the author of the WWW site of creating navigational aids, and allows users to orient themselves by returning to the TOC whenever they feel "lost in hyperspace.[4]"

---

[4] The position in the TOC is highlighted to assist in the orientation process.

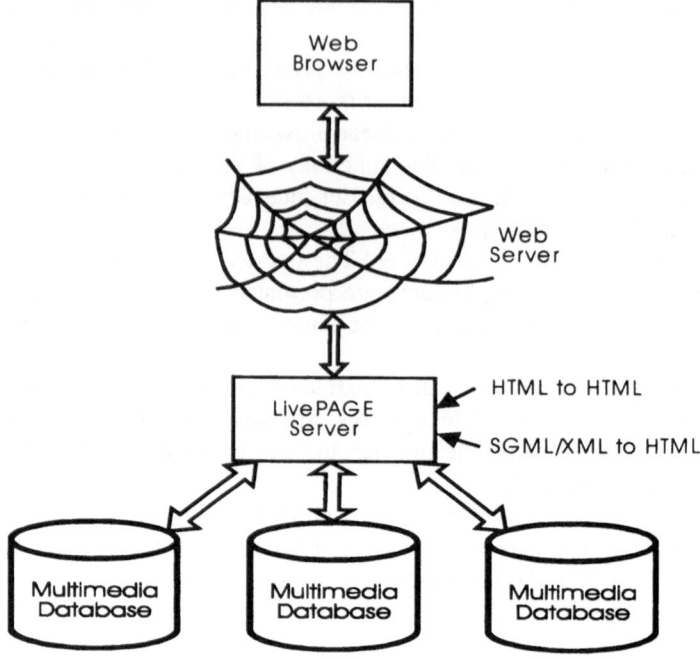

Figure 15.2. Accessing the database over the WWW.

The SGML/XML pages in the database can also contain embedded SQL commands that support access to structured relational databases. The LivePage Server intercepts these embedded SQL statements and passes them to the structured database. Thus we can combine multimedia and structured data in a single page. The LivePage Server module is not restricted to a single database, but can retrieve and search WWW pages from multiple tagged document databases as illustrated in Figure 15.2 .

The Publisher is a tool similar to the Server Administrator except that the Publisher generates a static Web site. The generation process creates a WWW site from the database at a specific point in time. Obviously, if the database changes after the last creation time, then the "publishing" process must once again be repeated.

Importing Legacy WWW Sites

There are many existing WWW sites that could benefit from the support of document databases. The LivePage toolkit provides a facility to import an existing WWW site, to attempt the correction of structural errors, and then to build a tagged document and multimedia database. Once the database is constructed, all the tools previously described can be used.

15.4.2 Extending the Base Implementation

The extensibility of the database and tagging approach to documentation systems is illustrated through features that have been added to the database through the LivePage toolkit.

We have often augmented a DTD with tags to support features within a document. For example, a document could contain a "rating" tag that is not visible but that describes the intended audience for the document.The database can be easily extended to provide new features in a document. For example, a history indicating dates on which a specific section of a document has been changed or comments describing those changes can be easily included.

We can also easily provide "views" of a document through the realm concept. A realm is a set of pages in the database with a user assigned to one or more realms through a database table. Thus a user can be excluded from browsing a specific set of pages by being excluded from a realm. Realms can be used to implement access control, or tables of contents for limited viewing.

We consider documents as composed of uniquely identified components that are organized into trees. Thus, database tables can specify the table of contents (TOC) or structure of a document. If we wish to create another document from the same set of components then we only need to create new database tables or TOCs to specify the new structure. Thus when a user switches contexts the system is only required to switch to a new TOC. This useful feature has been added to the original system in order to provide multiple structural views of the same contents.

In summary, current prototypes of the documentation system support:

- *Automatic dynamic translation of SGML documents into HTML*: Documents stored in a database are translated into HTML and served to the Web at the time they are requested. A table of contents (TOC) and context-sensitive navigation buttons are added to the document to provide the user with advanced navigation capabilities.
- *Conditional views (dynamic and static):* The same documentation is usually presented in different ways to different users depending on the user's interest or qualifications. For example, some documents have "conditional" sections that are displayed only under certain circumstances. "Static" views (e.g. author vs. user views) are password protected, while "dynamic" views (e.g. OS/2 vs. Windows 95 views) may be changed during navigation.
- *Structural views:* The document appears to be re organized with a different clustering of topics depending on the user's requirements. For example, the document could be presented in a tool rather than a task view.
- *Multiple table of contents (TOCs):* a different TOC is generated automatically for each conditional or structural view of a given document.
- *"Intelligent" searching:* the model provides support for searching where the results are organized according to a relevance ranking. Searching within

a context provided by SGML tags is also supported. Searching is restricted to the current view of the document.

- *Unicode documents:* the model supports documents written in Unicode allowing the display of documents written in other national languages.

15.4.3 Evaluation

The approach outlined in the previous sections has been applied to create webs of product information for several VisualAge products. This section presents a discussion about the results of applying our approach to some classes of technical documents.

The LivePage implementation retains the basic concepts of our underlying hypermedia model by maintaining the separation of the different concerns of Web-based documents. The structure of the database used in the LivePage model was optimized for retrieval rather than updates, since we expect that a document will be browsed more often than modified. The organization of the internal tables of the database allows fast retrieval of a subtree of the original document at the expense of slower updates; currently, an update is implemented as a deletion and then an insertion. We are investigating better algorithms to perform updates.

There is approximately a six-fold difference between the size of the original untagged document and its equivalent database. This increase in size is caused by a number of factors including: the system tables, the indexing associated with fast retrieval of information from the database tables, and the indexing of every word in the document (with the exception of stop words).

The implementation supports referential integrity. In the LivePage implementation referential integrity is inherent in the tagging since it is simple to verify that all the links and anchors of a document exist. Access and update control, locking mechanisms, and rollback are all inherent in the LivePage implementation, since LivePage uses an SQL relational database as its storage model. The LivePage tools provide extra navigational aids such as table of contents generation. Such a facility could also easily be provided in the model.A complete WWW site is stored in a single database that can be easily moved and does not have file system dependencies. LivePage is successful in solving many of the common problems inherent in WWW site development. However, there are a number of issues that need to be addressed.

As more and more information is made available on the WWW it becomes increasingly difficult to find the information that you want. Even search tools which use ranking to return only the results that are the most relevant, are nearing their limits as to how much text they can effectively index. One technique to increase the search effectiveness is to include in the ranking algorithm information that can be derived from the HTML tags about the structure of the document. Unfortunately, the HTML tagset is not very rich in its ability to describe the structure of all documents accurately. Augmenting HTML with additional SGML tags would be one way to overcome this problem.

Complex WWW sites do not just consist of static textual data with a few added graphics. It is often desirable to include other data, such as a stock market table, that is more dynamic and may be constantly changing. Frequently, this kind of data is also stored in relational databases. We have created a number of demonstrations of how this kind of data can be seamlessly integrated into the WWW site. Further analysis is needed to make this approach comparable to the process of building a simple WWW page.

Even the static textual data that makes up the majority of information in a WWW site is dynamic if looked at over a period of time. Frequently, a WWW site will go through several versions as it is enhanced and maintained. In some applications it is important to keep track of these different versions and to be able to recall an earlier version of the site. This form of version control could be added to the LivePage system.

Currently databases created for WWW sites are tagged with HTML, rather than SGML to avoid translating SGML tags to HTML tags and perhaps encountering incompatibilities. However, HTML may not adequately reflect the structure of the information, and SGML may be a better solution. However, it will be necessary to allow the database administrator to define sets of transformation rules to convert SGML code into HTML. Such a capability requires further study.

The LivePage document database tools only support a single DTD per document, whereas a document may have several different types of structures. This feature is supported by the SGML definition but is not currently available in the LivePage system.

15.5 Related Work

Different approaches have been tried to separate the content from its organization and presentation. We highlight some of them in this section.

Other Tagging Languages

Since HTML has limited structural components and is more oriented toward presentation, some authors have chosen to use another tagging language for the "master" of the information they maintain. The most common tagging system chosen uses SGML-compliant tagging languages which have a richer structure than HTML. These languages allow the author to characterize the structure of a set of documents, and to enforce this structure. Using ad-hoc filters, the SGML files can be converted to HTML. The advantage of such an approach is that the structure of the published information is kept separate from its presentation. If the user decides to change the master document's appearance, then only the filters need to be changed. A number of companies who publish the same information in various forms, have chosen SGML-compliant tagging languages as their master format. Other master formats have been proposed: LaTeX, word-processor based tags, and RTF. All these consider a WWW site as a text document, with well-specified rules to translate it into HTML. Properly used, this approach avoids inconsistencies, and separates presentation and navigation information from content. The main disadvantage of this approach is its focus on documents with a linear structure, such as books and articles, rather than the highly interconnected structures of objects typical in hypermedia applications.

Publishing SGML-Compliant Documents Directly on the WWW

Some WWW publishers make their documents only available for users with specific SGML browsers (such as Grif Symposia and SoftQuad's Panorama). They publish documents tagged with SGML-based tagging languages compliant with a standard DTD. A style-sheet is produced for the DTD, and is downloaded with the document to ensure proper rendering. SoftQuad is distributing copies of its browser to promote this concept.

Macroprocessor-Based Systems

In this approach the master information is stored in an ad-hoc tagging format, and a preprocessor or macroprocessor tailored specifically for HTML, is used to convert the files into HTML pages. A flexible macroprocessor can greatly assist in WWW development, reducing inconsistencies and separating content from presentation and navigation structure. Prior to defining the approach described in this chapter, we have used a macroprocessor-based system approach to create the WWW version of the "The University of Waterloo Undergraduate Calendar," which is composed of around 500 pages. The savings in development time were enormous compared to using plain HTML files. We have also developed a prototype macroprocessor system using the M4 preprocessor.

Page Image Systems

PDF and PostScript are popular formats used to publish information on the WWW. Both require special browsers to provide full control of the document typography.

Hypermedia-Based Systems

The success of the WWW has prompted the authors of some hypermedia systems such as Microcosm to adapt them to generate HTML pages. Hill et al. (1995) proposed to unify Microcosm and the WWW in three ways:
- Microcosm-aware WWW clients that is enhancing clients to support Microcosm primitives.
- Generating static pages out of a Microcosm system.

- Using CGI scripts to allow the interaction of a Microcosm server with typical WWW clients. The CGI scripts would convert Microcosm requests to HTML browsable files.

Other Systems

In all the previous cases, the information does not reside on a database. However, there are other implementations (Active Systems, Inc., 1996; EBT International, 1996) that use a database specialized for the storage and retrieval of tagged documents. However, these are proprietary in nature and not easily extensible by the user of the system. Other hypermedia systems (Hill et al., 1995) have been adapted to generate HTML tagged text. However the information does not reside in a database. Other authors have described using relations to represent hyperlinks (Lange, 1995; Isakowitz et al., 1995; Schwabe et al., 1996).

15.6 Conclusion and Future Work

In this chapter we discuss issues related to creating and maintaining large hyperlinked documents, a form of documentation that is becoming more common as the World Wide Web becomes increasingly pervasive. We describe a system that provides the tools necessary to create and maintain large, complex WWW sites. The system utilizes the power of SGML and relational database systems to solve many of the problems with which developers of large WWW sites are currently struggling. A clear separation is provided between the content, presentation, and navigational structure of the WWW site. This separation allows authors to focus on what they do best, writing content. On large WWW sites there will be other experts to focus on presentation and navigation. Even on smaller WWW sites, where there is only one expert, this separation can provide significant advantages by allowing the author to focus on each aspect of WWW development in turn.

We also claim that the database approach overcomes significant limitations of Web-based documentation systems related to openness, extensibility, consistency, and referential integrity. Finally we present an approach to documentation systems based on storing text marked with an SGML or XML compliant tagging language in a relational database. Style languages such as XSL are used to convert SGML tags into HTML for presentation using the Web. The implementation is open since it is based on standards in both tagging languages and databases. Further, these two standards are extensible. In addition, our approach leads to an implementation that is independent of specific storage structures. For this reason, the designer of a system can more freely make choices based on the available database systems and respective authoring tools.

Besides the technical advantages, adopting our approach also leads to benefits from a corporate perspective. The approach is cost-effective in terms of leveraging an organization's existing investment and expertise in RDBMS. There is also an ample supply of third-party (or outside) assistance. Because it is based on open standards, developers are not locked into a proprietary solution. In addition, text and data can be accessed using SQL across different vendors, and systems are easily portable to other vendors' systems. Furthermore, since relational database technology is a current *de facto* standard, relational databases are portable across different hardware vendors.

Indeed, the database support for our approach to documentation is scalable, flexible, extensible and proven. It scales from stand-alone PCs to mainframes. There is also a wide range of relational database vendors with excellent track records. In particular, relational databases have proven the test of time with respect to security, performance, and data replication.

Ongoing and future work will deal with topics related to modeling, and with verification and validation of software documents described using our approach, and include the following topics.

We are working on the definition of document models based on graphs that separate the concerns of Web-based documents, easily support the expansion of requirements, and can incorporate legacy material. These rigorous graph models will be used as a basis for the design and implementation of flexible and extensible documentation and help systems for large document sets. We also plan to use this model as a basis for the validation and verification of technical document descriptions.

We also want to take into account the roles of the different users that can access a dynamic document. Such roles can be related to various user characteristics, such as his/her level of expertise, hierarchical position in the organization, and access authorization level. A novice and an expert user, for example, would not normally have access to the same parts of a document. However, the objects in a page should be accessed based on user roles; that is, some information which is shown to a user belonging to a specific role may not be shown to a user belonging to a different role. Further, user access also depends on the navigational context: depending on the page a user is accessing, he/she may see (not see) parts of this page depending on his/her user role. This model provides a foundation for a user-based access control mechanism related to dynamic documents. Realms may be used as the basic implementation mechanism for this model.

Further, we are working on combining the verification of role-based access constraints with the verification through model checking (Clarke et al., 1986) of navigational properties of the dynamic document models. In this way, we are able to check if, based on a particular user role, a certain navigational constraint holds about the document model. As an example, one should be able to prove whether or not a user with a specific role is able to see a certain page.

With regard to implementation issues, we also plan to investigate the automation of the conversion process of legacy systems into our research model. Management tools will be implemented to automate the creation and maintenance of new document structures. Finally, new data models and tools will be investigated to improve our ability to manage concurrent updates of the several document structures.

Ideally, the information delivery system should provide multiple views into the information for the user depending on their level of expertise or the type of knowledge being requested. Meta-data about this information can be stored in the SGML or XML markup language, or in the database as attributes.

15.7 Acknowledgments

The authors wish to thank IBM Canada and the Consortium for Software Engineering (CSER) for their support.

15.8 References

ActiveSystems, Inc. (1996). *ActiveSystems—Reference Manual*.

Adler, S. (1994). ISO/IEC DIS 10179.2:1994. Information Technology - Text and Office Systems—Document Style Semantics and Specification Language (DSSSL), International Organization for Standardization.

Berners-Lee, T., Masinter, M., and McCahill, M. (1994). Uniform Resource Locators (URL), Request for Comments 1738.

Brereton, P., Budgen, D., and Hamilton, G. (1998). Hypertext: The Next Maintenance Mountain. *IEEE Computer*, 13(37), pages 49-55.

Clarke, E. M., Emerson, E. A., and Sistla, A. P. (1986). Automatic verification of finite-state concurrent systems using temporal logic specifications. *ACM Transactions on Programming Languages*, 8(2), pages 244-263.

EBT International. (1986). *DynaBase Reference Manual*.

Garzotto, F., Paolini, P., and Schwabe, D. (1993). HDMA: Model-Based Approach to Hypertext Application Design. *ACM Transactions on Information Systems*, 11(1), pages 1-26.

German, D. M., Cowan, D. D., and Alencar, P. S. C. (1999). A Framework for Formal Design of Hypertext Applications. In *4th Brazilian Symposium on Multimedia and Hypermedia Systems*, Rio de Janeiro, Brazil.

Goldfarb, C. (1990). *SGML Handbook*. Oxford University Press. Oxford.

Halasz, F. and Schwartz, M. (1994). The Dexter Hypertext Reference Model. *Communications of the ACM*, 37(2), pages 30-39.

Hill, G., Hall, W., Roure, D., and Carr, L. (1995). Applying Open Hypertext Principles to the WWW. In *Proceedings of the International Workshop on Hypermedia Design (IWHD'95)*, June 1995.

Isakowitz, T., Stohr, A., and Balasubramanian, P. (1995). RMM: A Methodology for Structured Hypermedia Design. *Communications of the ACM*, 38(8), pages 34-44.

Lange, D. (1995). An Object-Oriented Design Method for Hypermedia Information Systems, In *Proceedings of the 28th Hawaii International Conference on System Sciences*, January 1995.

Janna Systems, Inc. (1999). *LivePage Enterprise*. 158 University Avenue West, Waterloo, Ontario.

Mackie, E. and Zobel, J. (1992). Retrieval of Tree-structured Data from Disc. In *Databases '92, Third Australian Database Conference*, Melbourne, February 1992.

Microsoft Corporation. (1998). *XSL Tutorial*. Available: www.microsoft.com/xml/xsl/tutorial/tutorial.asp.

Pressman, R. S. (1992). *Software Engineering: A Practitioner's Approach*. McGraw-Hill, New York, 1992.

Schwabe, D. and Rossi, G. (1995). The Object-Oriented Hypermedia Design Model. *Communications of the ACM*, 38(8), pages 45-46.

Schwabe, D., Rossi, G., and Barbosa, S. D. J. (1996). Systematic Hypermedia Application Design with OOHDM. In *Proceedings of Hypertext 96*, pages 116-118.

Stieren, C. (1997). Add One Egg, a Cup of Milk and Stir: Single Source Documentation for Today. In *Proceedings of the SIGDOC*, pages 255- 262.

Tanenbaum, A. S. (1996). *Computer Network*. Prentice-Hall, Englewood Cliffs, NJ, 1996.

W3 Consortium. (1997). *Extensible Markup Language (XML)*. Available: www.w3.org/TR/PR-xml-971208.

W3 Consortium. (1998). *A Proposal for XSL*. Available: w3c.org/TR/NOTE-XSL.html.

Zobel, J., Wilkinson, R., Mackie, E., Thom, J., Sacks-Davis, R., Kent, A., and Fuller, M. (1991). An Architecture for Hyperbase Systems. In *1st Australian Multi-Media Communications Applications and Technology Workshop*, Sydney, July 1991.

16
Support for Geographically Dispersed Software Teams

Ivan Tomek

16.1 Introduction

Product development is typically a team effort involving information-related activities and intense communication. As projects increase in size and as economies become globalized, enterprises become geographically dispersed (Carmel, 1999). Walking over to another team member's desk first becomes difficult and then impossible. Chance encounters—known to play a very important role in product development (Harrison and Dourish, 1996; Huxor, 1998; Isaacs et al., 1996)—are restricted to meetings with collocated team members, and traditional face-to-face communication is replaced with various forms of telecommunication.

Although technology alleviates problems caused by geographic dislocation, team members still find it inadequate and much research has been dedicated to finding more effective collaborative environments for geographically dispersed work teams (Herbsleb, 1999; CSCW'98; CVE'98; ECSCW'99; CRIWIG'99; WACC'99). The topic is relevant to the software engineering community. As evidence of this, the International Conference on Software Engineering held its 3rd Workshop on Software Engineering over the Internet.

In this chapter, we first informally analyze the work performed by members of software development teams and use this analysis to formulate the desirable features of a collaborative work environment. We then explain why a text-based collaborative virtual environment (CVE) appears to be a very good fit for these requirements, and describe two pilot environments that we developed to address the issues of distributed software engineering (DSE). The chapter concludes with an outline of anticipated future work, concluding remarks relating our project to other recent research, and a list of references.

16.2 The Work of a Software Developer

The primary task of software developers is to *create and organize information*. The required information typically consists of formal documents such as requirements specifications, analysis and design documents, source code, and inspection, bug, and test reports. Although most development methodologists would let us believe that formal documents are all that is really worth creating and keeping, software developers consider informal information equally or more important (Kaiser 2000). They value informal notes, hand-drawn diagrams, e-mail records, URL links, references to trade journals, and mental notes gathered during formal meetings and conversation with colleagues and customers, and phone calls. The sum of this information and the knowledge gained by personal work experience forms the critically important context of work, and contributes to corporate memory. The quality, organization, and accessibility of this information greatly affect the quality and productivity of a team and the enterprise.

An essential part of the development process is communication. Software developers communicate with other team members, managers, and customers via face-to-face encounters, telephone conversations, e-mail, video conferencing, electronic chat, mail, fax, and other media. Communication may be planned or unplanned, and synchronous (occurs in real time), or asynchronous (does not require the participants to be present at the same time). The format of communication includes words, either spoken or textual, and documents such as requirement specifications, design diagrams, and code files. Whatever the means of communication, productive teams are always characterized by good communication.

As teams get larger and geographically dispersed, creation, gathering and access of information become increasingly difficult, and communication progressively shifts from synchronous face-to-face communication to asynchronous electronic communication. Meetings become more and more difficult to organize, particularly as teams span time zones, and cultural differences create additional problems where cross-cultural teams are involved (Raybourn and McGrath, 1999). In these cases, communication becomes less efficient and teams less productive.

To counter the negative effects of separation, a great amount of research has been dedicated to the study of its effects and to finding ways to minimize them. Computer networks are the natural technology of choice because much of the development process already takes place electronically, and the general direction of research has been to create shared environments in which team members can communicate and share common views of documents and tools. Two general approaches can be identified. One approach focuses on creating shared environments centred around projects (Steinfeld et al., 1999; Highsmith, 1999) while other researchers argue that if physical collocation is impossible, virtual collocation via software emulating essential aspects of the physical world is the best substitute (Churchill and Bly, 1999a; Roseman and Greenberg, 1996; Spellman et al., 1997). Our work belongs in the second category, and the rest of this chapter is dedicated to this approach.

16.3 Requirements on a Collaborative Virtual Environment

During the relatively long existence of groupware (software for the support of collaboration), many sophisticated environments have been developed only to be rejected by their intended beneficiaries (Baecker, 1993). The reasons for this can be traced to two main causes—lack of involvement of prospective users in their design, and difficulty of predicting all possibly required forms of collaboration. Before embarking on yet another groupware project, it is thus essential to determine what properties the environment should have. As we have already stated, our premise is that a collaborative environment should emulate and extend the essential properties of a physical workplace and substitute physical and temporal collocation with virtual ones. These properties include topological organization of disjoint work places, communication among collocated workers, navigation from one place to another, support for awareness of events, objects (primarily artefacts) and tools that can be moved from one virtual place to another, and unlimited extendibility and customizability. We will now give several reasons for this position.

Emulation of real-world topology is important because it is a very natural and easily understood metaphor, and appropriate metaphors are very important for usability and learnability, which are the prerequisites for successful software. The principle of emulation of physical space also provides a natural organizing principle—offices, meeting rooms, and document libraries are some of the natural types of places suitable for organizing a virtual space for software development teams. Besides, not only people, but information too can be organized in a spatial manner.

In the physical world, space is naturally allocated to a particular use, equipped for that use, and restricted for use by a particular group of people. A virtual environment should also exhibit these features and provide means for enforcing privacy and separation.

The importance of communication in the work process has already been discussed and allowing multiple simultaneous communications localized in disjoint scopes populated by team members or their software proxies provides a natural means for focused discussion and a basis for recording communication in context. Navigation is necessary for virtual displacement of users and their virtual holdings from one emulated place to another. It is required for both planned activities such as individual and group meetings, and to enable chance encounters.

An essential part of work-related communication is timely notification of the occurrence of work-related events such as the release of a new version of code by a team member. Team members should be able to register their interest in specific events, and their occurrence should be automatically broadcasted to them. Besides being aware of events, the environment should facilitate their automatic handling by subscriber-defined mechanisms. Emulation of the physical world provides a natural basis for event-driven operation.

Objects such as documents, and tools such as software development tools are at the heart of software development. Emulation of the physical world and the ability to move objects and tools around and share them provides a parallel to the way that we deal with objects and tools in the real world. To be truly useful, an emulated work environment should be all-inclusive like the real world, and provide seamless access to external tools. The CVE should thus form a universe interfacing to other software tools rather than be just another application disjoint from others.

Human needs and the nature of work are unpredictable and development and decision processes naturally evolve. Any environment that is closed and proprietary and can only be extended or modified by a small group of developers is thus doomed to fail. As a consequence, a useful work environment must be reconfigurable, customizable and extendible—just like the real world. In the physical world, we depend on our ability to rearrange or extend our offices, construct new buildings, use them for a variety of purposes, create new types of objects and tools, move them from one place to another, etc. A virtual environment can and should provide these facilities.

Teamwork is characterized by a multitude of dimensions whose study is the subject of several disciplines including Computer Supportive Collaborative Work (CSCW). These features include, for example, support for awareness, usage policies that control how tools and objects can be used according to the roles of individual team members, and work processes. A virtual environment emulating the physical world is a natural framework for supporting these concepts.

An important aspect of a physical environment is that it allows contact beyond the limits of the current work team. Physically collocated workers can talk not only to people who are working on the same project, but also to others. This allows exchange of ideas and sharing of valuable expertise. Project-centered groupware does not provide this facility, but emulated virtual spaces make it possible. In recent studies by Churchill (Churchill and Bly, 1999a, 199b) long-term CVE users reported that they commonly used the environment to meet co-workers working on other projects and even people who have left the enterprise, and used these virtual encounters to support their own project.

All the above arguments suggest that close emulation of those features of the physical world that are essential for collaboration, a CVE, seems an optimal candidate for a DSE environment. What other properties should such environments have? The environment must be easy to learn and use, responsive, and unobtrusive. An environment whose learning and use requires substantial effort or is slow and detracts from work will not be popular with busy software developers and will not be used. Churchill states that long-term CVE users report that the lightweight nature of the environment with its ease of use and rapid response is one of CVE's main advantages.

Besides involving geographically dislocated teams, today's work demands frequent individual displacement, both locally and over large distances. A CVE must therefore allow its users ubiquitous access to the environment and to other users, whether they are momentarily accessible or not. Churchill reports that the ability to access a CVE from virtually anywhere, and to find one's co-workers in predictable virtual locations, are among the main benefits cited by long-term CVE users.

Finally, to stimulate its users, the environment should be engaging, that is, preferably fun to explore and use. Long-term experience with virtual environments has shown that virtual environments satisfy these requirements (Haynes and Holmevik, 1998).

16.4   Which Type of CVE?

Having accepted the premise that a CVE provides a suitable basis for support of work teams, the next question is which of the several known CVE types is best suited for software developers. Available technologies include text-based, virtual reality-based, and augmented reality. VR-based environments can be further divided into low-technology desktop environments based on VRML and similar techniques (Ames et al., 1996; Damers, 1998), and high realism and high-cost environments (VRAIS'98; IEEE, 2000). Augmented reality combines text-based or virtual reality environments with information from sensors in the real world, possibly implemented as electronic objects in *collaborative*. We will now briefly evaluate the suitability of these technologies for our purpose.

Text-based collaborative virtual environments use GUI windows, possibly enhanced with graphics, audio, or even video input and output. Following others, we will refer to these environments as MUDs (an acronym to be explained later). One of the advantages of these environments is that they are easy to learn and use, allowing users to focus on contents rather than manipulation, and not distracting with additional visual context. MUDs are also low-tech and thus high-performance environments.

Users, via simple commands can easily extend MUDs through an extendible programming language. Another advantage of MUDs is that text-based information can be easily captured, organized, and searched. Their disadvantage is that a GUI is an incomplete approximation of the real world, but this is not a serious drawback when focus is on sharing textual and diagrammatic information. On the psychological side, experience shows that users quickly acquire a feeling of physical collocation with other occupants of the virtual space even without the visual cues.

Environments based on virtual reality (VR) of one kind or another have the advantage of providing a more accurate approximation of physical reality. They are, however, more difficult to use (requiring, for example, manipulation of the user's avatar on the screen via mouse buttons), thus distracting the user from communication. They are also much more difficult to expand and modify, and the additional visual cues enlarge the amount of information that must be processed by the user without providing a significant benefit in applications that don't require spatial models of reality.

Augmented reality is an extension of MUD and VR environments, still relatively little explored. Although it has potential benefits, we have not considered it appropriate at this stage of our research.

Our brief analysis suggests that MUDs are preferable to other virtual environments when the focus is on communication and textual or graphical artefacts, and when capturing and accessing verbal contextual information is important. VR-based environments have their place in applications in which access to visual information is essential, as in e-commerce, architectural design, etc. Since our focus is on the use of CVEs for software development teams whose interests are primarily in textual and graphical documents and exchange of ideas, the work reported below is restricted to text-based CVE environments. Our decision to focus on MUD-based environments has many precedents as numerous publications, commercial and experimental products, and periodicals dedicated to virtual environments attest (Fitzpatrick et al., 1996; Harrison and Dourish, 1996; *Journal of MUD Research*; Lindstaed and Schneider, 1997; Poltrock and Englebeck, 1997; Roseman and Greenberg, 1996; Spellman et al., 1997; Steed and Tromp, 1998; TeamWave).

16.5   What Is a MUD?

MUDs first appeared in the late 1970s. The acronym MUD originally stood for Multi-User Dungeons because the first MUDs were networked implementations of the popular fantasy game called Dungeons and Dragons. Eventually, the acronym acquired additional and more respectable interpretations including Multi-User Domains and Multi-User Dialogs, particularly when the environments were extended to support socialization rather than strictly game playing.

In the late 1980s, Paul White developed an object-based implementation of MUD referred to as MOO, for MUD Object-Oriented. Pavel Curtis then reimplemented the concept and created Lambda MOO (Haynes, 1998), which has since become the most common form of MUD. In the following, we will use MUD as a generic term representing both MUDs and MOOs.

A classical implementation of a MUD consists of a single server with multiple connected clients. Until relatively recently, MUD users used a simple Telnet client to connect to the server. After connecting, users would communicate, navigate, and perform other operations by typing commands that would be interpreted by the server, which would then update its database and return a response to the user using ASCII text. Recently, pure text Telnet interfaces have mostly been replaced with GUIs, most commonly based on HTML and Java and using a Web browser (TWUMOO). Beyond the changes in the user interface, the principle of the environment has remained essentially unchanged.

As we have already explained, a MUD emulates selected features of the physical world inhabited by user proxies (called agents or avatars), objects, and tools. The emulated world (universe) is divided into disjoint but possibly nested domains corresponding to interconnected rooms, buildings, and other real-world concepts. The consequences of this partitioning are that individual spaces may be dedicated to specific uses, restrict communication to groups of users, and serve as repositories of objects and tools with restricted access.

The avatars representing MUD users can move from one virtual place to another (navigate) carrying their possessions (objects and tools) with them. Autonomous software agents playing various roles and often automating mechanical tasks typically complement them. Agents of both kinds can pick up and drop objects and communicate with other agents, typically within the constraints of their current location. The environment is persistent and the database containing the universe with its interconnected places, objects, tools, and agents resides on the server

Avatars representing users are generally constrained by roles that authorize them to perform a variety of actions and prevent them from executing others. The main differences between different roles are typically in limits on how much an avatar can extend and customize the MUD universe. At the lowest level, avatars can instantiate a predetermined number of entities such as rooms, objects, and tools, whereas users with higher authorization can create new types (classes) of objects and functionalities, and add them to the environment.

This brief description shows that a MUD satisfies the CVE requirements postulated above. It is a persistent emulation of essential features of the real world, provides navigable scopes that can be used for separate activities using and producing tools and artefacts, incorporates the concepts of time and events, and provides means for synchronous and asynchronous communication. Its users can perform assigned roles and these roles may be used to define policies for the use of tools and other tasks. MUDs are easy to use and easily accessible and, most importantly, user-extendible and customizable at two levels: A user can instantiate an existing class of entity and—with proper authorization—extend the functionality of the universe by extending existing types of entities and defining new ones.

In the following sections, we will now present two environments that were developed and used to explore some of the requirements enumerated above.

16.6 Jersey: An Overview

Our interest in CVEs was sparked by Object Technology International (OTI), a recognized leader in the development of Object Oriented technology, particularly Smalltalk and later Java. Object Technology International has several offices around the world and their need to deal with geographic separation of team members led to the formulation of the problem addressed in our project.

To help us in our exploration of possible use of MUDs in distributed software development, OTI provided us with the skeleton of a non-commercial application called Jersey implementing a basic MUD architecture. The environment used a Telnet connection and all communication from a client had the form of Smalltalk messages transmitted as ASCII text and interpreted by a Smalltalk server. This was acceptable because the intended users were Smalltalk programmers and because of Smalltalk's simple syntax.

Since the server can process any Smalltalk messages, users can send not only Jersey-specific commands to perform usual MOO activities, but can also create new functionality on the fly and do anything that a Smalltalk environment permits. This provides great flexibility and lets users customize and extend the universe at run time. However it also violates basic security because it allows the user to use the Telnet client to program the server to do such things as capture all Jersey communication, damage or even destroy the whole Jersey universe and its engine or even the Smalltalk environment itself. In our pilot project, this was not an important consideration because security was low on our priority list.

The design of Jersey allows a flat layer of virtual rooms with no support for containment. In other words, users can create rooms but not rooms within buildings. A user's avatar always resides in a room and can move to any adjacent room via an exit or to any other room in the universe by *teleporting*. Users can communicate with standard MOO commands such as "whisper," "say," and "shout," and use simple built-in e-mail. Jersey also provides a basic framework for software agents and defines a hierarchy of *utility* and *information holding* objects whose examples are described below.

After installing Jersey, recovering its design from the undocumented source code, and correcting some problems, we embarked on experimentation and expansion (Tomek et al., 1998a; 1998b; Tomek et al, 1999a; 1999b). Our experiments were restricted to a small team of faculty and MSc students and to several software-engineering courses. We held class and team meetings on Jersey and used it for inspection of Jersey code. We also used the concept of disjoint domains to organize our project artefacts (see *Class Rooms* below).

When using Jersey for meetings, we quickly found the limitations of textual communication due to slow typing and network delays, and the importance of friendly user interfaces. The open nature of Jersey proved very beneficial here, as we were able to change the environment on the fly. As an example, we implemented simple meeting support while an actual meeting was in progress.

Our extensions of the original implementation included new user interfaces, new objects and tools, new types of agents, on-line help and query support, access to Smalltalk code for use in software inspections, and Development Clusters, templates of room combinations to accommodate development teams. The following section will describe this work.

16.7   Jersey: User Interfaces

As already mentioned the original Jersey user interface requires the user to enter commands as Smalltalk messages. This practice, common in conventional MUDs, is awkward and makes the use of the environment difficult for two reasons. Users must remember the exact syntax of all commands that they want to use (or find it via a primitive "help" command), and the sometimes-lengthy multi-argument commands must be entered with flawless spelling. To remove this annoying shortcoming, we designed an interface that allows the user to produce commands by filling in automatically generated templates.

The main window of the new user interface is shown in Figure 16.1. Besides providing buttons to perform the most common actions, the window contains several specialized fields and lists. The input field (lower left) is used to send commands to the server. Typing text into the field and sending it to the server is interpreted as a "say" message and causes the text to be displayed in the output pane (upper left) of a similar window seen by all users whose avatars are present in the same location. The screenshot shows the format of these notifications.

If the user precedes the text with the @ symbol, the line is interpreted as a

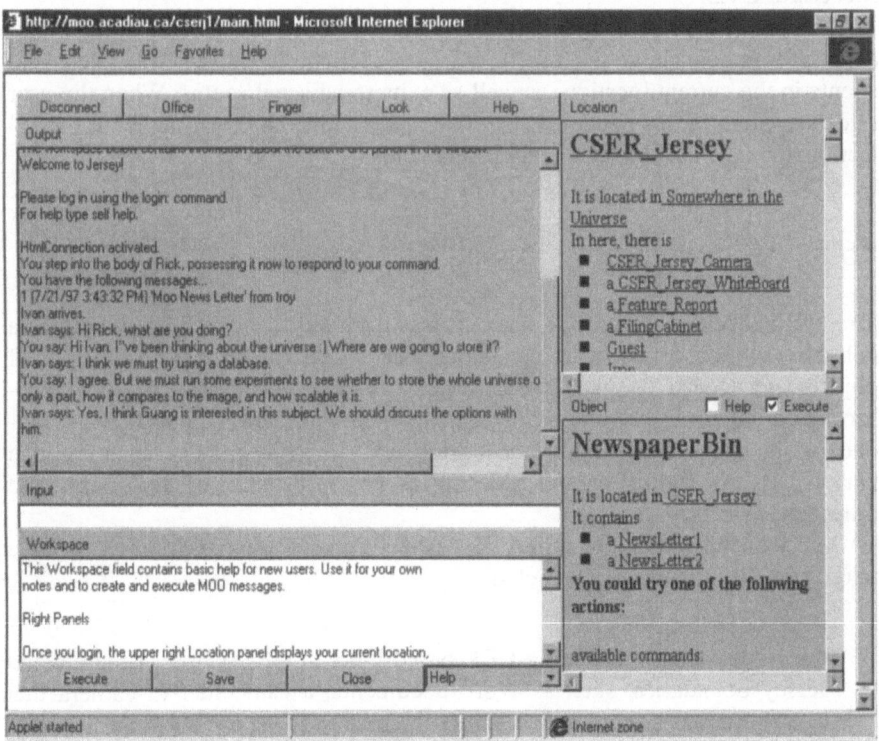

Figure 16.1. WWW main Jersey interface.

Smalltalk message. The server filters all arriving messages, ignores those that are illegal, and executes those that are valid. As mentioned earlier, the text is not restricted to Jersey messages and any Smalltalk message may be entered here. The input field can thus be used to program Jersey at run time, although not as comfortably as with a regular Smalltalk code browser.

As in any MUD, the total number of Jersey messages is large and their details difficult to remember. Jersey provides several ways to alleviate this problem. One is the workspace below the input field, which can be used as a repository of frequently used commands. Users can type commands into this pane and then copy and paste them into the input field. Another form of support is a special help facility that can be activated by the Help button; it displays help information in the upper part of the window. The Tree Help agent described below can also be used for environment help although its function is intended mainly for development support. Switching from command execution mode to command help mode via the radio buttons between the two lists on the right provides another form of help. In addition to direct command entry, commands associated with rooms and objects can be activated via clickable text as explained below. We found that these simple improvements greatly improved Jersey's usability ,and usability is, as we mentioned above, one of the critical requirements on a successful CVE.

The top of the right-hand side of the main window is a list containing clickable information about the user's current location. It shows all objects and agents in the current location, as well as exits to adjacent rooms. When the user selects an item in this pane, the list underneath shows information about the selection and its click able executable commands.

16.8   Jersey Objects, Tools, and Agents

The original Jersey was only a basic framework, and to make it interesting as a collaborative tool for software developers, we added a number of new classes of objects and agents. The new objects can be divided into utility objects and information-capturing objects. *Utility objects* include offices equipped with standard tools, desks consisting of a desktop and drawers, garbage cans emptied periodically by janitor agents, and copiers for duplication of documents and other text objects.

Many useful objects for capturing, organizing, and keeping information are a part of the framework. These include:

- filing cabinets,
- document objects providing URL-based links to information stored beyond Jersey boundaries, such as Word documents, a camcorder (a camera that can be carried around to record communication that occurs in the location of the agent carrying it—an extension of the stationary security camera, which is bolted to a wall),

- a whiteboard for recording and displaying information,
- and other objects.

To provide a flexible general-purpose query facility, we created an agent-based Help Tree, a variation on Answer Garden 2 (Ackerman et al., 1996). The Help Tree uses an autonomous software agent that processes queries from users and tries to match them against answers stored in folders in a *filing cabinet* (all of them Jersey objects). If the agent fails to find an answer, it sends the question to users who have registered as experts in the query area and the received answers are stored in folders for future use and delivered to the user who issued the query.

The Help Tree agent is an example of an autonomous agent. Autonomous agents in Jersey are software entities that can autonomously move from one place to another, interacting with the environment, and executing scripts. They are mobile, but only in a limited sense because they can only move within the universe running on the server machine. The scripts defining agents are Jersey objects and as in the case of such objects, they may be shared among different users and edited.

Agent actions are based on a combination of mission actions defining the purpose of the agent, autonomous random actions providing a semblance of free will, and finally response actions that allow the agent to respond to events in its environment.

Examples of Jersey agents include messenger agents who deliver messages, janitors who navigate through the universe and empty office trash cans, and an agent who makes copies of new issues of the Jersey newsletter and delivers them to each subscriber's office. Jerry is the Help Tree agent, and Tim is the notifier agent who notifies interested users whenever a new edition of a Smalltalk source code module to which they subscribed is released.

Tim is our solution to a problem that we faced when we wanted to use Jersey to support software development teams. Although Jersey is developed in Smalltalk, its user interface cannot access Smalltalk development tools such as code browsers and we thus implemented access to source code via Class Rooms, special rooms that allow viewing individual selected classes in the Smalltalk library. Class Rooms are an example of the use of Jersey's topological principle to organize project-related information. Tim's mission is to navigate Class Rooms, look for new code releases, and notify users who have registered an interest in them.

To provide software development teams with a simple way to create virtual spaces to support individual and teamwork, we created a template of a basic floor plan called the Development Cluster. A Development Cluster is a collection of rooms centered around a project room used mainly for meetings and providing access to the offices of the developers working on the project, the leader of the team, and a documentation used. A Development Cluster also includes Class Rooms providing access to project software modules.

16.9   Jersey Evaluation

Our observations can be divided into usage experience and design issue. The following two sections deal with both of these categories.

16.9.1. Functional Issues

When Jersey reached the state of a fully working environment, its functionality was still too primitive for industrial use and we thus had students in a senior Computer Science course use and evaluate it informally by completing a questionnaire. The results can be divided into general MUD experiences and an evaluation of Jersey-specific issues.

On the MUD side, we found that the powerful and user-friendly interfaces described above made the use of Jersey much easier to use than the original Telnet interface. It is worth noting, that other studies did not consider the effect of user interfaces—Churchill (Churchill and Bly, 1999a; 1999b) found that users considered even MUDs with primitive Telnet interfaces to be very useful. Our evaluation also showed that the use of the interface was surprisingly immersive in the sense that being in Jersey gave the physically separated users a profound sense of being together. We quickly got used to holding meetings in Jersey and recording them for later perusal and reference. After the initial chaotic experiences, we developed a meeting tool with simple support for agenda, chair and secretary roles, and floor control, and this greatly helped to make meetings more manageable and improve usability.

The relatively slow speed of typing and the resulting occasional lack of coherence of individual contributions complicate informal meetings in MUD. This, of course, is known for other forms of synchronous communication as well. Without some control, threads of communications quickly diverge, and following them becomes difficult. This problem has been noted and various approaches attempted. As an example, Highsmith (Highsmith, 1999) reports that Project Community Software uses sidebars for side dialogs during team meetings. Sidebar dialogs between two members are, of course, different from threads evolving in a multi-person communication, but it is possible that a similar approach might be used to deal with this problem as well. Another possibility is to banish multiple threads and follow a strict agenda as the Neometron product appears to expect.

As we started using Jersey, we quickly discovered the need to extend it with new objects and new functionality. The ability to extend and modify the environment turned out to be essential, and one of the most important features distinguishing MUDs from related environments such as chats, e-mail, or virtual environments based on predefined virtual space structures. This is because not even the most intelligent and creative designers can anticipate all the possibilities and create an environment that will satisfy all potential users in all possible applications, and provide all desirable features. Even providing users with a scripting language and customizable templates seems too restrictive in comparison with freely modifiable MUD environments.

Similar to other studies of MUDs in collaborative work, we found it useful to be able to use the same environment for both synchronous and asynchronous communication. Its persistence and continuous availability are two other important features.

A shortcoming of our experiment was that our test group was too small—fewer than ten users—well below a critical size required for an objective groupware test. In addition, our users were students rather than the targeted professional developers. We have also failed to take full advantage of one of the most important benefits of a MUD—that it can provide continuous access to all members in the group. Churchill reports on a longitudinal study of a work team that used a MUD over a period of several years. It found that its users have a MUD window open 24 hours a day, occasionally checking the ongoing informal exchanges, and jumping in when a relevant topic was addressed or when they needed to ask a question.

Among the weaknesses that Jersey shares with other MUDs is that it is isolated from other applications. To alleviate this shortcoming, we introduced the earlier-mentioned URL-based access to other forms of documents, but future MUDs should provide a seamless environment encompassing other applications such as word processors, spreadsheets, e-mail, and software development tools.

16.9.2. Design Issues

The design strengths of Jersey include its simple design resulting in relative understandability, and the possibility to modify and extend the design even at run time. These features make Jersey highly suitable for testing new concepts. This is essential for CVEs, particularly at this relatively early stage of research.

Our list of Jersey design weaknesses starts with its lack of uniform and universal support for events. This precludes, for example, subscription to events, such as new releases of code modules, and automatic notification of subscribers when these events occur. As mentioned above, we had to resort to the concept of Class Rooms periodically scanned for new releases by a specialized agent to solve this problem.

Another problem with Jersey is that, although its user interface is substantially more sophisticated than that of other MUDs, the client is still too primitive and the server does not provide any connection to the rest of the software environment. The lacks of support for shared viewing and shared manipulation of windows are also serious limitations.

Jersey's text-only communication between the client and the server is too restrictive since nothing but ASCII text can be downloaded. URL-based access to files alleviates this shortcoming but does not remove it.

The centralized nature of the architecture with a single server storing the universe and performing all processing is also a shortcoming. It makes the environment too vulnerable and has the potential of overloading both the processor and the network connection. The fact that the universe database is, in fact, a part of the Smalltalk environment rather than a true database is also a limitation.

As already mentioned, Jersey does not address security issues and leaves the whole system completely open to users who have full access to the source code of not only Jersey but of the whole Smalltalk environment. We did not consider this to be a problem because of the experimental nature of the project and the fact that more fundamental issues needed to be resolved first. Moreover, Jersey was intended for use in a limited and safe user community where security was not a problem. In a production environment, the question of reconciling security with openness and extendibility will be very important.

Finally, Jersey does not attempt to support advanced CSCW features such as groups, roles, policies, work processes, and tasks. These seemingly exotic features are very important in team activities such as meetings, which require support for roles such as chairperson, secretary, and meeting participant—sharing tools but having different authorizations. Another example of the need for CSCW features is code inspection where team members assume roles such as the moderator, reader, verifier, and developer and each uses both shared and individual tools but not with the same authorization. Concepts such as groups are also essential for creating flexible locking mechanism for rooms and objects, and for providing basic security. Questions of flexible specification of policies are being intensely explored by other researchers in projects such as COCO (Du and Muntz, 1999), and CVEs could use the proposed solutions.

16.10 MUM: Multi-Universe MOO

The previous section identified several of limitations of Jersey, but Jersey's architecture would make it too difficult to remove them. We thus decided to design a new MUD and we called it MUM for Multi-Universe MOO. Its main features are described next and further details are available in Tomek and coworkers (1999c, 1999d, 2000).

Clients, servers, and meta-servers. One of the limitations that we decided to explore was the fact that a MUD normally runs on a single server. We thus designed MUM as a network of interconnected clients and servers implemented as Smalltalk parcels (Cincom). Each parcel collection contains both a MUM server and a MUM client and each machine may thus be simultaneously a server providing access to a MUD universe installed on the machine, and a client accessing a universe implemented on the same or another machine. This means that while the avatar of the user of machine A may be in a universe on machine B, avatars of remote users may be using a universe on machine A. Since the universes are interconnected (see below), avatars can also move from one universe to another with all their holdings.

The possibility of having an unlimited number of servers and universes requires a higher-level coordinating server. This meta-server keeps track of the location of individual host machines and their universes. Information stored on the meta-server is dynamic, reflecting the momentary state of the network, and is automatically updated as host machines connect and disconnect their local universes.

Another issue addressed by MUM is alleviating the potentially high loads on the server and the network by letting the clients do as much work as possible and providing a framework for creating flexible and customizable user interfaces. This is achieved by creating *tool libraries* consisting of tool *manuals* and tool code on the server, and providing a mechanism for downloading them to the client and automatically extending the dictionary defining client-server communication. More information about this aspect of MUM is provided later in this section.

MUM also changes the nature communication between the client and the server and replaces text-based communication with a filter-based communication of binary data.

Our discussions with OTI software developers convinced us of the importance of awareness of events. As discussed in the Conclusion, several other researchers independently reached the same conclusion. We have thus decided to make MUM fully event-driven This means that everything that happens in a virtual MUM universe is an event and everything in the universe happens as a result of passing an event from one object to another. In other words, there is no direct messaging among MUM universe objects.

When everything happens by explicit processing of events by an event handler, any event associated with any object is *subscribable*. Any object, typically an agent representing a user, may then register interest in the occurrence of the event and is automatically notified when the event occurs. The notification has the form of a *notification event* that contains enough information to allow the subscriber's client to respond with an appropriate pre-programmed action.

The ability to subscribe to events must be restricted to authorized users and this is achieved by groups, allowing the owner of an object to specify who can subscribe to the events processed by the object. Groups can also be used in locking objects to lock rooms, controlling communication, defining features restricted to universe administrators such as creation of new users, and letting the owner of an object specify who can send commands to it. By providing such fine-grain control, groups and event-based operation also provide a certain amount of security.

The processing of an event may require a complicated sequence of operations whose order of execution may depend on context. As an example, an attempt to enter a room requires sending an event to the destination room object requesting a permission to enter, and the positive or negative response event determines how the processing of the requesting event continues. To make this possible, each event is described by an *event descriptor*, a finite-state automaton (FSA) whose discrete states allow chunking of event execution and specification of multiple alternative sequences of execution. This arrangement also solves the problem of asynchronous behaviours such as a request for a vote, which requires a response from one or more objects and cannot continue until the response (*confirmation*) events are received.

An interesting question related to the processing of events is how to deal with situations that require multiple confirmations. In the current implementation, the arrival of at least one *confirmation event* restarts the suspended event, but this solution cannot satisfy all situations. In the future, we will implement a more general mechanism in which each asynchronous state is associated with a *confirmation policy* that determines how to process incoming confirmation events.

We mentioned earlier that the poor quality of user interfaces and lack of integration with other applications are the main reasons why MUDs have not yet become a prominent groupware category (Churchill and Bly, 1999a; 1999b). Following the example of Jersey, MUM users may access the universe via commands displayed in the user interface. When activated, these commands dynamically create a user interface window to elicit required parameters, and produce events, which are then sent to the target object in the universe on the server side. More commonly, user actions are executed via specialized UIs. MUM thus goes beyond Jersey where users click commands and fill in arguments into message templates, and eliminates the need for a programming-language-based user interface.

MUM's user interface is implemented with *tools*, whose definitions reside on the server. When a user enters a universe, the main window automatically displays all the available tools and allows the user to open a selected tool. If the tool is not installed on the client, the code is automatically downloaded from the server and installed. Alternatively, when a tool is required for interaction with an object selected by the user, the tool is opened automatically, after possibly being automatically downloaded.

As MUM evolves, the user needs to use the latest versions of all code. MUM does this automatically as follows: When a user logs into a universe, the client notifies the server about its code versions and if the code is out of date, the server automatically downloads the new versions.

Snapshots of two examples of MUM user interfaces are shown in the next two Figures. Figure 16.2 shows the *launcher*, which is used to connect to a remote or local universe, log in with a user name and password, and log out. The launcher also allows opening of tools displayed in the list on the right, and its text pane on the left displays system messages.

Figure 16.3 shows the UniTool (the Universal Tool), the basic MUM user interface. The upper right list pane provides access to the essential information in the user's current virtual location and can be switched to show objects, occupants, or exits. When displaying occupants, the list also provides simple awareness support based on a server clock, which monitors the activity of each user and notifies the clients. The client's UniTool then uses different fonts to display user names and indicate their status. The bottom right list of the window dis-

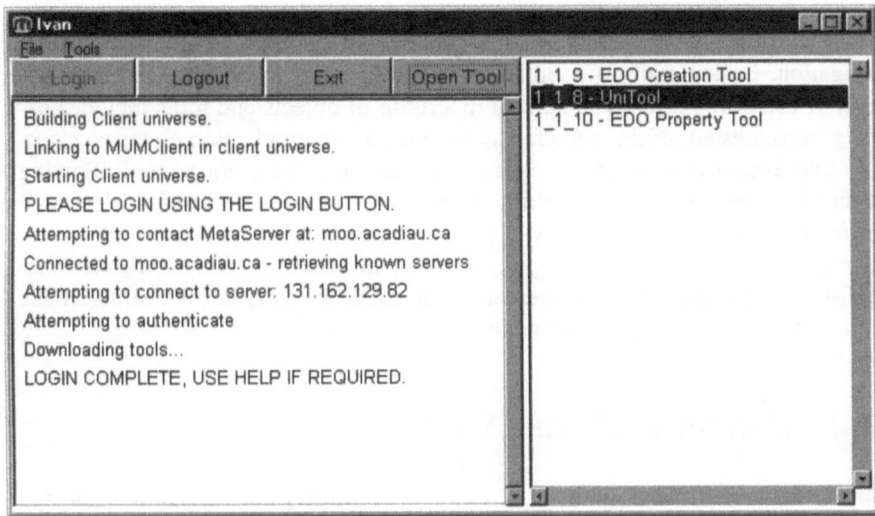

Figure 16.2. MUM Launcher.

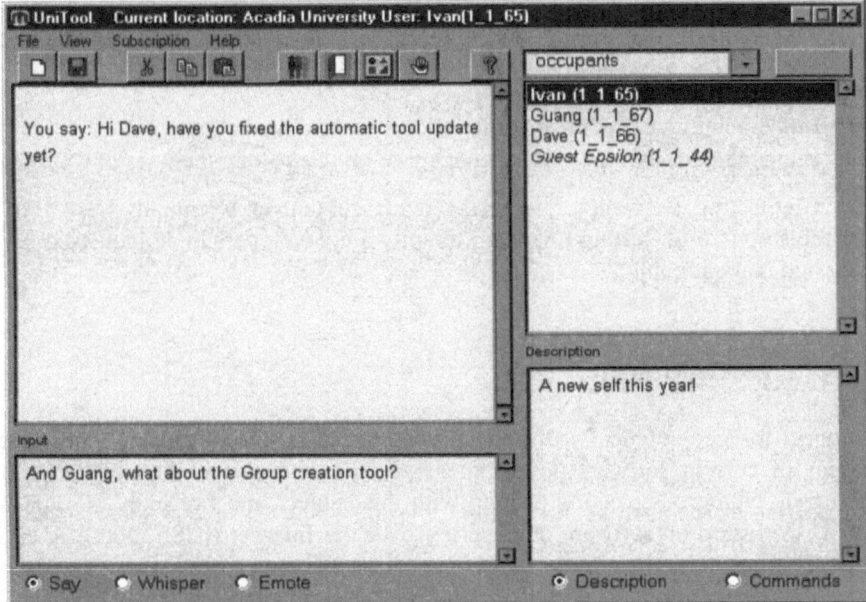

Figure 16.3. MUM UniTool.

Summary of current functionality. The existing functionality is still limited because most of our work to date focused on the development of the framework. MUM currently implements basic MOO operations such as communication, navigation, instantiation of a limited number of types of objects, and management of their properties. The current repertoire of objects and tools includes users, groups, nested places, cameras for recording communication on tapes, tapes, a simple e-mail system and, most recently, a code management tool allowing versioning and code membership (Yang and Tomek, 2000). An *electronic binder* with pages using a variety of page styles to hold assorted forms of project information including UML diagrams (Alshepani, 2000) is being integrated into MUM. Group definition, object creation, object properties, and the camera have their own tools with specialized windows.

16.11 Current and Future Work

Our current work and plans can be divided into three categories—design changes, extensions, and use and testing. Some of the anticipated design changes include the following:

- Relaxing the fully event-based MUM operation to reduce execution overhead.
- Moving from a collection of autonomous interconnected universe to a single universe whose extensions can be hosted on arbitrary servers.
- Better support for off-line operation.
- Implementation of confirmation policies as described above.
- Implementation of the CSCW concept of policies along the lines of COCO.

After testing, we want to use MUM in a larger course. Eventually we will offer the software for testing to a team of software developers in an industrial setting and make it public.

16.12 Conclusion

Support for geographically dispersed work teams is one of the most pressing issues of current software development practice and subject of much CSCW research. Numerous meeting dealing with this subject, most recently the ICSE-2000 workshop on software engineering over the Internet (ICSE, 2000) is evidence of this. The main focus of study is the development of collaborative virtual environments of one type or another. Several research and commercial products are based on the premise that if physical and temporal collocation is impossible, emulation of physical co-presence is the next best thing. These projects use the concepts introduced in recreational and educational MUDs and their extensions. Published studies of the use of even the most primitive existing text-based MUDs in industrial settings confirm the potential of this largely untapped paradigm.

In this chapter, we have described our exploration of the essential characteristics of MUDs that would make them useful for software development teams. We developed two functional environments including Jersey and MUM, Jersey's successor. Our work introduced several innovative concepts aimed at improving MUD usability including:

- flexibility,
- customizability,
- event awareness,
- subscribability,
- new type of user interfaces,
- the use of a powerful client to offload processing from the server and relieving network traffic,
- distribution of operation among multiple servers,
- implementation of selected CSCW features such as event awareness,
- and design for off-line operation.

We pointed out that many design and conceptual issues still remain unresolved and extensive testing is required.

To conclude, we will now survey some of the most recent published works to show how other researchers address issues of distributed software engineering and how their work relates to ours.

In a publication at the ICSE-2000 workshop on Internet-based software development, Cook focuses on the management of the development process in DSE (Cook, 2000). He stresses the role of monitoring of events and analysis of event traces and notes that because DSE is technology-based, automatic event capture and analysis are relatively easy. He describes several tools developed to test the usefulness of automatic analysis of events captured during the development process. In comparison with our holistic focus on support for team activities in the development process, Cook focuses on its analysis. The two subjects are complementary and the importance attached to events and their automatic capture is shared in both studies.

Another view of event-aware environments with shared distributed tools is presented by Grundy (Grundy, 2000). The project addresses issues including coordination, synchronous and asynchronous sharing and collaborative editing of a variety of artefacts, shared repositories, and integration of external components. It stresses the importance of flexibility and the role of events as a unifying mechanism. Event-handling and issues of formal and informal team communication and support for social aspects of collaboration are not addressed.

Harjumaa and Tervonen focus on software inspection in DSE (Harjumaa and Tervonen, 2000). Inspection is a prototypical social task and its implementation with geographically distributed teams is expensive and difficult because of the need for coordination, shared viewing of documents, communication, and enforcement of *process rigor*. The authors describe two experimental tools for Web-based inspection, and propose a model of the inspection process modified for use in DSE. Due to the limited scope of the project, they do not address issues of communication and ignore the important aspect of event notification. In the context of this chapter, it presents an example of an important software development process that cannot be implemented in a traditional way in DSE and requires emulation of collocation.

Kaiser (Kaiser, 2000) addresses the use of multimedia in DSE, describing work being done within CHIME, the Columbia University Hypermedia IMmersion Environment. In the words of the project's Web page (CHIME), "users are immersed in a 3D MUD (Multi-User Domain)-style virtual world where they encounter and communicate with other users' avatars (representations in the 3D world)." Its focus is on supplementing conventional types of artefacts with videos capturing, for example, requirements meetings with customers and team design meetings, replaying them collectively, and synchronizing their shared viewing across multiple platforms with varying connectivity and viewing parameters. The aspects most relevant to our work are the fact that CHIME is a MUD and that the author explores integration of a new medium, thus extending the existing environment. It is interesting that CHIME uses 3D graphical representation; this can be attributed to the fact that the environment is also used in other collaborative contexts, for example, by chemists who require shared viewing of 3D information. We mentioned earlier that this paradigm seems distracting in contexts where stress is on textual and diagrammatic artefacts, as in DSE.

Another prominent relevant recent development is Project Community Software. PCSW is a new commercial environment marketed by Neometron based on the premise that decision-making is the determining factor of the success of any team project. In a recent article describing PCSW, Highsmith (Highsmith, 1999) argues that project success depends on effective dynamic decision-making, and that the decision-making process cannot improve without access to the full context in which decisions are made. The context itself consists of both the formal artefacts produced during the project's lifetime and the communications that surround their creation. The article argues that since every project is unique and the process of decision-making must continuously evolve, no single environment can fit all needs. This implies the need for flexible environments allowing integration of special-purpose tools with standard applications and tools facilitating role-based communication, preserving project context, and allowing easy access to it. PCSW addresses these issues via project modelling including support for communication, interfacing to external tools, and scripting for automatic event capture and notification. Although PCSW deals with many of the issues listed in our introduction, it does not use the concept of customizable inteconnected and navigable spaces and easy extendibility.

We conclude that reports on the most recent developments demonstrate that DSE research focuses on development and testing of new development environments that are

- flexible and easily customizable,
- support synchronous and asynchronous communication and sharing,
- automatically capture and report events,
- integrate special-purpose and commercial tools,
- and capture and provide easy access to project context.

Whereas most of the reported research deals with a selection of these issues, our research is holistic and attempts to address the same issues in an integrated fashion. As the surveyed literature indicates, little is known about the real needs of geographically distributed teams and the best way of supporting DSE concerns, and further experimentation and practical validation are required to produce an environment that satisfies the needs of this increasingly common and important form of software development.

16.13 Acknowledgements

The first two-thirds of the project described in this chapter were undertaken in collaboration with Drs. Robin Nicholl and Rick Giles. For various reasons, they have not been able to participate in the writing of this chapter. Most of the implementation of Jersey has been done by a succession of students including Kenn Hussey, Francois Gagnon, Kevin Shu, Troy Saulnier, and Kevin Swan. Dave Murphy and Guang Yang implemented most of MUM.

16.14 References

Ackerman, M. S., and McDonald, D. W. (1996). Answer Garden 2: Merging organizational memory with collaborative help. In *CSCW '96, Proceedings of ACM Conference on Computer Supported Cooperative Work*, Pages 97-105.

Alshepani S. (2000). *A UML Development Tool.* MSc thesis, Acadia University.

Ames A.L., Becks, J., and Ralph, T. (1996). *VRML 2.0 Sourcebook,* John Wiley & Sons, New York.

Baecker R. M. (1993). *Readings in Groupware and Computer-Supported Collaborative Work*, Morgan Kauffmann Publishers.

Carmel E., (1999). *Global Software Teams Collaborating Across Borders and Time Zones*, Prentice-Hall, Englewood Cliffs, NJ.

CHIME. *Columbia University Hypermedia IMmersion Environment.* http://www.cs.columbia.edu/~sdossick/www/create.html

Churchill, E., and Bly, S. (1999a). Virtual environments at work: Ongoing use of MUDs in the workplace. In *Proceedings of WACC 99.*

Churchill, E., and Bly S. (1999b) It's all in the words: Supporting work activities with lightweight tools, In *Proceedings of Group 99.*

Cincom. http://www.objectshare.com/

Cook J.E. (2000). Internet-based software engineering enables and requires event-based management tools. In *Proceedings of Third ICSE '2000 Workshop on Software Engineering over the Internet.* Available at: http://www.ul.ie/~icse2000/workshops1.html#011.

CRIWG 99 (1999). *Fifth International Workshop on Groupware*, Cancún, Mexico, September 22-24.

CRIWG 2000 (2000). *Fifth International Workshop on Groupware*, Madeira Island, Portugal, 18-20 October.

CSCW 96 (1996). *ACM Conference on Computer Supported Cooperative Work*, Boston, Massachusetts, November 16-20, Available at: http://www.acm.org/sigchi/cscw96/

CSCW 98 (1998). *ACM Conference on Computer Supported Cooperative Work*, Seattle, Washington, November 14-18. http://www.acm.org/sigchi/cscw98/

CVE 98 (1998). *Collaborative Virtual Environments*, University of Manchester, UK, 17-19June. http://www.crg.cs.nott.ac.uk/~dns/conf/vr/cve98/

Damers, B. (1998). *Avatars!* Peachpit Press.

Du, Li., and Muntz, R.R., (1999) Runtime dynamics in collaborative systems. In *Proceedings of Group '99.*

ECSCW 99 (1999). *European Conference on Computer Supported Cooperative Work*, Copenhagen, Denmark, 12-16 September, http://www.cti.dtu.dk/CSCW/ECSCW99.html

ENVY/Developer (1998). Object Technology International Inc., http://www.oti.com/

Fitzpatrick, G., Kaplan, S., and Mansfield, T. (1996). Physical spaces, virtual places and social worlds: A study of work in the virtual. In *CSCW 96, Proceedings of ACM Conference on Computer Supported Cooperative Work.*

Group 97, International Conference on Supporting Group Work, Phoenix, Arizona, USA, November 16-19, 1997.

Group 99, *International Conference on Supporting Group Work*, Phoenix, Arizona, USA, November 14-17, 1999.

Grundy, J. (2000). Distributed component engineering using a decentralised, internet-based environment, In *Proceedings of Third ICSE ''2000 Workshop on Software Engineering over the Internet.* http://www.ul.ie/~icse2000/workshops1.html#011

Harjumaa, L., and Tervonen, I. (2000). Virtual software inspections over the Internet. In *Proceedings of Third ICSE 2000 Workshop on Software Engineering over the Internet.* http://www.ul.ie/~icse2000/workshops1.html#011

Harrison, S., and Dourish, P. (1996). Re-Place-ing Space: The roles of place and space in collaborative systems. In *CSCW '96, Proceedings of ACM Conference on Computer Supported Cooperative Work.*

Haynes, C., and Holmevik, J. R. (1998). *High Wired: On the Design, Use, and Theory of Educational MOOs*, University of Michigan Press.

Herbsleb, D., and Grinter, R.E., (1999). Architectures, coordination, and distance: Conway's law and beyond. *IEEE Software* (September/October).

Highsmith, J. (1999). Managing distributed project teams. *E-Business Application Delivery*, August 1999. http://cutter.com/ead/ead9908.html

Huxor, A. (1998). An Active Worlds interface for BSCW to enhance chance encounters. In *Proceedings of CVE'98*, pages 87-94. http://www.fxpal.com/cve/

ICSE 2000 (2000*). Third ICSE 2000 Workshop on Software Engineering over the Internet.* ICSE 2000, International Conference on Software Engineering, Limerick, Ireland, June 4-11, http://www.ul.ie/~icse2000/workshops1.html#011.

Isaacs, E.A., Tang, J.C., and Morris T. (1996). Piazza: A desktop environment supporting impromptu and planned interactions. In *CSCW '96, Proceedings of ACM Conference on Computer Supported Cooperative Work.*

Journal of MUD Research. http://journal.tinymush.org/~jomr/

Kaiser, G.. Ravages of Time: Synchronized Multimedia for Internet-Wide Process-Centered Software Engineering Environments, In *Proceedings of Third ICSE 2000 Workshop on Software Engineering over the Internet.* http://www.ul.ie/~icse2000/workshops1.html#011

Lindstaed, S., Schneider, K. (1997). Bridging the gap between face-to-face communication and long-term collaboration. In *Proceedings of Group '97.*

IEEE (2000). *Virtual Reality 2000.* New Brunswick, NJ, USA, March 18-22, 2000, http://www.caip.rutgers.edu/vr2000/

Neometron. *PCSW: Project Communities Software.* http://www.neometron.com/main/maincommunities.html

Poltrock, S.E., and Engelbeck, G. (1997). Requirements for a virtual collocation environment. In *Proceedings of Group '97.*

Raybourn, E.M., and McGrath, A. (1999). Designing from the interaction out: Using intercultural communication as a framework to design interactions in collaborative virtual communities. In *Proceedings of Group 99.*

Roseman, M., and Greenberg, S. (1996). TeamRooms: Network places for collaboration. In *CSCW '96, Proceedings of ACM Conference on Computer Supported Cooperative Work.*

Spellman, P., Mosier J.N., Deus, L.M., and Carlson, J.A. (1997). Collaborative virtual workspace. In *Proceedings of Group 97.*

Steed, A., and Tromp, J. (1998). Experiences with the evaluation of CVE applications. In *Proceedings of CVE 98* (D. Snowdon, E. Churchill, editors), pages 123-132.

Steinfeld C., Chyng-Yang, J., and Pfaff, B., (1999). Supporting virtual team collaboration: The TeamSCOPE system, In *Proceedings of Group 99.*

TeamWave. http://www.teamwave.com/

Tollmar, K., Sandor O., and Schömer A. (1996). Supporting social awareness @ work, design and experience. In *CSCW 96, Proceedings of ACM Conference on Computer Supported Cooperative Work*, Pages 298-307.

Tomek, I., Nicholl, R., and Giles, R. (1998a). Supporting software development teams. In *Proceedings of Advances in Concurrent Engineering, 5th ISPE International Conference on Concurrent Engineering*, Tokyo, Japan, July 15-17.

Tomek, I., Nicholl, R., Giles R., Saulnier, T., and Zwicker J. (1998b). A virtual environment supporting software developers. In *Proceedings of CVE 98.*

Tomek, I., Giles, R., (1999a). A Virtual environment to support software development teams, *Journal of Concurrent Engineering Research and Applications.*

Tomek, I., Giles R. (1999b). Virtual environments for work, study, and leisure. *Virtual Reality* 4(1).

Tomek, I., Murphy, D., and Yang, G. (1999c): MUM: A multi-universe MOO, In *Proceedings of WebNet 99* (October).

Tomek I., Murphy, D., and Yang, G. (1999d). Multi-user object-oriented environments. *Lecture Notes in Computer Science No. 174: Object-Oriented Technology ECOOP 99 Workshop Reader*, Springer-Verlag.

Tomek I. (2000). The Design of a MOO, *Journal of Network and Computer Applications*. (To be published).

TWUMOO (1999). *Texas Woman's Moo.* http://moo.twu.edu:7000/

VRAIS 98 (1998). *Virtual Reality Annual International Symposium*, Atlanta, Georgia, USA, March 14 - 18 1998, http://www.eece.unm.edu/eece/conf/vrais/

WACC 99 (1999). *International Joint Conference on Work Activities Coordination and Collaboration*, San Francisco, USA, February 22-25, 1999, http://www.cs.colorado.edu/wacc99/

WebNet 99, *World Conference on the WWW and Internet*, Honolulu, Hawaii October 25-28, 1999.

Yang G., Tomek I. (2000). Team Lab: A Collaborative Environment for Software Developers, *Proceeding of CRIWG 2000.*

17
Parsing C++ Code Despite Missing Declarations

Gregory Knapen
Bruno Laguë
Michel Dagenais
Ettore Merlo

17.1 Introduction

This chapter addresses the problem of parsing a C++ software system that is known to compile correctly, but for which some header files are unavailable. A C++ program file typically depends on numerous included header files from the same system, a third party library, or the operating system standard libraries. It is not possible with a conventional parser to analyze C++ source code without obtaining the complete environment where the program is to be compiled. This chapter studies the parsing ambiguities resulting from missing header files and proposes a special parser which uses additional rules and type inference in order to determine the missing declarations. This new parser has achieved 100% accuracy on a large system with numerous missing header files.

This project was conducted at Bell Canada, a telecommunications service provider. Bell Canada performs software source code assessment as part of its acquisition process. The complete process is described in detail by Mayrand and Coallier (1996). One major aspect of this process is the static analysis of the source code. This requires parsing the source code to build an abstract syntax tree (AST) from which various metrics can be extracted. The AST is also used to build the control flow graph (CFG).

Most systems being evaluated are written in C and C++, with C++ clearly becoming one of the main languages for system development. Over the course of a source code assessment, the supplier is responsible for providing all the files required for building the system. Very often, however, a certain number of files are missing. These are most often header files from third-party libraries or system-specific header files. These files are usually of little importance in the evaluation of the software, as they are usually beyond the scope of the software developed by the vendor of the system under consideration. Yet, in C++ these files are actually required to parse the code.

Parsing C++ programs is a challenging task. The language is not context-free and contains many ambiguities. These ambiguities arise due to the fact that it is not always possible to distinguish a type from a simple identifier (function or variable) from the syntax alone. Traditional parsers (as implemented in compilers) are not very fault tolerant and must resort to using a symbol table to keep track of which identifiers are types. Compilers require that the compilation unit be complete (no missing header files) in order to parse the code. This chapter discusses parsing C++ source code with missing header files, thus with a potentially incomplete symbol table.

17.2   Previous Work

The topic of parsing incomplete C++ source code is relatively new. The term "Fuzzy Parser" was introduced by Bischofberger to describe a fault-tolerant parser "which can deal with incomplete software systems containing errors" (Bischofberger, 1995). The parser in question is said to have only a partial understanding of C++. A more formal definition of Fuzzy Parsing is given by Koppler (Koppler, 1996). Both approaches allow only to recognize a subset of the language. This approach is fine for building a class browser or some other form of graphical representation of the class structure. But this is not adequate when trying to build an AST; the whole language must be considered in order to have an exact and complete abstract representation of the source code.

17.3   Problem Description

Parsing C++ is in itself a difficult task. It becomes even more difficult when header files are missing. In the context of this project, the suppliers are very often unable to provide the complete source code for the whole software system. The missing files are usually header files from third-party libraries or system specific header files.

The root of the problem is in the C++ grammar. The current grammar of C++ is given by Stroustrup (1997); an older version is also available from the same author (Stroustrup, 1991). The same names for the grammar rules are used here. This grammar contains many syntactic ambiguities that must be resolved in order for the parser to apply the proper production; otherwise a parsing error may result. Therefore, C++ requires additional semantic information during parsing to resolve these ambiguities.

Traditionally, C++ parsers keep most semantic information in a symbol table. In C++, an identifier can be a user defined type, a variable or a function. For the purpose of parsing, it is not always necessary to distinguish between a variable and a function. From a practical point of view, a function can be considered a special case of a variable. In this chapter, the term variable is used loosely to refer to a variable or a function. In the grammar (Stroustrup, 1997), a function declaration is viewed simply as a variable declaration with an argument list. Each symbol (or identifier) can have two different semantics associated with it: type or variable.

When a symbol is first declared, the symbol is saved in the symbol table along with its semantics. When the symbol is later encountered during parsing, it is possible to know if it is a type or a variable and then to select the correct production. The symbol table keeps track of the current scope since symbols from one scope can hide those of an outer scope.

When header files are missing, it is not possible to trust the symbol table to be complete since some declarations may be missing. Semantic information might be missing, making some statements difficult to parse. Consider the C++ statement in the following example.

Example 17.1.

```
T(a);
```

Assume that this statement is found inside the scope of a function. This statement is syntactically correct ,but it is ambiguous because it can have two interpretations. In the C++ grammar referenced above, there are two possible rules that can interpret this statement. This statement can be parsed as a variable declaration or a function call. It is not possible to determine which rule to use based on the syntax alone. A semantic test has to be performed to remove any ambiguity. A simple test can be performed based on the semantics of the symbol T. If T is a type, the statement is parsed as a declaration. If T is a function, the statement is parsed as a function call. Note that this semantic test is not used to verify the semantics of the code, but to determine how to parse this statement

It can be seen that if T was declared in a missing header file, T would be undefined. The ambiguity would remain because it would not be possible to determine which rule to use based on the semantics of T. On the other hand, it is not true to say that semantic information is required to recognize all statements. For example, consider the following code fragment.

```
T a;
```

It is obvious from the syntax that this is a declaration with T being a type and a variable that is declared. Therefore it is not necessary to check in the symbol table that T is actually a type. Semantic information is only necessary to parse ambiguous constructs.

An additional complication comes from the scope rules of C++.

> A class name may be hidden by the name of an object, function, or enumerator declared in the same scope. If a class and an object, function, or enumerator is declared in the same scope (in any order) with the same name the class name is hidden. (Stroustrup, 1991)

This statement implies that even if the symbol table appears to be complete, symbols in a missing header file could have hidden symbols in the current compilation unit. This is illustrated in the following example.

Example 17.2.

```
missing_header.h
int T(int);
extern int a;
main.C

#include <missing_header.h>
class T {  /* rest of code */ };
    int main() {
    T(a);   /* parser would incorrectly interpret this
as a declaration when header file is missing. This is
in fact a function call! */
}
```

This means that we cannot guarantee that the name of a type that is present in the symbol table was not hidden by a function or variable defined in one of the missing header files. This means that any type could in fact be a variable (or function). Only variables are guaranteed to be variables, since they have precedence over a class (type) that has the same name as the variable. This can possibly cause problems when trying to resolve ambiguities and will be discussed in later sections.

Also, it is not possible to parse C++ without infinite lookahead (or backtracking) due to the difficulty in recognizing between expression-statements and declarations (Ellis and Stroustrup, 1990; Stroustrup, 1991). This means that the parser may need to look at a whole statement before deciding how to parse it.

Another aspect that must be considered is the preprocessing. In the absence of header files, it is possible that some macro definitions will be missing. One of the consequences is that the undefined macros will not be expanded. This can result in syntax errors, if the syntax of the unexpanded macros are not recognized by the language. Another consequence is that source code in a conditional compilation block might be removed by the preprocessor because of a missing #define directive.

Within the context of this paper, it is possible to assume that the code is semantically correct. This is a valid assumption since the systems inspected have always been compiled successfully beforehand. It cannot be assumed that the code is syntactically correct because of the possibility of unexpanded macros. So if a construct is valid syntactically, it is assumed to be semantically correct. This will allow to resolve certain ambiguities and will be discussed in later sections. Very little emphasis is put on error reporting. Instead the emphasis is put on parsing the code correctly to eventually build an AST.

17.4   Impact of Missing Header Files on the Resolution of Ambiguities

The concept of ambiguities was introduced in the previous section. Ambiguities are syntactically correct constructs from a recognition point of view (i.e., it is possible to determine if a given string belongs to the language). On the other hand, translation is not possible since there are two (or more) possible semantics associated with that construct. Consider the ambiguity in Example 17.1 when building an AST. It would not be possible to determine if a node representing a declaration or a function call should be added to the abstract syntax tree. If we only wanted to get the list of class declarations, this ambiguity would be irrelevant since it has no effect on the translation. Therefore, this problem should not be considered a recognition problem but a translation problem. The distinction between recognition and translation was made informally by Parr (Parr and Quong, 1996).

A list of ambiguities was compiled from various sources (Stroustrup, 1997; Parr, 1995; The Draft C++ Standard, 1996), as well as from the news group comp.std.c++. This list is given in Table 17.1.

The first column defines the type of the ambiguity and the second column gives an example. Each ambiguity can include a large number of constructs. For example, ambiguity 1 also occurs in the following statements: T(*a); T(&a); T((a)); etc. Ambiguities are classified according to where they occur in the grammar, not according to a specific syntax. For example, even though the syntax for ambiguity 1 and 2 can be the same, they do not occur at the same point in the grammar and are two different ambiguities. Also different versions of the language may have different ambiguities. Ambiguity 2 only occurs in an older version of the grammar (Stroustrup, 1991) where it is not mandatory to specify the type of a variable in a global declaration. This ambiguity does not exist in the latest grammar (Stroustrup, 1997) since all variable and function declarations must have a type.

The third column shows a possible semantic test that could be used to resolve each ambiguity. In Table 17.1, it is assumed that the symbol table is complete, that is, there are no missing header files. Therefore, all ambiguities can be resolved. In all cases, this is accomplished by checking whether a given identifier is a type or not. Most parser generators have a mechanism to report ambiguities in a grammar.

The list in Table 17.1 does not include syntactic ambiguities that are inherent to the language. These ambiguities are inconsistencies in the C++ grammar that arise even if the symbol table is complete. These ambiguities are discussed by Stroustrup (Stroustrup, 1991), and are resolved syntactically as defined by the language. This is illustrated in Example 17.3.

Table 17.1. Most important ambiguities in the C++ language.

Ambiguity	Example	Semantic Test
1. Ambiguity between a function call and a variable declaration (at function scope).	T(a);	If T is a type then it's a variable declaration, else it's a function call.
2. Ambiguity between a typed variable declaration, an untyped function declaration and an untyped variable declaration with initializer (at global scope)	T(a);	If T is a type then it's a variable declaration, else if *a* is a type then it's a function declaration, else it's an untyped variable declaration with *a* as an initializer.
3. Ambiguity between a parameter list and an initializer	A f(T);	If T is a type then it is a parameter list, and the whole statement becomes a function declaration. If not, it is an initializer, and the whole statement becomes a variable declaration initialized with T.
4. Ambiguity between a C-style type cast and an expression.	a = (T) *b;	If T is a type then it is a type cast, else it is a multiplication.
5. Ambiguity between a declarator and an abstract-declarator	A f(B(T));	Assume B is a type. If T is a type, it is an abstract declarator, else it is a declarator.
6. Ambiguity between a type specifier and a declarator	const T(x);	If T is a type then it's a type specifier, else it is a declarator.
7. Ambiguity between a pointer declaration and a multiplicative expression	T * a;	If T is a type then it's a declaration, else it's a multiplicative expression.
8. Ambiguity between templates	A < T > C;	If A is a template (generic type) and T is a type then C is a template instantiation. Otherwise the whole statement is an expression.

Example 17.3.

```
int b =3;
float a(float(b));
```

The second statement can be interpreted as a function declaration with a redundant parenthesis around the name of the argument, or a variable declaration initialized with a function style type cast. In reality, the language specifies that this construct should always be interpreted as function declaration.

There are also more subtle ambiguities. Consider a call to an overloaded operator ( ) and function-style type casts. Both of these constructs have the same syntax as a function call. In this chapter, these are all parsed as a function call since the semantics are similar. Later, the actual case can be determined by examining the type of the target of the call.

There are also some pathological cases that are a combination or variation of the listed cases. Consider the syntax in Example 17.4. This can have three interpretations as given in Table 17.2.

Example 17.4.

```
A (B) (C);
```

Table 17.1 showed how a traditional compiler can resolve ambiguities. It typically resolves the ambiguity based only on the type of the current symbol being parsed. Note that traditional parsers do not resolve ambiguities explicitly. This is done implicitly by determining the type of every symbol encountered by doing a table lookup in the symbol table. It is assumed that the symbol table is complete; in traditional compilers, an error is reported when an undefined symbol is encountered.

When header files are missing, the symbol table is potentially incomplete. This will have an impact in the resolution of ambiguous constructs. The semantic tests shown in the third column of Table 17.1 are not valid anymore because they do not take into account the case where the symbol T is undefined. However, when a symbol is undefined inside an ambiguous construct, it may still be possible to deduce the meaning of a statement from the semantics of other symbols inside that construct. This can be illustrated by an example. If we consider again the ambiguity between a function call and a variable declaration:

```
T(a);
```

Suppose symbol T is undefined because it is declared in a missing header file. If *a* is a variable previously declared in the same scope as the statement, then the statement can only be a function call since re-declaration of a variable in the same scope is not permitted. It is then possible to infer that T is the name of a variable (a function in this case). This resolution is based on the assumption that the source code is semantically correct, which is realistic in a reverse engi-

Table 17.2. Various interpretations of Example 17.4.

Semantics of A	Semantics of B	Semantics of C	Interpretation
function	Variable	variable	function call followed by call to operator ()
type	Variable	variable	variable declaration initialized with C
type	Variable	Type	function declaration

neering context. It excludes the possibility that *a* was declared twice in the same scope which is an error.

Table 17.3 shows how the semantic tests listed in Table 17.1 can be modified to better cope with missing header files. The first and second columns remain the same. In column three, the resolution of the ambiguities are based on the partial semantic information. The semantics of all symbols are considered in an attempt to resolve each ambiguity. It can be seen that the semantic test is not

Table 17.3. Ambiguity resolution when header files are missing.

Ambiguity	Example	Semantic Test
1. Ambiguity between a function call and a variable declaration (at function scope)	T(a);	If T is a type then it's a variable declaration; else if T is a function then it's a function call; else if *a* is an identifier declared in the same scope then it's a function call (i.e., T is unknown); else it's ambiguous (i.e., T and *a* are unknown).
2. Ambiguity between a typed variable declaration, an untyped function declaration and an untyped variable declaration with initializer (at global scope)	T(a);	If T is a type then it's a variable declaration; else if *a* is a type then it's a function declaration; else if *a* is a variable then it's an untyped variable declaration with a as an initializer; else it's ambiguous.
3. Ambiguity between a parameter list and an initializer	A f(T);	If T is a type then it's a function declaration; else if T is a variable then the statement is a variable declaration; else it's ambiguous.
4. Ambiguity between a C-style type-cast and an expression	a = (T)*b;	If T is a type then it's a type-cast; else if T is a variable then it's an expression; else it's ambiguous.
5. Ambiguity between a declarator and an abstract-declarator	A f(B(T));	Assume B is a type. If T is a type then it's an abstract declarator; else it is ambiguous.
6. Ambiguity between a type specifier and a declarator	const T(x);	If T is a type then it's a type specifier; else if x is a type then T is a declarator; else if x is a variable then T is a declarator; else it's ambiguous (i.e. T and x are undefined).
7. Ambiguity between a pointer declaration and a multiplicative expression	T * a;	If T is a type then it's a declaration. If T is a variable then it's an expression; else it's ambiguous.
8. Ambiguity between a template instantiation and an expression	A < T > C;	If A is a template (generic type) then it's a template instantiation; else if A is a variable then it's an expression; else if T is a type then it's a template instantiation; else it's ambiguous.

guaranteed to resolve the ambiguity anymore. We ignore in Table 17.3 the possibility that a type could have been hidden by a function or variable declared in a missing header file. If this assumption is not made, all cases where T is a type become undefined. Ambiguity 5 shows the limits of ambiguity resolution. The case where T is really a declarator is always theoretically ambiguous. Since T would be a parameter declarator, it would be the first time this symbol is encountered and nothing can be deduced from it. There is always the possibility that there is a type T declared in one of the missing header files. In this case, the symbol table is complete, but because there are missing files we cannot exclude the ambiguous case. Therefore, some cases will always remain ambiguous. We could assume a default behavior, this will be discussed in the heuristics section. In ambiguity 5, it is important to note that if B is undefined it becomes a variation of ambiguity 3. In this case, it is possible that variable f is being initialized with a function call to B.

17.5   Parsing Incomplete Compilation Units

It was shown so far that it is not possible to know the semantics of all symbols when header files are missing. Yet, a large portion of the language can be parsed without this information. The solution proposed here is to add special rules to the grammar that only recognize ambiguous constructs. For simplicity, these rules are referred to as ambiguity rules. With the addition of the ambiguity rules, the grammar will be even more ambiguous than before, since there is now one more rule that contains the ambiguity.

Example 17.5 shows two simple ambiguity rules used to parse the ambiguity between a function call and a variable declaration. These rules are expressed in the syntax used in ANTLR (Parr, 1996), which is based on the BNF notation. The symbol I is used to separate alternatives and the parentheses are used to group symbols into subrules. The non-terminal symbol qualified_id is described in the C++ grammar (Stroustrup 1997). All symbols enclosed in double quotes represent terminal symbols. ID is a terminal symbol representing any non-qualified identifier in the C++ grammar.

Example 17.5.

```
func_call_or_var_decl :
    qualified_id "(" init_or_var_decl ")" ";" ;
init_or_var_decl :
    ID | ( "&" | "*" ) init_or_var_decl |
    "(" init_or_var_decl ")"  ;
```

The parser first checks if a given language construct is ambiguous. If it is not ambiguous, then it is possible to parse this construct based on the syntax alone. If the construct is ambiguous, then there are two possibilities. The ambiguity could be simply reported by the parser. The second alternative is to try to resolve the ambiguity based on the partial information available. Since ambiguities are parsed by special rules, semantic actions can be associated with these rules. The rules shown in Table 17.3 could be used to try to resolve the ambiguous constructs. In this case, a symbol table is needed, but only to resolve the ambiguous cases. This yields a simple algorithm:

1. if the syntax is ambiguous, perform special treatment;
2. else try other applicable rules;
3. else it is a syntax error.

Very often the parser will not be able to determine using finite lookahead if a construct is ambiguous or not. For this reason, the parser must be able to perform backtracking.

If no resolution of ambiguities is performed, the problem has been reduced. Translation could be performed only on the syntactically unambiguous constructs. This becomes a form of Fuzzy parsing since only the non-ambiguous subset of the language is considered.

It was shown that some ambiguous constructs will always remain ambiguous even if all the necessary semantic information is available. But other ambiguous constructs can be resolved with very little partial information. Consider the following example.

Example 17.6.

```
T x(A,B,C);
```

If we discover during parsing that C is a type then the parenthesized list becomes a parameter-declaration list, and the whole statement becomes a function declaration. Again, it is assumed that the code being parsed is semantically correct.

Generally, symbols are added to the symbol table only when they are declared. But since header files are missing, not all declarations will be available. Furthermore, if we assume that the source code is semantically correct, it is possible to obtain the type of a symbol from its use in a non-ambiguous construct.

Therefore, if an undeclared symbol is encountered in a non-ambiguous construct, it is possible to infer the type of that symbol, and add it to the symbol table. If the same symbol is later encountered in an ambiguous context, its type will be known and it will be possible to resolve the ambiguity. Of course, if the first encounter with the symbol is in an ambiguous context, it will not be possible to determine the type right away.

This concept can be illustrated in the following example.

Example 17.7.

```
T a; // non-ambiguous, T added to symbol table as type
a = (T) *b;  // this is a type cast (ambiguity 4)
```

Assume that T is declared in a missing header file. From the first statement, it can be seen that T is a type. Therefore, T can be added to the symbol table as a type. Even though the declaration of T was never seen by the parser, it was deduced that T was a type. This allows to resolve the ambiguity of the second statement.

It is also possible that symbols encountered later, will resolve previous ambiguities.

Example 17.8.

```
int x(v); // ambiguous
b = x+2; // x is a variable
```

In this example, it can be inferred from the second statement that x is a variable. This would make the first statement non-ambiguous. I.e., a variable declaration initialized with v.

From the point of view of ambiguity resolution, parsing incomplete source code can be done in one or two passes. In the one-pass approach, the ambiguity resolution is done during parsing. In the two-pass approach, an AST is built in the first pass, and the ambiguities are resolved during the second pass by performing some tree transformation operations on the AST. This requires AST nodes to represent ambiguous constructs.

17.6 Heuristics

It was shown in Table 17.3 that some constructs will remain ambiguous. Either because there is not enough information in the symbol table or because that case is always ambiguous. It is still possible to make an educated guess about what a given construct means. With this approach, heuristics have to be used to resolve the ambiguity. The heuristics are generally based on the syntax and the scope of a given ambiguous construct. But the partial symbol table information can also be used to try to determine the most likely meaning for that construct. Also heuristics could be based on known programming idioms and coding standards.

For example, consider the ambiguity between a declaration and a function call again. This syntax is generally used to write a function call. Parenthesis are usually only used around a declarator to declare a pointer to a function which is not ambiguous. Suppose the ambiguous function call or declaration is not in the global scope and that all symbols are undefined, then a good assumption would be to say that it's a function call. This heuristic is based on the syntax and the scope of the construct.

A second heuristic can be used to resolve the ambiguity between a parameter list and an initializer. If the ambiguity is in the global scope, assume it is a parameter list, since most functions are declared in the global scope. If the ambiguity is encountered in a local scope (function or block), assume it is an initializer since functions are rarely declared inside a function scope. These two heuristics are summarized in Table 17.4. The approach used in this paper was to use heuristics when it was not possible to resolve the ambiguity from the information available in the symbol table.

17.7   Implementation

A parser was generated with a tool called ANTLR (previously known as PCCTS). ANTLR is a predicated LL(k) parser generator. This tool was chosen because it allowed building parsers that perform backtracking through a mechanism called syntactic predicates. It was also possible to select rules according to semantic information with the help of semantic predicates. This made ANTLR appropriate to build a C++ parser. ANTLR is described by Parr and Quong (Parr, 1996; Parr and Quong, 1995). The parser was generated from a modified public domain C++ grammar. This grammar was modified to parse C++ as much as possible without the help of a symbol table.

The emphasis was put on the parsing phase. The one-pass approach was used for the prototype, and no AST was built. Rules were added to the grammar to recognize the ambiguous cases. Certain simplifications were made. Referring to Table 17.3, only ambiguities 1 to 6 were recognized. In the case of ambiguity 7, it was always assumed to be a declaration when T is undefined. Ambiguity 8 was always considered a template declaration. Also, problems due to the scope rules of C++ were ignored. Thus, if a type is present in the symbol table, it is assumed that it is not hidden by a function or variable in a missing header file. These simplifications can be considered as *a priori* heuristics. The rules shown in Table 17.3 were used to try to resolve the ambiguities.

Since they usually apply to very specific constructs, the ambiguities were easy to express and the associated grammar rules were easy to write. The resolution of ambiguities was performed directly during parsing, it was necessary to check in each ambiguity rule if enough semantic information was available to resolve the ambiguity. If enough information was available, the context would be non-ambiguous and the ambiguous rule would fail. Backtracking would be performed and the next non-ambiguous rule would be tried.

The problem with this approach is that it relies heavily on backtracking. Also, all rules that can match syntactically an ambiguous construct must perform

Table 17.4. Heuristics.

Ambiguity	Heuristic
Ambiguity between a function call and a variable declaration (function scope)	Always a function call.
Ambiguity between a parameter list and an initializer	If it's in the global scope, it's a parameter list. If it's in a function scope, it's an initializer.

many semantic checks. For example, if an ambiguous rule fails because enough information is available to resolve the ambiguity, then the next rule must check again all semantic conditions to make sure it applies.

Our symbol table did not take inheritance into account. Therefore symbols from a base class were not accessible to a derived class. This means that a public variable declared in a base class is not visible from the derived class. This only limits the amount ambiguity resolution that can be done.

The preprocessing step is still required. Unexpanded macros used to represent constants were interpreted as variables. Unexpanded macros that had a function style syntax were interpreted as function calls when their syntax was recognizable by C++; otherwise they were considered as syntax errors. Little emphasis was put on error reporting. Only the line where the error occurred was reported along with the line of the grammar rule that failed. Also, the parser was able resynchronize itself and continue parsing.

17.8 Experimental Work

A real system that had been evaluated before was used to test the prototype. This system was originally incomplete due to missing header files (as were all currently examined systems). The characteristics of the system are given below.

- 380 KLOC approximately
- 657 source (.C) files
- 740 header (.h) files
- 1238 classes
- at least 7 header files were known to be missing

The lines of code were counted by simply counting non-empty lines. The preprocessing was done as a separate step using the GNU preprocessor. The files that were reported missing were counted. Each unique header file was counted only once. Also, the number of compilation units that reported missing files was counted. The preprocessed files were then parsed using the experimental parser.

Three configurations were used to test the parser, as shown in Table 17.5. These configurations differ in the number of header files of the system made available for parsing.

In configuration 1, no header files were included except header files in the same directory as the C file. This configuration represents the extreme case, and was used to see how well the parser would perform in such circumstances.

In configuration 2, 104 header files were missing. These files were removed from the initial system. The files removed were the standard C++ files, the header files for the GUI, the operating system header files and other utility library files. These files are at the top of the dependency graph, as a lot of compi-

Table 17.5. Configurations used to test the parser.

Configuration 1	Configuration 2	Configuration 3
• No headers • 654/657 compilation units were affected. • Total preprocessed size: 532 loc	• Some header missing • 104/740 missing header files • 650/657 compilation units were affected • Total preprocessed size: 5M loc	• Initial configuration • Most complete • 7 missing header files • 17 compilation units were affected • Total preprocessed size: 8 M loc

lation units would include these files. This can be seen in the numerous compilation units affected. This configuration represents a possible scenario, where none of the third-party libraries or system files are available.

The third configuration represents the most complete system available. Even in that case, 7 files are known to be missing (note that the exact count cannot be known, as the identified missing include files may also require other header files). It took several iterations with the system vendor to obtain this almost complete system. In reality, most systems analyzed would lie somewhere between configuration 2 and 3.

Before doing the test, it was verified that the source code did not contain any of the pathological cases. This was done using UNIX tools such as grep, awk and a modified version of the parser used only to detect potentially difficult patterns. No such cases were discovered.

It should be mentioned that we selected this system for this empirical evaluation of the parser because its anterior source code analysis revealed many serious weaknesses. Of particular interest in the current context is that it lacked well-defined interfaces (no layering), it had a complex inheritance graph and showed a lack of coding standards. For these reasons, this system was particularly well suited to test the parser. It showed many different styles of programming and displayed many dependencies between the files. The tests were performed on a SUN Ultra-1 with one CPU running at 143 MHz and 64 MB of RAM, running Solaris 2.5.

17.9   Results and Discussion

The results for the various configurations are given in Tables 17.6 to 17.9. The first column indicates the type of the ambiguity found. Note that only three types of ambiguities were found in the code. These correspond to ambiguities 1, 3 and 4 from Table 17.3. The rules from Table 17.3 were used to resolve these ambiguities.

The second column indicates the total number of occurrences of each ambiguity. Since it is possible that many compilation units include the same header files, if ambiguities exists in those files, they will be repeated across all compilation units. This explains the large numbers obtained in the second column. The third column gives the number of ambiguities left unresolved. These are the ambiguities that could not be resolved from the information in the symbol table. The fourth column gives the distribution for each ambiguity. The fifth column gives the accuracy of the heuristic when applying it to *all* occurrences of each ambiguity. First, each case left unresolved after querying the symbol table was verified by visual inspection, in order to determine if the heuristic made the right choice. Second, it was possible to determine from the data whether the heuristics alone would have produced the same results as those obtained from the approach based on the queries to the symbol table.

Several observations arise from Tables 17.6 and 17.7. All cases of the first ambiguity are function calls and the heuristic is 100% accurate. This shows that even though the grammar is ambiguous, programmers tend to always use the same syntax. In this case, the variable declaration with redundant parentheses never occurs, as it is not intuitive and it makes the code less readable. The heuristic for the second ambiguity was similarly accurate. No function declarations were found inside function bodies. All function declarations were in the global

Table 17.6. Results for configuration 1.

Ambiguity	No. of occurrences	No. of unresolvable cases	Distribution	Accuracy of heuristic for all occurrences
Function call or variable declaration	2579	240	all were function calls	100%
Parameter or initializer	441	11	9 parameter lists; 432 initializer lists	100%
Type-cast or expression	5	0	1 type cast; 4 expressions	No heuristic

Table 17.7. Results for configuration 2.

Ambiguity	No. of occurrences	No. of unresolvable cases	Distribution	Accuracy of heuristic for all occurrences
Function call or variable declaration	3,648	36	all were function calls	100%
Parameter or initializer	441	11	9 parameter lists; 432 initializer lists	100%
Type-cast or expression	5	0	1 type cast; 4 expressions	No heuristic

scope. All initializer lists were found inside function bodies to initialize local variables. This allows ambiguity resolution based on the scope. Configuration 2 has the same values as configuration 1 for the second and third type of ambiguity. The number of occurrences of ambiguity 1 is lower in configuration 1 than in configuration 2. This may seem contradictory at first, given that the configuration with the most missing headers (and the least complete symbol table) has the least amount of ambiguities. The difference in the number of ambiguities is found in the header files. There were a lot of function calls with the ambiguous syntax inside inline functions in the header files. Since these were not included in configuration 1, the number of reported occurrences for ambiguity 1 was lower. It is possible that the number of non-resolvable cases could have been lower, had we used a more sophisticated symbol table. Remember that inheritance was not taken into account, and that this system had a very complex inheritance graph.

It is interesting to point out that only three syntax errors were reported due to syntactically incorrect macros that were not expanded. The parser was able to recover from these errors and continue parsing.

Even though configuration 3 had the least amount of missing header files, this configuration contained the most ambiguities. It can be noticed from Table 17.8 that most occurrences are of the type ambiguity between a parameter and an initializer (ambiguity 2). Again, these come from the declaration of inline functions and free functions in header files. Since the layering was poor, these ambiguities would be repeated across numerous compilation units. The 107 unresolvable cases are the result of the symbol table not being able to take inheritance into account. When a member variable from a parent class is used to initialize a local variable in an ambiguous way, the ambiguity can not be resolved. Had we used a more sophisticated symbol table, more ambiguities would have been resolved.

Since we are using the experimental parser to parse all compilation units, it is assumed that they are all incomplete. This is not true and it would suggest a

Table 17.8. Results for configuration 3.a (parsing all files with the experimental parser).

Ambiguity	No of occurrences	No of unresolvable cases	Distribution	Accuracy of heuristic for all occurrences
Function call or variable declaration	3648	0	all were function calls	100%
Parameter or initializer	36803	107	432 initializer; rest parameter	100%
Type-cast or expression	8	0	4 type cast; 4 expressions	No heuristic

hybrid parser that would be able to parse complete and incomplete source code. A second test based on configuration 3 was done by parsing only the incomplete compilation units. It was assumed that a traditional parser (or a hybrid parser) would be able to parse all other complete compilation units. The results are shown in Table 17.9.

This configuration produced fewer ambiguities. All ambiguities were resolved from the symbol table information and heuristics would not have been necessary. This is the ideal scenario where only a few header files are missing and only a few compilation units are incomplete.

The heuristics seem to apply very well to the code analyzed. Initially heuristics were incorporated into this project to try to resolve the cases that were not resolvable from the information available in the symbol table. But it was found that they were 100% accurate in resolving all ambiguities of a given type. The heuristics used seem to work well because they coincide with common programming idioms. For example, the syntax of ambiguity 1 was always used to make a function call. This syntax is used for function calls, so it will not be used for any other purpose. Violating this idiom would result in making the code less readable. This means that the two heuristics could potentially replace the semantic tests 1 and 3 in Table 17.3. A symbol table would not be necessary to resolve those two ambiguities.

No heuristic for the ambiguity between a type cast and an expression was developed at the time because all such ambiguities could be resolved from the symbol table information. Also, no heuristics were developed for the other ambiguities since there were no such ambiguities in the code to compare them against.

Although the two heuristics used did not rely on the symbol table to make their guess, this does not necessarily have to be the case. Consider the ambiguity between a C-style type cast and expression. It is not possible to guess the true meaning from the syntax alone. And since a type cast and an expression both occur at function scope, the scope cannot be used to discriminate among the

Table 17.9. Results for Configuration 3.b (parsing only the affected compilation units).

Ambiguity	No. of occurrences	No. of unresolvable cases	Distribution	Accuracy of heuristic for all occurrences
Function call or variable declaration	80	0	all were function calls	100%
Parameter or initializer	481	0	20 initializer; 461 parameter	100%
Type-cast or expression	0	0	N.A.	No heuristic

two. From Table 17.8, we can see that both possibilities are just as likely. So we cannot assume that it is always a type cast or always an expression. Yet, we can still develop a simple heuristic that takes into account the semantic information available.

Consider the rule in Table 17.3 used to resolve the ambiguity between a C-style type cast and an expression (ambiguity 4). If T is undefined, we could assume that it's a type cast since it is more likely that a type was declared in a header file (missing in this case). For this heuristic, a symbol table is still required. The assumption made is based on the fact that the symbol is undefined because it was declared in a missing header file, not because this information was not properly extracted. This shows that knowing that a symbol comes from a missing header is still valuable information that can be used to resolve ambiguities.

Ironically, this heuristic is not that useful. This can be observed from the results. All ambiguities between a type cast and an expression could be resolved from the information available in the symbol table. This has a very simple explanation. In all cases, when a type cast is present in a function, a variable of that type was previously declared in the same function. This results in the addition of the type in the symbol table prior to the parsing of the type cast, as illustrated in Example 17.7.

As mentioned previously, no other type of ambiguity was found. This is an interesting result that implies that only certain types of ambiguities arise in practice. While it might be interesting to detect all ambiguities, it is probably worthwhile to only try to resolve the frequent ones. The ideal solution (from an accuracy point of view) would be to first use the resolution based on the information available and then resort to heuristics when symbols are undefined.

The approach used was to parse the code in one single pass. The ambiguities were resolved with the current information available. If more semantic information would become available later, it was not possible to go back and make an ambiguous construct non-ambiguous. This is due to the fact that no AST was being built at the time.

Another disadvantage of this approach is that of complexity. For each type of ambiguity, there are at least three rules that apply, the ambiguous rule and the other potential rules. Since the resolution of ambiguities is done during parsing, the syntax and the semantics must be checked together. This can result in complicated predicates. In this case, backtracking occurs either when the construct is syntactically incorrect or semantically incorrect. Even with extensive backtracking, the performance was acceptable. It took around 2 minutes to parse all the files for configuration 1 and about 20 minutes for configuration 3.

With the two-pass approach, as soon as an ambiguous case is detected the ambiguous rule would be selected and an ambiguous AST node would be built. Backtracking would only be done to detect ambiguous constructs and to recognize certain difficult C++ constructs.

17.10 Conclusions

This paper demonstrates the ability to parse C++ compilation units despite missing header files. The proposed approach uses special grammar rules to handle ambiguities. All non-ambiguous constructs are parsed based on the syntax alone, eliminating the need to see all symbol declarations. Furthermore, symbols were added to the symbol table not only from declarations but from any non-ambiguous construct, helping to resolve more ambiguities.

Backtracking is necessary to check if a given construct is ambiguous or not. Most ambiguities can be resolved using the rules shown in Table 17.3 and a symbol table. This is confirmed by the results. The cases that can't be resolved from the information available in the symbol table can be resolved using heuristics. The simple heuristics used in this paper were 100% accurate, and could replace the corresponding semantic tests defined in Table 17.3.

As discussed earlier, heuristics could not entirely replace the approach based on the symbol table. Yet, heuristics can be used to make the parsing simpler and to resolve the difficult cases. Both approaches are complementary.

The parser could keep track of the number of ambiguities detected. From a metrics point of view, the number of ambiguities could be used as an indicator of the readability of the source code. Since it is possible for heuristics to guess wrong, it can be a good idea to have a metric that records the number of times a heuristic is used. It would then be possible to know the percentage of ambiguities resolved by heuristics, thus providing a confidence level for the results.

In the future, the second approach based on the AST should be tried. This approach would be simpler from the parsing point of view. Also it would be instructive to compare metrics extracted by a traditional parser and the ones obtained form the experimental parser when header files are missing. This could help determine the influence of missing headers on the resulting metrics.

In the discussion, a hybrid parser was suggested. If all the header files are available, all compilation units are complete, and the parser can make the same assumptions as a compiler. In this case, all symbols will be defined and all ambiguities should be resolvable. As soon as a header file is missing, the parser would work in the manner described. Such a parser would need to know if the preprocessor was able to include all files or not. This can be easily achieved using a #pragma directive, that is, the preprocessor would issue the directive in its output telling the parser that a header file is missing. The parser would use the rules in Table 17.1 when the compilation unit is complete and would switch to the rules in Table 17.3 when header files are missing.

17.11 References

Aho, A.V., Sethi, R., and Ullman, J.D. (1986). *Compilers—Principles, Techniques and Tools*, Addison-Wesley, Reading, MA.

Bischofberger, W.R. (1995). Sniff—A Pragmatic Approach to a C++ Programming Environment. In *Proceedings of the 4th International Workshop on Parsing Technologies* (Prague, Czech Republic).

Ellis, M.A., and Stroustrup, B. (1990). *The Annotated C++ Reference Manual*, Addison-Wesley, Reading, MA.

Koppler, R. (1996). A Systematic Approach to Fuzzy Parsing. *Software—Practice & Experience* (27)6: 637-649.

Mayrand, J., and Coallier, F. (1996). System Acquisition Based on Software Product Assessment. In *Proceedings of the 18th International Conference on Software Engineering* (Berlin, March 25-29).

Parr, T.J. (1996). *Language Translation Using PCCTS & C++: A Reference Guide*, Automata Publishing Company, San Jose, CA.

Parr, T.J., and Quong, R.W. (1996). LL and LR Translators Need k >1 Lookahead. *SIGPLAN Notices* 31(2).

Parr, T.J., and Quong, R.W. (1995). ANTLR: A Predicated-LL(k) Parser Generator. *Software—Practice & Experience* 25(7): 789-810.

Parr, T.J. (1995) PCCTS Workshop.
Available at http://www.antlr.org/1.33/workshop95

Sametinger, J., and Schiffer, S. (1995). Design and Implementation Aspects of an Experimental C++ Programming Environment. *Software—Practice & Experience* 25(2): 111-128.

Stroustrup, B. (1997). *The C++ Programming Language*, Addison-Wesley, Reading, MA.

Stroustrup, B. (1991). *The C++ Programming Language*, Second Edition, Addison-Wesley, Reading, MA.

Stroustrup, B. (1994). *The Design and Evolution of C++*, Addison-Wesley, Reading, MA.

The Draft C++ Standard (1996). *Working Paper for Draft Proposed International Standard for Information Systems—Programming Language C++*. (ANSI Document X3J16/96-0225, ISO Document WG21/N1043.)

18
Towards Environment Retargetable Parser Generators

Kostas Kontogiannis
John Mylopoulos
Suchun Wu

18.1 Introduction

One of the most fundamental issues in program understanding is the issue of representing the source code at a higher level of abstraction. Even though many researchers have investigated a variety of program representation schemes, one particular scheme, the Abstract Syntax Tree (AST), is of particular interest for its simplicity, generality, and completeness of the information it contains. In this chapter, we investigate ways to generate Abstract Syntax Trees that conform with a user-defined domain model, can be easily ported to different CASE tools, and can be generated using publicly available parser generators. The work discussed in this chapter uses PCCTS and yacc as parser generators, and provides an integration mechanism with the conceptual language Telos, and the CASE tools Rigi, PBS, and Refine^{TM}.

Extracting and representing the syntactic structure of source code is generally acknowledged to be one of the most important activities in program understanding. This activity is considered a prerequisite to both maintenance and reverse engineering of legacy source code (Tilley and Smith, 1996). Traditionally, the activity consists of two steps, parsing and lexical analysis. However, unlike traditional syntax-directed approaches used by compilers, parsing and lexical analysis for program understanding purposes are carried out with respect to a language-specific domain model which describes the syntactic and semantic constructs of the underlying programming languages. The use of domain models by parsers and parser generators is not new. Arango and Prietro-Diaz (1991) and Markosian (1994) discuss source code analysis techniques for legacy code that produce Abstract Syntax Trees (AST) on the basis of domain models.

In the literature one can find a wealth of parser generator environments (PC-CTS, Yacc, Eli, TXL, LLGen, Pgs, Cola, Lark, Genoa, and Dialect, to mention a few) (Malton, 1993; Fischer and LeBlanc, 1991; Breuer and Bowen, 1993; Parr,

1996). All of these environments provide a formalism to represent grammatical rules, and a mechanism to trigger semantic actions when a rule is applied successfully during the parsing process. Kotik and Markosian's (1989) Refine re-engineering environment allows for the development of parsers based on domain models. Similarly, GENOA, discussed in Devambu (1992) and Devambu et al. (1994), is a language independent application generator that can be interfaced to the front-end of a compiler, which produces an attributed parse tree. This can be achieved by writing an interface specification using a companion system to GENOA, called GENII. The advantage of GENOA/GENII is that tools for program understanding, metrics, reverse engineering and other applications can be built without having to write a complete parser/linker for the source language in which the application is written. Moreover, earlier versions of the `yacc` (Breuer and Bowen, 1992) parser generator allowed for the creation of a walkable data structure that represented an abstraction of the AST in dynamic memory. The major difference of the proposed approach with the one applied in `yacc` is that in the approach presented here, the user can customize the domain model and therefore the annotations and the shape of the generated AST to fit specific analysis objectives.

However, most commercial tools do not provide a programming interface (API) and therefore the generated Abstract Syntax Trees can only accessed and processed in a limited way for any complex re-engineering or program understanding task. Within this framework, the objectives of this chapter focus on three directions.

The first is to report on techniques which make it possible to generate annotated Abstract Syntax Trees at various levels of granularity with respect to the parsed source code.

The second is to propose a methodology for simplifying the process of developing a grammar and a parser for a given programming language.

The third is to report on an architecture that facilitates the exchange of source-code-related information, between different software engineering analysis tools through the use of domain models, schemata, and persistent software repositories.

Towards these objectives, we experimented with the use of domain models by different parser generator environments. The first one is the PCCTS (Parr, 1996; Stanchfield, 1997) parser generator environment. The second is the C public domain parser generator `yacc`. Ongoing work reported also in this chapter involves the use of XML for annotating source code using the JavaCC parser generator (Sun Microsystems, 2000).

The work discussed here was carried out within the context of a software re-engineering project whose ultimate objective is to establish a generic and open software re-engineering environment. The environment should allow for different CASE tools to be integrated in terms of suitable intermediate representations and a persistent repository of multi-faceted information about a legacy system. Earlier reports on this project can be found in Buss et al. (1994) and Finnigan et al. (1997).

This chapter is organized as follows. In Section 18.2 we report on different techniques for producing source code representations tailored for program analysis and program understanding. In Section 18.3 we discuss the rationale behind the use of the Abstract Syntax Trees (ASTs) as a representation of source code structure. In Section 18.4 we outline the approach we adopted in order to construct customizable and domain re-targetable ASTs, and discuss how our approach works by applying it to a small C code fragment. In Section 18.5, we discuss advantages and limitations of our approach. In Section 18.6 we present alternative parsing techniques based on XML. In Section 18.7 we discuss the design of an integration environment for communicating data between the system presented in this chapter and various CASE tools and offer experimental results by using the proposed approach. Finally in Section 18.8 we summarize the chapter and we provide a perspective for further work.

18.2   Parsing for Program Analysis

Traditionally, parsing has been seen as a tool for producing internal representations of source code with the purpose of generating executable binaries for a specific target operating platform. In contrast, parsing for program understanding aims on producing representations of the source code that can be used for program analysis and design recovery purposes. In this respect, program representation aims on facilitating source code analysis that can be applied at various levels of abstraction and detail, namely at:

- the physical level where code artifacts are represented as tokens, syntax trees, and lexemes,

- the logical level where the software is represented as a collection of modules and interfaces, in the form of a program design language, annotated tuples, aggregate data and control flow relations,

- the conceptual level where software is represented in the form of abstract entities such as, objects, abstract data types, and communicating processes.

These representations are achieved by parsing the source code of the system being analyzed at various levels of detail and granularity. Specifically, over the past years a number of parsing tools have been proposed and used for redocumentation, design recovery and, architectural analysis. Overall, the parsing technology for program understanding can be classified in three main categories.

The first category, deals with full parsers that produce complete ASTs of a given code fragment. The second category focuses on scanners that produce partial ASTs or emit facts related to control and data flow properties of a given source code fragment. Finally, the third category deals with regular expression analyzers that extract high-level syntactic information from the source code of a given system.

Full parsers are used for detailed source code analysis as they provide low-level detailed information that can be obtained from the source code. This includes data type information, linking information, conditional compilation directives, and pre-processed libraries and macros.

In this context, a full parser generator called Dialect is proposed in Kotik and Markosian (1989). The approach uses a domain model as well as yacc and lex to produce a parser, given a BNF grammar. The AST is represented in terms of CLOS objects in dynamic memory, and can be accessed by a LISP-like programming interface (API) written for the CASE tool Refine.

Datrix (Bell Canada, 2000) is another full parser for C++ source code. The parser emits an AST representation that is suitable for source code analysis and reverse engineering of systems written in C++. A domain model for C++ provides the schema that describes the structure of the generated AST. Moreover, programming interface provides access to the AST and the ability to export detailed information in the form of RSF tuples (Müller, 1993).

Similar to the approach above, Devambu (1992) presents a C/C++ parser generator that produces a fully annotated AST representation of the code. The source code representation can be accessed by GEN++ for specifying C++ analysis and GENOA that provides a language-independent parse tree querying framework.

Finally, another technique that is gaining popularity due to the emergence of mark-up languages is to annotate the source code using XML. Document Type Definitions (DTDs) can be automatically built by analyzing the grammar of a given programming language. Parser generators such as JavaCC can be used to emit XML annotated source code by altering the semantic actions in a given grammar specification. Currently, DTDs for C, C++, and Java have been proposed (Mamas, 2000) and are available through the Consortium for Software Engineering Research (CSER). Once XML annotated source code is parsed, AST-like representations can be generated. These AST-like structures are called DOM trees.

In the second category of parsing techniques, scanners are used for extracting high-level information from a software system. This includes information related to declarations, calls, fetches and stores of program variables as well as, high level directory and source code organizational information. Data obtained from scanners are particularly useful for high level architectural recovery of large systems and can be readily used by various visualization and analysis tools.

Müller (1993) proposes a source code representation scheme that is based on relation entity-relation tuples (RSF). The approach is based on parsers for which their semantic actions are modified and applied only to a selected set of grammar rules to emit facts in the form of entity-relation tuples. As a result information pertaining only to specific syntactic construct (i.e., declarations, function calls) is presented and the rest of the source code is treated effectively as whitespace to be skipped.

Similarly, Holt (1997) describes a modified gnu C parser that allows for attributed tuples to be emitted. The modified parser called CFX produces high-level source code representations that comply with the TA syntactic form and can be directly used by the PBS visualization toolkit described in Chapter 14.

In the third category, regular expression analyzers provide high-level syntactic information of a system. Their major strength is their simplicity and availability as they can be implemented using scripting languages such as Perl, TCL, and Awk.

18.3   Rationale for Using AST Representations

As programming languages become more and more complex, one-pass compilers which don't produce any intermediate form of the compiled code are becoming very rare. This is also true in the area of program understanding and software re-engineering (Tilley and Smith, 1996). This has led to a variety of intermediate representations of the syntactic structure of source code.

For program understanding and re-engineering purposes, a suitable representation must be able to represent syntactic information which persists and evolves through the entire life-cycle of a software system. This life-cycle typically begins with source code analysis during development, and continues throughout successive maintenance, reverse engineering and re-engineering phases (Chikofsky and Cross, 1990).

Often, such a representation limits what can be expressed and described within it for the source code. Hence, generating an intermediate representation is an extremely important aspect for program understanding.

Kontogiannis (1993) surveyed common program representations, such as Abstract Syntax Trees (AST), Directed Acyclic Graphs (DAG), Prolog rules, code and concept objects, and control and data flow graphs. Among these, the AST is the representation that is most advantageous, and is most widely used by software developers. The reason for the popularity of the AST as a program representation scheme is its ability to capture all the necessary information for performing any type of code analysis, as well as the neutral representation of the source code it offers with respect to data flow and control flow source code properties.

To justify the AST representation used here, we need to distinguish first between a parse tree and an AST.

A parser explicitly or implicitly uses a parse tree to represent the structure of the source program (Aho et al., 1986). In Figure 18.1(a) such a parse tree for an arithmetic expression is illustrated.

An AST is a compressed representation of the parse tree where the operators appear as nodes, and operands of the operator are the children of the node representing that operator. Figure 18.1(b) illustrates the AST for the the expression whose parse tree is given in Figure 18.1.

Figure 18.1(c) illustrates an annotated AST where the tree edges become annotated attributes between nodes.

The AST we adopted for our project is a variation of the AST shown above, called annotated AST. The following is an example of an annotated AST for the PL/X If-Statement illustrated in Figure 18.2:

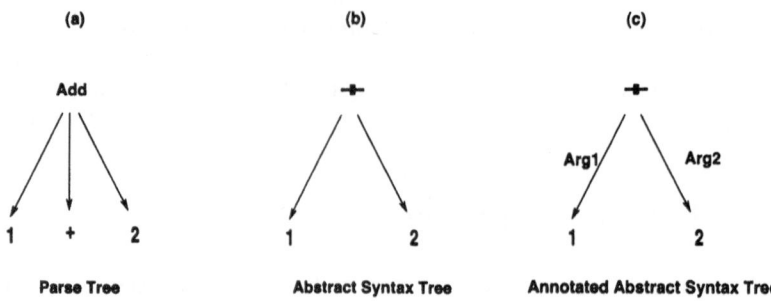

Figure 18.1. Parse tree and AST representation for the expression "1 + 2".

```
IF (OPTION > 0) THEN
   SHOW_MENU(OPTION)
ELSE
   SHOW_ERROR("Invalid option...")
```

Links of the AST are represented as attributes associated with (node) objects. In the If-Statement example, three attributes, are associated with the If-Statement node, and hold the fact that there are three components to an If-Statement (condition, then-part, else-part). The tree in Figure 18.2 is also annotated with a fanout attribute that denotes the number of function calls that appear in the AST node corresponding source code entity. The fanout attribute can be computed compositionally from the leaves to the root of the AST as illustrated in Figure 18.2. In the subsequent discussion, we use the term AST to denote an annotated AST.

18.4   The Domain Model Approach

In this section, we describe a domain-model based technique of generating an AST. The process of developing a domain model based parser is illustrated in Figure 18.3 and consists of three phases:

1. Identification and modeling of the syntactic structures of a programming language in the form of object classes in a domain model. Instances of the object classes along with their corresponding attributes form the actual AST nodes and edges, respectively,

2. Development of a grammar for the programming language by using the domain model object classes as grammar nonterminal symbols,

3. Integration of semantic actions with grammar rules so that the AST can be built during parsing in a customizable way.

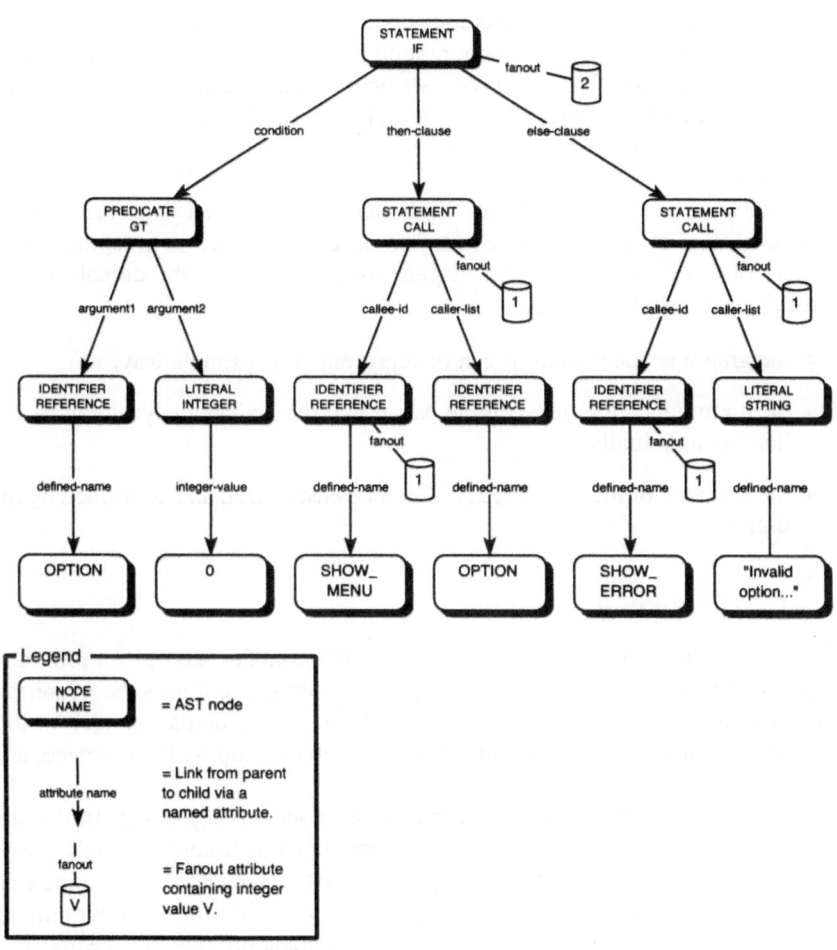

Figure 18.2. Annotated AST for an If-Statement.

For the overall AST generation process there are two levels of abstraction. The higher level focuses on the definition of the domain model using a modeling language and the specification of grammar rules using EBNF.

The lower level of abstraction focuses on utilities that allow for the generation of an AST in terms of a concrete programming formalism. For our work we have chosen to represent ASTs in terms of C++ objects, and the grammar to be specified in an off-the-shelf parser generator (i.e., PCCTS). Finally, the domain model is designed and implemented using the conceptual language Telos (Mylopoulos et al., 1990).

As indicated in the introduction, the domain model-based approach aims at the development of parsers that are easy to develop, and can be integrated with a variety of CASE tools. For this chapter, we examine how the domain model approach can be applied so that:

- the grammar specifications can be represented in a simple way,

- the communication between the parser and the lexical analyzer can be enhanced, and finally,

- the structure of the generated AST can be customized and controlled by the user.

18.4.1   Developing a Domain Model

There are two basic methods for building a domain model for a given programming language. One method is bottom-up, in the sense that it uses the nonterminals in the language grammar to obtain the classes of the domain model. In this approach each nonterminal symbol has a close relationship with the objects in a parse tree (Aho et al., 1986).

The other basic method for building domain models is top-down. In this approach, domain models are built in an incremental way where the higher-level schemata (domain model entities) are specified first, and then they are refined according to the syntactic and structural elements and relations of the programming language being modeled. The domain model schemata provide the specification for the objects with which ASTs are generated and composed.

In this context, a domain model defines a set of objects and the interrelationships among them. Overall, the domain model must be expressed in an environment which offers modeling capabilities and some persistent storage for the classes and objects of the domain model (which represent generated AST). For our work, we adopt Telos (Mylopoulos et al., 1990) to represent domain models, primarily because of its expressiveness and portability. Among other features, Telos allows an arbitrary number of meta-class hierarchy levels to be defined. This feature is exploited in dealing with different versions of the same language. Moreover, the AST generated by the parser generator can be persistently stored in a Telos repository or any other commercial database and exported to other tools

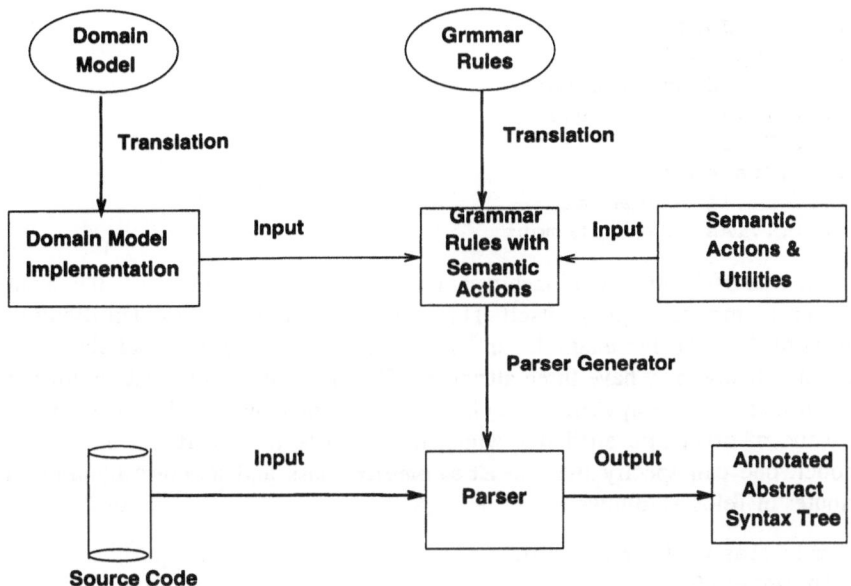

Figure 18.3. The AST domain-model based generation process.

for subsequent analysis (Buss et al., 1994). Modeling the application domain involves the discovery of objects classes that represent the AST nodes and their relationships which represent the AST branches.

For example, in the case of the C programming language, we may consider the following categories of schemata (classes) as part of the C domain model (Reasoning Systems, 1990(a); Kernighan and Ritchie, 1988):

```
Telos-Object
    - Program
    - Declaration-Object
    - File
    - Function
    - Statement
```

For each language domain model, there is an object hierarchy that can be implicitly imposed on schema entities by the structure of the programming language itself. Along these lines, further refinement of the C language object domain hierarchy is shown below (Kernighan and Ritchie, 1988):

```
ObjectClass
...Container
...Attribute
...C-object
......Program
......Declaration-Object
```

```
........Function
......Expression
........Identifier-Ref
........Function-Call
......File
......Statement
........If-Statement
........Assign-Statement
```

The task of defining relationships among objects is emanating from the syntax of a programming language itself. This task is directly related to identifying the edges of the AST. For example, an If-Statement domain-model class as illustrated below may have three attributes. The one is the condition attribute which maps to an Expression class, and the other two are the then-part and the else-part attributes which map to a Statement. In the domain model, one can specify the If-Statement class and its corresponding attributes in Telos as follows:

```
SimpleClass If-Statement
  in ObjectClass
  isA Statement
  with
    attributes
    condition        : Expression;
    then-part        : Statement;
    else-part        : Statement;
end
```

This can be read as follows: the class If-Statement is a subclass of a Statement domain model class; it has three arguments two of them map to the class Statement and one to the class Expression. A simple transformation program can translate the above domain model class definition to corresponding C++ classes, two of which are illustrated in the example below:

```
class If-Statement: public Statement,
                         ObjectClass
  {
  private:
    Condition *condition;
    Then-part *then-part;
    Else-part *else-part;
  public:
    Condition *getCondition();
    Then-Part *getThen-Part();
    Else-Part *getElse-Part();
    void      *putCondition(Condition *aCond);
    void      *putThen-Part(Statement *aStat);
    void      *putElse-Part(Statement *aStat);
```

```
};
```

and the sample attribute:

```
class Condition: public Attribute, ObjectClass
 {
  private:
   If-Statement *from;
   Expression   *to;
  public:
    C-Object  *getFrom()
    Container *getTo()
    void       *putFrom(If-Statement *aStat)
    void       *putTo(Expression *aExpr)
 };
```

The instantiations of the above C++ classes can be generated at parse time and form the nodes of the AST.

18.4.2 Defining the Grammar

To understand how the grammar specification associates with the domain model, consider the development of a grammar for three C language constructs (If-Statement, Assign-Statement, Block-Statement).

A domain model for the above constructs is specified in terms of an hierarchical schema as:

```
Statement
...If-Statememt
...Assign-Statement
...Block-Statement
```

In Telos,the constructs are specified as follows:

```
SimpleClass Statement
  in ObjectClass
  isA C-Object
end

SimpleClass If-Statement
  in ObjectClass
  isA Statement
  with
    attributes
    condition       : Expression;
    then-part       : Statement;
    else-part       : Statement;
end
```

```
SimpleClass Assign-Statement
  in ObjectClass
  isA Statement
  with
    attributes
    assign-lhs      : Identifier-Ref;
    assign-rhs      : Expression;
end

SimpleClass Block-Statement
  in ObjectClass
  isA Statement
  with
    attributes
    stat-list  : sequence-of(Statement);
end
```

The grammar for a given language can be built in two phases. The first phase is automatic and is used for emitting grammar rules that can be directly inferred from the domain model. These include rules that involve nonterminals that correspond to class-subclass hierarchies and to class-attribute relations in the domain model. An example is the rule R.4 and rules R.5–R.10 respectively as illustrated below.

The second phase is user-assisted and involves the user writing the grammar for a given programming language provided that he of she uses as non-terminals entities specified in the language domain model. Examples are the rules R.1–R.3 illustrated below. For example, the Assign-Statement domain entity, is used as a non-terminal in rule R.2 along with its attributes assign-lhs and assign-rhs. Attributes for which their target domain is a sequence of entities (such as in the case of stat-list attribute), are transformed into rules that involve the closure operations * or + as illustrated in the case of rule R.3.

Given these classes, the following grammatical rules can be specified as: [1]

```
R.1 If-Statement :   "if" "(" condition ")" "then"
                     the-part {["else" else-part]};

R.2 Assign-Statement : assign-lhs "=" assign-rhs;

R.3 Block-Statement : stat-list +;
```

---

[1]The grammar rules are given for clarity at a higher level that the one they will appear at the original PCCTS specification. An automatic translation to PCCTS or yacc rules from the given high-level rule specification is also possible. In these rules, curly brackets denote optional choice while square brackets indicate sequencing.

while the rules the following rules are generated automatically by the domain model,

```
R.4 Statement   : If-Statement | Assign-Statement |
                  Block-Statement;

R.5 condition   : Expression;

R.6 then-part   : Statement;
R.7 else-part   : Statement;


R.8 assign-lhs  : Identifier-Ref;
R.9 assign-rhs  : Expression;

R.10 stat-list  : Statement;
```

The coordination of grammar rules and the domain model in order to generate the desired AST is achieved only with a set of semantic actions that are invoked from within the parser generator. We do not put any restriction on the parser generator and therefore the same semantic actions can be invoked by a variety of parser generator tools requiring only minor or no modifications.

Defining a parser for a programming language can be a tedious exercise especially if the language contains context-sensitive structures.

18.4.3 Generating the AST

In order to fulfill the task of AST generation by using the machine described above, we need appropriate semantic actions to be inserted into the grammar.

We have defined three semantic actions that are associated with each rule. These are: `BuildRule`, `BuildTerm`, and `BuildAttr`. These actions operate on two global stacks `RuleStack` and `NodeStack`. The first stack keeps track of the current rule applied while the second stack stores the generated AST nodes that have still to be linked with their parent node during the AST generation phase. The semantic actions are automatically inserted in the grammar rules given the domain model specification. Only the rules for which their left-hand size part (i.e., the head of the grammar rule) corresponds to a domain model class that does not have any subclasses need to be annotated by the semantic actions described below. The reason is that all other rules are not used to generate AST nodes and are simply used to facilitate the parsing process for a given top-level non-terminal starting grammar symbol. These semantic actions are discussed in detail below:

`BuildRule(Rule)`: This action takes as a parameter the current rule name (i.e., the name of the non-terminal in the head of a rule). This action is inserted as the first semantic action to be carried out at the right-hand side of a given rule. It is actually invoked before the rule components are tried. In other words, the action is invoked before a rule recognizes anything in the input stream. More specifically, this action registers the rule as the current rule applied. Concretely, it creates an instance of the class `Rule` the pointer of which is pushed onto a RuleStack.

Once the rule succeeds (i.e., all right-hand-side non-terminals or terminal symbols have been resolved against the source text), the reference for this rule is popped from the RuleStack indicating that this is not anymore the current rule being tried. Hence, the only purpose of the `BuildRule()` action is to keep track which is the current rule being tried. In this respect, a stack data structure allows for keeping track of multiple nested invocations of the same rule–a frequent case that occurs during the parsing process.

As an example consider the rule:

```
Assign-Statement :
   assign-lhs "=" assign-rhs;
```

The rule above has two nonterminals (`assign-lhs, assign-rhs`) and one terminal (the token "=").

By examining the domain model, two more rules are automatically added. These are:

```
assign-lhs : Identifier-Ref;

assign-rhs : Expression;
```

The domain model is also used to recognize if a non-terminal is an attribute or a class. For the example domain model given in Section 18.4.2, `Assign-Statement` is defined as a class entity, while `assign-lhs` and `assign-rhs` are defined as attributes of the `Assign-Statement` class. The `Assign-Statement` rule shown above enhanced with the `BuildRule` semantic action and the additional rules obtained by the domain model becomes:

```
Assign-Statement:
   << BuildRule(Assign-Statement); >>
      assign-lhs "=" assign-rhs ;

assign-lhs:
   << BuildRule(assign-lhs); >>
   Identifier-Ref;

assign-rhs:
   << BuildRule(assign-rhs); >>
   Expression;
```

`BuildTerm(Term)`: This action takes as a parameter the name of the non-terminal symbol at the head of the rule as well. This semantic action is placed at the end of a rule, provided that the head of the rule is a class that has no subclasses in the domain model. If the head of the rule is an attribute then the `BuildAttr` semantic action is applied instead. The `BuildAttr(Attr)` action is discussed below. Examining whether or not a term corresponds to a `Class` or an `Attribute` takes only a simple look-up operation on the domain model specification. The `BuildTerm(Term)` action aims at building the AST node that corresponds to the latest term (head of the rule) succeeded. This action is implemented by incorporating a globally available stack called `NodeStack`.

Once the rule is successfully parsed the `BuildTerm(Term)` semantic action is invoked. An instance of an object of type `Term` is constructed and is pushed on the TermStack indicating that this is the most recent rule successfully tried. If the rule fails then a cleanup of the stacks occurs up to the last rule that had been successfully tried.

Augmented with both actions `BuildRule(Rule)` and `BuildTerm(term)`, our example rule looks like the following:

```
Assign-Statement:
   << BuildRule(Assign-Statement); >>
      assign-lhs "=" assign-rhs ;
   << BuildTerm(Assign-Statement); >> ;
```

In our example the `BuildTerm(Assign-Statement)` action will create an instance of the class `Assign-Statement`.

`BuildAttr(Attr)`: This action is placed at the end of a rule, provided that the head of the rule is recognized as an `Attribute` in the domain model and not as a class. The `BuildAttr(Attr)` action is used for creating the annotated edges of the AST. The most recent attribute created by the process becomes an incoming edge to the most recent created node. Augmented with the semantic actions `BuildRule(Rule)`, `BuildTerm(Term)`, and `BuildAttr(Attr)` our example rules become:

```
assign-lhs :
   << BuildRule(assign-lhs); >>
      Identifier-Ref
   << BuildAttr(assign-lhs); >>

assign-rhs :
   << BuildRule(assign-rhs); >>
      Expression
   << BuildAttr(assign-rhs); >>
```

For the above example the AST which will be created for the C statement "a = 1" is illustrated in Figure 18.4[2].

---

[2]We assume a domain model that contains `Identifier-Ref`, and `Integer` classes with attributes `name` and `value`, respectively

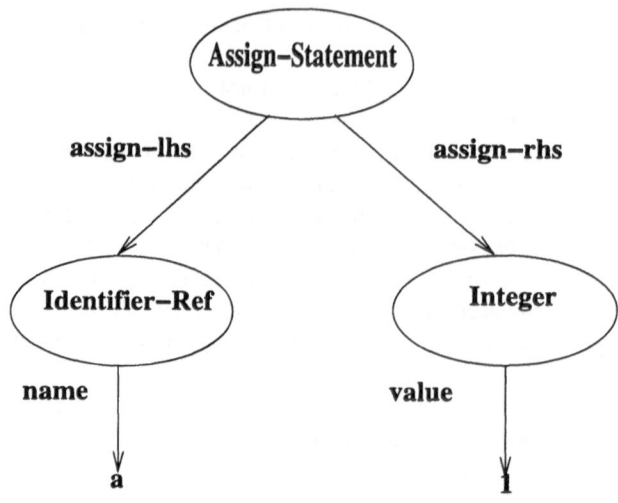

Figure 18.4. AST representation for the statement a=1.

This process allows for a customizable way to impose a structure in the AST, which can be used to port AST structures from one tool to another with minimal effort. In practice, the programmer is not even required to specify the actions BuildRule(Rule), BuildTerm(Term), and BuildAttr(Attr). These can be generated automatically by a transformation program that takes abstract grammar rules and generates legal code for the parser generator.

The following sections discuss the functionality of the semantic actions in more detail.

18.4.4   Semantic Actions

The three semantic actions sketched in the previous session are used in coordination with two global stacks to create the Annotated Abstract Syntax Tree. The following algorithms describe how the semantic actions are used in the AST generation process for a rule of the form NT_{Head} : $NT_1 NT_2 \cdots NT_k$, where NT_i is a a non-terminal. For clarity we omit terminals in our rule descriptions.

Procedure Initialize

Step 1 RuleStack ← NULL
Step 2 NodeStack ← NULL
Step 3 Exit

Procedure BuildTerm(NT_{head})

Step 1 RulePtr ← CreateRuleObject(NT_{Head})

Step 2 RulePtr.count ← 0

Step 3 Push(RulePtr, RuleStack)

Step 4 Exit

Procedure BuildAttr(NT_{head})

Step 1 Pop(RuleStack)

Step 2 Top(RuleStack).count++

Step 3 Exit

Procedure BuildTerm(NT_{head})

Step 1 Term ← CREATE-TERM(NT_{Head});
TheNonTerm ← Pop(RuleStack);

Step 2 IF RuleStack ≠ NULL THEN
AnAttr ← Top(RuleStack);
CurrentAttr ← CREATE-ATTR(AnAttr);
/* CREATE-ATTR builds a labeled AST edge */
/* with information obtained from CurrentAttr */
Term.IncomingAttr ← CurrentAttr
END IF

Step 3 FOR i = 1 TO TheNonTerm.count DO
aNode ← Top(NodeStack);
/* Link the incoming attribute to aNode */
/* with the parent of aNode, which is Term */
LinkIncomingWith(aNode, Term)
Pop(NodeStack)
END DO

Step 4 Push(Term, NodeStack);

Step 5 Return(Term)

18.5   Advantages and Limitations

In Section 18.4.4, we described a technique for incorporating the semantic actions for AST generation into a grammar. The basic difference between traditional approaches and the domain-model based approach is the level where the actions are embedded. Traditional approaches can be thought as syntax-directed while the domain-model approach as rule-directed.

In this section, we take a look at the grammars written by using the two different approaches, and we discuss the advantages and limitations of the domain model approach.

A version of grammar rules for generating an AST for a `Block-Statement` and an `Assignment-Statement` are shown below:

```
Block-Statement >
   << List* stat-list = NULL;
      Statememt * Stat; int i=0;>>
      (LC:LEFT-CURLY
      ( Statement >[Stat] SE:SEMICOLON
      << if (i==0)
          {stat-list=new List(Stat); i=i+1;}
          else stat-list -> append(Stat); >>)+
      RC:RIGHT-CURLY)

Assign-Statement >
   [Assign-Statement * Assign];
   << Expression* Expr; Identifier-Ref* Id-Ref;>>
   ID:ID-REF
   <<Ident=new Identifier-Ref($ID->getText());>>
   AS:ASSIGN-SIGN
   Expression > [Expression]
   << $Assign=new Assign-Statement(Id-Ref,Expr);>> ;
```

For the cases where the programming language has context-sensitive constructs the grammar above can be even more complex to design and develop. With the domain-model approach, by using the semantic actions discussed above the sample grammar can be rewritten and still perform the same task.

```
Block-Statement >
   << BuildRule("Block-Statement"); >>
   (LC:LEFT-CURLY
       ( stat-list SE:SEMICOLON )+
      RC:RIGHT-CURLY)
   << BuildTerm("Block-Statement"; >>

Assign-Statement >
   << RuleCount("Assign"); >>
      assign-lhs AS:ASSIGN-SIGN assign-rhs
   << BuildTerm("Assign-Statement") >> ;
```

A translation process takes the simplified grammar specification and generates PCCTS code (above) or `yacc` code. The translation process will generate valid PCCTS or `yacc` code using the simplified grammar and the domain model, and by adding more rules and attaching the semantic actions discussed above at the beginning and the end of each rule.

Therefore, in practice, the programmer needs only to define the following /break grammar:

```
Block-Statement :
    (LC:LEFT-CURLY
      (stat-list SE:SEMICOLON)+
    RC:RIGHT-CURLY)

Assign-Statement :
    assign-lhs AS:ASSIGN-SIGN assign-rhs;
```

The domain model is also used to automatically generate the header files that contain the C++ class instances which represent AST nodes. Our experiments suggest the following major advantages for the domain model approach.

First, the AST generation process can be easily applied to accommodate different programming languages. Most programming languages constructs can be modeled using the domain-model approach and any parser generator can be used when augmented with the proper semantic actions.

Second, once the AST is created, it is easy to make tree analyzers and pretty print utilities. This is of particular importance for re-engineering projects aimed at the migration of programs from one language version to another.

Third, the approach effectively hides implementation details for generating AST. It is notable that the domain-model-based grammar specification is much more concise than that generated by the traditional approach.

Finally, context-sensitive languages can be specified easier as the structure of the rules is simpler. This is of particular importance, since many programs that have to be re-engineered or migrated are written in highly specialized, context-sensitive languages.

The proposed approach has the limitation that when used with an LL parser generator, it may give rise to complex rules in the implementation due to the left-recursion restrictions (Aho et al., 1986). In this case the user has to be careful to write grammar rules, as discussed above, that are not subject to left-recursion. However, these restrictions do not apply when the proposed domain-model approach is used with an LALR parser. Moreover, an algorithmic process for eliminating left recursion in grammar rules has been presented in Aho et al. (1986).

18.6 Alternative Techniques

In this section we present alternative techniques for customizable domain-driven parsing using the extensible Mark-up Language (XML) (Mamas, 2000).

The objective is to develop program representations based on XML that provides information at the same level as ASTs. This alternative representation is simple but detailed enough to represent the complete syntax of a specific programming language. This mark-up language based approach aims on developing more generic representations suitable for domains with similar characteristics.

18.6.1 Annotating Source Code Using XML

Mapping ASTs to DTDs

Given a specific programming language we need to define a representation in which every valid source code program can be mapped to. To accomplish this mapping from ASTs to XML DOM trees we need to define a method to map the grammar of the programming language structure to a Document Type Definition (DTD). The mapping at this level will guarantee that all possible syntax trees defined by the grammar (and therefore any source code program), can be mapped to XML trees defined by the DTD. One of the requirements when defining new XML representations is to make them as easy to use as possible. Proposing a generic algorithm that maps a grammar to a DTD is something that result in hard to use representations. Instead, an alternative is to provide general guidelines that assist in implementing a good mapping from a grammar to a DTD.

Once a grammar is mapped to a DTD, the ASTs for a specific program can be mapped to XML files. These XML files can then be used in place of the ASTs or the original source files for maintenance tasks.

Java Mark-up Language (JavaML)

The generation of a program representation for Java is based on a parser generator tool called Java Compiler Compiler or JavaCC (Sun Microsystems, 2000) in short. This tool was initially developed by Sun Microsystems and it is the one of the most popular parser generators for Java. The popularity of JavaCC is most probably due to the grammar for Java that is shipped with the tool. The majority of Java source code parsers are built using JavaCC and the Java 1.1 grammar. The Java 1.1 grammar was developed by Sriram Sankar at Sun Microsystems and a copy of this grammar can be found in the distribution of JavaCC.

The complete DTD that we generated based on the Java 1.1 grammar is presented in Mamas (2000) and can be found at "http://swen.uwaterloo.ca/docs/javaml.html". Below we present a small example of a Java source file and its corresponding JavaML representation.

Java Source Code

```
public class Car{

 int color;

 public int getColor(){
  return color;}

}
```

JavaML Representation

```
<ClassDeclaration Identifier="Car">
 <FieldDeclaration>
  <PrimitiveType Type="int"></PrimitiveType>
  <VariableDeclaratorId Identifier="color"/>
 </FieldDeclaration>

 <MethodDeclaration Identifier="getColor">
  <ResultType>
   <PrimitiveType Type="int"/>
  </ResultType>
  <Block>
   <ReturnStatement>
    <PrimaryExpression>
     <Name Identifier="color"></Name>
    </PrimaryExpression>
   </Block>
  </MethodDeclaration>
</ClassDeclaration>
```

The above annotated source code can be parsed by an XML parser such as IBM's XML4J parser and produce a DOM tree that corresponds in this context to an Annotated Abstract Syntax Tree.

C++ Markup Language (CppML)

The generation of a representation for the C++ programming language is based on a different approach than that for Java. Instead of using a parser generator such as JavaCC, we took advantage of a compiler product that maintains the intermediate representation of the code and provides access to it through an API. This product is the IBM VisualAge C++ (IBM Corp., 1999) IDE which is developed at the IBM Toronto lab. VisualAge contains a repository which is called Codestore in which all the information generated during the compilation process is stored. Parsing, processing and code generation information can all be accessed using the provided APIs. The goal behind the architecture of VisualAge is to allow developers to maintain and analyze C++ source code. Our goal in using VisualAge is to demonstrate that a commercial product can be integrated and used as a tool in a more complex environment. The complete representation for C++ that was generated using IBM's VisualAge C++ can be found at "http://swen.uwaterloo.ca/docs/cppml.html". Sample source files and their representations are also available. The grammar on which CppML is based was implicitly extracted from the Codestore APIs, which was in turn obtained from the VisualAge development team. This grammar is expressive enough to represent ANSI C++ compliant source files.

18.7   Experiments

In this section we provide experimental results related both to the performance of the generated parser using the proposed domain-model-based approach, and to the performance of the architecture used for tool integration.

18.7.1   Parser Performance

The experimental results presented here focus on two main categories namely, parse time performance and, space requirements for the generated Abstract Syntax Tree. The results were obtained by evaluating a parser developed for the C programming language, using the domain-model approach discussed in this chapter. Ongoing work focuses on developing parsers for PL/IX, PL/X, and PL/I.

In Table.18.1, the time and space performance statistics for the C parser are illustrated. These results indicate that the parser developed is scalable with respect to the time required to parse source code and build the corresponding Abstract Syntax Tree.

In particular, the results indicate a linear complexity between the number of statements to be parsed and the time spent to actually parse these statements. The same linear relationship holds between the number of lines of code to be parsed and the actual parse time. On average, the parser parsed 44.43 statements, or 235 lines of code (LOC) per second, on a Sparc 128 MB Ultra 1 machine.

Similarly, the space requirements for the generated Abstract Syntax Tree indicate that the size of the tree in terms of the number of nodes is linear when compared to against the number of source code statements and the lines of source code (LOC) parsed.

Ongoing work focuses on the use of XML and DOM for representing the Abstract Syntax Trees and DTD domain models have already built for Java and C++.

18.7.2   Tool Integration

In developing a portable program representation environment, the following problems have to be considered:

- Data integration is essential to ensure data exchange between tools.

- Control integration enhances inter-operability and data integrity among different tools.

The first can be accomplished through a common schema, while the second can be accomplished with a server that handles requests and responses between tools in the environment.

A solution to the data integration problem is based on a system architecture in which all tools communicate through a central software repository that stores,

Table 18.1. Time and space statistics for the prototype parser.

LOC	# of Statements	Parse Time (sec)	# AST Nodes (thousands)
1	1	0.04	0.008
15	1	0.05	0.005
49	1	0.14	0.038
40	1	0.2	0.068
101	1	0.32	0.113
203	1	0.92	0.409
371	1	1.71	0.713
302	1	2.41	1.085
76	2	0.85	0.406
122	4	0.23	0.068
38	16	0.16	0.055
54	25	0.38	0.165
65	50	0.46	0.202
196	89	1.28	0.603
178	110	1.46	0.701
240	131	1,92	0.907
238	153	1.59	0.846
365	248	2.86	1.401
960	476	8.52	4.214
1,002	728	8.07	4.125
8,050	4,723	92.99	39.89
16,203	7,486	149.1	63.53
34,271	14,240	277.19	114.622

normalizes and makes available analysis results, design concepts, links to graph structures, and other control and message passing mechanisms required for the communication and cooperative invocation of different tools. Such integration is achieved by using a local workspace for each individual parser or tool in which specific results and artifacts are stored, and a translation program for transforming tool-specific software entities into a common and compatible form for all environments entities.

The translation program generates appropriate images in the central repository of objects shared with local workspaces. For the program representation scheme proposed in this chapter (i.e., annotated ASTs based on a domain model) this translation is a straightforward process, as the AST nodes and links correspond to classes that can be mapped from one tool to the other (CLOS in Refine, C++ for PCCTS etc.) A system architecture for such an integrated reverse engineering environment that uses common program representation interchange data is illustrated in Figure 18.5

Communication in this distributed environment is achieved by scripts understood by each tool using a shared schema data model for representing data from the individual local workspaces of each tool and, a message passing mechanism

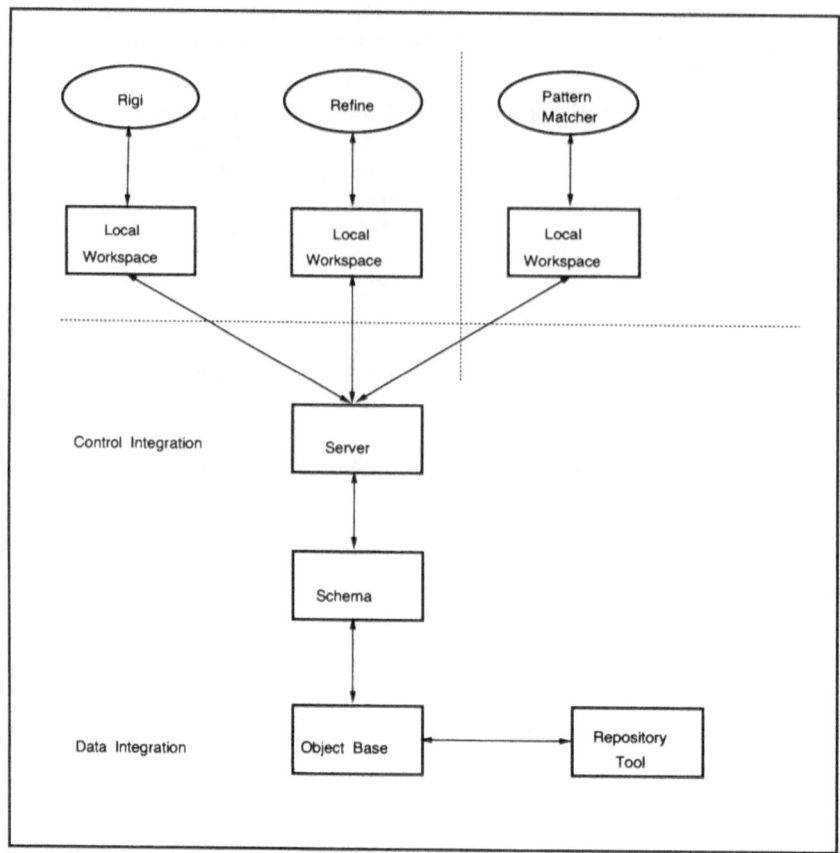

Figure 18.5. The implemented system architecture for tool integration. Dashed lines distinguish computing environments, usually running on different machines.

for each tool to request and respond to services.

A message server allows all tools to communicate both with the repository and with each other, using the common schema. These messages form the basis for all communication in the system.

The central repository is responsible for *normalizing* these representations, making them available to other tools, and linking them with the other relevant software artifacts already stored in the repository (e.g., documentation, architectural descriptions).

Finally, communication scripts are in the form of s-expressions. Each s-expression is wrapped in packets called *network objects* and sent via a message server to the appropriate target machine (Buss et al., 1994). The message server uses UNIX sockets for the communication and utilizes the TCP/IP network infrastructure.

An example s-expression for a `Function` called `hostnames-matching` is given below.

This s-expression is used to represent an annotated (yet simplified) AST node corresponding to a C `Function`. Annotations in this example include call information, metrics information and, data flow information.

```
(Function-176 Token
  (Function)
  ()
  (((objectId)
    (("#176")))
   ((cyclomaticComplexity)
    ((5.0)))
   ((calls)
    ((Function-175)
     (Function-174)))
   ((definesLocals)
    (("word")
     ("yylval")))
   ((definesGlobals)
    (("shell-input-line")
     ("shell-input-line-index")))
   ((functionName)
    (("hostnames-matching")))))
```

The shared schema facilitates data integration and encodes program artifacts (i.e., the AST), as well as analysis results (e.g., the call graph, the metrics analysis).

The schema has been implemented in Telos and allows for multiple inheritance and specialization of the attribute categories for each object. In this way, an AST entity (i.e., File) may have attributes that are classified as *Refine-Attributes*, *Rigi-Attributes*, and *PBS-Attributes*. The schema is populated by tools that may add, or retrieve values for the attributes in the objects to which it has access to.

Similarly, data integration for analysis results was achieved by designing schema classes for every type of analysis a tool is able to perform. Each such class is linked via attributes to the actual AST entities and this is visible to all the other tools that may request it.

At run-time, the user may request and select repository entities according to specific object types or attribute values.

In addition to the Data Integration aspects discussed above, Control Integration is based on designing and developing a mechanism for:

- uniquely registering tool sessions and corresponding services,

- representing requests and responses,

Table 18.2. Storage statistics (only File and Function object types are stored).

LOC	# of Functions	# of Files	# of Objects
943	38	3	920
13,615	235	39	1,089
27,393	632	63	1,606
32,807	705	40	1,694
44,754	658	46	3,340

- transferring object entities to and from the repository, and

- performing error recovery.

At the Application layer (Stallings, 1991) a message server is used to facilitate inter-networking. The message server, offers an environment to manage the transfer of data via TCP/IP using a higher-level language to represent source and destination points, processes, and data. Essentially, the server offers an environment to access lower-level UNIX communication primitives (i.e., sockets), in order to manage the transfer of data via TCP/IP using a higher-level language to represent source and destination points, processes, and data.

Each tool generates a stream of *network objects* encoded as a stream of s-expressions. A parser analyzes the contents of each it network object and performs the appropriate actions (e.g., respond to a request, acknowledge the successful reception of a *network object*).

Tool integration statistics are discussed and in particular the relationship between source code size, total number of repository-generated objects, data retrieval performance as well as upload and download times.

Our experiments for time and space statistics related to the integration architecture involved five software systems. For each system we have measured the number of objects generated for the reduced AST as well as the upload and download times from the repository to the individual tools.

The total number of objects generated for the reduced AST that correspond to files, functions and declarations is illustrated in Table 18.2. These measurements indicate that the approach of storing only the necessary parts of the AST results in a large potential for scalability, as major increases in the size of the source code do not affect dramatically the total number of objects generated.

The upload times are illustrated in Figure 18.6. These statistics indicate a relatively linear relation between the upload time and the total number of objects to be loaded in the repository.

Similarly, the download statistics are shown in Figure 18.7. These statistics indicate that download time relates in a linear manner to the number of objects dowloaded from the repository to the CASE tool. This is an important observation as it is directly connected with the scalability of the system.

The server has been extended to handle more complex messages and respond automatically to events using a rule base and the *Event, Condition, Action*

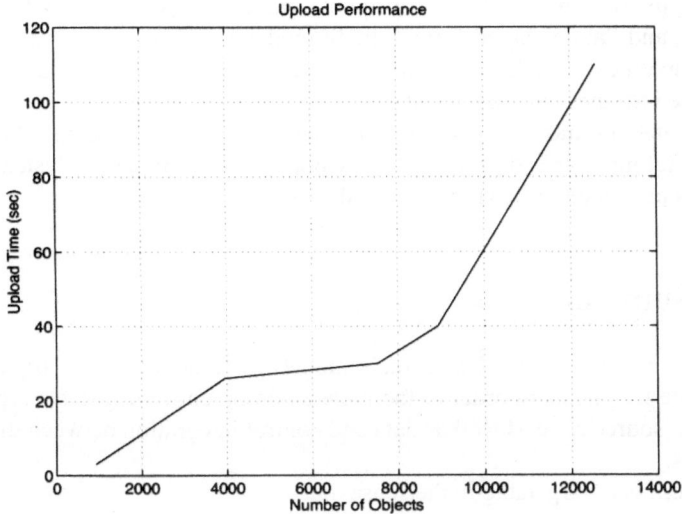

Figure 18.6. Upload AST performance.

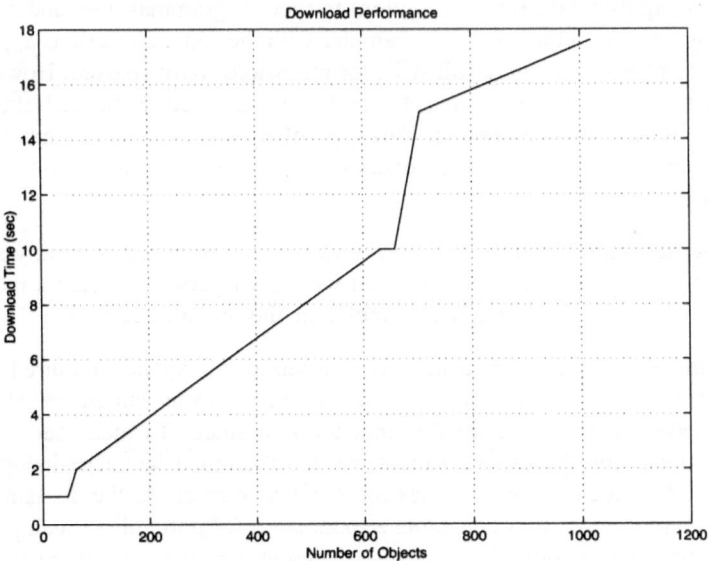

Figure 18.7. Download AST performance.

paradigm (Mylopoulos et al., 1996).

A prototype system that allows for the integration of the CASE tools Refine, Rigi, Telos, and data obtained from domain-model based Abstract Syntax Trees has been implemented at the University of Waterloo, and the IBM Canada, Center for Advanced Studies (Mamas, 2000).

This architecture has also been used to facilitate control and data integration between different tools and processes in a Cooperative Information System Environment, as presented in (Mylopoulos et al., 1996).

18.8   Summary

This chapter examines the use of domain models for generating AST representations of code fragments in order to facilitate environment re-targetable representation of the source code as well as data and control integration between different CASE tools.

The system is re-targetable in the sense that:

- The ASTs generated by the technique discussed in this chapter can be easily traversed, and can easily be ported to another tool or stored in an object-oriented database or relational database.

- The level of granularity source code parsed can be easily modified by selectively applying the semantic actions to specific grammar rules and by omitting them from the others. A grammar with the semantic actions applied to every rule will create a full AST for the whole source parsed. However, if the user decides to apply selectively the semantic actions then a lightweight partial AST can be created. This type of lightweight AST is most useful for analysis related to the recovery of high level architectural views of the code.

- The development and the specification of the grammar is greatly simplified and the approach can be used with most parser generators requiring minimum modifications to accommodate the semantic actions.

Domain models are used to infer the semantic information required by the parsing process for transforming the parsed input into an annotated AST, and provide a common schema for different tools to share. To make such a common schema usable by different tools, we have adopted language-independent and tool-independent representations for ASTs as well as for the domain model itself. Such representations constitute a foundation for portability. Such portability is of particular importance as it allows different parsers to export the generated AST to CASE tools that are very powerful on analyzing source code.

Ongoing work for this project includes stress-testing the control and data integration of different reverse engineering tools by using the common data interchange formats such as XML, RSF, TA, and ASTs as well as enhancements for the AST and DOM tree traversal,and pattern matching utilities.

18.9   Acknowledgements

The authors would like to thank Bill O'Farrell and Steve Perelgut of IBM Canada Ltd., Center for Advanced Studies, for their support and valuable insights related to this work. Also the authors would like to thank Adam Zimmer and Evan Mamas of University of Waterloo, for the implementation of the prototype parser generator, and their technical views related to the use of XML as source code representation formalism for program understanding. Finally the authors would like to extend their gratitude to the Center for Information Technology Ontario and Formal Systems, Inc. for their financial support.

NOTE: Refine is a trademark of Reasoning Systems, Inc.

18.10   References

Aho, A.V., Sethi, R., and Ullman, J.D. (1986). *Compiler Principles, Techniques, and Tools.* Addison-Wesley Publishing Company, Reading, MA.

Arango, G., and Prieto-Diaz, R. (1991). Domain Analysis Concepts and Research Directions. In *Domain Analysis and Software Systems Modeling*. Prieto-Diaz and Arango (eds.). IEEE Computer Society Press.

Bell Canada Datrix Group. (2000). *Abstract Semantic Graph: Reference Manual.* Bell Canada Ltd., Version 1.3, January.

Breuer, P.T. and Bowen, J.P. (1993). The PRECC Compiler-Compiler. In *Proceedings UKUUG/SUKUG Joint New Year 1993 Conference*. St. Cross Centre, Oxford, UK, January 6-8.

Breuer, P.T., and Bowen, J.P. (1992). A PREttier Compiler-Compiler: Generating Higher Order Parsers in C. *Oxford University Computing Laboratory Technical Report PRG-TR-20-92*. November.

Buss, E., De Mori, R., Gentleman, W.M., Henshaw, J., Johnson, H., Kontogiannis, K., Merlo, E., Müller, H., Mylopoulos, J., Paul, S., Prakash, A., Stanley, M., Tilley, S.R., Troster, J., and Wong, K. (1994). Investigating Reverse Engineering Technologies for the CAS Program Understanding Project. *IBM Systems Journal*, 33(3).

Chikofsky, E.J., and Cross, J.H. (1990). Reverse Engineering and Design Recovery: A Taxonomy. *IEEE Software*, January.

DeBaud, J., and Rugaber, S. (1995). A Software Re-Engineering Method using Domain Models. Technical Report, College of Computing, Georgia Institute of Technology, Atlanta, GA.

Devambu, P., Rosenblum, D., and Wolf, A. (1994). Automated construction of testing and analysis tools. In *Proceedings of 16th, International Conf. on Software Engineering*, Los Alamitos, CA. IEEE Computer Society Press, May.

Devambu, P. (1992). Genoa–A language and front-end independent source code analyzer generator. In *Proceedings of 14th, International Conf. on Software Engineering*, Los Alamitos, CA. IEEE Computer Society Press, May.

Fischer, C. and LeBlanc, R. (1991). *Crafting a Compiler With C*. Addison-Wesley, Reading, MA.

Holt, R. (1997). An Introduction to TA: The Tuple-Attribute Language. http://plg.uwaterloo.ca/ holt/cv/papers.html. Dept. of Computer Science, University of Waterloo, March.

IBM Corporation. (1999). Visual Age C++.
Online at http://www.ibm.com/software/ad/vacpp.

Kernighan, B., and Ritchie, D. (1988). *The C Programming Language*. Prentice Hall, Englewood Cliffs, NJ.

Kontogiannis, K. (1993). Program Representation and Behavioural Matching for Localizing Similar Code Fragments. In *Proceedings of CASCON'93*. Toronto, Ontario, Canada, October.

Kotik, G., and Markosian, L. (1989). Automating Software Analysis and Testing Using a Program Transformation System. Reasoning Systems, Inc., Palo Alto, CA.

Malton, A. (1993). The Denotational Semantics of a Functional Tree-Manipulation Language. *Computer Languages*, 19(3).

Mamas, E. (2000). Design and Development of a Code Base Management System. M.Sc. Thesis, Dept. of Electrical & Computer Engineering, University of Waterloo, Canada, June.

Markosian, L. (1994). Using an Enabling Technology to Reengineer Legacy Systems. *Communications of the ACM*, 37(5).

Müller, H. (1993). Understanding Software Systems Using Reverse Engineering Technology Perspectives from the Rigi Project. In *Proceedings of CASCON '93*, Toronto, Canada, October 22-24. pp. 217-226.

Mylopoulos, J., Borgida, A., Jarke, M., and Koubarakis, M. (1990). Telos: Representing Knowledge About Information Systems. *ACM Transactions on Information Systems*, 8(4).

Mylopoulos, J., Gal, A., Kontogiannis, K., and Stanley, M. (1996). A Generic Integration Architecture for Cooperative Information Systems. In *Proceedings of Co-operative Information Systems '96*, Brussels, Belgium.

Parr, T. (1996). Language Translation Using PCCTS & C++ - A Reference Guide. Automata Publishing Company.

Purtilo, J. and Callahan, J. (1989). Parse-Tree Annotations. (1989). *Communications of the ACM*, 32(12).

Reasoning Systems, Inc. (1990a). *Dialect User's Guide, Version 2.0*. Palo Alto, CA, July.

Stanchfield, S. (1997). *A PCCTS Tutorial.*
Online at http://www.scruz.net/thetick/pcctstut/.

Stallings, W. (1991). *Data and Computer Communications*. MacMillan, Toronto, Canada.

Sun Microsystems. (2000) JavaCC: The Parser Generator. Online at http://www.metamamta.com/JavaCC. Sun Microsystems.

Tilley, S., and Smith, D. (1996). Coming Attractions in Program Understanding. Technical Report CMU/SEI-96-TR-019 ESC-TR-96-019, Software Engineering Institute, Carnegie-Mellon University, Pittsburgh, PA, December.

Annotated Bibliography

Aho, A., Sethi, R., and Ullman, J.D. (1986). *Compilers: Principles, Techniques, and Tools*. (Addison-Wesley). This classic text provides a detailed perspective on compiler construction with an emphasis on parsing techniques, lexical analysis, data flow analysis, optimization, and code generation. The theory behind parsing is well described, but there is little information on backtracking.

Anquetil, N., and Lethbridge, T.C. (1999b). A comparative study of clustering algorithms and abstract representations for software remodularization. In *Proceedings of the Working Conference on Reverse Engineering*. (IEEE Press). pp. 235-255. *Presents more details of many experiments with hierarchical clustering algorithms for remodularization. The two main aspects of this article are that it is specifically geared toward remodularization and it is an experimental study.*

Baker, S.B. (1995). On finding duplication and near duplication in large software systems. In *Proceedings of the Working Conference on Reverse Engineering, Toronto, Canada*. This paper describes Dup, which is the program developed at AT&T to locate instances of duplication or near-duplication in software systems. Dup detects sections of code which are textually identical or which are mostly textually identical but with systematic substitutions of one set of variable names and constants for another. Further processing locates longer sections of code which are the same except for other small modifications. Experimental results from running Dup on millions of LOC's from two large software systems show the effectiveness and the execution speed of the tool.

Basili, V.R., Briand, L.C., and Melo, W.L. (1996). A validation of object-oriented design metrics as quality indicators. *IEEE Transactions on Software Engineering*. 22(10). pp. 751-761. This work is an attempt to validate the C&K metrics as indicators of fault proneness. While the experiment was carried out only on small software systems, developed by students, the results are nonetheless encouraging. The authors show that some of the metrics in the suite can be used as fault-proneness predictors. An interesting feature of the paper is the rigor of the statistical approach.

Booch, G., Jacobson, I., and Rumbaugh, J. (1999). *The Unified Modeling Language User Guide*. (Addison-Wesley). Reference manual and guide book alike. The principal authors of the UML (sometimes referred to as "the three amigos") describe the UML modeling language.

Buhr, R.J.A. (1998). Use case maps as architectural entities for complex systems. *IEEE Trans. Software Engineering*. 24(12). pp. 1131-1155. A concise and extremely readable introduction to Use Case Maps. Those who want to learn about case maps without reading an entire book can read this first. It includes some updates to the notation and some interesting examples.

Buhr, R.J.A. and Casselman, R.S. (1996). *Use Case Maps for Object-Oriented Systems*. (Prentice-Hall). The definitive book by the originators of Use Case Maps (UCMs). Describes the Use Case Map notation in detail and gives many examples. The preface to the book shows an example of a UCM used for a human activity (reading the book).

Buschmann, Meunier, R., Rohnert, H., Sommerlad, P., and Stal, M. (1996). *Pattern-Oriented Software Architecture—A System of Patterns*. (Wiley). Well-known book on patterns and similar concepts, covering architectural patterns, design patterns, idioms, pattern systems, and their relation to software architecture. Compared to the Gang-of-Four pattern book, the emphasis is on patterns at a higher-level of abstraction, i.e., on architectural patterns, and coarse-grained design patterns.

Buss, E. (1994). Investigating reverse engineering technologies for the CAS program understanding project. *IBM Systems Journal*, 33(3).

Buss, E., DeMori, R., Gentleman, W.M., Henshaw, J., Johnson, H., Kontogiannis, K., Merlo, E., Müller, H.A., Mylopoulos, J., Paul, S., Prakash, A., Stanley, M., Tilley, S.R., Troster, J. and Wong, K. (1994). Investigating reverse engineering technologies for the CAS program understanding project. *IBM Systems Journal*. 33(3). pp. 477-500. This paper discusses techniques related to reverse engineering, automatic defect filtering, and automatic clone detection. It summarizes the experiences on analyzing large legacy systems, focussing on IBM's database management system UDB/DB2. It also describes the scope and results of a research project on program understanding undertaken by the IBM Toronto Software Solutions Laboratory Centre for Advanced Studies (CAS). The project involved a team from CAS and five research groups working cooperatively on complementary reverse engineering approaches. All the groups were using the source code of SQL/DS* (a multimillion-line relational database system) as the reference legacy system. Also discussed is an approach adopted to integrate the various tools under a single reverse engineering environment.

Chaumun, M.A. (1998). *Change impact analysis in object-oriented systems: conceptual model and application to C++*. Master's Thesis. Université de Montréal, Canada. (November). This report, in French, describes in detail the change impact model presented in this book. The C++ expressions defining every change are described as are the impact formulas before and after simplification. The proof of feasibility experiment presented in Chapter 10 is also described in detail.

Chidamber, S.R. and Kemerer, C.F. (1994). A metrics suite for object-oriented design. *IEEE Transactions on Software Engineering*. 20(6). pp. 476-493. This is the last of a series of papers describing the Chidamber and Kemerer (C&K) suite of metrics. The theoretical foundations of the metrics are presented. Details of the metrics are described and validated on two industrial-strength systems. This is recommended reading for any work in object-oriented design metrics.

Chikofsky, E.J., and Cross, J. (1990). Reverse engineering and design recovery: a taxonomy. *IEEE Software*, 7(1). pp. 13-17. This article provides definitions and terminology used in software reverse engineering and related fields. The definitions given in this paper are widely adopted by the research community and officially adopted by IEEE.

CHIME, the Columbia Hypermedia IMmersion Environment. Online at: http://www.cs.columbia.edu/~sdossick/www/create.html. The main value of CHIME in the context of this article is that it illustrates a MUD environment designed and used for collaboration. An interesting aspect of CHIME is that it is built on top of an extensible, XML-based Metadata server. Thus artifacts in CHIME virtual worlds continue to reside in their original locations, be they legacy database systems, document management systems, or source code configuration management repositories.

Churchill, E. and Bly, S. (1999). It's all in the words: Supporting work activities with lightweight tools. In *Proceedings of Group '99*. Describes and analyzes long-term work experience with a simple text-based MUD and provides evidence of the usefulness of the concept for collaborative work in geographically dispersed teams.

Denzin, N.K., and Lincoln, Y.S. (eds.). (1994). *Handbook of Qualitative Research*. (Sage). This book is an edited collection of readings on the practice of qualitative research. The handbook gives an excellent overview of the various paradigms for doing qualitative work, the strategies developed for studying people in their natural settings, and a variety of techniques for collecting, analyzing, interpreting, and reporting results. It covers everything from theoretical approaches to ethical issues. Contributing authors were selected from a variety of disciplines.

El-Emam, K., Benlarbi, S., Goel, N., and Rai, S. (2001). The confounding effect of class size on the validity of object-oriented metrics. *IEEE Transactions on Software Engineering*. (To appear). This paper conjectures that size has a confounding effect in most past validation studies of OO metrics, and comments on the methodology of these studies. It argues that future empirical validation should control for the correlation between size and the metric being evaluated to eliminate this effect.

Gamma, E., Helm, R., Johnson, R., and Vlissedes, J. (1995). *Design Patterns: Elements of Reusable Object-Oriented Software*. (Addison-Wesley). Capturing a wealth of experience about the design of object-oriented software, the four authors (often referred to as the Gang-of-Four) present a catalog of proven and succinct solutions to commonly occurring design problems. Previously undocumented, these 23 patterns allow designers to create more

flexible, elegant, and ultimately reusable designs without having to redis-
cover the design solutions themselves.

German, D.M., Cowan, D.D., and Alencar, P.S.C. (1998). A Framework for
formal design of hypertext applications. In *Proceedings of the 4th Brazilian
Symposium on Multimedia and Hypermedia*. The design of hypertext applications is currently specified in notations, which are not formal. The result
is the inability to verify their correctness. In this paper, the authors propose
a formal specification language for hypertext design, Hades, which separates content, organization, linking and typesetting information. This language permits the verification of properties such as completeness, referential integrity, node layout of a hypertext application. Hades will permit the
analysis of hypertext applications before these are actually implemented.

Gropp, W., Lusk, E., and Skjellum, A. (1994). *Using MPI: Portable Parallel
Programming with the Message-Passing Interface*. (MIT Press). This book
is a good introduction to the Message Passing Interface (MPI), the proposed standard for writing message-passing programs. MPI aims at establishing a practical, portable, efficient and flexible standard for message
passing.

Harrison, S., and Dourish, P. (1996). Re-Place-ing Space: The roles of place and
space in collaborative systems. In *Proceedings of CSCW '96. A classical
paper using experimental evidence to justify the usefulness of communication scopes in collaborative work.*

Henderson-Sellers, B. (1996). *Object-Oriented Metrics: Measures of Complexity*. (Prentice-Hall). This book gives an overview of object-oriented metrics
and proposes new ones. It is one of the few books that proposes a cognitive
theory for their justification. Includes references to work on cognitive complexity.

Herrera, F. (1999). *A Usability Study of the "TkSee" Software Exploration Tool.*
M.Sc. Thesis. School of Information Technology and Engineering, University of Ottawa, Canada. Online at: http://www.site.uottawa.ca/
~tcl/gradtheses/fherrera/. This thesis discusses in much more depth the usability evaluation work presented in this book.

Highsmith, J. (1999). Managing distributed project teams. *E-business Application Delivery* (August). Online at: http://cutter.com/ead/ ead9908.html. Explains motivation, conceptual foundation, and architecture of Project Communities Software, a current state-of-the-art CSCW product by Neometron
designed for use in collaborative applications including possibly Distributed
Software Engineering.

Hutchens, D.H., and Basili, V.R. (1985). System structure analysis: clustering
with data bindings. *IEEE Transactions on Software Engineerin* (August).
pp. 749-757. One of the early works that used structural information (data
bindings) and a hierarchical algorithm to cluster software systems. The results were compared to the developer's mental image of the system's struc-

ture. They categorize different systems depending on the output of their algorithm on them. Interesting issues such as algorithm stability and modularity deterioration are raised.

Jain, A., and Dubes, R. (1988). *Algorithms for Clustering Data.* (Prentice-Hall). One of the best texts on cluster analysis. A good book for someone that wants to understand the issues and difficulties a clustering project presents. They present a comprehensive survey of algorithms found in the cluster analysis literature, including hierarchical, partitional, and graph-theoretic ones. They discuss issues such as cluster validity and stability. They also present a framework for a cluster analysis project.

Johnson, J.H. (1993). Identifying redundancy in source code using fingerprints. In *Proceedings of the 1994 Centre for Advanced Studies Conference (CASCON' 93)*, Toronto, Canada. (IBM and NRC). This paper reports about the implementation of a mechanism, which uses fingerprints to identify exact repetitions of text in large programs. Fingerprints have been defined as short strings which can be used for comparison purposes to stand in for larger data objects. A fingerprint is a mapping function from some data object domain into the set of fingerprints. Experiments involved the construction of source trees and the successful identification of repetitions in a legacy software system of over 300 megabytes. This redundancy identification system has provided useful information as well as establishing the scalability of the approach, which may form the basis of a suit of tools for the visualization and understanding of programs. The paper employs a technique similar to a string searching method of Karp and Rabin.

Johnson, J.H. (1994). Substring matching for clone detection and change tracking. In *Proceedings of International Conference on Software Maintenance (ICSM)*, Victoria, Canada. (September 19-23). pp. 120-126. This paper elaborates the method of textual redundancy to include clusters and components. Components become a useful way to structure the searches for interesting matches in an example based on gcc.

Johnson, J.H. (1994). Visualizing textual redundancy in legacy source. In *Proceedings of 1994 Centre for Advanced Studies Conference (CASCON '94)*, Toronto, Canada. (IBM and NRC). pp. 9-18. Introduces a method of visualizing the structure of components and clusters is presented. The method explores some more complex features of the gcc example.

Keller, R.K., and Schauer, R. (1998). Design components: towards software composition at the design level. In *Proceedings of 20th International Conference on Software Engineering*, Kyoto, Japan (April). pp. 302-310. Introduces the notion of design component. Design components are reified design elements, such as patterns, idioms, or application-specific solutions, and their provision as software components. Design components play a key role in the SPOOL approach to design pattern recovery and engineering.

Kontogiannis, K. Program representation and behavioral matching for localizing similar code fragments. In *Proceedings of the Centre for Advanced Studies Annual Conference (CASCON '93)*, Toronto, Canada. (IBM and NRC). This paper presents pattern matching techniques for the identification of cloned components in very large software systems. The pattern matching is based on dynamic programming, data flow and source code properties, and software metrics.

Kontogiannis, K., et al. (1998). Code Migration Through Transformations: An Experience Report. In *Proceedings of Centre for Advanced Studies Conference (CASCON '98)*, Toronto, Canada (IBM and NRC). One approach to dealing with spiraling maintenance costs, manpower shortages and frequent breakdowns for legacy code is to migrate the code into a new platform or programming language. This paper explores the feasibility of semi-automating such a migration process in the presence of performance and other constraints for the migrant code. In particular, the paper reports on an experiment involving the migration of several modules of a medium-size software system from PL/IX to C++. The paper reports on the transformation techniques used by the transformation process, the effectiveness of the prototype tools developed, and some preliminary evaluations of the experiment.

Kung, D., et al. (1994). Change impact identification in object-oriented software maintenance. In *Proceedings of International Conference on Software Maintenance (ICSM)*, Victoria, Canada (September). pp. 202-211. One of the few papers dealing with change impact in object-oriented systems, although with a different purpose in mind. The objective here is to define the testing set. Changes are enumerated, a classification of impacts is provided, and the change impacts are calculated by using a firewall calculation approach.

Laguë, B., Proulx, D., Mayrand, J., Merlo, E., and Hudepohl, J. (1997). Assessing the benefits of incorporating function clone detection in a development process. In *Proceedings of International Conference on Software Maintenance (ICSM)*. The objective of the experiments presented in this paper is to bring insights in the evaluation of the potential benefits of introducing function clone detection in an industrial software development process. Two modifications to the software development process are presented namely preventive control and problem mining. Experiments are presented that consists of evaluating the impact of proposed changes on a large telecommunication software system of a about 89 MLOC of analyzed code. The studies are applied over a three years development period in which six subsequent versions of the software under study were released consuming an effort of about 10,000 person-months. Results showed that a significant number of clones are removed from the system over time. However, this clone reduction is not enough to prevent the growth of the overall number of clones in the system under study. In this context, preventive control would have been very appropriate. Experiments also indicate that problem mining would have provided programmers with a significant number of opportunities for correcting problems before customers experience them. These results show a potential for improving the software system quality and customer satisfaction.

Lakhotia, A. (1997). A unified framework for expressing software subsystem classification techniques. *Journal of Systems and Software*, 36(3). pp. 211-231. Presents an excellent framework for comparing various aspects of clustering in the context of software remodularization including clustering algorithms and descriptive features.

Lethbridge, T., Singer, J., Vinson, N., and Anquetil, N. (1997). An Examination of Software engineering work practices. In *Proceedings of Centre for Advanced Studies Conference (CASCON '97)*, Toronto, Canada. (IBM and NRC). pp. 209-223. This paper presents work practice data of the daily activities of software engineers. Four separate studies are presented; one looking longitudinally at an individual SE; two looking at a software engineering group; and one looking at company-wide tool usage statistics. The paper also discusses the advantages in considering work practices in designing tools for software engineers.

Lethbridge, T.C., Lyon, S., Perry, P. (2001). The management of university-industry collaborations involving empirical studies of software engineering In *Empirical Studies in Software Engineering*, Khaled El-Eman and Janice Singer (eds.) (MIT Press). This chapter discusses the pragmatic considerations that university researchers and companies should consider when establishing collaborative software engineering research projects; in particular, those involving empirical studies of software engineers. The chapter is illustrated with a case study describing the research collaboration between the authors, one of whom is an academic and the other two are from industry.

Li, W., and Henry, S. (1993). Object-oriented metrics that predict maintainability. *Journal of Systems and Software*, 23. pp. 111-122. The work presented in this paper is one of the first attempts to relate some object-oriented design metrics to maintainability. The metrics considered are a prior version of the C&K suite, enhanced by several metrics proposed by the authors. An empirical study on two industrial-strength software systems enabled them to show that a subset of the metrics is indeed a predictor of maintainability.

Markosian, L. (1994). Using an enabling technology to reengineer legacy systems. In *Communications of the ACM*, 37(5). This paper provides experimental results from the analysis and re-engineering of COBOL legacy systems. The analysis tool presented is based on Annotated Abstract Syntax Trees and a specialized language called Refine.

Mayrand, J., Leblanc, C., and Merlo E. (1996). Experiment on the automatic detection of function clones in a software system using metrics. In *Proceedings of the International Conference on Software Maintenance (ICSM)*.

This paper introduces the basic philosophy of detecting clones by using metrics and the Datrix environment. The clone identification technique, presented in this paper, uses 21 function metrics grouped into four points of comparison. Each point of comparison is used to compare functions and determine their cloning levels. An ordinal scale of eight cloning levels is defined. The levels represent clones ranging from exact copies to distinct functions. The metrics used, the thresholds employed and the detection process are fully described. Results of applying the clone detection technique to two telecommunication-monitoring systems of about one MLOC in size are provided as examples.

Meszaros, G., and Doble, J. (1997). A pattern language for pattern writing. In *Pattern Languages of Program Design-3, Software Patterns Series.* (Addison-Wesley). The article discusses the commonly accepted format presently used for writing patterns. The "Pattern Languages of Program Design'" series of books are good references for anyone interested in pattern-related topics that cover a diverse range of disciplines.

Müller, H., Orgun, M., Tilley, S., and Uhl, J. (1993). A reverse engineering approach to subsystem structure identification. *Journal of Software Maintenance: Research and Practice,* 5(4). pp. 181-204. This paper describes a reverse engineering approach to creating higher-level abstract representations of a subject system, which involves the identification of related components and dependencies, the construction of layered subsystem structures, and the computation of exact interfaces among subsystems. The authors show how top-down decompositions of a subject system can be (re)constructed via bottom-up subsystem composition. This process involves identifying groups of building blocks (e.g., variables, procedures, modules, and subsystems) using composition operations based on software engineering principles such as low coupling and high cohesion. The result is an architecture of layered subsystem structures.

Mylopoulos, J. (1990). Telos: representing knowledge about information systems. *ACM Transactions on Information Systems,* 8(4). This paper discusses a conceptual modeling language that allows for schemata and domain models to be specified. The language allows for schemata or meta-schemata to be specified in terms of object-like entities. Attributes can be classified in categories and treated as first class entities.

Mylopoulos, J. (1996). A generic integration architecture for cooperative information systems. In *Proceedings of Co-operative Information Systems.* This paper discusses a data and control integration system that allows for CASE tools to coordinate in order to assist software engineers perform software maintenance tasks.

Nielsen, J. (1994). Heuristic evaluation. In *Usability Inspection Methods,* J. Nielsen and R. L. Mack (eds.) (Wiley). pp. 25-62. An easy-to-read overview of heuristic evaluation, in a book that covers a wide range of issues related to usability evaluation.

Opdyke, K. (1992). Refactoring object-oriented frameworks. Ph.D. Thesis. University of Illinois at Urbana-Champaign. This thesis defines a set of program restructuring operations (refactorings) that support the design, evolution and reuse of object-oriented application frameworks. Its focus is on the automation of these refactorings that preserve the behavior of a program. It provides a catalog of refactorings, explains under what circumstances they are behavior preserving (preconditions) and defines three complex refactorings in detail.

Parr, T. (1996). *Language Translation Using PCCTS and C++: A Reference Guide.* (Automata Publishing Company). This book provides an overview of compilation and parsing technology and focuses on the inner workings of a novel top-down parser generator called PCCTS.

Parr, T.J. and Quong, R.W. (1995). ANTLR: A predicated-LL(k) parser generator. *Software: Practice & Experience,* 25(7). pp. 789-810.   This article describes the parser generator ANTLR. It discusses the use of predicates as form of backtracking.

Schwanke, R.W. (1991). An intelligent tool for re-engineering software modularity. *Proceedings of the 13th International Conference on Software Engineering (ICSE '91).* pp. 83-92. This paper presents ARCH, a software tool that provides heuristic modularization advice for improving existing code. It introduces the shared neighbors principle. The tool learns and adapts to the architect's preferences. It can also perform corrective clustering through its maverick analysis.

Singh, A., Schaeffer, J., and Szafron, D. (1998). Experience with parallel programming using code templates. *Concurrency: Practice and Experience,* 10(2). pp. 91-120. The authors of this paper have been working on pattern-based models and systems in parallel computing for over a decade. The paper outlines their experiences in developing and using these systems. A list of desirable characteristics of pattern-based approaches in parallel computing is also discussed. The observations are discussed from the perspective of their own systems, Frameworks and Enterprise. They are equally relevant to other pattern-based parallel programming models and systems.

Sneath, P.H.A. and Sokal, R.R. (1973). *Numerical Taxonomy.* (W.H. Freeman and Company). San Francisco. A book that presents many aspects of clustering in depth. Algorithms are described and their statistical properties discussed, many distance metrics are p resented, etc. The viewpoint is that of taxonomy (the mother area of clustering), but many conclusions apply to remodularization.

Stallings, W. (1991). *Data and Computer Communications.* (MacMillan). This book provides a comprehensive view of networking technology and communication protocols. Particular emphasis is placed on Internet protocols and inter-process communication mechanisms. The definitive work on usability engineering by the leader of the field.

Tilley, S., Wong, K., Storey, M.A., and Müller H. (1994). Programmable re-verse engineering. *International Journal of Software Engineering and Knowledge Engineering,* 4(4). pp. 501-520. This paper describes a pro-grammable approach to reverse engineering. The approach uses a scripting language that enables users to write their own routines for common reverse engineering activities such as graph layout, metrics, and subsystem decom-position, thereby extending the capabilities of the reverse engineering tool set to better suit their needs. A programmable environment supported by this approach subsumes existing reverse engineering systems by being able to simulate facets of each one.

Weinand, A., Gamma, A., and Marty, R. (1989). Design and implementation of ET++, a seamless object-oriented application framework. *Structured Pro-gramming,* 10(2). pp. 63-87. ET++ is a well-known object-oriented applica-tion framework that is based on the architecture of MacApp and imple-mented in C++. It was one of the first of its kind, excels in the application of design patterns, and is available in the public domain. These characteris-tics make it a prime guinea pig system in the domain of design pattern re-covery and engineering.

Wiggerts, T. (1997). Using clustering algorithms in legacy systems remodulari-zation, In *Proceedings of the Working Conference on Reverse Engineering.* (IEEE Press). pp. 33-43. Presents an overview of the general literature of clustering as applied to remodularization. Lists and describes the principal choices in the domains of clustering algorithms, distance metrics and link-age rules. The approach is theoretical as opposed to experimental.

Wiggerts, T.A (1997). Using clustering algorithms in legacy systems remodu-larization. In *Proceedings of the Fourth Working Conference on Reverse Engineering.* (IEEE Computer Society Press). pp. 33-43. A very good sur-vey of cluster analysis techniques covering the most important classic clus-tering algorithms, as well as publications on software clustering. A good starting point for someone interested in learning more about software clus-tering. Contains a number of good references.

Zobel, J., Wilkinson, R., Mackie, E., Thom, J., Sacks-Davis, R., Kent, A., and Fuller, M. (1991). An architecture for hyperbase systems. In *Proceedigns of First Australian Multi-Media Communications Applications and Technol-ogy Workshop,* Sydney (July). In this paper, the authors propose a struc-tured architecture for hyperbase systems. A hyperbase system is a system that manages databases that store hypermedia information. Amongst its ad-vantages, the proposed architecture is based on the well-established data-base techniques.

Glossary

Abstract Syntax Tree (AST)—A tree that offers a translation of an input stream in terms of operands and operators, omitting superficial details such as which grammar productions were used and syntactic properties of the input string.

Agglomerative clustering algorithms—A type of hierarchical clustering algorithms that operate in a bottom-up fashion; i.e., they initially assign each object to a cluster, and then they start joining the most similar clusters.

Ambiguity—The situation that results when two or more grammar rules can be applied at the same time when parsing a language construct. To decide which rule to apply, we need additional rules (usually based on semantics of the language) to resolve the ambiguity.

Backus-Naur form—A grammar whose production rules are of the form $A \leftarrow A_1, ..., A_n$, or of the form $A \leftarrow A_1 \mid ... \mid A_n$, where A_i are terminal or non-terminal symbols.

Black hole configuration—A pathological situation in clustering in which an algorithm continuously adds elements to one large cluster instead of creating smaller clusters of more moderate size. See also *gas cloud configuration*.

Bottom-up parser—A parser that generates parse trees starting from their leaves and working towards the root. See also *parser generator* and *parse tree*.

Browser—A tool for viewing and navigating hypertext documents. In particular, Web pp. are meant to be viewed through an interactive browser.

C&K suite of metrics—Chidamber-and-Kemerer suite of metrics. Chidamber and Kemerer are the authors of an object-oriented design metrics suite that has become a benchmark in the field.

CASE—See *Computer-Aided Software Engineering Environment*.

Change impact—The set of classes which have to be changed if a given class is modified.

Changeability—The extent to which a piece of software can be easily modified, regardless of the purpose of the change.

Clone(s)—Sections of program source code, often complete functions, which are nearly identical. Clones are typically created when programmers copy functions or files which they need for a new application, perhaps with slight modifications. During the maintenance of large software systems under time pressure, it is often quicker to copy and modify a working software component. Cloning leads, over time, to systems that grow exponentially as a function of time, and consequently, have serious difficulties with maintenance.

Clustering—The process of grouping together similar entities. In the context of software engineering, it is used for remodularization.

Code Base Management System—A computer-sided software engineering (CASE) environment (CASE) that allows for the integration of various tools that facilitate software maintenance tasks.

Cognitive complexity—The mental burden of the individuals (for example, the developers, testers, inspectors, and maintainers) who have to deal with a particular software component or subsystem.

Cohesion—The extent to which aspects of a software system that are logically related are kept closer together, and are therefore easier to find and manipulate. High cohesion is a goal of good design.

Cohesion metric—A value that measures the extent of cohesion in a software component.

Collaborative Virtual Environment (CVE)—Networked environment designed for team collaboration and providing a semblance of collocation

Common Gateway Interface (CGI)—A mechanism that allows a Web server to launch and convey requests to arbitrary external programs.

Computer-Aided Software Engineering (CASE)—Refers to a support environment or a set of tools. The support of software development through a set of (often-integrated) software tools that help automate certain tasks and processes and manage the underlying complexity. These may include support for editing, compilation and linking; management of dependencies among software artifacts; visualization of software artifacts; navigation through software artifacts; access control; documentation production; detect ion of inconsistencies and error reporting; and reverse engineering.

Control integration—The process of allowing tools to be synchronized with respect to their invocation in order to perform a given task.

Corrective clustering—A procedure that refines an existing taxonomy by rearranging some of the objects.

Coupling—The amount of linkage among various components of a software system. Lower coupling is a goal of good design.

Coupling metric—A value that measures the extent of coupling in a software component.

Cyclomatic number–Measure of a code section's, e.g., a function's, control flow graph complexity, defined as the number of regions in the planar graph.

Data integration—The process of allowing tools and processes to exchange data in a transparent way.

Descriptive feature—The characteristic used to describe entities to be clustered (see also *similarity metric*). In the context of remodularization, types of descriptive feature include software components referred to by an entity (e.g., inclusion of files, calls to routines) and words contained in the entity's name. For each entity, data corresponding to the descriptive feature is represented as a vector of attributes.

Design component—A design component is the reification of design elements, such as patterns, idioms, or application-specific solutions, and their provision as software components (JavaBeans, COM objects, or the like), which are manipulated via specialization, adaptation, assembly, and revision. For the purpose of Chapter 8, the term *design component* is used as a package of structural model descriptions together with informal documentation, such as intent, applicability, or known uses.

Design pattern—Design patterns capture the rationale behind proven design solutions and illuminate the trade-offs that are inherent in solutions to a non-trivial, recurring design problem. The notion of design pattern has become widely popular by the book on that subject written by Gamma et al.

Design pattern recovery—Detection and description of instantiations of design patterns occurring in a software system. Note the difference from design pattern mining, where the goal is to identify recurring design solutions and provide them as design pattern templates.

Design repository—See *repository*.

Distributed Software Engineering (DSE)—Software development performed by geographically distributed teams.

Divisive clustering algorithms—A type of hierarchical clustering algorithms that operate in a top-down fashion, i.e., they start with all the objects in one cluster, and then they start splitting it.

Domain model—A schema for the conceptual modeling of a given domain (i.e., the syntactic structures of a programming language).

Empirical study—The study of a phenomenon through observation or measurement.

Extensible Markup Language—A W3C standard for marking text so that semantic content can be associated with syntactic text entities.

First-degree empirical study—An empirical study in which those being studied are directly involved, for example, by answering questions.

Fuzzy parser—A fault-tolerant parser.

Gas cloud configuration—A pathological situation in clustering in which an algorithm leaves many leftover unclustered elements. See also *black hole configuration*.

Heuristic evaluation—A technique for evaluating the usability of software in which one or more usability experts walk through the software, determining whether a set of guidelines have been adhered to. The technique was invented by J. Nielsen.

Hierarchical clustering algorithm—An approach to clustering in which a hierarchy of clusters is formed, with all the elements in a single cluster at the root, and all the elements as singleton clusters at the leaves. A category of algorithms that produce a nested sequence of partitions, and then choose one of them as their output.

Hypermedia—Hypertext systems where the nodes can contain multimedia data, such as text, graphics, audio, video, as well as source code or other forms of data. See also *hypertext*.

Hypertext—An approach to information management in which text is stored in a network of document nodes connected by links (also called hyperlinks). A link is something that connects a piece of text to a destination piece of text; the source and destination areas are usually marked on a display by highlighting or special graphics. The World Wide Web (WWW) is an example of a set of distributed hypertext documents. See also *hypertext* and *World Wide Web*.

Hypertext Markup Language (HTML)—A composite document model. The document may contain references to other documents that are rendered in line by the client (e.g., tags, pictures, audio, video) and links to external documents. See also *markup language* and *hypertext*.

Hypertext Transfer Protocol (HTTP)—The common protocol for client-server communication on the Web. See also *hypertext* and *World Wide Web*.

Incremental clustering—A procedure that adjusts an existing taxonomy when the object set is modified.

Internet—A world-wide network of interconnected networks that supports host-to-host communication that adhere to open protocols and procedures defined by Internet standards. The Internet is based on the TCP/IP protocol suite, a set of protocols that allow multiples networks to be connected together in a seamless way.

Left recursion—The problem of creating infinitely long parse tree branches when top-down parsing is involved in rules of the form $A \leftarrow A, B$.

Legacy software system—A large, old, and mature software system that constitutes a massive asset to a business. The proper functioning of the software and the ability to add functionality is essential for the survival of the business.

Linkage rule—A rule used in clustering to determine how to compute the distance between two clusters. Two extreme cases are single linkage, which uses the distance between the closest elements in the two clusters, and complete linkage, which uses the furthest elements.

Logistic regression—A statistical modeling technique that is used when the dependent variable is binary.

Maintenance—The set of activities involved in modifying a piece of software once it is in operation. The modification can be of any kind and for any purpose.

Markup Language—A language that uses tags or labels to mark or distinguish different types of text in a document. These tags add information to the text indicating the logical components of a document, or instructions for layout of the text on the page. The word markup originated from the words and symbols that editors wrote on the printed page as instructions to the typographers.

Message Passing Interface Forum (MPIF)—An organization formed with the participation of over 40 organizations . The forum has been meeting since January, 1993 to discuss and define a set of library interface standards for message passing. See http://www.mpi-forum.org/.

MIMD (Multiple Instruction Multiple Data)—A computer architecture for parallel processing, defined by Flynn's taxonomy. A multiple-instruction multiple-data stream (MIMD) computer is a multi-processor system where each processor is capable of executing a different program independent of the other processors.

Model/View/Controller (MVC) —A software architecture, or design pattern, first described for Smalltalk, in which the parts of the software are divided into the model, holding the actual data; the view, which displays the data; and the controller, which allows the data to be manipulated.

Module—Source code file, which is at the same time a lexical scoping unit.

MOO (MUD Object-Oriented)—A MUD implemented with object-oriented technology

MPI (Message Passing Interface)—A communication standard for writing parallel programs. It aims at establishing a practical, portable, efficient and flexible standard for communication among parallel programs using the message -passing paradigm.

MUD (Multi-User Domains)—Collaborative virtual environment emulating selected features of the real world such as places, objects, tools, and inhabitants, designed for social or work interactions of multiple users over a network.

Multimedia—Multimedia usually refers to computer presentation of documents involving text, graphics, voice, video, and other types of media.

Multipurpose Internet Mail Extensions (MIME)—Refers to an Internet standard that specifies how messages must be formatted so that they can be exchanged between different email systems. Specifically, MIME messages can contain text, images, audio, video, or other application-specific data.

Object-oriented database management system (OODBS)—A database management system that stores, retrieves, and updates objects using transaction control, queries, locking, and versioning.

Package—Set of modules forming a library or program, and possibly relying on other library packages.

Parse tree—A parse tree for a grammar G with terminal symbols T, and nonterminal symbols V, applied to text S is a labeled ordered tree such that: (a) its root is the start symbol of G; (b) every leaf node has a label from the set T; (c) every internal node has a label from the set V; (d) if there is an internal node labeled A and its children are labeled a_1, a_2, ..., a_n, there must be a production rule of the form $A \leftarrow a_1, a_2,..., a_n$ in the grammar G; and (e) if a leaf is labeled by an empty label then it must be the only child of its parent.

Parser generator—A tool that generates a parser from a grammar.

Parsing—The process of determining if a string of tokens can be generated by a grammar. See also *parse tree*.

Partitioning (partitional) clustering algorithms—A category of algorithms that start with an initial partition, and attempt to modify it in order to optimize certain measures that represent the quality of the given partition.

Precision—A metric from information retrieval that measures the percentage of retrieved data items that are valid. See also *recall*.

Product metric—Usually refers to a quantitative description of an internal attribute of a piece of software, such as level of coupling between subsystems, cohesion within subsystems, and depth of the inheritance hierarchy. See *software metric*.

Program representation—A collection of techniques and methodologies to represent the source code at a higher level of abstraction than source text. These include among others, Abstract Syntax Trees, call graphs, data flow graphs, control flow graphs, program dependency graphs, program summary graphs.

Qualified identifier—Identifier (e.g., type, variable or procedure name) qualified with the module name (e.g., M1.P2 for procedure P2 in module M1). The module name can be omitted when the identifier is used within the module where it is defined.

Quality metric—Usually refers to a quantitative description of an external attribute of a piece of software, such as number of faults, down-time, speed of computation, and maintenance effort. See *software metric*.

Quality model—A quantitative model relating software product metrics with measures of external quality attributes, such as number of faults and maintenance effort.

Recall—A metric from information retrieval that measures the percentage of valid data items that are retrieved. See also *precision*.

Re-engineering—As applied to software. The examination and alteration of the subject system to re-constitute it in a new form and subsequent implementation of that form.

Refactoring—A restructuring operation that supports the design, evolution and reuse of object-oriented application frameworks. This restructuring operation preserves the behavior of a program.

Relational database management system (RDBMS)—A software system that supports the construction and management of relational databases. An RDBMS allows the definition of data structures, storage and retrieval operations, and integrity constraints using the relational model. DB2, IN-GRES, Sybase, and Oracle are well known examples.

Relational database—A database based on Codd's relational model. Such a database has its data and relations between them organized in tables.

Remodularization—The process of dividing software into a more understandable set of modules or subsystems.

Repository—A centralized database that contains all diagrams, form and report definitions, data structure, data definitions, process flows and logic, and definitions of other organizational and system components; it provides a set of mechanisms and structures to achieve seamless data-to-tool and data-to-data integration. The term *design repository* refers to an object-oriented database management system, together with a repository schema of reverse engineered models that comprise structure, behavior, and mechanisms at the design level.

Reverse engineering—As applied to a software system. The process of analyzing a subject system to (a) identify the system's components and interrelationships among the components, and (b) create representations of the system in another form or at a higher level of abstraction. The analysis of a given system in order to understand its structure and its behavior.

Safe programming language—Language for which the runtime system cannot be corrupted, thus insuring that the execution is faithful to the language semantics.

Second-degree empirical study—An empirical study in which those being studied are only indirectly involved, for example, by logging the use of tools.

Similarity metric (measure)—A class of metrics used in clustering to compute the similarity of two elements by comparing vectors of each element's attributes. Important types of similarity metrics include association coefficients, distance coefficients and correlation coefficients.

Software clone(s)—See *clone(s)*.

Software documentation—The task of producing a set of documents describing the construction, operation and use of software and produced throughout the software development lifecycle.

Software metric—A quantitative description of a piece of software, of a design artifact, or of the process of its development or maintenance. May refer to an internal attribute (such as internal complexity, coupling, cohesion) that is measured through analysis of the source code or another software artifact, or an external attribute (such as reliability, maintainability, performance) that is measured during development, operation, or maintenance of the software in its intended environment. See also *product metric* and *quality metric*.

Synchronized shadowing—A technique for observation wherein two people using clock-synchronized laptop computers record different aspects of people's work. The recording is done using a program that provides a set of *buttons* that allow specific information to be recorded and time-stamped. The output of the two computers is later combined and analyzed to discover work patterns.

Think-aloud usability testing—A technique for evaluating the usability of software in which one or more users is asked to perform specific tasks with the software while constantly talking about what they are thinking and doing. The sessions are normally videotaped and later analyzed to detect usability problems.

Third-degree empirical study—An empirical study in which information is gathered by studying artifacts left by those being studied, for example, looking at reports written by people being studied.

Three-tier architecture—A software architecture proposed back in the 1970s providing a storage (internal) schema, which is the database design; an external schema representing the applications; and a conceptual schema, which constitutes the domain tier and captures the semantics of the enterprise.

Threshold—A metric value below which the probability of a fault in a software component is steady, and above which the probability of a fault in the component increases.

Tool integration—The process of allowing tools and processes to collaborate for accomplishing a given task. Tool integration entails data and control integration.

Top-down parser—A parser that generates parse trees starting from the root and working towards the leafs.

Transliteration—The conversion of a software system at the source code level, from one programming language into another. Transliterations maintain the original architecture and data and control flow in the target system to a high degree.

UML metamodel—A metamodel is a model that includes types whose instances are also types. Metamodels are often used to specify other models. Specifically, the UML metamodel defines the types ModelElement, Class, Method, Feature, Package, and many others, as found in the UML notation.

Unified Modeling Language (UML)—The UML is an international standard for capturing analysis and design information through a set of well-defined models and diagrams. It comprises use cases, class and scenario diagrams, state and activity diagrams, as well as component and deployment diagrams. The UML is specified by the UML metamodel. See also *UML metamodel*.

Uniform Resource Locator (URL)—A link that designates the location and the identity of a resource on the World Wide Web.

Usability—The ability of software to be easily learned, to be efficiently exploited, to handle errors effectively and to satisfy users when used by particular classes of users performing particular classes of tasks. An important factor contributing to a software system's usefulness that should be considered independently of utility.

Use Case Map (UCM)—A graphical notation invented by R.J.A. Buhr showing multiple causal flows of responsibilities (paths) interacting with various contexts (shown as boxes, possibly nested). The notation was designed to represent the high-level architecture of real-time systems, but it can be used in other contexts, such as representing work patterns.

Utility—An abstract measure of the degree to which software has the computational capabilities to perform a given task, independent of its usability. An important factor contributing to software's usefulness.

Validation—Validation is the process of evaluating software during all phases of the software development process to ensure compliance with software requirements.

Variant—Variants of software components are developed to meet the requirements of different platforms. Often they express the same or similar functionality in different languages or in different environments.

Verification—Verification is the process of determining whether a software system retains specific properties when development moves from one phase to another in the software development lifecycle.

Version—Versions of software components are brought together to form a release of a system. A version is a frozen-in-time snapshot of the component. Maintenance activities produce new versions by making corrections to older versions.

VR (Virtual Reality)—Usually, interactive software typically modeling 3D aspects of the real world.

Work pattern—A sequence or graph of activities that occurs repeatedly in the work of an individual or group. Identifying work patterns can help in the process of automating or facilitating it.

World Wide Web (WWW)—A software application developed in 1989 at CERN (the European Center for Nuclear Studies) aimed at providing hypertext-style access to information from a wide range of distributed sources. The WWW can be seen as a web of linked documents distributed worldwide. See also *hypertext*.

Index